Encounters in the Rubble

American Interactions with German Children in Postwar Germany

Inaugural-Dissertation

zur Erlangung des Doktorgrades der Philosophie
der Ludwig-Maximilians-Universität München

vorgelegt von
Erica Jade Lansberg
aus
Sellersville, Pennsylvania
2025

Referentin: PD Dr. Charlotte Lerg
Korreferent: Professor Dr. Michael Hochgeschwender
Tag der mündlichen Prüfung: 20. Februar 2024

Erica J. Lansberg

Encounters in the Rubble

De Gruyter Studies in Military History

Edited by
Jörg Echternkamp and Adam Seipp

Volume 12

Erica J. Lansberg

Encounters in the Rubble

American Interactions with German Children and Youth in Postwar Germany

DE GRUYTER
OLDENBOURG

Diss., Ludwig-Maximilians-University Munich, 2024

Erica J. Lansberg is not an employee of DPAA, she supports DPAA through a partnership. The views presented are those of the author and do not necessarily represent the views of DPAA, DoD, or its Components.

ISBN 978-3-11-158702-8
e-ISBN (PDF) 978-3-11-158815-5
e-ISBN (EPUB) 978-3-11-158922-0
ISSN 2701-5629

Library of Congress Control Number: 2025936549

Bibliographic information published by the Deutsche Nationalbibliothek
The Deutsche Nationalbibliothek lists this publication in the Deutsche Nationalbibliografie; detailed bibliographic data are available on the internet at http://dnb.dnb.de.

Cover image: An infantryman makes friends with a dog belonging to these German children. US Army Signal Corps, National Archives, 111-C-867
Typesetting: Integra Software Services Pvt. Ltd.
Printing and binding: CPI books GmbH, Leck

www.degruyterbrill.com
Questions about General Product Safety Regulation:
productsafety@degruyterbrill.com

To Linda,
And to my grandfather Earl, whose story I never got to know

Acknowledgments

This work is an updated version of my dissertation submitted to the Ludwig-Maximilians-University Munich in October 2023 and defended in February 2024. Over the past few years, this project has profoundly shaped me and has also been shaped by global events in ways that I could have never imagined when my doctoral studies began. Stretching across an ocean and taking place within the context of a pandemic, this project has come to its end only through the support of so many people.

Firstly, I would like to extend my thanks to those who have supported and helped me with this project, especially Professor Dr. Michael Hochgeschwender for his enthusiasm about my project and for serving as my second advisor. Many thanks go to Professor Dr. Uwe Lübken for his role as third evaluator for the defense. Moreover, I would like to thank Professor Dr. Silke Hackenesch, Professor Dr. Katharina Gerund, and Dr. Christopher Knowles for their help on various aspects of the project. I would like to extend a special thanks to Dr. Nadine Klopfer for her encouragement with my project. Moreover, Dr. Kaete O'Connell provided me with advice on working with the collections of the Truman Library, and her work on food aid in occupied Germany was especially helpful for my research. For my chapter on the Bremen Enclave, I had the kind assistance of various people, including Dr. Anna-Maria Pedron, Lutz Rode, and Peter Strotmann. A special thanks goes to Margaret Wood for sharing her personal records and talking to me about her experiences as a child in Bremen and Bremerhaven. I would like to extend my heartfelt thanks to Theodor Wild, whose openness in sharing his life experiences including his incredible diary collection fundamentally enriched this work. A special thanks also extends to all of those whose voices and stories made it into my work, especially for allowing their personal records to be seen and read by others through publication, online, or in the archives. Any mistranslations or mistakes made in documenting the details of their personal stories are entirely my own.

In addition, I would like to thank the archivists, librarians, and staff of the archives, institutions, and libraries I visited over the years, including the National Archives at College Park, Maryland, the National Archives at St. Louis, Missouri, the United States Army Heritage and Education Center, the Harry S. Truman Presidential Library, the Amerikahaus Munich, the Library of Congress, and the Deutsches Tagebucharchiv. A special thanks goes to Megan Harris, librarian at the Veterans History Project at the Library of Congress. I would also like to thank Jutta Jäger-Schenk at the Deutsches Tagebucharchiv. In addition, many thanks to my former colleagues in the Interlibrary Loan department at the Bethlehem Area

https://doi.org/10.1515/9783111588155-202

Public Library for their help with acquiring materials for my research. I would also like to thank my colleagues at The National WWII Museum for their support with the final stages of this project. Thank you to Rabea Rittgerodt-Burke and the team at De Gruyter for their assistance in making this book happen.

Moreover, I would like to thank the various organizations that helped fund this project. These have included the Graduate Center of the Ludwig-Maximilians-University Munich, the German Historical Institute Washington, DC, the Studienstiftung des deutschen Volkes, and the Truman Library Institute. Without this financial support, this project could not have been completed.

Finally, I am grateful for the support of my family and friends, a group stretching around the world who I am lucky to have in my life. Thank you to all my friends, both new and old, who have supported me through this project. I especially want to thank Linda for her unwavering support, kindness, and generosity through the past years, from Williams first days to today. I also want to thank David for staying by my side as a supportive force since meeting that day in the Austrian Alps. A special thanks goes to Kathleen for helping me so much, including for her assistance with German and for taking on bureaucratic tasks. Many thanks to Alexandra for her assistance and advice. A special thanks to Fabienne for her dedication and support, and her willingness to travel through all of Germany to attend my dissertation defense. Amy and Khanh, thank you. Heather, thank you for your support during the in-between phase. A special thanks goes to my parents, who dealt with my long absence while I was living in Europe and who supported me during the pandemic. Thank you as well to all the teachers, professors, and school staff who have encouraged me over the years. I especially would like to extend my thanks to Magnús Bernhardsson, who has always been willing to extend a helping hand or a wise word of advice. My time in his history classes at Williams College made this adventure and this project possible in the first place. Finally, thank you to my grandparents.

Last but not least, I would like to extend my deepest thanks to my advisor, PD Dr. Charlotte Lerg, whose enthusiasm and support never wavered through these years. Thank you for your excitement about this project, from its earliest phases of reading a certain war diary to its completion while we were on opposite sides of the Atlantic. This project would not have come to fruition without you. Thank you.

Contents

Abbreviations

ACLU	American Civil Liberties Union
AFN	American Forces Network
AFSC	American Friends Service Committee
AMZON	American Zone
AYA	Austrian Youth Activities
BBC	Bremen Boys Club
BDM	*Bund Deutscher Mädel* (League of German Girls)
CARE	Cooperative for American Remittances to Europe
CIC	Army Counter Intelligence Corps
CRALOG	Council of Relief Agencies Licensed to Operate in Germany
DP	Displaced Persons
DTA	Deutsches Tagebucharchiv (German Diary Archive), Emmendingen
ECA	European Cooperation Administration
ERP	European Recovery Program
EUCOM	United States European Command
FDJ	*Freie Deutsche Jugend* (Free German Youth)
FDP	*Freie Demokratische Partei* (Free Democratic Party)
FRG	Federal Republic of Germany
GDR	German Democratic Republic
GRFPL	Gerald R. Ford Presidential Library
GYA	German Youth Activities
HICOG	United States High Commission for Germany
HJ	*Hitlerjugend* (Hitler Youth)
HQ	Headquarters
HSTP	Harry S. Truman Papers
HSTPL	Harry S. Truman Presidential Library
ICD	Information Control Division
IRO	International Refugee Organization
JCS	Joint Chiefs of Staff
KGF	*Die Kampfgemeinschaft gegen den Faschismus* (Action Group against Fascism)
MG	Military Government
MP	Military Police
NACP	National Archives at College Park, Maryland
NASL	National Archives at St. Louis, Missouri
NATO	North Atlantic Treaty Organization
NSDAP	National Socialist German Workers' Party
NS	National Socialist, National Socialism
PBS	Public Broadcasting Service
POW	Prisoner of War
PSF	President's Secretary's Files, in Harry S. Truman Papers
PX	Post Exchange
OF	White House Central Files: Official File, in Harry S. Truman Papers
OKW	*Oberkommando der Wehrmacht* (Wehrmacht High Command)
OLV	Operation Little Vittles

https://doi.org/10.1515/9783111588155-204

OMGBR	Office of Military Government for Bremen
OMGBY	Office of Military Government for Bavaria
OMGH	Office of Military Government for Hesse
OMGUS	Office of Military Government, United States
OMGWB	Office of Military Government for Württemberg-Baden
RAF	Royal Air Force
RG	Record Group
SA	*Sturmabteilung* (Storm Troopers)
SPD	*Sozialdemokratische Partei Deutschlands* (Social Democratic Party)
SS	*Schutzstaffel* (Protection Squads)
UNICEF	United Nations Children's Fund
USAF	United States Air Force
USAHEC	United States Army Heritage and Education Center, Carlisle, PA
USFET	United States Forces European Theater
USIA	United States Information Agency
VD	Venereal Disease
VE	Victory in Europe
VHP	Veterans History Project, Library of Congress
WAC	Women's Army Corps
YMCA	Young Men's Christian Association

Illustrations

https://doi.org/10.1515/9783111588155-205

Introduction

For the first time in the history of the world a victor was willing to restore the vanquished as well as to help its allies.
–President Harry S. Truman[1]

In early June of 1945, Lieutenant Melvin J. Lasky, a combat historian in the Seventh Army, jotted down a scene in his diary that he observed in the rubble of occupied Nuremberg. It involved a leisurely American soldier (also known as a GI) and innocent looking German children, both of whom had become ubiquitous in the ruins of a devastated Germany in the aftermath of World War II. He wrote, "And there was the ineluctable pathos of the rubble; children playing in the ruins, a GI sitting in the skeleton of a bombed-out building, sitting in an improvised easy chair, reading a novel."[2] Lasky's diary entry depicted members of two groups who had a marked presence in the rubble of the German nation after the madness of the Third Reich: a soldier of the occupation forces, perched as conqueror among the wreckage, and German children, a visible remnant of a destroyed society left to deal with the lingering consequences of the war.

The American soldier was thus here to stay in the aftermath of World War II, with his casual pose marking his sense of belonging among the ruins of Germany in the American occupation zone.[3] German youngsters also made their mark on occupied Germany, and their presence in the postwar rubble went beyond that of silent victims of war. German children and youth fundamentally impacted occupation-era relations, playing a role in shaping policies in the American occupation zone as well as spurring wide-ranging, long-term impacts on transatlantic relations. Moreover, the postwar presence of both American occupiers and German youngsters led to interactions that shaped personal experiences of the occupation. Above all, these transatlantic and multi-generational encounters between Ameri-

1 Harry S. Truman, *Memoirs of Harry S. Truman: Years of Trial and Hope*, vol. 2 (Da Capo Press, 1956), 110.

2 Charlotte A. Lerg, ed., *The Diary of Lt. Melvin J. Lasky: Into Germany at the End of World War II* (Berghahn Books, 2023), 211. After his service as a combat historian for the Seventh Army, Melvin J. Lasky remained in Europe and became a prominent figure in the Cultural Cold War, publishing the intellectual magazines *Encounter* and *Der Monat*.

3 The American presence during the occupation was predominantly male, but there were also American female military personnel present, members of the Women's Army Corps (WAC), as well as American female civilians employed by the occupation forces and American military wives.

https://doi.org/10.1515/9783111588155-001

can soldiers and young Germans provide an important lens for examining the history of the American occupation zone.

Throughout the occupation, American military personnel came into contact with young Germans in diverse ways, including in informal situations such as chance encounters on the streets or living nearby as neighbors in German cities, towns, and villages. These interactions on the ground helped lead to shifts in the occupation sphere, as the occupation authorities increasingly realized that these informal encounters could be harnessed for official occupation purposes, including for reeducation and democratization. Moreover, friendly relations between Americans and Germans, including children and youth, helped contribute to the wider shift of occupation policies away from punitive measures toward embracing (West) Germans as friends and allies rather than enemies, a shift that then fit well with the emerging geopolitical situation of the Cold War. It was the youngest of Germans who played a fundamental role in this shift. Their postwar needs and desires shaped an image of Germans as innocents in need of aid, and also impacted individual Americans in their interactions with youngsters.

As American occupation policy moved away from punishment toward the rehabilitation of Germany, young Germans emerged as especially central figures within occupation navigations, seen as the future of a democratic (West) Germany. Occupation authorities thus increasingly encouraged encounters between Americans and young Germans, and the Army-sponsored German Youth Activities (GYA) program became a major occupation measure that aimed at teaching youngsters positive behaviors and democracy within the space of youth centers and youth clubs run by GI sponsors. Moreover, as the Cold War began to emerge, the focus on (West) German children and youth fit American geopolitical aims. American benevolence toward Germans (especially the youngest Germans) led to an infrastructure of German gratitude for American aid, which included CARE packages and a school feeding program, the *Schulspeisung*. The Berlin Airlift and the candy bombing initiative of Lieutenant Gail Halvorsen cemented this relationship, a moment in history that has become a staple in transatlantic collective memory practices, with reenactments continuing into the present day.[4] Placing the youngest of the German population as the central focus of the period thus enables a greater understanding of the everyday lived realities of occupation, as it highlights the complexity of navigations made between the occupiers and the occupied, and shows how this transatlantic exchange made an impact on both per-

4 On collective memory, see Jeffrey K. Olick, Vered Vinitzky-Seroussi, and Daniel Levy, eds., *The Collective Memory Reader* (Oxford University Press, 2011), 3–5. For a foundational text on collective memory, see Maurice Halbwachs, *On Collective Memory* (University of Chicago Press, 1992).

sonal and political levels. The encounter between the GI and the young German not only shaped individual experiences of the immediate postwar era in Germany for both GIs and young Germans but also fundamentally molded the face of the occupation.

This work digs into the layers of the lived realities of the American occupation that have been obscured behind dominant collective memory narratives. Overall, a success story has emerged about the postwar occupation of Germany, which seems to be proven by Germany's transformation into a strong democracy. This success story narrative tends to especially highlight the supposedly undoubted goodness of the American presence in postwar Germany, in the process transforming the complexities of occupation into a simplified narrative of the "good occupation."[5] This narrative shift has also occurred to a certain extent with World War II itself, as it has been transformed from the most devastating war in human history into the "good war" that has become "sanitized and romanticized almost beyond recognition," as literary scholar Paul Fussell argues.[6] Within the United States, a trend of nostalgia remains common in narratives of World War II, which glosses over the high costs of the war and the challenges of its aftermath, and often ignores the complex lived realities of combatants and civilians during the war.

The postwar American occupation of Germany has thus gained a purified and celebratory image. Susan L. Carruthers marks this shift a "radical reconstruction" of the image of the occupation, furthered by a focus on positive stories rather than on complexities such as "the boredom, bafflement, and boorishness that pervaded daily life for occupation's often reluctant foot soldiers."[7] Werner Sollors also notes that today's image of the occupation as a success has overshadowed the reality that in postwar Germany, "the temptation of despair was omni-

---

5 Susan L. Carruthers, *The Good Occupation: American Soldiers and the Hazards of Peace* (Harvard University Press, 2016), 5. President George W. Bush and his administration also referenced the success of the occupation of Germany as a means of building up support for the invasion of Iraq (1–2).

6 Paul Fussell, *Wartime: Understanding and Behavior in the Second World War* (Oxford University Press, 1989), ix. See also Thomas Childers, *Soldier from the War Returning: The Greatest Generation's Troubled Homecoming from World War II* (Houghton Mifflin Harcourt, 2009). For a more recent examination into the "good war," see Elizabeth D. Samet, *Looking for the Good War: American Amnesia and the Violent Pursuit of Happiness* (Farrar, Straus and Giroux, 2021). Samet argues, "World War II left behind the dangerous and seemingly indestructible fantasy that our military intervention will naturally produce (an often underappreciated) good. Each succeeding conflict has led to the reprise and reinvention of the Good War's mythology in order to justify or otherwise explain uses of American power" (9–10).

7 Carruthers, *The Good Occupation*, 311–312.

present and exerted quite a powerful pull." He argues that this reality is surprising "only in the retrospective glow of the success story."[8] Memory narratives about the American occupation tend to highlight positive, glowing stories including those that highlight the generosity showered upon young Germans by Americans, such as gifts of sweets, CARE packages, and the *Schulspeisung*. Popular narratives and images of the American occupation often focus on the friendliness of GIs, such as a friendly African American GI in a jeep handing out candy, or during the Berlin Airlift, children catching candy parachutes that dropped from American planes.[9] According to this rhetoric, the Allies (and most especially the Americans) had arrived in Germany as liberators from fascism, with the Eighth of May serving as a Day of Liberation, which continues to be celebrated today and linked to Western values such as freedom and democracy.[10] This selective focus on liber-

---

8 Werner Sollors, *The Temptation of Despair: Tales of the 1940s* (The Belknap Press of Harvard University Press, 2014), 5–6.

9 For an example in *Der Spiegel Geschichte*, see an interview with a contemporary witness, Diether Sieghart, who was a refugee from Upper Silesia who participated in GYA and worked as a newspaper boy for the Americans in Moosburg. "Mit der Seifenkiste zur Demokratie," *Der Spiegel Geschichte* 1 (2018), https://www.spiegel.de/geschichte/deutschland-nach-1945-wie-us-soldaten-deutsche-kinder-beeindruckten-a-1198446.html. Sieghart highlights the generosity of Americans, including gifts of sweets and the *Schulspeisung*. The introductory text notes that Sieghart learned how to love the "American way of life" as an 11-year-old. See also Petra Goedde, *GIs and Germans: Culture, Gender, and Foreign Relations, 1945–1949* (Yale University Press, 2003), 167. Petra Goedde notes that American soldiers giving candy to young Germans has "become as much a staple of German recollections about American GIs as the reception of CARE packages from the United States."

10 In a May 8, 2023 press release, Federal Government Commissioner for Culture and the Media of Germany Claudia Roth characterized the Eighth of May as an important day of liberation from the National Socialist reign of terror throughout Europe. She noted that the Eighth of May stands for the daily commitment to peace, freedom, democracy, and self-determination in a common, united Europe. See Die Bundesregierung, Presse- und Informationsamt der Bundesregierung (BPA), "Kulturstaatsministerin Claudia Roth zum Tag der Befreiung: '8. Mai steht für das notwendige Eintreten für Frieden, Freiheit, Demokratie und Selbstbestimmung in einem geeinten Europa,'" Pressemitteilung 93, May 8, 2023, https://www.bundesregierung.de/breg-de/service/archiv/kulturstaatsministerin-claudia-roth-zum-tag-der-befreiung-8-mai-steht-fuer-das-notwendige-eintreten-fuer-frieden-freiheit-demokratie-und-selbstbestimmung-in-einem-geeinten-europa–2188844 On May 8, 2023, the Brandenburger Tor in Berlin was illuminated in honor of the Day of Liberation, with the word "Danke," appearing in Russian, English, French, and German. See "08. Mai: Tag der Befreiung," Berlin.de: Das offizielle Hauptstadtportal, May 8, 2023, https://www.berlin.de/kultur-und-tickets/tipps/tag-der-befreiung/. May 8, 2025 was designated as an official holiday in Berlin to mark the eightieth anniversary of liberation from National Socialism and the end of World War II. See "Einmaliger Feiertag am 8. Mai 2025," Berlin.de: Das offizielle Hauptstadtportal, September 26, 2024, https://www.berlin.de/aktuelles/9188766-958090-einmaliger-feiertag-am-8-mai-2025.html.

ation is represented in the ubiquitous occupation encounter of the American soldier and the German child, which has become a common trope about the era. This encounter seems to portray the benevolent role of American occupiers, who were handing out Hershey bars to German children and providing helpful guidance to Germans on reorienting towards democracy.

A focus on encounters between German children and GIs proves particularly powerful today, as it appears to provide a sense of proof that World War II was worth the fight, since it rescued the youngest of the Germans from Nazism and sent them in the direction of democracy. In addition, such success stories imply that the American presence denoted that a new, fresh postwar era had dawned in Germany, one in which the horrors of the war and complicated grappling with the crimes of the Holocaust were left behind. In its place, Germany had become a land where a benevolent soldier could ensure that innocent children, including the children of the former enemy, were not denied a sweet, simple pleasure of life, such as chocolate or chewing gum, as (West) Germany moved on a straight line toward its democratic future. This implies that the encounter between the GI and the child represented all that was possible during *Stunde Null*, zero hour. Moreover, focusing on the benevolence of GIs toward youngsters furthers narratives of the occupation as a time of goodness, in which Americans acted with kindness towards the youngest members of the former enemy population who had caused the horror in the first place. According to such narratives, Americans active in the postwar occupation seemed to be continuing their duties and sacrifices as part of the "Greatest Generation."[11]

Although young Germans serve a prominent role in present-day memory culture about the occupation, their actual lived experiences have received little consideration, including in historical research. This work aims to complicate the dominant success story narrative by centering everyday experiences of both the occupiers and the youngest of the occupied, focusing on the wide range of their experiences during the time. The American occupation was more than just a time of goodness; it proved often quite chaotic and complex, a reality that can be grasped at through examining the folds of daily life.[12] Lived experiences of the occupation thus complicate present-day collective memory and its simplified version of the postwar occupation of Germany. Interactions between American mili-

---

11 See Tom Brokaw, *The Greatest Generation*, Random House trade pbk. ed. (Random House Trade Paperbacks, 2005), xi-xii.

12 See John Willoughby, *Remaking the Conquering Heroes: The Social and Geopolitical Impact of the Post-War American Occupation of Germany* (Palgrave, 2001), 5–6.

tary personnel and young Germans did indeed frequently occur during the American occupation, but it is essential to move beyond simplistic narratives that focus on the supposedly undoubted success, greatness, and goodness of the occupation and its occupiers. Instead, a deeper examination of interactions between American occupation personnel and German youngsters provides a sharper view into the complex transition period of the occupation. Rather than serving as silent players, for example in the trope of the benevolent GI gifting chocolate to an innocent child, both Americans active in the occupation and German children need to be considered as important historical actors who documented the interactions with each other in materials ranging from diaries to drawings. In the background of kind gestures lurks a more complex reality, one of both sides undergoing ambivalent navigations made in the rubble of ruined cities and towns. Young Germans carved their own mindsets and interpretations about the occupiers, their behaviors, and their policies. Americans also viewed young Germans in diverse ways, not always merely as innocent victims in need of gifts of benevolence. Above all, although the kindness of American soldiers toward young Germans was undoubtedly often very real, the lived realities of the time highlight a more complicated story.

Moreover, not all encounters between Americans and Germans were unequivocally positive within the power structure of the occupation. The occupation was a time in which Americans had power over Germans of all ages, including in a gendered context through a masculine military government run by victorious occupiers.[13] According to Petra Goedde, "American power over Germans extended from the military government's ability to set policy and appoint political officials in the American zone to the relationships between individual soldiers and German civilians." GIs provided a masculine presence, filling the void left behind by the shortage of German men and stepping into the role of paternal provider. Goedde argues, "Women and children were often more willing to accept the presence of American soldiers, in part because they benefited most from the GIs' relative economic wealth, but also because the soldiers' presence did not challenge their role within German society." Eventually, Goedde notes, postwar (West) Germany took on a new identity "of a feminized, victimized, and most importantly pacific, client state."[14] Within this framework of the hierarchies of a society under military occupation, GIs and Germans encountered each other in a wide range of ways, which could also include fraternization in a sexual context with unequal

13 See Heide Fehrenbach, "Rehabilitating Fatherland: Race and German Remasculinization," *Signs* 24, no. 1 (Autumn 1998): 109, http://www.jstor.org/stable/3175674.
14 Goedde, *GIs and Germans*, xxi–xxiii. On GIs as paternal providers, see Goedde, 149, 164.

power dynamics. Fraternization between GIs and German women, although banned in the first months of occupation, took place at extremely high levels, and was mostly of a sexual nature. German women, including young women such as teenagers, experienced everyday life within this highly sexualized terrain in which the occupiers had access to material plenty (and thus easy access to women's bodies), which stood in stark contrast to the deprivations that the occupied German civilians faced. Within this sexualized landscape, Germans had to navigate power structures and negotiate for their needs. For example, some German women traded sexual favors or provided non-sexual services such as washing clothes in order to get access to more food or other goods, navigating complexities including hierarchies of unequal power and hunger, desire, and need.[15] Moreover, German children and youth navigated the power dynamics of occupation in diverse situations, for example in informal contexts such as begging GIs for chocolate that they could later trade on the black market, or in formal spaces such as in American-sponsored youth clubs, where American occupiers served as providers of material benefits as well as mentors.

Overall, the occupation led to shifts in what was considered acceptable behavior in German society, with morally ambivalent practices taking place such as German women having sexual relations with GIs in exchange for goods, or youth participation in the black market, behaviors that often were linked to German attempts to provide for their needs.[16] The occupation authorities aimed to push back against this moral ambivalence, and for example encouraged young Germans to behave properly, as they were seen as both the future hope and as a problem group. Occupation attempts to reeducate young Germans into future democratic citizens aimed at simultaneously decreasing juvenile delinquency and bringing about societal order.[17] For example, this meant encouraging participation in youth clubs (in GYA or in German-run clubs such as religious or trade union clubs), where youngsters could participate in positive activities, including music, sports, and civic engagement. Moreover, for the authorities, proper behav-

---

15 See Atina Grossmann, *Jews, Germans, and Allies: Close Encounters in Occupied Germany* (Princeton University Press, 2007), 70–72, 76, 79; Petra Goedde, "Gender, Race, and Power: American Soldiers and the German Population," in *The United States and Germany in the Era of the Cold War, 1945–1990: A Handbook*, Volume 1, ed. Detlef Junker (Cambridge University Press, 2004), 516. On the concept of "sexual barter" taking place within the hierarchies of the ghetto society of Theresienstadt, see Anna Hájková, "Sexual Barter in Times of Genocide: Negotiating the Sexual Economy of the Theresienstadt Ghetto," *Signs* 38, no. 3 (Spring 2013): 503–533, https://doi.org/10.1086/668607.

16 See Paul Steege, *Black Market, Cold War: Everyday Life in Berlin 1946–1949* (Cambridge University Press, 2007), 121–124. Also, Hájková, 525.

17 See Goedde, *GIs and Germans*, 127.

ior meant engaging in non-sexual activities. This also extended to GIs, who for example were encouraged to take part in GYA as a positive form of fraternization in contrast to sexual relations with German women, highlighting the attempts of the authorities to regain a sense of order and bring about the rebuilding of morals in postwar occupation society.[18] Encounters between Americans and Germans took place within constant navigations of power and control among the occupiers and the occupied in a postwar society under transition. The lives of young Germans were thus caught up within the wider context of the power structures and hierarchies of occupation.

This study places the everyday experiences of children and youth at the center of examining the history of the US occupation zone. It focuses on the multilayered experiences of young Germans and their contributions to the American occupation on personal and political levels, as well as the ways in which they came up against the contradictions and ambivalences of the time. Overall, the category of age was of major relevance during the occupation. The work considers the everyday experiences of young Germans of a range of ages, from young children to young adults. Moreover, this study will use various terms to describe young Germans, including children, youth, youngsters, and young people, unless a specific focus is on a certain term in original source material or regarding certain occupation policies and developments. For example, clubs were specifically designed for German youth (usually for those Germans around ten to eighteen years old). In addition, juvenile delinquency was frequently referred to as a major societal issue during the occupation. The term "teenager" will also be used in this book, although it was not yet in common usage in the late 1940s.

---

18 See Willoughby, *Remaking the Conquering Heroes*, 113–114; Martin Kalb, *Coming of Age: Constructing and Controlling Youth in Munich, 1942–1973* (Berghahn Books, 2016), 17–54; Jennifer V. Evans, *Life among the Ruins: Cityscape and Sexuality in Cold War Berlin* (Palgrave Macmillan, 2011). Evans's work looks into the intersections of sexualities, modernity, and anxieties about social control in postwar Berlin. Her work focuses on "moral rebuilding as linked to the process of policing encounters in the various spaces where men, women, and youths came into contact with one another, and where transactions often ensued of a distinctly (if not overtly) sexual character." She notes that this policing ascribed "distinctions between 'good' and 'bad' sexual practices and identities," and served to form a "foundation for heterosexuality as a supposedly natural condition of successful social and political rebuilding" (13). For more on policing male sex in postwar Berlin, including intergenerational sex, see Jennifer V. Evans, "Bahnhof Boys: Policing Male Prostitution in Post-Nazi Berlin," *Journal of the History of Sexuality* 12, no. 4 (October 2003): 605–635, https://doi.org/10.1353/sex.2004.0026.

On Occupation and Age

The American occupation of Germany included an infrastructure of official policies that impacted the daily existence of German youngsters, ranging from rationing levels based on age groups, denazification, and an initial ban on fraternization to reeducation. These policies were part of official plans for the governance of Germany after the war. At the end of the war, the Allies divided the former enemy nation into four occupation zones: American, British, French, and Soviet. The American zone included the states of Bavaria, Greater Hesse, and Württemberg-Baden, as well as the American sector of Berlin and the Bremen Enclave. At the Potsdam Conference in July and August 1945, the Allies established the Four Ds as the basis for occupation policies: demilitarization, denazification, decentralization, and democratization.[19] In the US zone of occupation, the American military served as the supreme power. Military government was administered through the Office of Military Government, United States (OMGUS), a structure with a military governor at its head, which lasted until the official establishment of the West German state, the Federal Republic of Germany (FRG), in 1949.[20]

After the end of military government in the Western Allies' zones of occupation, the Allied High Commission through the United States, Great Britain, and France took over supervision of the new state. American participation was handled by the US State Department through a civilian US High Commission for Germany (HICOG). The FRG was not yet a fully sovereign state, as an occupation statute continued to apply, lasting until May 1955, when it expired and the United States established formal political relations with the FRG through the US embassy in Bonn.[21] John J. McCloy, who served as the first US High Commissioner for Germany, described the circumstances of the role of the occupation's military gover-

19 Decartelization was another aim of the Allies.

20 The Soviet zone of occupation became the German Democratic Republic (GDR) in 1949, known as East Germany, which lasted until German reunification on October 3, 1990. For more on OMGUS and its structure, see *OMGUS-Handbuch: Die amerikanische Militärregierung in Deutschland 1945–1949*, ed. Christoph Weisz (Oldenbourg, 1994), https://doi.org/10.1524/9783486587777; Earl F. Ziemke, *The U.S. Army in the Occupation of Germany 1944–1946*, Army Historical Series (Center for Military History, United States Army, 1990), 425–443, https://purl.fdlp.gov/GPO/LPS33225. Military governors included General of the Army Dwight D. Eisenhower, General George S. Patton, General Joseph T. McNarney, General Lucius D. Clay, and Lieutenant General Clarence R. Huebner.

21 Carruthers, *The Good Occupation*, 7; Adam R. Seipp, "Donuts, Cab Drivers, and Gold Rush Towns: Germans Encounter the US Army, 1945–1952," in *The Berlin Airlift and the Making of the Cold War*, ed. John M. Schuessler, Adam R. Seipp, and Thomas D. Sullivan (Texas A&M Press, 2022), 126.

nor as "a pretty heady job. It was the nearest thing to a Roman proconsulship the modern world afforded . . . It was a challenging job to an ambitious man. Benevolent despotism."[22]

American occupation policies were modeled on Joint Chiefs of Staff (JCS) directive 1067 from April 1945, which was largely based on the plan of Treasury Secretary Henry Morgenthau Jr.[23] Overall, JCS 1067 aimed at punitive measures, including ensuring that the living standard for Germans would remain below that of its neighboring countries. The directive noted that "Germany will not be occupied for the purpose of liberation but as a defeated enemy nation." In addition, the directive stated, "The principal Allied objective is to prevent Germany from ever again becoming a threat to the peace of the world." The text highlighted that the destruction of the German economy and the inevitable suffering and chaos that emerged was caused by the Germans themselves due to their "ruthless warfare and the fanatical Nazi resistance." Germans, thus, were responsible for facing the consequences of their warmongering, destruction, and fanaticism, and the Allies were present as occupiers to impose a new system that would prevent Germany's powerful rise again. For the world's safety, Germans could not be allowed to create a new system on their own.[24] Early official American occupation rhetoric and policies emphasized collective guilt, claiming that all Germans were undoubtedly guilty, including the youngest of the Germans.[25] These policies remained officially in effect in the US zone until July 1947, when a new directive, JCS 1779, was released. This directive reflected the shift that had already been occurring in the American occupation sphere, with official policies moving away from punishment toward the rehabilitation of Germany into a democratic state,

22 Jean Edward Smith, ed., *The Papers of General Lucius D. Clay: Germany 1945–1949*, vol. 1 (Indiana University Press, 1974), xxv. General Lucius D. Clay served as deputy military governor from 1945 to 1947, then as military governor from 1947 to 1949. For more on John J. McCloy and his wide-ranging influence on postwar American foreign policy towards Germany, see Thomas Alan Schwartz, *America's Germany: John J. McCloy and the Federal Republic of Germany* (Harvard University Press, 1991).

23 The Morgenthau Plan focused on the punishment of Germans for the war and Nazism, and even aimed at pastoralizing Germany into an agrarian state so it would never again be a threat to the world. See "Program to Prevent Germany from starting a World War III," in Henry Morgenthau, *Germany is Our Problem* (Harper & Brothers Publishers, 1945).

24 JCS 1067, in Carl J. Friedrich and Associates, *American Experiences in Military Government in World War II* (Rinehart, 1948), 381–402.

25 For more on collective guilt, see Karl Jaspers, *Die Schuldfrage: Von der politischen Haftung Deutschlands* (Piper, 2012).

and focusing on "a stable and productive Germany," which could contribute to order and prosperity in Europe as a whole.[26]

For many German civilians, Americans emerged as the preferred occupiers among the four Allies, especially in comparison to the Soviets. The results of an official OMGUS survey from October 29, 1947 indicated that "of the four Allies, the Germans most trusted the United States to treat Germany fairly." In addition, "an overwhelming number of AMZON [American zone] Germans (84%) would have picked the United States as an occupying power if history could have been turned back." Respondents also believed that they were better off in the American zone than Germans in the other three zones.[27] This survey, taken after the official shift in policies toward rehabilitation rather than punishment, perhaps reflects the increasing role of friendly relations between (West) Germans and Americans, in which Germans were seen as allies rather than enemies within a few years after the end of the war.

Overall, encouraging encounters between young Germans and American soldiers was not an official part of the initial Allied planning for the occupation of Germany after World War II. Moreover, in the first months of occupation, these encounters were even illegal, as a fraternization ban was in place between American soldiers and German civilians, including children. The ban was put in place to help protect occupation soldiers from potential German sabotage, subversion, and resistance, as well as to serve to punish Germans and point out their total defeat. The policy was also meant to prevent German propaganda from influencing the minds of individual occupation soldiers. In addition, military planners be-

---

26 JCS 1779, in Friedrich and Associates, *American Experiences in Military Government in World War II*, 402–415. By the time JCS 1779 was released, the occupation had already shifted away from punitive policies on the ground, especially after Secretary of State James F. Byrnes gave the Stuttgart Speech, known as the "Speech of Hope," on September 6, 1946. Byrnes's speech highlighted the policy shifts in the American occupation away from punitive toward reconstruction and presented the prospect that Germans would one day regain authority over their domestic affairs and form their own government on a democratic basis. "Stuttgart Speech ('Speech of Hope') by James F. Byrnes, United States Secretary of State (September 6, 1946)," in *Occupation and the Emergence of Two States, 1945–1961*, ed. Volker Berghahn and Uta Poiger, volume 8, German History in Documents and Images, German Historical Institute, Washington, DC, https://ghdi.ghi-dc.org/pdf/eng/Allied%20Policies%209%20ENG1.pdf.

27 See Report No. 76 (October 29, 1947) in Anna J. Merritt and Richard L. Merritt, eds., *Public Opinion in Occupied Germany: The OMGUS Surveys, 1945–1949* (University of Illinois Press, 1970), 180–181. See also Richard L. Merritt, *Democracy Imposed: U.S. Occupation Policy and the German Public, 1945–1949* (Yale University Press, 1995), 260.

lieved that nonfraternization could evoke respect from Germans, who would be impressed by the aloofness of the American troops.[28]

Being friendly to Germans, including children, was contrary to the initial punitive aims of the occupation, and such encounters were even seen as dangerous and worrisome. Early plans for the postwar occupation assumed that German civilians would not easily lay down their arms and give up their seeming propensity toward militarism and authoritarianism. Moreover, Americans worried about whether the German mindset and their "alarming" behavior could even be cured.[29] German youngsters were seen as especially dangerous, as they had grown up only knowing life under the National Socialist regime, and they had been indoctrinated in Nazi values in the *Hitlerjugend* (HJ) or the *Bund Deutscher Mädel* (BDM). Allied troops anticipated facing heavy German resistance at the immediate end of the war, including stiff fights by *Werwolf* resistance groups, made up of fanatical Hitler Youth and SS members. Initial occupation polices such as nonfraternization were put in place upon the basis of the assumption that the safety of the occupiers would constantly be in danger, including due to indoctrinated youngsters who grew up during the Nazi regime.[30]

However, these predictions about civilian resistance did not become a reality, and troops were surprised at the lack of fight that ordinary Germans put up. Instead, during the occupation, most Germans tended to focus on getting their daily needs met, and they largely came to accept that cooperation was the best option for them.[31] By and large, although there were isolated instances of sabotage, they did not fundamentally impact the occupation, and fraternization between the population and troops occurred at increasing levels.[32] Americans at home sup-

---

28 See a detailed list of reasons for the nonfraternization policy in Joseph R. Starr, *Fraternization with the Germans in World War II* (Office of the Chief Historian, European Command, 1947), 10–14. See also Goedde, *GIs and Germans*, 45–46; Ann Elizabeth Pfau, *Miss Yourlovin: GIs, Gender, and Domesticity during World War II* (Columbia University Press, 2008), 5, http://www.gutenberg-e.org/pfau/.

29 Richard M. Brickner, *Is Germany Incurable?* (J.B. Lippincott Co., 1943); Richard M. Brickner, "Is Germany Incurable?" *The Atlantic*, March 1943, 84–93; Richard M. Brickner, "Is Germany Incurable? The Treatment," *The Atlantic*, April 1943, 94–98.

30 See Pfau, *Miss Yourlovin*, 5.

31 Merritt, *Democracy Imposed*, 268–269.

32 Merritt, *Democracy Imposed*, 239. See also Perry Biddiscombe, *Werwolf!: The History of the National Socialist Guerrilla Movement, 1944–1946* (University of Toronto Press, 1998). Biddiscombe notes that there was indeed some *Werwolf*-fueled resistance. One major act of resistance conducted by SS and Hitler Youth members was the shooting of the American-appointed mayor of Aachen, Franz Oppenhoff, in March 1945. See Gerhard Rempel, *Hitler's Children: The Hitler Youth and the SS* (University of North Carolina Press, 1989), 244–245.

ported the fraternization ban, and reports of friendly GIs and German civilians mingling as early as September 1944 caused uproar within the United States.[33] However, the ban soon became a nightmare for American public relations due to the lack of adherence to the policy on the ground, especially regarding fraternization between German women and GIs, which reached extremely high levels after the war was over. In June 1945, the policy was overturned for troop fraternization with small children (no specific age was given, and thus the term "children" was interpreted widely, defeating the purpose of continuing to have a nonfraternization policy in force, according to an official United States European Command (EUCOM) report).[34] By October 1, 1945, the policy was completely abandoned, allowing fraternization with Germans of all ages.[35] Overall, as the occupation progressed and shifted away from punitive policies, young Germans were no longer seen as dangerous elements, but as a group that could even help aid the occupation and its increasingly forward-looking aims.

In addition, the Allies crafted policies that defined age and innocence under denazification procedures, with a Youth Amnesty enacted in the American, British, and French zones. In the American zone, beginning in August 1946, anyone born after January 1, 1919 was released from denazification procedures, which included bureaucratic measures such as filling out a questionnaire (known as the *Fragebogen*) and potentially attending a tribunal. The amnesty applied to all young Germans born after that date unless they were chargeable under the categories of "Major Offenders" or "Offenders." Together with the 1946 Christmas Amnesty in the US zone, which released Germans of low income and those with a disability of at least 50%, the amnesties greatly reduced the number of Germans still being processed under denazification, with over two million people coming under the amnesties by June 1, 1948.[36] Thus, young Germans who were affected

---

33 Pfau, *Miss Yourlovin*, 1; Ziemke, *The U.S. Army in the Occupation*, 97–99. See Henry T. Gorrell, "Hostility of Some Waning," *New York Times*, September 16, 1944. See also photograph of a German family gathering around a jeep: "As American First Army Entered Soil of the Reich," *New York Times*, September 17, 1944.

34 Starr, *Fraternization with the Germans in World War II*, 93–95.

35 Starr, 2; Ziemke, *The U.S. Army in the Occupation*, 322–327.

36 See OMGUS, "Denazification (Cumulative Review), Report of the Military Governor no. 34, 1 April 1947–30 April 1948," 5, Germany under Reconstruction, University of Wisconsin-Madison Libraries, https://search.library.wisc.edu/digital/ANFEGQAS34M52B8R; "The Present Status of Denazification (December 31, 1950)," in *Occupation and the Emergence of Two States, 1945–1961*, ed. Berghahn and Poiger, volume 8, German History in Documents and Images, German Historical Institute, Washington, DC, 3–4, https://ghdi.ghi-dc.org/pdf/eng/Denazification%203ENG.pdf. Also, James F. Tent, *Mission on the Rhine: Reeducation and Denazification in American-Occupied Germany* (University of Chicago Press, 1982), 68, 98–99. For an overview of the *Fragebogen* and its

by the Youth Amnesty would have included young adults up to 26 years old at the end of the war. This policy was significant to the everyday lives of young Germans, marking levels of culpability for Nazism by age.

The Youth Amnesty illustrates the shifting logic of official occupation policies, which increasingly saw German youth as an audience for its efforts. By mid-1946, it had become more important to focus on the reeducation of young Germans toward democracy rather than require them to go through occupation denazification processes. The majority of young Germans were thus seen as not at fault for coming of age and only knowing life under National Socialism. This contrasted with earlier occupation rhetoric, which marked all youngsters as potential dangers and as part of a collectively guilty Germany. A July 1946 article in the *New York Times* included a statement from Deputy Military Governor Lucius D. Clay, who declared:

> It is the desire of the United States military government in Germany to offer encouragement to the youth of Germany to understand and to develop a democratic way of life, which was denied to them under the Nazi regime. We are fully aware of the insidious indoctrination in Nazi ideology to which this age group was subjected during its impressionable years. We expect the penalties fixed under the law for Class 1 and Class 2 offenders to provide punishment for those in this age group who were eager to accept the Nazi ideology and to assist in fostering its growth and power among the German people.[37]

Clay's statement highlights the shift of the occupation's focus, which increasingly aimed to reeducate youngsters, turning them toward the democratic way of life. The official focus of occupation policies regarding youth thus shifted by mid-1946 toward the rehabilitation of the vast majority of German youth who had been indoctrinated yet were not high-level offenders who had profited from or played a leading role in Nazism. Occupation authorities saw German youth increasingly as a potentially highly receptive audience for their aims. They realized that American interactions with youth could be used "as a tool of re-education," as Petra Goedde argues. Goedde notes how the authorities aimed to "regain control over the process of interaction" between American soldiers and German youth.[38] This played a role in the official decision to create the Army Assistance to German Youth Activities (GYA) program beginning in April 1946.[39] Interactions between

impacts on everyday lives in the occupation, see Mikkel Dack, *Everyday Denazification in Postwar Germany: The Fragebogen and Political Screening during the Allied Occupation* (Cambridge University Press, 2023), https://doi.org/10.1017/9781009216326.

37 Kathleen McLaughlin, "U.S. Gives Amnesty to Youth Germans," *New York Times*, July 3, 1946.

38 Goedde, *GIs and Germans*, 130, 137.

39 Youth clubs were not a new phenomenon in Germany. Before 1933, a strong tradition of youth organizations had developed, which included youth groups of political parties, churches,

Americans and Germans were thus co-opted for their potential as a means of re-education, taking on a central role in official occupation policies. Encounters between German youngsters and Americans, which had been occurring since the first moments of contact despite the initial fraternization ban, became a major part of the occupation.

Overall, young Germans' lives were wrapped up in the circumstances of the occupation and were impacted by their previous wartime experiences, which were dependent on their age at the time. The generation born under National Socialism and shortly before had a unique and challenging role in postwar German society. As Rolf Schörken notes, they were too young to have had voted for Hitler, too young to have had a major influence in German politics or the military, and thus had only really known Nazi Germany.[40] Age therefore determined not only the shape of experiences during the period of Nazism, such as membership in the Hitler Youth or the BDM, but also marked the level of exposure to violence and indoctrination. Recently, various categorizations of a German generation with similar experiences of growing up under National Socialism and war have emerged, such as the Hitler Youth generation or the *Flakhelfer* generation, those born between 1926 and 1929, who were recruited in the last years of the war to assist the Luftwaffe, a task which became increasingly dangerous in the last weeks of the war.[41] Germans born in 1929 had the potential to experience significant roles in the war years, as they were ten years old in 1939, when membership in Hitler Youth organizations became mandatory for all Germans between ten and 18, and then were 16 years old at the end of the war, thus able to serve as

and more. Many organizations tended to be nationalistic and increasingly militaristic. In addition, there was a strong youth movement in the early twentieth century, including the *Wandervogel*, which focused especially on outdoor activities such as hiking. See Helen Liddell, "Education in Occupied Germany: A Field Study," *International Affairs* 21, no. 1 (January 1948): 33–34, https://doi.org/10.2307/3016951. See also Dirk Schumann, "Introduction: Child-Rearing and Citizenship in the Twentieth Century," in *Raising Citizens in the "Century of the Child": The United States and German Central Europe in Comparative Perspective*, ed. Dirk Schumann (Berghahn Books, 2010), 8. Schumann argues that the youth movement was "politically highly ambiguous" and that "this attempt at developing youth's own agency led many participants to volunteer as soldiers in 1914 and later on to join the ranks of the National Socialists." See also Walter Laqueur, *Young Germany: A History of the German Youth Movement* (Basic Books, 1962).

40 Rolf Schörken, *Die Niederlage als Generationserfahrung: Jugendliche nach dem Zusammenbruch der NS-Herrschaft* (Juventa, 2004), 21. See also David Phillips, *Educating the Germans: People and Policy in the British Zone of Germany, 1945–1949* (Bloomsbury Academic, 2018), 147–148.

41 See Malte Herwig, *Die Flakhelfer: Wie aus Hitlers jüngsten Parteimitgliedern Deutschlands führende Demokraten wurden* (Deutsche Verlags-Anstalt, 2013).

Flakhelfer or in the *Volkssturm*.[42] Many of the young Germans in this work did grow up within the context of National Socialism and played a role in the fascist system in various ways, such as taking part in Hitler Youth activities. Depending on their age, they also had various levels of awareness of Nazism and participation in Nazi wartime efforts. With this in mind, however, the focus of this work is on the complexities of a broad range of young Germans' experiences in postwar interactions with Americans and shifts in official occupation policies, rather than on drawing wide-reaching conclusions about common generational experiences.

Age is a shifting category based on societal needs, including for wartime purposes. In addition, young people themselves could use age to serve their own purposes. For example, underage boys who wished to serve in World War II sometimes lied about their ages while enlisting. In 1942, the draft age in the United States was lowered from 21 to 18, sending countless young adult males into the battlefield, although boys had already often historically been used to serve in armies in various wars, including in the American Revolutionary War and the Civil War.[43] Paul Fussell examines the nature of age and combat, citing Herman Melville, who in 1861 wrote, "All wars are boyish, and are fought by boys" in his poem "The March into Virginia."[44] Fussell argues that "war must thus rely on the young, for only they have the two things fighting requires: physical stamina and innocence about their own mortality . . . Knowledge will come after a few months, and then they'll be used up and as soldiers virtually useless—scared, cynical, debilitated, unwilling."[45] The phenomenon of the militarization and mobilization of youth thus reached high levels in World War II. In Germany in August 1944, 70% of German 16-year-old Hitler Youth members signed up for military service in response to a call from Artur Axmann, Reich Hitler Youth

---

42 See Mary Fulbrook, "'Normalisation' in the GDR in Retrospect: East German Perspectives on Their Own Lives,'" in *Power and Society in the GDR, 1961–1979: The 'Normalisation of Rule'?*, ed. Mary Fulbrook (Berghahn Books, 2009), 288–289, 292.

43 See Caroline Cox, *Boy Soldiers of the American Revolution* (University of North Carolina Press, 2016); James Marten, ed., *Children and Youth during the Civil War Era* (New York University Press, 2012). Interestingly, not until July 1971, with the ratification of the Twenty-Sixth Amendment, was the voting age lowered from 21 to 18. The lowering of the draft age in 1942 quickly led to the birth of the slogan, "Old enough to fight, old enough to vote." See Gemma R. Birnbaum, "'Old Enough to Fight, Old Enough to Vote': The WWII Roots of the 26th Amendment," The National WWII Museum, October 28, 2020, https://www.nationalww2museum.org/war/articles/voting-age-26th-amendment

44 Herman Melville, "The March into Virginia Ending in the First Manassas (July, 1861)," quoted in Fussell, *Wartime*, 52.

45 Fussell, *Wartime*, 52.

Leader. This followed in October 1944 with mandatory service in the *Volkssturm* for those 16 and older.[46]

This work centers on the intersections of childhood and war, highlighting the tensions between militarized societies and modern notions of a protected childhood based on conceptions of age. Age is not simply a number: as Corinne T. Field and Nicholas L. Syrett point out, age is "both a biological reality and a social construction."[47] In their work on modern warfare and childhood, Mischa Honeck and James Marten highlight that a paradox of modern societies is that a central aim is to protect children from harm, yet also "to integrate them into the body politic," which may even include mobilization of children for war.[48] Thus, they argue, "modern warfare would not have been possible without modern childhood," noting that children served not only as victims of war but as "future citizens, as future defenders, as one of the objects about which wars were fought, and as one of the resources for fighting them."[49] Honeck and Aaron William Moore have explored the diverse range of children's wartime and postwar experiences, noting that it was adult decisions that sometimes caused children to become "soldiers, evacuees, refugees, orphans," despite simultaneous "discourses that celebrate young people as precious or invaluable for the future."[50] During World War II, American children were also actively encouraged to help out on the home front, highlighting the all-encompassing nature of the war in American society.[51] With such an active militarization of youngsters common during the war and the war's often brutal consequences impacting youngsters' lives throughout the world, childhood was hardly the protected status it was claimed to be.

46 Nicholas Stargardt, *Witnesses of War: Children's Lives Under the Nazis* (Alfred A. Knopf, 2006), 290.
47 Corinne T. Field and Nicholas L. Syrett, "Introduction," in *Age in America: The Colonial Era to the Present*, ed. Corinne T. Field and Nicholas L. Syrett (New York University Press, 2015), 1. See also Howard P. Chudacoff, *How Old Are You? Age Consciousness in American Culture* (Princeton University Press, 1989).
48 Mischa Honeck and James Marten, "More than Victims: Framing the History of Modern Childhood and War," in *War and Childhood in the Era of the Two World Wars*, ed. Mischa Honeck and James Marten (Cambridge University Press, 2019), 1–4.
49 Honeck and Marten, "More than Victims," 14.
50 Mischa Honeck and Aaron William Moore, "War and Conflict," in *A Cultural History of Youth in the Modern Age*, ed. Kristine Alexander and Simon Sleight (Bloomsbury Academic, 2022), 211–212, https://doi.org/10.5040/9781350033085. On missing, lost, and displaced German children after World War II, see Michelle Mouton, "Missing, Lost, and Displaced Children in Postwar Germany: The Great Struggle to Provide for the War's Youngest Victims," *Central European History* 48, no. 1 (March 2015): 53–78, https://doi.org/10.1017/S0008938915000035.
51 See William M. Tuttle, *Daddy's Gone to War: The Second World War in the Lives of American Children* (Oxford University Press, 1993).

The war also disrupted the system of knowledge about age, highlighting its fragility despite its centrality to modern Western societies. After the war, restoring this system of the certainty of age enabled nation states and humanitarian organizations to attempt to rebuild postwar normalcy.[52]

This study acknowledges the significance of age for occupation policies such as nonfraternization, denazification, and reeducation, in addition to influencing on-the-ground, personal reactions of Americans toward Germans. American soldiers behaved in ways that were dependent on the age of the Germans they encountered, with younger German children and youth often spurring American soldiers' desire to help or give a gift of candy. In addition, the age of the Americans themselves may have impacted their relations with German youngsters, with younger men perhaps reacting in a way that yearned for a sense of boyhood to ease the tensions of grappling with the aftermath of a terrible war. In addition, American men who had their own families at home perhaps wished to take on a fatherly role towards the young Germans they encountered to provide a temporary substitute for their children back home. Above all, in the postwar era, German children and youth experienced the occupation in ways that were shaped by their age at the time and by their wartime experiences, which influenced the level of understanding about what they were witnessing. Even the youngest German children could be aware of occupation circumstances that affected their daily lives, such as the presence of American soldiers. The category of age during the occupation thus molded both personal experiences and occupation policies.

A New Approach to the History of the Occupation of Post-World War II Germany

Overall, this book takes a multilayered approach to explore the role of German children and youth during the US military occupation of Germany after World War II, using the lens of cultural history to attempt to capture a glimpse of lived realities and cultural dynamics during the period of the occupation. In addition, it blends this approach with the history of children and youth, *Alltagsgeschichte* (the history of everyday life), occupation studies, and new military history. Taking this combined path merges the everyday experiences of children with the context

52 Antoine Burgard, "Contested Childhood: Assessing the Age of Young Refugees in the Aftermath of the Second World War," *History Workshop Journal* 92 (Autumn 2021): 174, https://doi.org/10.1093/hwj/dbab016. Burgard explores the fluidity of the category of age during the aftermath of World War II, including the lack of clarity about the age of displaced persons (DP) child survivors.

of a military occupation, providing a new look into a postwar society. This work thus takes on an innovative approach to explore the sphere of the US military occupation of Germany, also examining the experiences of ordinary occupation soldiers and highlighting the interactions of these military personnel with young German civilians. Above all, it centers young Germans' roles in the immediate postwar era in Germany.

This study thus contributes to the field of new military history through its approach of linking everyday cultural dynamics and the history of children within a postwar occupation landscape. New military history denotes the decades-long attempt to bring innovation to the field of military history, moving beyond a focus on analyzing battlefield operations towards an examination of the intersections of war and society, such as military-civilian relations.[53] In addition, this work marks the occupation of Germany as a specific historical period in need of deep examination, following the work of scholars in the emerging field of occupation studies, who highlight the importance of looking into "military occupation as a subject in its own right," as Camilo Ehrlichman and Christopher Knowles argue.[54] Examining the power structures and the relations on the ground between foreign occupiers and the occupied population portrays the complexities of everyday relations in a dynamic time period, providing a glimpse into lived realities.[55]

Within the United States during the 1940s, the idea of a military occupation of a foreign country was not without debate. The concept of conducting an occupation made some Americans uncomfortable due to its imperial-seeming nature and its requirement of a large standing army. With its anti-colonial past, many Americans distrusted these factors, despite the fact that the US had indeed already engaged in empire-building activities, for example in the Pacific Islands

53 See Robert M. Citino, "Military Histories Old and New: A Reintroduction," *The American Historical Review* 112, no. 4 (October 1, 2007): 1070–1071, https://doi.org/10.1086/ahr.112.4.1070. Citino notes that new military history is not necessarily new anymore, but instead is "an integral, even dominant, part of the parent field from which it emerged." See also John Whiteclay Chambers II, "Conference Review Essay: The New Military History: Myth and Reality," *The Journal of Military History* 55, no. 3 (1991): 397, https://doi.org/10.2307/1985686. At the annual meeting of the Society of Military History in March 1991, Peter Paret of the Institute for Advanced Study in Princeton defined new military history as "an expansion of the subject of military history from the specifics of military organization and action to their widest implications, and also a broadening of the approaches to the subject, [and] of the methodologies employed."

54 Ehrlichman and Knowles, "Introduction: Reframing Occupation as a System of Rule," in *Transforming Occupation in the Western Zones of Germany: Politics, Everyday Life and Social Interactions, 1945–55*, ed. Camilo Ehrlichman and Christopher Knowles (Bloomsbury Academic, 2018), 4.

55 Ehrlichman and Knowles, 5–7, 10, 18–19.

and in Central America. Susan L. Carruthers examines the debates within the United States about having the US military serve as occupiers of Germany, rather than civilian experts, such as welfare and municipal administrative personnel. As Carruthers notes, imperialism, empire, and the occupation of foreign places went against the country's "self-understanding as a nation that repelled oppressive British rule to establish itself as a shining beacon of republican liberty." The notion of occupation was "inescapably entwined with thorny questions of national history and self-image, particularly with regard to imperialism overseas and the Civil War and Reconstruction at home," and was thus linked to "uncomfortable issues of race and empire," Carruthers notes.[56]

However, the end of World War II came about in a time when the United States was evolving into a world power rather than an isolated country, a time denoted as the American Century, as publisher Henry Luce termed America's rise.[57] The American Century was partially forged by the strength of the US military in foreign lands after World War II, including in the occupation of Germany. After the end of the occupation, the new West German state largely accepted the continued US military presence. US power thus gained a permanent presence in Europe, represented through the US military, a relationship that continues today. American citizens at the time also began to view their military in shifting ways: John Willoughby argues that military and civilian life increasingly looked like each other, as the military became domesticated. Furthermore, Willoughby states, "Americans became used to the idea that the world required their military presence," and the US military became a "legitimate and popular institution essential to the maintenance and extension of contemporary American power."[58] Overall, the US occupation of Germany was thus a phase of transition in twentieth-century history, a time period shaped by occupiers and ordinary citizens grap-

56 Susan L. Carruthers, "Preoccupied: Wartime Training for Post-War Occupation in the United States, 1940–5, in *Transforming Occupation in the Western Zones of Germany: Politics, Everyday Life and Social Interactions, 1945–55*, ed. Ehrlichman and Knowles, 26–28. See also Carl J. Friedrich, "Preface," v, and Merle Fainsod, "The Development of American Military Government Policy during World War II," 23, in Friedrich and Associates, *American Experiences in Military Government*. On the linkages between reeducation and imperialism, see Jana Aresin and Katharina Gerund, "Civilization, Democratization, Containment: Strategies of Re-Education in Imperial Settings and Beyond," *The International History Review* 46, no. 3 (2024): 263–270, https://doi.org/10.1080/07075332.2024.2298035.

57 Henry Luce, "The American Century," *Life*, February 17, 1941, 61–65.

58 Willoughby, *Remaking the Conquering Heroes*, 150–151. Willoughby notes that the years of the American occupation of Germany marked the beginnings of a fundamental change toward the normalization of the belief in the United States as a global military power with a "large, peacetime standing army" as an asset and symbol of this power (2–3).

pling with notions of military occupation, empire, and democracy. This work enables a glimpse at the occupation developments that molded German society and everyday experiences in the latter half of the 1940s, some of which continue to impact German-American relations to this day. The very foundations of present-day democratic Germany were created in the midst of the occupation with the presence of the Allies among the rubble.

This book examines the experiences of young Germans in the aftermath of World War II, focusing on the young German population in general, not on the experiences of the surviving victims of the Holocaust and the National Socialist regime. During the war, non-“Aryan” and “Aryan” children experienced differing levels of violence. Children marked as non-“Aryan” by the National Socialist system experienced extreme levels of atrocities and high rates of death in the Holocaust. “Aryan” children who were able to remain in Germany during the war did experience violence and traumatic events such as Allied bombings but escaped the levels of systematic violence and genocide that Holocaust victims experienced. Despite the fact that “death and violence were ubiquitous” throughout Europe during World War II, scholars such as Dirk Schumann have argued that describing non-victim German children as “collectively traumatized would be going too far and would gloss over crucial differences between the causes of their losses and wounds.”[59] Although some of the young victims of the Nazi regime survived in hiding or by being sent abroad, for example to Great Britain through the *Kindertransport*, children who were victims of the Nazis were the least likely group to survive in concentration and death camps. Over one million children died as a consequence of the Final Solution.[60] Holocaust diaries such as Anne Frank’s as well as material culture from Holocaust victims including children’s drawings from the Theresienstadt camp provide an unsettling view into children’s creative work during the mass atrocities of the Holocaust.[61] On the whole, however, in contrast to the victims of the Holocaust and the Nazi euthanasia program who did not survive, the majority of non-victim “Aryan” German witnesses of the war survived, and were able to record down their experiences of the war and the

---

59 Dirk Schumann, “Childhood and Youth in Nazi Germany,” in *The Routledge History of Childhood in the Western World*, ed. Paula S. Fass (London: Routledge, 2013), 464.

60 Stargardt, *Witnesses of War*, 9. 1.1 million children died in the Final Solution.

61 State Jewish Museum, *Children’s Drawings from the Concentration Camp of Terezín* ([Praha]: n.d.); Anne Frank, *Anne Frank: The Diary of a Young Girl*, trans. B. M. Mooyaart-Doubleday (Bantam Books, 1993). In addition to the famous diary of Anne Frank, see also other materials from young Holocaust victims and survivors: Thomas Geve, *Es gibt hier keine Kinder: Auschwitz, Gross-Rosen, Buchenwald: Zeichnungen eines kindlichen Historikers* (Wallstein Verlag, 1997); Laurel Holliday, ed., *Children in the Holocaust and World War II: Their Secret Diaries* (Pocket Books, 1995).

postwar occupation. Later in their lives, they also were able to decide whether to donate items such as their diaries to archives for preservation, or whether to give interviews, write memoirs, or participate in oral histories about their experiences of war and occupation.

The purpose of this study is not to focus on wartime suffering or on debates on levels of victimhood as a consequence of the war but rather to examine the roles of young Germans under the immediate postwar American occupation in ways that explore the complexities of life in the aftermath of a war of one's society's own making. "Aryan" German children grew up in a regime that marked them as safe from deportation and mass murder during the war, which led to complicated navigations in the aftermath of war when they came face-to-face with the former enemy, Allied soldiers. This work looks at how both sides of the occupation encounter, Americans and Germans, had to grapple with memories of the war and face challenging questions over guilt. It highlights German youngsters' roles under occupation, while also acknowledging the fact that German children did face traumatic experiences during the war, which could include Allied bombings, loss of parent(s) and family members, loss of housing, and being uprooted from their hometowns. In addition, some children did pass away during the postwar occupation period. For example, there were high rates of infant mortality, and sometimes children were killed or injured when playing in the ruins, where dangers such as bombs that had not yet exploded were aplenty.[62]

This work thus links the *Alltagsgeschichte* of a military occupation to the history of children, youth, and childhood. This dynamic lens highlights the interplay of personal experiences, agency, and the emotions of occupation actors including both Americans and Germans, and also explores societal developments regarding categories based on age. *Alltagsgeschichte* "attempts to show how 'ordinary people' refused to accept their assigned roles as the passive 'objects' of impersonal historical developments and attempted, instead, to become active historical 'subjects,'" as David F. Crew writes.[63] Through an analysis of the personal experiences of individual actors, this work considers the agency and personal judgments of

62 Berlin diarist Ruth Andreas-Friedrich wrote on October 3, 1945 that official reports state that the infant mortality rate in the state of Brandenburg was 80 to 90%. In addition, she wrote that there were still 10,000 orphaned children roaming around Germany, surviving from begging and stealing: Ruth Andreas-Friedrich, *Battleground Berlin: Diaries 1945–1948* (Paragon House, 1990), 96. Hilke Lorenz writes that around 74,000 children were killed in the Allied bombings of Germany: Hilke Lorenz, *Kriegskinder: Das Schicksal einer Generation* (List, 2003), 19.

63 David F. Crew, "Alltagsgeschichte: A New Social History 'From below'?'" *Central European History* 22, no. 3/4 (Sep.-Dec. 1989): 396, http://www.jstor.org/stable/4546159. See also Alf Lüdtke, "Was ist und wer treibt Alltageschichte, in *Alltagsgeschichte: Zur Rekonstruktion historischer Erfahrungen und Lebensweisen*, ed. Alf Lüdtke (Campus Verlag, 1989), 9–47.

both Americans and Germans, examining understudied populations including children and youth in addition to racial and ethnic minorities. It aims to capture the individual lived-ness of the occupation and the ways in which regular citizens navigated encounters, centering the experiences and views of ordinary American soldiers and young Germans. The individual stories of young Germans serve to highlight the complexity of childhood at that time as an experience dependent on many individual factors, from family situation to lingering wartime memories.

Remarkably, childhood has only recently emerged as a significant factor in the examination of the past. Although scholarly studies about children occurred earlier in other fields such as psychology, historical study of children's roles and childhood remained overlooked. Scholars of the humanities only began to seriously consider children's history as important in the second half of the twentieth century with the rise of social history about marginalized groups.[64] Colin Heywood notes that, previously, childhood had been marked as unimportant to research, being seen as a "'natural' phenomenon" of little interest. In addition, the assumption "that the biological immaturity of children would be the overriding influence on this stage of life" impacted researchers' disinterest, as children remained seen as "deficient" in comparison to fully developed adults. This lack of interest in studying childhood in ways that admit to the role of children as actors rather than "passive receptacles of adult teaching" began to shift, especially in the 1990s. Heywood highlights that the category of childhood is a "variable of social analysis," intersecting with other factors such as class, race, ethnicity, and gender. Finally, he notes, children play an active role in "determining their own lives and the lives of those around them."[65]

Childhood itself has undergone transformations in the past centuries. Paula S. Fass, whose work has been foundational for the field of children's history, notes that "modern views of children and the values we attach to childhood" are mutable.[66] In addition, she argues, everyone has a childhood, when "defined as a period of growth—physical, emotional, and cognitive," but that childhood "as a realm of protected development, an extended time of leisured maturation . . . has historically been enjoyed by few" since the Ancient World. In addition, the "belief

64 The first major text on childhood history was written by a French historian, published in 1960 and translated into English in 1962, which argued that childhood was an invention of early modern Europe, not something natural: Philippe Ariès, *Centuries of Childhood: A Social History of Family Life* (Vintage Books, 1962).

65 Colin Heywood, *A History of Childhood: Children and Childhood in the West from Medieval to Modern Times* (Polity Press, 2001), 2–4.

66 Paula S. Fass, "Is There a Story in the History of Childhood?" in *The Routledge History of Childhood in the Western World*, ed. Fass, 5.

in the possibilities of childhood for all children" only began to emerge beginning in the eighteenth century.[67] Moreover, Fass argues that both children's experiences and the linkages between childhood and cultural, economic, and political changes are of great importance to historical study. She highlights, "Just as no understanding of the past is now complete if we leave out women, so too no real understanding of the past is possible if children are excluded as participants in the events."[68] Steven Mintz also argues for the importance of historical analysis of childhood, highlighting that childhood "is the true missing link: connecting the personal and the public, the psychological and the sociological, the domestic and the state."[69] Children are not isolated from the shifting circumstances they live in and the changing social, political, and cultural dynamics.[70]

The history of children and youth continues to be a dynamic field, and present-day historians continue to debate the role of children in history and their level of agency.[71] However, Mintz counteracts debates that question children's roles in history, highlighting the importance of children's history and the necessity of seeing children as historical actors. He argues that just as adults do, children take on a range of roles, take various actions, experience different emotions, and make a diverse array of choices, even though their "agency exists along a spectrum or continuum, and their ability to make choices and decisions and exert influence varies widely depending on a child's age and on social and cultural context." Mintz highlights that children remain essential to historical study, as they "clearly are social actors, who attempt to make sense of the world around them and who are capable of various kinds of action."[72] The focus of this work is not to argue about the level of agency of children in postwar Germany but to examine the intersections of childhood with war and its aftermath during an occupation.

67 Fass, "Is There a Story in the History of Childhood?" 12.

68 Fass, "Is There a Story in the History of Childhood?" 9.

69 Steven Mintz, "Why the History of Childhood Matters," *The Journal of the History and Childhood and Youth* 5, no. 1 (Winter 2012): 17, https://doi.org/10.1353/hcy.2012.0012.

70 See Steven Mintz, *Huck's Raft: A History of American Childhood* (The Belknap Press of Harvard University Press, 2004), vii.

71 Recently, scholars have been debating about the utility of the concept of "agency" regarding the history of children and youth. This work continues to use the term to note the importance of seeing youngsters as important historical actors whose everyday experiences are valuable for historical research, while also acknowledging the concept's imperfections. For a debate on agency by scholars of the history of children and youth, see Stephanie Olsen et al., "A Critical Conversation on Agency," *The Journal of the History of Childhood and Youth* 17, no. 2 (Spring 2024): 169–187, https://dx.doi.org/10.1353/hcy.2024.a926862.

72 Steven Mintz, "Children's History Matters," *The American Historical Review* 125, no. 4 (October 2020): 1291, https://doi.org/10.1093/ahr/rhaa382.

This project centers German children and youth as actors, and explores not only official policies and adult-generated discourses about children and childhood but also aims to consider the nuanced picture of the experiences of German children themselves. This includes not only how they were depicted in adult sources but also how they themselves viewed, interpreted, depicted, and felt about their complex circumstances and everyday lives.

Ego-documents including diaries play a central role in this work. Diaries are usually written as a sort of individual performance, often for personal usage, not to be read by strangers. They are often written in secret, to be re-read, perhaps also edited and commented on later.[73] Diaries highlight the ways that people directly witnessed and interpreted events in complicated, individual ways, creating their own narratives of the past. Thus, such personal materials can lead to a better understanding of individual experiences within a larger framework, enabling analysis of common reactions to and depictions of events during that time period itself. Children's diaries are especially fascinating in the often-unexpected ways young people conceptualized and described their experiences and emotions, as well as in how they portrayed adults' reactions to events. As Sarah Wallis and Svetlana Palmer write in the introduction to their collection of children's World War II diaries, children's diaries are "intimate and often more direct than those of adults." In addition, Wallis and Palmer write, "these diaries were a place to confide and to question, to preserve one's dignity, or maintain independence of spirit and thought."[74]

Sources from the time including diaries enable a glimpse into personal experiences of a society under military occupation. The set of young Germans considered in this work is in no way representative of an entire generation, nor do their materials provide a pure autobiographical picture into their inner lives. Nicholas Stargardt, who has explored children's drawings made during the Holocaust, argues that these materials, created in the historical moment they were living in, should be seen as "frozen moments of a social history lived in a very particular time and location," as "snapshots" rather than as "individual biographies," as we do not know if these were the only stories they wanted to tell.[75] Alexandra Zap-

73 See Sollors, *The Temptation of Despair*, 54. Sollors writes, "Diaries are texts that are written privately but are probably kept for the purpose of rereading—why else would they be written? —and of adding on corrections, afterthoughts, and new events that make a past expectation seem false or justified. Hence they provide opportunities for revising."

74 Sarah Wallis and Svetlana Palmer, *We Were Young and at War: The First-Hand Story of Young Lives Lived and Lost in World War II* (Collins, 2009), 1.

75 Nicholas Stargardt, "Children's Art of the Holocaust," *Past & Present* 161, no. 1 (November 1998): 234, https://doi.org/10.1093/past/161.1.191.

ruder, who has researched and published a collection of children's Holocaust diaries, also notes the fact that a diary is but a "fragment" out of the life of the writer. However, despite this, she believes that these "historical fragments" can "shed light on aspects of the Holocaust as it was lived by individual young writers," and that they stand "as a mark of the writer's place in the world, a gesture taken against obliteration."[76] Although written in a completely different context than Holocaust diaries, young Germans' occupation diaries provide insight into their lived realities and their places in the world. In their own words, they described their experiences of life under occupation in the aftermath of a devastating war, allowing for a glimpse into the ways that wider events impacted the lives of young Germans.

In addition, scholars must consider the tension between considering children's directly documented experiences and the (adult) interpretations and descriptions of their experiences, including the scholar's own. A major difficulty for historians of childhood is the role of materials, since children often leave behind few items that make their way into official archives and records. However, this work aims to use as many sources from the time as possible, including everyday records from children and youth such as diaries and drawings. This approach ensures that present-day discourses about the past such as collective memory narratives do not influence the sources, since the witnesses were describing their navigations within that historical moment. However, care must be taken when using these materials. Scholars create their own subjective interpretations of a text, creating a discourse that produces knowledge and meaning about the text from a position of power as the interpreter.[77] In addition, adults or even other children may also have directly intervened in the making of children's documents.[78] However, despite these limitations, such materials still provide crucial knowledge about society at a certain moment and the everyday lives lived within those times. In addition, using sources such as diaries and letters highlights pieces of evidence that depict events at the time within the folds of ordinary people's lives, without the knowledge of what was to come next.

This work analyzes encounters between young Germans and American GIs using materials written at the time, as well as memoirs and oral histories created

76 Alexandra Zapruder, ed., *Salvaged Pages: Young Writers' Diaries of the Holocaust* (Yale University Press, 2002), 8–12. See also Laura Hobson Faure, "Exploring Political Rupture Through Jewish Children's Diaries: *Kindertransport* Children in France, 1938–1942," *Journal of Modern European History* 19, no. 3 (2021): 259, 261, 272, https://doi.org/10.1177/16118944211017765.
77 See Michel Foucault, *The History of Sexuality*, 1st American ed., vol. 1 (Pantheon Books, 1978), 11.
78 Faure, "Exploring Political Rupture," 260, 265, 271–272.

later on. Materials created after the end of the occupation, although potentially impacted by the knowledge of what came next, as well as by dominant collective memory narratives, still can provide evidence into lived experiences. Many of these materials document the confusion and chaos of the aftermath of the war, and attempt to grapple with the complexities of trying to describe the level of destruction and devastation the witnesses experienced. These sources are important yet are considered with care, because they were created after the time of the occupation, when witnesses were remembering and recollecting about the occupation. Overall, various modes of remembrance and forgetting not only play a role in crafting collective memory and national narratives of history but also shape what individuals remember about a historical period.[79]

This study uses a diverse set of sources from witnesses of the period of the occupation of Germany, with authors cutting across a wide range of ages, religions, and racial and ethnic backgrounds, from German children as young as seven years old to American GIs, to American and German Jews employed in the occupation forces, to American military family members, to German teenagers. These sources include the published memoirs of major figures such as President Harry Truman and Military Governor Lucius Clay.[80] Also examined are the published diaries of soldiers active in the immediate aftermath of the war, including the diaries of Melvin J. Lasky and Forrest C. Pogue.[81] The photographs of Tony Vaccaro and those of Signal Corps photographer Malcolm L. Fleming enable an additional glance into the time.[82] Memoirs and reflections by Germans who were

79 Aleida Assmann, *Erinnerungsräume: Formen und Wandlungen des kulturellen Gedächtnisses*, Fünfte, Durchgesehene Auflage (C.H. Beck, 2010), 18–23; Olick, Vinitzky-Seroussi, and Levy, "Introduction," in *The Collective Memory Reader*, ed. Olick, Vinitzky-Seroussi, and Levy, 18–21, 37.

80 Truman, *Memoirs of Harry S. Truman*, vol. 2; Lucius D. Clay, *Decision in Germany* (Doubleday, 1950).

81 Lerg, ed., *The Diary of Lt. Melvin J. Lasky*; Forrest C. Pogue, *Pogue's War: Diaries of a WWII Combat Historian* (University Press of Kentucky, 2001). See obituary of Melvin J. Lasky: Richard Bernstein, "Melvin J. Lasky, Cultural Cold Warrior, Is Dead at 84," *New York Times*, May 22, 2004; obituary of Forrest C. Pogue: Bart Barnes, "Forrest C. Pogue Dies at 84," *The Washington Post*, October 8, 1996.

82 Tony Vaccaro, *Entering Germany: 1944–1949* (Taschen, 2001); Malcolm L. Fleming, *From War to Peace in 1945 Germany: A GI's Experience* (Indiana University Press, 2016). See obituary of Tony Vaccaro: Richard Goldstein, "Tony Vaccaro, 100, Dies; Photographed War From a Soldier's Perspective," *New York Times*, December 30, 2022, updated January 10, 2023, https://www.nytimes.com/2022/12/30/arts/tony-vaccaro-dead.html. See Malcolm Fleming World War II Photographs, Indiana University Archives, Bloomington, Indiana, Image Collection Online, https://webapp1.dlib.indiana.edu/images/splash.htm?scope=archives/VAD2888. Fleming received training to be an official Army photographer. See interview with Malcolm L. Fleming (AFC 2001/001/27926), Veterans History Project (VHP) Collection, American Folklife Center, Library of Congress.

young during the time of the occupation also provide various perspectives about their childhoods, such as Henry Beissel's long poem memoir.[83] Jürgen Kleindienst's published collections of reflections of German adults who were children and youth in postwar Germany depict diverse stories of life in the postwar era.[84] Unpublished items held at the Veterans History Project at the Library of Congress provide extra insight for this project, including oral histories, letters, and diaries from American soldiers. Moreover, this study uses unpublished German children's diaries from the collection of the Deutsches Tagebucharchiv (German Diary Archive) in Emmendingen, Germany. In addition, a variety of children's letters, drawings, school essays, and other creative work are used from both published and unpublished sources, including from the records of the Harry S. Truman Presidential Library, which for example holds various children's drawings and letters sent as a gesture of thanks to President Truman. This work also examines materials including official American military government documents to explore the discourses which demarcated official occupation roles for American soldiers and German children and youth.

Using this wide range of primary sources in a critical way enables a better understanding of the complexity of historical experiences and provides a fuller picture of the past that moves closer to "history which Happens [sic] to people," in the words of Melvin J. Lasky in his diary.[85] As Paul Fussell mentions, quoting Walt Whitman, "The real war will never get in the books."[86] This work does not claim to provide an examination of the occupation as truly lived by all witnesses, but it attempts to get closer to the lived realities of historical experiences, for example through its usage of diaries. Without such sources, voices such as those from historically marginalized and less powerful groups including children would be weakened and potentially even erased from interpretations and documentation of the past. Moreover, a rich variety of sources from witnesses of various ages enables an exploration that complicates present-day collective memory narratives. In addition, these sources portray how processes of exchange and

---

83 Henry Beissel, *Coming to Terms with a Child: Ein Kind kommt zur Sprache* (Verlag Literatur-Wissenschaft.de, 2015).

84 These works include Jürgen Kleindienst, ed., *Hungern und hoffen: Jugend in Deutschland 1945–1950: 48 Geschichten und Berichte von Zeitzeugen* (JKL Publikationen, 2000); Jürgen Kleindienst, ed., *Lebertran und Chewing Gum: Kindheit in Deutschland 1945–1950: 55 Geschichten und Berichte von Zeitzeugen* (JKL Publikationen, 2000); Jürgen Kleindienst, ed., *Nachkriegs-Kinder: Kindheit in Deutschland 1945–1950: 67 Geschichten und Berichte von Zeitzeugen* (JKL Publikationen, 1998); Jürgen Kleindienst, ed., *Der Traum ist aus: Jugend im Zusammenbruch 1944–1945: 31 Geschichten und Berichte von Zeitzeugen* (Zeitgut, 2005).

85 Lerg, ed., *The Diary of Lt. Melvin J. Lasky*, 295.

86 Fussell, *Wartime*, 290.

transfer occurred not only on an official level during the occupation but in multidirectional ways between both Germans and Americans. This focus on lived experiences also helps grapple with the wide-ranging effects of the tensions apparent even at a grassroots level of the contradictions of the US military occupation and debates over understandings of concepts of democracy and liberty, and also allows for a critical lens to the growth of global American military power.[87] All in all, this work aims to delve into the complexities of the lived experiences of the occupation by centering young Germans' experiences in the aftermath of World War II.

Previous Studies of Occupation

This book examines the US occupation in a way that moves away from a top-down examination of the occupation through its focus on personal encounters. Numerous early scholarly studies of the US occupation examined official policies in Germany, but few engaged with everyday experiences under the occupation, with a few exceptions, such as John Gimbel's 1961 examination of experiences in the city of Marburg during the occupation.[88] More recent scholarship has examined case studies of specific locations and the effects of the American presence, including in the cities of Heidelberg, Berlin, Wiesbaden, and the small town Wildflecken.[89] Dewey A. Browder's work provides a thorough glimpse into the various

87 See Dewey A. Browder, *Americans in Post-World War II Germany: Teachers, Tinkers, Neighbors and Nuisances* (The Edwin Mellen Press, 1998), xvi; Carruthers, "Preoccupied," in *Transforming Occupation in the Western Zones of Germany*, eds. Erlichman and Knowles, 27–28. See also Carl J. Friedrich, "Military Government and Democratization: A Central Issue of American Foreign Policy," in Friedrich and Associates, *American Experiences in Military Government*, 3–22. See also a guide for American occupation soldiers about what exactly they were portraying as representatives of the United States, "the greatest democracy in the world": "What is Democracy," *Troop I & E Bulletin* 2, no. 47 (November 23, 1947): 4–15; Folder Troop I & E Bulletin, 1947 [3 of 3], Printed Materials File, 1924–1975; Box 16; Paul L. Webb Papers; Harry S. Truman Presidential Library (HSTPL).

88 John Gimbel, *A German Community under American Occupation: Marburg, 1945–52* (Stanford University Press, 1961).

89 A small sampling of recent scholarship on the impacts of Americans in specific locations during the occupation period (and beyond) includes Anni P. Baker, *Wiesbaden and the Americans 1945–2003: The Social, Economic, and Political Impact of the U.S. Forces in Wiesbaden* (Magistrat der Landeshauptstadt Wiesbaden, Kulturamt-Stadtarchiv, 2004); Steege, *Black Market, Cold War*; Stefanie Eisenhuth: *Die Schutzmacht: Die Amerikaner in Berlin 1945–1994* (Wallstein Verlag, 2018); Theodor Scharmholz, "German-American Relations at the Local Level: Heidelberg, 1948–1955," in *GIs in Germany: the Social, Economic, Cultural, and Political History of the Ameri-*

roles of the American occupiers of Germany and the impacts on German-American relations, looking at the "human dimensions" of the occupation.[90] Recent scholarship has also focused on gender and the experience of German women during the occupation in ways that critically examine postwar German women's roles.[91] Petra Goedde's work provides a valuable study of the effects of everyday encounters between American soldiers and Germans, including women and children. Goedde argues that it was these very encounters that helped shift American views of Germans from enemies into that of infantile, feminized citizens in need of protection by the US Forces, a process that began even before the emergence of the Cold War.[92] Atina Grossmann has focused on the triangular, entangled relationship between Americans, Germans, and the victims of the Nazi regime.[93]

There are few major studies that use an age-focused lens of the German-American postwar encounter. Most works examine adult-created policies and official rhetoric that affected children's lives during the occupation period, rather than highlighting the personal experiences of children and young people themselves. This focus has occurred despite the fact that youth were essential for American occupation efforts. Studies published in the decades immediately after the war focused more on childhood development, educational studies, and community case studies.[94] Scholarly research into official occupation policies that impacted children and youth tends to examine topics such as food policies, humani-

---

can Military Presence, ed. Thomas W. Maulucci Jr. and Detlef Junker (German Historical Institute; Cambridge University Press, 2013); Adam R. Seipp, *Strangers in the Wild Place: Refugees, Americans, and a German Town, 1945–1952* (Indiana University Press, 2013).

90 Browder, *Americans in Post-World War II Germany*, xi.

91 See Maria Höhn, *GIs and Fräuleins: The German-American Encounter in 1950s West Germany* (University of North Carolina Press, 2002); Pfau, Chapter 3: "Fraternization and the Uncensored Occupation," in *Miss Yourlovin*; Leonie Treber, *Mythos Trümmerfrauen: von der Trümmerbeseitigung in der Kriegs- und Nachkriegszeit und der Entstehung eines deutschen Erinnerungsortes* (Klartext, 2014).

92 Goedde, *GIs and Germans*, xxi–xxiii, 205.

93 Grossmann, *Jews, Germans, and Allies*, 2, 9.

94 Carl Coerper, *Deutsche Nachkriegskinder: Methoden und erste Ergebnisse der deutschen Längsschnittuntersuchungen über die körperliche und seelische Entwicklung im Schulkindalter* (Thieme, 1954); Wilhelm Hagen, "Deutsche Nachkriegskinder," *Sozialer Fortschritt* 4, no. 7/8 (Juli/August 1955): 169–171, https://www.jstor.org/stable/24498368. See also community case studies of the Institut für sozialwissenschaftliche Forschung Darmstadt, including Gerhard Baumert, *Jugend der Nachkriegszeit: Lebensverhältnisse und Reaktionsweisen* (Eduard Roether Verlag, 1952).

tarian aid, schools, and formal education, rather than navigations on the ground or children's direct experiences.[95]

As the occupation developed, reeducation (later termed reorientation) became one of the central tenants of the US occupation, especially after JCS 1779 shifted the focus of occupation to the rehabilitation of Germans.[96] Scholarly research on American reeducation policies includes works by James F. Tent and Karl-Heinz Füssl, which examine various occupation policies affecting youth, including attempts at school reform, which largely failed in the American zone due to strong German educational traditions. Tent argues that this failure exposed the "naiveté" of American attempts to reeducate another population toward democracy.[97] Moreover, stemming from psychiatry, the term reeducation itself never even "received a precise definition," Tent notes.[98] Füssl discusses American reeducation policies and the American sponsored youth activities program, GYA.[99] Most works on reeducation in the immediate postwar era tend to mention GYA merely in passing (if at all).[100] Some previous studies have even included misleading information about the American efforts to impact youth on the ground, for example stating that one GI founded GYA in 1945, which is incorrect.[101] Soldiers on the ground did indeed engage in youth work as early as 1945, but they did not found GYA. Their early work with youth activities provided a model which was then taken on as an official military policy and, by mid-1946, GYA became one of the central tenants of occupation reeducation work aimed at children and youth.

---

95 The literature on these topics is vast. Some examples include Browder, *Americans in Post-World War II Germany*, 55–81, 95; Brian M. Puaca, *Learning Democracy: Education Reform in West Germany, 1945–1965* (Berghahn Books, 2009); Alice Weinreb, *Modern Hungers: Food and Power in Twentieth-Century Germany* (Oxford University Press, 2017), especially 88–121; Sara Fieldston, *Raising the World: Child Welfare in the American Century* (Harvard University Press, 2015).

96 JCS 1779, in Friedrich and Associates, *American Experiences in Military Government*, 402–415. The term reorientation reflected the shift away from a punitive occupation.

97 Tent, *Mission on the Rhine*, 318. See also, 12, 312–313.

98 Tent, 13.

99 On GYA, see Chapter 6, "Der Erziehungsbeitrag der US-Armee: Das GYA-Programm," in Karl-Heinz Füssl, *Die Umerziehung der Deutschen: Jugend und Schule unter den Siegermächten des Zweiten Weltkriegs 1945–1955*, 2., Unveränd. Aufl. (Ferdinand Schöningh, 1995), 148–167.

100 In addition to Karl-Heinz Füssl's work, some works do include a brief overview of GYA: for example, see Merritt, *Democracy Imposed*, 278–282.

101 Hermann-Josef Rupieper, *Die Wurzeln der westdeutschen Nachkriegsdemokratie: Der amerikanische Beitrag 1945–1952* (Westdeutscher Verlag, 1993), 156: Rupieper mistakenly states that GI Patrick Moriarty started the GYA program through his private initiative to help malnourished and "degenerate" youth at the end of 1945.

However, in addition to Füssl's work, there is some scholarship that has explored reeducation efforts such as GYA and the direct impacts on German youth. For example, Heather L. Dichter has provided a valuable look into youth sports clubs and their role in American and British democratization aims.[102] Additionally, a 1987 work in German exclusively examined GYA.[103] More recent scholarship has provided a fresh lens into reeducation and also has examined the intersections between humanitarianism and young Germans. A volume edited by Katharina Gerund and Heike Paul examines various tenants of American reeducation policies, including the *Amerikahäuser*, documentary films, and the role of humanitarian aid through organizations such as CARE.[104] In addition, Kaete O'Connell has provided impactful studies of American humanitarian food aid in postwar Germany, focusing on the role of this aid in attempts to win the peace after World War II and in portraying the power of American democracy in a heightening Cold War context, especially when aid was directed toward German children.[105]

Scholarly studies have also focused on children's societal roles in postwar Germany, including in families. For example, children played a central role as the female-centric German family was shaped into a major actor of the postwar period: Dorothee Wierling has shown that having children in postwar German soci-

102 Heather L. Dichter, "Sporting Democracy: The Western Allies' Reconstruction of Germany through Sport, 1944–1952" (PhD diss., University of Toronto, 2008), https://central.bac-lac.gc.ca/.item?id=NR57981&op=pdf&app=Library&oclc_number=755208434; Heather L. Dichter, "Game Plan for Democracy: Sport and Youth in Occupied West Germany," in *Transforming Occupation in the Western Zones of Germany*, ed. Erlichman and Knowles, 133–150. Dichter argues, "The Allied attempt to reform German sport was therefore a significant part of 'doing occupation', as they sought to translate their geopolitical aims for a new Germany into practical activities that could directly reach individual Germans" (147). See also Wolfgang Buss, "Reeducation durch Sport – Ein Gescheiterter Versuch Amerikanischer Besatzungspolitik im Nachkriegsdeutschland?" *STADION* 37, no. 1 (2011): 109–126, https://doi.org/10.5771/0172-4029-2011-1-109. Buss argues that American reeducation efforts in regards to sports were not a total failure but did not have a lasting effect on the development of sports in the Federal Republic of Germany. Germans did not need American role models and standards when the most popular sport was soccer (119, 121–122).
103 Gerhard Rathfelder, Ulrich Schubert, and Margarethe Wild, *GYA Das Jugendarbeitsprogramm der amerikanischen Armee im Nachkriegsdeutschland* (Verlag Burkhard Fehrlen, 1987).
104 Katharina Gerund and Heike Paul, eds., *Die amerikanische Reeducation-Politik nach 1945: Interdisziplinäre Perskeptiven auf "America's Germany"* (Transcript, 2015).
105 See Kaete O'Connell, "The Taste of Defeat: Food, Peace and Power in US-Occupied Germany," in *Food, Culture and Identity in Germany's Century of War*, ed. Heather Merle Benbow and Heather R. Perry (Palgrave Macmillan, 2019), 201–225; Kaete M. O'Connell, "Weapon of War, Tool of Peace: U.S. Food Diplomacy in Postwar Germany" (PhD diss., Temple University, 2019), http://dx.doi.org/10.34944/dspace/489.

ety became seen as a *Glücksauftrag*, a task of happiness.[106] In addition, Tara Zahra has examined how children played a role in postwar humanitarian rhetoric, which focused on the central role of the family in returning Germany to normalcy.[107] Young Germans were also placed at the center of contentious postwar societal debates over juvenile delinquency. German fears of juvenile crimes intersected with American aims of controlling crime during the occupation, including youth crime. Martin Kalb and Jaimey Fisher have both explored how postwar discourse about controlling youth was essential to harnessing a sense of societal order and recovery in Germany. Fisher argues that this postwar focus on "youth and particularly youth crises served as discursive sites onto which to displace, and with which to distract from the wider challenges of coming to terms with Germany's burdensome past," shifting postwar discussions "from difficult questions of guilt to manageable challenges of generational discipline."[108] Kalb argues that "juvenile delinquency was never about crime. Instead, it had become an almost mystical symbol embodying a variety of societal fears: disorder, disillusionment, and destitution."[109] In addition, Thomas Kehoe's work on criminality during the American occupation includes a section on "juvenile disorder" as a major social problem in the fraught aftermath of the war. American occupation authorities especially viewed Edelweiss Piraten youth gangs as a threat, conducting raids

---

106 Dorothee Wierling, "Mission to Happiness: The Cohort of 1949 and the Making of East and West Germans," in *The Miracle Years: A Cultural History of West Germany, 1949–1968*, ed. Hanna Schissler (Princeton University Press, 2001), 113–116. For more on wartime and postwar German families, see Hester Vaizey, *Surviving Hitler's War: Family Life in Germany, 1939–48* (Palgrave Macmillan, 2010).

107 Tara Zahra, *The Lost Children: Reconstructing Europe's Families after World War II* (Harvard University Press, 2011), 93–95. Similarly, Lynne Taylor has explored the intersections between unaccompanied minor refugees in the US occupation zone, adult agents determining the supposed "best interests" of the children, and the role of citizenship and nationality in determining the children's fates. See Lynne Taylor, *In the Children's Best Interests: Unaccompanied Children in American-Occupied Germany, 1945–1952* (University of Toronto Press, 2017). Christian Höschler has also added an important contribution to the field of humanitarian aid and children in Germany after the war by looking at unaccompanied displaced persons children and the role of humanitarian organizations such as the International Refugee Organization (IRO) in child welfare work at the Bad Aibling Children's Village outside of Munich. See Christian Höschler, *Home(less): the IRO Children's Village Bad Aibling, 1948–1951* (Epubli, 2017).

108 Jaimey Fisher, *Disciplining Germany: Youth, Reeducation, and Reconstruction after the Second World War* (Wayne State University Press, 2007), 2, 14. See also Frank Kebbedies, *Außer Kontrolle: Jugendkriminalpolitik in der NS-Zeit und der frühen Nachkriegszeit* (Klartext, 2000).

109 Martin Kalb, "'The Youth is a Threat!' Controlling the Delinquent Boy in Post-WWII Munich," *The Journal of the History of Childhood and Youth* 6, no. 2 (Spring 2013): 283, https://doi.org/10.1353/hcy.2013.0022. Also, Kalb, *Coming of Age*.

and even allowing for Army Counter Intelligence Corps (CIC) surveillance (code named “Operation Valentine”). The Edelweiss Piraten had been a youth resistance movement during the war, but after the war, the term referred to gangs that supposedly formed a subversive, pro-Nazi, anti-occupation faction. American surveillance did not lead to any proof of a highly organized, centralized crime network, but rather the Edelweiss Piraten members appear to have been petty criminals or youth who were having difficulties such as homelessness or dealing with life as an orphan.[110]

Young Germans who may have been struggling with their circumstances in the aftermath of the war were thus seen by adults as a threat that needed to be taken care of in order to establish a stable postwar status quo. American occupation policies also tended to focus on the symbolic role of German youngsters, who gained a central status in democratization efforts. In the view of American officials, the occupation could be seen as successful if only the youngest Germans, the future of Germany, embraced the offerings of American-style democracy, rather than the dangers of youth criminality and juvenile delinquency. Thus, American reeducation policies were double-edged: they focused not only on impacting German youth in a positive manner, with youth playing a role as future democratic citizens, but they also illustrated the occupiers’ anxieties about juvenile criminality’s potential societal harms and disruption to order.

Rather than focus on the symbolic nature of the category of youth and adult-focused views of the potential negative societal impacts of youth, this work shifts its focus instead to the actual experiences and navigations of German young people during the occupation. Nearly all studies of *Kriegskinder* (children of war) have only been published in German. Since the 2000s, there has been an increasing number of works about personal experiences of growing up during and after the war in Germany, which are often memoirs and recollections aimed at readers from the same generation, written late in life usually as a reflection of their personal histories.[111] A growing field of research has also examined *Besatzungskinder*, the children of occupation soldiers, who were especially stigmatized and

110 Thomas J. Kehoe, *The Art of Occupation: Crime and Governance in American-Controlled Germany, 1944–1949* (Ohio University Press, 2019), 100, 103–107. Also, Thomas Boghardt, *Covert Legions: U.S. Army Intelligence in Germany, 1944–1949* (Center of Military History, United States Army, 2022), 210–212, https://purl.fdlp.gov/GPO/gpo183492. See also Norman M. Naimark, *The Russians in Germany: A History of the Soviet Zone of Occupation, 1945–1949* (The Belknap Press of Harvard University Press, 1995), 382–384, for information on Soviet policing of German young people, who “were the most resistant to Soviet rule in the East” (382).

111 For example, see Sabine Bode, *Die vergessene Generation: die Kriegskinder brechen ihr Schweigen*, 2. Aufl. (Klett-Cotta, 2004).

excluded from postwar German society, especially those with African American fathers.[112] Above all, the main focus of this work is to center young Germans within the history of the occupation, focusing especially on lived experiences of encounter, rather than focusing on adult discourses or a collection of biographies of experiences. Instead, it aims to examine the tensions and complexities of the occupation and the ways that young people's lives impacted personal and political relations.

Beyond the US Zone: The Occupations

The period of the US occupation of Germany after World War II was not the first time that Americans and Germans encountered each other in the context of a postwar occupation. American troops were also present during the occupation of the Rhineland after World War I.[113] This work remains limited in its focus on World War II's aftermath in Germany, excluding other post-World War II American occupations, for example the occupation of Japan.[114] Moreover, Germans encountered Allied soldiers belonging to one of four different nationalities depending on which of the four occupation zones they were located in: the American, British, French, or Soviet.[115] Some Germans migrated between zones, especially from the Soviet zone, or they were in an area that shifted hands after the end of the war, such as in certain areas in Berlin. This study focuses on the US zone of occupation, thus remaining limited in overarching conclusions about all occupa-

112 The topic of children born of war is a growing field but not a main focus of this work. Some of the major works on the children born of World War II and occupation include Elke Kleinau and Ingvill C. Mochmann, eds. *Kinder des Zweiten Weltkriegs: Stigmatisierung, Ausgrenzung, Bewältigungsstrategien* (Campus Verlag, 2016); Silke Satjukow and Rainer Gries, *Bankerte!: Besatzungskinder in Deutschland nach 1945* (Campus Verlag, 2015); Heide Fehrenbach, *Race after Hitler: Black Occupation Children in Postwar Germany and America* (Princeton University Press, 2005).

113 See Brian F. Neumann and Shane D. Makowicki, *Occupation and Demobilization 1918–1923* (Center of Military History, United States Army, 2019).

114 Other occupations in World War II and its aftermath with an American presence included occupations in North Africa, Korea, and Austria. The occupation of Austria will be touched upon briefly in this work.

115 For an overview of British, French, and Soviet occupation policies (as of August 1947), see United States Department of State, *Occupation of Germany: Policy and Progress 1945–46* (United States Government Printing Office, 1947), 223–241. The publication noted that the "prime objective of United States policy is to achieve the demilitarization and democratization of Germany to the end that Germany may ultimately take its place in the community of peaceful and law-abiding nations," iii.

tion zones, instead honing in on German-American exchanges in the US zone of occupation.

Developments in the Soviet zone of occupation provide the greatest contrast to the US zone. In the Soviet zone, youth were mobilized into one state-sponsored youth organization, the *Freie Deutsche Jugend* (FDJ), which was used as a means of Soviet political control.[116] In addition, fraternization between Soviet troops and German civilians proved complex. Fear of soldiers and resentment were both common among the German population, especially due to the lingering memories of the experience of mass violence at the immediate end of the war, including women who experienced rape at the hands of Soviets.[117] Regulations on relations between Soviet troops and the Germans were initially lax, with no ban on fraternization, in contrast to the strict initial restrictions in the other zones. Later on during the occupation, Soviet officials created more restrictions on fraternization between their soldiers and Germans, ultimately isolating their troops from the German population by the summer of 1949, in an attempt to deal with various problems by reducing contact.[118]

Occupation troop violence was not limited to the Soviet zone. Wide-scale looting was common especially in the immediate aftermath of the war, and there were violent acts committed against Germans by Western Allied soldiers, including Americans, such as rape.[119] Overall, however, Germans viewed the troops of

---

116 Naimark, *The Russians in Germany*, 272. For a history of the FDJ, see Alan McDougall, *Youth Politics in East Germany: The Free German Youth Movement 1946–1968* (Clarendon Press, 2004). In addition, Osmar White noted in 1945 that Russians were "unconcerned with problems of 'humanitarianism' as it was defined by the British or the Americans." Osmar White, *Conquerors' Road: An Eyewitness Report of Germany 1945* (Cambridge University Press, 2003), 206.

117 See Naimark, Chapter 2, "Soviet Soldiers, German Women, and the Problem of Rape," 69–140.

118 Naimark, 92–97.

119 Final numbers regarding rape are difficult to assess, but perhaps up to two million German women were raped by Soviet soldiers at the end of the war. See Atina Grossmann, "A Question of Silence: The Rape of German Women by Occupation Soldiers," *October* 72, Berlin 1945: War and Rape "Liberators Take Liberties" (Spring 1995): 46–47, https://doi.org/10.2307/778926. Also, Naimark, Chapter 2, "Soviet Soldiers, German Women, and the Problem of Rape," 69–140; Goedde, "Gender, Race, and Power," in *The United States and Germany in the Era of the Cold War*, ed. Junker, 517–518. Goedde notes that even American occupation officials acknowledged that rapes by GIs occurred more often than official records showed; however, in German regard, American offenses appeared mild in comparison to the behavior of the Soviets. See also Starr, *Fraternization with the Germans in World War II*, 80–84; Browder, *Americans in Post-World War II Germany*, 12, 158; Edward N. Peterson, *The American Occupation of Germany: Retreat to Victory* (Wayne State University, 1977), 155; White, *Conquerors' Road*, 97–98. See Miriam Gebhardt, *Als die Soldaten kamen: Die Vergewaltigung deutscher Frauen am Ende des Zweiten Weltkriegs*, 3. Auflage

the Western Allies as friendly, "even attractive," according to journalist Harald Jähner, in contrast to the largely negative German views of the Soviets. Jähner notes that many Germans were especially relieved when the first troops to arrive in their towns were not the Soviets, despite the fact that Nazi propaganda had also attempted to arouse fear about what the Western Allies would do to Germans.[120] At the same time, a monolithic view of Soviet soldiers as a mass of violent men is complicated by accounts of Soviet soldiers' kindness toward children, as well as the fact that there were female Soviet soldiers serving in the Red Army as well.[121] Norman M. Naimark argues that although the Soviet troops did commit acts of violence toward the German population, Soviets and Germans still engaged in acts of "consensual fraternization" and that the German Democratic Republic (GDR) "was created primarily out of the interaction of Russians and Germans in the Soviet occupied zone."[122]

The British zone of occupation also provides a contrast to the US zone, although policies did overlap. In 1947, the two zones merged into an economically unified Bizone (in 1948, the French zone merged with the Bizone, creating the Trizone). According to Christopher Knowles, British occupation officials shifted toward a policy based on the "'Three R's,' – physical and economic Reconstruction, political Renewal, and personal Reconciliation" rather than the Four Ds agreed to at the Potsdam Conference.[123] In comparison to the Americans, British authorities focused less attention on punitive policies such as denazification, which they believed to be relatively futile in the wake of the entrenched Nazism of all Germans.

(Deutsche Verlags-Anstalt, 2015), for an examination of the widespread nature of sexual violence, which extended to all Allied troops as perpetrators and continued beyond the end of the war. An instance of rape by an American in Kassel is recorded in Elfrieda Berthiaume Shukert and Barbara Smith Scibetta, *War Brides of World War II* (Presidio Press, 1988), 124. See also Chapter 2: "Flaccid Fatherland: Rape, Sex, and the Reproductive Consequences of Defeat," in Fehrenbach, *Race after Hitler*, 46–73.

120 Harald Jähner, *Aftermath: Life in the Fallout of the Third Reich 1945–1955*, trans. Shaun Whiteside (Alfred A. Knopf, 2022), 147–148.

121 Fulbrook, "'Normalisation' in the GDR in Retrospect,'" in *Power and Society in the GDR*, ed. Fulbrook, 293; Naimark, *The Russians in Germany*, 75, 82–83, and image from 1945 of a Russian soldier on a bike with two children, captioned: "Russian soldiers were noted for their indulgent behavior toward German children." For images of Soviet female soldiers, see Fleming, *From War to Peace*, 78–79. Also, Fleming, 86: a banner hung in Ichterhausen read stated "We Greet the Red Army" in German and Russian. Fleming commented, "'We Fear the Red Army' would be more literally true of the German sentiment."

122 Naimark, 470.

123 Christopher Knowles, *Winning the Peace: The British in Occupied Germany, 1945–1948* (Bloomsbury Academic, 2017), 1.

However, in both the American and British zones, there was a consistent focus on the role of German youth as a potential threat to occupation order and simultaneously as an opportunity for the occupiers relating to their occupation reeducation goals. Youth participation in voluntary recreational, religious, and cultural clubs was also encouraged in the British zone, and Field Marshal Bernard Law Montgomery prioritized youth matters, even as early as July 1945. In addition, early on during the occupation, German *Kreis* youth offices were recreated, with British occupation personnel participating in an advisory capacity. The official guidelines for German youth activities in the British zone were released in August 1945, which encouraged British-style clubs with a focus on a wide variety of activities. Summer camps were also set up with the purpose of fostering democratic ways of thinking. Interestingly, the British did not allow youth scouting groups until mid-1948, due to fears over the wearing of uniforms and other potential similarities to the Hitler Youth.[124] According to Dewey A. Browder, however, the "biggest difference" between the US and British zones was related to youth activities policies. The British had fewer resources to devote to youth work in comparison to the American authorities, who encouraged active engagement from all levels of military personnel and even from military families as the occupation progressed. British authorities also tended to focus on more formal reeducation policies, such as schooling.[125] Moreover, as Helen Liddell noted in 1948, the British occupation authorities tended to have a "'colonial' attitude," even regarding youth and education work, working "in the best British tradition of a kindly, tolerant, efficient superiority."[126] However, despite contrasts in some policies and a differing level of active troop assistance to youth, both the US and British occupation authorities did establish the fact that German youth participation in organized, positive groups was of importance for their occupation goals and for the stability of the occupation order.

The French occupation authorities also enacted youth programs, but overall, their policies tended to focus more on de-Germanization. Denazification was less strict, since the French believed that all Germans were guilty and thus could not be reformed; instead, German national traits needed to be reformed. The German population in the French zone tended to be more resentful of the French presence, as Browder notes.[127] Overall, the French occupation zone has remained understudied, and arguably even forgotten. The pioneering work on the French

---

124 Phillips, *Educating the Germans*, 146–156.
125 Browder, *Americans in Post-World War II Germany*, 94.
126 Liddell, "Education in Occupied Germany," 50.
127 Browder, *Americans in Post-World War II Germany*, 83–84, 87–88.

zone by F. Roy Willis was published in 1962.[128] However, there has been more recent scholarship, for example explorations of German-French occupation relations during the twentieth century using a comparative and transnational lens.[129] The French zone of occupation after World War II also provides a fascinating, understudied parallel to the US zone and navigations of race: colonial soldiers including Africans were present in the French zone as occupiers, thus impacting power structures, conceptions of race, and understandings of occupier and occupied, which had effects on social relationships on the ground.[130]

Historical research of the postwar occupation of Germany as well as collective memory narratives both follow the trend of highlighting the American occupation zone and the role of the Americans, despite the presence of four Allied troops and the fact that there were four occupation zones, each with unique circumstances. This work acknowledges this tendency of unequal emphasis on the US zone, while also asserting the importance of exploring encounters between German youngsters and Americans. Hopefully, the conclusions drawn about these intergenerational encounters in the US zone can be further explored in future literature about the other three zones of occupation. Above all, focusing on the US zone highlights the ways in which interactions with young Germans helped shape wide-reaching developments and policies in the postwar historical moment when the United States rose to a global power. Moreover, it looks into the consequences of the American troop presence in Germany, and examines the roles that young Germans played within these shifting geopolitical spheres.

****

128 F. Roy Willis, *The French in Germany 1945–1949* (Stanford University Press, 1962).

129 Frank Engehausen, Marie A. Muschalek, and Wolfgang Zimmermann, eds., *Deutsch-französische Besatzungsbeziehungen im 20. Jahrhundert* (Verlag W. Kohlhammer, 2018). Jessica Reinisch's study of public health in occupation Germany includes the French zone. See Chapter 8, "The Forgotten Zone: Public Health Work in the French Occupation Zone," in Jessica Reinisch, *The Perils of Peace: The Public Health Crisis in Occupied Germany* (Oxford University Press, 2013), https://doi.org/10.1093/acprof:oso/9780199660797.001.0001.

130 For a study of encounters between French and Germans in Freiburg including an examination of race, see Ann-Kristin Glöckner, "Shared Spaces: Social Encounters between French and Germans in Occupied Freiburg, 1945–55," in *Transforming Occupation in the Western Zones of Germany*, ed. Ehrlichman and Knowles, 191–210. For an examination of the contributions of black African infantry to both the British and French war efforts during World War II, see John H. Morrow Jr., "Black Africans in World War II: The Soldiers' Stories," *The Annals of the American Academy of Political and Social Science* 632, Perspectives on Africa and the World (November 2010): 12–25, http://www.jstor.org/stable/27895945.

This book highlights the shifting navigations regarding German youngsters in the sphere of the US occupation in the aftermath of World War II, moving away from a top-down approach. The main goal of the study is to portray the wide-ranging impacts of the exchange between young Germans and Americans, while highlighting the centrality of children and youth to the fabric of the occupation. The study explores personal experiences of the encounter and examines sources from the time documenting individual interpretations of the occupation, the occupied, and the occupiers, as well as the ways in which the occupiers and German youngsters influenced each other. It also examines on-the-ground developments that impacted occupation policies, including reeducation aims. Using a multilayered approach that links military history, the history of children and youth, occupation studies, and *Alltagsgeschichte*, each chapter delves into various aspects of the role of young Germans during the occupation in ways that illustrate the dynamism of personal experiences and the evolving nature of official policies that were relevant to youth and that youth themselves also impacted.

Chapter One explores the particularities of American perspectives and narratives about German youngsters. Views of the occupation from GIs themselves have been overlooked in the wake of powerful collective memory narratives and the mythologization of the occupation of Germany into a story of undoubted success. By looking at the complexities of their encounters with the youngest citizens of the former enemy population, this chapter examines the shifting and often contradictory role of GIs during the occupation, explores the ways in which circumstances on the ground impacted higher policies, and also portrays the various roles that GIs played for children and youth. The chapter delves into themes including tensions over collective guilt, the failure of early nonfraternization policies, and debates over democratization. Moreover, this chapter focuses on the complex power structures within occupation dynamics that were impacted by categories including race, which played out in encounters. African American soldiers played a major role in the occupation, including through their benevolence toward German children, a story often featured in collective memory narratives of the occupation. The chapter examines this trend while also highlighting black GIs' actual experiences of occupation and encounter.

Chapter Two explores the lived experiences of German young people and their views of Americans. Exploring the realities of childhood during occupation and its shifting meanings for children at the time enables a move beyond official discourses and a top-down focus on adult actions that impacted children. This chapter examines the roles of children and youth in the occupation as actors able to impact everyday life in the occupation. This enables an individualized glance into children's experiences, examining the various factors that molded the lives of young people after the war. These factors included memories of war experiences (such as the *Kinderlandverschickung* to rural areas or experience of bombings), location/region including rural or urban areas, gender, role during National Socialism including Hitler Youth or BDM membership, family status including the loss of a parent (or parents), health, class, language skills (especially English), schooling level, and even age itself, with some differences between older teenagers who may have had military combat experience, younger teens, and children. This chapter examines texts written by children and youth, for example the diaries of a boy in Amberg in Bavaria. His experience proves a fascinating case study, because of his early recording of his daily life in his diary, even as young as age seven. As the son of a single mother, he often wandered around town, encountering GIs in various circumstances. This chapter avoids generalizations and sweeping conclusions about generational experiences, highlighting instead the diverse nature of the experiences of German children and youth who witnessed the war and its aftermath. These experiences were contingent on specific factors in each child's life, and the chapter aims to avoid claiming to know the truth of all young Germans' experiences in all areas of the American occupation zone.

Chapter Three takes on a study of youth in the Bremen Enclave, an overlooked part of the US occupation zone, and also a prominent location for official American military government policies regarding youth. American soldiers in Bremen proved particularly active in creating constructive youth programs, even as early as summer 1945, spurring Bremen to take on a leading role in the development of the official US military-sponsored German Youth Activities program, which officially began throughout the US zone in April 1946. Early individual initiatives of GIs profoundly shaped official military government policies, helping lead to the creation of youth clubs for Germans, which became an official part of occupation reeducation goals. In Bremen, Sergeant Patrick Moriarty's engagement in founding the Bremen Boys Club gained transatlantic attention. In addition, the military government also actively supported German-run youth clubs (such as religious or trade union clubs), although this sometimes led to tensions between the American-sponsored clubs and German clubs. The creation of official American-sponsored youth clubs, youth centers, and other programs for youth was impactful yet also sometimes contradictory. Young Germans were occupied with activities seen as meaningful and positive by the Americans, and they were taught a specific type of democracy under the guide of GIs, yet were living within a military occupation. In addition, occupation authorities also aimed to use the clubs as a way to combat juvenile delinquency and bring about societal order. GYA illustrates the shifting nature of the occupation, which turned away from punishing Germans toward embracing them as allies and friends to be assisted. German youth were seen by the American military government as the future of a democratic Germany, yet the clubs were sometimes limited in their actual practice of democracy within the restrictive spheres of the military government. The case of the Bremen Boys Club makes apparent the increasingly central nature of youth activities to official occupation goals of reeducation and democratization, while also highlighting the ambivalences of these very policies. The chapter also looks into potential differences between boyhood and girlhood in American-sponsored youth programs. In addition, the chapter touches upon the role of American dependent children in German-American postwar interactions, exploring the experiences of a young American girl whose father was stationed in the Bremen Enclave.

American products including Hershey bars and Coca-Cola played a central role in occupation navigations, as Chapter Four makes clear. These products became linked with a geopolitics of gratitude that especially emerged in the heightening Cold War context, in which American military humanitarianism and acts of benevolence were intertwined with German gratitude for the acts of kindness. These kind acts ranged from individual gifts such as candy bars for German children to official actions such as the *Schulspeisung* school feeding program and shipments of CARE packages for needy Germans. These individual and collective acts of kindness thus aligned with larger American geopolitical aims of creating a unified, economically prosperous Europe as a bulwark against communism and as a way to help ensure security for the United States. The Truman Doctrine and the Marshall Plan both cemented the belief that economic prosperity in Europe achieved American security. Reports of GIs' benevolence toward German youngsters became great publicity for these wider geopolitical aims. Reeducation thus became increasingly focused on anti-communism rather than anti-Nazism. In addition, Germans learned a particular type of democracy, one in which freedom and democratic rights meant consumption and access to non-essential goods such as sweets. In young Germans' conceptions of democracy, freedom thus became linked to sensory memories such as the taste of a first candy bar or a Coca-Cola drink at a GYA youth center.

The Berlin Airlift from June 1948 to September 1949 illustrated the culmination of the embrace of (West) Germans as friends to be protected and provided for. The Western Allies provided for the West Berlin population, delivering supplies via the *Rosinenbomber* (raisin bombers, as the Airlift planes became known as) for over a year during the Soviet Blockade. Chapter Five explores the collective memory of the Berlin Airlift, honing in on the action known as the candy bombing. This action was initiated by one American pilot, Lieutenant Gail Halvorsen, as an individual desire to help a group of German children he met near the runway at Tempelhof Airport in Berlin. Halvorsen became known as the

Candy Bomber, or Uncle Wiggly Wings.[131] The candy bombing initiative was an act of individual benevolence that was taken on as a collective military action, which shaped the entire Berlin Airlift and even continues to impact present-day German and American memory narratives of the occupation period. The candy bombing also served as a valuable source of Cold War propaganda for the Americans, providing tangible proof of their benevolent power. West Berliner children and youth emerged as central figures in this discourse, as they proved willing beneficiaries of American (and Western Allied) support, thus cementing their friendship. In addition, the recipients of the Airlift, especially those who remember Halvorsen the Candy Bomber, were profoundly impacted by the events, in which their early lives were shaped by a geopolitical crisis and the excitement of candy falling from the sky. The chapter also examines memorialization practices around the Airlift and candy bombing, which continue to the present day. It explores the 2019 celebrations of the seventieth anniversary of the Airlift at the Lucius D. Clay Kaserne in Wiesbaden, Germany, where Halvorsen was present and reenacted the candy bombing.

Overall, this work highlights the centrality of young Germans to the period of the US occupation after World War II. Children and youth were more than the obvious victims of the war. Instead, they were central figures at the frontlines of navigations undertaken in the aftermath of the war, a time fraught with fear over the future, the trauma of the past, and perhaps even sometimes excitement at the imagined possibilities of a new life after war. In addition, youngsters played a role beyond that of serving adult purposes. Everyday encounters amidst the rubble involved young Germans in diverse ways. Young Germans impacted the occupation experiences of US soldiers and also influenced American policies and personal views of Germans, including those of Americans back home. Personal interactions between German children and American soldiers were at the forefront of these changes. Many GIs behaved towards youngsters in ways that broke with official policies and rhetoric, especially early on during the occupation. Moreover, GIs also impacted the daily lives of German youngsters, who viewed the soldiers and the occupation as a whole in dynamic ways. These exchanges illustrate the ambivalent role of the occupation's foot soldiers, who were given abundant goods such as chocolate and challenging tasks as a democratizing force among a devastated and defeated former enemy population. Young Germans were also seen as an important group for occupation aims, simultaneously

131 Halvorsen became known as Uncle Wiggly Wings because he would wiggle the wings of his plane, so the children below would know which plane was his. After wiggling his wings, his crew would drop the candy parachutes over the children below.

as both a problem group and as the hope for a democratic future. Young Germans and GIs both viewed each other in unique and shifting ways, leaving behind descriptions in sources from the time, including diaries. These interactions highlight the singularity and complexity of the postwar era in the US occupation zone. The postwar occupation of Germany after World War II was a time of deep transition within the lingering aftershocks of a terrible war. The impacts of the occupation continue on into the present day, highlighting the potential for long-lasting aftermaths resulting from humanity's capacity for waging war and committing acts of mass violence. This work remains especially relevant in a time when war has returned to Europe and continues to play a role in modern society, having a profound impact on the children and youth faced with navigating the rubble that continues to be formed by the darker side of humanity.

Chapter 1
The Encounter: Soldiers and Children in the Ruins

We come as conquerors, but not as oppressors.
–General Dwight D. Eisenhower[1]

American soldiers entering Germany in 1944 and 1945 as the war progressed were constantly warned about the dangers prevalent among the German population. These first encounters with Germans were influenced by a US military propaganda campaign, which aimed to educate GIs about the lurking danger of entrenched Nazism within the German population in an attempt to prevent fraternization. One of these cautionary announcements, which aired on the Allied Forces Network, noted that even pretty German girls and adorable German children could serve as a subversive force, harming the war efforts: "If, in a German town, you bow to a pretty girl, or pat a blond child . . . you bow to Hitler and his reign of blood . . . you caress the ideology that means death and persecution. Don't fraternize!"[2] Much of the German population that GIs encountered were young women, children, and the elderly, since combat-age German men were away fighting the war, were dead or missing, or had been taken as prisoners. Thus, the German civilians who Americans encountered on the ground contrasted with what Americans had imagined of the "Aryan" master race superfighters. American soldiers who had fought Germans on the battlefield were sometimes tempted to spend time with pretty women and cute children in Germany, but official war aims needed to prevent that human temptation to make contact with the local population. A 1945 War Department training film, *Your Job in Germany*, noted that "every German is a potential source of trouble." In addition, the film argued that Germans were tainted by their Nazi beliefs:

> Don't clasp that hand. It's not the kind of a hand you can clasp in friendship . . . Some day the German people might be cured of their disease. The super race disease. The world conquest disease. But they must prove that they have been cured, beyond the shadow of a

1 See United States Holocaust Memorial Museum, "A sign in front of a U.S. military installation in Berlin features a quotation by General Dwight D. Eisenhower that reads: 'We Come as Conquerors . . . Not as Oppressors,'" United States Holocaust Memorial Museum Collections, Photograph Number 26311, courtesy of Aviva Kempner, https://collections.ushmm.org/search/catalog/pa1086512.
2 Starr, *Fraternization with the Germans in World War II*, 22.

https://doi.org/10.1515/9783111588155-002

> doubt, before they ever again are allowed to take their place among respectable nations. Until that day, we stand guard.[3]

As the war came to a close and Germany became a landscape of military occupation divided under the four Allied powers, interactions between the local population and the troops proved impossible to control in the US zone of occupation. The fraternization ban failed to prevent interactions between American soldiers and German civilians. By June 1945, American troops were allowed to fraternize with German youngsters, and by October 1945, the fraternization policy was completely scrapped.[4]

Although fraternization between the German population and American soldiers was allowed for the remainder of the occupation, young Germans continued to be marked as a suspicious population in need of oversight: they were former members of the Hitler Youth who had grown up only knowing Nazism, thus they needed a guiding hand (and a watchful eye) to turn them toward values such as democracy and decency. In November 1945, US official Byron Price, former director of censorship during World War II, visited Germany and reported on conditions to President Truman. His report marks the contradictory response of American officials about the state of German youth: on the one hand, youngsters were still dangerous, potentially plotting sabotage of the occupation in a desire to return to the days of Nazism, and yet they were also seen as the future of a democratic, peaceful Germany. Price wrote, "The former Hitler Youth — young people of their teens, — are potentially the most dangerous single element of the population. It may be hoped that the current effort to organize these crooked-minded children into non-military societies and clubs after the American fashion will help turn them away from idleness and subversion." Price also claimed that these former Hitler Youth members had linkages to the German soldiers who were recently discharged, in addition to Nazis forced out of office and criminals among the DP population. He argued that dangerous conditions could emerge in postwar Germany, as "the suffering sure to come with winter may be expected to bring into the open whatever threat of real disorder and rebellion may now lie buried

---

3 Frank Capra and Theodor Geisel, *Your Job in Germany* (1945); 111-OF-8; Orientation Films, 1942–1949; Records of the Office of the Chief Signal Officer, Record Group (RG) 111; National Archives and Records Administration, National Archives at College Park, Maryland (NACP); available at https://catalog.archives.gov/id/4529712. Theodor Geisel was better known as Dr. Seuss.

4 Starr, *Fraternization with the Germans in World War II*, 2; Ziemke, *The U.S. Army in the Occupation*, 322–327. For a detailed examination of fraternization between Germans and Americans during the fraternization ban and after, see Johannes Kleinschmidt, *Do Not Fraternize: die schwierigen Anfänge deutsch-amerikanischer Freundschaft 1944–1949* (WVT Wissenschaftler Verlag, 1997).

beneath the surface." Thus, to deal with such threats, he advocated for continued troop presence rather than demobilization.[5]

In contrast to his dire statements about the potential dangers lurking among young Germans, Price also wrote about the positive effects of the American encounter with German children: "Fraternization, which has come about naturally and inevitably, has made some friends, particularly among the young children who are the hope of the long future; for the American soldier is the world's best salesman of democracy."[6] American intelligence officer Saul K. Padover also marked the young as the only hope for Germany: "Only the coming generation of Germans can redeem their country. One must hope and pray that they will not fail."[7] Thus, American officials marked young Germans simultaneously as a problem group to be fixed and as the hope for a democratic future. American soldiers were put in the position of educating, policing, and selling democracy to German youth and children. Both groups thus were prescribed with undertaking massive tasks within an occupation environment where German youngsters were seen both as the problem and the solution. Young Germans needed to behave properly and work toward their place as future democratic citizens of a peaceful Germany, and GIs were supposed to shape them, moving them from criminality toward democracy. This ambivalent messaging regarding young Germans impacted encounters on the ground, where GIs were faced with contradictory policies and rhetoric about German youngsters. Later on, as the occupation shifted toward the rehabilitation of Germans as allies and friends to be protected, especially against the new Soviet enemy, policies shifted even further, moving toward the embrace and support of young Germans. In addition, relations between young Germans and GIs shifted as newly recruited American troops arrived in Germany, who did not bring the experience of combat, which could play a role in their views of German youngsters, viewing them in a more innocent lens.

GIs had to navigate complex everyday judgments about Germans in the context of a military occupation involving a German civilian population that was highly female and young. Occupation troops thus traversed a shifting landscape of official occupation policies that fluctuated from early attempts to punish Germans into policies largely aiming at rehabilitating Germany within the wider context of

5 Byron Price, Memorandum to President Truman, November 9, 1945, p. 12; Folder OF 198 1945–April 1950 [1 of 2] Germany; White House Central Files: Official File (OF) 198; Harry S. Truman Papers (HSTP); Box 738; HSTPL.

6 Byron Price, Memorandum to President Truman, p. 2; Folder OF 198 1945–April 1950 [1 of 2] Germany; OF 198; HSTP; Box 738; HSTPL.

7 Saul K. Padover, *Experiment in Germany: The Story of an American Intelligence Officer* (Duell, Sloan and Pearce, 1946), 400.

power over Germans as members of the occupation forces. It was in this in-between phase of military occupation during a period of major global transformation and transition that individual American soldiers encountered young Germans. The two interlinking layers of views of German children as both problem and solution played a role in military government policy purposes, while also impacting personal encounters on the ground. Both of these interlinking layers of adult views about young Germans as well as youngsters' actual experiences as actors during the occupation are relevant to soldiers' everyday experiences of occupation.

Millions of American soldiers have had contact with Germans since 1945. Since the end of World War II, over 15 million Americans have lived and worked in (West) Germany, the majority of whom were military members.[8] At the end of World War II, around two million American soldiers occupied Germany. Numbers decreased by 1950, when about 80,000 troops remained in Germany, but grew to over 300,000 in 1952 during the period of the Korean War. Over the decades, until the early 1990s, troop presence numbered around 200,000. In 2000, around 60,000 American troops were present in Germany.[9] The American military has thus continued to play a role in Germany even beyond the end of the Cold War and the reunification of East and West Germany, remaining today during a time of heightening tensions in Europe. In addition, as Petra Goedde notes, over the decades, "Germans never seriously challenged the legitimacy of the American military presence on their soil," regarding the "troops' presence as a vital element of their nation's security," despite periods of tensions, such as during the late 1960s, when American "economic and political prestige declined."[10] American and German partnership was thus cemented especially through the decades-long presence of the US military in Germany.

Statistics about encounters between German civilians and American troops in the aftermath of World War II highlight the increasing prevalence of personal interactions after the end of combat in May 1945. The exact number of encounters can never be fully known, but according to informal polls of US troops taken between VE Day and September 30, 1945, the majority of American soldiers had frat-

---

8 Höhn, *GIs and Fräuleins*, 5. Number from US Information Service.
9 Dewey A. Browder, "Appendix: Population Statistics for U.S. Military in Germany, 1945–2000," in *GIs in Germany*, ed. Maulucci and Junker, 351–352. Troop strength figures also in Daniel J. Nelson, *A History of U.S. Military Forces in Germany* (Westview Press, 1987), 45, 81, 103. Also, Goedde, "Gender, Race, and Power," in *The United States and Germany in the Era of the Cold War*, ed. Junker, 515. See Höhn, *GIs and Fräuleins*, for more on Korean War era German-American encounters in the state of Rhineland-Palatinate, which became the site of large US military bases.
10 Goedde, "Gender, Race, and Power," 520–521.

ernized in some form with the local German population.[11] Moreover, according to an official EUCOM report on fraternization, children played a central role: "Violation of the rule of fraternization began with children."[12] Official OMGUS and HICOG surveys of the German population included surveys on relations between the German population and Americans. A survey taken in September 1946 showed that 14% of the German respondents in the US zone knew an American "well" or "fairly well," 20% had talked to an American, and 66% had experienced neither situation, having "no relations with the American forces."[13] By November 1947, numbers grew: around one in four Germans knew an American personally, mostly in casual relationships, made by chance or through professional networks, and half of those knew more than four Americans.[14] In December 1949, the number of Germans in the US zone acquainted with an American had grown to around one-third of Germans, and the majority of respondents thought Americans had good conduct.[15] Furthermore, a survey conducted of 226 Mannheim adults in September 1946 reported that 20% of the adults had some sort of relationship with white soldiers, 8% had personal relations with black soldiers, and 8% both. In addition, 36% of the respondents claimed that black soldiers were friendlier toward the German population than white soldiers, especially toward children.[16] These surveys were taken within the context of official occupation goals; thus, the responses should be interpreted cautiously, as Germans may have tried to answer based on what they believed the American authorities wanted to hear.[17] However, the surveys indicate the fact that an increasing percentage of German civilians admitted to having contact with American troops, including with African American soldiers.

---

11 Goedde, "Gender, Race, and Power," 516; Starr, *Fraternization with the Germans in World War II*, 45–46.

12 Starr, *Fraternization with the Germans in World War II*, 46.

13 See Report No. 27 (November 13, 1946) in Merritt and Merritt, eds., *Public Opinion in Occupied Germany*, 111–112; Merritt, *Democracy Imposed*, 253.

14 Report No. 94 (February 24, 1948) in Merritt and Merritt, eds., *Public Opinion in Occupied Germany*, 202–203; Merritt, *Democracy Imposed*, 253–254.

15 Report No. 6 (March 6, 1950) in Anna J. Merritt and Richard L. Merritt, eds., *Public Opinion in Semisovereign Germany: The HICOG Surveys, 1949–1955* (University of Illinois Press, 1980), 58; Merritt, *Democracy Imposed*, 255–256.

16 Report No. 24 (October 22, 1946), in Merritt and Merritt, eds., *Public Opinion in Occupied Germany*, 107–108; Merritt, *Democracy Imposed*, 258–259.

17 See Foreword by Frederick W. Williams (Director of the survey unit) in Merritt and Merritt, eds., *Public Opinion in Occupied Germany*, xvii–xxi for a discussion of the survey unit for more details about its organization and structure. Authorities especially aimed to find proof as to the changes occurring among the German people during the occupation.

Overall, especially after the end of the fraternization ban in October 1945, the occupation evolved into an atmosphere in which German-American encounters were commonplace. Germans tended to accept the American troop presence, and the American-German "victor-vanquished relationship" shifted into a partnership, in which (West) Germans viewed the United States "as the defender of their freedoms," as Richard L. Merritt terms it.[18] In addition, the US military government had gained a reputation among Germans for "competence and fairness," according to Merritt.[19] German survey respondents also noted the friendliness of American troops, with three-quarters of respondents in September 1946 agreeing that "Amis" were friendly.[20] Thus, personal encounters under a military occupation with troops as representatives of the United States had become a widely accepted circumstance in postwar Germany.

Common narratives about the occupation tend to focus on American troops' interactions with German women and children. However, the OMGUS postwar surveys of Germans paint a more complex picture about relations among the US soldiers and German population: the surveys indicate that instead of mostly young German women from lower socioeconomic classes fraternizing with Americans, overall more German men than women had some type of relationship with an American, and Germans from a higher socioeconomic status encountered Americans at a higher rate than those of lower classes.[21] The role of gender in the frequency of encounters is especially interesting due to the fact that women outnumbered men in postwar German society: according to Petra Goedde, in the age group of 20- to 40-year-olds, there were 160 women per 100 men.[22] The September 1946 OMGUS survey of nearly 3,000 people in the US Zone and of 404 people in the US and British sectors of Berlin did indicate that younger Germans were more likely to have had some form of contact with Americans, with 59% of men under age 20 and 30% of young women under 20 having had contact. In addition, 43% of women in their twenties had interacted with Americans (again, in comparison, 66% of the total survey respondents of all ages had no relations with US troops).[23] Thus, young men and women were interacting with soldiers at higher

18 Merritt, *Democracy Imposed*, 259, 267, 269.

19 Merritt, *Democracy Imposed*, 261.

20 Merritt, *Democracy Imposed*, 254.

21 Report No. 27 (November 13, 1946) and Report No. 94 (February 24, 1948) in Merritt and Merritt, eds., *Public Opinion in Occupied Germany*, 111–112, 202–203.

22 Goedde, "Gender, Race, and Power," in *The United States and Germany in the Era of the Cold War*, ed. Junker, 516.

23 Report No. 27 (November 13, 1946) in Merritt and Merritt, eds., *Public Opinion in Occupied Germany*, 111–112.

levels than older Germans: age played a decisive role in determining the rate of German contact with Americans. The November 1947 OMGUS survey, which interviewed 3,000 Germans from 225 cities, towns, and villages in the US zone, as well as 500 people in Berlin, also showed that younger Germans had higher levels of American acquaintances: 43% of men under 30 years of age and 25% of women under age 30 had friendships with Americans. This contrasted with those aged 60 or older, with only 25% of men and 11% of women being acquainted with Americans. Rates of contact were higher among members of higher classes of both genders. In addition, 12% of those surveyed had received gift packages from Americans.[24] However, again, the conclusions drawn from the surveys should be taken with some caution. Especially for German women survey respondents, the negative stigma of female interactions with American soldiers may have impacted their willingness to admit to acquaintanceships with the mostly male occupying forces. German women who had relations with American soldiers were known as *Fräuleins* and mostly looked upon unfavorably by German society. The study also did not include information on the frequency of the contacts, such as whether Germans met regularly with their American contact or whether the interaction was a onetime event. Undoubtably, however, with the presence of over a million Americans in the US zone of occupation at the end of the war, a wide variety of encounters occurred between American troops and Germans of all ages, classes, and genders.

The lived experiences of Americans thus brushed up against young Germans in the changing cultural landscape of postwar Germany, spurring transatlantic encounters under an array of circumstances. This chapter centers on the experiences of ordinary Americans to gain insight into their roles, opinions, and experiences relating to German children and youth in the immediate postwar sphere. Over time, the interaction between the youngest Germans and American GIs has become a cliched, simplistic narrative of the American occupation of Germany after World War II, one that implies that generous Americans were readily gifting German children the material benefits of American-style democracy and freedom, including goods such as candy. However, in reality, the encounter between young Germans and Americans was complex and took place within the context of an ambivalent occupation sphere, one in which policies and official rhetoric were constantly in flux and even contradictory. Occupation power structures influenced the perceptions of and the actions of the populations toward each other.

24 Margaret L. Geis and George J. Gray Jr., *The Relations of Occupation Personnel with the Civil Population: 1946–1948*, Occupation Forces in Europe Series (Historical Division, European Command, 1951), 12; Report No. 94 (February 24, 1948) in Merritt and Merritt, eds., *Public Opinion in Occupied Germany*, 202–203.

Wider global geopolitical developments also shaped shifting perceptions, impacting the encounter between young Germans and Americans. In addition, individual, personal encounters between Americans and German youngsters were affected by adult views about the proper behavior of German youngsters in postwar German society. Overall, interactions between American troops and young Germans shaped everyday life during the occupation, and even spurred shifts in official American military government policies. The meeting of the GI and the German child was not as simplistic as it has been portrayed.

First Impressions of the Children of the Enemy: Setting the Stage of Encounter Under Occupation

On September 11, 1944, the first American troops entered Germany in the area of Landkreis Bitburg-Prüm, for the first time directly encountering civilians of the enemy German population. The battle for Aachen began shortly after.[25] American officials debated about what to do with the German civilians they would inevitably encounter as troops entered Germany, putting into place nonfraternization orders. According to an official EUCOM report, the nonfraternization policy "was a favorite subject of conversation wherever Americans gathered in the European Theater of Operations. It was heatedly justified by the proponents of a 'hard peace,' and severely criticized by those who saw possibilities for the early regeneration of the Germans." Moreover, as it became clear that the policy was not working, it was seen as a "noble experiment" that was "doomed to failure," like prohibition, as it went against certain American character traits and habits.[26] However, in the first months of contact during the war and the first months of occupation, nonfraternization remained in place, and American soldiers entering Germany were faced with signs that were posted warning, "YOU ARE NOW ENTERING GERMANY—NO FRATERNIZING!," as Australian war correspondent Osmar White (who was attached to the US Third Army) observed posted on a bridge leading into Germany in early March of 1945.[27]

In Roetgen, the first German town that was captured, the American press quickly picked up on instances of fraternization: German children had emerged from the rubble "to demand—and receive—gifts of gum and candy from Ameri-

25 Starr, *Fraternization with the Germans in World War II*, 18; Seipp, "Donuts, Cab Drivers, and Gold Rush Towns," in *The Berlin Airlift and the Making of the Cold War*, ed. Schuessler, Seipp, and Sullivan, 127.
26 Starr, *Fraternization with the Germans in World War II*, 1–2.
27 White, *Conquerors' Road*, 9.

can soldiers," according to the EUCOM report on fraternization. In response to such reports, General Eisenhower responded, "This must be nipped in the bud immediately."[28] A *Stars and Stripes* article from September 15, 1944 on the incident was entitled, "German Kids Are Asking for Gum, Chums." The article noted that the children of Roetgen had appeared just a few hours after the troops took the area, once the German civilians realized that Americans were not harming the civilians as they passed through. Children apparently appeared lining the village streets and asking the soldiers, "*Haben sie gum, kamerad*? *[sic]*" (Do you have gum, comrade?). The civilians, although scared, were apparently not unhappy, and the article noted that German children seemed just like the children of England and France. The article quoted a GI stating, "The kids of all nations seem to be internationalists, minus fear or hate, with love for candy and gum," as he threw a K-ration chocolate bar to a German boy.[29] Officials including President Franklin D. Roosevelt and members of the War Department in addition to the American public were disturbed by such reports of the friendliness displayed by American troops toward German civilians. Thus, officials tried to clamp down on fraternization by ensuring images and news reports of troop fraternization were censored and that those soldiers breaking the ban on fraternization were punished. In addition, a media campaign was enacted to educate soldiers about the reasons for the policy, which included training films such as *Your Job in Germany*, which warned against any kind of contact with German, including cute children.[30] A troop guide, the *Pocket Guide to Germany*, was also widely distributed among troops, which explained nonfraternization and the types of conduct that was allowed and prohibited. The guide stated that German youth between the ages of 14 and 28 were especially dangerous, as they have "been carefully and thoroughly educated for conquest, killing, and treachery."[31] In the first weeks and

---

28 Starr, *Fraternization with the Germans in World War II*, 19–20. Also, Browder, *Americans in Post-World War II Germany*, 4; Peterson, *The American Occupation of Germany*, 154.

29 Andy Rooney, "German Kids Are Asking for Gum, Chums," *Stars and Stripes*, September 15, 1944.

30 Starr, *Fraternization with the Germans in World War II*, 19–22. Capra and Geisel, *Your Job in Germany* (1945).

31 Army Information Branch, Army Service Forces, *Pocket Guide to Germany* (US Government Printing Office, 1944), 7, Historic Government Publications from World War II, Southern Methodist University Libraries, https://digitalcollections.smu.edu/digital/collection/hgp/id/686/. Also, Starr, *Fraternization with the Germans in World War II*, 5–6, 8, 14–15. The *Pocket Guide to Germany* apparently caused some confusion as it included a guide to conversational German. To correct the impression that conversations were allowed, the guide included a sticker on its cover pointed out the nonfraternization orders. Starr, 14–15. For the British guide to soldiers, see *Instructions for British Servicemen in Germany 1944* (Bodleian Library, 2007). First published by the

months of contact, the act of gifting candy to children or even speaking to them was thus *verboten* for American soldiers, and they were liable for punishment. Images and reports of this illegal encounter also had the potential to spark outrage and anxiety among the American public and American officials, who worried about the negative harm the encounter could have on the gains of the troops during the war and later on, on the developments during the occupation, even by a cute child reaching out for a bar of chocolate.

In contrast to expectations of fierce resistance among the German population, such as a *Werwolf* movement led by "bands of fanatic youths," the German population put up very little resistance, besides isolated instances such as sniping and sabotage.[32] Instead, the first troops in towns and cities were met with a variety of reactions among the German population, from indifference and fear to even being welcomed as liberators.[33] Confusion and ambivalence often reigned in these first encounters of victors and vanquished, and Americans often projected an image of ease and health, appearing well-fed with a laid back mannerism, some chewing gum while a cigarette dangled from their mouths.[34] War correspondent Osmar White described the reaction of a German family in a village during the moment of surrender. The family had been eating dinner when the American troops arrived, and the two children came running at the sound of the tanks, holding their hands up in surrender while still wearing their bibs. The tank commander waved to them to put their hands down, and "the children's faces split into timid smiles." White wrote, "the last I saw of them, their hands were still raised, but they were now waving frantically."[35] German children responded to the arrival of American troops in a variety of ways: for example, they could run out and ask for candy, as they apparently did in the town of Roetgen, or they could hide cowering in bombed-out apartments as the first enemy entered. One of combat historian Melvin J. Lasky's first direct conversations with Germans occurred on a trip to Heidelberg on April 18, 1945. He recorded in his diary,

> On the road I could make out only friendliness. The old people smiled at you and always volunteered information eagerly. At crossroads directions were given with warm endless detail. The young ones waved at us and a few called out for "chocolate." (So the last dignity of Nazi fanaticism passes away—the vaunted loyalty of the Hitlerjugend! lost for the pangs

---

Foreign Office, 1943. The guide warned British soldiers about German civilians, and told soldiers to "do go easy on Schnaps" (back cover).

32 Merritt, *Democracy Imposed*, 239.

33 Starr, *Fraternization with the Germans in World War II*, 18.

34 See Sollors, *The Temptation of Despair*, 25–27.

35 White, *Conquerors' Road*, 26.

> of a sweet tooth . . .) In Lützel-Sachsen I stopped at a fence along a field and asked the family group what was being grown. (I was perfectly curious about what we had been calling "the host of golden daffodils.") "*Löwenzahnen*" [sic] [dandelions], the father said. "*Ach, ja!*" [Oh yes!] the children shouted, "*die gelben Blumen . . . Löwenzahnen!*" [the yellow flowers . . . dandelions!] (No we were not referring to the dandelions, but for now we would have to be content with that intelligence.) I drove off, and felt a little put out when I saw the father come back to the fence with a handful of "*gelbe Blumen*" [yellow flowers] for me. We had left too soon.[36]

GI documentation of early encounters often depicted children in scenes of rubble and destruction, sometimes shoeless or in wayward attire, yet brave enough to speak to the conquerors, the American soldiers. Forrest C. Pogue, a combat historian like Lasky, wrote in his diary on March 29, 1945 that "German children begin to ask for cigarettes as we pass."[37] On March 20, 1945, while still in the Alsace region of France, Melvin Lasky described an encounter made in the rubble and noted down his thoughts about the children's presence in the ruins of war:

> The children in the rubble everywhere, playing their games, but never so absorbed as not to run out to greet us with their universal "*shawkalahd?* [sic]." I wonder what their childhood memories of these times will be; what flavor of reminiscence there will be to their recollection of growing up and playing and making first youthful friends and enemies. (What happens to an Alsatian Tom Sawyer in all this degradation of a world . . . ?)[38]

As the war came to an end on May 8, 1945 and the occupation began, the nonfraternization policy became nearly impossible to enforce. Suddenly overnight, combat troops had become occupation soldiers, thus having more leisure-time and no longer serving in battle.[39] Soldiers "were hungry for the company of women, curious about their defeated foes, sympathetic to those who suffered, intent on obtaining souvenirs, and desirous of what comforts could be found in the German homes left standing," as Dewey A. Browder writes. Browder notes that both sides were ready and willing to fraternize.[40] In addition, Germans noticed the material wealth of GIs: many Germans participated in bartering activities with the sol-

---

36 Lerg, ed., *The Diary of Lt. Melvin J. Lasky*, 157–158.

37 Pogue, *Pogue's War*, 355. For a study of the relationship between the US military and the cigarette, see Joel Richard Bius, "The Soldier and the Cigarette: 1918–1986" (PhD diss., University of Southern Mississippi, 2015), 3, https://aquila.usm.edu/dissertations/63: Bius notes that his research is a study in modern American corporatocracy; he examines the role of the cigarette in programs such as the Berlin Airlift and the Marshall Plan, leading Europe to value American tobacco in new ways (139), and how there was a campaign to link smoking to freedom (141).

38 Lerg, ed., *The Diary of Lt. Melvin J. Lasky*, 114.

39 Starr, *Fraternization with the Germans in World War II*, 25, 45–46.

40 Browder, *Americans in Post-World War II Germany*, 5–6. Also, Starr, *Fraternization with the Germans in World War II*, 29–32.

diers, trading material items to GIs such as watches or offering services such as washing soldiers' clothes. Some German women performed sexual favors in order to get chocolate, cigarettes, or food from GIs.[41] Overall, the ban on fraternization caused a prohibition-like atmosphere, which made issues such as high rates of venereal disease even worse and harder to control. Lasky termed fraternization during the ban "'bootleg' love, 'bootleg' sex, and 'bootleg' social life."[42] After the ban on fraternization with German children was lifted in June 1945, *Life* magazine reported that GIs would use this as an excuse to talk to German women, telling them "Goodday [sic], child," highlighting how widely the fraternization ban was continuously violated due to GIs' "desire to associate with German women."[43]

The ban also impacted American reactions to German children. For example, as Melvin J. Lasky moved into Germany with his unit on March 29, 1945, he commented on the confusion about responding to children's greetings: "The trucks were setting a fierce pace. Children were still around waving at the convoy going by, but this time there was no response. Were we still in France? Wasn't this German territory? No one would risk a gesture of fraternization, and the new coldness was a little bewildering."[44] Lasky regularly defied the fraternization ban and interacted with Germans while the ban was still in place, often seeking out German citizens to gain insight into their personal stories of the war and occupation. Similarly to Lasky, Signal Corps photographer Malcolm L. Fleming also noted his interest in learning the stories of the "steady procession of wandering people" in postwar Germany.[45] During the last days of the war on April 22, 1945 while in Darmstadt, Lasky described the uncomfortable nature of the nonfraternization policy for GIs:

> 'Non-fraternization' has made us all a little cold; and it has not been an easy thing to live with. For most of the troops it means first, no source for souvenirs and street-life, for everything German (a whole nation!) is off-limits; second, no women, and in every outfit but a combat-line-company most of the day is devoted to hopes, reminiscences, jokes, plans, doggerel, art-work, and assorted folk-lore of fornication; and third, a rather uncomfortable per-

41 Browder, *Americans in Post-World War II Germany*, 5–6. On the concept of "sexual barter," see Hájková, "Sexual Barter in Times of Genocide."

42 Starr, *Fraternization with the Germans in World War II*, 1; Lerg, ed., *The Diary of Lt. Melvin J. Lasky*, 218.

43 "German Girls: U.S. Army boycott fails to stop GIs from fraternizing with them," *Life*, July 23, 1945, 35–36.

44 Lerg, ed., *The Diary of Lt. Melvin J. Lasky*, 124.

45 Fleming, *From War to Peace*, 120.

> sonal feeling, staring past passers-by on an avenue, rudely ignoring occasional smiles of old folk and the playful greetings of children waving at the columns going by.[46]

GIs such as Lasky thus navigated shifting landscapes regarding fraternization, a policy that in the end was doomed to fail as interactions increased after the end of the war. Soldiers also chose to defy the ban based on their own reasonings, such as a desire for sexual intercourse, a wish to help a hungry child, or for other personal reasons, such as those of Melvin Lasky, who wished to hear the stories of a wide range of German citizens in an attempt to understand Germans' responses regarding National Socialism. In doing so, soldiers conducted political acts in encounters with Germans, acting in ways that defied the fraternization ban.

American responses on the ground highlight the ambivalent nature of early encounters with Germans among a landscape of ruins. Soldiers encountered a devastated Germany, a place returned to the "Bicycle Age," as *Army Talks* correspondent Julian Bach Jr. termed it.[47] Americans described the unsettling nature of the destruction in Germany, of a devastation that was "monumental," even "majestic" in its immense scope, as *Time/Life* journalist Percy Knauth wrote. Knauth described the absurdity of the immediate postwar era, of humans living among rubble of their own making: "And yet, in all these ruins, people stirred, and lived, and some of them were not even changed by the war and their own personal defeat."[48] Soldiers were impacted by the level of destruction that they witnessed in Germany, where every city seemed to reach a new level of "wasteland," as Lasky termed the destruction.[49] Cities including Berlin, Frankfurt am Main, Dresden, and Nuremberg especially shocked soldiers. Signal Corps photographer Malcolm Fleming described Frankfurt am Main as a site that looked like "the crumbling habitation of an ancient civilization."[50] On Nuremberg, Fleming wrote, "somehow people are living in that jungle of wrecked buildings."[51] Foreign correspondent William L. Shirer noted in his diary in November 1945 that the US Army described Nuremberg as "91 per cent dead."[52] While in Germany for the Potsdam Conference, President Harry Truman wrote a letter to his wife Bess, noting his impres-

46 Lerg, ed., *The Diary of Lt. Melvin J. Lasky*, 166.
47 Julian Bach Jr., *America's Germany: An Account of the Occupation* (Random House, 1946), 14.
48 Percy Knauth, *Germany in Defeat* (Alfred A. Knopf, 1946), 11.
49 Lerg, ed., *The Diary of Lt. Melvin J. Lasky*, 124, 136.
50 Fleming, *From War to Peace*, 109.
51 Fleming, 113.
52 William L. Shirer, *End of a Berlin Diary* (Alfred A. Knopf, 1947), 287.

sions of Berlin: "This is a hell of a place," he wrote.[53] In his diaries from the Potsdam Conference, Truman described seeing "old men, old women, young women, children from tots to teens carrying packs [,] pushing carts, pulling carts, evidently ejected by the conquerors and carrying what they could of their belongings to nowhere in particular."[54] John McCloy, later US High Commissioner under HICOG, described the aftermath in Germany as a "complete economic, social, and political collapse" at a scope that was unparalleled since the fall of the Roman Empire.[55] Swedish journalist Stig Dagerman described the German postwar state as a "mute German agony."[56] Historian Richard Bessel argues that Germans experienced a level of defeat in World War II that could never be forgotten, spurred by the failure of the thousand-year Reich and the subsequent societal rupture.[57] Within this context of defeat, most Germans tended to focus solely on matters of day-to-day survival.[58] Rather than facing challenges such as dealing with the Nazi past, many Germans were content to focus on the everyday, choosing repression over confrontation.[59] American soldiers encountered Germans facing a historic defeat, and they had to navigate their own reactions to the German past and their views on collective guilt and on the German population's complicity in the crimes of National Socialism. Those who had witnessed some of the atrocities of Nazism, such as through the liberation of concentration camps, were especially faced with complex navigations.

The official EUCOM report on fraternization from 1947 hinted at the complexities of the encounter between the victor and the vanquished: "The perplexities of the American soldier on finding that the enemy whom he had been taught to hate and fear was a people with a culture and living habits so much like his own had already become evident."[60] American soldiers were impressed with German hab-

53 Harry S. Truman, letter to Bess Truman, July 20, 1945; Folder Correspondence from Harry S. Truman to Bess Wallace Truman, 1921–1959: July 20, 1945; Family Correspondence Files; Harry S. Truman Papers Pertaining to Family, Business, and Personal Affairs; Box 14; HSTPL; online at https://catalog.archives.gov/id/155226635.

54 Diary of Harry S. Truman, July 16, 1945, in Barton J. Bernstein, ed., "Truman at Potsdam: His Secret Diary," *Foreign Service Journal* 57, no. 7 (July/August 1980): 33.

55 John J. McCloy, quoted in Tony Judt, *Postwar: A History of Europe since 1945* (The Penguin Press, 2005), 39.

56 Stig Dagerman, *German Autumn*, trans. Robin Fulton Macpherson (University of Minnesota Press, 2011), 120.

57 See Richard Bessel, *Germany 1945: From War to Peace* (Harper Perennial, 2009), 4–7, 9, 385–386, 389–397.

58 Bessel, 6.

59 See Jähner, *Aftermath*, 323.

60 Starr, *Fraternization with the Germans in World War II*, 20.

its such as "cleanliness and industriousness," and many felt connected to Germany due to common heritage such as ancestors from Germany or an interest in German culture. Surveys even indicated that Americans preferred spending time with Germans over the Allies such as the French.[61] Sergeant Walter C. Krause spent four years as a soldier in occupation Germany, and he noted in his memoir that the lifestyle of Germans was similar to that of his own family, and that even though he was an American, "the German culture, which was supposed to be different from mine, was much the same as I had found in my hometown."[62] Krause could speak German and his parents were German-American, yet many other Americans also felt similarly at home in occupied Germany, whether due to family ties or simply feeling that German culture was familiar. Moreover, as will be explored further in greater detail, many African American soldiers felt freer in German society than back at home in the United States. Military service in Germany, despite taking place in the former land of National Socialism, was an experience of freedom for many black military personnel, who were free to mingle among the white German civilian population. This was especially significant for those soldiers from the segregated South, and served to highlight the contradictions of segregation within the US military, which lasted until 1948.[63]

Overall, the main reason for the initial ban on fraternization was security, reflecting a general fear among American authorities that German civilians, including women and youngsters, would put up fierce resistance.[64] Another potential reason for the policy, however, was due to high officials' beliefs about the supposed simple nature of the average soldier. Soldiers were viewed as being potentially susceptible to subversive influence after becoming friendly with Germans. Official policies thus also aimed at controlling the behavior of troops on the ground. According to the EUCOM report on fraternization, some officials may have believed that GIs were "not conditioned for contact with the German population and for duty in a military occupation," and needed to be guided in their conduct toward the conquered Germans.[65] This official logic implied that the simple doughboy was thus incapable of occupation tasks without a guiding hand.

61 Ziemke, *The U.S. Army in the Occupation*, 327. See also Browder, *Americans in Post-World War II Germany*, 4–5; Bertram Schaffner, *Father Land: A Study of Authoritarianism in the German Family* (Columbia University Press, 1948), 95.

62 Walter C. Krause, *So I Was a Sergeant: Memoirs of an Occupation Soldier* (Exposition Press, 1978), 196.

63 See Maria Höhn and Martin Klimke, *A Breath of Freedom: The Civil Rights Struggle, African American GIs, and Germany* (Palgrave Macmillan, 2010).

64 Starr, *Fraternization with the Germans in World War II*, 10–11.

65 Starr, 13–14.

They could be led astray by the beckoning gaze of a German women or a friendly young boy asking for candy, who may have actually been plotting to conduct acts of sabotage that would harm occupation aims.

Early fraternization violations began with troop contacts with German children, including giving young Germans gifts such as chocolate, causing worries about losing the peace among higher officials and Americans at home. German children thus brought along the potential to harm American wartime and occupation aims, because they provided a friendly image to the enemy German population that was actually potentially dangerous and who had allowed for the rise of National Socialism. In this early phase of occupation, German children played a role as a population to be feared and controlled, and also were part of the reason that Germany needed to be punished for its warmongering and occupied by a foreign military power. This logic implied that a seemingly innocent child with his or her hand stretched out for a chocolate bar could actually be waiting with a grenade in the other hand, taught by the Hitler Youth to be a fanatic who hates Americans. In contrast to GIs like Lasky, who wanted to fraternize to try to learn from Germans and their experiences, some Americans present during the end of the war and early occupation continued to see young Germans as part of the enemy population. *Life* photographer Margaret Bourke-White was present in Germany to document the war and its end. In her 1946 publication on her experience in Germany, she often mentioned German youth participating in fanatical behaviors, such as youth holding onto a bridge into Bremen at the end of the war, and "ferocious youngsters" shooting concentration camp survivors. She also stated that the former Hitler Youth members were even more fanatical than the SS.[66] Correspondent Julian Bach Jr. also described the supposed fanaticism of German youth. An excerpt of his 1946 book *America's Germany* in *Life* magazine on May 13, 1946 included an illustrated image of "a German kid, still imbued with nationalism," who goose-steps when Allied troops drive by.[67] Bach noted that the boy did this because "he thinks he is being cute . . . You think so, too . . . Until you remember that unless he is taught to stop goose-stepping, your son may be doing close-order drill."[68] Bach noted the confused state of German youth, mentioning that German "kids are in a muddle," while also referring to them as "very sour 'krauts.'"[69] Helga Dudman, an American civilian working for the Denazification Unit who was

---

66 Margaret Bourke-White, *"Dear Fatherland, Rest Quietly": A Report on the Collapse of Hitler's "Thousand Years"* (Simon & Schuster, 1946), 10, 34, 48, 79.

67 Julian Bach Jr., "America's Germany," *Life*, May 13, 1946, 106.

68 Bach Jr., *America's Germany*, 25.

69 Bach Jr., *America's Germany*, 151.

preparing evidence for the Nuremberg Trials, also saw German children from a similar angle, noting their cuteness in a letter sent to her parents from Berlin on November 1, 1945, yet never forgetting the children's Germanness:

> There are indeed lots of German children around, all of them very blond, as I think I've told you. The ones under 7 are quite cute . . . They come running after you saying "Yes, you have some tchewing [sic] gum for me?" and I dislike them all . . . You see groups of boys on the streets at night now—about 12–16 yrs [sic] old—the cute little junior werewolves.[70]

Dudman, who was Jewish and had to work with high-level Nazis in preparation for the Nuremberg Trials, contrasts with Melvin Lasky, who also was Jewish, but aimed at giving individual stories of Germans a voice in his diary. Dudman also noted that some military government employees kept pictures of concentration camps to look at whenever they felt themselves "getting soft toward individual Germans."[71] Malcolm L. Fleming described the confusion at the end of the war when encountering Germans of around 15 to 18 years of age who had taken part in combat roles. He noted that these young prisoners were young officers in the making, and that the "doughs [infantry] hadn't decided whether to bother taking them back to the Regt [sic] or not when I left."[72] German youth, especially boys of teenaged ages, evoked complex reactions and even confusion among Americans about their role in the Nazi war machine and whether they also were complicit despite their young age. These navigations were never simple and clear-cut.

Overall, more positive encounters with young Germans may have also helped troops deal with the everyday challenges of the war and postwar. The presence of youngsters amidst the rubble enabled soldiers to perform small acts of humanity and may have provided soldiers with a sense of normalcy in an abnormal time among grim realities that lingered into the occupation. In June 1945, Lasky met a group of children near Innsbruck in Austria (also under Allied occupation), who were dressed in their "church finery" after a Corpus Christi procession. He got the children to sing for him, which they agreed to after he promised them "sweets, chewing gum and chocolate" (Figure 1.1).[73] The EUCOM report on fraternization noted that German children "crowded around their [soldiers'] jeeps, haunted their mess lines, and frequented the company areas. All regulations to the contrary, the soldiers were soon passing out candy and gum, and seeking the company of children as one means to recapture some aspects of a normal home

70 Helga Dudman, *Letters Home to San Francisco from Occupied Germany 1945–1946* (Carta, 2007), 96.

71 Dudman, 48.

72 Fleming, *From War to Peace*, 64.

73 Lerg, ed., *The Diary of Lt. Melvin J. Lasky*, 205.

life."[74] In addition, German children had quickly learned that American soldiers would readily give them items such as candy and cigarettes, and they mastered tactics such as trailing Americans, picking up cigarette stubs, and hanging out and even searching through trash near US Army spaces such as the Post Exchange (PX), officer clubs, and mess halls.[75] Robert Baird, who enlisted after graduating from high school in 1945, served as an occupation soldier in Berlin in a Quartermaster Trucking Company. When Baird drove a garbage truck to the dump, Germans, including "children and older adults," would sort through the "load of discarded food scraps and assorted junk." Baird wrote in his memoir, "It was a sad thing to see and to experience . . . It was difficult and sad to believe that human beings in a civilized country living in the twentieth century would be required to humiliate themselves to such an extent." As for his role as the American truck driver, he wrote, "it was an embarrassing position to be in and you wished that there would have been a rock nearby that you could have crawled under."[76]

While in Augsburg a few weeks after the end of the war on June 13, 1945, Lasky had a conversation with a group of children. He recorded in his diary what he learned from the youngsters: "The competition for American cigarettes was fierce, but . . . each was averaging about ten a day, and the oldest boy remarked proudly that most of his butts (salvaged), which were turned over to his father, were picked up while they were still burning. We made some facial sign of appreciation for the alertness and speed, and walked on."[77] Young Germans' needs and requests penetrated the everyday experience of GIs: as Lasky wrote in August 1945 in Kassel, "Kids were on the mound of ruins and shouted 'chewing gum' at us as we passed."[78] This had quickly become the norm in the American occupation zone. The decision of members of the troops to give children food implies that these soldiers saw the children as innocent of the Nazi crimes, despite their Germanness. GIs had to navigate their own personal views of Germans and opinions on their guilt for the Nazi past and the war when coming face to face with young Germans' needs.

74 Starr, *Fraternization with the Germans in World War II*, 46–47.

75 Emmy E. Werner, *Through the Eyes of Innocents: Children Witness World War II* (Westview Press, 2000), 181. For more on existing from food found in American trash cans, see Rosemarie Köhler, *Brennesselsuppe und Rosinenbomber: Das Berliner Notkochbuch. Rezepte, Erfahrungen und Hintergründe 1945–1949* (Eichborn, 1999), 12–13.

76 Robert Walter Baird (AFC/2001/001/73816), VHP Collection, American Folklife Center, Library of Congress.

77 Lerg, ed., *The Diary of Lt. Melvin J. Lasky*, 218.

78 Lerg, ed., 244.

Figure 1.1: Children along the road near Innsbruck in front of Lt. Melvin J. Lasky's jeep, June 1945 (Lasky Center for Transatlantic Studies Munich).

Melvin Lasky also noted the complexities of the role of children in postwar Germany. For example, children could create a sense of normalcy through their play, but it often remained tinged by the war. On April 9, 1945, he spotted a small German boy playing with a huge balsa-wood model airplane onto which the boy had painted the German cross: "This was the last token of Wehrmacht and Luftwaffe power: a child zooming and dive-bombing with a miniature in his hand, winning endless plaything victories."[79] Sometimes, grim realities proved inescapable for Lasky, when he encountered ragged and sometimes injured children and youth, as on July 30, 1945:

> The war, and sometimes even the occupation, is fled, gone, and for my own part recoverable only by special effort—or betimes by the accidental turn of a street-scene. Young German boys, without an arm or leg, making their way down the avenue. Another former Wehrmacht soldier, hopping off a truck, dirty, weary, weighted down by the fantastic collection of front paraphernalia strapped to his back (blankets, gas mask, canteens, souvenirs), suddenly running into a girl, his sister perhaps, or his wife, and she screams and embraces him

79 Lerg, ed., 142.

> and kisses him and helps him with his pack. Two miserable pitiful boys wandering along in the square, their ragged clothes barely suggesting the field-gray of the army uniform, skinny, red-eyed, with the most terrible expression of emptiness and hopelessness and confusion on their faces. And yesterday: a young man, who looked Jewish, stuffing books into a little briefcase, and under his rain-coat you could see the zebra-striped jacket of the concentration camp, now neat and laundered. So the black days return for a moment.[80]

Jella Lepman, a German Jewish children's author who had returned to Germany from exile in England to work as an advisor in cultural and educational affairs for the US military authorities, observed similar disconcerting scenes, which she recorded in her memoir, which was first published in German in 1964. As she traveled around Germany with her American jeep driver, Joe, she noticed many children on the roads, including ones who "clung to our jeep in clusters when we stopped. Their thin, half-savage faces showed their hunger. They snatched at everything we offered them. They even babbled in American-style English, but it was easy enough to understand them without words." Lepman spoke to the children, asking about their parents, and she "got the same answer each time. 'No home . . . don't know where mother and father are. On the road . . . somewhere on the road. Or dead, dead . . .'"[81] Lepman noted that what was astonishing was that although they had witnessed terrible experiences, "crimes of the basest kind," and that "nothing had been kept from them," they still had "the eyes of children, and that was the astonishing thing." Lepman wrote that many of these wandering children stayed together in bands in spaces such as bombed out buildings. She witnessed one adorable little girl, who received many gifts from Americans, give all the goods to "two big toughs," who were the ring leaders who then sold the items on the black market.[82] However, Lepman, who was Jewish and had survived the Nazi regime in exile, also grappled with the children who were no longer there, the victims of the Holocaust:

> Nevertheless, I could not forget the millions of children who were small shadowy figures behind these others. The thought of them tormented me night after sleepless night. Hadn't they been torn from their mothers and fathers, or shut up with them in camps unfit for human beings? Hadn't they been humiliated, tortured, beaten, starved, finally to end up in the gas chamber? Compared with them, even these children of the ruins were lucky.[83]

---

80 Lerg, ed., *The Diary of Lt. Melvin J. Lasky*, 236.

81 Jella Lepman, *A Bridge of Children's Books: The Inspiriting Autobiography of a Remarkable Woman*, trans. Edith McCormick (O'Brien Press, 2002), 29. Memoir first published in German in 1964: Jella Lepman, *Die Kinderbuchbrücke* (S. Fischer, 1964).

82 Lepman, *A Bridge of Children's Books*, 30.

83 Lepman, *A Bridge of Children's Books*, 31.

The horrors of the war and the Holocaust lingered on in occupation Germany, impacting how occupation personnel responded to German citizens, including youngsters. These navigations were always complex in a space where "black was not black, white not white," as Lepman wrote in her memoir.[84] Lepman dealt with the complexities by aiming to help German children by developing a traveling exhibition of children's books from around the world. Lepman believed that children would "show the grown-ups the right way to go," and that it was important to "set this upside down world right again by starting with the children."[85]

Despite an early focus on fraternization with children, as the occupation developed, debates about fraternization shifted toward focusing on troop sexual relations with German women. After VE Day, venereal disease rates rose steadily, with a 235% increase between May 1945 and December 1945.[86] "Going frattin'" meant going out to meet German women, not other activities such as giving gum to children, for example, and usually implied engaging in sexual behaviors with women.[87] An official United States Forces European Theater (USFET) troop survey from the fall of 1945 suggested that during a typical week, over one-quarter of the troops were having sexual contact with German women.[88] During the entire occupation, around 94,000 children from sexual relations between German women and

84 Lepman, *A Bridge of Children's Books*, 28.

85 Lepman, *A Bridge of Children's Books*, 33.

86 Kevin Conley Ruffner, "The Black Market in Postwar Berlin: Colonel Miller and an Army Scandal," *Prologue Magazine* 34, no. 3 (Fall 2002), https://www.archives.gov/publications/prologue/2002/fall/berlin-black-market-1.html; Willoughby, *Remaking the Conquering Heroes*, 34–39. See also Starr, *Fraternization with the Germans in World War II*, 76–80; Oliver J. Frederiksen, *The American Military Occupation of Germany 1945–1953* (Historical Division, Headquarters, United States Army, 1953), 109; Peterson, *The American Occupation of Germany*, 155; Browder, *Americans in Post-World War II Germany*, 6–7; Goedde, *GIs and Germans*, 91–93; Shukert and Scibetta, *War Brides*, 135–136. On July 1946, the VD rate reached over one in four soldiers, most likely the highest in US military history (Shukert and Scibetta, 135). VD rates reached especially high levels among black troops. According to an official report, "Negro soldiers, who comprised only nine percent of EUCOM's total strength, contributed 25 – 30 percent of the venereal disease patients." However, the report also noted that rates were still abnormally high among white troops and even among officers. Geis and Gray Jr., *The Relations of Occupation Personnel*, 36. See also Fehrenbach, *Race after Hitler*, 64. Fehrenbach argues that "American officials tended to *record* and *assess* African American masculinity nearly exclusively in terms of negative undisciplined, sexual, or unsoldierly qualities."

87 Bach Jr., *America's Germany*, 76; Percy Knauth, "Fraternization: The Word Takes on a Brand-New Meaning in Germany," *Life*, July 2, 1945, 26.

88 Ziemke, *The U.S. Army in the Occupation*, 327; Willoughby, *Remaking the Conquering Heroes*, 34.

the Western Allies were born; these children were known as *Besatzungskinder*, children of the occupation.[89] Sabine Lee estimates the number of children born of US soldiers to be about 37,000.[90] Once the fraternization ban was no longer in place, restrictions remained on certain types of fraternization with Germans, such as marriage. Eventually, after petitions to the US government from servicemen, American troops were allowed to marry Germans in December 1946.[91] By the end of 1945, fraternization between American soldiers and German women had become the norm during the occupation. On December 5, 1945, Melvin J. Lasky wrote in his diary, "The large picture of US-German relations is not the 'resistance of Germans' but the 'acceptance of the Americans.' They have been taken into their beds."[92]

Fraternization with German women remained a major issue during the occupation among both Americans and Germans. German women who associated with GIs were known as *Fräuleins* as well as "furlines," "fraternazis," "*Amizonen*," or even "Ami-whores."[93] Venereal disease also became nicknamed *Veronika Dankeschön*. German women were viewed as potential dangers who could harm the body, mind, and family life of the average GI.[94] *Life* magazine reported in May 1945 that GIs who had liberated Dachau were on "the very next day being kissed and wreathed in flowers by the German women of Munich."[95] Julian Bach Jr. even blamed the behavior of GIs on the supposedly attention-seeking and demanding American women at home, thus placing the burden of improper behavior on women, not on the male sexual misconduct that was taking place.[96] Germans responded to the sexual behavior of women in various ways, with extreme reactions including hanging up posters denouncing the women for betraying the so-called Fatherland, and even sometimes cutting women's hair off.[97] Often, young German

89 Hans Habe, *Our Love Affair with Germany* (Putnam, 1953), 10. See also Goedde, *GIs and Germans*, 94; Fehrenbach, *Race after Hitler*, 2; Peterson, *The American Occupation of Germany*, 155.
90 Sabine Lee, "A Forgotten Legacy of the Second World War: GI Children in Post-War Britain and Germany," *Contemporary European History* 20, no. 2 (2011): 170, http://www.jstor.org/stable/41238351.
91 Shukert and Scibetta, *War Brides*, 144.
92 Lerg, ed., *The Diary of Lt. Melvin J. Lasky*, 287.
93 See Shukert and Scibetta, *War Brides*, 125–127, 132; Bach Jr., *America's Germany*, 76.
94 Pfau, *Miss Yourlovin*, 58; Goedde, *GIs and Germans*, 93–94.
95 Sidney Olson, "End of War: Defeated Land," *Life*, May 14, 1945, 110.
96 Bach Jr., *America's Germany*, 73; Pfau, *Miss Yourlovin*, 3.
97 Starr, *Fraternization with the Germans in World War II*, 73–76; Lerg, ed., *The Diary of Lt. Melvin J. Lasky*, 283–284; Bach Jr., *America's Germany*, 78–81. See also Tamara Domentat, *"Hallo Fräulein": Deutsche Frauen und amerikanische Soldaten* (Aufbau-Verlag, 1998), 183–190.

men and teens were the ones responding in this manner.[98] Women's bodies and the types of relationships remained regulated: the GI was quite free to explore his pleasures, while German women were often unable to do the same without repercussions, such as becoming the targets of blame or being forcibly searched for VD.[99] GIs usually had no legal responsibility for their actions, while women entered relationships for a variety of reasons, from economic need to yearning for romance. Moreover, it is important to remember that most of the sexual relationships between German women and American soldiers were temporary ones in the context of "sex as a commodity" during a military occupation.[100] John Willoughby argues that fraternization with German women became an essential part of the occupation, as the "stabilization of intimate relations between conqueror and conquered went hand-in-hand with the establishment of 'normalized' German-American relations."[101] Women provided a variety of services for American soldiers, not only sexual services, from laundry and sewing to working as household servants or even in military posts. In return for their work, they often received gifts of food, ration cards, or cigarettes and chocolate, which they could trade on the black market.

The war had thus destroyed the German nuclear family model, as fathers were missing or dead, and overwhelmed single mothers were commonplace. Children themselves often helped run the family.[102] US occupation personnel thus increasingly began to play a role as substitute providers and protectors for Germans, with German children especially helping enable this shift toward viewing Germans as a dependent victim population in need of protection.[103] Fraternization with all ages of Germans continued, and soldiers' encounters with young Germans impacted their personal experiences and played a role in the evolving relations and navigations of the occupation. Americans took on a shifting role as

---

98 Starr, *Fraternization with the Germans in World War II*, 74; Bach Jr., *America's Germany*, 80–81. Bach Jr. claimed that most of the poster hanging and hair clipping incidents were conducted by male youths, some as young as 12 years old.

99 Willoughby, *Remaking the Conquering Heroes*, 37, 44.

100 Pfau, *Miss Yourlovin*, 61. For more on gender, military masculinity, and the occupation, see Katharina Gerund, "(Military) Masculinity and a Feminized Europe," in *The Diary of Lt. Melvin J. Lasky*, ed. Lerg, 48–58. Also, Shukert and Scibetta, *War Brides*, 132, 136. The estimated number of German women who were prostitutes during the occupation was around 10 to 20% of women. The sexual nature of the occupation was so intense for all women that American dependent women and daughters needed to wear a brassard with an American flag to protect them from the types of greetings that German women got from GIs.

101 Willoughby, *Remaking the Conquering Heroes*, 39.

102 Vaizey, *Surviving Hitler's War*, 123, 129–131.

103 Goedde, *GIs and Germans*, 164; Goedde, "Gender, Race, and Power," in *The United States and Germany in the Era of the Cold War*, ed. Junker, 516.

punishers turned into protectors, and their presence in postwar Germany was normalized. As the occupation progressed, fraternization evolved from a *verboten*, dangerous activity to one that was actively encouraged by official policies, which reflected the role of Americans as a protective force aiming at rehabilitation rather than punishment. Within the context of the heightening Cold War, American policies became increasingly focused on setting up a bulwark against communism in Western Europe, including in West Germany. Aid toward suffering Germans played a role in attempts to win over hearts and minds, and GIs as well as Americans at home largely came to see the vanquished Germans as victims. GIs navigated this geopolitical context and used their agency and privilege as conquerors to make decisions about the conquered.

The GI and the German child had become omnipresent in the aftermath of the war, as Americans solidified their power and presence in the postwar German landscape. GIs interacted with young Germans for a variety of reasons, for example out of a desire to help and show their humanity, or from boredom in an occupation where many troops simply wanted to return home. Moreover, American assistance toward the German population normalized German-American relations. Young Germans played a role in this shift through their very child-ness: they provided Americans with an image that furthered views of Germans as victims. How could a German child, perhaps eight years old, who had known nothing but war, bombings, uprooting, and maybe had lost a parent, be a Nazi? This question and more entered the minds of GIs in their navigations of the postwar landscape, for example as they handed over a bar of chocolate to a pleading child.

After Nonfraternization: Reeducation of the Future of German Society

As early as the first moments of contact between Germans and Americans as World War II drew to its end, young Germans impacted official American policies and molded GIs' experiences. Encounters between German children and American military personnel drew attention across the Atlantic and shifted understandings of the conquered enemy population. Troop interactions with German youngsters were first interpreted with fear, with worries about young fanatic Germans who continued to cling to Nazism. However, as the occupation progressed, views of Germans shifted toward a mindset focused on German victimhood, represented especially by German children and women. Fraternization thus became normalized and even encouraged, and US military members became providers and protectors, especially for German children who also represented the future of German democracy. Instead of fearing and forbidding troop interactions with young Germans, occupation officials started to encourage and embrace fraternization as a means of reeducating, democratizing, and rehabilitating Germany. The GI had thus stepped into his role as "the world's best salesman of democracy," as Byron Price described the role of the average soldier in his November 1945 report for President Truman.[104] On-the-ground interactions between GIs and young Germans especially enabled this official shift. German children and youth were increasingly seen as a solution to occupation issues and as the hope for the future of Germany, as long as they followed the correct path toward democratic reeducation based on the example of the GI. According to Petra Goedde, this focus on the youngest Germans helped avoid contradictions inherent in the occupation aims of forcing democratization, as young Germans provided an image of the German population as "infantile citizens" in need of teaching about democratic citizenship.[105] Geopolitical relations between Germany and the United States also shifted toward a strong partnership, and a sort of "love affair" developed between the former enemies, as Ralph Willett argues.[106]

Encounters between Germans and Americans often became highly personal, taking place in ways such as living next to Germans or entering into relationships, and ranging from casual conversations and sexual exchange to marriage. The populations encountered each other in both regulated and illicit spaces, for example the beer hall, black market, workplace, the street, churches, and in official occupation spaces such as German Youth Activities or German-American clubs.[107] Black market participation often required some form of German involvement with GIs, as cigarettes were the main form of currency of the occupation until the currency reform in June 1948. Children even sometimes traded with cigarettes on the black market.[108] Soldiers were granted multiple packs of cigarettes in their weekly PX ration, in addition to candy bars. For example, according to a letter sent from GI Bernard Bolf to his sister in March 1945, GIs received seven packs of

104 Byron Price, Memorandum to President Truman, November 9, 1945, p. 2; Folder OF 198 1945–April 1950 [1 of 2] Germany; OF 198; HSTP; Box 738; HSTPL.

105 Goedde, *GIs and Germans*, 128.

106 Ralph Willett, *The Americanization of Germany, 1945–1949* (Routledge, 1989), 2.

107 Browder, *Americans in Post-World War II Germany*, 15–20. See also Geis and Gray Jr., *The Relations of Occupation Personnel.* A recent work examines encounters in Western Allied officers' and soldiers' clubs from 1945 to 1955: Lena Rudeck, *Vergnügen in Besatzungszeiten: Begegnungen in westalliierten Offiziers- und Soldatenclubs in Deutschland, 1945–1955* (Transcript, 2023).

108 Geis and Gray Jr., 40–45; Browder, *Americans in Post-World War II Germany*, 15; Ziemke, *The U.S. Army in the Occupation*, 336–339. On the black market in Berlin, see Malte Zierenberg, *Berlin's Black Market: 1939–1950* (Palgrave Macmillan, 2015). For an image of German children selling cigarettes in Schöneberg in Berlin, see Zierenberg, 184.

cigarettes, seven sticks of gum, and seven candy bars in their weekly rations.[109] GIs thus came from a land of material prosperity in contrast to Germans, and found that their status as well-off conquerors in Germany enabled them access to material benefits: they could get souvenirs or sex for a few cigarettes or a candy bar.

In a letter to Hannah Arendt recorded in his diary, Melvin Lasky categorized his experience in the occupation as "an unbelievable unreal adventure!"[110] However, despite this positive feeling of adventure, he also noted an ambivalence present in the occupation experience: there was a "general tourist-unsettledness" to the experience for Americans in the in-between phase of the occupation.[111] Most soldiers who had served in combat especially wished to return home rather than remain in Germany now that the war was over. Jella Lepman described how her jeep driver, Joe, yearned to return home to his fiancée in his hometown in the Midwest. He even had a calendar where he would cross off the days left until his discharge. Lepman wrote in her memoir that Joe did not care about his special privileges among German women. Instead, he "was suffering agonies of homesickness." Joe said, "I wish I'd never seen this d— Germany . . . I want to go home. I want to go home."[112] Another soldier in occupation Germany, James Gustavus Smith, wrote to his wife back home on July 18, 1945: "It has been nice sitting out here in the country doing absolutely nothing but is getting rather tiresome. I have enjoyed my stay here and it has lasted just long enough. Now if I can catch that boat [home] in about three weeks I will be satisfied." On July 16, 1945, he also wrote to his wife how when he finally came home, his son, who was turning nine months old, would probably not "understand who this strange man is that is making his Mummy cry."[113] Instead of fighting for their lives in combat, occupation troops spent the hours on more monotonous tasks, such as guard duty or administrative tasks. Many were also able to take advantage of trips arranged especially for GIs, for example to Paris or the Alps.

Overall, Germans gained an impression of American soldiers as easygoing, informal, equal to their superiors, and comfortable anywhere, for example, put-

109 Bernard R. Bolf (AFC/2001/001/25786), VHP Collection, American Folklife Center, Library of Congress.
110 Lerg, ed., *The Diary of Lt. Melvin J. Lasky*, 271. On similar feelings of excitement in personal experiences of female officials in the Control Commission for Germany (British Element) (CCG (BE)) in the British Zone, see Daniel Cowling, "Gosh . . . I Think I'm in a Dream!," in *Transforming Occupation in the Western Zones of Germany*, ed. Erlichman and Knowles, 211–229.
111 Lerg, ed., 281.
112 Lepman, *A Bridge of Children's Books*, 21–22, 29.
113 James Gustavus Smith (AFC/2001/001/106804), VHP Collection, American Folklife Center, Library of Congress.

ting down their machine guns after entering Erfurt on April 14, 1945 and starting to play soccer on the street corner, which Annemarie Meckel described in her diary as her first impression of Americans.[114] GIs thus appeared to have the power to show Germans what was possible in the new era of postwar. They showed Germans that the average American had a relatively prosperous life, and for German youth, the example of the American soldier showed a glimpse into another sort of life, different from the Nazi era and wartime. Harald Jähner terms the GI as showing "relaxed masculinity," which contrasted sharply with the strict hierarchies and norms of Nazism.[115] The mannerisms and behaviors of GIs thus impacted German impressions of life in the United States and their views about American-style democracy, which seemed to imply material prosperity. American soldiers provided a glimpse into the so-called "good life" that Americans increasingly enjoyed in the years after the war.

The material wealth and mannerisms of GIs had the potential to impact German youngsters, who chose to approach GIs for various reasons, whether due to curiosity or hunger, or a mix of both. Young Germans learned that GIs were often generous to youngsters, and they acted accordingly based on this awareness, calling out to soldiers, asking for anything, or following them around. In addition, occupation policies of food rationing often left many children hungry. Thus, the very cause of their hunger was a direct result of Allied policies of rationing, which remained restrictively low due to food shortages and to ensure that Germans would not receive more rations than their neighboring countries, since they were the perpetrators of the war. One major factor that spurred GI benevolence toward children was this hunger. Children also navigated GI encounters in ways that would provide them with more food than their rations allowed. Official rationing policies were often not mentioned in rhetoric about the difficult conditions of the young. Overall, the challenging state among youth is what increasingly spurred American humanitarian actions, especially later during the occupation.

Above all, the physical, mental, and moral condition of young Germans worried observers, including GI Tony Vaccaro, who took countless photographs of children among the physical devastation that was postwar Germany. He remarked in the introduction to his published photograph collection that in the midst of the rebirth of a new Germany, children were often left to fend for themselves. He worried about what was to become of "these orphans of war," espe-

---

114 Gerhard Hirschfeld and Irina Renz, eds.,*"Vormittags die ersten Amerikaner": Stimmen und Bilder vom Kriegsende 1945* (Klett-Cotta, 2005), 133.
115 Jähner, *Aftermath*, 150–152.

cially boys, who often lacked male role models. He wrote, "Often I saw children without shoes and poorly clothed. It was a perfect scenario for an entire schizophrenic or depressed state in the male line of future generations. I tried to capture with the camera what I saw of those children."[116] Melvin Lasky also described the utter need he witnessed in the occupation on December 16, 1945 in Berlin: "On the roads: old men, and young kids, waving hundred-mark bills at passing Allied vehicles, hoping for some bargain on cigarettes or chocolate or sugar or breakfast-dinner-supper rations, or anything."[117] Even later on in Germany, children continued to trail GIs and ask for goods. Richard W. Fabian, who served in Germany from 1952 to 1954, noted that two children in Stuttgart were following him around. Fabian gave the children candy and ice cream regularly and "took them around," because he missed his sister's children at home. Fabian viewed these children as a "substitute for my nieces and nephews," and helping them out was "a morale builder" for him.[118]

Many GIs were quite young themselves and had their own children or other young relatives back home, thus having potential commonalities with young Germans. For example, Robert Edward Wilson befriended the neighborhood German kids, noting in his memoirs that they "looked just like the kids down the block at home." Wilson became a soldier in 1943 at age 18, and a veteran at age 21. He noted that he had matured through his service, but "had not reached full manhood" at the end of his service on January 1, 1946.[119] Some observers remarked on the childishness of GIs: Swedish journalist Stig Dagerman described a group of soldiers as "drunk American boy-soldiers, each one his own hit-song. They fight another playfully."[120] Furthermore, many GIs increasingly saw children as victims, which could have enabled them to better handle the complexities of judgments about German guilt.

Views of childhood in the 1940s also impacted soldiers' perceptions of young Germans. Americans at the time held diverse views of childhood, especially in the wake of the militarization of American childhood during World War II as part of the home front effort, which encouraged constant preparedness. Children were to prepare for the potential of being future soldiers, as well as participate in activi-

116 Vaccaro, *Entering Germany*, 22.
117 Lerg, ed., *The Diary of Lt. Melvin J. Lasky*, 292.
118 Interview with Richard W. Fabian (AFC/2001/001/62498), 37:00–37:35, VHP Collection, American Folklife Center, Library of Congress.
119 Robert Edward Wilson (AFC/2001/001/2210), VHP Collection, American Folklife Center, Library of Congress. Wilson's work in occupation Germany included preparing the prison in Nuremberg for the prisoners before the Nuremberg Trials.
120 Dagerman, *German Autumn*, 102.

ties such as collecting scrap for the war effort.[121] Angelo Patri's *Your Children in Wartime*, published in 1943, even stated that American children were "enlisted for the duration of the war as citizen soldiers."[122] Despite this militarization of childhood, American children in World War II were removed from directly experiencing wartime violence, coercion, and the threat of death as faced by children elsewhere during the war.[123]

Simultaneously to being militarized, childhood was also increasingly seen as a special and protected age period, with children meant to enter the standardized schooling system, not work in factories or assist in wars. In addition, attention to the fields of developmental psychology, social work, and psychiatry had increased, as well as a focus on the potential detrimental effects of war on children.[124] American experts also came to occupation Germany to study German children and families in an attempt to understand the indoctrination that had occurred under the Nazis. For example, American psychiatrist Bertram Schaffner ran the Information Control Division (ICD) Screening Center, which screened Germans who were applying for Information Control licenses.[125] Schaffner researched authoritarianism in Germans, arguing that authoritarianism was the central factor in German life, which began "from its starting point in the family, into the education of the children and the political life of the adult."[126] Schaffner highlighted the role of the father as the dominant figure in the family, and noted that despite the defeat and failure of both National Socialism and Hitler, the ultimate father figure, German youth may still "have an unfulfilled need for a substitute for the lost father-symbol," noting their continued susceptibility toward authoritarian figures due to their Germanness.[127] Schaffner argued that "without skillful and patient help," German youth would not be able to "strip themselves of the emotional authoritarian patterns and traditions in which they have been reared since early childhood."[128] For American experts such as psychiatrists and

---

121 See Ross F. Collins, *Children, War and Propaganda* (Peter Lang, 2011), xiii–xvi, 274–277. See also Tuttle, *Daddy's Gone to War*.

122 Angelo Patri, *Your Children in Wartime* (Doubleday, Doran, & Co., 1943), 89.

123 Collins, *Children, War and Propaganda*, 274.

124 See Anna Freud and Dorothy T. Burlingham, *War and Children* (Ernst Willard, 1943) for one of the first studies of the psychological effects of war on children. Anna Freud was the daughter of Sigmund Freud. Americans increasingly turned to pediatrician Dr. Benjamin Spock's work on guidance for child care, first published in 1946. Benjamin Spock, *Common Sense Book of Baby and Child Care* (E.P. Dutton, 1985).

125 See Schaffner, *Father Land*, ix, 117.

126 Schaffner, 5.

127 Schaffner, 15, 89–90, 93.

128 Schaffner, 93.

psychologists, the reeducation of Germans was a necessary yet wide-ranging task, dependent on modifying traits that had been ingrained in Germans since early childhood.[129] Attempting to interrupt negative patterns of German child rearing became relevant for military government tasks, and German youth were placed in the role of figures in need of modification so that Americans could reach their occupation goals of reeducation.

Young Germans' physical and spiritual states began to draw the attention of both occupation officials and outside observers, who worried about the impacts of both Nazi indoctrination and the challenging postwar conditions. The condition of youngsters became central factors in critiques of the postwar occupation. For example, occupation critic Victor Gollancz, a British Jewish publisher, wrote in his work *In Darkest Germany* that "the worst thing in Germany—worse than the malnutrition, the overcrowding, the gaping footwear in the schools—is the spiritual condition of the youth."[130] Gollancz's work included images of malnourished children, with such shocking images serving to evoke recent crimes of the Holocaust as a reason for feeding Germans.[131] In 1947, former President Herbert Hoover visited Germany as head of the Famine Emergency Committee at the request of President Truman to study the conditions there and provide recommendations to Truman. Hoover apparently was appalled by what he found in Germany, also evoking references to the Holocaust while demanding improvements: "We do not want the American flag flying over nation-wide Buchenwalds."[132] Hoover also equated American values to human decency such as providing enough food. He believed that with the raising of the American flag in Germany, "We accepted the responsibility to maintain human values."[133] He also argued using the logic of anti-communism, noting that hungry bellies could lead populations to become susceptible to communist influence.[134] Thus, according to Alice Weinreb, German postwar hunger enabled Germans to become "legitimate targets of international sympathy."[135] Hoover's work in postwar Germany helped lead to the introduction of an extra meal given at schools, the *Schulspeisung* (also called the *Hoover-Speisung* or *Quäker-Speisung*), which helped many children, since many came to school hungry and could not concentrate due to hunger. The *Schulspeisung* had

129 See Schaffner, 5.

130 Victor Gollancz, *In Darkest Germany* (Henry Regnery Company, 1947), 230.

131 Gollancz, 233–238. See also Weinreb, *Modern Hungers*, 107–108.

132 Weinreb, 109; Amy Bentley, *Eating for Victory: Food Rationing and the Politics of Domesticity* (University of Illinois Press, 1998), 150.

133 Clay, *Decision in Germany*, 267.

134 Goedde, *GIs and Germans*, 122.

135 Weinreb, *Modern Hungers*, 109.

started in the British zone in 1946, but Hoover's work led to its spread to the US zone in 1947.[136] Dialogue around American food aid increasingly focused on the suffering of hungry Germans (especially the youngest Germans) and the goodness of benevolent Americans, including the GI as a representative, rather than focusing on official occupation policies such as rationing.

Relatively quickly after the end of the war, it had become common knowledge among Americans that German children were hungry. Beginning in June 1946, American citizens sent CARE packages to Germany. In 1946, over 300,000 CARE packages were sent to Germany, and in 1947 this number rose to over 1.8 million packages.[137] Sending a package was fairly easy: Americans could place their order for a CARE package for the price of $10 at department stores such as Macy's or through civic and religious organizations in their hometowns.[138] Americans could also indicate who the package would go to. For example, they could choose to send it to orphaned children or single mothers.[139] Within the first five years of its operation, CARE sent ten million packages across the Atlantic, with six million of those going to Germany.[140] Overall, over the years, "Germany received more CARE Packages than any other nation in Europe," according to David Morris. Around 40 million Germans (two-thirds of the population) received these packages, sent from regular American citizens to the citizens of a former enemy nation.[141]

---

136 See Herbert Hoover, *Freedom Betrayed: Herbert Hoover's Secret History of the Second World War and its Aftermath*, ed. George H. Nash (Hoover Institution Press, Stanford University, 2011), 805–806. Quakers in the aftermath of World War I and World War II were active in providing meals for children, especially through the American Friends Service Committee (AFSC). Herbert Hoover, also a Quaker, was also the initiator the post-World War I food aid. See Achim von Borries, *Quiet Helpers: Quaker Service in Postwar Germany* (Quaker Home Service and the American Friends Service Committee, 2000), https://afsc.org/sites/default/files/documents/Quiet%20Helpers%20%28Quaker%20Service%20in%20Postwar%20Germany%202000.pdf. For more on Quaker humanitarian and international work beginning in 1917, see Daniel Maul, *The Politics of Service: US-amerikanische Quäker und internationale humanitäre Hilfe 1917–1945* (De Gruyter, 2021). Quaker aid to German children after World War I also provided millions of meals for hungry children.

137 Statistics are for packages sent to the American, British, and French zones and to Berlin. Klaus-Jörg Ruhl, *Neubeginn und Restauration: Dokumente zur Vorgeschichte der Bundesrepublik Deutschland 1945–1949* (Deutscher Taschenbuch Verlag, 1982), 516. Aid also came through CRALOG, the Council of Relief Agencies Licensed to Operate in Germany, beginning in April 1946.

138 Werner, *Through the Eyes of Innocents*, 191, 193. In 1946, the price of CARE packages was reduced from $15 to $10, which led to a surge in purchases.

139 Philipp Baur, "From Victim to Partner: CARE and the Portrayal of Postwar Germany," in *Die amerikanische Reeducation-Politik nach 1945*, ed. Gerund and Paul, 120.

140 Maximilian Klose, *Why They Gave: CARE and American Aid for Germany after 1945* (Franz Steiner Verlag, 2024), 16.

141 See David Morris, *A Gift from America: The First Fifty Years of CARE* (Longstreet Press, 1996), 21; Werner, *Through the Eyes of Innocents*, 193.

American postwar food aid to Germany became part of the shifting realm of occupation policies, and the focus turned to the Soviet Union as a new enemy, rather than on punishing the Germans for past crimes. Food aid to Germany thus had both "practical and symbolic power," as Kaete O'Connell argues. Rhetoric about American actions, such as feeding hungry stomachs, highlighted the generosity of Americans and became especially useful in the escalating Cold War and American attempts to win over hearts and minds.[142] German children became aware that Americans were their benefactors, and some wrote thank you letters to Americans, including to Herbert Hoover and President Harry Truman, as well as to Quakers who led food relief programs in the American and British zones.[143] The challenging occupation circumstances among young Germans played a central role in shifting discussions about Germans from punishment for the crimes of the Nazi past to a focus on assistance and recovery. Thus, German youngsters and their hunger helped spur major shifts in the politics of the occupation. Increasingly, Germans were viewed as friends to be helped rather than enemies dealt the inevitable fate of hunger due to their responsibility for the war.

Young Germans also emerged at the forefront of future hopes for Germany during the occupation. On May 10, 1945, Melvin Lasky spoke to a former political prisoner in Laufen concentration camp, who stated, "I have no hope for Germany. A little hope for the new generation, the children who will grow up. But new 'human beings' have to be created."[144] The plight of young Germans and their hunger helped shift views of Germans into victims, especially as Americans worried about potential negative, lasting effects of Germans' challenging state of hunger and suffering. German youngsters needed to be helped in order to ensure a positive future, rather than punished. In addition, assistance toward German children and youth helped Americans illustrate their humanity while also shifting the focus from the Nazi past and questions of guilt toward a focus on the present-day needs and hopes for the future of a democratic German nation, as Petra Goedde notes.[145] Young Germans thus became major figures in US occupation aims, as their education could help ensure future world peace, if it was under-

---

142 Kaete O'Connell, "Washington, D.C., 1946: Humanitarian Food Relief for Occupied Germany," in *Online Atlas on the History of Humanitarianism and Human Rights*, ed. Fabian Klose, Marc Palen, Johannes Paulmann, and Andrew Thompson, October 2017, https://hhr-atlas.ieg-mainz.de/articles/oconnell-washington-dc.

143 See Kaete O'Connell, "Benevolent Diplomacy," *Perspectives on History*, American Historical Association, December 4, 2017, https://www.historians.org/perspectives-article/benevolent-diplomacy-childrens-art-and-us-food-relief-in-occupied-germany-december-2017/. See also Chapter 4 of this work.

144 Lerg, ed., *The Diary of Lt. Melvin J. Lasky*, 186.

145 Goedde, *GIs and Germans*, 164.

taken in a positive, democratic manner. Encounters on the ground between youngsters and US soldiers became part of an official occupation drive to rehabilitate Germans and reeducate them into democratic citizens.

The official occupation aim to reeducate German youngsters was bolstered by the fact that encounters on the ground were already focused on impacting youth in positive ways. As early as the summer of 1945, GIs had noticed the needs of German youth, creating youth programs for Germans to partake in various organized activities, from baseball to discussion groups. After watching two Army teams playing a football game in Berlin in October 1945, James K. Pollock, a political scientist and special advisor to the military government, wrote in his diary that young Germans should be taught about [American] football as a way to improve this younger generation and teach American-style qualities, such as "excellent team play, good sportsmanship."[146] Such initiatives were already happening on the ground by then, spurred on by the individual desire of GIs to help young Germans. Occupation authorities realized that this work could be of use for occupation aims of reeducation and democratization. Thus, they actively encouraged the formation of voluntary clubs and other activities for youth, and beginning in April of 1946, the Army Assistance to German Youth Activities was created.[147] GYA provided an infrastructure that aimed toward the rehabilitation of youth as democratic citizens, with the GI serving as role model. Helen Liddell, who researched education in occupied Germany, wrote in 1948 that "no one can be in the American zone for any length of time without being made aware of these G.Y.A. [sic] activities of the United States Forces," noting that over a million German youth had received Army assistance in February 1947. Moreover, she highlighted the particular generosity of the US military personnel, writing that "the vitality and generosity of the average American is nowhere more clearly seen than in these G.Y.A. activities." However, she noted that there were challenges, including a lack of awareness about the program among many youths and competition between civilian and military authorities. She also noted that other initiatives such as exchange programs to other countries such as England were

146 James K. Pollock, *Besatzung und Staatsaufbau nach 1945: Occupation Diary and Private Correspondence 1945–1948*, ed. Ingrid Krüger-Bulcke (R. Oldenbourg, 1994), 111–112.

147 15 April 1946 HQ USFET; Folder USFET Youth Directives 15 April 1946; Records RE the Work of the Youth Activities Section; Records for the Community Education Branch, Records of the Education and Cultural Relations Division; Box 148; Office of Military Government, United States (OMGUS); Records of U.S. Occupation Headquarters, World War II, RG 260; NACP. For more on GYA, see Chapter 3 of this work.

essential, as these visits would be to places "where democracy works and is not a ridiculous parrot-cry, synonymous with hunger and military occupation."[148]

Above all, despite the challenges of democratic reeducation within a military occupation, Army-sponsored GYA clubs, GYA youth centers, and other organized activities impacted youth, even though not all German youth were aware of the offerings of the program. Military government authorities also actively encouraged non-GYA, German-organized youth clubs, including scouting clubs, trade union groups, and religious clubs. These clubs also had to undergo democratic practices, such as holding elections and writing a constitution. Other youth reeducation programs such as leadership schools also aimed to teach Germans about democratic values, and exchange programs to the United States helped further notions of democratic global citizenship.[149] Thus these measures of positive programs for youth contrasted with the methods of the Hitler Youth, which aimed to militarize and indoctrinate youth into National Socialists, focusing on paramilitary activities and preparation for wartime service, including military drills, weapons practices, camping exercises, National Socialist songs, and competitive sports.[150] Girls in the BDM were also indoctrinated and socialized for roles of serving the *Vaterland*, for example as future National Socialist wives and mothers, although BDM activities also emphasized physical fitness.[151] In contrast, the US aim for occupation youth activities aimed to demonstrate democracy through hands-on programs. Club membership was voluntary, and clubs were to focus on civic engagement, open discussions, team work, and building positive relationships, with activities such as sports, music, discussions, dancing, and more. Youth activities served a political aim for the American occupiers, the reeducation of German youth, who were the future democratic citizens of German society. Encounters between GIs and young Germans became a major part of the fabric of occupation policies and its official aims through the GYA program.

The focus on young Germans among American occupation authorities did contain a level of continuity with the Nazi past. Youngsters during National Socialism were also a focus group for official attempts to bring about societal con-

148 Liddell, "Education in Occupied Germany," 48–49, 52. See also Browder, *Americans in Post-World War II Germany*, 94.

149 Browder, *Americans in Post-World War II Germany*, 69–70.

150 Michael H. Kater, *Hitler Youth* (Harvard University Press, 2004), 28–37. Kater argues "that the hallmark of HJ socialization was militarization, with a view to a war of territorial expansion and, as its predetermined goal, the neutralization of Europe's Jews" (28–29).

151 See Birgit Retzlaff and Jörg-Johannes Lechner, *Bund Deutscher Mädel: Fakultative Eintrittsgründe von Mädchen und jungen Frauen in den BDM* (Kovač, 2008), 135–211; Dagmar Reese, ed., *Die BDM-Generation: Weibliche Jugendliche in Deutschland und Österreich im Nationalsozialismus* (Verlag für Berlin-Brandenburg, 2007).

trol. Youth were thus central to National Socialism, and the last picture of Hitler before his suicide was of him greeting children during the Battle of Berlin in April 1945.[152] In a similar manner, postwar American officials focused much attention on their worries about youth, including fears that wayward boys could turn into criminals and young women into prostitutes. Activities such as GYA participation would help ensure proper behavior, American officials believed. To these officials, proper reeducation was the cure to the plague of Nazi ways of thinking. Theodor Geisel (better known as Dr. Seuss), who had worked on propaganda measures during the war, had illustrated a political cartoon in 1942 which depicted the "'psychological disarmament' of Axis youth," which required clearing their minds to create new ways of behaving and thinking, such as "peace thoughts," as the caption noted.[153] His cartoon vividly depicted what became American reeducation aims during the occupation: American occupation authorities hoped reeducative policies, which essentially were policies focused on cleansing the minds of youth, would shape German youth toward proper behavior. This view was based on seeing youth as simultaneously innocents in need of protection and as potential criminals in need of prevention from delinquency. Molding youth properly furthered the official occupation policies of reeducation and democratization. On-the-ground encounters between GIs and German youth thus became part of the official occupation goals, made to serve a larger purpose. Young Germans served a larger geopolitical purpose for American authorities, who may not have always had the best interests of youngsters in mind but rather were concerned with how to use the needs of young Germans to further their own purposes. For example, rehabilitation and reeducation of youngsters fit well with American goals in the heightening Cold War context, in which Americans needed West Germans as allies. In addition, focusing on positive actions toward youth allowed Americans to avoid discussions of the contradictions of these very policies, in which an occupation run by foreign military personnel was making democracy mandatory for the German population.

However, it is important to remember that in contrast to Nazi youth programs, German youngsters were not forced to join in new measures such as GYA clubs or American-sponsored camping trips. Youth had the voluntary choice to participate in and quit such activities, and the focus was on increasing young Ger-

---

152 Fisher, *Disciplining Germany*, 1–2.

153 Richard H. Minear, *Dr. Seuss Goes to War: The World War II Editorial Cartoons of Theodor Seuss Geisel* (The New Press, 2001), 64. The cartoon was from December 30, 1942. In 1941 and 1942, Dr. Seuss drew political cartoons for *PM*, a New York daily newspaper. Later, he left *PM* and accepted a commission with the Army in Frank Capra's Signal Corps unit, helping make propaganda films for military and civilian purposes. See 6, 259.

mans' democratic skills, such as participative citizenship through elections and discussions. When GYA and other youth activities measures were conducted well, German youth got to enjoy new experiences that focused on their individual wishes and interests, which could vary from learning English to writing club newspapers. This contrasted with the compulsory, follow-the-leader focus of the Hitler Youth and BDM, whose main purpose was to train young Germans to be the future upholders of the National Socialist regime. Although fraught with tensions, with American adults aiming to use the reeducation of German youth for their political purposes, American occupation programs such as GYA did enable some youth a glimpse into a different way of living. In addition, youth gained opportunities to interact with representatives of the United States, GIs, who could embody a different way of living. Americans were to be mentors and role models of German youth rather than leaders demanding compulsory obedience.

Other American reeducative programs included the *Amerikahäuser*, which provided access to libraries and information, including for youth, and were first financed by the US military government until the US Information Agency (USIA) took over.[154] The *Amerikahaus* in Munich opened on July 12, 1948 and was the largest *Amerikahaus* in the US zone. The first visitor was a young girl, who was depicted in a newspaper article reading a picture book with General George P. Hays, the deputy military governor of the US zone.[155] The *Amerikahaus* Munich not only contained a collection of thousands of books and magazines designed to give insight into democratic life but also held programs for special audiences, including events specifically for children and young people.[156] In addition, in July 1946, the first international exhibition returned to Germany, the International Exhibition of Children's Books, which was held at the Haus der Kunst in Munich, run by the children's author Jella Lepman.[157] Lepman went on to found the first International Youth Library in Munich in September 1949. Lepman believed that children's books were especially important in postwar society, as they played a role as the "first messengers of peace," and that German youngsters were in no way responsible for the war.[158] She aimed to do something to help Germany's children, who were "just as innocent as children all over the world," in order to prevent them from falling "into the wrong hands if no help came from the world

154 See "The History of the Amerikahaus," Amerikahaus Munich, accessed January 4, 2025, https://www.amerikahaus.de/en/about-us/history.

155 "Eröffnung des größten Amerikahauses der US-Zone," *Frankfurter Rundschau*, July 15, 1948. Clipping in Amerikahaus Munich archives, Munich, Germany.

156 See Amerikahaus programs from 1948, available at Amerikahaus Munich archives.

157 See Lepman, *A Bridge of Children's Books*, 13, 55.

158 Lepman, *A Bridge of Children's Books*, 36.

outside."[159] Overall, young Germans faced a shifting landscape in which they could choose their level of participation (or lack thereof) in activities that served American occupation aims, and they had access to resources that could expand their horizons, such as the *Amerikahaus* library or a visit to Lepman's International Exhibition of Children's Books in 1946.

In addition to worries about German youth, American authorities were also worried about troop behavior during the occupation, thus creating an interesting parallel in which reeducation activities for German youth also served to control American troop delinquency.[160] Much attention was paid to controlling the behavior of GIs, which was sometimes especially rowdy in the wake of occupation boredom and easy access to sex and alcohol. In an attempt to combat high venereal disease rates, "Pro" stations became a common sight in occupation Germany, where GIs could get condoms. Although German women were often the ones blamed for their willingness to have sex with GIs, for example in exchange for a candy bar, authorities did also discuss GI delinquency. Programs that focused on German youth rather than German women enabled officials to get GIs to participate in activities that were aimed at a more innocent sector of the German population, and also provided great publicity for the cause of occupation. Images of GIs working together with young Germans showed that something constructive was coming out of the occupation, helping soothe American worries about promiscuous *Fräuleins* and portraying German youth as the democratic future.

In addition, GIs' work with young Germans could help boost occupation troop morale, which was often an issue during the postwar occupation. Soldiers who had participated in combat and were waiting to return home were often caught in a challenging waiting game, in which their departure from Germany depended on how many points they had accrued during the war, with factors such as length of service, battle wounds, and decorations impacting point levels.[161] Many combat troops remained in Germany as occupiers into 1946. Working with or helping young Germans enabled soldiers to regain a sense of purpose to their service, and perhaps helped ease yearnings for their own families back home as they spent their time in the waiting game. Troops also viewed work with German youngsters as a rewarding occupation duty. For example, Robert Allen

159 Lepman, *A Bridge of Children's Books*, 14.

160 See Geis and Gray Jr., *The Relations of Occupation Personnel*, 46–47; also, 4–5. On GI delinquency in 1950s Germany, see Gerhard Fürmetz, "Insolent Occupiers, Aggressive Protectors: Policing GI Delinquency in Early 1950s West Germany," in *GIs in Germany*, ed. Maulucci Jr. and Junker, 189–211.

161 See for example, the journal of Sergeant Henry Giles: Janice Holt Giles, ed., *The G.I. Journal of Sergeant Giles* (Boston: Houghton Mifflin, 1965), 356–358.

Macon was proud to have worked with the local German population, including helping bring food to German children, and to see Germany coming back from the ruins. His work with Germans even inspired him to stay in the military, and he later served in the Korean War.[162] In addition, John Junji Katsu, who during World War II had been interned in Japanese internment camps before he enlisted, worked for the military government during the occupation of Germany. As part of his occupation duties, he helped teach German youth about democracy by organizing youth activities, which entailed traveling to different villages and towns, getting religious leaders to sponsor activities for youth, and helping them with material assistance such as sports equipment. In addition, he helped organize movie nights and craft shows for youth. In an oral history interview, Katsu said that as part of the "everyday operation" of his office, they were trying to teach kids democratic practices, such as "organizing a team or organizing an activity," or voting. He also tried to encourage American soldiers to volunteer to help out with youth activities, so that there was "a mixing of American soldiers and German children." Katsu noted that the "kids . . . were very impressed by these guys," and the "soldiers were just as nice as you can imagine." Katsu was free to work on youth activities programs as he liked, without supervision, with the knowledge that the aim "was to democratize" the youth, and "to teach them what we all grew up with."[163] Although John Junji Katsu had directly experienced the contradictions of American democracy, which led to the racist practice of Japanese internment during the war, he still seemed excited and motivated about his experience teaching American democratic practices to German youth as part of his official occupation duties.

Birch Bayh, who later became a Senator of Indiana, was sent to serve in Germany in 1946. During his service in the occupation, Bayh started a gardening project for hungry German youth in Hungen, near Frankfurt am Main. The German children there reminded him of American children he had worked with through 4-H. He also noted that they were not just physically hungry, but were also "hungry for something else. Something to live for . . . and they just didn't know what to make of us Americans."[164] He aimed to help children grow their own food, teaching American democratic values such as personal responsibility and com-

162 Interview of Robert Allen Macon (AFC/2001/001/90477), 40:30–43:35, VHP Collection, American Folklife Center, Library of Congress.

163 Interview of John Junji Katsu (AFC/2001/001/89308), 1:37:35–1:44:28, VHP Collection, American Folklife Center, Library of Congress. Katsu even went skiing with German youth, who waxed his skies for him.

164 Karl Detzer, "GI Ambassador," *Reader's Digest*, November 1948, quoted in O'Connell, "Weapon of War, Tool of Peace" 234–235.

munity work. Bayh was glad to have helped Germans and serve as a representative of the United States.[165] Occupation work with German youngsters thus helped rationalize and normalize the ongoing presence of American troops in Germany, providing proof that occupation forces were capable of making a positive impact in Germany. Americans at home also increasingly saw Germans as victims in need of assistance, a view that the focus on young Germans helped shape. In addition, work with young Germans gave occupation troops a morale boost, which was essential to an occupation that initially seemed to have no end date. German youth thus had reached a central place within occupation navigations and geopolitical developments, as encounters became part of the very fabric of the occupation and its aims.

Mediators of Hope, Democracy, and Chocolate? The Role of the GI in Encounters with Young Germans

American soldiers were at the forefront of the US occupation of Germany, playing a fundamental role through their official occupation tasks, while also serving as the main contact that the German population had with Americans. Since the beginning of the occupation, GIs juggled their official roles and the often informal roles that sprang up though encounters with German civilians, including women and children. Influenced by interactions with civilians in various spaces, GIs may have chosen to take on roles including as lovers to German women, providers to German families (for example, by giving them some of their rations), and father figures to German children. Signal Corps photographer Malcolm L. Fleming was especially interested in the situation among German civilians. A photograph from September 1945 taken in Regensburg depicts young children near a GI, who is perched next to a wall, hugging a child in an affectionate, fatherly way. Fleming captioned this photo, "Children everywhere it seems, and many of them. Fellows like them and find most are intelligent and surprisingly healthy" (Figure 1.2).[166] In addition, Fleming photographed situations in which children's hunger was very clear. In another photo from Regensburg in September 1945, children cling onto the windows of an Army mess hall begging for food. Another image of the mess hall shows a GI handing food out the window to a barefoot girl, who had climbed

165 O'Connell, "Weapon of War, Tool of Peace," 235–236.

166 Fleming, *From War to Peace*, 153; Malcolm Fleming World War II Photographs, Indiana University Archives.

up on some bricks to be able to reach up through the window (Figure 1.3). Fleming wrote in the caption for the photo:

> GI hands a morsel of food out to eager child. In many places they haunt mess-gear laundries, carrying a can for food and one for coffee. The fellows soon get used to pouring the leftover coffee from their cups into the container held out and allowing the food in their mess gear to be picked over before dumping into garbage cans.[167]

Figure 1.2: "Children everywhere it seems," Regensburg, September 1945 (Malcolm Fleming Collection: Indiana University Archives).

Fleming's images provide a haunting look into the aftermath of war, with a May 11, 1945 image of an elderly woman and a young boy in Sangerhausen captioned, "War's Residue, the Very Old and Very Young."[168] None of these observations of German civilians were easy for Fleming, who witnessed some of the Nazi atrocities, including the aftermath of the Gardelegen atrocity, in which over a thousand forced laborers were burned to death and shot, including by local Hitler

167 Fleming, 152–153; Malcolm Fleming World War II Photographs, Indiana University Archives.
168 Fleming, 135.

Figure 1.3: "GI hands a morsel of food out to eager child." Regensburg, September 1945 (Malcolm Fleming Collection: Indiana University Archives).

Youth.[169] Fleming, like many other GIs, grappled with a range of emotions on the subject of German culpability for Nazi crimes, including in encounters with young Germans. On March 27, 1945, Fleming shot a photo of a family in Obereip outside of their house going through their belongings, which had already been picked over by troops and moved outside. Fleming was staying with the troops in the family's house, and watched the family, wondering what they were thinking. As the caption of the photo, he wrote, "Mixed emotions were mine."[170]

169 Fleming, 89–91.
170 Fleming, 42.

Above all, GIs emerged as central figures of occupation navigations, charged with monumental and contradictory tasks to be undertaken in their interactions with German civilians, including children. As representatives of the United States, they were to serve as an example to guide Germans "along the right road," as an OMGUS poster termed it.[171] They were to be agents of democracy, salesmen of the American way, and "ambassadors of the American way of life" to the German population, in addition to serving as teachers of young Germans, mentors, role models, and even parental figures who would provide for the youngest of Germans.[172] These roles were shaped by the tensions inherent in the occupation, including occupation realities such as chaos, a militarized masculinity shaped through access to easy sex with German women, and high levels of alcohol consumption. In addition, soldiers were often disillusioned, wondering about the purpose of occupation and a longing to return home. These tasks were a lot to expect from both the initial battle-hardened troops and the new fresh recruits who came later in the occupation. In addition, tensions frequently emerged due to the realities of a still segregated military, which ultimately harmed occupation goals and created further chaos.[173] Interactions between GIs and young Germans were thus impacted by these tensions, and the goals of military occupation proved to have limitations. However, decisions made by individual GIs continued to play a role in the occupation, even having the potential to shape official policies. GIs also navigated these encounters in their own individual ways. For example, in seeing German children with sympathy and behaving toward them in a similar manner as they would to American children, GIs could better cope with the daunting and complex tasks of occupation. In addition, they were able to show their humanity in certain ways, which provided distraction for them from the grim realities of life in postwar Germany, and could serve to create a sense of normalcy.

Even as early as September 1944, GIs had taken on the role as providers of moments of joy for German youngsters, gifting items for children such as sweets. GI benevolence to Germans thus emerged strong during the occupation, espe-

---

171 See OMGUS poster, which noted, "Germany is at the Crossroads: Is Your Example Guiding Them Along the Right Road?" in Katharina Gerund, "Reeducation und Reorientation," Historisches Lexikon Bayerns, August 5, 2020, https://www.historisches-lexikon-bayerns.de/Lexikon/Reeducation_und_Reorientation.

172 Geis and Gray Jr., *The Relations of Occupation Personnel*, 4. Also, Byron Price, Memorandum to President Truman, p. 2; Folder OF 198 1945–April 1950 [1 of 2] Germany; OF 198; HSTP; Box 738; HSTPL. Susan Carruthers argues that American soldiers underwent a "postwar incarnation as agents of democratization." Carruthers, *The Good Occupation*, 10.

173 See Willoughby, *Remaking the Conquering Heroes*, 58–72. See also Thomas A. Guglielmo, *Divisions: A New History of Racism and Resistance in America's World War II Military* (Oxford University Press, 2021).

cially evoked in encounters with young Germans. In October 1945, Melvin J. Lasky wrote of coming across a group of young Germans in Bremen. One of the girls wore a patch over her eye, which had been blinded by an artillery splinter during the April assault on Bremen. Another boy was 17 and had apparently served on the Eastern Front for three years despite his young age. Lasky ended up chatting with them about the movies and then they sang to each other in German, causing everyone to laugh before saying goodnight.[174] He thus shared a moment of joy in an exchange with young Germans, who were still visibly affected by the war, exchanging knowledge of culture and language with each other. Benevolent acts undertaken by GIs did not need to include gifting of sweets but could simply be a fun moment providing distraction from an injury or wartime memories.

However, not all American interactions with German children and youth fit the narrative of the benevolent soldier being welcomed by the local population. John Tomikel, a member of the US Forces in Germany in the early 1950s, detailed a violent incident between his fellow GIs and local Germans in his diary. A group of German youth responded aggressively to the GIs' presence in a tavern:

> They sat staring at us and mumbling sideways to each other. Buckland [a fellow GI] decided that we would have to fight our way out and he had judged the situation correctly. The youths stood up in a row and started toward us. Like a scene from a movie Buck grabbed a wine bottle and broke the end off on the table, leaving a perfect piece of jagged glass in his hand . . . He snarled and enticed the "bastards" to come forward and fight. They backed off and went out the door.[175]

In addition, once while on a walk with his wife, who had joined him in Germany, two boys who they had waved at ended up following them, "hollering 'pussy' and 'cowgummie' [sic] at the top of their voices."[176] These young boys were thus aware of the sexualized nature of the American presence, assuming that Tomikel's American wife was his German lover. In addition, American GIs were not only known among Germans as kind soldiers but also were sometimes viewed with caution. Throughout the occupation, GIs often violated traffic laws, had frequent car accidents, were involved in bar fights, assaulted taxi drivers, conducted illegal black market activities even into the 1950s, and were seen as being boorish,

---

174 Lerg, ed., *The Diary of Lt. Melvin J. Lasky*, 265. See also Fleming, *From War to Peace*, 133, which depicts a group of children waiting for milk in Gardelegen; one of the girls has an eye patch.

175 John Tomikel, *A German Journal: The Diary of a Soldier in the Army of Occupation of Germany Shortly After World War II: The Occupation Diary of Cpl. John Tomikel* (Allegheny Press, 2000), 86.

176 Tomikel, 145.

looking for sex.[177] Crime and policing thus intersected with the American presence and impacted the encounters between Americans and Germans.[178]

However, overall, positive encounters between Americans and young Germans quickly became a central tool for official occupation aims. American occupation authorities realized encounters based on aiding German youth could play a role in reeducation and democratization, with GIs taking on the role of agents of democracy. They would be able to sell democracy's benefits through their demonstration of its qualities through positive forms of fraternization with German youth, which Byron Price had commented on in his November 1945 report.[179] Individual American soldiers could serve as ambassadors of democracy, with their mere presence in occupation Germany providing a force of instruction in democracy for Germans.[180] The average soldier could provide Germans a glimpse into the benefits of American-style democracy due to his role as a citizen in a people's army representing his nation. For Germans, the personal characteristics of the GIs they encountered could create an impression of what democracy was like, with the result often being an average soldier who was generally likeable, laid back, and kind.[181] The behavior of the soldier could provide an example to Germans who searched to understand what the purpose of American occupation goals was, including democratization.

However, not everyone was satisfied by the simple doughboy's new postwar role as democratizing agents: there were debates about soldiers' adequacy in this position, with somewhat patronizing claims that most regular GIs could not explain what exactly democracy was and what their feelings were about it. Psychiatrist Bertram Schaffner argued that GIs remained "enthusiastic but still amateur educators" who did not have the words (nonetheless the German words) that could describe the complexities and challenges of American democracy, nor the ability to explain the ironies of a military government rule under the occupation attempting democratization of its subject peoples. In addition, Schaffner argued, Americans were perhaps hesitant about teaching democracy to the German population, because there were obvious flaws in American democratic life, in which

177 Browder, *Americans in Post-World War II Germany*, 155–162. Also, Willoughby, *Remaking the Conquering Heroes*, 16–28.

178 Kehoe, *The Art of Occupation*, 3.

179 Byron Price, Memorandum to President Truman, p. 2; Folder OF 198 1945–April 1950 [1 of 2] Germany; OF 198; HSTP; Box 738; HSTPL.

180 See Browder, *Americans in Post-World War II Germany*, 19, 167; Geis and Gray Jr., *The Relations of Occupation Personnel*, 4; Peterson, *The American Occupation of Germany*, 155.

181 See Gimbel, *A German Community*, 210–212. Gimbel claims that Marburg citizens' overall impressions of Americans were favorable but that American policies left an unfavorable impression.

"not every facet of American life was democratic. Americans could not hide their treatment of the Negro soldier."[182] Thus not all military personnel members were equal, with distinctions in power based on race, gender, or ranking, and their roles within the hierarchal military limited their abilities to prove the benefits of democracy.[183] Germans could most clearly observe the poor treatment of black GIs, who remained segregated from white soldiers. In addition, the military government itself provided a clear irony, with American power over Germans causing resentment among the German population. John Gimbel argues that the policies and power structures of the US occupation as a whole ensured a "different code of justice for Germans than for themselves." American policies such as the requisitioning of homes, the demands for city neighborhoods for use by Americans only, and the segregation of facilities including trains into American troops and German sections had the potential to harm American attempts of democratization.[184] As mentioned previously, the boredom and privilege of occupation soldiers had the potential to cause chaos. However, soldiers remained the first and main contact that average Germans had with Americans.[185] GIs knew and had experienced something young Germans who grew up during the war and under Nazi rule had never experienced: life in a democracy under relative prosperity. American military personnel remained impressive and enticing for many young Germans who were curious about the American presence and wished to learn more about what exactly democracy was about and what the United States stood for. Thus, through their role as average soldiers, GIs remained in the occupation role as the best possible models of the democratic, American way of life to average German citizens. Soldiers could embody a different way of life, even the future, through their utter presence as embodiments of democracy.[186]

In addition, American military personnel took on roles in official programs of reeducating youth, including GYA. Their role in clubs was to be that of sponsors and teachers, guiding children and youth rather than leading them. GYA club sponsors helped guide youth to form the club by helping them fill out the official application for approval from the military government, which required attaching a constitution. The aim was to teach German youth how to run the club themselves, rather than have the GIs control the club. Despite possible shortcomings, military personnel could be role models and mentors for youth.[187] Military wives

182 Schaffner, *Father Land*, 100. See also, 95.
183 See Carruthers, *The Good Occupation*, 10.
184 Gimbel, *A German Community*, 202–203.
185 Schaffner, *Father Land*, 95.
186 See Jähner, *Aftermath*, 324.
187 See Browder, *Americans in Post-World War II Germany*, 152–153.

and female military members were also encouraged to play a role in GYA, especially to increase girls' participation in these official reeducation efforts and serve as positive female role models.[188]

Finally, American military personnel took on parental roles during the occupation, often through interactions that led them to provide for young Germans. Petra Goedde argues that GIs saw themselves as "surrogate fathers . . . just as they had become surrogate husbands to German women."[189] Encounters involving gifts of food played a role in feeding young Germans' stomachs, and American aid aimed at youngsters became a major part of the occupation, such as Christmas parties and the *Schulspeisung*. Young Germans were thus aware that Americans had stepped into the provider role, and navigated the circumstances based on their needs, for example, waiting for food handouts outside an Army mess hall or directly asking a soldier for candy. Neighborhood children approached Robert Edward Wilson, a young GI, who helped them with gifts of food because they reminded him of the kids back home in the US. To him, it was not difficult to befriend children and step into a provider role.[190] In his memoir, Walter C. Krause described noticing "the present want and suffering of the women and children" while on a train journey south through Germany. When the train "slowed down or stopped, children would come and line up near the train, begging for candy, for gum, or for food, and the softhearted GIs gave them their sandwiches or some of their C-rations." Krause, who could speak German, was disturbed by the suffering he witnessed among the population as well as the devastating effects of the war. However, he also tried to put the reasons for German suffering in context, as they had cheered on Hitler during the war, and he also "remembered the Jews, who had been killed like cattle—exterminated."[191] In addition, he depicted a scene in which a woman with a small child also approached the train as it stopped. She asked the soldiers for food or cigarettes, and Krause described that a soldier behind him stated, "She reminds me of my wife and baby. How sad." Seeing the suffering woman with a child could thus spur a desire to act toward Germans in a fatherly manner, for example wanting to help the woman by providing her with food for her young child. However, Krause noticed that one of the soldiers approached the woman, gave her a sandwich, but also gave her an unwanted embrace and touched her in a degrading manner. Krause noted that "the needs of the child dictated her actions," with the child's hunger spurring her to

188 Geis and Gray Jr., *The Relations of Occupation Personnel*, 52–54.

189 Goedde, *GIs and Germans*, 164. See also, 139.

190 Robert Edward Wilson (AFC/2001/001/2210), VHP Collection, American Folklife Center, Library of Congress.

191 Krause, *So I Was a Sergeant*, 50.

engage with GIs in a humiliating situation.[192] Krause's depiction of this scene highlights that GI responses to youngsters could thus vary from viewing the children from the lens of sympathy, a yearning for their own children, to also self-interest in wanting something in return from the child's mother.

Official occupation authorities policies increasingly aimed at providing substitute father figures for young Germans via the example of the GI, especially in regards to beliefs that German parenting played a role in the rise of Nazism: Bertram Schaffner, for example, argued that the German father was especially to blame for holding up authoritarianism as the central family trait.[193] According to this logic, American soldiers thus could be better father figures than Germans, with GIs providing a contrast to the authoritarian father and to the ultimate Nazi father figure, Adolf Hitler.[194] Some GIs also informally adopted German children. Dewey A. Browder, who researched the impacts of the American presence in the city of Zweibrücken, noted that in the 1950s, the city had a "Dad for a Day!" program in which American military personnel "adopted" German children for a day, such as on Christmas.[195]

In addition, some GIs became actual biological fathers during the occupation. Tens of thousands of the children of the occupation, the *Besatzungskinder*, had American fathers, although many of course never met their biological fathers. GIs who fathered children in Germany may have never known of their birth, or they did not have the resources to bring them to the United States, or sadly, perhaps they lacked the desire to have a connection. Moreover, some of the children may have been born in the context of non-consensual relationships. Some of these children were adopted or raised in foster families. Mixed race children of black GIs and German women had particularly challenging lives in postwar German society. Estimates of how many of these children were born are uncertain, but numbers ranged around 3,000 by 1950. The presence of these children spurred a debate in Germany regarding national identity, race, and female sexuality. Public announcements about equality existed simultaneously with racially exclusive

---

192 Krause, 51.

193 Schaffner, *Father Land*, 15.

194 On Hitler as father figure, see Tiia Sahrakorpi, "Memory, Family, and the Self in Hitler Youth Generation Narratives," *Journal of Family History* 45, no. 1 (January 2020): 99, https://doi.org/10.1177/0363199019880254.

195 Browder, *Americans in Post-World War II Germany*, 145. British occupation soldiers also "adopted, or become adopted by" German families and visited them, bringing them food, according to Fenner Brockway in his diary. Brockway was a British socialist politician who visited as a correspondent Germany in 1946. Fenner Brockway, *German Diary* (Victor Gollancz, 1946), 57.

ideas of German identity.[196] Some of these children were adopted by families both in Germany and the United States.[197] The African American press covered the situation of these "brown babies," including in *Ebony* and *Jet* magazines. On November 8, 1951, an article was published in *Jet* magazine entitled "Brown Babies Adopted by Kind German Families." The article documented the lives of two mixed race children who were adopted by an elderly couple in Munich, who "are symbolic of the warm human concern of an increasing number of Germans for orphan 'brown babies.'" However, the article explained that most of these mixed race children still lived with their mothers, who "live on in the hope that either their lover or some other American Negro will marry them and take them to the rich and well-fed U.S."[198] Thus, these articles noted the tensions over the children's identity: they indicated that they belonged to the African American community while also simultaneously belonging in a Germany that did not usually welcome them with open arms in the way that the family in the article did.

****

Overall, Americans in the occupation navigated their encounters with young Germans in ways dependent on their own individual identities and backgrounds. Various factors influenced their perceptions of young Germans and their desire to participate in the official and unofficial roles they took on during the occupation. These included roles as benevolent providers, ambassadors of democracy, GYA youth club sponsors, and more. A willingness to interact with the youngest of Germans was shaped by military personnel's service during the war, family background at home (including marital status and fatherhood), religion, military ranking, gender, class, and race. For example, some military personnel were assigned to be GYA officers as their official duty, thus ensuring them a major role in occupation youth activities.[199] Although the American presence in occupation Germany was heavily masculine, there were women present as well. In addition,

196 Fehrenbach, "Rehabilitating Fatherland," 108, 117, 121–123. See Chapter 3, "'Mischlingskinder' and the Postwar Taxonomy of Race," in Fehrenbach, *Race after Hitler*, 74–106. Also, Browder, *Americans in Post-World War II Germany*, 164.

197 On US adoption of children of German women and African American GIs, see Yara-Colette Lemke Muniz de Faria. "'Germany's "Brown Babies" Must Be Helped! Will You?': U.S. Adoption Plans for Afro-German Children, 1950–1955," *Callaloo* 26, no. 2 (2003): 342–362, http://www.jstor.org/stable/3300857.

198 "Brown Babies Adopted by German Families," *Jet*, November 8, 1951, 14–16.

199 For example, John Junji Katsu was assigned to work on youth activities within the military government, ensuring plenty of contact with the local youth: see John Junji Katsu (AFC/2001/001/89308), VHP Collection, American Folklife Center, Library of Congress.

female military members also worked directly with German youth. For example, beginning in October 1946, Women's Army Corps (WAC) servicewomen were also assigned to work with GYA.[200] In addition to WACs, American women also played roles as civilian military government employees and as Red Cross workers. American military wives also became an important population during the occupation, and they were encouraged to invite German children to their homes.[201] American female journalists and photographers such as Marguerite Higgins, Lee Miller, and Margaret Bourke-White were also present, especially as the war came to an end and the occupation began.[202] Although female figures played a smaller role in occupation developments, their experiences are as significant as male figures. Most focus tends to remain on male military experiences, and the term "GI" tends to evoke the notion of a male soldier, eliminating the presence of American women in the occupation sphere.

Moreover, soldiers' personal backgrounds and family life at home affected their service in Germany. Some military personnel especially loved kids in general, or they had kids or young relatives at home who they missed, and German children provided a temporary substitute. Religion also could play a role: Gail Halvorsen, who served as a pilot in the Berlin Airlift and became known as the Candy Bomber after he decided to drop candy from his plane to the children of Berlin, was influenced by his experience in the Mormon church, which taught him the importance of service to others.[203] Some GIs were close in age to German youth, for example only 18 or 19 years old, which may have allowed them to sympathize with young Germans, who were coming of age in challenging circumstances. GIs from all socioeconomic classes also experienced a high economic status in postwar Germany, with access to plenty of consumer goods through military institutions such as the PX. Cigarettes served as the currency, which ensured GIs had a high status and a powerful role due to their access to an abundance of cigarettes.[204] GIs made vari-

200 5 October 1946 Directive, HQ USFET; Folder USFET Directive 5 October 1946; Records RE the Work of the Youth Activities Section; Records for the Community Education Branch; Records of the Education and Cultural Relations Division; Box 148; OMGUS; RG 260, NACP.

201 Browder, *Americans in Post-World War II Germany*, 20; Geis and Gray Jr., *The Relations of Occupation Personnel*, 54. See also Chapter 3 of this work for more on American dependents.

202 See Bourke-White, *"Dear Fatherland"*; Antoinette May, *Witness to War: A Biography of Marguerite Higgins* (Beaufort Books, 1983); Lee Miller, *Lee Miller's War: Beyond D-Day* (Thames & Hudson, 2014).

203 See Gail S. Halvorsen, *The Berlin Candy Bomber* (Horizon Publishers, 2017), 142. See more on the Berlin Airlift and Gail Halvorsen in Chapter 5.

204 See Jähner, *Aftermath*, 191.

ous decisions about what to do with their material wealth. Some soldiers aimed to gain even more money by trading on the black market, for example trading cigarettes with Germans for material items such as watches, and then selling the watches to Russian soldiers, which was especially common early on.[205]

Race proved a central factor in influencing encounters between Americans and Germans. In 1946, around 9% of the US Armed Forces in Europe was African American.[206] Black troops were often placed in service positions, including as drivers and cooks.[207] The military remained segregated until July 26, 1948, when President Truman officially desegregated it with Executive Order 9981.[208] However, integration of military units proved slow to develop, with only 7% of black soldiers in 1952 serving in integrated units.[209] In addition, racist practices within the US military remained common after desegregation, with black soldiers often charged with offenses at higher rates, or being denied permission to marry German women once marriage between American troops and Germans was again allowed. Germans during the occupation could thus clearly see the contradictions of American-style democracy, which did not grant full democratic rights and privileges to all of its citizens. As Petra Goedde notes, American racism thus reinforced German racist mindsets at the very moment when Americans were attempting to teach Germans about democracy and reeducate them to prevent the return of Nazi ideology, which had preached racial superiority itself.[210] German women who dated black soldiers were often characterized as prostitutes, receiving scorn and even sometimes legal troubles within German society.[211] Prostitution cases in local courts in the 1950s mostly involved black GIs, and German police sometimes raided bars commonly patronized by black soldiers.[212] Germans

---

205 See Ziemke, *The U.S. Army in the Occupation*, 337.

206 Geis and Gray Jr., *The Relations of Occupation Personnel*, 36; Willoughby, *Remaking the Conquering Heroes*, 65.

207 Sollors, *The Temptation of Despair*, 186.

208 For the full text of Executive Order 9981, see "Executive Order 9981," Executive Orders, Library Collections, HSTPL, https://www.trumanlibrary.gov/library/executive-orders/9981/executive-order-9981.

209 Höhn, *GIs and Fräuleins*, 95. Also, Fehrenbach, *Race after Hitler*, 18–19. See also Höhn and Klimke, *A Breath of Freedom*, 2. On integration in Germany, see Chapter 4 in Höhn and Klimke, "Setting the Stage for Brown: Integrating the Military in Germany," 63–88.

210 Goedde, "Gender, Race, and Power," in *The United States and Germany in the Era of the Cold War*, ed. Junker, 517.

211 For more on German women and black GIs, see Timothy Schroer, *Recasting Race after World War II: Germans and African Americans in American-Occupied Germany* (University Press of Colorado, 2007), 83–147.

212 Goedde, "Gender, Race, and Power," in *The United States and Germany in the Era of the Cold War*, ed. Junker, 519.

also may have been influenced by collective memories of the occupation after World War I, when France used colonial black African occupation soldiers to occupy the Rhineland, the so-called "Black Horror on the Rhine," which Germans saw largely as a humiliation.[213] The American occupiers thus did not eliminate societal racism among Germans. American racial practices also increased tensions during the occupation, leading to clashes between black and white soldiers, and most likely increased German resentment toward German women who had relations with black soldiers. Occupation encounters were taking place within this complex context of occupation and the presence of tensions between the past ideology of Nazi racial superiority and German awareness of the Americans' unequal treatment of black soldiers. The clear contradictions of American aims of democratization while retaining unequal treatment of their own citizens only served to harm the fabric of the occupation itself and condoned continuing German racism.[214] In his diary on December 4, 1945, Melvin Lasky described a visit to a VD clinic, where he talked to a German woman, a wife of a former German officer, who may have been having sexual relations with an African American GI, and who challenged the American racial mindset. Lasky wrote that this woman "was asked if she knew that social intimacy not to mention sexual relations with Negroes was normally frowned on. She replied—'I don't see anything wrong. They're Americans. Same as you—are they not? Your democracy says all men are the same. I see nothing wrong . . .'" Her sentence was a VD check and a fine for violating curfew and trespassing on US property.[215]

However, despite initial fears and racist ideas about black people common among Germans, on the whole, many Germans tended to treat both black and white GIs with equal regard during the occupation.[216] African American soldiers usually had an overwhelmingly positive experience during their time stationed in Germany, even experiencing their time there as a "breath of freedom."[217] For many black GIs, they experienced less discrimination than in their homeland, especially for those from the South, who lived under the realities of Jim Crow segregation. For example, black soldiers were able to date white German women and

213 Keith L. Nelson, "The 'Black Horror on the Rhine': Race as a Factor in Post-World War I Diplomacy," *The Journal of Modern History* 42, no. 4 (December 1970): 606–627, https://doi.org/10.1086/244041.

214 See Fehrenbach, *Race after Hitler*, 18–19, 45.

215 Lerg, ed., *The Diary of Lt. Melvin J. Lasky*, 288.

216 Goedde, "Gender, Race, and Power," in *The United States and Germany in the Era of the Cold War*, ed. Junker, 517; Fehrenbach, *Race after Hitler*, 32–35.

217 Höhn and Klimke, *A Breath of Freedom*, 39–40. See also Oliver R. Schmidt, *Afroamerikanische GIs in Deutschland 1944 bis 1973: Rassekrieg, Integration und globale Protestbewegung* (Münster: Monsenstein und Vannerdat, 2013), 140–161.

go to bars and nightclubs. As Petra Goedde notes, black GIs, in particular those from the South, experienced Germany as a place of "racial tolerance and personal freedom."[218] Some black soldiers even had white German household staff. German women even wrote to African American magazines such as *Ebony* "requesting" black husbands. In April 1952, *Jet* magazine published an article on "Why German Women Want Negro Husbands." Some of the women featured already had a mixed-race child, while some wanted to come to the US. The article mentioned the current shortage of German men, and also noted that letters requesting marriage were not legally binding.[219] Lawrence Johnson, an African American who served in Berlin in 1945 as a guard, had a very positive experience in occupation Germany, and did not recall any instances of discrimination from the German population. He recalled that Germans "were very mannerly and even hospitable." One day he helped a girl carry her groceries home, and she invited him home, where they had dinner together with her mother. According to Johnson, when he headed home after dinner, it was dark and he got lost, but a German policeman was "very courteous" and helped him with directions.[220] Thus in the former homeland of National Socialism, African American GIs often received kinder and more tolerant treatment than what they had experienced at home. Many black GIs wished to reenlist to remain in Germany, causing military officials to worry about high numbers of black troops in Germany. Many military leaders had racist attitudes and actively tried to reduce black troop service in the occupation. For example, Lieutenant General Geoffrey Keyes, commander of the Third Army (and later commander of the US Forces in Austria and High Commissioner of Austria), worked to reduce the number of African American troops in Germany.[221]

One fascinating factor of the black GI occupation service experience is that black soldiers were generally known among Germans as the most generous group of Americans, especially to German children.[222] Many Germans mention the kindness of black soldiers as they look back in memoirs and other writings about the occupation.[223] For example, Werner Sollors, who was born in 1943 and witnessed

218 Goedde, "Gender, Race, and Power," in *The United States and Germany in the Era of the Cold War*, ed. Junker, 520.
219 "Why German Women Want Negro Husbands," *Jet*, April 3, 1952.
220 Lawrence Johnson; "A Lot of Pleasure in Berlin"; interview by Maggi Morehouse, Cleveland, Ohio, 1998; AACVR: The Civil Rights Struggle, African-American GIs, and Germany; excerpt available at http://digitales-archiv.aacvr-germany.org/.
221 Höhn and Klimke, *A Breath of Freedom*, 41; Willoughby, *Remaking the Conquering Heroes*, 69–72.
222 Fehrenbach, *Race after Hitler*, 33; Schroer, *Recasting Race*, 121.
223 Höhn and Klimke, *A Breath of Freedom*, 47–48.

the occupation as a child, describes his personal experience with black soldiers in his book on the occupation. Sollors comments:

> The particular kindness of black soldiers toward German children may be a stereotype, but if so, it is a cliché that I experienced as a child: black G.I.s [sic] driving by in trucks and jeeps were always smiling at us children, and a black man who worked for the occupation authorities on several occasions gave me delicious Marabou chocolate, which one could not then get in Germany.[224]

Sollors and Maria Höhn both argue that African American GIs may have felt less vindictive toward the German population. African Americans were a marginalized population, just like Germans could be perceived as being treated by the US Army as second-class citizens during the occupation.[225] Black soldiers may have empathized with the German population, especially the youngest of them, who suffered from hunger and impoverished conditions. Thus, it may have seemed natural to black soldiers to conduct acts of humanity toward Germans, especially toward the youngest, most innocent-seeming members of the population.[226] Many black soldiers were from the South, and may have been especially religious, which could impact their views of the German population, despite Germans' roles in the racist Nazi past. In conducting a spontaneous act of kindness, a black GI thus could gain a "fuller sense of humanity that is denied [to] him in America," as Sollors terms it.[227] Black soldiers often served as jeep drivers and were thus mobile, enabling them to use their rations and goods in ways such as gifting them to German children.

In 1951, novelist Kay Boyle wrote a fictional story entitled "Home," which was first published in *Harper's*. The story features an unnamed African American GI from Mississippi, who commits an act of kindness by buying a German boy new clothes and shoes. In the story, the boy had been standing in the rain outside the American PX. The soldier and the boy went inside together, where the soldier bought him a rodeo shirt, blue jeans, and shoes. The German saleswoman protested, claiming that the boy got dropped off at the PX by his family every day, and that he should take the clothes off the boy and send him back outside, to which the black GI responded, "At home, ma'am, I never had much occasion to do for other people, so I was glad to have had this opportunity offered [to] me." This

224 Sollors, *The Temptation of Despair*, 201.
225 Sollors, 201; Höhn, *GIs and Fräuleins*, 90–91. Also, Alexander Stephan, "A Special German Case of Cultural Americanization," in *The Americanization of Europe: Culture, Diplomacy, and Anti-Americanism after 1945*, ed Alexander Stephan (Berghahn Books, 2006), 79.
226 Sollors, 201. See also Höhn and Klimke, *A Breath of Freedom*, 47–48.
227 Sollors, 201.

fictional soldier "had known only leaning Negro shacks," and was elated at becoming "the provider, the protector at last, the dispenser of white-skinned charity."[228] Black service in the occupation thus challenged traditional racial roles in both American and German societies. Kindness toward German children was one way that black soldiers were able to use their status as occupation soldiers of the victorious Army and their personal free agency to conduct acts based on their individual wishes and needs. In a way, ironically, for many African American soldiers, life in postwar Germany was in reality more democratic, free, and equal than life at home in the United States.

Black service in World War II and the immediate postwar period fundamentally impacted American politics at home, as stories of violence against returning black soldiers reached an audience all the way to President Truman. The experience of a black serviceman, Sergeant Isaac Woodard, who was attacked and blinded by a South Carolina policeman a few hours after his honorable discharge from the US Army on February 12, 1946, played a major role in President Truman's decision to desegregate the military via Executive Order 9981 in July 1948.[229] In response to Woodard's blinding, Truman launched a federal investigation of the attack and a committee on civil rights. The attack also mobilized the civil rights movement in the United States. The "Double V" campaign (short for "Victory Abroad and Victory at Home"), which was launched by the *Pittsburgh Courier* in 1942, was not over in the postwar era. The end of World War II had only led to victory over fascism but not over Jim Crow and inequality back home.[230] Black soldiers who had experienced life in an unsegregated society such as Germany played a role in these developments. In September 1959, journalist William Gardner Smith was interviewed in the *New York Post*, stating, "Do you know what it's like for a Negro to be among the 'conquerors' instead of the defeated? We learned about it for the first time when we 'occupied' Germany and none of us ever got over it. We will never go back to the old way again."[231] Smith had been drafted in 1946; in Ger-

---

228 Kay Boyle, "Home," *Harper's*, January 1951, 78–83; also in Kay Boyle, *The Smoking Mountain: Stories of Germany During the Occupation* (Knopf, 1963), 149–162.

229 See Richard Gergel, *Unexampled Courage: The Blinding of Sgt. Isaac Woodard and the Awakening of President Harry S. Truman and Judge J. Waties Waring* (Sarah Crichton Books/Farrar, Straus and Giroux, 2019).

230 See "Double Victory: The African American Military Experience," Smithsonian National Museum of African American History and Culture, accessed September 17, 2023, https://nmaahc.si.edu/explore/exhibitions/double-victory.

231 William Gardner Smith, in Joseph Barry, "An American in Paris-III," *New York Post*, September 29, 1959, quoted in Maria Höhn, "'We Will Never Go Back to the Old Way Again': Germany in the African-American Debate on Civil Rights," *Central European History* 41, no. 4 (December 2008): 619, https://doi.org/10.1017/S0008938908000861.

many, he worked in Berlin as a clerk-typist for the 661st Trucking Company. In 1948, Smith published a novel that drew upon his experiences in Germany, entitled *Last of the Conquerors.*[232]

Finally, African Americans also made an impact on Germans, including young Germans. Some German youth were drawn toward black soldiers, for example as a way to rebel against German societal norms. Young Germans were also attracted to African American influenced music such as jazz, swing, and, later, rock n' roll.[233] Germans did sometimes view black Americans in stereotypical ways, including as exotic non-Western type figures, and the cliched narrative of the kind black GI itself has a level of continuity with racist tropes about smiling, simple, naïve, even child-like black people.[234] However, as Sollors commented from his experience as a child, that kindness was undoubtedly very real and had the potential to make a profound impact on young Germans.[235] African Americans therefore made their mark on the encounter with young Germans, proving to be central figures in the complex and contradictory occupation sphere, in which members of the conquering forces may have for the first time been allowed to conduct a simple act like passing candy or gum to a hungry white child, who was a member of the society that had allowed some of the worst crimes against humanity to occur based on an ideology centered around racial superiority.

****

Overall, occupation encounters between Americans and young Germans were ever-shifting. Americans of all backgrounds viewed, acted toward, and described German youngsters in diverse ways, navigating the changing landscape of the occupation to the best of their abilities. From the very beginning of contact with

---

232 William Gardner Smith, *Last of the Conquerors* (Farrar, Straus, 1948). See also Sollors, *The Temptation of Despair*, 190–198.

233 Goedde, "Gender, Race, and Power," in *The United States and Germany in the Era of the Cold War*, ed. Junker, 519–520. Also, Uta G. Poiger, *Jazz, Rock, and Rebels: Cold War Politics and American Culture in a Divided Germany* (University of California Press, 2000), 1–2; Schroer, *Recasting Race*, 151; Stephan, "A Special German Case of Cultural Americanization," in *The Americanization of Europe*, ed. Stephan, 79–80. Stephan argues, "Young Germans quickly identified with the unauthoritarian behavior of the victors" (79). See also Uta G. Poiger, "Rebels with a Cause? American Popular Culture, the 1956 Youth Riots, and New Conceptions of Masculinity in East and West Germany," in *The American Impact on Postwar Germany*, ed. Reiner Pommerin (Berghahn Books, 1995), 93–96. On black jazz musicians as artists and occupiers in postwar Germany, see Kim Nalley, "GI Jazz: African Americans as Artists and Occupiers in Post-World War II Germany" (PhD diss., University of California, Berkeley, 2021), https://escholarship.org/uc/item/9wx3s83d.

234 See Goedde, "Gender, Race, and Power," 519–520; Schroer, 121.

235 Sollors, *The Temptation of Despair*, 201.

Germans as the war made its way to its end, American views of Germans were always ambivalent and complicated. Thus, there was no simple switch on the ground from a belief in a hard peace and a view of Germans as collectively guilty toward a belief in a benevolent peace aimed at understanding, rehabilitation, and material support for Germans. Instead, American interactions with Germans were always fraught with complex individual interpretations. American views of the youngest of the Germans provide a glimpse into the navigations made in the aftermath of war and the ways in which Americans attempted to understand an encounter that was bilingual, transatlantic, multi-generational, and often complicated. GIs were assigned and took on various roles relating to work with young Germans, from GYA officer to informal parent. On July 4, 1945, Sergeant Henry E. Giles wrote in his journal while in Munich that "there are an awful lot of kids in this city & [sic] I guess the civilians aren't having a very easy time. We're suckers for the kids, as usual. As much as you might hate the Nazis for what they've done, you can't hold it against a bunch of innocent children. All of us give them the candy & gum we get in rations & whatever else we can pick up."[236] Giles, who had served in combat including in the Battle of the Bulge, thus noted the everyday tensions among occupation soldiers, who saw the daily suffering of civilians. The decision of the GIs to give children candy hints at the hidden complexity of the situation, where soldiers who had fought against Germans in combat were met with the hunger and wishes of the youngest of the population. In response to complex navigations regarding the guilt, hunger, and need of a former enemy, many soldiers chose to take on the simple act of giving.

236 Janice Holt Giles, ed., *The G.I. Journal of Sergeant Giles*, 373.

Chapter 2
Survival Among Chaos and Change: Occupation Childhoods

As American troops entered Germany in late 1944 and early 1945, young Germans got their first glimpse of *der Feind,* the enemy. On April 13, 1945, Edeltraud Großjohann (born in 1926) wrote in her diary about seeing the Americans marching into the town of Eisleben in Saxony-Anhalt:

> There they were, the enemy tanks! . . . In no time the local population also was there and gaped at the Americans (me too) and like a sign from heaven it began to rain . . . Hour after hour tanks and automobiles rolled by. Our people waved at the enemy and gave them cigarettes. Most people see our liberators in the Americans, but I don't know. Almost all of them look well-fed. They have ample weapons and are naturally in good spirits. Each one has a cigarette hanging from the corner of his mouth or is chewing his gum from one side to the other. It looks disgusting, but I guess one will have to get used to it. (*Da waren sie, die feindlichen Panzer! . . . Im Nu war auch die Bevölkerung da und gaffte die Amerikaner an (ich auch) und wie ein Zeichen des Himmels begann es zu regnen . . . Stunde um Stunde rollten Panzer und Autos vorbei. Unsere Leute winkten den Feinden zu und schenkten ihnen Zigaretten. Die meisten sehen in den Amerikanern unsere Befreier, aber ich weiß nicht. Sie sehen fast sämtlich gut genährt aus. Ihre Bewaffnung ist reichhaltig und sie sind natürlich guter Dinge. Jeder hat eine Zigarette im Mundwinkel hängen oder schiebt den Kaugummi von einer Seite zur anderen. Das sieht zum Kotzen aus, aber man wird sich ja wohl daran gewöhnen müssen.*)[1]

The population of Eisleben thus responded to the arrival of Americans with a mix of curiosity, generosity, and skepticism. Edeltraud's description notes that some locals even gave Americans gifts of cigarettes, which contrasts with the common collective memory narrative of Americans as the ones giving Germans goods such as chocolate and cigarettes at the end of the war. Young Edeltraud, born in Breslau in Silesia, seemed mostly skeptical at this first moment of contact, and she did not feel entranced by the healthy, relaxed nature of the GIs. However, some youngsters felt enraptured by the arrival Americans, finding their foreignness, easy-going manner, and material prosperity exciting, providing a contrast to the usually wretched state of German soldiers returning home. In postwar Germany,

1 Diary of Edeltraud Großjohann, Deutsches Tagebucharchiv (DTA) Reg. Nr. 185/I 1–4 Abschrift. The original German text is included in parentheses following the English translation to bring the focus onto the original words of the witnesses, and the texts are kept as in original with misspellings and other errors. Any mistakes in translation and transcription from the original records are entirely the author's.

https://doi.org/10.1515/9783111588155-003

many children found GIs to embody a "new and different adult figure they could then try to imitate," as Werner Sollors describes the allure of the GI.[2]

Theodor Wild (born November 5, 1937) was seven years old on April 22, 1945 when the Americans arrived in Amberg, a town in Upper Palatinate in Bavaria.[3] In a book of short autobiographical stories from his life published in 2015, Wild depicted the excitement of seeing Americans for the first time while out in the streets with his mother. He noted that the first American he saw was an African American perched on the turret of a tank. Many Germans who witnessed the first contact with American soldiers at the end of the war often mentioned seeing black soldiers. For many Germans, this was the first time they had ever seen people of color. The depiction of a friendly African American GI providing candy for the children has become a cliché in memory culture; however, many African American soldiers did indeed have visible positions as tank drivers. In his story of his first encounter with a soldier, Theodor Wild described his fascination with the exotic appearance of the GI, who shouted to Wild to move "*geradeaus*," straight ahead. When Wild did not move because he was so busy gazing at the fascinating soldier up above, the GI threw him a pack of gum and a bar of Hershey's chocolate. On the walk home, he asked his mother, almost in a reproachful manner, why he was not black.[4] After the American troops took over Amberg, Wild's neighbor took a picture of Wild next to an American tank. His neighbor still had a camera despite the command to give them up to the Americans.[5] Images of children next to a tank (see for example Figure 2.1), a huge machine of warmaking, provide a contrast to more benevolent depictions of the encounter with the American military, such as friendly GIs handing out food.

2 Sollors, *The Temptation of Despair*, 217.

3 The author wishes to extend her special thanks to Theodor Wild for his willingness to share information about his childhood and his excitement about this project. The author reached out to him after reading his childhood diaries at the Deutsches Tagebucharchiv in Emmendingen. He passed away in 2021, but previously, the author had been able to speak to him multiple times over the phone and he was kind enough to answer two questionnaires the author sent him in 2019 and 2020, in addition to sending the author his books of stories from his life and poems from his travels around the world. His openness has enriched this work in so many ways.

4 Theodor Wild, *Wo der "Müde" war, war immer was los* (Verlag Leben in der Sprache, 2015), 19–20. On the imagery of black soldiers as drivers of jeeps and tanks, see Sollors, *The Temptation of Despair*, 186.

5 Theodor Wild, in phone calls with the author, February 10, 2020, January 15, 2020, and March 11, 2019. Author has notes from all interviews with Wild and a recording of the March 11, 2019 phone call. See the image of Theodor Wild next to a tank in Andreas Ascherl, "Die Schlinge zieht sich immer enger: Amberger warten auf das Eintreffen der Amerikaner," in *Sie kommen!: Die letzten Kriegstage in der Oberpfalz 1945*, ed. German Vogelsang (Buch & Kunstverlag Oberpfalz, 2005), 68; also in Andreas Ascherl, "Mutige Menschen retten unsere Stadt," *Amberger Zeitung*, April 22, 2015.

Figure 2.1: German children watch as a member of the US Second Armored Division drives his tank through a rubble-strewn street in Berlin, Germany, July 1945 (National Archives, 111-SC-293155).

Throughout the years since he was a boy, Theodor Wild kept a diary, including during the occupation years in Amberg. He described various scenes of occupation encounters in his diaries, which provide a captivating look into the impressions of the occupation and of the occupiers from the lens of a small boy. Wild started writing a diary at the age of five, beginning with jotting down his nickname (Toto) and all of his possessions such as books and toys. Then he started to write down the names of the people around him, and also the names of train stations where he traveled to with his parents, including Berlin, Hof, and Como in Italy. By early 1945 at age seven, he was writing descriptive entries in his diary, and he also began to sometimes date the entries.[6] Young Germans such as Theodor Wild and Edeltraud Großjohann depicted their views of the encounter with Americans in their own unique ways, providing a glimpse into the lived experiences of youngsters during the US occupation of Germany.

6 Theodor Wild, answer to question 1 in first questionnaire sent from author on January 21, 2019. See his three diaries from the occupation period, Diaries of Theodor Wild (then Theodor Gruschka), DTA Reg.-Nr. 540,1–3.

Sources including young Germans' diaries from the time are not representative of all German children's experience in the US occupation zone, but they can provide pieces of knowledge of how young people lived through, understood, and dealt with the transition period of the occupation, and also of how they viewed their encounters with American soldiers. Including sources from young Germans themselves moves beyond a top-down or an adult-focused lens of the US occupation, enabling a view of children as historical actors rather than simply as statistics or objects impacted by adult decisions. Young Germans were not simply victims faced with hunger and challenging circumstances, or objects in need of state protection, but they played an essential role in the occupation of Germany. They were "co-creators of everyday life who gave their own meaning to the policies affecting them by way of their practices," as Machteld Venken and Maren Röger describe children's historical roles in the aftermath of World War II.[7] Children's everyday lives thus intersected with postwar policies and developments in diverse ways, and young people described these intersections in their own ways, in works which ranged from drawings, letters, and school essays to diaries. Alexandra Zapruder argues that children's diaries are "repositories of information" and "intentional records" that can play a role in contributing to historical understandings of daily life at that time.[8] Nicholas Stargardt writes, "Children established their own chronologies of the war through key events; the moment when *their* war became real."[9] Moments of rupture in children's lives could be the moment of separation from family members, or, in the case of the end of the war and the beginning of the occupation, the first moment that children saw the enemy troops, such as Theodor Wild's first sighting of an American GI.

Materials written by young people come about in diverse ways and for various purposes, ranging from a desire to write a diary since young childhood, such as Theodor Wild's, to a response written in a classroom based on a teacher's instruction. Youngsters' materials were also impacted by the societal context in which they were produced. Laura Hobson Faure notes that "adults and fellow children prove determinant to children's writing." For example, one of the *Kind-*

7 Machteld Venken and Maren Röger, "Growing up in the Shadow of the Second World War: European Perspectives," *European Review of History: Revue Européenne d'histoire* 22, no. 2 (March 4, 2015): 200, https://doi.org/10.1080/13507486.2015.1008410. See also Jürgen Zinnecker, "Zur Einführung in Teil I: Erfahrungsräume von Kriegskindheiten," in *Erinnerungen an Kriegskindheiten: Erfahrungsräume, Erinnerungskultur und Geschichtspolitik unter sozial- und kulturwissenschaftlicher Perspektive*, ed. Hans-Heino Ewers, Jana Mikota, Jürgen Reulecke, and Jürgen Zinnecker (Juventa, 2006), 12.
8 Zapruder, *Salvaged Pages*, 11.
9 Stargardt, *Witnesses of War*, 12.

ertransport children's diaries she analyzes was illustrated by another child, and in the context of the *Kindertransport*, adult educators often encouraged children to write in their diaries as a way of processing that helped children cope with their difficult circumstances.[10] Similarly, adults in the postwar era sometimes encouraged young people to write about their wartime experiences, including schoolteachers, welfare workers, and doctors.[11] Thus, young Germans' diaries, drawings, and other items from the time of the occupation may have been created for a variety of reasons, including in response to adult wishes, hopes, and actions, such as trying to help children deal with trauma, or they could have been made out of a child's own personal initiative, for example as a way to provide comfort within a difficult time.

Young people's sources are of equal value and importance to those made by adults, as they can equally shed light on the history of everyday life for Germans during the US occupation. Instead of viewing materials from youngsters as unimportant due to the nature of children not being at the same stage of development as adults, these items are undoubtedly essential for a better understanding of German views of and responses to occupation. Focusing on the unique ways in which young Germans described their experiences during the occupation can lead to fascinating glimpses into life under occupation in ways that are not possible when examining only sources from adults. In general, young people can cut through to the truth and highlight the contradictions of war and human nature on a level that adults may not be able to reach. For example, as Eleanor Roosevelt wrote in the introduction to Anne Frank's diary, "Written by a young girl—and the young are not afraid of telling the truth—it is one of the wisest and most moving commentaries on war and its impact on human beings that I have ever read."[12] Moreover, in the context of the occupation, German children and youth tended to evoke a different response among the American occupiers in comparison to German adults, as GIs often viewed German youngsters in an especially positive light. American reactions to Germans thus varied by the age of the Germans involved. Young Germans were able to capture their lived experiences of the Americans' responses to their youngness. Sources from young Germans them-

---

10 Faure, "Exploring Political Rupture," 260, 265, 271–272.

11 For an example from postwar Poland, see Corinne Matthews, "The Right to Resist: Childhood Agency in Julian Kulski's World War II Diary," *Journal of the History of Childhood and Youth* 16, no. 1 (Winter 2023): 140, https://doi.org/10.1353/hcy.2023.0012. Julian Kulski was active as a youth in the Polish resistance in Warsaw. He wrote his journal after the war based on the recommendation of a doctor as a way of coping with what we now classify as post-traumatic stress disorder.

12 Frank, *The Diary of a Young Girl*, xiii.

selves are thus of essential nature to a deeper understanding of the interactions undertaken in the occupation.

In addition, memoirs and oral histories from these adults looking back on their childhood also add context for analyzing childhood experiences during the occupation, despite being influenced by the knowledge of what events occurred afterwards, as well as by collective memory narratives. Testimonies from former children can provide a "gateway" into the past childhood experiences of witnesses, as Machteld Venken and Maren Röger argue about the value of oral histories.[13] In Germany, recent discussions surrounding *Kriegskinder*, children of war, the generation who grew up affected by the Second World War, have led to a boom in that generation's personal reflections on the past, attracting media coverage. Historians, psychologists, and journalists turned their attention to these witnesses of total war as they entered their last decades of their lives, examining issues such as trauma and potential life-long impacts of the war.[14] Overall, this chapter focuses on those young Germans who were present during the occupation, not focusing on the victims of the Holocaust nor on children born as a result of the consequences of the interactions of the war, the *Besatzungskinder*, the children of occupation soldiers.

Many of these Germans who grew up in the war and occupation spent their whole adult lives trying to understand what they had witnessed when they were young. Wolfgang W. E. Samuel, who immigrated to the United States with his mother in 1951, published his childhood experiences in 2000 in the book *German Boy*. He writes that "it took fifty years, nearly a lifetime, for me to be able to look back and re-create those days of darkness and terror."[15] Henry Beissel, who immi-

13 Venken and Röger, "Growing up in the Shadow," 204. See also Sahrakorpi, "Memory, Family, and the Self in Hitler Youth Generation Narratives," 89.

14 See Zinnecker, "Zur Einführung in Teil I," in *Erinnerungen an Kriegskindheiten*, ed. Ewers, Mikota, Reulecke, and Zinnecker, 13–16; Sabine Bode, "Trümmerkinder—erwachsene Kinder," in *Erinnerungen an Kriegskindheiten*, ed. Ewers, Mikota, Reulecke, and Zinnecker, 49–50; Venken and Röger, "Growing up in the Shadow," 202–203; Lu Seegers, *"Vati blieb im Krieg": Vaterlosigkeit als generationelle Erfahrung im 20. Jahrhundert—Deutschland und Polen* (Wallstein Verlag, 2013), 14–27; Lu Seegers, "'Dead Dads': Memory Narratives of War-Related Fatherlessness in Germany," *European Review of History: Revue Européenne d'histoire* 22, no. 2 (2015): 259, https://doi.org/10.1080/13507486.2015.1008417. See also Lorenz, *Kriegskinder*; Bode, *Die vergessene Generation*. For a psychosocial study, see Christa Müller, *Schatten des Schweigens, Notwendigkeit des Erinnerns: Kindheiten im Nationalsozialismus, im Zweiten Weltkrieg und in der Nachkriegszeit* (Psychosozial-Verlag, 2014).

15 Wolfgang W. E. Samuel, *The War of Our Childhood: Memories of World War II* (University Press of Mississippi, 2002), xii; Wolfgang W. E. Samuel, *German Boy: A Refugee's Story* (University Press of Mississippi, 2000).

grated to Canada in 1951, published a poetic memoir in 2015 looking back on his childhood, written in both English and German. He wrote the long reflection poem about his youth in Nazi and postwar Germany in order to come to terms with his past, as well as for his newly born grandson. Beissel's memoir is shaped both by the person he was at that moment looking back at his past and by the child who he remembers and has come to terms with, one that "finds its own language." The child in his memoir "is Henry Beissel, but not the Henry Beissel who remembers his past but above all the child that the octogenarian remembers and has to come to terms with. There is the perspective of the remembering *I*, but also that of the remembered *it*," as Martin Kuester writes in the introductory remarks.[16] Beissel writes that he sometimes cannot distinguish between actual past experiences and the projections of fear, writing that he remains haunted by the continuance of wars throughout the world:

> Here vast solitudes are invaded only by the wind
> and the dark skies flash only with dying comets
> and the ghostly dances of northern lights. Night
> now brings forgetting, offers coveted oblivion.
> The bloodthirsty beasts of war swoop down on me
> in broad daylight instead. They bear different names:
> Bosnia, Chechnya, Iraq, Rwanda, Afghanistan
> and Gaza, each of them recalling reenacting reviving
> the surreal scenes I witnessed in those years of terror
> and tyranny so bone-chillingly beyond belief and bearance
> I can no longer be sure what fevered fear projects
> on the walls of memory and what I experienced,
> what panic stampedes into images and what I saw
> turn ten thousand childhoods into one long nightmare.[17]

In 1965, Klaus Granzow, who was a member of the Hitler Youth and eventually became a prisoner of war (POW) of the Soviets at age 17, published his diaries from the years 1943 to 1945. He noted in the foreword to the publication that he had reread his diaries with a sense of shame, thinking of another girl his age at the same time hidden in a house in Amsterdam, Anne Frank, whose war experience turned out so different than his own, ending with death in the Holocaust. Granzow published his diary with the hope that following generations would never have to grow up with war.[18] German adults looking back on the past thus could have gained different conceptions of their childhoods from later in life due

16 Beissel, *Coming to Terms with a Child*, 7.

17 Beissel, *Coming to Terms with a Child*, 19.

18 Klaus Granzow, *Tagebuch eines Hitlerjungen: 1943–1945* (C. Schünemann, 1965), Vorwort.

to their knowledge of the impacts of Nazism and their thoughts about their role in that system. However, their depictions of their childhoods still can provide important context to what everyday life was like for young Germans during the occupation, and enable researchers to analyze the life-long impacts of war, violence, and major disruptions during childhood.

Age thus shaped personal experiences of the postwar occupation, and childhood during the occupation in the US zone went through various shifting meanings. For example, American authorities viewed German childhood increasingly as a phase in which youngsters needed to be molded and protected, rather than punished for the crimes of the past. Moreover, the centrality of the recent war, National Socialism, and defeat molded the lives of young people. Occupation policies also imprinted youngsters' everyday experiences, including policies centered around access to food, formal education, and democratization. Within the transition from war to peace under a military occupation, young Germans' experiences were shaped not only by their age but also by their various individual circumstances, such as gender, location, and family situation. Young Germans played an active role in the historical moment of the occupation and were aware of the ways the occupation impacted them.

Above all, young Germans' voices emerge in unexpected ways, searing through simplified narratives about the American postwar occupation of Germany that portray it as undoubtedly good and the time of *Stunde Null*, zero hour, as a moment in which difficulties ended through liberation and a fresh start. Instead, young Germans' everyday experiences of the postwar occupation were marked by complex personal moments of rupture, confusion, and resilience. These personal histories of occupation can help depict what it was like to be human and young in the aftermath of the fracture of World War II, a war that sent babies to gas chambers and armed children to defend cities in the last days of a total war. On April 14, 1945 in Erfurt, German housewife Annemarie Meckel recorded the arrival of American troops that morning. She wrote that especially children were full of burning interest in everything that was going on after the arrival of the Americans. The children would say, "Now it is peace (*Nun ist Frieden*)," in a dazed manner.[19] The postwar occupation encounter with members of the American Armed Forces evoked complex emotions among youngsters ranging from guilt, loss, misery, and hope to curiosity. Young Germans navigated these circumstances with various levels of awareness and a wide range of interest in the events taking place. German children and youth thus played a central role in

19 Hirschfeld and Renz, eds., *Vormittags die ersten Amerikaner*, 133.

the postwar occupation sphere, impacting Americans and their personal experiences of the occupation, as well as influencing official occupation policies.

Meeting the Enemy: The Rupture

On August 17, 1945, *Yank, the Army Weekly* magazine published an article entitled "Germany's Steep Road," which depicted the moment of rupture for the German population as the first Americans arrived: "When the Americans first came, the Germans hid in their homes. They had heard Goebbels warn again and again that the Americans would murder the men and rape the women. Instead the Americans played with the German kids, looked wistfully at the German girls, and helped old Germans when their carts broke down." The article declared Germany "a guilty land trying to hide from its own guilt," where "German children still play soldier" despite seeing the remnants of the Wehrmacht returning home utterly defeated.[20] However, the moment of the first encounter with American troops proved significant as a personal moment of rupture for most young Germans, some of whom recorded the event in their diaries, such as Edeltraud Großjohann, or remembered the moment vividly later on while looking back on their lives, such as Theodor Wild. Those looking back upon the past often indicate the liberatory nature of the arrival of the Americans, most likely influenced by collective memory discourses common today in Germany.[21] Betty Qui (a pseudonym), born in 1928, recollected about her first glimpse of American soldiers. As the Americans arrived, Qui was in Hanau in the state of Hesse, watching from the window, hidden behind the curtains. She saw dark-skinned soldiers of the US Fifth Army handing out sweets to the girls and boys loitering around them. She wrote that the German children did not know what candy bars were, and were happy about getting other American goods such as chewing gum and peanut butter as well. The children had been told during Nazi times that Americans would kill them all, and now they cheerfully stood around the tanks and the GIs even let them climb about the tanks. Qui wrote that the African American GIs laughed and played with the youngsters, who had lost all of their shyness. The war had come to an end, she wrote, thus drawing a connection between children receiving American goods and the end of the war.[22] Winfried Weiss, born in 1937, wrote in his memoir that he had fallen in love with Americans, as he watched them mov-

20 Pfc. Debs Myers, "Germany's Steep Road," *Yank, the Army Weekly*, August 17, 1945, 2–3.

21 For example, Theodor Wild stated that the time of the occupation was one of liberation for him. Wild, in questionnaire 1, answer 2.

22 Betty Qui [pseudonym], "Der Traum von Amerika," in *Hungern und hoffen*, ed. Kleindienst, 122.

ing quickly to install telephone lines a few days after their arrival in Kitzingen in April 1945. He wrote, "The Americans moved with speed, precision, and powerful bodies: I fell in love with them."[23] In addition, he noted the moment of change: "One moment we were citizens of Hitler's Reich, and in the next we belonged to a new world."[24]

This moment of personal rupture meant that young Germans were faced with the transitions of meeting the enemy, the end of the war, the German military loss, the end of National Socialism, and also encountering men of different skin color, usually for the first time. The depiction of the first encounters with American troops often revolve around black GIs and their kindness, as Betty Qui wrote about in her recollection. Harald Jähner argues that this reaction was influenced by Nazi propaganda, which had provoked fear about black people, but then when Germans met black Americans for the first time, they were surprised and relieved by the reality of their kindness. Thus, the reality of their behavior contrasted with what the propaganda had claimed, making a strong impression among Germans.[25] The arrival of American soldiers played a role in shattering many young Germans' world views, with the appearance of the enemy soldiers including black Americans in German cities and towns marking that the present and future would be a very different reality than what they had grown up with. This transition was sometimes quickly adapted among the youngest Germans, who had "made a fast comeback," for example flashing the V-sign for victory while asking GIs for "Chocolate, onckle [sic]," according to a July 20, 1945 *Yank* article.[26] Some children such as Theodor Wild viewed the time period as exciting. He met many American soldiers in Amberg, and even began trading souvenirs with them. All of the soldiers treated him well, except for one mean red-haired GI who confiscated his rare Siemens model electric locomotive.[27] After the end of the war, Theodor wrote in his diary, capturing the changes that the arrival of the Americans brought:

> As the German soldiers were gone, we were very sad, because they were better than the enemy. Maybe Hitler is not dead after all, many people say. For God's sake, my mother says. I saw him once in Berlin. I liked that. Who says Hitler whispers while doing so. I always listen to the radio . . . Before everyone called out "Heil Hitler" and raised the hand and now one must not say Hitler loudly. (*Als die deutschen Soldaten wegwaren waren wir sehr traurig, weil die besser waren als die Feinde. Vielleicht ist Hitler gar nicht tot sagen viele*

23 Winfried Weiss, *A Nazi Childhood* (Capra Press, 1983), 171.

24 Weiss, 169.

25 Jähner, *Aftermath*, 150.

26 Pfc. Debs Myers, "Re-education of Germany," *Yank, the Army Weekly*, July 20, 1945, 10.

27 Wild, in questionnaire 1, answer 4.

> *Leute. Um Gottes Willen sagt meine Mutter. Ich habe ihn einmal in Berlin gesehen. Das hat mir gefallen. Wer Hitler sagt flüstert dabei. Ich höre immer Radio . . . Früher haben alle heil Hitler gerufen und die Hand gehoben und jetzt darf man Hitler nicht laut sagen.*)[28]

Theodor thus captured the moment of transition with the arrival of the occupiers in Amberg, when Germans now had to whisper "Hitler." Although he had written in his diary that he was sad when German soldiers departed and enemy soldiers arrived, and that he had liked seeing Hitler, once the occupation began, Wild chose to spend much time with American soldiers.

While Wild and other children often approached GIs, viewing their presence with excitement, some children viewed the Americans from afar, or continued to view Americans as enemies. Some young Germans encountered Americans in more difficult circumstances such as during the requisitioning of their apartments or homes. Other young Germans, including Edeltraud Großjohann, who was over ten years older than Wild, were skeptical about whether the arrival of the Americans meant liberation. She was not impressed with the way the GIs behaved, chewing gum and dangling a cigarette from the corner of their mouths.[29] The opinion of another young German, Dietrich Volker (a pseudonym) of Augsburg, born in 1929, highlights the fact that not all youngsters were pleased about the end of the war and the arrival of Americans, and hints at the higher levels of indoctrination among older youths, in comparison to young children. Dietrich remained convinced about the validity of National Socialist beliefs even into the occupation. On April 20, 1945, Dietrich had noted down Hitler's birthday in his diary, including his portrait and writing that Hitler was leading the decisive battle for the capital of the Third Reich, Berlin. As the war came to an end, Dietrich recorded his personal feelings about the capitulation of Augsburg. On April 28, 1945, he wrote down that he was ashamed that the city decided not to defend itself against the Americans. On May 1, 1945, he wrote, "With revulsion I looked at the many white flags. (*Mit Abscheu betrachtete ich die vielen weißen Fahnen.*)" Dietrich's experience in the immediate postwar aftermath was impacted by his belief and active participation in National Socialism, the seizure of his family's apartment by the Americans, and also the arrest of his father by the Americans right after the end of the war. His diary is marked by portraits of Hitler inserted into the pages, as well as sketches of militaristic images, including weapons, tanks, and even an American jeep with the name "Mary" drawn onto it, showing his awareness of the American military presence.[30] Similarly, Wolfhilde von König of

28 Diary 1 of Theodor Wild, DTA Reg.-Nr. 540,1.

29 Diary of Edeltraud Großjohann, DTA Reg. Nr. 185/I 1–4 Abschrift.

30 Diary of Dietrich Volker [pseudonym], DTA Signatur-Nr. 1950,1.

Munich, born in 1925 and active in the *Bund Deutscher Mädel*, described in her diary on April 30, 1945 how quickly white flags starting appearing on her street in Munich once the Americans arrived. She wrote, "I thought the population of Munich would have been capable of having more honor. (*Etwas mehr Ehre hätte ich den Münchnern schon zugetraut.*)"[31] Overall, not all youngsters viewed the arrival of the Americans as a liberatory, exciting, and fresh start, nor were they all enticed by the American presence and offers of candy and gum. Some remained convinced in their beliefs in National Socialism. Young Germans reacted to the arrival of the first Americans in complex ways, highlighting that not all youngsters embraced actions such as asking GIs for candy or playing on tanks.[32]

In addition, some young Germans who lived in the US occupation zone during the occupation had experience with other Allied troops at the immediate end of the war, as the borders for the four occupation zones were not yet cemented, especially in Berlin. For example, young Germans in Berlin encountered Soviet troops during the final Battle of Berlin and its aftermath, and women of all ages were at risk of being a target for the mass rapes that took place there, from girls who may not have yet entered puberty to elderly women.[33] Berlin diarist Ruth Andreas-Friedrich wrote about visiting an acquaintance who had been raped seven times in a row.[34] The presence of young children, however, could serve as a protective force against rape for some women. In the 1945 diary *A Woman in Berlin*, the anonymous narrator wrote about a female acquaintance who was lodging with a mother of two small children. Once the soldiers saw the baby and the four-year-old son, they left the two women alone.[35] Werner Sollors was about two years old when his mother fled with him from Silesia; she used him as a deterrent from rape, holding him on top of her at night.[36] However, the presence of children did not always deter rapes. Karl Brach, then 11 years old, recalled that he

31 Sven Keller, ed., *Kriegstagebuch einer jungen Nationalsozialistin: Die Aufzeichnungen Wolfhilde von Königs 1939–1946* (De Gruyter, 2015), 213, https://doi.org/10.1515/9783110405378.

32 See Benjamin Möckel, *Erfahrungsbruch und Generationsbehauptung: die "Kriegsjugendgenerationen" in den beiden deutschen Nachkreigsgesellschaften* (Wallstein Verlag, 2014), 196–197, for more examples of German youth who had negative first impressions of American soldiers, viewing them as sloppy, weak, and arrogant.

33 On Soviet troops and rape, see Naimark, *The Russians in Germany*, Chapter 2, "Soviet Soldiers, German Women, and the Problem of Rape," 69–140.

34 Andreas-Friedrich, *Battleground Berlin*, 16.

35 Anonymous, *A Woman in Berlin: Eight Weeks in the Conquered City: A Diary*, trans. Philip Boehm (Picador/Henry Holt, 2005), 131–133. For more on the diary and debates over its authenticity, see Sollors, *The Temptation of Despair*, 36–55.

36 Sollors, *The Temptation of Despair*, 47.

and his younger sister witnessed his mother and grandmother getting raped repeatedly in April 1945 in Jüterbog, south of Berlin.[37] Christa Ronke, born in 1929, was raped as a teenager by Soviets in Dahlem in Berlin, which later became part of the American sector of Berlin.[38] On July 8, 1945, Ronke wrote in her diary that a former schoolmate was pregnant as a result of being raped six to seven times. She noted that this fate could have happened to any of them. Later in 1945, after Dahlem became part of the US sector of Berlin, Ronke paused going to school and worked with her mother at a US officers' mess hall in order to be fed and warm through the winter. Her father remained imprisoned as a prisoner of war, a common situation for many German families, and he ultimately passed away from typhus in a POW camp in the Urals.[39] Germans including women thus navigated their circumstances within the shifting context of occupation encounters with the various Allied troops. Ronke noted in her diary that an acquaintance, whose husband died in the war, had to beg a Russian soldier to help her get milk for her children, because one was ill. He did so, but expected something from her in return. He started to often come over to bring her food and play with the children, which the neighbors were unhappy about.[40] These navigations highlight the complex nature of postwar encounters with the Allies and the variety of decisions made in the shifting contexts and power dynamics.

Although Americans usually have been portrayed for their generosity to young Germans even in the immediate aftermath of the war, all of the Allied troops reacted to the presence of German youngsters. Soviet troops commonly reacted with kindness toward German children, which provides a more complex image of Red Army soldiers in contrast to the dominant, monolithic narrative of the initial encounter between Russians and Germans, which depicts violent, drunk Russians looting German homes and raping the women, including young teenage girls. Moreover, sexual violence by the Western Allies was also common, as Miriam Gebhardt's work has shown.[41] The Soviet soldiers' response to young Germans highlights the complex nature of encounters made in the rubble of for-

37 Samuel, *The War of Our Childhood: Memories of World War II*, 168.

38 Christa Ronke, "Christa Ronke: Auszüge aus meinem Tagebuch 1945," Lebendiges Museum Online, Stiftung Haus der Geschichte der Bundesrepublik Deutschland/Deutsches Historisches Museum/das Bundesarchiv, December 2008, https://www.dhm.de/lemo/zeitzeugen/christa-ronke-auszuege-aus-meinem-tagebuch-1945.html.

39 Christa Ronke, "Keep Smiling!" in *Hungern und hoffen*, ed. Kleindienst, 114–117, 121. See also Christa Ronke, "Nun sind wir amerikansich!: Aufzeichnungen einer Sechzehnjährigen im Berlin der Stunde Null," in Tamara Domentat, *Coca-Cola, Jazz & AFN: Berlin und die Amerikaner* (Schwarzkopf & Schwarzkopf, 1995), 80–81.

40 Ronke, "Keep Smiling!" in *Hungern und hoffen*, ed. Kleindienst, 112.

41 Gebhardt, *Als die Soldaten kamen.*

mer Nazi Germany. Theodor Wild noted that during the occupation, Russian soldiers were sometimes present in Amberg in addition to Americans, and they wanted to chat and laugh with youngsters like himself, but that they had nothing to give to children. They also begged to the Americans, just like the German youngsters. In addition, they even begged for cigarettes from the children. Wild wrote in his diary about an encounter with Russian soldiers: "I say 'Towaresch' [comrade] to them, then they laugh and want to speak with me. From the Russians you don't get anything. They also beg with the Americans. Cigarettes. (*Ich sage: 'Towaresch' [Kamerad] zu ihnen, dann lachen sie und wollen sich mit mir unterhalten. Von den Russen bekommt man nichts. Sie betteln selbst bei den Amis. Zigaretten.*)"[42] Before the war had ended, some Amberg children who lived near a camp of Russian prisoners of war and forced laborers tried to help them by passing them food through the fence. As a sign of thanks, the Russian prisoners made homemade toys for them. Sometimes the camp guards chased the children away, but the older guards tended to look away, allowing this exchange to occur, highlighting the possibilities for acts of kindness even within wartime encounters.[43]

Initial encounters had the potential to show Germans unexpected glimpses of the occupiers' humanity, including acts of kindness from Soviet soldiers. Ingeborg Schreib-Wywiorski, born in 1936 and living in Berlin at the end of the war, described in her recollections how a Russian soldier was emotionally touched when he encountered her family. He witnessed an idyllic family image: he saw Ingeborg with a doll in her arms, her younger brother with a wooden toy train, and her grandfather with a cold pipe in his mouth. This soldier then gave her mother a watch, which she gave later on to another Russian soldier who threatened her. The soldier who had been so impacted by the family had started crying and attempted to tell them that his children were waiting for him in the same way at home. He had not seen them in years. Ingeborg thus realized from this encounter that not all of the Russians were "*Unmenschen*," brutes.[44] Dietwart Nehring, 14 years old at the end of the war, was living with his parents in Rostock in the state of Mecklenburg-Vorpommern with his four other siblings between six months old and 17 years old. His father was the head of an agricultural testing station there, which had an institute and a villa where the family lived. In his recollections, Dietwart noted the turbulence of the first weeks after the arrival of the Red Army

---

42 Diary 1 of Theodor Wild, DTA Reg.-Nr. 540,1.

43 Andreas Ascherl, "'Aus seinem Mund und Rücken sickert Blut': Täglich Luftalarm in Amberg: Bomber und Tiefflieger über der Stadt," in *Sie Kommen!*, ed. Vogelsang, 30. These Russians were unable to take shelter during air raids during the war, and many died during Allied bombings.

44 Ingeborg Schreib-Wywiorski, in "Gemischte Gefühle und Schokolade," *Der Spiegel Geschichte* 1 (2018): 56.

but also that the military patrols who searched the institute and the air raid shelter were mostly friendly, especially to the children. At one point as Russians came in and out, a young soldier, perhaps around 17 years old, went up to the baby stroller that Dietwart's youngest brother was in. In the one hand, the soldier held his weapon, and with the other, he stroked the child. This soldier attempted to tell the children that the war was over, repeating "Chitler kaput [sic]," and he also tried to let them know that it was safe for them to go to sleep. Dietwart also stated that many of the Russian troops themselves behaved like little children, for example, being fascinated by modern conveniences such as telephones and bicycles. They allowed one soldier to use the telephone and he dialed a random number, speaking Russian. The caretaker then took the phone and explained to the man on the other line, the owner of a paper store, that the Russian who called only wanted to learn how to use a telephone. However, Dietwart also noted that less lighthearted encounters were common: he wrote that despite the common friendliness of Russians, the neighborhood women hid away in a secret hiding place in the institute's library, as rape was still an issue.[45] Encounters with the various Allied troops thus brought various levels of violence, which young Germans were a witness to, and young women could become victims of sexual violence in ways that boys and men mostly did not have to deal with. This was a consequence of the troop behavior of all the Allies, not only that of Soviets, as other Allied troops committed acts of violence including rape. However, soldiers' reactions to the youngest of Germans tended toward benevolence or kindness, including the most feared of the Allies, the Russians. Children and youth faced complex first encounters in the rubble with the foreign troops, ranging from a girl witnessing a Russian soldier breaking down at the sight of her family to a small boy trading souvenirs to American GIs.

Occupation Roles: Being Young Under Occupation

After the end of the war, the Allied troops settled into their role as occupiers, and young Germans experienced life in a society under military occupation. Many factors impacted young Germans' experiences of the postwar occupation sphere and their views of the occupiers. These included aspects of young people's identities such as age itself, class, health, religion, and gender, in addition to wartime roles such as military service, prisoner of war status, Hitler Youth/BDM participation, a role in resistance to the NS regime, refugee status, and more. In addition, family

45 Dietwart Nehring, "Besiegte und Sieger," in *Der Traum ist aus*, ed. Kleindienst, 299, 302–307.

status molded many youngsters' experiences in the postwar era, including the absence of fathers (or a mother, or both parents), and the attempt of some children to take on a parental role for younger siblings, or the role of a substitute partner for overwhelmed mothers.[46] Housing status also played a role in postwar experiences, especially impacting those whose houses or apartments were requisitioned by the Americans. English abilities could also spur encounters with GIs or could enable young Germans to take on roles such as working for the Americans. In addition, hunger often served as the central motivating factor for many youngsters, who noticed the relative luxury of the GIs, which stood in stark contrast to the difficult situation among the German population. Many young Germans thus attempted to interact with soldiers in order to gain more food. Overall, these factors all molded the roles that young Germans took on during the US occupation and shaped how they reacted to the presence of Americans.

Young Germans thus took part in occupation life in diverse ways, navigating encounters with Americans within occupation power structures. German children and youth became witnesses of occupation and the neighbors of the American occupiers who had moved in to their cities and towns. Theodor Wild was the child of a single mother who had not yet married his father, who had not yet returned to the family after the war. She was raising him alone in Amberg after being evacuated from Berlin. After his father's eventual return, his parents did marry, and Theodor took on his father's last name, Wild, instead of Gruschka, his mother's family name. Wild's occupation diaries are full of his youthful adventures throughout Amberg, and in them, he depicted his life experiences with a clear awareness of the distinctiveness of the occupation atmosphere. Theodor would often wander around town, talking to and trading souvenirs with GIs. Some GIs would ask him whether they were in Hamburg (not Amberg), and wondered where the water was, since Hamburg is a port city.[47] Theodor would also run to watch occupation *Razzien*, raids, because they were exciting. He wrote in his diary that during these raids, American men would jump out of jeeps, storm into a building, and sometimes naked women would run out of the building being

46 Seegers, *"Vati blieb im Krieg"*, 10, 88; Seegers, "Dead Dads," 259; Venken and Röger, "Growing up in the Shadow," 205; Vaizey, *Surviving Hitler's War*, 123, 129–131. The return of fathers was not always easy as well. Many former German soldiers returned home in a terrible state, and many youngsters did not recognize their fathers. Hans Herzmann of Remagen, then 12 years old, notes that after the release of his father in May 1945, they had conflicts, because his father "had to establish that he was running the show, not his twelve-year-old son," whereas Hans "wasn't ready to again become just an obedient little boy." In Samuel, *The War of Our Childhood: Memories of World War II*, 121.

47 Diaries of Theodor Wild, DTA Reg.-Nr. 540,1–3; Theodor Wild, in phone call with the author, January 10, 2019.

raided, wrapped only in blankets. He was aware that the women, who he called "*Amischicksen*," went with the Americans; around Russians, he noted, women ran away.[48] The raids were mainly conducted either to catch the women or to catch soldiers who had stolen goods. Sometimes a soldier would yell at him to get away from the raid if he stood too close. Once a soldier shouted, "Hau ab [*go away*] you facken [sic] boy." Wild wrote, "My mother says that is something obscene. (*Meine Mutter sagt das ist was unanständiges.*)" In mid-1946, Theodor Wild wrote in his diary about the "*Amischicksen*" getting picked up by the American Military Police and checked so they did not infect GIs with sexually transmitted diseases. After describing this, Theodor then wrote in this diary entry about how his mother calls the music Americans play "*Negermusik*," and that he does not like jazz, preferring organ music in the church. Then he went on to describe a new language system he created with symbols, which enabled him to write secret messages to his friend on the street with chalk. He also went on to write in the entry that he wished he had a brother.[49]

Thus, the occupation imprinted the everyday of Theodor Wild's childhood, in which, at a very young age, he was aware of the often chaotic, sexualized, and sometimes violent nature of the encounters between American soldiers and German women. Later in the summer of 1948, while playing on the Mariahilfberg outside of town with some friends, the group of boys heard a strange noise in the bushes, and thinking it was a wild boar, Wild threw a big rock into the bushes. A naked black American man suddenly appeared shouting, causing the boys to run in all directions. Wild however, remained hidden and witnessed the man having sex with a German woman, and he wrote that he would later describe what he saw in detail to his friends but that he could never tell his mother, who would respond by saying that he is "*verdorben*," corrupted.[50] Young Germans such as Theodor thus frequently stumbled upon Americans in their daily lives, gaining exposure to the sexualized and chaotic occupation landscape. In 1945, Theodor recorded a violent instance in his diary in which a German girl was killed by an American soldier: she had shouted "Nigger" at a black GI, and he had responded

48 The term "*Amischicksen*" was used as a pejorative term for German women who had relationships with GIs, among other terms such as "Ami-whores." See Shukert and Scibetta, *War Brides*, 125–127, 132. Interestingly, the word *Schickse* is a Yiddish term that refers to a non-Jewish woman, but probably by the time of the occupation, the meaning had shifted in Germany to refer to supposedly easy or loose women.

49 Diary 1 of Theodor Wild, DTA Reg.-Nr. 540,1. Anne Frank also invented secret codes in her diary. See Frank, *The Diary of a Young Girl*.

50 Diary 1 of Theodor Wild, DTA Reg.-Nr. 540,1; Theodor Wild, answer to question 9, in questionnaire 2, sent from author on August 22, 2020.

by slapping her face so hard that she died. Theodor wrote that the GI was sent back to the United States to be imprisoned. This situation provided a grave lesson to the local children to never say that word.[51] Despite the continuation of legal segregation in the US military until 1948, black GIs had status as occupiers amidst the power structures of postwar Germany. Black American occupation soldiers thus had the ability to impact the everyday fabric of life in postwar Germany, taking actions ranging from relations with German women and kindness to youngsters to a violent response to hearing a racial epithet from a young German.

Ingrid Picker, born in 1932, also showed awareness of the circumstances of the occupation as a young teenager. Her family's apartment in Lenggries in Upper Bavaria was requisitioned by the Americans and her father, an officer in the Wehrmacht, remained imprisoned until March 1947, thus impacting her everyday experiences during the occupation. In the diary, she remained skeptical about the American presence, most likely due to her father's continued imprisonment and the loss of her family's apartment. Like Theodor Wild, she observed the chaos of occupation raids, claiming that the most "*Amischixen* [sic]" are in her town of Lenggries.[52] In contrast to Theodor, however, she viewed the raids less as exciting and more as a sign of the dysfunction caused by the American presence, which to her was mostly negative. Older German youth may have been less entranced by the excitement and were more influenced by the negative factors of the occupation, such as the loss of housing or the absence of fathers. Younger children may have thus reacted differently to the encounters of the times, viewing the presence of American soldiers as exciting, because they could get sweets from them or learn some eye-opening early lessons in human relationships.

Gender also profoundly impacted occupation encounters, especially for German girls who were teenagers. Young German women had to navigate the unique circumstances and the complexities of a sexualized occupation sphere. Some German women chose to avoid Americans as much as possible, while others decided to take on relationships with the occupiers for a variety of reasons. In addition, young German women including teens took on work such as doing laundry for the Americans or working in American establishments.[53] While working in an American officer's mess hall in Berlin in 1945, Christa Ronke became known as "Coffee-Christel," and was the youngest worker there. She described in her diary that a GI guard tried to ask her on a date, but she refused, because it could be the grounds for dismissal from her job. On November 3, 1945, a friendly American

51 Diary 1 of Theodor Wild, DTA Reg.-Nr. 540,1.
52 Diary of Ingrid Picker, DTA Signatur-Nr. 3853,1.
53 See Shukert and Scibetta, *War Brides*, 128–130, 137–138.

officer took her home, which was at first uncomfortable for her, because she was worried others would talk of her as an *"Amiliebchen,"* an American sweetheart. The officer could speak German well and was half Jewish, and he had previously worked for the *Frankfurter Zeitung*. She learned from him about how millions of Jews had been murdered by the Nazis, and she wrote in her diary after this encounter that she was ashamed to be a German and would like to emigrate.[54] Her interaction with this American officer, which came about through her job at the American mess hall, thus shifted her view of her Germanness and her knowledge of the Nazi past.

Karin Finell also witnessed the end of the war and occupation in Berlin as a teenager. She was able to escape rape by Soviet soldiers by wearing a disguise.[55] Finell published a memoir of her childhood in 2006, which depicts her childhood and teenage years in Berlin. Finell was motivated to publish her story by the desire to break the silence about what it was like for German women and children in Berlin during and after the war.[56] Finell eventually dropped out of high school in 1950, entered drama school, and also began to work for the Americans in the PX, where she was a salesgirl and also helped out in the American movie theater next door. For Karin, who could speak "perfect English," working at the PX was "a dream job" with a "dream boss," Mr. Arnsen, an American civilian who had previously been in the military. She was even able to watch new American movies while eating candy bars in the movie theater. She became "the mascot of the PX," and also went on a date with an American officer from Puerto Rico.[57] Her grandmother had previously lived in the United States, where she still had a sister-in-law, and they had resumed their correspondence after the war. The relative extended an invitation to Karin to move to the United States. After this, Karin decided that her "future was clear: I would go to America."[58] In October 1951, she received her visa to immigrate to the United States, leaving Germany in January 1952.[59] Karin Finell's connections to the United States, including American family members, her job working for the Americans, English fluency, and interest in American culture such as movies spurred her to make the decision to leave behind her home country and travel alone to the United States.

54 Ronke, in *Hungern und hoffen*, ed. Kleindienst, 117–119.
55 Karin Finell, *Good-bye to the Mermaids: A Childhood Lost in Hitler's Berlin* (University of Missouri Press, 2006), 162. Karin Finell passed away in June 2023. See "Obituary: Karin Finell," *Santa Barbara Independent*, June 22, 2023, https://www.independent.com/obits/2023/06/22/karin-finell/.
56 Finell, 1–3.
57 Finell, 310–313, 321–325.
58 Finell, 236.
59 Finell, 338, 346.

Some young German women chose to become the lovers of Americans, and some even immigrated to the United States as war brides once marriage was allowed again between Germans and Americans in late 1946.[60] German women who were lovers of soldiers were often seen in a negative light, portrayed as a monolithic group of promiscuous *Fräuleins* who were abandoning moral values and traditions. However, in reality, German women entered into relationships with American GIs for a variety of reasons and in diverse circumstances.[61] These reasons could range from an economically-motivated decision, such as access to more food, to a desire for a bit of fun in the aftermath of a terrible war, and also due to falling in love with a soldier. Future war bride Hilde Robichaud of Vienna, Austria, then 18 years old, stated how attractive American soldiers seemed to her during the occupation of Vienna, where all four Allied troops were present. The Americans acted joyful and child-like, with their behavior providing a stark contrast to the challenges of the past years of war and the continuing difficulties of the occupation. Hilde described her impressions of American occupation soldiers in a 1988 study of the war brides of World War II. Hilde stated,

> Long before I met my husband-to-be [an American soldier] I was fascinated by these young men; they seemed so carefree, happy, and well fed, friendly, gentle with children and animals. At an outdoor cafe, they would sit and drink their Coca-Cola from a straw, while reading "Funny-Books." I wished that I could erase all the sad memories of the past years and act as young and spirited as they did.[62]

60 The first German war bride was Katharina Trost. GI Daniel Militello, then 24 years old, and Katharina, then 16 years old, met while Militello was on patrol in Bad Nauheim in April 1945, and the two fell in love. Trost got pregnant in the fall of 1945. They were denied a marriage license, and Militello was sent back to the United States. However, he continued petitioning Congress members, politicians, General Eisenhower, and even President Truman, without success. He then snuck back into Germany by enlisting as a mess steward for the Merchant Marine then jumped ship in Bremerhaven, sneaking back to Bad Nauheim. They married there in June 1946, and when Militello went to the American consulate in Frankfurt am Main, he was arrested. Militello was able to get media attention while imprisoned for 30 days. The intervention of New York Congressman Edward Elsaesser enabled Trost to receive an exit permit, and she arrived in the US as the first German war bride on November 11, 1946. On December 11, 1946, the ban on marriages between Germans and American soldiers was officially repealed, although bureaucratic hurdles still remained, especially for African American GIs. However, thousands of GIs did successfully marry Germans during the occupation. By the end of December 1946, 2,500 GIs had submitted an application for marriage permission. Shukert and Scibetta, *War Brides*, 125, 139–140, 144, 150–151; Domentat, *"Hallo Fräulein"*, 70–78.

61 See Domentat, *"Hallo Fräulein"*; Annette Brauerhoch, *Fräuleins and GIs: Geschichte und Filmgeschichte* (Stroemfeld, 2006); Shukert and Scibetta, *War Brides*, 130–131, 136–137.

62 Shukert and Scibetta, *War Brides*, 128.

The easygoing, well-fed, even joyous postwar American warrior also contrasted directly with the German soldier, who began to reappear after the end of the war. Ruth Andreas-Friedrich described in her diary in July 1945 how these men "shamble around like walking ruins," and had "wretched, pitiful looks."[63]

Betty Qui, then 17 years old, had been working at the American telephone central switchboard in Hanau in Hesse when she was summoned by a colonel, who needed a translator and writer for the dry cleaning facilities. She became the lover of the colonel, who brought her everything she needed from the PX, and they had a good time together. He even taught her how to drive his Cadillac. However, one day, the colonel informed her that he was being relocated to Garmisch-Partenkirchen. He promised Betty that his wife back home wanted a divorce and that he would find a way to bring Betty to the United States. However, for Betty, the dream of "*Amerika*" stayed a dream, never seeing the colonel, Joe, again. In contrast, her friend Irmgard married her GI lover and left for the United States.[64] Young German women thus navigated occupation circumstances, sometimes becoming active participants through their work or relationship choices. Encounters with American soldiers could even lead to the life-changing decision to immigrate to the United States.

Another occupation role that young Germans took on was as business partners of the Americans. Young Theodor Wild wrote in his diary, "The first word from the Americans was moneymaking. I don't know at all what they want. But now I also do moneymaking with everything that they want to buy, like medals and Hitler stuff. (*Das erste Wort von den Amis war moneymaking. Ich weiß gar nicht was die wollen. Aber jetzt mache ich auch moneymaking mit allem, was die Amis kaufen wollen, z.B. Orden, Hitlerkram.*)"[65] Wild would gather up and then trade Nazi souvenirs to the GIs, for example anything with Nazi symbols such as Hitler Youth medals, iron crosses, and even the *Mutterkreuz* (Cross of Honor of the German Mother), which he sold for the price of $50, with his main goal "moneymaking."[66] The money he made from his haggling would help his mother buy food and also enabled him to secretly save some money for himself.[67] In the first

63 Andreas-Friedrich, *Battleground Berlin*, 78. See also Shirer, *End of a Berlin Diary*, 149. Shirer described the demobilized German soldiers, the former "Herrenvolk," hobbling about, young yet toothless, begging for cigarettes.

64 Betty Qui [pseudonym], in *Hungern und hoffen*, ed. Kleindienst, 124–129.

65 Diary 1 of Theodor Wild, DTA Reg.-Nr. 540,1.

66 Diary 1 of Theodor Wild, DTA Reg.-Nr. 540,1; Wild, in questionnaire 1, answer 7; Wild, in questionnaire 2, answers 2 and 7.

67 Diary 1 of Theodor Wild, DTA Reg.-Nr. 540,1.

half year of the occupation, he made around $500 from his trading.[68] Wild's favorite spot to spend time in Amberg was at the Marktplatz in the center of the town, where he met school friends and many GIs, who would often ask the children for information. Wild did his trading business with the GIs there, and there was also a PX nearby, which meant GIs would often bring children sweets from there.[69] On May 20, 1947, Theodor wrote in English that "my mother says I am a 'kupzik' (=it is polish) a dealer with the Amis because I sell all the Amis need. I get Dollars and that is better than chocolate. The best customers are the negros [sic], they love children and give am meisten (mostly?) [the most]."[70] In his diary entry, Wild thus recorded the commonality of the high level of generosity of black American soldiers. Wild's mother knew Polish because her family was from Upper Silesia and she would sometimes sing Polish songs to him. When they had lived there previously when he was younger, Theodor had also been able to speak some Polish. Theodor also noted the differences between Americans and Russians in Amberg. Russian soldiers had nothing to offer to the children besides a friendly greeting. To Theodor, Russians smelled like sweat and sour soup (such as "Borscht"), while Americans smelled like soap and American gasoline, "*Ami-Benzin*," he wrote.[71]

Similarly to the German civilians who were employed by Americans, Wild had particular skills that enabled him to interact and trade with Americans: he had learned English from his aunt in Berlin since he was small.[72] In addition, he was a particularly curious child, and was brave enough to approach soldiers. He wrote in his diary, "I am not scared of the Americans, because I can speak English. (*Ich habe keine Angst vor den Amerikanern, weil ich ja englisch kann.*)" Theodor described an interaction with a GI one day in 1945: "How are you? Oh, very well! My name is Theodor. Oh, like our president Rosewelth [sic], sagte ein Ami zu mir" (an American said to me). Furthermore, Theodor highlighted the way that he dealt with American soldiers, "When I speak English with them they are friendly again (*Wenn ich mit ihnen english speak sind sie wieder freundlich*)," and he described that he did not beg the American soldiers for goods, "But when they give something out to all the children, I also stand there. (*Aber wenn sie an alle Kinder was verteilen, stelle ich mich auch hin.*)"[73] However, instead of getting gifts of sweets from American soldiers, he preferred to haggle with them. When his

68 Wild, in questionnaire 1, answer 4; Wild, in questionnaire 2, answer 7.
69 Wild, in questionnaire 2, answer 2.
70 Diary 2 of Theodor Wild, DTA Reg.-NR. 540,2.
71 Diary 1 of Theodor Wild, DTA Reg.-Nr. 540,1.
72 Diary 1 of Theodor Wild, DTA Reg.-Nr. 540,1; Wild, in questionnaire 1, answers 3 and 8.
73 Diary 1 of Theodor Wild, DTA Reg.-Nr. 540,1.

younger cousin Aimée was visiting Amberg, black soldiers would often want to touch her blonde hair, which was long and golden, and they would give her entire bags of sweets from the PX in return.[74] In addition, Theodor had to wear a bandage on his head for nearly a year due to a surgery he had for an ear infection earlier in 1945, and many GIs felt increased compassion for him, because they thought he had been wounded in the war, which led to him getting a double amount when they gave out gifts to the children.[75]

These interactions appeared to be especially exciting for Theodor Wild, who chose to navigate the occupation scene in ways that would provide adventure and enable him to have access to more food. As Harald Jähner writes, during the aftermath of World War II, "A lot of younger people in particular changed worlds daily; they moved in social spheres shaped by completely different sets of values. Whether they were dealing with their families, with black markets or with occupying soldiers, they always acted according to differently coded systems. That could be exciting and profitable."[76] Hans Magnus Enzensberger, a German author who was 16 years old in late 1945, worked as an interpreter for the Americans and then the British, and had experiences on the black market that were "character building" for him, Jähner notes. In a similar manner to Wild, Enzensberger saw Americans as business partners, trading Nazi souvenirs for American cigarettes, and then trading the cigarettes for more souvenirs. At some point, he apparently had 40,000 cigarettes stored at his parent's house, a value of about 400,000 Reichsmarks then.[77] Trading "in these symbols from two worlds, Lucky Strikes for Golden Party Badges, sharpened the senses and presence of mind" of the teenage boy, as Jähner describes.[78] Youngsters were aware of and affected by the hard facts and policies of the occupation, such as rationing and the black market. Moreover, they were active and aware of the circumstances of the time, with young Germans such as Wild and Enzensberger taking on roles during the occupation that psychologist Emmy E. Werner describes as part of "a game of survival" among challenging circumstances as children growing up in the aftermath of war.[79] For some youngsters in the occupation, this role could even be thrilling to them.

---

74 Wild, in questionnaire 1, answer 6; Wild, in questionnaire 2, answer 5.

75 Wild, *Wo der "Müde" war, war immer was los*, 24; see also Diary 1 of Theodor Wild, DTA Reg.-Nr. 540,1.

76 Jähner, *Aftermath*, 185.

77 Jähner, 185–186; Matthias Matussek and Markus Brauck, "Phantastischer Gedächtnisverlust," *Der Spiegel* 45 (2008).

78 Jähner, 186.

79 Werner, *Through the Eyes of Innocents*, 181.

Many youngsters entered into encounters centered around food as part of that survival game. Their young age ensured they were able to gain from the presence of the GIs because of soldiers' generosity toward children, which could help their families. For example, Theodor Wild took on a provider role for his mother. He traded with the Americans so that his mother could buy more food with his earnings, writing in his diary, "When there is a lot of money, my mother can buy more. (*Wenn es viel Geld gibt, kann meine Mutter mehr einkaufen.*)" In his diary, he wrote about a time when after playing in the warm bakery with his friends, the baker's son snatched some bread for them all. Theodor ended up saving some of the bread to bring home to his mother. He wrote, "I then don't eat everything and bring something for my mother. (*Ich esse dann nicht alles auf und bringe meine Mutter was mit.*)"[80] The fact of his mother's hunger was thus a central part of Theodor's daily existence. Interestingly, the family was Catholic and his mother seemed especially worried about Theodor's moral state due to him having a childhood during an occupation by foreign troops in the aftermath of war, for example often scolding him for committing sins in ways such as haggling with the Americans. However, many of his antics were indeed undertaken to try to help her. Theodor's diary was a way for him to keep some of his actions a secret: He sometimes wrote his secrets in the code he developed, and sometimes he wrote in English so his mother could not read what he wrote. In 1948, he wrote that he had two diaries, because his mother searched through his diary and sometimes took it away. She apparently wanted to know all his secrets, especially regarding girls.[81]

On June 1, 1947, Theodor wrote that "my mother is often sad because I am rare[ly] (selten?) at home," implying that he was often roaming around the town, away from her.[82] His mother's suffering extended beyond her hunger, a fact Theodor was aware of, writing in 1946, "Since my mother is so anxious, I have to do a lot . . . If I do something by myself my mother must not know about it. (*Weil meine Mutter so ängstlich ist, mußs [sic] ich viel machen . . . Wenn ich was alleine mache darf es meine Mutter nicht wissen.*)"[83] Theodor reflected in his diary on his mother's view about the family's condition, and noted his yearning to be back in the family home in Berlin with all his relatives, a place he seemed to idealize. Before the war, the family had been well off, but the Nazis and later the Soviets had

80 Diary 1 of Theodor Wild, DTA Reg.-Nr. 540,1.
81 Diary 3 of Theodor Wild, DTA Reg.-Nr. 540,3.
82 Diary 2 of Theodor Wild, DTA Reg.-Nr. 540,2.
83 Diary 1 of Theodor Wild, DTA Reg.-Nr. 540,1.

dispossessed the family of their wealth.[84] On Christmas of 1945, Theodor wrote about his feelings about his family situation:

> My mother says we are poor. I don't know that. I always have something to eat. Only no good shoes. My feet often hurt. I always run around barefoot. My mother is sad because we are evacuated [from Berlin]. The Russians are now in Berlin in our apartment. They took or broke everything, wrote Annuschka. I play with my electric train Siemens [later stolen by a mean GI, according to Wild] . . . I also am a little sad. I prefer to be now in our apartment in Berlin with my mother, my father, with Annuschka, Aunt Heide and Aimée and Grandfather. (*Meine Mutter sagt wir sind arm. Ich weiß das nicht. Ich habe immer ein Essen. Nur keine guten Schuhe. Meine Füße tun mir oft weh. Ich laufe immer barfuß rum. Meine Mutter ist traurig weil wir evakuiert sind. Die Russen sind jetzt in Berlin in unserer Wohnung. Sie haben alles weggenommen oder kaputt gemacht hat Annuschka geschrieben. Ich spiele mit meiner Elektrischen Eisenbahn Siemens . . . Ich bin auch ein bisschen traurig. Lieber will ich jetzt in unserer Wohnung in Berlin sein mit meiner Mutter, mit meinem Vater, mit Annuschka, Tante Heide und Aimée und Großvater.*)[85]

Young Germans often described the various challenges of their family members during the occupation in their diaries, and they were often aware of the great effort that was made to care for them within the challenging circumstances. For example, Ingrid Picker's father remained imprisoned after the war, but she noted in her diary how her mother still made sure the children had enough to eat and provided for them in other ways, such as ensuring that they had a good Christmas in 1945. On June 10, 1945, Ingrid wrote that her mother had become so gaunt from a sickness in May as well as due to strain that her dresses no longer fit and she looked like a young girl. Ingrid also described her grandmother's struggles, who lived in Ingolstadt and who had a nervous breakdown in November 1945. Her mother came home depressed after visiting the grandmother in December 1945, who apparently kept making statements such as "Alas, if only I could go into the Danube River! I am responsible for all of your misery! (*Ach, wenn ich nur in die Donau gehen könnte! Ich bin an all eurem Elend Schuld!*)"[86] Young Germans thus faced a period in which adult figures such as parents were showing signs that they were struggling with the circumstances of the time. Young Germans themselves noticed this struggle and sometimes tried to mitigate the adults' suffering. Youngsters often had to take on distinct roles within their families to cope with the challenges of the time.

Overall, hunger especially permeated the childhood experience in the occupation, as American rationing policies remained restrictive until the currency re-

84 Wild, in questionnaire 1, answer 14.
85 Diary 1 of Theodor Wild, DTA Reg.-Nr. 540,1; Wild, in questionnaire 1, answer 4.
86 Diary of Ingrid Picker, DTA Signatur-Nr. 3853,1.

form of June 1948. Rationing policies allotted children above age six and teenagers to receive higher rations than the regular adult ration of around 1,400 to 1,550 calories, but this higher rate still was often not enough for youngsters' growing bodies, often leaving them hungry.[87] Theodor Wild stated that he was undernourished, like most children, but he was not unhappy.[88] Young Germans commonly navigated the occupation scene in ways that would ensure gaining more food, as Theodor Wild did when he traded souvenirs with American soldiers for money so his mother could get more food. Peter Grell in Berchtesgaden recounted in a collection of reflections of contemporary witnesses about his "stealing phase" from 1945 to 1948, when he was only caught once. He usually searched through the Americans' trash cans for food, sometimes finding loot such as half a piece of white bread with a small bit of mold on a corner.[89] Peter stated that hunger hurt, and that pride was something that you could have only when you were not hungry. He recalled an incident during school vacation in the summer of 1946 when he was invited to pick up tennis balls for the Americans playing on two new tennis courts built across from the Berchtesgadener Hof. He had intended to try to steal some of their possessions, which they had left on the benches at the courts, but he failed. Afterwards, as he was about to leave after helping during the game, a couple of soldiers asked him, "Peter, what [do] you want?" and offered him a Coke, to which he responded in German that he was hungry. The soldiers eventually understood the word "Hunger" and returned with a huge plate with six pieces of bread covered with spread, two of which disappeared with incredible speed into his mouth, to the pleasure of the three adults. He took the rest home to have later, as he told the Americans, not indicating that he was bringing it to his family at home, who were hungry too. If he had told them this, he believed they would not have given him so much and let him get away with the rest. After eight days at his "job" picking up the tennis balls, he was told that Germans were not allowed at the tennis courts anymore.[90] Christa Ronke and her family in Berlin also made the decision about her employment in the American officer's mess hall based on the fact that she would have food and heating there to get her through the winter, although she would have to pause her schooling. However, she had

---

87 For an example of calories for rationing by age in the state of Bremen, see Imke Ehlers, *Die Ernährungssituation nach dem Zweiten Weltkrieg am Beispiel des Landes Bremen* (Universitätsbuchhandlung, 1995), 67.

88 Wild, in questionnaire 1, answer 11.

89 Peter Grell, "Ganze acht Tage in 'Lohn und Brot,'" in *Nachkriegs-Kinder*, ed. Kleindienst, 224.

90 Grell, in *Nachkriegs-Kinder*, ed. Kleindienst, 223–226.

trouble concentrating in school anyway because she was so hungry. Her mother was fired while working at the same mess hall for being caught sneaking food out, but despite this, Christa continued to sneak food for her family out of the mess hall, never forgetting their needs as well.[91]

Young Germans' descriptions of the time were often imbued with certain flavors and tastes, sometimes marked by an obsession with food. Many children saw and ate foods such as white bread and peanut butter for the first time. The *Schulspeisung* was introduced in 1946 in the British zone and then also in the US zone in 1947 through the initiative of former President Herbert Hoover, which provided pupils in the Bizone with an extra warm meal.[92] The *Schulspeisung* was often the highlight of the day for many youngsters. Ingrid Picker noted in her diary about the start of the *Schulspeisung* in her school in 1947, which featured chocolate in many of the meals.[93] In 1947, Theodor also mentioned the *Schulspeisung*, writing that summer vacation was fun but that there was no *Schulspeisung*.[94] Ingrid Picker described the *Schulspeisung* menu during the first week, which included:

1. Chocolate (1–2 bars)
2. Hot chocolate and cookies
3. Oatmeal (thin) with fine fruits and dried egg . . .

(1. Schokolade (1–2 Tafel)
2. Kakao u. Keks
3. Haferflockenbrei (dünn) mit feinen Früchten u. Eipulver . . .)

Ingrid was not completely pleased by the contents of the meal, which tended to upset her stomach, but she was glad to be a little bit less hungry before she came home.[95] Meals thus permeated many young Germans' childhoods: Another diary of a boy during the occupation consisted nearly only of lists of what he ate that day.[96]

Encounters with American soldiers also often involved more complicated aspects, in contrast to the mostly positive encounters based around youngsters re-

91 Ronke, in *Hungern und hoffen*, ed. Kleindienst, 115–116, 121.
92 Ehlers, *Die Ernährungssituation*, 30–33. Also, Borries, *Quiet Helpers*.
93 Diary of Ingrid Picker, DTA Signatur-Nr. 3853,1.
94 Diary 2 of Theodor Wild, DTA Reg.-Nr. 540,2. Theodor Wild described that whole families lived on the leftovers from the *Schulspeisung* in Amberg. Sometimes GIs gave out chocolate in addition to the main meal. GIs were at first the ones supervising the school meals, then the teachers took over as supervisors of the *Schulspeisung* a few months later. When the German teachers took over, the chocolate bars disappeared and would turn up later on the black market. Wild, in questionnaire 1, answer 12.
95 Diary of Ingrid Picker, DTA Signatur-Nr. 3853,1.
96 Diary of Wolfgang K. in "Vereinte Tagebücher 1945–46," DTA Reg.-Nr. 1414-I.

ceiving extra food. Complex negotiations about German guilt affected young Germans, even those as young as Theodor Wild. Young Germans had to deal with questions regarding the Nazi past and their participation (and their family's participation) in the National Socialist regime. Youngsters also reacted to the presence of Americans in different ways based on their wartime roles and whether they continued to find meaning in National Socialist beliefs. On October 19, 1946, Dietrich Volker wrote in his diary that he told his teacher that he would like to do a presentation in class on Adolf Hitler, to which the teacher apparently responded with deep astonishment. Dietrich appeared to remain convinced about the heroism of Hitler, even over a year after the end of the war.[97]

Theodor Wild, who had initially written that he preferred the presence of German soldiers to that of enemy soldiers, and who had liked seeing Hitler in Berlin, dealt with conversations with GIs around guilt, even though he was a young boy. Theodor wrote that his mother told him, "We are not Nazis (*Wir sind keine Nazis*)," but he noted, "The Americans also say Nazis to us. (*Die Amis sagen zu uns auch Nazis.*)"[98] Often, American GIs asked him about his father, as he wrote about on May 16, 1947, in English:

> Where is your father? me ask an american [sic] officer [an American officer asked me]. I told him that my father in [sic] prison from russian [sic]. He was a nazi? No, I say, he was a [sic] officer too; in the OKW—you know I think, he do [sic] not know. I say this is the hight [sic] commando of military. Ah, your father is a nazi. No, the nazis will kill my father because he was not a nazi. Pah! All Amis think all german [sic] are nazi [sic]. That is stupid.[99]

Wild's father had been in the *Oberkommando der Wehrmacht* (OKW) (the Wehrmacht High Command), but the SS had apparently been after his father and the family had been placed under house arrest in Berlin. After the war, Wild's mother was able to get a certificate right away from the commandant's office stating that they were not Nazis.[100] In his diary, Theodor professed to know who the local Nazis of Amberg were. He also noted the American efforts to find Nazis: In December 1945, the Americans were still running around the streets searching for Nazis, according to Theodor.[101] Interestingly, Wild later recollected that black GIs never asked German children if their parents were Nazis, highlighting the differ-

97 Diary of Dietrich Volker [pseudonym], DTA Signatur-Nr. 1950,1.
98 Diary 1 of Theodor Wild, DTA Reg.-Nr. 540,1.
99 Diary 2 of Theodor Wild, DTA Reg.-Nr. 540,2.
100 Diary 1 of Theodor Wild, DTA Reg.-Nr. 540,1; Wild, in questionnaire 1, answers 13 and 16.
101 Diary 1 of Theodor Wild, DTA Reg.-Nr. 540,1.

ent views of Germans among the Americans themselves.[102] This furthers the interpretation that black soldiers seemed to view German children in an especially innocent light, focusing more on their present needs than on the Nazi past.

Theodor Wild's childhood writings thus highlight the complexity of navigations about German guilt. Due to the fact that he was a child, Theodor seemed innocent to the Americans, and he was thus often the recipient of benevolence. However, some soldiers still wondered about his father's wartime role, especially since his father had been high up in the military. However, Theodor asserted to American soldiers that his father had not been a Nazi, despite his high position in the Wehrmacht, providing a contrasting opinion to the common American belief that all Germans were tainted by Nazism and needed to go through the denazification process. Individual soldiers could also react ambivalently about guilt, for example not questioning the innocence of the youngest Germans such as Theodor. Many GIs also wanted a German girlfriend even if they believed in collective German guilt. According to a June 24, 1945 journal entry by Sergeant Henry Giles, a fellow GI even called his German girlfriend "his little Nazi."[103] Overall, Americans tended to view older German youth as more indoctrinated by Nazi beliefs than young German children. American military government especially focused on reeducating youth aged ten and above. This group of young Germans was seen as the main audience for democratization efforts, with American officials responding to German juvenile delinquency in ways such as organizing youth committees or encouraging youth to join the Army-sponsored GYA clubs, which aimed to transform former Hitler Youth into the future democrats of Germany.[104]

For Henry Beissel, born in 1929 and a teenager in Hamburg after the war, the occupation period made him realize his feelings of guilt as a German, playing a role in his decision to immigrate to Canada. In his poetic memoir, he wrote about his attempts to "negotiate the desperate emptiness between yesterday and tomorrow" while working as an interpreter for the Allied troops during the occupation, including for the Americans:

> In a world of contradictions he became aware
> of his guilt. He had done nothing to merit
> survival, and now he was living in luxury
> while the others struggled with misery.
> Cigarettes and whiskey, coffee
> and chocolate were the currency
> of the new world. His army

102 Wild, in questionnaire 2, answer 5.
103 Giles, ed., *The G.I. Journal of Sergeant Giles*, 370.
104 See Ziemke, *The U.S. Army in the Occupation*, 438–439.

> rations were the safe conduct
> to survival for his mother and his brother
> as he interpreted and negotiated
> between occupiers and occupied . . .
> It was a *danse macabre* that brought
> conqueror and conquered together
> In an unacknowledged admission
> Of their common folly. And he was cock
> Of the dunghill, straddling both
> Sides of the equation, indulging
> An appetite for life that became more
> ferocious as he lost it to the horrors
> of the thousand-year childhood.
> That stole his soul.[105]

For Beissel, learning of the horrors of the Holocaust through films that were shown to the German population about the camps was a turning point, leading him to flee the land of his past and his childhood in search of a new homeland. He wrote,

> Something broke inside this 16-year-old
> And he knew his heart could never forgive
> Himself for not doing what he could
> Not have done. It would never stop
> weeping till it stopped beating.[106]

Therefore, the occupation served as an awakening to the horrors of National Socialism for Beissel, leading him to no longer see a future for himself in Germany, although he was aware that his memories would probably follow him wherever he went.[107] Young Germans thus played a role as mediators between American soldiers and their questions about guilt, attempting to explain their fathers' wartime roles and, sometimes, their own active or passive participation in National Socialism. Some youngsters, such as Henry Beissel, grappled with their feelings of guilt as Germans and questioned whether they saw a future staying in Germany. Also, some young Germans even departed Germany, whether on their own initiative, due to family connections, or as a war bride.

German youth also began to take on roles as active participants in developments spurred by American occupation policies. For example, occupation reeducation and democratization goals encouraged German participation in youth

105 Beissel, *Coming to Terms with a Child*, 109–111.
106 Beissel, 121.
107 Beissel, 122–123.

clubs, including the Army-sponsored GYA program. Some youth became active members of these democratically oriented clubs, or visited the clubs, youth centers, and other American-sponsored youth events. Ingrid Picker described in her diary the events organized by the Americans for the local youth and children, including various festivals for children, a sports race, a trip to Garmisch, and a Christmas party on December 21, 1946. Ingrid participated in some of the events but claimed to keep a distance from the Americans, because she knew the real purpose of the events: "They think it's now important to ingratiate themselves with German children. I will not take part in that! I will not let myself be blinded like so many others. (*Die haben's jetzt wichtig, sich bei den deutschen Kindern einzuschmeicheln. Da mach' ich nicht mit! Ich laß mich nicht verblenden, wie so viele andere.*)" After attending the Christmas party, which she attended and where she received a present of fruit, chocolate, chewing gum, and toothpaste, she wrote, "It would all be good and nice, if on the other side, they weren't doing so much harm and taking things away. In this way, they also only just want to ingratiate themselves with the youth. (*Es wär ja alles gut und schön, wenn sie uns nicht auf der anderen Seite wieder so viel antäten u. wegnähmen. Sie wollen sich ja auch dadurch nur bei der Jugend einschmeicheln.*)"[108] For Ingrid, receiving benefits such as presents from the Americans could never be separated from her awareness that there was a purpose behind the benevolent acts of the occupiers, of trying to bring youngsters to their side. She did not seem to be convinced that the American occupation presence would spur anything beneficial.

However, other young Germans were excited by the possibilities that opened up in the occupation, such as partaking in the youth activities program in their free time. Karin Finell's mother worked for a GYA girls' club in Berlin starting in 1948 during the time of the Berlin Airlift. In her memoir, Karin described her mother explaining to her that the club was "a place for young girls to go after school . . . It's a terrific idea. The [US] military is keeping the children off the streets while teaching them to do useful things and about democracy." Karin's mother explained that she would keep the girls busy after school, teaching arts and crafts, for example, and starting a choir. One day in late fall, Karin visited the GYA club, which was in Zehlendorf, two stops away by *S-Bahn* from where they lived. When she arrived, she smelled apples and cinnamon, which made her mouth water: It was the smell of apple pie. She then tried her first ever slice of apple pie, provided by the "soldiers in charge of teaching German boys about America, baseball, and democracy." On top of the pie, there was vanilla ice cream, which was strange for Karin to eat since it was cold outside. For Karin,

108 Diary of Ingrid Picker, DTA Signatur-Nr. 3853,1.

"the taste combination was sheer heaven." In the GYA club, the children had English lessons, learned about American customs, and even ate hot dogs during baseball games. To Karin, the apple pies "symbolized an appropriate supplement to the lessons on democracy: democracy tasted sweet."[109] For Finell, her visit to the GYA club provided another example of the positive aspects of the United States, and she remained certain about her desire to immigrate there. She was aware that not every aspect relating to the Americans was positive; for example, she dealt with two invasive male doctors at the US Army hospital during the medical examination required for her visa to immigrate to the United States, but she was steadfast in her decision to seek a new life abroad in the homeland of the occupiers.[110] For other young Germans, participation in GYA clubs could provide a variety of experiences, from lessons in English to having fun playing new sports such as baseball, to going home with a full stomach, to learning about democracy. As the occupation developed and the Americans shifted their aim toward the rehabilitation of Germans rather than punishment, encounters between Americans and German youngsters became a central part of occupation aims, especially those in controlled spaces such as GYA clubs.[111]

Young Germans also began to become school pupils again during the postwar occupation. As 1945 progressed, schools reopened, usually beginning with the elementary schools in the fall of 1945 and then the higher classes later in 1945. Both teachers and textbooks went through denazification processes. Young Germans thus began to spend more time in the structured space of the classroom. This stood in contrast to the immediate end of the war, when schools remained shut and children roamed around the ruined cityscapes. As a young boy during the war while still in Berlin, Theodor Wild had been unable to start with regular schooling, instead receiving private tutoring after his school in Berlin was bombed.[112] Some postwar German school officials and teachers reacted with awareness to the singularity of the time period and the challenging circumstances of having to grow up in wartime and living in its aftermath. Teachers sometimes assigned school assignments that required the reflection of their pupils about their war years. For example, thousands of German pupils submitted responses from 1946 to 1949 about their life stories, part of a requirement for registering for

109 Finell, *Good-bye to the Mermaids*, 268–272.
110 Finell, 339–341.
111 See Chapter Three for more information on GYA and a case study of a GYA boys club in Bremen.
112 Wild, *Wo der "Müde" war, war immer was los*, 11–13; Diary 1 of Theodor Wild, DTA Reg.-Nr. 540,1.

the *Reifeprüfung*, the school leaving examination.[113] These reports provide a glimpse into how young Germans dealt with their personal situations.[114] Udo K., 21 years old at the time of his report, had been a prisoner of war in a British camp in Belgium, returning home on Christmas of 1945. Udo recorded his thoughts about being young: for him, if being young meant having traits such as enthusiasm and freshness, then he no longer felt young. Instead, he was still searching for the meaning of this life, which he had been searching for ever since he saw the first person die for no reason.[115] For this young direct witness of war, he felt robbed of his youth in the face of seemingly senseless violence. In contrast, Ursula V., 19 years old at the time of writing her report, wrote about the difficulties of the *Zusammenbruch*, the collapse of Germany, but that she realized that life goes on. She had regained a positive outlook on her life. After initial disinterest in politics, the young woman had started to read the news and listen to the radio, realizing that now she could make her own informed opinions. She had thus managed to navigate the shifting dynamics of immediate postwar German society, going from numbness in the wake of defeat to disinterest in politics and then active engagement in the evolving German society.[116]

In 1946, Otto Barthel, a school inspector (*Schulrat*) for the upper classes in Nuremberg schools, started an initiative aiming at helping pupils with *Vergangenheitsbewältigung*, coming to terms with the past, by writing about their wartime experiences. Overall, as a result of Barthel's initiative, Nuremberg school pupils, mostly from *Volksschulen* and *Berufsschulen*, created around 7,000 items including reports and drawings. These items provide testimony of the lived experiences of youth under National Socialism, during World War II, and its immediate aftermath, and the ways youth interpreted their lives.[117] Beate Müller notes that the reasoning behind Barthel's decision to undertake the project is unclear; however, he had claimed that he hoped the results could be used for further studies into the status of the youth, for example for usage by historians, psychologists, or pedagogues. However, in the end, the results were not disseminated, instead landing only in Barthel's private papers. According to Müller, the items give a glimpse

---

113 See excerpts of responses in Kurt Haß, ed., *Jugend unterm Schicksal: Lebensberichte junger Deutscher 1946–1949* (Bern: Aare-Verlag, 1950). It is unclear whether this was a requirement for all German pupils or whether it was limited to certain occupation zones or regions.

114 Haß, ed., 9.

115 Haß, ed., 144–145.

116 Haß, ed., 178–179.

117 The collection of pupils' items can be found in Otto Barthel's personal papers, which are now located at the Nuremberg Stadtarchiv: E 10/1 Nachlass Otto Barthel, Stadtarchiv Nürnberg. On Otto Barthel, see "Otto Barthel: Biografien: Menschen aus Bayern," Haus der Bayerischen Geschichte, accessed on August 31, 2023, https://hdbg.eu/biografien/detail/otto-barthel/2295.

into the "coping strategies" that young people forged in the wake of an "acute crisis of consciousness" of the collapse of the Third Reich.[118] These coping mechanisms included withdrawal from politics, idealizing the past before the war, and relativizing German guilt by pointing out the negative effects of the Allies, such as wartime bombings and occupation policy. In addition, school students often focused on their young age, professing innocence regarding the crimes of the Nazi regime.[119]

In 1980, Hannes Heer published a selection of some of the Nuremberg pupils' reports, as a warning against war by depicting its gruesome impacts on youngsters in their own words.[120] The reports depict the variety of experiences of the war and immediate postwar, which in 1946 were still fresh on the pupils' minds. In addition, they were created in school, not for publication, although teachers may have affected how the texts were written or what the pupils thought they should write about. However, despite this, they are "more direct and spontaneous than any text carefully composed and edited for publication," as Beate Müller notes.[121] The published selection includes reports that document the range of experiences of various young Germans during the war and immediate postwar era, including experiences such as the loss of a father, returning home from the *Kinderlandverschickung*, having one's home being destroyed by bombs, witnessing Holocaust victims on death marches near Flössenburg concentration camp, and the return of a father from a concentration camp, where he had been imprisoned for 11 years.[122]

Especially fascinating are the school students' early impressions of American soldiers, with many of them commenting on seeing black American soldiers, highlighting how much of an impression this made on school pupils, enough to write it in their reports. In a similar manner to young Theodor Wild's first impression of Americans, one 13-year-old pupil wrote about the arrival of the American troops and seeing black GIs driving the tanks. The school pupil noted how the soldiers went looking for SS members and soldiers, searching through the houses. The boy then went out onto the street, and got a gift of a bar of chocolate,

---

118 Beate Müller, "'Der Mann, den ich vergötterte, hat uns ins Unglück geführt': The Post-War Crisis of Consciousness as Mirrored in Essays and Questionnaires by Nuremberg's Schoolchildren in 1946," *German Life and Letters* 69, no. 4 (October 2016): 453–457, 459–460, https://doi.org/10.1111/glal.12130.

119 Müller, "Der Mann, den ich vergötterte, hat uns ins Unglück geführt," 453, 459–467.

120 Hannes Heer, ed., *Als ich 9 Jahre alt war, kam der Krieg: Schüler-Aufsätze 1946: ein Lesebuch gegen den Krieg* (Prometh, 1980), 7–8, 189.

121 Müller, "Der Mann, den ich vergötterte, hat uns ins Unglück geführt," 457.

122 Heer, ed., *Als ich 9 Jahre alt war*, 72, 151, 153, 157.

which made him very happy.[123] Another 13-year-old pupil witnessed black American soldiers shooting SS troops who had been hiding in the woods. When the three black GIs came into the house, they were nice to the children, giving them cigarettes and sweets.[124] A report by a 14-year-old boy noted the evacuation of families with children from Nuremberg to neighboring villages at the end of the war; there they also hid in a nearby trench shelter as the American troops arrived. Rumors from retreating SS groups claimed that Nuremberg had been taken by the Americans and that all youth there between 13 and 17 years of age had been abducted by black soldiers. Once the Americans arrived on April 18, 1945, a black GI told the children that they would not do anything to them, and to return to the village. However, shots were fired again, and one hit the boy's arm; an American soldier wrapped up the boy's wound.[125] A girl wrote in her report about taking walks with her friend while they were evacuated in Weißenburg in Bayern, south of Nuremberg. On a beautiful Sunday morning, they decided to visit the Bismarckturm, a tower which had a good view. Suddenly, while on top of the tower, they heard a foreign language: two black Americans were coming up the stairs to the tower. She and her friend were apparently appalled by their black faces, claiming they looked hideous. The GIs started to talk to the girls, wanting to know everything, and they spoke for a while, and one of them offered them a bar of chocolate. However, the girl who wrote about this incident was so scared of the black soldiers that she could not take the chocolate, although she would have liked to eat it. She was glad when the soldiers left.[126] One 12-year-old boy wrote a short report about the end of the war, saying that when the Americans came, they shot his mother, not writing the reason why, highlighting the possibilities for violence in the context of war and its aftermath.[127] This collection of reports provides a glimpse into the diversity of young Germans' experiences, who were not a monolithic group, and highlights the ways in which school pupils described their experiences in the context of a postwar school assignment.

Werner Schütz, born in 1929, was a pupil at the *Realgymnasium* in Heppenheim in Hesse when it reopened in October 1945. He reflected on his experiences as a school pupil in the early months of occupation, recorded in a collection of reflections of contemporary witnesses published in 2000. Similar to the Nuremberg school pupils under Otto Barthel, Werner also was given a school assignment

123 Heer, ed., 145. The witness' information: initials G.G., boy, age 13, in the *Volksschule* [all following witnesses were also attending the *Volksschule*].
124 Heer, ed., 145–146. L.W., boy, age 13.
125 Heer, ed., 146–147. G.H., boy, age 14.
126 Heer, ed., 147–148. J.A., girl, no age listed.
127 Heer, ed., 151. H.H., boy, age 12.

to reflect on his postwar experiences by his first German teacher in the new postwar times. His teacher appeared odd to the teenage boys: he had an Upper Silesian accent and wore an old Wehrmacht uniform, like many other destitute teachers in the postwar years. This teacher assigned the first major class essay of the postwar period, to write a report about their personal experience of the invasion of the Americans and the thoughts that came about from that experience. They had five class hours to complete the assignment. However, Werner, then 16 years old, wrote one sentence: "I do not remember how I experienced the invasion of the Americans. (*Ich weiß nicht mehr, wie ich den Einmarsch der Amerikaner erlebt habe.*)" He received the worst possible grade on the essay. In reality, Werner did remember the events, but October 1945 was too early for him to be able to recall his traumatic experiences and be able to clarify his thoughts. In March 1945, as the American troops had arrived at his family's farm, they set fire to it, fulfilling his worst childhood fear, besides the death of his parents: the farm burning down. Werner and his family spent the next minutes trying to stop the fire and rescue their farm animals; some of the animals had to be shot, while some survived, but most had to be put down anyway from smoke poisoning. American soldiers apparently watched the scene while chewing gum and laughing. The surrounding buildings were also badly damaged. The Americans also ended up taking over the family house for months. Werner believed that none of his classmates had such an experience as his during the arrival of the Americans. Werner reflected that he remained angry and in grief for many years, hating anything from American culture. He noted in his reflections that he had grown up indoctrinated under National Socialism, and did not realize that the arrival of Americans meant more than "*Chesterfield und Boogie-Woogie*," Chesterfield cigarettes and boogie-woogie music. Only slowly did Werner realize that a terrible system based on terror had ended, and that despite the chaos, restrictions, regulations, and military government of the postwar occupation, it brought about a new value system and political culture, a new liberal-democratic *Grundordnung*, the basic order of the German constitution. For Werner, 1945 was like a vacuum: a year of traumatic experiences, the collapse of the National Socialist system, and a sense of skepticism regarding the changes brought about by the Americans. A school assignment that may have been meant to help the school pupils reflect on their past experiences instead led Werner to react with silence. Decades later, Werner was able to reflect upon his past and understand why he reacted that way; this postwar school assignment seemed to remain a major event in his memories of his occupation experiences.[128]

---

128 Werner Schütz, "Der Klassenaufsatz," in *Hungern und hoffen*, ed. Kleindienst, 24–31.

Reports of first impressions of Americans highlight how much these experiences remained imprinted in young Germans' minds, months after the end of the war and start of the occupation. They depict the level of violence that young Germans were exposed to in ways that narratives that focus on American soldiers arriving as liberators gloss over, and they also portray the lingering aftermath of Nazi propaganda about Americans, which especially centered around race-based fear of black Americans, for example having tails or kidnapping children.[129] Some young Germans, such as Theodor Wild, were fascinated by their sight of the first black Americans, while others such as the young girl school pupil in Weißenburg in Bayern remained terrified, although she and her friend did talk to the soldiers. Personal encounters show that the first interactions between young Germans and Americans were indeed often complex, with a blend of emotions ranging from fear to curiosity arising among young Germans. Many youngsters noted down the arrival of the Americans, aware that the presence of the foreign troops marked a new phase in their personal life histories. Encounters between Americans and young Germans played a central role in the occupation, causing shifts to take place on the ground through personal interactions. These shifts were then later reflected and even modeled in higher policies, which focused increasingly on building positive German-American relations, with Americans increasingly serving in the role of protectors of the German population within the budding Cold War atmosphere.

A Town Under Occupation: Amberg Childhoods

Theodor Wild spent the occupation years living with his mother in one room in Amberg on Gabelsbergerstrasse, nearby to the train station. The town had an interesting occupation blend of buildings and people, including multiple barracks for American troops, with one specifically for black American GIs, as well as a military hospital. Present in the town were also Russians, including former POWs or forced laborers, Serbians, who were former collaborators with the Germans, and liberated Jews.[130] The population of Amberg grew from around 27,000 to over 50,000 during the occupation due to the arrival of many German refugees from

---

129 Fehrenbach, *Race after Hitler*, 32. A propaganda cartoon in the Nazi newspaper *Völkischer Beobachter* from January 1945 depicted American soldiers as marauding, degenerate gangsters, kidnappers, and convicts who would torment German children. In Frederick Taylor, *Exorcising Hitler: The Occupation and Denazification of Germany* (Bloomsbury Press, 2011); Biddiscombe, *Werwolf!*

130 Wild, in questionnaire 1, answers 8, 9; Diary 1 of Theodor Wild, DTA Reg.-Nr. 540,1.

the East.[131] As a young boy, Wild reacted to this occupation mix with curiosity, especially regarding the antics of American troops, such as their occupation raids and sexual encounters with German women.

Wild's diaries of his childhood provide a fascinating glimpse into the unique blend of occupation encounters in Amberg, which he often witnessed as a child running around the town, and also through his seeking out of American troops for the purpose of moneymaking. His descriptions of his life at the time depict a mix of adventures undertaken by himself and with other children in the aftermath of World War II. His diary entries hint at the lingering impacts of the past, portray the worries of adults such as his mother, illustrate the times when he got in trouble with adults, highlight his sexual curiosity, and show his wide range of emotional responses in his life, from loneliness to excitement. In 1945, Wild wrote entries about often being lonely and described his desire to have a brother, in addition to the fact that he missed his extended family members back in Berlin. He also wrote that he wanted to be a Native American or an African American, and he also wanted to become a priest but was worried he could not become one because he was an illegitimate child, since his parents were not yet married. He wrote that he wanted to do something special, but not in Amberg, instead in Africa, showing his fascination with foreign lands. He had already traveled widely in Europe with his parents. Like many youngsters of the time and most likely influenced by growing up during a war, Theodor was fascinated by militaristic types of play, such as playing "Cowboys and Indians." In 1948, he recorded down in his diary a list of his weapons, which included an air pistol, a bow and arrows, a sling shot, knives, a spear, a medieval pistol, munition, and even a bomb, which he drew a picture of.[132]

This bomb may have been the same one Wild had discovered in 1947, which he wrote about as one of the short stories in his memoir. One day, he had found an unexploded American bomb in a field, which he carefully picked up and hid in his hiding place in the old brickyard. Due to his discovery of the bomb, he was excited that he would become the top of his schoolmates, who were all zealous collectors of the dangerous leftovers from the American troops, who often left munition lying around after their practice troop movements in and around Amberg during the occupation. As his friends were trying to figure out who had the best finds of the dangerous items, Theodor boasted about his bomb. His friends did not believe him, so he took two of them to his hiding place where the bomb

131 Ascherl, "'Aus seinem Mund und Rücken sickert Blut': Täglich Luftalarm in Amberg: Bomber und Tiefflieger über der Stadt," in *Sie kommen!*, ed. Vogelsang, 29.
132 Diary 1 of Theodor Wild, DTA Reg.-Nr. 540,1.

was. They then decided they would try to get the bomb to explode, and put it on top of a dense blackthorn hedge in a way that would allow the wind to spin the propellor, causing it to detonate. They then hid in a big ditch, waiting for it to explode, but it did not seem to detonate. Checking on it would have been too dangerous, so they just stayed in the ditch and chatted about their knowledge of these dangerous "toys," which they continued to gather and play with, even though in school and in the news, children were warned against touching such things. Instead, they were to report the find and let it sit where it was. However, as Wild described in his short story memoir, nearly every one of his friends had a dangerous "toy" in his or her collection, and one of his friends had lost his middle finger, and another had suffered from burns from such "toys." While in the ditch, Wild had continued to chat with his friends, forgetting about his bomb. Thus, they were shocked when there was suddenly an immense explosion nearby, causing sand and pieces of dirt to fly into their necks. Once it was over, they saw that the bomb had not just made a small crater, but it had completely wiped away the hedge where they had placed it. They heard a siren from the direction of the barracks, and two jeeps with GIs raced in their direction. They ran away as fast as they could, using their best method of escape: scattering in every direction. During the next day of school, the main topic was the bomb. Wild's teacher, who suspected that many of his pupils played with old munitions despite all warnings against this, succinctly told the children that they would be able to continue going to school with a ripped off finger, but with a ripped off head, the only direction they would go to was the cemetery.[133]

Theodor had also witnessed violence during the war itself. Before coming to Amberg, while still in Berlin with his extended family, his school had been destroyed by a bomb. In addition, while on the Mariahilfberg in Amberg one day during the war, he witnessed a low level air attack on Amberg, in which he saw a nearby bicyclist get killed from the shots of the aircraft cannon, while he hid in the underbrush behind a tree.[134] In addition, a bad ear infection required him to have a surgery, and he had to lie in a field hospital with wounded German soldiers for days, witnessing some of them passing away from their injuries.[135] Wild thus had early exposure to the closeness of death and directly witnessed the violent impacts of war. However, he remained curious about the interplay of war,

133 Wild, *Wo der "Müde" war, war immer was los*, 35–37.

134 Wild, *Wo der "Müde" war, war immer was los*, 25–26; Ascherl, "'Aus seinem Mund und Rücken sickert Blut': Täglich Luftalarm in Amberg: Bomber und Tiefflieger über der Stadt," in *Sie kommen!*, ed. Vogelsang, 31.

135 Wild, *Wo der "Müde" war, war immer was los*, 21–24; Diary 1 of Theodor Wild, DTA Reg.-Nr. 540,1.

violence, and excitement, highlighting his way of dealing with the challenges of the time, in which his curiosity never diminished. During the war, he had witnessed the man being killed during an air raid, yet after the war, he still wanted to top his classmates with the best war-related "toy," a bomb. Wild stated in a 2006 article in *FOCUS* that the war was a fascinating time for children like him.[136] The postwar occupation seemed extra exciting for him, with its blend of Americans, chaos, and dangerous remnants of the war lying around.

Wild attended school in Amberg, and he noted down his antics in the classroom and his complaints about school, for example about getting a bad grade in history. In September 1946, he entered the *humanistisches Gymnasium* for a "*Probezeit*," a trial period, due to his desire and that of his mother that he become a priest. Theodor wrote in his diary that this school smelled bad because there was also a hospital for German soldiers located inside, and they could hear soldiers screaming in pain. The professor told the pupils that they would have to get used to that noise, since the soldiers were yelling, because they were getting an arm or leg amputated. The limbs were then thrown into a pit in the schoolyard, where the pupils were told not to go (in addition, some of the soldiers in the hospital were also war criminals, so the pupils were not to interact with them), but Theodor Wild wrote in his diary, "I still went there, because I want to know everything. (*Ich bin doch hingegangen, weil ich alles wissen will.*)" This statement encapsulates his reaction to the unique aspects of the postwar occupation sphere in Amberg: he viewed everything with a high level of curiosity and inquisitiveness. He even took action with these German soldiers in the school, going into their rooms (even though that was forbidden too) to help them by mailing letters for them.[137]

Theodor Wild quickly adapted to the new circumstances of the occupation in Amberg, marked by the presence of American soldiers. In addition to encountering GIs during his business deals when he traded Nazi souvenirs, young Theodor also met Americans in other contexts. There was a "*Jugendcasino*," a youth center run by the Americans, where he went nearly every day. Wild stated that the atmosphere there was high quality, pristine even, and the GIs, American female civilians, and an older female soldier (a "GI mum") in charge would make sure everything was running smoothly and the children were behaving. There they held various activities for the children such as group games, English lessons, and they would also screen movies. In contrast, Wild noted that sporting events that were

136 "Wir wissen nicht, ob sie noch leben," *FOCUS Magazin*, December 22, 2006. See also Theodor Wild, "Vielleicht ist Hitler gar nicht tot, sagen viele Leute," *FOCUS Magazin*, December 22, 2006.
137 Diary 1 of Theodor Wild, DTA Reg.-Nr. 540,1.

organized by the Americans were often chaotic, and many times they had to be cancelled because older boys would steal the equipment. Wild was mostly too young to join in the sports events, and he got annoyed at those who stole the supplies, but he did enjoy playing billiards and shuffleboard.[138] Special events such as holiday celebrations were also a chance for Wild to interact with soldiers and bring home candy. At these events, children were allowed to bring home as much as they could carry (bags were not allowed). At the first Fourth of July celebration in 1945, which was technically only for German refugees, but to which a GI who served as his mentor brought him, Theodor was able to stuff his pockets full of candy.[139] In addition, he noted that he saw American soldiers at church attending mass, noting that there were usually more black soldiers in attendance, who were often more religious than white soldiers.[140] Theodor thus interacted with GIs in various circumstances that led to him viewing a wide range of soldiers' behaviors and their attitudes about Germans, ranging from witnessing their sexual relationships with German women to answering questions about his family's role during the National Socialist regime, attending the regulated space of the American youth center after school, and seeing GIs at church.

Friedrich Brandl also wrote about his experiences growing up in Amberg after the war, where he lived in Ziegelgasse in the historic center of the town. His reflections, published in 2009, included a section entitled, "Dubble Bubble." Brandl wrote about how chewing gum was a "*Reizwort*," an emotive word for the local children. If they heard American tanks, they then ran out into the alleyway and gawked at the Americans in their jeeps and tanks, waving and shouting to them, "Tschewengum plies, Tschewengum plies! [sic]." The older children had taught the younger ones how to do this, and soldiers did sometimes throw gum to the kids. That was the best experience for the children, who imagined that all soldiers had their pockets full of gum and sweets. Sweets remained special for Brandl as a child, as they were not everyday things but were available via the Americans or on special occasions, such as festivals on the Mariahilfberg (the hill where Theodor Wild had seen the bicyclist get hit by a bomb and where he had discovered the black GI having sex with a German woman). Brandl wrote that even the sound of the words "Dubble Bubble" spurred great excitement among the children. They could do so much with the gum, such as grow the largest bubble, or make the largest pop when it burst, and the smell of it made it clear to others that a kid was chewing Dubble Bubble, not just any kind of gum. Having

138 Wild, in questionnaire 2, answer 4. Also, Diary 2 of Theodor Wild, DTA Reg.-Nr. 540,2.
139 Wild, in questionnaire 1, answer 5; Wild, in questionnaire 2, answer 6.
140 Wild, in questionnaire 1, answer 6.

some Dubble Bubble was one of Brandl's secret wishes, but his mother never bought any, he never had any given to him as a gift, and he had no money himself. He was jealous when his friends were chewing Dubble Bubble, and really wanted to try the special gum. One day, he stumbled upon an unwrapped Dubble Bubble on the street. It did not seem that fresh anymore, with its wrapper lying next to it, and it was a bit flattened. He took it home, hiding it in the washhouse, and let it sit in water filled in a tin pot for two days as a way of sanitizing it. Two days later, he put it in his mouth, first cautiously, and then full of joy, attempted to blow his first bubble with a Dubble Bubble. After a few minutes, he put it back in the water, hiding it, since his mother would notice if he came into the house chewing gum. Over the next days, he took his piece of gum from the pot of water and chewed it while out on the streets, successfully popping the gum with a loud pop. After a few days, his piece of gum did not taste like much anymore, but he was happy.[141] Americans and the products they brought with had thus become a central part of postwar Amberg childhoods. American chewing gum could impact the actions of youngsters, who developed a taste for the product and were aware that closeness to Americans would increase the chances of access to it. Theodor Wild did not really like chewing gum, preferring instead Hershey bars.[142] Wild also knew that being close to Americans, for example spending time in the town center at the Marktplatz, would enable him to meet GIs who would buy Hitler souvenirs from him, or allow him to get sweets from them as they came out of the nearby PX. Young Amberg citizens thus made conscious decisions to seek out the occupiers, the Americans, based on their desires and needs.

Young Germans in Amberg played roles beyond recipients of American candy and observers of American antics, instead often entering an active role in everyday encounters, such as Theodor Wild and his trading deals with soldiers. The actions of a teenage boy in Amberg also proved decisive during the end of the war and the arrival of American soldiers. On April 22, 1945, the Americans took over Amberg. It was a teenage boy, Wolfgang Babl Jr., who was responsible for successfully raising the first white flag of surrender in Amberg, thus saving the town from further destruction as the American troops arrived, members of the Third Battalion, 14th Infantry Regiment, 71st Infantry Division.[143] Babl Jr., then 15 years old, was part of a local anti-defense group in Amberg, which had planned

141 Friedrich Brandl, *Ziegelgassler: Eine Kindheit nach dem Krieg* (Ed. Lichtung, 2009), 41–48.
142 Wild, in questionnaire 2, answer 8.
143 For a report on American combat actions in Amberg, see Samuel Campanella, "'Operations of the Third Battalion, 14th Infantry, 71st Infantry Division, at Amberg, Germany, 22 April 1945' (Central Europe Campaign)," Advanced Infantry Officers Course 1948–1949, General Subjects Section, Academic Department, The Infantry School, Fort Benning, Georgia, in World War II Student

for the defenseless surrender of Amberg since the beginning of 1945, going against Heinrich Himmler's order to defend all cities against the Allied troops. Members of the anti-defense group included Babl's father, Wolfgang Babl Sr., Josef Kerschensteiner, and a *Volkssturm* instructor, *Oberfeldwebel* (Staff Sergeant) Julian Keppner, the main leader of the group. The group worked to actively resist the Amberg NSDAP *Kreisleiter* Dr. Artur Kolb's calls for defending Amberg with all means, which had become a suicidal act as the war drew to its end. Dr. Kolb had promised that anyone who raised a white flag would be shot.[144] However, he himself was suddenly shot by American troops on April 22, 1945, according to the official version of the story. Babl Jr., however, claims that Keppner may have actually been the one who shot Dr. Kolb, who was on the way to pick up remaining SS divisions to defend Amberg.[145] Then, also on April 22, anti-defense group member Wolfgang Babl Jr. with the help of Josef Kerschensteiner raised the first white flag on the tower of the Dreifaltigkeitskirche. The Amberg mayor, Sebastian Regler, surrendered the town without a fight to the Americans the next day. Babl Jr. was an altar boy at the Dreifaltigkeitskirche and thus was given the task of raising the flag there, as he was able to get the key to the church. Babl Jr.'s father had been the one to recommend him for the task. During the flag raising, Kerschensteiner had a pistol with for protection, as it was an incredibly dangerous action: Across the street from the church lived a SA-*Obersturmbannführer* (lieutenant colonel of the SA Storm Troopers). Three other white flags in Amberg were supposed to be raised in addition to the one at the Dreifaltigkeitskirche, but they failed to be raised despite the plans of the anti-defense group. Thus, Babl Jr.'s white flag was the deciding factor that led to the Americans ceasing their fire in Amberg and preventing widescale destruction. In addition, on Keppner's orders, Babl Jr. had also previously helped with the collection and disappearance of *Volkssturm* weapons, which helped prevent their usage in a defense of the city. The actions of a teenage boy, under risk of his life from both American gunfire and discovery by Nazi party officials, thus changed the history of Amberg, bringing the war to an end there.[146] In April 2015, then 85-year-old Wolfgang Babl Jr., who in 1945 was

---

Papers Collection, Maneuver Center of Excellence Libraries, Fort Benning, Georgia, https://www.benning.army.mil/Library/Donovanpapers/wwii/index.html.

144 Leonie Sanke, "Sein Tod war die Rettung Ambergs," *Mittelbayerische Zeitung*, May 1, 2015. Also, Theodor Wild, in questionnaire 2, answer 3.

145 Sanke, "Sein Tod war die Rettung Ambergs"; "Ein Bub und das Kriegsende in Amberg," *Mittelbayerische Zeitung*, April 22, 2015; Andreas Ascherl, "Mutige Menschen retten unsere Stadt," *Amberger Zeitung*, April 22, 2015.

146 Sanke, "Sein Tod war die Rettung Ambergs"; "Ein Bub und das Kriegsende in Amberg"; Ascherl, "Mutige Menschen retten unsere Stadt."

nicknamed "Junior" or "*der Boum*" ("the boy" in Bavarian dialect), initiated a special seventieth anniversary commemoration of the events, and since then, the white flag has been raised again yearly on the church tower of the Dreifaltigkeitskirche as a renewed symbol of peace.[147] In 2019, the white flag was raised again on the church tower, and Babl, then turning 90 years old, was honored by the town of Amberg and its mayor.[148] As a teenager, Babl was thus active in resisting the destructive wishes of the local Nazis, and he used his agency as a choir boy to gain access to the church to spur a major development in Amberg's history, the capitulation to the Americans. Young Germans were thus capable of fundamentally molding the shape of history as the war came to an end and the era of occupation began.

****

Overall, American occupation officials were especially interested in young Germans' views about the occupation and the occupiers, as they were an important group for their occupation goals. On June 28, 1946, the Surveys Branch of the OMGUS Information Control Division published the results of a survey entitled "Attitudes of Some Bavarian Schoolchildren." Two hundred and fifty Bavarian schoolchildren between the ages of 12 and 18 filled out questionnaires during school in the villages, towns, and cities of Regensburg, Kelheim, Pirkensee, and Burglengenfeld, which are all within 50 miles (about 80 kilometers) of Amberg. The survey aimed to get a representative look of the situation in the selected areas: Around half of respondents were from the middle class, the rest were from working class families, and 16% were sons and daughters of refugees and evacuees. The survey asked the youth about their opinions on daily life during the occupation, such as questions about living conditions, orientation toward school, thoughts on the war, expectations, and attitudes about the American occupiers. Some 88% of respondents had belonged to a Hitler Youth organization, and around 37% of the respondents' parents had belonged to the NSDAP, which the

---

147 "Ein Bub und das Kriegsende in Amberg"; Ascherl, "Mutige Menschen retten unsere Stadt"; "Amberg hat wieder eine Friedensfahne," *Amberger Zeitung*, April 28, 2015. Also, Adele Schütz, "72 Jahre Frieden dank der weißen Fahne: Pfarrei Dreifaltigkeit segnet Gedenktafel," *Oberpfalz Medien*, May 3, 2017, https://www.onetz.de/amberg-in-der-oberpfalz/vermischtes/72-jahre-frieden-dank-der-weissen-fahne-pfarrei-dreifaltigkeit-segnet-gedenktafel-d1746884.html.
148 "Friedensfahne weht wieder," *Amberger Zeitung*, May 14, 2019; "Amberg mit Mut und Verstand gerettet," *Amberger Zeitung*, May 15, 2019.

survey stated was usually the proportion of party membership found in the population in the US zone. Only 12% were members of a new postwar youth organization, such as the *Katholische Pfarrjugend* (Catholic Parish Youth). Some 84% of the respondents were Catholic, and most respondents would vote for the newly founded Christian Social Union (CSU) political party (48%), if they could vote, while 29% said they would not vote even if they were able to. For the youth, "the principal concern" of the present was food, but shoes and clothing were also mentioned. The survey noted that the youth were asked directly about the state of their footwear, and half of the youth said they had only one pair. Additionally, their greatest wish was to be given more food, 26%, while 20% wished for "peace." According to the survey, the health of the youth seemed good, and 98% of respondents said they liked going to school. The survey claimed that most of the youngsters displayed an "inadequate realization of the reasons which brought about Germany's present condition as a defeated nation," for example a lack of awareness about the "weakness of the dictatorial system of government." Instead, the young survey respondents referred mainly to Germany's loss as a result of the strength of the enemy and Germany's lack of materials (36%). The survey indicated a hopefulness for better, peaceful times, but 41% of respondents still believed that there would soon be another war, with most expecting it to "arise with Russia." The survey noted that the Soviet occupation zone was not too far away, thus rumors were often present in the region near the border area. Interestingly, the survey also depicted the complexity of the youngsters' feelings about the American troops:

> The American occupation soldier was not well regarded by many (39%) of the youth. However, nearly as many (35%) said they did like our soldiers, and the rest (26%) held no opinion. More than half of those who disliked the American soldier spoke with feeling about his general behavior—lack of discipline, immoral activities, drunkenness. Others pointed at instances of careless jeep-driving, complained about the requisitioning of homes, unkept promises, the lack of interest in the Germans, and the drive toward denazification.
>
> Among those who liked the American soldier about one-fourth spoke appreciatively about gifts they had received, and as many remarked about his friendliness and pleasant disposition. Others praised him for having "liberated" them, for his good discipline, his handsome uniform, his military qualities compared with those of other occupying powers, and his inclination toward order and cleanliness.
>
> More displeasure with the occupation soldier was voiced by girls (41%) than by boys (26%). Conversely, more than half [of] the boys (53%) but less than one-third [of] the girls (29%) liked the American soldier.[149]

149 "Attitudes of Some Bavarian Schoolchildren," Surveys Branch, Information Control Division, OMGUS, June 28, 1946; Folder ICD Opinion Surveys; Records RE the Work of the Youth Activities Section; Records of the Education and Cultural Relations Division: Records of the Community Ed-

Although the results are specific to these locations in Bavaria (located in Upper Palatinate and Lower Bavaria), and the survey was conducted by American military government officials who may have been aiming for certain responses, which the children may have realized, the survey still gives a fascinating glimpse at the complexity of encounters between German youth and soldiers. The results were especially divided based on gender, with many more boys than girls liking the American soldier. This could be a result of the heavily sexualized nature of occupation encounters between soldiers and young women, in which teenaged girls may have had to deal with challenging situations such as unwanted advances or harassment from GIs. The results also do not portray the opinions of children below ten years of age, which might not have been as divided between gender and may have been more favorable, since younger children might not have been active in the Hitler Youth, nor been as influenced by Nazi propaganda regarding the enemy troops. They may also have been the recipients of more benevolence from the soldiers, such as gifts of candy. They perhaps even sought out GIs themselves for these gifts or for the purpose trading with them, as Theodor Wild did in Amberg. However, overall, most youngsters in the survey did have an opinion about the occupying soldiers, highlighting their awareness of the presence of foreign military personnel. Sources from young Germans themselves enhance the picture that the data in the survey portrays, adding layers to show what an official survey alone cannot show. For example, their writings depict the ways in which they navigated the singularity of growing up in a defeated nation under a foreign military occupation. German children and youth were not only directly affected by the facts and policies of the occupation, they were active and aware of the circumstances of the time.

For some young Germans, keeping a diary helped them cope with the challenges and ambivalences of the time, giving them a place to reflect on loss and grief, and enabled them to explore their emotions, both positive and negative.[150] Young Germans were often aware of the unique nature of growing up under military occupation, in addition to the loss often inherent in their experiences as chil-

---

ucation Branch; OMGUS; Box 142; RG 260; NACP. See also Report No. 12 (28 June 1946), in Merritt and Merritt, eds., *Public Opinion in Occupied Germany*, 86–87.

150 For Anne Frank, who was born in 1929 in Frankfurt am Main, and whose life took on a different trajectory than those young Germans in this chapter, as she was a victim of the Holocaust who did not survive the war, her diary served as a real friend she could confide in about anything while in hiding. On June 20, 1942, she wrote, "In order to enhance in my mind's eye the picture of the friend for whom I have waited so long, I don't want to set down a series of bald facts in a diary like most people do, but I want this diary itself to be my friend, and I shall call my friend Kitty." Frank, *The Diary of a Young Girl*, 3. Her diary remains one of the most popular works of nonfiction worldwide.

dren and youth during this time. Diary writer Edeltraud Großjohann wrote about her feelings of the loss of the happy days of being young: “And the fear for the little bit that was left, the naked life, that is now my sunny time of youth, which I once dreamed of. Me and millions of unhappy brothers and sisters. (*Und das Angsthaben um das bisschen was geblieben ist, um das nackte Leben, das ist nun meine sonnige Zeit der Jugend, von der ich einmal träumte. Ich und Millionen von unglücklichen Brüdern und Schwestern.*)”[151] Ingrid Picker recorded her thoughts about the importance of having a diary during this time as she wrote to her diary itself: “Yes, if I hadn't had You . . ., then I would have often been desperate. (*Ja, wenn ich Dich nicht gehabt hätte . . ., dann wäre ich oft verzweifelt.*)”[152]

The direct experiences of young Germans in the aftermath of World War II depict the wide range of encounters made within the occupation, as children, teenagers, and young adults became active participants in the postwar sphere. Whether as neighbors, business partners, or for those who were older, lovers of Americans, young Germans played a fundamental role in everyday occupation developments. Personal experiences of the encounter with Americans portray the centrality of age in the aftermath of the war. Youngsters were not simply innocent actors with limited agency, victims of war, dangerous elements, or the future hope of the nation, as adults often viewed them, but they were central figures capable and ready to navigate and respond to the complex dynamics of the postwar in diverse ways, often with great awareness of the realities and intentions of the American occupiers. Their very real, complex, and sometimes contradictory experiences provide a glimpse into the lived realities of the past in ways that adult-focused narratives gloss over or are unable to portray. Young boys who traded with American soldiers, young women who decided to work for Americans, or those youngsters who simply were attempting to navigate the challenges of their experiences while living under occupation all are witnesses whose experiences must be considered as of equal value to those of adults. Moreover, without sources created by young people such as diaries, historical knowledge of the past would be lacking, ignoring a central element of the human population, the young. Historical research would remain limited in its portrayal of the wide-ranging effects of human decisions and the ways people of all ages have coped with the challenges of their everyday lives. Above all, encounters among the rubble stamped personal histories of the occupation and impacted higher transatlantic geopolitical policies, with attention to the fate of young Germans reaching all the way across the Atlantic.

151 Diary of Edeltraud Großjohann, DTA Reg. Nr. 185/I 1–4 Abschrift.
152 Diary of Ingrid Picker, DTA Signatur-Nr. 3853,1.

Chapter 3
From Little Nazis to Democrats? The Bremen Enclave and German Youth Activities

"Officials had nothing to do with it. It was the inspiration of G.I.s [sic] themselves," proclaimed an article in *Time* magazine on October 7, 1946 about the youth-oriented engagement of GIs in Bremen. In August of 1946, Sergeant Patrick J. Moriarty and nine of his fellow soldiers from the 104th Labor Supervision Center had taken action and decided to form a boys club in Bremen after seeing hungry, scared, and begging German children.[1] On August 17, 1946, these GIs had placed an ad in the local newspaper, the *Weser-Kurier*, stating that local boys who were interested in joining the club could write a letter to the Haus des Reichs, the headquarters of military government in Bremen. Instead of a few responses to the ad, as Moriarty and his fellow soldiers had anticipated, thousands of boys answered the ad: some sources speak of 2,500 and others of as many as 7,000 responses.[2] Out of these thousands, around 100 boys between the ages of ten and 17 were chosen to be members of the newest American-sponsored youth club in town, the Bremen Boys Club (BBC). The Club gained a level of fame that even

1 "The Nations: Democracy at Work," *Time*, October 7, 1946.

2 The *Weser-Kurier* was one of the first licensed newspapers in the American zone, appearing for the first time on September 19, 1945. The *Time* article speaks of 6,500 to 7,000 responses; Moriarty stated that "kids were climbing in windows, telephoning, crowding at the door." A *Reader's Digest* article also mentioned 7,000 responses: Frederic Sondern Jr., "GI Teachers for German Children," condensed from the *Kiwanis Magazine*. Read into the Congressional Record by Robert Joseph Twyman, Representative from Illinois, in United States: Congress, Congressional Record (Bound), House, 80th Congress, 1st Session, April 3, 1947, Vol. 93, Part 3 (March 31, 1947 to April 29, 1947), US Government Publishing Office, 3118–3119. Article also in Folder Bremen Boys Club 1946/47; Records of the Education Division: Records Relating to German Youth and Sports Clubs, 1947–49; Records of Office of Military Government Bremen (OMGBR); Box 316; OMGUS; RG 260; NACP. Also, "Bremen Boys Club: U.S. Sergeant Finances a Lesson in Democracy," *Life*, December 9, 1946, 36–37; *The U.S. Armed Forces German Youth Activities Program 1945–1955* (Historical Division, Headquarters, United States Army, Europe, 1956), 20. Other sources speak of around 2,500 responses: "'Boys-Club' in Bremen," *Weser-Kurier*, August 24, 1946, 3; Fritz Peters, *Zwölf Jahre Bremen 1945–1956: Eine Chronik* (H.H. Hauschild, 1976), 62; Kleinschmidt, *Do Not Fraternize*, 226. In a September 26, 1946 press release written by Percy Knauth for *Time*, Knauth wrote that the club "is more promising than anything I've personally seen anywhere in Germany." Percy Knauth, Bremen Press Camp release, September 26, 1946; Folder YXXI Army Assistance Program A. Bremerhaven Military Community 1947 (formerly Grohn Military Community); Records of the Education Division: Gen Corresp & Rel Recs of Youth Activities Branch, 1945–47; OMGBR; Box 315; OMGUS; RG 260; NACP.

https://doi.org/10.1515/9783111588155-004

made its way across the Atlantic. German Youth Activities (GYA) clubs such as the BBC symbolized a new era of occupation policies, which now aimed more at a positive policy of reorientation, treating Germans as victims to be helped rather than enemies. Moreover, GYA contributed to a new phase of youth experiences in the immediate postwar sphere. Additionally, the societal role of German youth began to emerge clear as the democratic future of Germany.[3]

This chapter explores how the actions of individual GIs such as Patrick Moriarty shaped assistance toward German youth, which began even as early as a few months after the end of the war in 1945 and developed into the Army Assistance to German Youth Activities program in 1946.[4] Early individual initiatives toward assisting German youth took place despite the ban on fraternization with Germans, which lasted until October 1945 and included children until it was modified in June 1945.[5] As the occupation progressed, troop fraternization with children increasingly occurred, and Army assistance for German youth gradually evolved into an official occupation policy, spurring GYA clubs such as Moriarty's Bremen Boys Club. Moreover, there was engagement among military officials in assistance to German youth, even as early as 1945: on September 14, 1945, the commander of the Seventh Army, Lieutenant General Geoffrey Keyes, issued a directive that encouraged active participation of all units (including chaplains) in the Western Military District (Greater Hesse and Württemberg-Baden) in sponsoring organized, scout-like youth activities such as woodcrafts and sports for the goal of assisting "in the regeneration of German youth." No difference was to made between children of Nazi and anti-Nazi youth, as the main goal was reeducation, not punishment.[6] According to an official report, Keyes believed that "the

3 See Goedde, *GIs and Germans*, 127–128, 164–165.

4 In 1948, the GYA program was renamed Armed Forces Assistance Program to German Youth Activities due to the unification of the Armed Forces in 1947. The Air Force had participated in GYA when it had been part of the Army and it continued to participate in GYA as a separate service. See *The U.S. Armed Forces German Youth Activities Program 1945–1955*, 10. The term Army Assistance to German Youth Activities will still be used throughout this work. The abbreviation GYA became common for referring specifically to the assistance program.

5 Ziemke, *The U.S. Army in the Occupation*, 327; *The U.S. Armed Forces German Youth Activities Program 1945–1955*, 4.

6 14 September 1945, Seventh Army Directive; Folder GYA Program 1946–48; Records of the Education and Cultural Relations Division: Group Activities Branch Records of German Youth Assoc. 1945–49; Records of the Office of Military Govt, Bavaria (OMGBY); Box 43; OMGUS, RG 260; NACP. Directive also in *German Youth Activities of the United States Army*, Occupation Forces in Europe Series (Frankfurt am Main: Office of the Chief Historian, European Command, 1947), 31–32. In 1947, Keyes became commander of the US Forces in Austria and US High Commissioner of Austria. He encouraged and supported the Austrian equivalent of German Youth Activities, the Austrian Youth Activities program. See Historical Outline: The Armed Forces Assistance Program to

friendliness of the American soldier could be used to great advantage in demonstrating democracy to German youth."[7] Keyes' initiative thus provided the foundation for the creation of an official Army assistance program for German youth, GYA, in April 1946.[8]

In addition, the US authorities quickly worked to reinstate German-run, voluntary youth groups, which would provide a contrast to the militaristic, authoritarian Hitler Youth of the Nazi regime. In October 1945, a USFET directive created the American zone-wide procedure for organizing and supervising German-run youth groups. The directive set up the infrastructure for German engagement in youth activities, including the creation of *Kreis*-level youth committees, which were to be made up of German educators, religious leaders, and trade union representatives; these committees would coordinate the German-run youth activities programs, although they remained under the ultimate control of the American military government. The directive also encouraged the formation of voluntary German-led youth groups for "cultural, religious, and recreational purposes." The groups were to "strive to develop and maintain high moral standards among German youth," modeling themselves after international organizations such as the YMCA and scouting groups. According to the directive, these groups were to be mainly for German girls and boys ages ten to 18, and they were to "aim to make possible the successful development of democratic ideas, to develop independence of thought, and to cultivate ideals of fair play, tolerance and honesty."[9]

On April 15, 1946, a zone-wide directive officially established the Army Assistance to German Youth Activities program, ensuring an active role of the American occupation forces in youth activities.[10] On October 5, 1946, another directive

---

Austrian Youth; Folder AYA-Reports. Consolidated. USACA. 1950; Box 1; Records Relating to Austrian Youth Activities 1946–1952; Box 1; Department of State/Office of the U.S. High Commissioner for Austria; RG 260; NACP.

7 *German Youth Activities of the United States Army*, 5–6.

8 Harald Leder argues that Keyes' September 1945 directive became the "nucleus" for German Youth Activities. See Harald T. Leder, "Americans and German Youth in Nuremberg, 1945–1956: A Study in Politics and Culture" (PhD diss., Louisiana State University, 1997), https://digitalcommons.lsu.edu/gradschool_disstheses/6430, 125.

9 25 October 1945, HQ USFET, in *German Youth Activities of the United States Army*, 35–37, also, 8–10. Also, *The U.S. Armed Forces German Youth Activities Program 1945–1955*, 5–7; Starr, *Fraternization with the Germans in World War II*, 140. See also Goedde, *GIs and Germans*, 135.

10 15 April 1946 Directive, HQ USFET; Folder USFET Youth Directive 15 April 1946; Records RE the Work of the Youth Activities Section; Records for the Community Education Branch; Records of the Education and Cultural Relations Division; Box 148; OMGUS; RG 260; NACP. April 15, 1946 directive also in *German Youth Activities of the United States Army*, 38–42.

was issued, which served as the basis of the GYA program for several years.[11] GYA included military personnel sponsored youth clubs (such as Moriarty's Bremen Boys Club), GYA youth centers set up throughout the US zone, and additional assistance to German youth such as community events or recreational activities. The total structure of youth activities thus bridged the military government, German youth authorities, and the US Forces. OMGUS was responsible for crafting and enforcing the policies for all youth activities, with duties including screening applications of new groups, appointing Germans for organizational duties, approving group sponsors, group leaders, and members of youth committees, and cooperating with German youth authorities. In addition, OMGUS maintained oversight over German-run youth programs through the *Kreis* committees. Meanwhile, the Army was responsible for the program of Army Assistance to GYA, in which military personnel were encouraged to play a role, such as helping to establish youth centers and sponsoring GYA youth clubs as Moriarty had done in Bremen. Some military personnel were also appointed as official GYA officers.[12] This wide-ranging structure for youth activities sometimes led to competition between German youth clubs and GYA clubs, in addition to spurring tensions between OMGUS and the Army. Germans were also sometimes resentful of the Army GYA program, since it had more resources and also requisitioned German properties for its youth clubs and youth centers. In addition, military personnel did not tend to coordinate with German authorities on youth matters, and sometimes did not follow the military government regulations regarding youth activities.[13]

However, GYA undoubtedly quickly became a central factor in American occupation policies. Major occupation actors including Military Governor General Joseph McNarney endorsed the importance of the Army Assistance to German Youth Activities program. In a speech in August of 1946 at a conference on youth activities, McNarney claimed that the program "is an extremely important job—

11 5 October 1946 Directive, HQ USFET; Folder USFET Directive 5 October 1946; Records RE the Work of the Youth Activities Section; Records for the Community Education Branch; Records of the Education and Cultural Relations Division; Box 148; OMGUS; RG 260; NACP.

12 See *German Youth Activities: Army Assistance Program Guide* (United States Army, European Command, OPOT Division, Training and Education Branch, 1948), 15, for the Functional Organization of GYA. See also *German Youth Activities of the United States Army*, Chart 1; *The U.S. Armed Forces German Youth Activities Program 1945–1955*, 8–9, 15–17; Geis and Gray Jr., *The Relations of Occupation Personnel*, Chart 1; 5 October 1946 Directive; Records RE the Work of the Youth Activities Section; Box 148; OMGUS; RG 260; NACP.

13 See *The U.S. Armed Forces German Youth Activities Program 1945–1955*, 17; Liddell, "Education in Occupied Germany," 49; Rathfelder, Schubert, and Wild, *GYA Das Jugendarbeitsprogramm*, 88; Merritt, *Democracy Imposed*, 279–280.

perhaps more important than any other one job that we today can do." Additionally, he stated that the end goal of the program would be that "a great number of German youth will absorb our democratic ideals and that they in turn will become the future leaders of the German nation . . . and that they will lead the German nation along the paths we wish them to learn so that it will not be necessary for us [to] again come to Europe to wage war."[14] German youth thus had emerged as the core population for occupation reeducation goals, with their absorbing of the values of democratization through programs such as GYA contributing to securing a future democratic, peaceful Germany. Moreover, not only would the reeducation of German youth contribute to a positive future, but it would also help reduce youth criminality, which remained a fear in postwar German society, even though it had become clear that fears of a large *Werwolf* resistance movement led by former SS and radical Hitler Youth were unfounded.[15] The April 15, 1946 directive on Army Assistance to German Youth Activities emphasized the role of "positive youth activities" in preventing delinquent behavior, claiming that similar programs in other countries had led to a "low rate of juvenile delinquency."[16]

Despite its role as one of the central components of occupation reeducation policies, the German Youth Activities program has been overlooked by scholars, and those who examine reeducation and policies toward youth tend to claim that GYA did not play a central role in occupation developments. Many scholars who have examined GYA often question the program's success, including whether the program had any bearing on the democratization of German youth. They note that GYA was heavily publicized but claim that the program had little impact on German youth as a whole. For example, Petra Goedde argues that "the GYA program's contribution to the democratization of the German youth was negligible." However, she notes that those who participated did seem to have gained a better

---

14 Transcript of General McNarney's address opening the conference on Army Assistance to German Youth Activities held at USFET Headquarters, 7–9 August [1946]; Folder GYA Program-1946–48; Records of the Education and Cultural Relations Div: Group Activities Branch Recs of German Youth Assoc. 1945–49; OMGBY; Box 43; OMGUS; RG 260, NACP. See also *German Youth Activities: Army Assistance Program Guide*, 13–14.

15 See Fisher, *Disciplining Germany*; Kalb, "'The Youth is a Threat!' Controlling the Delinquent Boy in Post-WWII Munich"; Kalb, *Coming of Age*. See also Peterson, *The American Occupation of Germany*, 157–158.

16 15 April 1946 Directive, HQ USFET; Folder USFET Youth Directive 15 April 1946; Records RE the Work of the Youth Activities Section; Box 148; OMGUS; RG 260; NACP. Also, Sondern Jr., "GI Teachers for German Children," in Congressional Record, April 3, 1947, Vol. 93, Part 3, 3118–3119. Sondern claims that juvenile delinquency and anti-Americanism have dropped in areas where GIs have been busy with youth programs.

understanding of democracy, based on the results of an official OMGUS survey, although she argues that the survey itself had its faults, such as not defining the term "democracy."[17] Moreover, Edward N. Peterson claims that GYA "expanded very slowly," and he also argues that Army-sponsored events such as Christmas parties "brought much publicity but little real personal contact." Some of the soldiers apparently were not very enthusiastic. For example, he mentions that soldiers in Nuremberg ended up handing children sporting equipment and disappearing to chase *Fräuleins*, "the more interesting youth activity."[18] Karl-Heinz Füssl notes that the program did not significantly contribute to the overall political socialization of German youth, who remained largely apathetic. However, he argues that GYA did help reduce the level of crisis in the immediate postwar sphere, for example providing food, warm rooms, and meaningful structured activities, which created a starting point for future societal developments.[19]

Arguments critical of GYA's impact highlight the fact that the majority of German youth did not take part in GYA activities: A March 1947 OMGUS survey of 1,021 boys and girls in various cities noted that around 45% of the youth questioned had heard of the "American Youth Program" but only 11% had taken part in the program. Moreover, most of the children took part in the program in order "to get candy and food" (40%), with "a chance for sports and games" the second greatest reason (26%), followed by "to show our former enemies what Germans really are" (23%). In addition, they were aware that democratization was a factor in the program: Around 22% stated they had gained "either a little better or a much better idea of democracy from the youth activities."[20] Interestingly, an OMGUS survey of youth and adults from March 1948 showed that the majority of youth between 13 and 25 years old "thought that the leader should be chosen by majority vote." This number was even higher among "youngsters belonging to youth clubs that elected their leaders [who] supported democratic principles (71%) to a greater extent than members of clubs that appointed their leaders (49%)."[21] This survey shows that democratic practices within the space of youth clubs (both Army-sponsored and German-led) could have a bearing on the democratic outlook of German youth. Yet another survey made in December 1947 ana-

17 Goedde, *GIs and Germans*, 158. Goedde is referencing OMGUS Report No. 56 (26 April 1947), in Merritt and Merritt, eds., *Public Opinion in Occupied Germany*, 155–157.
18 Peterson, *The American Occupation of Germany*, 158–159.
19 Füssl, *Die Umerziehung*, 166–167.
20 Report No. 56 (26 April 1947), German Children Appraise the Youth Program, in Merritt and Merritt, eds., *Public Opinion in Occupied Germany*, 155–157.
21 Report No. 96 (3 March 1948), German Youth Versus Adults on Questions of Democracy, Merritt and Merritt, eds., *Public Opinion in Occupied Germany*, 205.

lyzed occupation youth club participation, and noted that "of those club members who had also belonged to the Hitler Youth, 63 per cent contrasted the militarism of the earlier group with the freedom and democracy of the new."[22]

Official statistics do indicate that high levels of German youth were participating in youth activities during the occupation, which included both Army-sponsored GYA clubs and German-run clubs. By February 1948, 1,256,712 youth were members of organized youth groups in the US zone out of a population of around 2,300,000 young people aged 10 to 18. Clubs included religious, sports, hiking, trade union, political, scouting, and cultural groups. Moreover, a survey focused solely on GYA participation showed that in September 1947, 409,570 German youth had participated in the various activities of the Army Assistance GYA program; in February 1948, this number was 366,496.[23] The GYA program included Army-sponsored events such as holiday parties and GYA youth centers located in towns and cities, which had the potential to reach more youth, including those not members of youth clubs.[24]

Critical interpretations of the GYA program note that most youth in organized groups were participating in German-organized youth programs, such as religious or trade union clubs, not in Army-sponsored GYA clubs. However, the US military government maintained oversight over these clubs as well and was ensuring that they were partaking in democratic practices, such as writing a constitution. At the time during the occupation, the GYA program also received criticism, including from the American press: An article in the *Stars and Stripes* on February 5, 1947 mentioned a "failure to teach democracy to young Germans," as youth remained overwhelmingly demoralized and juvenile delinquency high.[25] However, GYA had emerged as undoubtedly a central part of occupation policies for the Americans, and had an impact on both Germans and Americans. Examining the program should move beyond searching for definitive conclusions about its success in preventing supposed delinquent behavior or whether it led to tangible changes in the mindset of young Germans. Moreover, GYA played a role among

---

22 Report No. 99 (5 March 1948), A Report on German Youth, in Merritt and Merritt, eds., *Public Opinion in Occupied Germany*, 208–209.

23 *German Youth Between Yesterday and Tomorrow, 1 April 1947–30 April 1948* (Berlin: Office of Military Government, Education and Cultural Relations Division, 1948), Statistics. See also Goedde, *GIs and Germans*, 155–156. Population data is from the October 29, 1946 Census.

24 GYA also included initiatives such as mobile libraries: Frederiksen's 1953 official study of the occupation includes an image of a GYA mobile library: Frederiksen, *The American Military Occupation*, 133.

25 "State Dept. Calls Zone Youth Still Generally Demoralized," *Stars and Stripes*, February 5, 1947; in Folder Y.A.-VI General Publicity; Records of the Education Division: Gen Corresp and Rel Recs of Youth Activities Branch, 1945–47; OMGBR; Box 313; OMGUS; RG 260, NACP.

adults as well. For example, German adults indicated some approval of GYA: In a November 1946 OMGUS survey of German adults about the GYA program, 55% of the respondents had heard of the program, and "even among parents whose children had not yet participated in the program, 84 per cent said they would give permission to participate."[26] In addition, for American military personnel, GYA was a positive form of engagement with Germans. A report on the opinions of the occupation forces on GYA indicated a high level of troop participation: 24% of enlisted men and 41% of officers were participating in the Army's GYA program, mostly in a voluntary capacity. Those who participated tended to be better educated, had previous experience in club work, had knowledge of German, "were more favorably disposed towards the Germans, and had been in the command longer." Those who participated had learned about it through "troop information and education orientation," in addition to through the *Stars and Stripes* newspaper. Most thought GYA "was a fairly good idea," and that it was helping prevent delinquency and teach "democratic principles." In addition, troop participants noted that both sides benefited: The troops were able to discuss "world problems" and it would "help with their education." Most participants also thought that the youth liked the program, although the desire among youth for a "handout" and a "place to keep warm" was mentioned. Finally, "a large percentage of those interviewed wanted to take part in the program."[27]

Rather than attempt to reach clear conclusions around the program's success or failure in the reeducation and democratization of German youth, this chapter aims to highlight GYA's undoubted centrality to American occupation aims. Encounters between German youth and American military personnel became central to the US occupation of Germany, in which American troops became educators of democracy for the future democratic citizens of Germany. In addition, examining GYA in the Bremen Enclave enables a look into a particularly active GYA scene, in which the interactions undertaken in GYA clubs reached a high level of publicity. The situation in the Enclave also portrays the tensions and ambivalences of the program itself. Edward T. Ladd, the director of the youth and sports division in the Bremen military government, wrote a letter on June 25, 1947 that although "the vast majority of young people . . . have little or no interest in public affairs," around 50% of youth aged 10 to 25 participating in organized non-school groups in Land Bremen had been impacted by the Army's assistance

---

26 Report No. 46 (19 February 1947), Army Aid to German Youth Activities Evaluated by German Adults, in Merritt and Merritt, eds., *Public Opinion in Occupied Germany*, 142–143. See also Goedde, *GIs and Germans*, 158–160.
27 *The U.S. Armed Forces German Youth Activities Program 1945–1955*, 28.

to GYA, which was "more highly developed in Bremen than any other Land of the U.S. Zone."[28]

Exploring GYA in the Bremen Enclave using the case study of the Bremen Boys Club illustrates the direct, face-to-face everyday interactions that were taking place between GIs and German youth in an official occupation space, a GYA club. The central role of individual GIs in youth activities continued on after the beginning of the occupation, in which GIs contributed to the development of youth work through their own initiatives. Early initiatives that had aimed at helping German youngsters led to the official creation of GYA, which spurred a shift in official military policies toward youth, and enhanced the emerging role of military personnel as protectors and teachers of Germans, rather than punishers. Assistance toward German youth especially contributed to the shift of seeing Germans as victims to be helped in a dependent role, with American military personnel as providers.[29] Individual soldiers were thus essential to youth activities in the occupation. Moreover, the GYA program impacted the occupation itself, gaining a central place in official goals of reeducation and democratization. German youth also became major actors in the occupation sphere, taking on leadership roles within youth clubs. Encounters between Americans and Germans in the sphere of American-sponsored GYA youth clubs rose to the forefront of the occupation goal of rehabilitating Germany into a free, peace-loving nation. The Bremen Enclave proves a particularly fascinating case study due to its pioneering role in youth activities within an often-chaotic occupation setting as the Port of Embarkation for US troops.

The Enclave of Bremen emerged early on as a major shaper in the field of activities for German youth, with the famous Bremen Boys Club and its founder Moriarty at center stage in occupation developments toward youth beginning with the club's founding in August 1946. Even earlier, beginning in summer of 1945, troops stationed in the Bremen Enclave played an active role in assisting German youth. Official reports mentioned the trailblazing work of these GIs, who created youth clubs despite the fraternization ban. An official report on fraternization noted that efforts in the Enclave "were apparently successful to a consider-

28 Letter from Edward T. Ladd to Director, Education Division, "Plans for youth activities work in coming months," June 25, 1947; Folder Youth Activities-Bremen; Records RE the Work of the Youth Activities Section; Records of the Community Education Branch; Records of the Education and Cultural Relations Division; Box 149; OMGUS; RG 260; NACP.

29 See Goedde, *GIs and Germans*, 164; Goedde, "Gender, Race, and Power," in *The United States and Germany in the Era of the Cold War*, ed. Junker, 516. See also Leder, "Americans and German Youth," xi.

able degree, considering that they had no official backing."[30] Overall, the GYA program generated positive press for the "cause" of the occupation among soldiers and domestic American audiences. Moreover, soldiers' work with youth portrayed the wide range of roles that American military personnel took on after World War II, including as the protectors of allies, especially within the escalating Cold War context.[31] Additionally, young German members of American-sponsored youth clubs learned a particular type of democracy that was especially based on material plenty, yet they also were confronted head on with the limitations and contradictions of practicing democracy under a military occupation.[32] Youngsters emerged not merely as beneficiaries of American prosperity but as actors in the occupation scene. American personnel served as counselors and sponsors in GYA clubs, while German youth gained the role of future leaders of the country, learning hands-on about democracy. GYA clubs were not simply spaces to get candy, although that remained a central draw for many children: The encounters undertaken in the clubs were at the frontline for the future of German democracy and even world peace. Before delving into the specificities of youth activities in the Enclave, this chapter first examines the specific factors of the occupation in Bremen and the surrounding area, in addition to the everyday challenges that Germans and Americans faced.

Bremen: The Overlooked Enclave

Overall, the Bremen Enclave has remained an understudied part of the American occupation zone.[33] This has occurred despite the fact that during the occupation

---

30 Starr, *Fraternization with the Germans in World War II*, 139. Also, *The U.S. Armed Forces German Youth Activities Program 1945–1955*, 4.

31 See Willoughby, *Remaking the Conquering Heroes*, 2–3.

32 On youth's association of democracy with materialism, see Goedde, *GIs and Germans*, 158.

33 There are some studies that have focused on occupation policies in the Bremen Enclave: About denazification, see Bianka Adams, *From Crusade to Hazard: The Denazification of Bremen Germany* (Scarecrow Press, Inc., 2009); Hans Hesse, *Konstruktionen der Unschuld: die Entnazifizierung am Beispiel von Bremen und Bremerhaven 1945–1953* (Selbstverlag des Staatsarchivs, 2005); and Wiltrud Ulrike Drechsel and Andreas Röpke, eds., *"Denazification": zur Entnazifizierung in Bremen* (Edition Temmen, 1992). For a study of the reform of formal education, see Denzil Tim Clifton, "Bremen Under U.S. Military Occupation, 1945–1949: The Reform of Education" (Microfilm facsimile (1974) of PhD diss., University of Delaware, 1973). Other studies in German have focused on topics such as the role of the black market as well as the food and nutrition situation: Stefan Mörchen, *Schwarzer Markt: Kriminalität, Ordnung und Moral in Bremen 1939–1949* (Campus Verlag, 2011); Ehlers, *Die Ernährungssituation*. One study also focuses on the US soldiers during the 1950s in Bremerhaven: Rüdiger Ritter, *Vorort von New York?: Die Amerikaner in Bremerhaven: Ergebnisse einer Studie am Museum der 50er Jahre Bremerhaven* (Wirtschaftsverlag NW, Verlag für neue Wissen-

itself, Bremen's famous Bremen Boys Club was featured in major publications, including *Time* and *Life* magazines. Moreover, the Bremen Enclave had a central role as the port of transit for Americans arriving and departing Germany beginning in 1945. Before VE Day during planning for the occupation of Germany, Americans had fought hard for port access: President Franklin D. Roosevelt especially desired northern Germany for its ports and supply lines.[34] However, Roosevelt was unsuccessful in his bid for the northern region of Germany as the American occupation zone, but he was successful in reaching an agreement about the creation of the Bremen Enclave at the Quebec Conference on September 16, 1944. Bremen thus would become the American Port of Embarkation and received special status as an Enclave during the occupation of Germany.[35] Americans would have control over Bremen, the seaport of Bremerhaven, and the immediate vicinity, and they would have access to the Enclave through the British controlled area.[36] In April 1945, Bremen surrendered to the British Forces, and in May 1945, they turned the city over to the 29th Infantry Division of the US Army.[37] Youngsters in the Bremen Enclave grew up in a complex societal context as members of a defeated people under a military government within an Enclave of the US zone, surrounded by the British zone and living in the presence of arriving and departing US troops. Various official occupation policies affected their daily existence, including policies toward youth activities.

Anna-Maria Pedron's work *Amerikaner vor Ort: Besatzer und Besetzte in der Enklave Bremen nach dem Zweiten Weltkrieg* is one of the few scholarly studies of the American presence in Bremen after World War II. This published dissertation, which heavily draws upon archival materials from the Bremen State Archive, provides a fascinating look into the many spaces of contact between Americans and Germans, and it explores the diversity of German-American encounters and exchange in everyday Bremen life.[38] Interestingly, Bremen has not only been understudied in present scholarship but also was relatively forgotten during the occupation itself, creating great challenges for occupation goals such as denazifi-

---

schaft, 2010). See also a photo essay on Bremerhaven and the US Army from 1945–1993, Horst-Eberhard Friedrichs, *Bremerhaven und die Amerikaner: Stationierung der U.S. Army 1945–1993; eine Bild-Dokumentation* (Wirtschaftsverlag NW, Verlag für neue Wissenschaft, 2008).

34 Anna-Maria Pedron, *Amerikaner vor Ort: Besatzer und Besetzte in der Enklave Bremen nach dem Zweiten Weltkrieg* (Selbstverlag des Staatsarchivs Bremen, 2010), 25–29; Adams, ix.

35 Pedron, 23–35.

36 Pedron, 48, 51–53; Lutz Rode, "Zwischen Re-education und Freizeitvergnügen: Die Jugendarbeit der US-Armee in der Besatzungszeit, der Bremen Boys Club und seine Zeitschift 'Die Brücke'" (Magisterarbeit, Universität Bremen, 2002), 28. The Enclave included the state of Bremen including Bremerhaven, the city and district of Wesermünde, and the districts of Osterholz and Wesermarsch.

37 Adams, *From Crusade to Hazard*, x–xi.

38 Pedron, *Amerikaner vor Ort*, 14.

cation. Despite being a central part of Allied debates during pre-occupation planning, after the war was over, the actual administration of the Enclave was often overlooked, often causing bureaucratic chaos. In addition, the administration was especially complex, as the American military government in the Enclave was to enforce the directives of the British occupation zone beginning in December 1945, in an attempt to improve coordination with the surrounding British authorities in the British zone. In 1947, the military government in Bremen switched back to enforcing American directives (at this time the American and British zones also merged into the Bizone). American occupation troops were always present in the Enclave but would enforce whichever zone's rules were in effect. Thus, the ensuing administrative chaos impacted American occupation objectives. According to Bianka J. Adams, the first years of occupation in the Enclave were "tumultuous," and Bremen "remained the poor, unloved relation of the main US zone in the south of Germany." This meant that official occupation programs including denazification "lagged a year behind other states," and were negatively impacted by the shifting administrative control and different views of the American and British military governments. For example, Americans believed that Nazism could be uprooted through the removal of all members of the Nazi party in public, semi-public, and private enterprises. The British, on the other hand, believed that Nazism was inescapable and only the worst flaws could be corrected through the removal of Nazis from public office.[39] For the occupiers of Bremen, this meant great challenges and administrative chaos, which contributed to demoralization among the German public. For example, there was resentment over the denazification process: in contrast to lower-level Nazi party members, many cases of higher-level Nazis were not tried until later in the occupation, when denazification had less priority, and some of these Nazis simply passed into the British zone where denazification policies were more lenient.[40]

As time passed, throughout the US zone, the early punitive occupation goals of JCS 1067 gained less traction and the realities on the ground took precedence, including in the unique situation in the Bremen Enclave. The factor of military personnel encountering the need of German youngsters helped change and shape occupation policies: Individual soldiers decided they needed to take action to improve the situation of youth, and military officials realized material aid and recre-

39 Adams, *From Crusade to Hazard*, ix–xi. See also Ian D. Turner, "Denazification in the British Zone," in *Reconstruction in Post-War Germany: British Occupation Policy and the Western Zones, 1945–55*, ed. Ian D. Turner (Berg, 1989), 239–240; 242–244. On the administration of the US military government in Bremen, see Andreas Röpcke, "Office of Military Government for Bremen," in *OMGUS-Handbuch*, ed. Weisz, 608–637.

40 Adams, xi–xii, 85–86, 104–105; Hans G. Jansen and Renate Meyer-Braun, *Bremen in der Nachkriegszeit: 1945–1949: Politik, Wirtschaft, Gesellschaft* (Bremen: Steintor, 1990), 150–151.

ation would help further the democratization of youth. Interestingly, aid for German youngsters including the GYA program predated the official switch towards the reorientation and rehabilitation of Germany, which officially occurred in July 1947 with the issuing of the new directive, JCS 1779.[41] Personal encounters on the ground helped create this shift. Again, the Bremen Enclave was unique in being especially active in this turn toward assisting needy German youth, including Patrick Moriarty's famous Bremen Boys Club, in addition to soldiers' work with youth as early as summer of 1945. In June 1945, Sergeant Wilson Ballard of the 660th Field Artillery Division received special permission to create a youth club in Brake in the northern area of the Bremen Enclave. In this early phase of the occupation, only a few weeks after the end of the war, months before the official founding of GYA in April 1946, and over a year before Patrick Moriarty's founding of the Bremen Boys Club in August 1946, Ballard aimed to do something that would create productive activities for girls and boys and also encourage them to learn basics about democracy. Activities in his club included handicrafts, sewing, softball, dances, forums with US soldiers about democracy, and a governing board run by the youths themselves. Even after Ballard was redeployed, his club continued and even grew stronger, as the children themselves began to take charge of the club. In contrast to official occupation rhetoric about nonfraternization, which included German children in notions of collective guilt, Ballard believed that youth did not internalize Nazi ideas. Using Ballard's initiative as a model, dozens of other GIs founded sports and youth clubs in the Bremen Enclave.[42] Within this context of an especially active youth scene during the occupation, young Germans in Bremen were still confronted with the challenges of everyday life in a defeated nation.

As with many other large German cities with a strategic location, as well as due to its port access, Bremen was heavily bombed during the war, with an estimated 60% of residential quarters destroyed.[43] On VE Day, *Life* photographer Margaret Bourke-White was on an airplane tour photographing the bombed ruins of Germany, including of Bremen. She remarked on the "urban cadavers" of the Bremen region, and her photo of central Bremen from above included the

---

41 JCS 1779, in Friedrich and Associates, *American Experiences in Military Government*, 402–415. See also Tent, *Mission on the Rhine*, 10–11; Goedde, *GIs and Germans*, 125–126.

42 *German Youth Activities of the United States Army*, 5; "Experiment Bremen," *I & E Bulletin*, May 26, 1946, pgs. 3–4; Folder Y.A.-VI General Publicity; Records of the Education Division: Gen Corresp & Rel Recs of Youth Activities Branch, 1945–47; OMGBRE; Box 313; OMGUS; RG 260; NACP. Also, Rode, "Zwischen Re-education und Freizeitvergnügen," 32–33, 38–39; Pedron, *Amerikaner vor Ort*, 277; Füssl, *Die Umerziehung*, 149–150.

43 Jansen and Meyer-Braun, *Bremen in der Nachkriegszeit*, 27.

caption "Bremen was a desert. A few landmarks told you it had been a city. St. Stephani's Church at left, Weser River in background."[44] Bremen faced a housing shortage after the war was over, and the presence of increasing numbers of refugees increased the housing crisis. As the occupation developed, American confiscation of properties for the troops also led to increased tensions between the occupiers and local population.[45] In 1939, the population of Bremen was around 450,000; in April 1945 it was around 300,000. In 1946, the population grew to about 386,000, and in 1947 it was around 400,000.[46]

Interestingly, Bremen was never a hotspot of National Socialism during the 1930s or 1940s, despite the decision of Nazi officials to defend the city to the very end in April 1945. Hitler only visited the city once to tour the industry there. In the elections of 1933, National Socialists received 32.6% of the vote in Bremen compared to an average of 43.9% throughout Germany.[47] Immediately after the war, an antifascist movement called *Die Kampfgemeinschaft gegen den Faschismus* (KGF) quickly gained strength and played a role in ousting the first American-appointed mayor Erich Vagts, who had apparently been a collaborator with the Nazis.[48] Additionally, Bremen had a few politicians who had experience in democracy before the rise of Hitler, including Theodor Spitta (*Deutsche Demokratische Partei*, then later a member of *Freie Demokratische Partei*, FDP) and Wilhelm Kaisen (*Sozialdemokratische Partei Deutschlands*, SPD), both of whom were members of the Bremen Senate before 1933. Kaisen was a major force in postwar Bremen, serving for decades as mayor of Bremen from August 1, 1945 until July 17, 1965.[49] Kaisen was also an ally of the American occupiers. For example, he reminded the Bremen citizens that the reason for the requisitioning of property was not the fault of Americans but rather the fault of Germans for starting a war; he

---

44 Bourke-White, *"Dear Fatherland,"* 55, 58–60. Image of Bremen in "Section IV. Urban Germany: What Our Bombs Left."

45 Pedron, *Amerikaner vor Ort*, 348; Jansen and Meyer-Braun, *Bremen in der Nachkriegszeit*, 27, 29.

46 Rode, "Zwischen Re-education und Freizeitvergnügen," 30; Klaus Wedemeier, "Vorwart," in *Kriegsende in Bremen: Erinnerungen, Berichte, Dokumente*, ed. Hartmut Müller and Günther Rohdenburg (Edition Temmen, 1995), 7; Peters, *Zwölf Jahre Bremen*, 19. In the state of Bremen in 1946, there were 1,154 women to 1,000 men. In the age group from 20- to 25-year-olds, there were 1,556 women to 1,000 men. In Jansen and Meyer-Braun, 197.

47 Jansen and Meyer-Braun, 247, footnote 1.

48 Jansen and Meyer-Braun, 134–136. For more on the KFG, see Heinz-Gerd Hofschen, "Zum ersten Male nach zwölf Jahren der Knechtung können wir wieder frei atmen": Bremer Antifaschisten und der Neuaufbau 1945, in *Kriegsende in Bremen*, ed. Müller and Rohdenburg, 161–175.

49 For a biography of Kaisen, see Karl-Ludwig Sommer, *Wilhelm Kaisen: eine politische Biographie*, 2., Durchges. Aufl. (Dietz, 2000).

also noted that Germans chose their fate by choosing National Socialism.[50] His wife Helene Kaisen also took on an active role in postwar Bremen society, and she encouraged Bremen women to help in political reconstruction. She also reminded Germans that women had played a complicit role under National Socialism.[51]

Another unique factor in the Bremen Enclave was the role of the region as a seaport, meaning that the Bremen region had centuries-long global ties due to the ship industry and its Hanseatic past. This factor impacted the population's views of the post-World War II foreign occupiers, since the citizens were more used to a blend of peoples who had descended upon the port area over the centuries. The Bremen region also had previous transatlantic trading ties to the United States, and many European migrants started on their journey to the "New World" on passenger ships in the Bremen region; Bremen was thus seen as a gateway to the United States.[52] Thus, the centuries-long presence of Americans and of people of various races, ethnicities, and nationalities impacted the Bremen population's views of the occupation soldiers, since they were more used to diversity than Germans in other areas in the US zone, such as rural Bavaria, where African American GIs were often the first people of color the population had ever encountered.[53] The Bremen population did not react as strongly to the arrival of black GIs compared to other areas of the US occupation zone, although in general, a certain level of racism and resentment was still present.[54]

The challenges facing the occupiers in the Bremen Enclave were similar to that in other areas under American occupation, but occupation chaos often occurred on a ramped-up scale due to the realities of the port of Bremerhaven as the first and last stop of Americans. As John Willoughby has shown, the heroic conquerors of the US Army took part in an occupation that was often less than orderly, with Army attempts to control the behavior of soldiers often falling flat. Alcoholism, brawls, and even violence between soldiers and German civilians oc-

50 Jansen and Meyer-Braun, *Bremen in der Nachkriegszeit*, 31; Hartmut Müller, "Einleitung," *Kriegsende in Bremen*, ed. Müller and Rohdenburg, 10.

51 Renate Meyer-Braun, "Wie Bremer Frauen das Kriegsende erlebten," in *Kriegsende in Bremen*, ed. Müller and Rohdenburg, 146.

52 Pedron, *Amerikaner vor Ort*, 170–171. See also Ritter, *Vorort von New York?*, on the impact of Americans in Bremerhaven.

53 Peter Martin, "Schwarze Sowjets an Elbe und Spree?" in *Zwischen Charleston und Stechschritt. Schwarze im Nationalsozialismus*, ed. Peter Martin and Christine Alonzo (Dölling und Galitz, 2004), 181; Pedron, 214.

54 Pedron, 214–215; Fehrenbach, *Race After Hitler*, 45.

curred, as did troop black market participation.[55] Sergeant Walter C. Krause described in his memoir about his experience arriving in Germany on July 16, 1946 via ship, docking at Bremerhaven. He noted how GIs were calling out to the women on the docks, from those over 60 years of age to little girls as young as 13, "and to all those in-between," sometimes making obscene gestures and whistling. Krause wrote, "The Germans must certainly have asked, 'What uneducated, uncivilized savages are being sent to Germany?'" In addition, he noted that the local children had appeared, gathering on the dock, as "the news had spread in the city that a new ship had arrived." These youngsters "gathered and waited for small pieces of candy, for gum, for canned rations, or for the cookies that the soldiers brought from the mess, the PX. Most of the men gave with charity and compassion." However, he did note that some GIs did perversely enjoy watching Germans scrambling and even getting into fights over cigarette butts or candy.[56] In his diary, John Tomikel also described chaotic scenes among American soldiers stationed in Germany, noting in his diary that "many soldiers drink to oblivion."[57] While stationed in Camp Grohn in the Bremen Enclave, he never left the camp to go into Bremerhaven, but many of his fellow soldiers did. Tomikel wrote, "and there are horror stories of fights, prostitution and general disorder." Tomikel thus wrote a "soldier's toast" to Bremerhaven:

> Here's to the city of Bremerhaven
> The beautiful stadt [sic] on the cold North Sea
> Where a woman's pass and a whisky glass
> Made a horse's ass out of me.[58]

Moreover, the factor of sexualized fraternization emerged strongly in Bremen: Women often followed their GI lovers around Germany, and once the soldiers sailed home to the United States, many of these women, known as Camp Followers, ended up in Bremen. Many of these women apparently were from the

55 Willoughby, *Remaking the Conquering Heroes*, 5, 29–31. Also, Pedron, 316–317, see also 294–311 for a discussion of the bar scene in Bremen. In April 1946, 33 attacks on German civilians were reported. Also, Fürmetz, "Insolent Occupiers, Aggressive Protectors: Policing GI Delinquency in Early 1950s West Germany," in *GIs in Germany*, ed. Maulucci Jr. and Junker, 190, 195–199, 210, Kleinschmidt, *Do Not Fraternize*, 147–151; Jansen and Meyer-Braun, *Bremen in der Nachkriegszeit*, 26; Dewey A. Browder, "The Two Faces of the American Soldier in Germany," in *Amerika in Rheinland-Pfalz: Beiträge zu einem halben Jahrhundert deutsch-amerikanischer Nachbarschaft*, ed. Winfried Herget (Wissenschaftlicher Verlag, 1996), 99–107; Mörchen, *Schwarzer Markt*, 141–147; Gimbel, *A German Community*, 203.
56 Krause, *So I Was a Sergeant*, 35–36.
57 Tomikel, *A German Journal*, 71.
58 Tomikel, 24.

Rhineland region and some were as young as 14. Some lived outdoors in “caverns” in the ground near the Huckelriede barracks, a barracks for black troops.[59] Women who had relationships with black GIs often received criticism from the local population, who sometimes found a sympathetic ear among white American officers.[60] American Military Police, the German police, and the Bremen public relief office (*Wohlfahrtsamt*) worked together to try to mitigate the issue of the Bremen Enclave Camp Followers.[61]

Within this sexualized atmosphere, many German women avoided Americans as a result of fear of repercussions, contempt, and jealousy from other Germans, as well as fear of drunk American soldiers.[62] Additionally, the venereal disease rate was significantly higher in the Breman Enclave than in other areas of the US zone, with rates even double that of Berlin’s, especially due to the realities of transitory port life.[63] German women in the Enclave bore the consequences of this issue, and could be forced to undergo random searches for sexually transmitted diseases, especially if they were out after curfew. By the end of 1945, the policy was changed to search only women they had apparent reasonable cause to suspect of disease; meanwhile male soldiers received informational brochures and only in October 1948 were soldiers who had contact with a case of venereal disease required to be treated.[64]

---

59 Report from Bremen signed by Schmidt, Krim. Sekretärin, June 18, 1946; Folder CIC-CID; Records of the Public Safety Division: General Correspondence & Other Records, 1945–49; OMGBRE; Box 224; OMGUS; RG 260; NACP. For more on Camp Followers during the occupation, see Willoughby, *Remaking the Conquering Heroes*, 63.

60 Pedron, *Amerikaner vor Ort*, 302. On white officers and black troops, see Mary Penick Motley, *The Invisible Soldier: The Experience of the Black Soldier, World War II* (Wayne State University Press, 1975), 78; also, 346. Many white military officers were from the Jim Crow South. Also, Matthew F. Delmont, *Half American: The Epic Story of African Americans Fighting World War II at Home and Abroad* (Viking, 2022), 230. Often white southerners were assigned as officers of black troops under the premise that white southerners could supposedly understand and control black people.

61 On Bremen Camp Followers, see Pedron, 216–220.

62 Regina Bruss, ed., *Mit Zuckersack und Heißgetränk: Leben und Überleben in der Nachkriegszeit Bremen 1945–1949*, Hefte des Focke-Museums, Nr. 83 (Bremer Landesmuseum für Kunst- und Kulturgeschichte, 1989), 22–23. In the Bremen Enclave, as in other areas in Germany, there were cases of punishment of German women who fraternized with GIs, which included incidents of German men cutting fraternizing women’s hair. Pedron, *Amerikaner vor Ort*, 318.

63 Pedron, 300.

64 Pedron, 318–321. Male prostitution also occurred during the occupation in Bremen, including in the area around the main train station; the consequences were severe for those caught: see Pedron, 300–301. See also Peters, *Zwölf Jahre Bremen*, 43: on December 18, 1945, 423 women in the train station area were searched for VD, which 114 were found to have. Some 51 of these women were apparently not from Bremen, but mostly from the Rhineland. Peters claimed that

Another major challenge that impacted daily life in the Bremen Enclave was the fact that racial segregation among the troops led to increased chaos and tension, ultimately harming the military's prestige and its occupation goals in Germany.[65] Black soldiers' experiences in the occupation thus took place within the context of officially sanctioned segregation. For troops in the Bremen Enclave, a booklet entitled *Bremen Port Command's "GI Paradise"* aimed to advertise the recreational facilities available in order to help the soldiers feel more at home. The booklet lauded all the available facilities, reminding GIs that the ultimate goal was to "enjoy yourself!" One of the special service clubs advertised was the Schwanewede Service Club, which apparently was "the focal point for colored troops in the Enclave," and it was "an extremely remote, out-of-the-way place about five miles from Blumenthal."[66] This serves as a stark reminder that Army facilities were segregated, meaning that the resources available to black and white soldiers were often extremely different, impacting their service experiences.

Moreover, the GYA program throughout the US zone was impacted by the continuance of racial segregation in the military. The image that emerged of GIs sponsoring German youth clubs was a predominantly white one. For example, the Bremen Boys Club GI sponsors were all white male troops. The level of black troop participation in GYA is unclear, although (white) women were encouraged to be active in GYA. Troops of various racial and ethnic backgrounds may have also played a part in GYA: Some photos of GIs involved in Bremen youth activities depict Asian American soldiers working on youth activities projects or donating rations for children.[67] However, despite few official records, there is some evidence that black soldiers played a role in youth activities. A January 1947 report from Marcus H. Ray, civilian aide to the Secretary of War, noted that in areas of

---

these girls, who were mostly 19 to 21 years old, sauntered through the streets and tried to attract attention in a boisterous manner. See also Georg Schmidt, *Als Bremen amerikanisch war: zwischen Krieg und Wirtschaftswunder: Bilder von 1945 bis 1950* (Johann Heinrich Döll Verlag, 1989), for images of German female police officers who aimed to solve the issue of VD.

65 See Willoughby, *Remaking the Conquering Heroes*, 58–64; Fehrenbach, *Race after Hitler*, 45.

66 *Bremen Port Command's "GI Paradise"* (Public Relations Office, Bremen Port Command, 1946), 35.

67 Images in "Youth Program Teaches German Tots Democracy," *Stars and Stripes*, September 20, 1946; in Folder Reports on GYA from Other Sources (e.g. Press); Records RE the Work of the Youth Activities Section; Records of the Community Education Branch; Records of the Education and Cultural Relations Division; Box 145; OMGUS; RG 260; NACP. Image of ration donation box, "Can you spare part of your rations for children in the Bremen area"; Folder German Youth; Records of Bremerhaven Liaison and Security Detachment: Records of Clubs and Youth Activities, 1947–49; OMGBRE; Box 589; OMGUS; RG 260; NACP.

Germany such as Grafenwöhr "where only Negro soldiers are located, the German youth program is progressing as well under the direction of colored soldiers as in other parts of Germany where only white troops are stationed." Ray wrote, "to accept the racial prejudices of the German people as a reason for the nonutilization of the American soldier who happens to be nonwhite is to negate the very ideals we have made a part of our reeducation program in Germany."[68] Ray thus pointed out the contradiction of military occupation policies, in which racist American practices fundamentally harmed occupation goals such as reeducation through the youth activities program. Maria Höhn and Martin Klimke note that the black press in the US especially highlighted the role of black troops in their contributions to the democratization of German youth through GYA, marking the fact that they did indeed play an important role in working with youth within the realm of the organized youth activities program.[69] For example, an article in the *Chicago Defender* from April 10, 1948 highlighted examples of "hundreds of Negro officers and soldiers," who were "winning the hearts of German children through their efforts in the GYA . . . A million children are being democratized." The article included an example of a sergeant in a village near Mannheim, who led "four hundred boys and girls in special training," focusing on "games which highlight the give-and-take principle of democracy," learning "useful activities" and "parliamentary procedure in their own youth councils." Moreover, the article noted the importance of black soldiers teaching German youth: "The little race-conscious Nazis trained by the Hitler Youth Corps are being challenged by the new GYA program much of which is directed by colored soldiers."[70] An official document reporting on the results of a study conducted by German and American GYA workers in Munich did mention that "Negro units" were sponsoring youth centers. This document stated that there had been complaints from GYA participants regarding different treatment of the GYA centers. The report noted that this different treatment was because "the American groups sponsoring GYA centers such as the German-American Women's Club, the Military Police, WAC units, Negro units etc. [sic] differ in means, enthusiasm, and generosity," which sometimes led to "envy and dissatisfaction between GYA participants."[71] Thus, the vari-

---

68 Marcus H. Ray, Memorandum to Sec. of War Robert P. Patterson for deputy chief of staff, January 7, 1947, in Bernard C. Nalty and Morris J. MacGregor, eds., *Blacks in the Military: Essential Documents* (Scholarly Resources Inc., 1981), 217.

69 Höhn and Klimke, *A Breath of Freedom*, 42.

70 Louis Martin, "Negroes Play Vital Reconstruction Role," *Chicago Defender*, April 10, 1948.

71 Report entitled "The Armed Forces Assistance Program"; Folder Germans on GYA; Records RE the Work of the Youth Activities Section; Records of the Community Education Branch; Records of the Education and Cultural Relations Division; Box 140; OMGUS; RG 260; NACP.

ous resources of the different units impacted the quality of GYA clubs and activities. It can only be assumed that black troops had less means for youth activities due to the continuation of segregation and racist practices in the military, but perhaps black soldiers' enthusiasm towards German children, as examined previously, perhaps made up for it. However, unfortunately, at least among the records relating to Bremen Enclave youth activities, official military government records are lacking on the contribution of African American soldiers in GYA. This may be a reflection of official practices of continuing racism within the military and the view that black contributions were less significant and not as worthy of documentation.

Official Policies and Youth: A Turn Toward Aid

The occupation sphere for youngsters in the Bremen Enclave was also shaped by American military government policies toward schools, food, humanitarian aid, and notions about the collective guilt of Germans. These policies and rhetoric played a central role in everyday life for youngsters, determining their daily schedule, including school participation, and whether they had to undergo denazification processes. Bremen schools remained closed until September 1945, when the *Volksschulen* reopened. In December 1945, secondary schools reopened. Vocational schools reopened in February 1946.[72] Thus, for the first months of peace, children had no structured educational activities to occupy their time. Even after reopening, school conditions were often dire, with many school facilities unavailable due to bomb damage, and with textbook and teacher shortages due to denazification processes. In June 1946, the teacher to student ratio in Bremen was 1:74 in elementary schools, 1:38 in secondary schools, and 1:61 in vocational schools.[73] Additionally, schools had to close due to coal shortages from January to March 1947 during one of the coldest winters ever recorded in Germany.[74] Humanitarian aid for German civilians began to arrive in 1946, with the first CARE packages arriving in the Bremen Enclave that year in July.[75] The *Schulspeisung* began in the Bremen Enclave through the British on March 25, 1946; the Americans took over responsibility in June 1947.[76] Common food in the *Schulspeisung* was soup: Pea soup, bread soup, and even choco-

72 Peters, *Zwölf Jahre Bremen*, 28, 40, 49; Clifton, "Bremen Under U.S. Military Occupation," 135, 140, 142.

73 Clifton, 132–138, 140, 142, 167–168.

74 Rode, "Zwischen Re-education und Freizeitvergnügen," 30.

75 Peters, *Zwölf Jahre Bremen*, 60; Ehlers, *Die Ernährungssituation*, 38.

76 Peters, 51, 86; Ehlers, 30–33.

late soup.[77] Outside of school, many children faced difficult home situations, including crowded conditions, and their "playground" was often the rubble.[78] Many children were orphans or half-orphans whose fathers had not survived the war or were not yet back from imprisonment after the war.[79] According to a 1947 study about the economic, social, and familial circumstances of around 50,000 Bremen schoolchildren from age six to 20, around a quarter of children were without a father in Bremen. Overall, around 10% of the fathers of the respondents were dead, 4% were missing, and 6% were prisoners of war. Moreover, the study noted the 42.7% of all the schoolchildren did not have a family situation where both the mother and father were present.[80] Schooling took place in challenging circumstances, and youth in general faced a context of deprivation and disruption, including challenging personal situations such as loss in their families. GYA facilities thus could provide a welcome space for youngsters to have a reprieve from the challenges of postwar life.

In addition, food rationing led to high rates of hunger among Germans, and growing children were especially affected.[81] According to a public health report on nutrition in the US zone in November 1946, children aged eight to 15 throughout the American zone suffered the most from caloric deficiency out of the entire population; the school feeding program helped but did not reach all children at that point. During that month, children aged six to nine in the US zone officially received 1,765 calories a day, while ages ten to 19 received 1,940 calories, more than the average adult consumer's ration of 1,550 calories a day but also not enough to ensure proper weight and nutrition for growing children and adoles-

---

77 Bruss, ed., *Mit Zuckersack und Heißgetränk*, 177. For statistics and menus for the Bremen *Schulspeisung*, see Ehlers, 69–72.

78 Phillips, *Educating the Germans*, 127–129; Lutz Rode, "Manche nannten sie nur 'Schokoladenclubs': Die Jugendarbeit der US-Armee in der Besatzungszeit," *Arbeiterbewegung und Sozialgeschichte, Zeitschrift für die Regionalgeschichte Bremens im 19. und 20. Jahrhundert* 13/14 (2004): 35; Bruss, ed., 162–165; see images in Schmidt, *Als Bremen amerikanisch war*.

79 See Seegers, "Dead Dads," 259; Seegers, *"Vati blieb im Krieg"*, 88–96.

80 Karl Kurz, *Lebensverhältnisse der Nachkriegsjugend: Eine soziologische Studie* (F. Trüjen, 1949), 15–17, 114. This sociological study was conducted by the Senator for the Schools and Education in Bremen. Schoolchildren in the summer of 1947 were asked 40 questions. Also includes information on housing, nutrition, and clothing situations. The study noted that 4,500 of the school pupils came to school without breakfast, and 1,400 of them did not have a warm meal during the day, besides the *Schulspeisung*.

81 See Manfred J. Enssle, "The Harsh Discipline of Food Scarcity in Postwar Stuttgart, 1945–1948," *German Studies Review* 10, no. 3 (Oct. 1987): 500–501, https://doi.org/10.2307/1430898. Also, "Hungerkinder," *Weser-Kurier*, August 24, 1946. The article includes an image of a malnourished boy in Hamburg, where around 10% of all illnesses were spurred by hunger-related causes.

cents.[82] Children often suffered from issues such as anemia stemming from malnutrition, and malnutrition had the potential to cause permanent cognitive and physical defects.[83] This impacted Bremen's children and youth: A report from 1947 stated that around 19% of Bremen's schoolchildren were undernourished and urgently needed more food, for example in the form of additional school meals.[84] Sometimes school pupils had to stay home from school as they were too weak to attend. Another issue was supplies: Many children did not have adequate clothing nor anything for the school day such as paper.[85] A Bremen contemporary witness recollected that boys often wore patched up clothes and whatever was available; he even had to go to school in high heeled women's boots, which was especially shameful for him at age 14.[86] To Bremen mayor Wilhelm Kaisen, the war's devastating effect on the German educational system was especially tragic, and he apparently wept during visits to the local schools.[87]

In addition to difficult physical conditions such as hunger, youngsters also faced psychological challenges. Children had to grapple with the rupture of the end of National Socialism, and also had to deal with traumatic memories of war. In Bremen, however, not all children had directly witnessed war-related violence such as bombings, since many children had been evacuated to the countryside through the *Kinderlandverschickung*.[88] Overall, OMGUS authorities were concerned about the psychological condition of youth in occupied Germany. From June 28 to July 3, 1947, a conference on youth matters was held at the University

82 Charles E. Brown, MD, Nutrition Summary Report, U.S. Zone, November 1946; Folder OMGUS IA&C Public Health Nutrition Summary Rpt Nov 1946; The Control Office: Activities of Internal Affairs & Communications Div.; Records of the Executive Office; Box 460; OMGUS; RG 260; NACP. See also Ehlers, *Die Ernährungssituation*, 59–60, 62–68, 75–81 for statistics on rationing and public health in Bremen.

83 Ryer III (first name unclear), Nutrition Summary Report, U.S. Zone, November 1947; Folder OMGUS IA&C Public Health Nutrition Summary Rpt Nov 1947; same location as previous file in Box 460; RG 260; NACP. Also, Enssle, "The Harsh Discipline," 501; Ehlers, 45–56.

84 File on Religion and Education, 1947?; Folder Youth Activities-Bremen; Records RE the Work of the Youth Activities Section; Records of the Community Education Branch; Records of the Education and Cultural Relations Division; Box 149; OMGUS; RG 260; NACP.

85 For an overview of the terrible conditions in Bremen schools in the early postwar years: Bruss, ed., *Mit Zuckersack und Heißgetränk*, 172–177; Clifton, "Bremen Under U.S. Military Occupation," 125–126, 137–138. See also Werner, *Through the Eyes of Innocents*, 179, 181–182.

86 Bruss, ed., 163.

87 Adams, *From Crusade to Hazard*, 148.

88 See Sylvelin Wissmann, "Ohne den Krieg wäre sie nicht nötig gewesen—Die Verschickung von Bremer Kindern 1941 bis 1945," *Am Roland hing ein Hakenkreuz: Bremer Kinder und Jugendliche in der Nazizeit: Katalog zur Ausstellung der Schulgeschichtlichten Sammlung Bremen*, ed. Schulgeschichtlichte Sammlung Bremen (Hauschild, 2002), 93–101.

of Munich. A report from the conference noted that "the German speakers emphasized the fact that they were undernourished spiritually as well as physically, that it was difficult to believe and hope for a better world after they had been indoctrinated with false ideologies for so long." They were willing to cooperate "in any constructive efforts to better the world, but . . . they would never let themselves be used as pawns in any future war."[89] Thus, many young Germans felt disillusioned about the empty promises of adults who had led the country to destruction and had used youth to further their aims. Many youngsters also had great difficulty in seeing a positive future.

Moreover, young Germans were implicated in the crimes of the Nazis, especially during the early phase of the US occupation, when the focus was on the punishment of collectively guilty Germans of all ages. One incident in Bremen occurred that reflected this focus: In May 1945, a few hundred German girls from Bremen learned an early lesson in atonement for German guilt, as they were sent to the nearby liberated concentration camp Sandbostel, where they worked for weeks cleaning the camp. According to the women who had experienced this, the German police had collected a group of young women in Bremen, took them to the camp to replace the nurses, and at first did not allow them to inform their parents about where they were. The women were supposed to have been BDM members and members of the *SS-Frauen/NS-Frauenschaft*, but it seems that the young women were arbitrarily chosen to take part in this activity as an act of reeducation.[90] Thus, a young age did not prevent Germans from being labeled as guilty in the early phases of the occupation. However, occupation policies shifted away from a focus on guilt and punishment, including the Youth Amnesty in August 1946, highlighting the growing focus on reeducation and democratization of youth through methods such as GYA clubs. Therefore, children emerged as the central figures of the democratic reconstruction of Germany, and they had to be reoriented to ensure a hopeful future.

89 Bavaria—Semi-Monthly Report, 10 July 1947; Folder Reports Land YA Section 1947; Records RE the Work of the Youth Activities Section; Records of the Community Education Branch; Records of the Education and Cultural Relations Division; Box 143; OMGUS; RG 260; NACP.

90 Bruss, ed., *Mit Zuckersack und Heißgetränk*, 178–179; Peters, *Zwölf Jahre Bremen*, 1. Peters writes that the 400 girls were members and leaders in the Hitler Youth (BDM). British Generals Sir Brian Horrocks and Allan Adair discovered the camp. Horrocks writes in his memoir that he was "so angry" that he ordered the mayors of the surrounding towns and villages to supply a quota of German women to clean up the camp and look after the prisoners. Brian Horrocks, *A Full Life* (L. Cooper, 1974), 264–265; Burchard Scheper, *". . . You Must Learn Democracy": Ende und Anfang 1944–1945* (Nordwestdeutsche Verlagsgesellschaft, 1995), 87–88. See also Theodor Spitta, *Neuanfang auf Trümmern: Die Tagebücher des Bremer Bürgermeisters Theodor Spitta 1945–1947*, ed. Ursula Büttner and Angelika Voß-Louis (R. Oldenbourg, 1992), 133.

Direct personal encounters between German children and American soldiers in the Bremen Enclave took place in a complex landscape of power relations between the occupied and the occupiers in a transitory port region. In general, adult Germans were more distanced from American soldiers, except for Germans who worked for the Americans, Germans active on the black market, and women who had relationships with soldiers.[91] However, young Germans often came into contact with members of the occupying forces during exchanges of benevolence, and youngsters often gained a positive view of soldiers. In the first weeks of contact between American military personnel and German civilians, US soldiers were observed handing out food and sweets to the hungry children of Bremen, despite the ban on fraternizing with all Germans. A Bremen witness (born in 1933) who described herself as a "*Kindernazi*" as a child described her first encounters with "the enemy," who gave her chocolate and bread. She noted that through this generosity of the soldiers (she did not mention whether they were Americans or British), her "*Feindbild*," her image of the enemy, became unsettled.[92]

Young Germans thus directly sought out contact with soldiers for material benefits such as chocolate, and as the occupation progressed, to participate in organized fraternization opportunities such as sports events or youth club activities including GYA. In addition, they even sometimes sought GIs for cigarettes, which they could deal with on the black market. Due to this, children were sometimes seen as partaking in troublesome behaviors with the occupation soldiers, and their behavior came under criticism in a similar manner to that of critiques of fraternizing German women. Children often gathered in crowds around soldiers to pick up the cigarette butts that soldiers had dropped, which would be collected and most likely sold on the black market. In Bremen, the streets that were especially lucrative for this "business" were the ones most often frequented by GIs, which became known as "Tobacco Road."[93] Sometimes soldiers even gave entire cigarettes to children.[94] Fears about children's troubling behavior led to warnings to the parents to monitor the behavior of their children, for example through an

91 Pedron, *Amerikaner vor Ort*, 316; Mörchen, *Schwarzer Markt*, 141–147. Black market participants were often young men and youth. See Schmidt, *Als Bremen Amerikanisch war*.

92 Bruss, ed., *Mit Zuckersack und Heißgetränk*, 20.

93 Pedron, *Amerikaner vor Ort*, 322–323; Ritter, *Vorort von New York?*, 127–128.

94 Erwin Bochnig, "Kindheit unter amerikanischer Besatzung," in *Kriegsende 1945: Vegesack und umzu: das Kriegsende erlebt und aufgeschrieben von Bewohnern aus Vegesack und umliegenden Ortschaften*, ed. Museum Schloß Schönebeck (J.H. Döll, 1994), 85: According to this eyewitness, born in 1939, black GIs gave children barely smoked or even whole cigarettes, so the kids often followed them, while white GIs apparently saw the kids coming and stomped out the cigarette butts. The kids also quickly learned to ask GIs, "Giff mi Schewingum . . . oder Bonbons!"

article in the *Weser-Kurier* on March 16, 1946, which informed readers about a notice from the police president reminding parents that they could be held responsible for children found begging. The article mentioned that many children had been observed begging soldiers for sweets in a bothersome manner.[95] Thus, children's behavior came under scrutiny within the context of the occupation. Notably, the reality remained that children's hunger was often a driving force in the yearning for sweets and even a desire for cigarettes, which could be traded on the black market for actual food. GIs in Bremen reacted with benevolence and sympathy when they saw the hunger of the children, and took individual action such as gifting sweets. However, the situation under the occupation was often dire and chaotic, and some Bremen families were so desperate that they traded the chocolate and sweets that their children had received from GIs on the black market.[96] According to an article in the *Port Reporter* in June 1947, youth in a GYA club staged a picket to stop cigarette butt collecting, indicating the fact that children were still engaging in this action in the Bremen Enclave in mid-1947.[97] Under such conditions of material want, need, and even a hunger for information after years of life under the National Socialist regime, German Youth Activities emerged as a major factor in postwar life for youngsters, with individual initiatives of American soldiers spurring a larger program aimed at reeducation of the youngest of the Germans. GYA provided a new model for democratic reform with the individual GI as the example of democratic life and the German youngster as the future of the German nation. As a September 1945 US Group Control Council letter termed it, German youth were thus the "raw material out of which a regenerated Germany can be built."[98]

Army Assistance to GYA evolved as a form of "guided fraternization," in which GIs gained a sense of responsibility through the concrete task of assisting German youth in a way that moved beyond the normally "dull business" of occupation duties.[99] GI behavior had also come under scrutiny and the development

95 "Bettelnde Kinder," *Weser-Kurier*, March 16, 1946.

96 Pedron, *Amerikaner vor Ort*, 339.

97 "GYA Youth State Picket to Stop Butt Collecting," *Port Reporter*, End of June; Folder YXXI Army Assistance Program A. Bremerhaven Military Community 1947 (formerly Grohn Military Community); Records of the Education Division: Gen Corresp & Rel Recs of Youth Activities Branch, 1945–47; OMGBR; Box 315; OMGUS; RG 260; NACP.

98 M.C. Stayer, Letter "Directive for the Control of Youth Activities" to the Chief of Staff, September 26, 1945; unnamed folder; Records RE the Work of the Youth Activities Section; Records of the Community Education Branch; Records of the Education and Cultural Relations Division; Box 145; OMGUS; RG 260; NACP.

99 "Experiment Bremen," *I & E Bulletin* 1, no. 9, May 26, 1946, pg. 4; Folder Y.A.-VI General Publicity; Records of the Education Division: Gen Corresp & Rel Recs of Youth Activities Branch, 1945–47; OMGBRE; Box 313; OMGUS; RG 260; NACP.

of Army Assistance to GYA emerged as a factor in encouraging positive behavior, away from negative behavior such as sexual relations with German *Fräuleins* and alcohol-heavy activities. Thus, the program would control both the delinquency of German youth and of GIs, since soldiers now could engage in positive, meaningful activities that had the potential to boost morale and reduce disillusionment. GYA had evolved into a means of encouraging positive activities not only for its audience, the German youth, but also for its sponsors, the American military personnel. Thus, in the warm rooms of GYA club homes and youth centers, German youth could learn positive behavior, learning a type of democracy under the guide and example of GIs, with sports and other activities encouraging teamwork and fair play, furthering the role of Americans as protectors, teachers, and even father figures, as well as embodiments of democracy.[100] Moreover, GIs would be engaging in positive occupation activities that had the potential to make a concrete impact, and they would be off the streets with their tempting *Fräuleins* and black markets. Instead, they were pitching baseballs and handing out Coca-Colas as youth took part in democratic discussions.

Bremen Stands for GYA

By 1946, Bremen had emerged as a central location of the Army Assistance to German Youth Activities program in the American zone. As it developed, the GYA program moved beyond material benevolence and aimed at filling the "vacuum" in children's lives through meaningful, engaging club activities and "positive" fraternization.[101] In turn, youth activities became a centerpiece of American reeducational policy. In addition, GYA provided a new model of pedagogical usage of free time activities.[102] The Bremen Enclave's pioneering role in this development began to take shape as early as June 1945 through Sergeant Wilson Ballard's youth club in Brake. This early engagement of GIs in youth work attracted wider attention beyond the Bremen Enclave, eventually impacting youth activities policies of the occupation military government. This work with youth happened even before the creation of clubs for adults and the founding of cultural institutions

100 See Goedde, *GIs and Germans*, 128, 164–165.

101 Goedde, *GIs and Germans*, 159–160; Willoughby, *Remaking the Conquering Heroes*, 113.

102 Füssl, *Die Umerziehung*, 20–22; Karl-Heinz Füssl and Gregory Paul Wegner, "Education under Radical Change: Education Policy and the Youth Program of the United States in Postwar Germany," *History of Education Quarterly* 36, no. 1 (Spring 1996): 1–2, 5, 12–13, 17–18, https://doi.org/10.2307/369298.

such as the *Amerikahäuser*.[103] In Bremerhaven, military personnel including those in the Navy were also active early in the occupation in promoting German youth activities, including a Navy chief who organized a Christmas party for 800 young Germans in 1945. In addition, this American officer invited all local youth above age 12 to a meeting at a school in order to start a youth movement, according to Burchard Scheper, then 17 years old. Scheper got to know many American officers beginning in 1945, because his father worked at their riding stable. Scheper also was able to use his school-level English to communicate with Americans, and even formed a friendship with a Jewish GI who had lost relatives in a concentration camp.[104] Soldiers' early initiatives with youth activities usually focused on their individual desire to help the youth, not on official reeducative purposes, but as momentum emerged, the military government realized the reeducative value of GYA clubs, and starting in April 1946 created the official directives to guide the program.[105] It had not been part of official occupation planning to have the US Army play a role in shaping German youth activities. However, developments on the ground showed that many GIs, working on their own initiative, had taken on new roles in a manner that could impact youth, as teachers of democracy and as the embodiment of the American way of life.[106] Scheper, for example, noted that the Navy chief who had been very active early on in trying to form a youth movement in Bremerhaven was often a guest at his home along with other officers. This officer would often tell him, "Burchard, but you must learn democracy." Scheper was aware that this demand was the most important concern of the Americans at that time and was the main reason for the many activities aimed at youth.[107] Thus, personal contact between American military personnel and German children rose to the forefront of reeducation work.

Officials within the Bremen military government also served to encourage the development of GYA in Bremen: For example, the commander of the Bremen Port Command, Colonel Bion C. Welker, recommended a youth activities directive in March of 1946. In addition, Bremen youth activities personnel created multiple pamphlets as guides for units about GYA, including an April 1946 pamphlet called "The German Youth: An Orientation for Army Units."[108] An official campaign thus

103 See Rode, "Zwischen Re-education und Freizeitvergnügen," 114; Pedron, *Amerikaner vor Ort*, 276–277.
104 Scheper, ". . . *You Must Learn Democracy*", 74.
105 See Rode, "Zwischen Re-education und Freizeitvergnügen," 114.
106 See Rode, "Zwischen Re-education und Freizeitvergnügen," 19, 34–36.
107 Scheper, ". . . *You Must Learn Democracy*", 75.
108 The German Youth: An Orientation for Army Units; Folder YI. Policies and Directives . . . This Headquarters; Records of the Education Division: Gen Corresp & Rel Recs of Youth Activities

emerged in Bremen in early 1946, aiming at attracting soldiers to GYA work.[109] This helped contribute to the continuing expansion of GYA in the Enclave, and the formation of the Bremen Boys Club in August 1946 brought even more attention to the Bremen youth activities scene. By mid-1946, the Bremen Enclave had the most active and best youth program in the entire American zone. By early 1947, the word "Bremen" had come to mean GYA in the US zone.[110] Statistics show that youth activities programs were making an impact in Bremen. In April 1947, there were 58 GYA youth clubs in Bremen with around 1,900 members, sponsored by 40 Army members.[111] In May 1947, around 24% of Bremen's youth were in a youth organization, which included both organized German youth clubs and Army-sponsored GYA clubs; around one in 30 youths were GYA club members. GYA clubs included the Bremen Youth Club, Metropol, Atlantic, Astoria, Bremen Girls Club, Bremen Baseball Club, Mosquito, Swing Freunde, and more, but the Bremen Boys Club remained the most well-known GYA club in Bremen.[112] In De-

---

Branch, 1945–47; OMGBR; Box 311; OMGUS; RG 260; NACP. Pamphlet also available in Folder German Youth Program; Post-Occupation Correspondence and News Articles; Military Government in Bremen; Box 3; Bion C. Welker Papers; U.S. Army Heritage and Education Center (USAHEC), Carlisle, PA. Also, "Experiment Bremen," May 20, 1946, p. 4; Folder Y.A.-VI General Publicity; Records of the Education Division: Gen Corresp & Rel Recs of Youth Activities Branch, 1945–47; OMGBR; Box 313; OMGUS; NACP. Untitled article, *Bremen Port Commander*, March 15, 1946; same location as previous file.

109 See Rode, "Zwischen Re-education und Freizeitvergnügen," 33–35; Rode, "Manche nannten sie nur 'Schokoladenclubs,'" 24; Pedron, *Amerikaner vor Ort*, 277–278. See also Füssl, *Die Umerziehung*, 150.

110 Rode, "Zwischen Re-education und Freizeitvergnügen," 31; Rode "Manche nannten sie nur 'Schokoladenclubs,'" 23–24, 26.

111 "Diskussion um die deutsche Jugend: Konferenz der im Jugendhilfswerk tätigen Amerikaner," *Weser-Kurier*, April 12, 1947.

112 Rode, "Zwischen Re-education und Freizeitvergnügen," 42–43; Rode, "Manche nannten sie nur 'Schokoladenclubs': Die Jugendarbeit der US-Armee in der Besatzungszeit," 26, 31; Pedron, *Amerikaner vor Ort*, 279. See a list of Army-sponsored clubs in the Bremen Enclave: William H. Marthinsen, OMGBR Education Division, Subject: Utilization of Army Sponsored German Youth Clubs and Buildings, December 10, 1947; Folder Y.A. XII. Club buildings, A. General and other Property of German Youth Organizations in Bremen; Records of the Education Division: Gen Corresp & Rel Recs of Youth Activities Branch, 1945–47; OMGBR; Box 314; OMGUS; RG 260; NACP. See also Goedde, *GIs and Germans*, 151. Goedde argues that the Bremen Boy's Club's impact on the reeducation of 64,000 youth in Bremen was minimal, as it only reached a few hundred boys at most. However, in contrast, Rode argues that overall, organized youth activities in Bremen did reach a significant number of youths, and those members of Army-sponsored clubs were impacted by the club's offerings, even if the number of youths in Army-sponsored GYA clubs was limited to approximately every thirtieth child aged six to 18. Rode, "Zwischen Re-education und Freizeitvergnügen," 43.

cember 1947, Army-sponsored Christmas parties for German youth reached tens of thousands of youngsters in the Enclave, who received 60,000 gift bags, highlighting the extensive reach of Army youth work in Bremen.[113]

Throughout the entire US occupation zone, and shaped by early troop engagement in the Bremen Enclave, GYA emerged as a major shaper in the field of youth reeducation. In 1990, Lawrence E. Norrie was interviewed about his life experiences in diplomacy and foreign relations, including his work on the reorientation of German youth as the Chief of the OMGUS Group Activities Branch, Education, Culture, and Religious Affairs during the occupation. Norrie brought along previous work experience with youth as an employee of the YMCA, where he for example worked with youth street gangs in Honolulu. In the interview, he highlighted the importance of GYA, stating that the development of Army assistance to German youth led to a US zone-wide growth of organized youth groups, both German and Army-sponsored: "This was the beginning of the friendship between the military and the German youth organizations, and it grew like wildfire. In that little pamphlet I showed you yesterday, 'Youth Between Yesterday and Tomorrow,' you will find how fast they grew from 83,000 to a million and a half in two years, i.e., youth in democratically organized groups."[114] By mid-1947, over one million youth in the entire US zone were members of organized youth groups and hundreds of thousands of youths were participating in the Army-sponsored program. In addition, in September 1947, 134 full-time military personnel and 1,313 volunteer military personnel were participating in GYA, as well as 25 full-time civilians, 586 volunteer civilian personnel, and 935 German civilians.[115] Occupation youth activities thus had a widespread impact, affecting both youth experiences as well as the experiences of the members of the occupation forces.

The goals of the GYA program are clearly depicted in a troop orientation pamphlet created by the Bremen military government in March 1946 entitled "The German Youth-A Joint Responsibility," which was published in German and English and contained information about the British occupation laws, which the Enclave was currently following. For the most part, British and American occupation policies regarding youth activities were similar, aiming at a rejuvenation of

113 Pedron, 283; Peters, *Zwölf Jahre Bremen*, 104. See also Goedde, *GIs and Germans*, 148–150.
114 Interview of Lawrence Norrie, interview by G. Lewis Schmidt, January 18, 1990, Frontline Diplomacy: The Foreign Affairs Oral History Collection of the Association for Diplomatic Studies and Training, Manuscript Division, Library of Congress, https://www.loc.gov/item/mfdip bib000874. See *German Youth Between Yesterday and Tomorrow*, 1. The numbers of members of organized youth groups grew from less than 200,000 in April 1946 to over 1,200,000 members in March 1948.
115 *German Youth Between Yesterday and Tomorrow*, Statistics 5 & 7.

voluntary, democratically-minded cultural, religious, and recreational youth groups. The pamphlet stated that “the best way” to achieve German democracy “is through the youth,” with youth activities as the “training ground . . . in the principles of democratic living.” The pamphlet explained democratization politics as well as the various duties of the Army, military government, and German administration, and also included concrete suggestions for Army units for positive youth work. The pamphlet proved quite popular and received a positive reception from its audience, which included Army units and German youth leaders.[116] In a letter introducing the pamphlet, Youth Activities Officer Lt. David Brown wrote that it was to serve as “a general guide,” with the hope “that it will arouse in all of you a consciousness, a feeling of personal responsibility toward the German youth and an active desire to help them in their efforts to find a place for themselves as future citizens of Germany and of the world.”[117] Bremen’s military government continued to encourage youth activities through its campaign to “sell” the idea, and new pamphlets were published in February 1947 entitled “Questions and Answers on Army Assistance to German Youth Activities in the State of Bremen,” and “A Guide for Youth Activities—Discussion Groups” (in both German and English), both of which aimed at increasing personnel participation.[118]

Edward T. Ladd was also a central figure in the program in Bremen. He was chief of the youth and sports division of the Office of Military Government Bremen (OMGBR) from July 1946 to August 1948.[119] Ladd was an educator who had

116 The German Youth-A Joint Responsibility; Folder YI. Policies and Directives . . . This Headquarters; Records of the Education Division: Gen Corresp & Rel Recs of Youth Activities Branch, 1945–47; OMGBR; Box 311; OMGUS; RG 260; NACP. Also available in Folder German Youth Program; Post-Occupation Correspondence and News Articles; Military Government in Bremen; Box 3; Bion C. Welker Papers; USAHEC, Carlisle, PA. See also Rode, “Zwischen Re-education und Freizeitvergnügen,” 35–37; Pedron, *Amerikaner vor Ort*, 278.

117 David Brown, OMGBR Sports and Youth Activities, Subject: Youth Booklet, March 2, 1946, in Folder German Youth Program; Box 3; Bion C. Welker Papers; USAHEC, Carlisle, PA.

118 Questions and Answers on Army Assistance to German Youth Activities in the State of Bremen, February 14, 1947; Folder YI. Policies and Directives; Records of the Education Division; OMGBR; Box 311; OMGUS; RG 260; NACP. Discussion Groups: A Guide for Youth Activities Discussion Leaders, February 21, 1947; Folder YXXI Army Assistance Program; Records of the Education Division; OMGBR; Box 315; OMGUS; RG 260; NACP. See also Rode, “Zwischen Re-education und Freizeitvergnügen,” 38, 45.

119 Edward T. Ladd, Curriculum Vitae; Folder 13; Box 2; bMS 16029; Unitarian Service Committee; Administrative Records, 1946–1950; Harvard Divinity School Library, Harvard University, Cambridge, Mass.; online at https://iiif.lib.harvard.edu/manifests/view/drs:12724213$1i.

graduated from Harvard and Yale universities.[120] He was especially engaged with the youth clubs, and would assist clubs in their process of applying for approval from the military government, for example helping them write their constitutions. Official records indicate that once he missed an appointment because he was so busy talking to members of the Ann Fitzgerald Girls Club about what a constitution does.[121] At a meeting on the German youth program in November 1946, Ladd stated that it was important to encourage Germans "to start a healthy democratic youth movement which will help to make this country stay in the nations," and that it was up to Americans "to assist Germans in finding their way to real democracy."[122] Ladd's engagement thus played a role in impacting the Bremen youth activities scene.

However, Army Assistance to GYA was not without critique, including from within the military government. As mentioned previously, the division of responsibilities for youth activities between military government, Army units, and German administrative and youth workers led to competition, internal conflict, and confusion.[123] In addition, there were debates about the ability of GIs to be educators of democracy to youth in the GYA program, rather than experts such as youth specialists, highlighting the complexities of military participation in a "non-military mission."[124] Despite then Deputy Military Governor Lucius Clay's praise of the individual goodwill behind Army personnel active in GYA, he was not completely convinced about the program in the early stages of the occupation, as he wished to turn over control to Germans as the occupation progressed, including youth activities. He believed that Americans should thus be providing indirect rather than direct assistance.[125] Lieutenant General Keyes' 1945 Seventh Army

120 Obituary, "Prof. Edward Ladd," *New York Times*, January 26, 1973. Ladd was later a professor of education at Emory University and the first president of the Georgia American Civil Liberties Union (ACLU) chapter.

121 Handwritten note, "AFN Girls Club," October 15, 1947; Folder Ann Fitzgerald Girls Club; Records of the Education Division: Records Relating to German Youth and Sports Clubs, 1947–49; OMGBR; Box 320; OMGUS; RG 260; NACP.

122 German Youth Program, fourth meeting (November 6, 1946); Folder YIII Reports from Other Offices D. USFET and other Army Units; Rcs of Bremerhaven Liaison & Security Detachment: Records of Clubs & Youth Activities, 1947–49; OMGBR; Box 592; OMGUS; RG 260; NACP.

123 Pedron, *Amerikaner vor Ort*, 278; Füssl, *Die Umerziehung*, 148–154; Rode, "Zwischen Re-education und Freizeitvergnügen," 35–36.

124 *The U.S. Armed Forces German Youth Activities Program 1945–1955*, 10–11. See also "Experiment Bremen," *I & E Bulletin*, May 26, 1946, p. 4; Folder Y.A.-VI General Publicity; Records of the Education Division: Gen Corresp & Rel Recs of Youth Activities Branch, 1945–47; OMGBRE; Box 313; OMGUS; RG 260; NACP.

125 *The U.S. Armed Forces German Youth Activities Program 1945–1955*, 14–15; Füssl, *Die Umerziehung*, 151–154; Rode, "Zwischen Re-education und Freizeitvergnügen," 24. See "249. German

youth program had also been met with criticism from the Office of Military Government in Hesse (OMGH), which argued that Keyes' encouragement of Army engagement "ran counter to Military Government's policy of making the Germans responsible for organizing youth groups."[126] Worries about overworking the soldiers also emerged, as well as concerns about the redeployment of soldiers, since the clubs would be impacted by the departure of soldiers and their replacement with new recruits.[127] Additionally, not all military personnel were enthusiastic about being encouraged to interact with German youngsters, with criticism about having to take on a new role as a "scoutmaster" along with all of their other duties in the occupation.[128]

In Bremen, however, the occupation atmosphere was marked by increasing engagement in youth activities from both the military government and Army personnel. On August 17, 1946, Sergeant Patrick Moriarty and nine of his fellow GIs placed the ad about their new boys club in the *Weser-Kurier*.[129] The ad promised a club based on the boys' own interests, complete with supplies such as games, sporting equipment, movies, English classes (if the boys so desired), and boxing and gym teachers. According to the ad, they would even provide rides home to boys who lived far away from the club house. That's the way the "crazy Americans" are, stated the ad. The main principles of the club were to be freedom, inde-

---

Youth Program," August 12, 1947, From Clay Personal for Noce, CC 1239, in Smith, ed., *The Papers of General Lucius D. Clay*, vol. 1, 400–401: Clay noted that GYA was an addition to the German youth program and served the voluntary role of "good neighbor," rather than for "applied instruction in democracy." Clay thus focused on the role of GYA in assisting the development of a democratic German youth movement, rather than being the foundation of such a movement. However, later on in the occupation, Clay's role in directly aiding youth increased, and he believed that GYA played a central role in the occupation. The General Clay Fund for German Youth Activities, formed in 1948, became one of the most important aid programs for German youth, led by Catherine Shouse. This fund was the first private group ever allowed to assist an Army activity. See Letter Catherine Shouse to President Truman, October 11, 1949; Folder OF 198 1945–April 1950 [1 of 2] Germany; OF 198; Box 738; HSTP; HSTPL. For more on the General Clay Fund and Catherine Shouse, see Chapter 4.

126 *German Youth Activities of the United States Army*, 6; *The U.S. Armed Forces German Youth Activities Program 1945–1955*, 5.

127 "Experiment Bremen," *I & E Bulletin*, 4; Folder Y.A.-VI General Publicity; Records of the Education Division: Gen Corresp & Rel Recs of Youth Activities Branch, 1945–47; OMGBRE; Box 313; OMGUS; RG 260; NACP. Also, Pedron, *Amerikaner vor Ort*, 277; Rode, "Zwischen Re-education und Freizeitvergnügen," 34–35.

128 Frederic Sondern Jr., "GI Teachers for German Youth," in Congressional Record, April 3, 1947, Vol. 93, Part 3, 3118–3119.

129 Peters documents this date in his *Chronik* of important dates in postwar Bremen history: Peters, *Zwölf Jahre Bremen*, 62.

pendence, and generosity. There were no membership fees, and any boy between ten and 17 was able to apply by writing a letter with his name, birthday, and the profession of his father to the military government (MG) headquarters at the Haus des Reichs in Bremen.[130]

According to a *Weser-Kurier* article from August 24, 1946, Moriarty had already founded youth clubs in the United States.[131] Additionally, some of his ancestors from his mother's side had been from the Bremen area, and thus he had linkages to the region and the German language and culture (although most reports noted his "Irish" background, marked by his red hair).[132] Again, Moriarty and his fellow GI founders received thousands of responses to their ad; the *Time* article spoke of children climbing through windows trying to join the club.[133] The selection process seemed to have been a collaborative effort between the GIs and three pupils of the *Oberschule* (secondary school) in the Schwachhausen neighborhood of Bremen, Martin Girschner Jr., who would be elected the first club president, Hans-Robert Spiecker, and Günther Holst.[134] Members were apparently chosen based on answers to a questionnaire, and traits such as intelligence and openness were important. Moreover, selections were made without regard to Hitler Youth roles or the Nazi activities of their parents; they aimed to choose youth from all backgrounds to have a cross-section of youth as members.[135] However, some reports indicated that most members were middle class, although President Girschner wrote in a 1947 article in the club newspaper that the members came from all backgrounds.[136] Girschner Jr., Spiecker, and Holst had all learned English

130 "Jungens!," *Weser-Kurier*, August 17, 1946.

131 "'Boys-Club' in Bremen," *Weser-Kurier*, August 24, 1946.

132 Pedron, *Amerikaner vor Ort*, 288. It is uncertain whether Moriarty could speak German. A letter from the Secretary of War Robert P. Patterson mentions that Moriarty wrote the War Department requesting German language books that could be of help for his club; he also stated that one of his assistants was a former POW who had been through War Department reeducation courses. Letter from Robert P. Patterson, Secretary of War, to Barrett Herrick, October 16, 1946; Folder AG 353.81 Welfare Activities 1-1-46 to 12-31-48; Army-AG Decimal File 1946–48 353.81 to 354.1; Box 1238; Records of the Adjutant General's Office, RG 407; NACP.

133 "The Nations: Democracy at Work," *Time*.

134 "The Nations: Democracy at Work"; Rode, "Zwischen Re-education und Freizeitvergnügen," 57–59. In contrast, *Life* magazine spoke of members being chosen by pulling names out of a hat. "Bremen Boys Club: U.S. Sergeant Finances a Lesson in Democracy," *Life*, 37.

135 "The Nations: Democracy at Work"; Sondern Jr., "GI Teachers for German Children," in Congressional Record, April 3, 1947, Vol. 93, Part 3, 3118–3119; Rode, "Zwischen Re-education und Freizeitvergnügen," 58.

136 "Bremen Boys Club: U.S. Sergeant Finances a Lesson in Democracy," 36; Martin Girschner Jr., "Ziele des Bremen Boys Club"; Folder Bremen Boys Club; Records Relating to German Youth and Sports Clubs, 1947–49; OMGBR; Box 316; OMGUS; RG 260; NACP.

and had a teacher who taught them a neutral worldview.[137] Girschner Jr., age 16, was the son of a Bremen lawyer and was talented in public speaking. He was also working as a translator for a military government office.[138] Moriarty and his fellow GIs' roles were to be sponsors and counselors of the BBC, while the boys would learn to run the club themselves. Moriarty stated that "the club's purpose . . . was simply to teach democratic ways of life."[139] The BBC was started without any concrete pedagogical goals in place but rather had the general goal of hands-on lessons in democracy.[140] This approach fit with the growing occupation development that focused on German youth as an audience for occupation aims, linking benevolent aid to children to German rehabilitation toward a democratic future.[141] Boys joined the club for various reasons. A report by a visitor to the club in April 1947 states that the visitor asked the boys why they joined. One boy told the visitor his reason for joining was an interest in developing his accordion-playing skills, another mentioned he planned to emigrate from Germany, and another stated that he had moved to Bremen from the Russian zone of occupation and did not have any friends when he arrived.[142]

Moriarty and his new boys club skyrocketed to fame, with articles about him and the club appearing in American media including *Time*, *Life*, and *Reader's Digest*, as well as being mentioned in the US House of Representatives on April 3, 1947.[143] The club also led to a further increase in other youth clubs. For example,

---

137 Interview of Hans-Robert Spiecker, interview by Lutz Rode, Bremen, May 13, 2002, interview quoted in Rode, "Zwischen Re-education und Freizeitvergnügen," 58.

138 Ernie Reed, "Experiment in Bremen," *Stars and Stripes*, January 19, 1947; Folder Bremen Boys Club; Records Relating to German Youth and Sports Clubs, 1947–49; OMGBR; Box 316; OMGUS; RG 260; NACP. Confidential ICD Intelligence Source, "Besuch beim Bremen Boys Club," April 1, 1947; same location as previous record. See also Rode, "Zwischen Re-education und Freizeitvergnügen," 57–59, 70.

139 "Bremen Boys Club: U.S. Sergeant Finances a Lesson in Democracy," *Life*, 37.

140 See Manfred H. Burschka, "Re-Education und Jugendöffentlichkeit: Orientierung und Selbstverständnis Deutscher Nachkriegsjugend in der Jugendpresse 1945–1948: ein Beitrag zur politischen Kultur der Nachkriegszeit" (PhD diss., Georg-August-Universität Göttingen, 1987), 21.

141 See Goedde, *GIs and Germans*, 127–130, 151.

142 Confidential ICD Intelligence Source, "Besuch beim Bremen Boys Club," April 1, 1947; Folder Bremen Boys Club; Records Relating to German Youth and Sports Clubs, 1947–49; OMGBR; Box 316; OMGUS; RG 260; NACP.

143 Sondern Jr., "GI Teachers for German Children," in Congressional Record, April 3, 1947, Vol. 93, Part 3, 3118–3119. Representative Robert Twyman of Illinois included the article from the April 1947 issue of *Reader's Digest*, and stated: "I want to commend Gen. Joseph T. McNarney for a forward step. The best way to combat communism, racial prejudice, and other substitutes for true Americanism is through education. I am seriously considering making an extended speech suggesting that an educational program should accompany any assistance which we give

right after the founding of the BBC, an article in the *Weser-Kurier* from September 7, 1946 noted that a new "Baseball-Club Bremen 1946" had been founded and that the head of the Bremen Boys Club had given his word of support.[144] The Bremen military government even helped sponsor press coverage about the club in the US media. The *Time* article from October 7, 1946 and the *Life* magazine article from December 9, 1946 served to increase awareness of the club even more.[145] Thus, Moriarty and the BBC had emerged as the model GYA group, with the potential to impact the entire GYA program in the US zone.[146]

Moriarty, who had served in the South Pacific during the war and had lost a younger brother who was in the Air Force during the war, stated his reasons for taking initiative and founding the club in the article in *Time* magazine:

> I saw kids in the streets picking up cigaret [sic] butts and begging. They all looked hungry, backward, scared. You know, they got an awfully dirty deal in this war; never had anything to look forward to. Me, I lost a redheaded kid brother, and I looked at these kids and at our job over here, and, by God, I don't ever want to think he died in vain. So I decided to do something.[147]

An article in the *Stars and Stripes* from January 19, 1947 highlighted that Moriarty "saw children running wild," who "looked frightened, hungry," and that "he wanted to do something about it."[148] Furthermore, Moriarty did not believe that collective guilt applied to German youngsters: "I don't want these kids to feel that the sins of their fathers are being visited on them."[149] According to the articles in the press, in the club, Moriarty aimed at "no politics except boys' politics," with

---

in connection with loans, military assistance, or any other aid. Unless we establish some such policy, communism will move in when we move out." See also Rode, "Zwischen Re-education und Freizeitvergnügen," 41–42, 68–69, 71; Pedron, *Amerikaner vor Ort*, 289.

144 "Bremer Jugend will Baseball spielen," *Weser-Kurier*, September 7, 1946.

145 Rode, "Zwischen Re-education und Freizeitvergnügen," 41–42, 68–69. Also, Reinald Ihler (Founder of Astoria GYA Club in 1949, participated in BBC events), interview by Peter Strotmann, Bremen, September 24, 2015.

146 Rode, "Manche nannten sie nur 'Schokoladenclubs,'" 26; Rode, "Zwischen Re-education und Freizeitvergnügen," 42, 71.

147 "The Nations: Democracy at Work," *Time*. On Moriarty's wartime service, see Official Military Personnel File of Patrick Joseph Moriarty, 36707703; Official Military Personnel Files; Records of the Army Staff, RG 319; National Archives and Records Administration, National Archives at St. Louis, Missouri (NASL). According to his November 20, 1945 discharge papers, he had served during the war in Guam. After the war, he reenlisted, serving in Germany until November 1948.

148 Reed, "Experiment in Bremen"; Folder Bremen Boys Club; Records Relating to German Youth and Sports Clubs, 1947–49; OMGBR; Box 316; OMGUS; RG 260; NACP.

149 "The Nations: Democracy at Work," *Time*.

"no racial discrimination" and "no racial discussion" and "no talk of concentration camps," as "several club members are Jewish."[150] The focus was on teaching "the independent, democratic way of life based on the Four Freedoms."[151] Good conduct of the members was required, with delinquent behaviors such as begging, cigarette butt picking, the "practice of grab-and-run" (theft), and "taking food out of the club" forbidden.[152] Club members were thus to learn hands-on about democracy, while also learning proper behavior.

Although Moriarty's official Army position was as a sergeant in the 104th Labor Supervision Center, which included work with displaced persons, such as former forced laborers, his work with the club was focused solely on helping Germans.[153] By 1946, US occupation aid tended to focus exclusively on assisting Germans, which was in contrast to the first year of occupation when aid from GIs often focused on young displaced persons, such as Christmas parties and donations of gifts in 1945 for DP children. However, displaced persons children were not completely forgotten and Christmas parties continued to help both German and DP children.[154] GIs from the beginning volunteered their time and contributed with their own resources: Much of the aid for German children, such as materials needed for the BBC, came out of the pockets of the GIs themselves.[155] A quarterly report of operations of the 104th Labor

150 "The Nations: Democracy at Work"; Reed, "Experiment in Bremen"; Folder Bremen Boys Club; Records Relating to German Youth and Sports Clubs, 1947–49; OMGBR; Box 316; OMGUS; RG 260; NACP. "Bremen Boys Club: U.S. Sergeant Finances a Lesson in Democracy," *Life*, 37.

151 Reed, "Experiment in Bremen"; Folder Bremen Boys Club; Records Relating to German Youth and Sports Clubs, 1947–49; OMGBR; Box 316; OMGUS; RG 260; NACP.

152 Reed, "Experiment in Bremen"; "The Nations: Democracy at Work," *Time*; "Bremen Boys Club: U.S. Sergeant Finances a Lesson in Democracy," *Life*, 36.

153 For example, former Polish forced laborers or prisoners of war were often used as guards of camps of German POWs. See records on the 104th Labor Supervision Center: Folder LACT-104 Rpt of Operations Jul–Dec 46; Army Command Reports 1949–54; Box 4703; RG 407; NACP. See also Rode, "Zwischen Re-education und Freizeitvergnügen," 39–40, footnote 144.

154 Goedde, *GIs and Germans*, 150. See also Dana Adams Schmidt, "German Children to Have a Big Yule," *New York Times*, December 16, 1946. Goedde argues that DP children were often forgotten by 1946. However, in 1946, according to an official report, DP children "were not forgotten" in Christmas celebrations, with each DP child receiving toys and special goods from Army stocks. A total of 47,786 DP children came to Christmas parties throughout the US zone (out of a total of 84,500 DP children). 794,023 German children participated in the parties. There is no mention in the sources of the fact that some of the displaced persons were Jewish and did not celebrate Christmas. In *The U.S. Armed Forces German Youth Activities Program 1945–1946*, 25. In 1947, Army-sponsored Christmas parties served 1,050,000 German children and 68,700 DP youth: Geis and Gray Jr., *The Relations of Occupation Personnel*, 53.

155 "The Nations: Democracy at Work," *Time*.

Supervision Center from October 20, 1946 noted that Moriarty's engagement in GYA was producing high morale in the entire unit. According to the report,

> Evidence of the high morale existing in this command is the formation and supervision of the "Bremen Boys Club" . . . Each man devotes a large part of his off-duty hours to the club and under the leadership of the Sgt. Major of Headquarters it has become probably the outstanding German Youth activity in the American zone. Full cooperation and encouragement is given by this command to all its activities.[156]

Thus, through engagement in GYA, such as the engagement of Moriarty and his fellow GIs, American occupation soldiers increasingly saw themselves as providers rather than as occupiers of Germany.[157] This shift was wide-reaching, impacting both personal experiences and political transatlantic relations during the occupation and beyond. Reporter Ernie Reed noted the early success of the club in his *Stars and Stripes* article from January 1947: "The German kids are learning democracy and liking it."[158] The December 1946 article in *Life* also noted that Moriarty admitted "that many of his boys came at first because of the food and the warmth, [but] they come now, he believes, because they are learning to like these strange new democratic ways."[159] Reports praised Moriarty for taking action based on his own individual initiative: One article noted that the best campaign so far "to affect the German mind" had been launched by a regular GI, not by experts such as psychologists or teachers.[160]

Activities in the Bremen Boys Club included sports, music, dances, theater, a photography group, discussions, excursions, hikes, carpentry, vacations on Juist Island, and even a big band.[161] At its peak in October 1947, the club had 370 members.[162]

156 James N. Luton, Quarterly Report of Operations (July, Aug and Sept); Folder LACT-104 Rpt of Operations Jul-Dec 46; Army Command Reports 1949–54; Box 4703; RG 407; NACP.

157 See Goedde, *GIs and Germans*, 149, 164.

158 Reed, "Experiment in Bremen"; Folder Bremen Boys Club; Records Relating to German Youth and Sports Clubs, 1947–49; OMGBR; Box 316; OMGUS; RG 260; NACP.

159 "Bremen Boys Club: U.S. Sergeant Finances a Lesson in Democracy," *Life*, 37.

160 Sondern Jr., "GI Teachers for German Children," in Congressional Record, April 3, 1947, Vol. 93, Part 3, 3118–3119.

161 Girschner Jr., "Ziele des Bremen Boys Club," *Die Brücke*, April 23, 1947, p. 2; Folder Bremen Boys Club; Records Relating to German Youth and Sports Clubs, 1947–49; OMGBR; Box 316; OMGUS; RG 260; NACP. Also, Pedron, *Amerikaner vor Ort*, 279–280; Rode, "Zwischen Re-education und Freizeitvergnügen," 40–41, 60–61; Peter Groth, "Bremer Jungs im Jahre Sechsundvierzig," in *Vom Trümmerkind zum Teenager: Kindheit und Jugend in der Nachkriegszeit*, ed. Doris Foitzik (Edition Temmen, 1992), 26; Christian Markwort, "Wo Hitlerjungen zu Demokraten wurden," *Weser-Kurier*, November 5, 2015.

162 Monthly Report, November 1, 1947; Folder Bremen Boys Club; Records Relating to German Youth and Sports Clubs, 1947–49; OMGBR; Box 316; OMGUS; RG 260; NACP.

Thus, boys in the club gained positive experiences and had the ability to choose free time activities. It provided boys with a respite from the misery and hardships of private life in postwar German society, with crowded, cold dwellings and little food.[163] The aim of the club was to create cosmopolitan citizens of the world, as Martin Girschner Jr. wrote in an article about the club's goals.[164] The club even aimed at creating opportunities for global exchange, for example through pen pal programs including with American children; there also was an interest in the world language Esperanto.[165] Additionally, the club held a dance every three weeks to which girls were invited.[166]

Besides taking part in such free time activities, club members also began to take over the running of the club, learning how to elect officers in a secret ballot under the guidance of Moriarty and the other GI sponsors. For the youth, this was the first time voting in their lives.[167] Martin Girschner Jr. was elected as the first president of the club. Club members also created a constitution.[168] Additionally, the club formed committees, including a social welfare committee, which helped needy boys and the wider community.[169] The club was active in charity work: In October 1947, members donated about $61 raised from a GYA benefit performance to the "Stop the Polio" drive in Berlin. The club voted unanimously to send the money to the polio fund, rather than using it for buying shoe leather for repairing their own shoes. Military government officials including Lawrence

---

163 Bruss, ed., *Mit Zuckersack und Heißgetränk*, 192–194; Rode, "Manche nannten sie nur 'Schokoladenclubs,'" 35.

164 Girschner Jr., "Ziele des Bremen Boys Club," *Die Brücke*, April 23, 1947, p. 1; Folder Bremen Boys Club; Records Relating to German Youth and Sports Clubs, 1947–49; OMGBR; Box 316; OMGUS; RG 260; NACP. See also Constitution, Bremen Boys Club; same location as previous record.

165 Gerald C. Fisher, Report of German Youth Activities, December 15, 1947; Folder Bremen Boys Club; Records of the Education Division: Records Relating to German Youth and Sports Clubs, 1947–49; OMGBR; Box 316; OMGUS; NACP. Rode, "Zwischen Re-education und Freizeitvergnügen," 68.

166 "Bremen Boys Club: U.S. Sergeant Finances a Lesson in Democracy," *Life*, 37; Markwort, "Wo Hitlerjungen zu Demokraten wurden," *Weser-Kurier*, November 5, 2015.

167 See a photo of the election in the *Life* article, "Bremen Boys Club: U.S. Sergeant Finances a Lesson in Democracy," 37. According to the article, "Some of them had a difficult time understanding that they did not have to sign their ballots." The election also had a poll watcher. See also Rode, "Zwischen Re-education und Freizeitvergnügen," 59–60.

168 Girschner Jr., "Ziele des Bremen Boys Club," *Die Brücke*, April 23, 1947, p. 1; Folder Bremen Boys Club; Records Relating to German Youth and Sports Clubs, 1947–49; OMGBR; Box 316; OMGUS; RG 260; NACP. Also, Constitution, Bremen Boys Club, same location as previous record.

169 Reed, "Experiment in Bremen"; Folder Bremen Boys Club; Records Relating to German Youth and Sports Clubs, 1947–49; OMGBR; Box 316; OMGUS; RG 260; NACP. Groth, "Bremer Jungs im Jahre Sechsundvierzig," in *Vom Trümmerkind zum Teenager*, ed. Foitzik, 26–27.

E. Norrie, Chief of Adult and Youth Activities section, commended the efforts of the club; Norrie wrote that their contribution is "evidence of a spirit of self-sacrifice, of thoughtfulness and concern for others."[170] Additionally, in February 1947, the American ship SS William S Cody arrived in Bremen with a large donation of food, which the club members distributed to the neediest in the Bremen population.[171] The ship's captain had seen the *Life* article about the Bremen Boys Club and collected donations from the San Francisco community, which he loaded on his ship to bring to Bremen's needy families via the boys club. The parcels were to have the sticker on them, "From a friend in U.S., distributed by Bremen Boys Club—People of U.S. do care!"[172] Thus, the Bremen Boys embodied a model of a new type of postwar youth: An active, democratic youth who focused on the greater good over personal interests and needs. Delinquent behaviors such as cigarette butt picking and begging, as well as subservience to higher-ups, were not allowed, as seen in BBC election campaign posters which had satirizing caricatures of "the Rider," who "bows with servility to his superior and kicks his subordinate," and "lazy Hans, who begs, picks up cigarette butts on the street, and steals food scraps."[173] Morality and decency were some of the club's main tenets.[174] Additionally, the club had a court run by the youths themselves, which would hold a trial of those who did not follow the membership rules. For example, the court ruled to expel a boy who had stolen a crust of bread from another member, highlighting the seriousness with which the youth took the club rules and how much they aimed to embody a new type of youth who was neither delinquent

---

170 See L.E. Norrie, Donation by Army Sponsored German Youth Activities Club, October 14, 1947; Harold H. Crabill, Donation by Army Sponsored German Youth Activities Club, October 2, 1947; Dr. Eugene E. Schwarz, Donation for Victims of Poliomyelitis, October 22, 1947; "GYA Gives for Polio," *The Port Reporter*, October 10, 1947; all in Folder Bremen Boys Club; Records Relating to German Youth and Sports Clubs, 1947–49; OMGBR; Box 316; OMGUS; RG 260; NACP.

171 Weekly report: Youth and Sports Branch, Bremen, March 6, 1947; Folder Reports Land YA Section 1947; Records RE the Work of the Youth Activities Section Folder Reports Land YA Section 1947; Records of the Community Education Branch; Records of the Education and Cultural Relations Division; Box 143; OMGUS; RG 260; NACP.

172 "Bremen Boys Club Receives Needy Gifts of Food, Clothes, From U.S. Seamen," *Port Reporter*, February 28, 1947; Val Bowman, "Bremen Needy to Get Relief From 'Frisco," February 28, 1947; both in Folder Bremen Boys Club; Records Relating to German Youth and Sports Clubs, 1947–49; OMGBR; Box 316; OMGUS; RG 260; NACP. Captain Paul E. Cole was also named an *Ehrenmitglied* (honorary member) of the Bremen Boys Club: see "Capt. Cole Ehrenmitglied des 'Bremen Boys Club,'" *Weser-Kurier*, March 8, 1947; same location as previous.

173 Sondern Jr., "GI Teachers for German Children," in Congressional Record, April 3, 1947, Vol. 93, Part 3, 3118–3119; "Bremen Boys Club: U.S. Sergeant Finances a Lesson in Democracy," *Life*, 37.

174 Groth, "Bremer Jungs im Jahre Sechsundvierzig," in *Vom Trümmerkind zum Teenager*, ed. Foitzik, 26.

nor subservient as the Hitler Youth had been taught to be.[175] An article in the US troop information *I & E Bulletin* included a photo of Girschner giving a speech and noted, "this German boy, president of the Bremen Boys' Club, typifies those being aided by German Youth Program," highlighting the BBC members' new role as the archetype of the future democratic German youth.[176]

Additionally, the club encouraged German parents to be active through parents' evenings and an advisory board, which included German mothers, German fathers, and American dependents, as well as the wife of an American Vice-Consul.[177] This also provided a contrast to the Hitler Youth and *Bund Deutscher Mädel*, which did not operate with parental consent and encouraged separation of youth from family life.[178] Encouraging parental involvement also aimed to help reduce German criticism of the American-run clubs; the BBC was often the target of criticism due to its fame.[179] GYA clubs such as the BBC received criticism from members of the German public that the only purpose of the clubs was to Americanize its members through material handouts such as chocolate and Coca-Cola.[180] Members of non-GYA German youth clubs even argued that the BBC club was a club for "chocolate servitude," and Bremen Senator Hermann Wolters described GYA clubs as "chocolate clubs."[181] In 1947, mistrust about American-sponsored clubs was widespread among the Bremen popula-

175 Reed, "Experiment in Bremen"; Folder Bremen Boys Club; Records Relating to German Youth and Sports Clubs, 1947–49; OMGBR; Box 316; OMGUS; RG 260; NACP. See also Rode, "Zwischen Re-education und Freizeitvergnügen," 61.

176 "German Youth," *I & E Bulletin* 2, No. 7, February 16, 1947, 8; Folder Y.A.-VI General Publicity; Records of the Education Division: Gen Corresp & Rel Recs of Youth Activities Branch, 1945–47; OMGBR; Box 313; OMGUS; RG 260; NACP.

177 Girschner Jr., "Ziele des Bremen Boys Club," *Die Brücke*, April 23, 1947, p. 2; Folder Bremen Boys Club; Records Relating to German Youth and Sports Clubs, 1947–49; OMGBR; Box 316; OMGUS; RG 260; NACP. See also Rode, "Zwischen Re-education und Freizeitvergnügen," 65.

178 Reed, "Experiment in Bremen"; Folder Bremen Boys Club; Records Relating to German Youth and Sports Clubs, 1947–49; OMGBR; Box 316; OMGUS; RG 260; NACP.

179 Pedron, *Amerikaner vor Ort*, 289–290; Rode, "Zwischen Re-education und Freizeitvergnügen," 48–49.

180 Pedron, 285–286; Markwort, "Wo Hitlerjungen zu Demokraten wurden," *Weser-Kurier*, November 5, 2015.

181 Bremen Area Intelligence Office, Monthly Political Summary No. 1, Copy No. 33, March 1947, p. 11; Records of the Executive Office: Security-Classified General Records, 1945–49; OMGBR; Box 23; OMGUS; RG 260; NACP. OMGBR, Civil Government Division, Youth Activities Branch, "Historical Report, January-March 1947," p. 5–6; Folder Historical Reports from Laender, 1946–48; Records RE the Work of the Youth Activities Section; Records of the Education and Cultural Relations Division: Records of the Community Education Branch; OMGUS; Box 146; RG 260; NACP. See also Rode, "Manche nannten sie nur 'Schokoladenclubs,'" 33; Rode, "Zwischen Re-education und Freizeitvergnügen," 48; Pedron, 285.

tion, and resentment due to the requisition of properties for GYA club house purposes served to further the negative image.[182] The BBC's club home was a stately residential property at Slevogtstrasse 17 in the Bremen city district of Schwachhausen. The owner of a nearby property that had been requisitioned for the GYA Bremen Girls Club, at Händelstrasse 7, requested the home back in 1947, but the request was denied, as the Army would have had to requisition another property for the club anyway if they gave up the original one.[183]

In addition, societal fears abounded about conditions in GYA clubs, with youth members supposedly beyond the control of German society, listening to "*Negermusik*" (such as jazz), dancing behind closed doors with girls, building close relationships with GIs, and drinking Coca-Cola. Among older Bremen residents, there were rumors of clubs as a "*Sündenbabel*," a den of vice, notes Peter Groth.[184] BBC club president Girschner even received negative press claiming that he had only joined the club for personal material gain. A US newspaper apparently characterized him and his looks and clothes as clearly a Hitler Youth type, a criticism to which he responded in the club's own newspaper, *Die Brücke*. Girschner wrote that he had bought his clothes from a US shop through his employment as a translator but that the journalist who wrote the article in question had the right to exercise free speech and criticize him.[185] Additionally, other club members responded to critiques of Americanization, with one member writing an article in *Die Brücke* entitled, "*Warum ich mir die Amerikaniseriung gefallen lasse*" ("Why I Let Americanization Happen to Me"). This member, who had been a member of the Hitler Youth and was initially skeptical about the BBC and Americans until a friend persuaded him to join the club, wrote that the turning point for him was the opportunity to exchange letters with American youth. He also

---

182 Rode, "Zwischen Re-education und Freizeitvergnügen," 25, 47–48; Pedron, 287. Critics argued that instead of taking over homes for small groups of children in the youth clubs, they could focus instead on using the Army's resources on efforts to reach a greater number of children.

183 William H. Marthinsen, OMGBR Education Division, Subject: Utilization of Army Sponsored German Youth Clubs and Buildings, December 10, 1947; Folder Y.A. XII. Club buildings, A. General and other Property of German Youth Organizations in Bremen; Records of the Education Division: Gen Corresp & Rel Recs of Youth Activities Branch, 1945–47; OMGBR; Box 314; OMGUS; RG 260; NACP.

184 Groth, "Bremer Jungs im Jahre Sechsundvierzig," in *Vom Trümmerkind zum Teenager*, ed. Foitzik, 26. See also Rode, "Manche nannten sie nur 'Schokoladenclubs,'" 29, 31–33. The Club House Meierei in the Bürgerpark was rumored to be a party house with alcohol drinking. It was the home to six clubs. Groth, 26.

185 Girschner Jr., "Und was meint die Redaktion dazu?" *Die Brücke* Nr. 13, January 15, 1947, 5–6; Folder Bremen Boys Club; Records Relating to German Youth and Sports Clubs, 1947–49; OMGBR; Box 316; OMGUS; RG 260; NACP. See also, Rode, "Zwischen Re-education und Freizeitvergnügen," 70.

praised the Americans' willingness to help and their idealism.[186] Another article written in the club newspaper to the club's opponents stated that the club did not pose any dangers to the "Germanness" of its members, as critics had claimed.[187] Many of the members did indeed show great interest in material goods such as Coca-Cola and candy (especially before the currency reform in 1948), and these benefits were readily supplied to them, yet the reality of the exchange occurring in the clubs was more complicated.[188] In the atmosphere of the occupation and within youth clubs, youth adapted American ideas and culture to their own needs and environments.[189] As one member stated decades later in 1998, the Americans showed the club members a way to live democratically; however, he said that the members remained at heart German youths.[190] The official aim of GYA clubs was not necessarily about Americanization but rather to serve reeducation goals of impacting young Germans' social behavior and to encourage youth to take on new democratic roles, as became exemplified by the BBC.[191]

The Bremen Boys Club also made a transatlantic impact: Media about the club in the American press increased American benevolent actions aimed toward Germans, for example the donations of food from San Francisco. In addition, Patrick Moriarty's parents in Minnesota were also active in encouraging aid for German youth. His father Joseph J. Moriarty was a judge of the Eighth Judicial District of Minnesota. He contacted politicians including President Truman regarding sending humanitarian aid for youth clubs. Joseph Moriarty also had the cooperation of Minnesota Representative Joseph P. O'Hara. In March 1947, Judge Moriarty wrote to President Truman noting the importance of friendship between American and German youth, stating that German children needed aid packages including clothing. He described his plan to have American schoolchildren collect items

186 "Warum ich mir die Amerikanisierung gefallen lasse," *Die Brücke* Nr. 18, April 8, 1947; Folder Bremen Boys Club; Records Relating to German Youth and Sports Clubs, 1947–49; OMGBR; Box 316; OMGUS; RG 260; NACP. See also Rode, "Manche nannten sie nur 'Schokoladenclubs,'" 30; Rode, "Zwischen Re-education und Freizeitvergnügen," 90, 95–96.

187 Pedron, *Amerikaner vor Ort*, 286; Rode, "Zwischen Re-education und Freizeitvergnügen," 95.

188 Pedron, 280, 286.

189 Leder, "Americans and German Youth," 724–725. Also, Kaspar Maase, *BRAVO Amerika: Erkundungen zur Jugendkultur der Bundesrepublik in den fünfziger Jahren* (Hamburg: Junius, 1992), 13–14.

190 Birgit Köhler, "Deutsche Jungs: Treffen des Bremen Boys Club nach 52 Jahren: Chewing-gum und Demokratie-Training," *Taz die Tageszeitung*, January 26, 1998.

191 Burschka, "Re-Education und Jugendöffentlichkeit," 22–23. There were apparently rumors that the CIC was behind the club. However, as Peter Groth argues, this narrative did not play a role in the everyday life of the club: Groth, "Bremer Jungs im Jahre Sechsundvierzig," in *Vom Trümmerkind zum Teenager*, ed. Foitzik, 25–26.

and send the aid packages to young Germans, and asked the president whether they could be shipped free of charge through the Army.[192] In April 1947, Joseph Moriarty received a response from the president's secretary denying his request for free transportation of relief packages for distribution to German youth: Despite the "merit of the boys' clubs," the Army was "not in a position to assume additional shipping responsibilities at this time."[193] Patrick Moriarty's mother also was active in spreading the story of the Bremen Boys Club in the local press: She put a story in the local paper of Shakopee, Minnesota encouraging shipping gift parcels for the members of the BBC for Christmas in 1946. The story was picked up by news agencies and spread across the country, and "from all over the U.S. [Patrick] Moriarty got 35,000 letters asking for the boys' addresses," according to the October 1946 *Time* article.[194] Additionally, Jordan High School in Jordan, Minnesota sent aid to Bremen in December 1946 due to the work of the Moriarty family: Pupils of the school apparently founded a "US Club Bremen" based on the example of the BBC, with the goal of raising clothing donations to send for Bremen's youth.[195] In a pamphlet about the school's aid, Judge Joseph Moriarty praised the dignity and goodwill of the school pupils, and wrote that "hate, jealousy, spite and revenge never did and never will find refuge in the heart of a true American." He also wrote that the "gallant" pupils of Jordan High School were sending Bremen youth "needed articles of clothing and letters of hope and good cheer as a token of their zeal for a solution of the mutual problems of their day and generation."[196] This early engagement of the Moriarty family later became commonplace as regular American citizens increasingly aided Germany through shipments of goods such as CARE packages.[197] In addition, humanitarian aid to Germans became a central part of American foreign policy during the Berlin Airlift and through the Marshall Plan.

In addition, press reports about the BBC reached the highest levels of American society. In October 1946, Barrett Herrick of Herrick, Waddell & Co., Inc. wrote

192 Letter from Joseph J. Moriarty to President Harry Truman, March 12, 1947; Folder OF 198 Misc. 1947 [1 of 2]; OF 198; Box 738; HSTP; HSTPL.

193 Letter to Joseph J. Moriarty from Matthew J. Connelly, Secretary to the President, April 3, 1947; Folder OF 198 Misc. 1947 [1 of 2]; OF 198; Box 738; HSTP; HSTPL.

194 "The Nations: Democracy at Work," *Time*. Also, Percy Knauth, Bremen Press Camp release, September 26, 1946; Folder YXXI Army Assistance Program A. Bremerhaven Military Community 1947 (formerly Grohn Military Community); Records of the Education Division: Gen Corresp & Rel Recs of Youth Activities Branch, 1945–47; OMGBR; Box 315; OMGUS; RG 260; NACP.

195 Rode, "Zwischen Re-education und Freizeitvergnügen," 69.

196 "Children of America are Sending Clothing to Children in War-Torn Lands: Jordan Sends Aid to Bremen"; Folder OF 198 Misc. 1947 [1 of 2]; OF 198; Box 738; HSTP; HSTPL.

197 See Klose, *Why They Gave*.

to his Phi Delta Theta fraternity brother, the Secretary of War Robert P. Patterson, about reading the article in *Time* magazine on the Bremen Boys Club. Herrick commended Patrick Moriarty for being an "ingenious and sincerely patriotic soldier." Herrick desired to have his American Legion Post get busy helping support boys clubs like Moriarty's that taught youth "something of the way of a Republican form of Government [sic]." Herrick, who had served as an officer in World War I, mentioned that one of his company's partners had a son who had been killed during World War II, and he also mentioned "brother officers of mine in World War I" who did not make it through the Second World War. Thus, Herrick connected with Moriarty's experience of losing a loved one in war, and commended the role of Moriarty's initiatives in cutting "down the risk of still further war."[198] Herrick's letter shows that Moriarty was seen as a patriotic figure taking practical action and participating in needed assistance to the youngest of the German population. The stakes of such a venture were high: It could help determine the future of war versus peace. Thus, Germans were no longer seen as enemies but as victims to be assisted and taught democratic values through actions such as GYA clubs. The Bremen Boys Club played a major role in this shift through Moriarty's concrete action in aiding youth. The club members themselves also helped shape a new model of democratic German youth.

Overall, however, the goal of GYA clubs such as the BBC was to teach Germans how to help themselves, as American material benevolence would not be indefinite. Patrick Moriarty highlighted his goal of teaching Germans to run the democratic club themselves: "When we leave here, we want these kids to be able to go on running the club on their own. So we keep out of things and leave it to them."[199] Besides elections, the club also held discussion groups, which were seen as particularly important for teaching democracy. One topic of a "Round Table Conference" in the boys club was on "What Can German Youth Do Toward World Peace," with the speaker Prince Hubertus zu Loewenstein, who was an early opponent of Hitler. At this round table discussion, the boys were able to direct questions toward the guest speaker, who would serve as discussion leader.[200] How-

198 Letter from Barrett Herrick to Robert P. Patterson, Secretary of War, October 4, 1946; Folder AG 353.81 Welfare Activities 1-1-46 to 12-31-48; Army-AG Decimal File 1946–48 353.81 to 354.1; Box 1238; RG 407; NACP.

199 "The Nations: Democracy at Work," *Time*.

200 HQ USFET, "Discussion Groups: A Guide for Youth Activities Discussion Leaders, December 12, 1946; Folder Y.I. Policies and Directives, D. USFET and other US Army Units; Records of the Education Division: Gen Corresp & Rel Recs of Youth Activities Branch, 1945–47; OMGBR; Box 311; OMGUS; RG 260; NACP. Education Division, Office of Military Government for Bremen, "Historical Report, 1 July 1946 to 30 June 1947," 9–10; Folder Historical Reports from Laender 1946–48; Reever, despite such successes in getting German youth active in democratic processes in various ways, the official aims of the BBC were ambivalent, as Moriarty did not allow party politics nor discussion of the past in the club.[201] Arguably, in order to have discussions and to debate the future, German youth needed to deal with political issues and the past in a critical way. American officials aimed to create a supposedly apolitical atmosphere for youth reeducation, which meant that political youth groups run by German political parties were not allowed in the American zone until 1947, highlighting Americans' cautions about having youth directly partake in politics.[202] The consequences of the precarious balancing act of creating a club based on democratic principles within the sphere of a military occupation emerge through the example of the club newspaper, *Die Brücke*. BBC members wrote articles and visited other clubs throughout Bremen in a journalistic role. The boys played a role as a new model of postwar boyhood with members exercising personal agency and actively participating in positive club and societal activities such as writing articles, yet they were also confined in practicing what they had learned, as they remained members of a society living under a military government. The contradictions of this fact came to the forefront for members of the boys club through the publication of their club newspaper, *Die Brücke*.

Die Brücke: Is This a Democracy?

During the occupation, the official youth press in the American zone grew rapidly and included various newspapers and magazines aimed at children, teens, and young adults, such as *Pinguin*, which was edited by author Erich Kästner.[203]

cords RE the Work of the Youth Activities Section; Records of the Community Education Branch; Box 146; OMGUS; RG 260; NACP.

201 "The Nations: Democracy at Work," *Time*. Reed, "Experiment in Bremen"; Folder Bremen Boys Club; Records Relating to German Youth and Sports Clubs, 1947–49; OMGBR; Box 316; OMGUS; RG 260; NACP. "Bremen Boys Club: U.S. Sergeant Finances a Lesson in Democracy," *Life*, 37.

202 Burschka, "Re-Education und Jugendöffentlichkeit," 21. The communist youth group *Freie Deutsche Jugend* (FDJ), which was the only group allowed in the Soviet zone, existed in the Western zones until 1951 when it was banned: "Weekly Highlights, Youth and Sports Affairs," June 26, 1951; Folder 572.02 Youth Activity-Weekly and Monthly Reports; Records Relating to Youth Affairs, Bremen Land Commissioner Field Operations Division U.S. Resident Officer; Box 128; Records of the U.S. High Commissioner for Germany (HICOG), RG 466; NACP.

203 OMGUS Office of the Director of Information Control, Publications Control Branch, "Periodicals for German Youth: Survey Made and Action Taken by Publications Control Branch, ODIC," July 24, 1946; Folder OMGUS IA&C E&RA Br Giving Youth New Goals Aug 46; The Control Office:

Youth in the occupation especially hungered for information through mass media and books. Youth clubs such as the BBC also began to print their own newspapers, which often focused on club life and were modeled in the style of American school newspapers, with articles similar to the style of school essays, for example articles about (pre-Nazi era) history and about famous German *Dichter und Denker*, poets and thinkers.[204] Overall, the youth press was supposed to remain unpolitical. Manfred H. Burschka describes GYA youth club newspapers as generally unpolitical informational newspapers, often focusing on the future.[205] The first issue of the Bremen Boys Club's newspaper *Die Brücke* came out shortly after the club was founded, on August 22, 1946, and it started out as a paper exclusively for members, focusing on inner club developments. Club members who were journalists for the paper had a press pass, which enabled them to visit other GYA clubs. Club president Martin Girschner also served as chief editor. The BBC was the first club in Bremen to have a license for publishing a newspaper, although there were restrictions on the format and amount they were printing.[206] The front page of the BBC's newspaper had an image of a bridge between the United States and Bremen, portraying the interconnections forged through GYA.[207] Ernie Reed's report on the BBC in the *Stars and Stripes* in January 1947 included an image of club journalists interviewing GIs, noting how youth clubs had bridged the divide between German youngsters and American military personnel.[208] However, despite the many positive factors of the newspaper, a sense of the youth's fears about the future still emerged, including fears about Germany's future and worries about another war, this time an atomic one.[209] In his Master's thesis from 2002 about the Bremen Boys Club and *Die Brücke*, Lutz Rode

---

Activities of Internal Affairs & Communications Div.; Records of the Executive Office; Box 460; OMGUS; RG 260; NACP. Also, *German Youth Between Yesterday and Tomorrow*, 24–25 & Statistics 9. See also Rode, "Zwischen Re-education und Freizeitvergnügen," 27.

204 Rode, "Zwischen Re-education und Freizeitvergnügen," 26–27, 78–79.

205 Burschka, "Re-Education und Jugendöffentlichkeit," 24.

206 Edward T. Ladd, Chief, Youth Activities Branch, "Evaluation of the Achievement of 1st. Sgt. Moriarty," June 11, 1947, 3; Folder Bremen Boys Club; Records Relating to German Youth & Sports Clubs, 1947–49; OMGBR; OMGUS; Box 316; RG 260; NACP. See also Rode, "Manche nannten sie nur 'Schokoladenclubs,'" 26.

207 See issues of *Die Brücke* in Folder Bremen Boys Club; Records Relating to German Youth & Sports Clubs, 1947–49; OMGBR; Box 316; OMGUS; RG 260, NACP.

208 Reed, "Experiment in Bremen"; Folder Bremen Boys Club; Records Relating to German Youth & Sports Clubs, 1947–49; OMGBR; Box 316; OMGUS; RG 260; NACP.

209 Rode, "Zwischen Re-education und Freizeitvergnügen," 84–87.

argues that, overall, the newspaper articles showed the young generation's search for an identity in a time marked by a sense of disorientation and confusion.[210]

Over time, the BBC's newspaper *Die Brücke* evolved beyond a newspaper about inner club workings, and became a newspaper by the Bremen Boys for Bremen youth.[211] In 1947, the *Weser-Kurier* company printed the paper, making up to 2,000 copies per issue, reaching an audience beyond the BBC itself.[212] Articles focused on youth dialogue and exchanges of opinions, with authors including their political opinions about democratic ideals versus the realities of life in Germany.[213] The authors thus wrote about political issues, including a belief that democracy and youth were the future, fears about the Moscow Conference from March to April 1947 being a death sentence for Germany, a rejection of the Communist one-party system in the Soviet zone and its corresponding one-party youth movement, and also a general skepticism regarding adults.[214] One author wrote about his belief that youth already instinctively knew about democracy whenever they made compromises with each other, noting the irony of the reeducation process that was occurring under duress with strict controls.[215] Another author also wrote about the American Civil War and how Abraham Lincoln's act of freeing the slaves was what set up true democracy in the United States.[216] Thus, the authors showed an active political interest within the borders of the US zone in Germany and beyond, with an ability to critically examine international past and present events and write about them in an open, reflective manner.

However, the young journalists soon reached the limits of tolerance from the American military government. Multiple articles reached the attention of the Information Control Division of the military government, which took away the Bre-

---

210 Rode, "Zwischen Re-education und Freizeitvergnügen," 80.

211 Rode, "Zwischen Re-education und Freizeitvergnügen," 87–90.

212 Letter from James R. Case, HQ OMGBR, "Boy's Club Publications," May 13, 1947; Folder 17 Die Brücke; Records of the Information Control Division: Reports & Other Records, 1946–49; OMGBR; Box 81; OMGUS; RG 260, NACP; See also Rode, "Zwischen Re-education und Freizeitvergnügen," 75.

213 Rode, "Zwischen Re-education und Freizeitvergnügen," 89–91.

214 *Die Brücke*, Nr. 17, March 22, 1947, 5, quoted in Rode, "Zwischen Re-education und Freizeitvergnügen," 92–94. "Moskauer Konferenz," "Wolf," "Im Gleichschritt marsh-unter anderer Fahne," *Die Brücke*, Nr. 20, May 8, 1947; Folder Bremen Boys Club; Records Relating to German Youth & Sports Clubs, 1947–49; OMGBR; Box 316; OMGUS; RG 260; NACP. See also Rode, "Zwischen Re-education und Freizeitvergnügen," 96–97.

215 *Die Brücke*, Nr. 17, March 22, 1947, 5, quoted in Rode, "Zwischen Re-education und Freizeitvergnügen," 92–94.

216 Otto Dunst, "Der Bürgerkrieg der USA: 1861 bis 1865," *Die Brücke*, Nr. 20, May 8, 1947; Folder Bremen Boys Club; Records Relating to German Youth & Sports Clubs, 1947–49; OMGBR; Box 316; OMGUS; RG 260; NACP.

men Boys Club's publication license on May 13, 1947.[217] Through its newspaper, the club had overstepped its boundaries, moving beyond an apolitical youth activities group which only focused on positive aspects of the present, instead investigating official problems of occupation life. Their violations also extended beyond political involvement. Not only did they publish articles critical of the occupation and three members of the United Nations, France, the Soviet Union, and Poland, violating the youth activities directive of October 25, 1945 which specifically forbade such behavior, they also violated the military government publication policy of not publishing for an audience beyond the youth club.[218] The critical articles in question that led to the revoking of their license included a series that began on April 8, 1947 regarding France and the Saarland, which claimed that France treated the Saarland better out of their own economic interests of having access to coal. Another article from April 23, 1947, "*Gebt uns eine Chance*" ("Give Us a Chance"), dealt with German reparations to the Soviet Union, which argued that the reparations mostly hurt the young generation who were not responsible for National Socialism. The article noted young people's doubts over the future of Germany, and asked about whether German youth would be able to make decisions themselves or whether they would always be the pawns of others. The author wrote, "We want to be free and not slaves! (*Wir wollen frei sein und keine Sklaven*!)"[219] Finally, the last article, "*Wer klagt an, wer richtet?*" ("Who Accuses, Who Judges?"), reported on terrible conditions suffered by a 16-year-old German in a Polish camp in 1945 and aimed at an assessment of human tragedy, dealing with the question of whether it would be considered a crime against humanity if a German was the victim of tragedy.[220] Club President Girschner wrote another article in the next issue of *Die Brücke* on May 8, 1947 entitled "*Unser Standpunkt*" ("Our Standpoint"), writing to justify the publication of "*Wer klagt an, wer richtet?*," arguing that he did this out of his duty as an editor under the aims of democratization.[221] Thus, the affair of the BBC's club newspaper highlights the cen-

---

217 Letter from James R. Case, "Boy's Club Publications," May 13, 1947; Folder 17 Die Brücke; Records of the Information Control Division; OMGBR; Box 81; OMGUS; RG 260; NACP. See also Rode, "Zwischen Re-education und Freizeitvergnügen," 99; 102–103.
218 See October 25, 1945 directive in *German Youth Activities of the United States Army*, 37. Also, Rode, "Zwischen Re-education und Freizeitvergnügen," 99–100; Pedron, *Amerikaner vor Ort*, 291.
219 "Gebt uns eine Chance," *Die Brücke*, Nr. 19, April 23, 1947; Folder Bremen Boys Club; Records Relating to German Youth & Sports Clubs, 1947–49; OMGBR; Box 316; OMGUS; RG 260; NACP.
220 "Wer klagt an, wer richtet," *Die Brücke*, Nr. 19, April 23, 1947; Folder Bremen Boys Club; Records Relating to German Youth & Sports Clubs, 1947–49; OMGBR; Box 316; OMGUS; RG 260; NACP.
221 "Unser Standpunkt," *Die Brücke*, Nr. 20, May 8, 1947; Folder Bremen Boys Club; Records Relating to German Youth & Sports Clubs, 1947–49; OMGBR; Box 316; OMGUS; RG 260; NACP.

tral contradiction inherent in reeducation and democratization policies: How could a foreign power's military government and military personnel teach the youngest of Germans about democracy when the society the youth were living in was not a democracy but a military occupation? When youth pushed the limits and took the democracy they learned about into action through exercising freedom of press, they were then punished in an undemocratic manner through the revoking of their right to publish. The case of *Die Brücke* reached a high level of scrutiny. In a Monthly Political Summary of the Bremen Area Intelligence Office from May 1947, the "interesting" case of *Die Brücke* was listed, noting that "potential Subversive [sic] influence is being investigated."[222]

Members of the BBC decided to take democratic action regarding the revoking of their publication license and organized a strike at the Haus des Reichs, the central office of the military government in Bremen. Wolfgang Steinert, age 15, was a schoolmate of the three founding members of the BBC: President Martin Girschner (at the time age 16), Vice President Hans-Robert Spiecker (age 15), and club secretary Günther Holst (age 17) at the *Oberschule* Kaiser Friedrich Strasse. Steinert gave a testimony on May 14, 1947 regarding the events of the day before, May 13, the day of the strike and the revoking of the license for the club newspaper. Upon arriving at school, Girschner apparently told Steinert about the morning's events. He said that he was nearly arrested by the Information Control Division due to his articles "*Wer klagt an, wer richtet?*" and "*Unser Standpunkt,*" and that "only by half an hour of discussion he managed that only the newspaper has to cease." Steinert reported that that morning, Girschner had also said that he had met with Moriarty "concerning 'freedom of press, democracy for all, though we have a military dictatorship, humanity for all!'" Girschner had also sent a telegram to General Robert A. McClure at the Allied Control Council, ICD in Berlin (but McClure actually had already left for the United States, so it is uncertain where the telegram ended up). The text of the telegram had been developed together with Moriarty but was signed by Girschner. Girschner's teachers even allowed him to leave school two hours early to go on strike at the Haus des Reichs, since the teachers said they had a "paedagogical [sic] interest in the magazine [*Die Brücke*] to which they have subscribed." At 2:45 PM, according to Steinert's testimony, Girschner met with the staff members of *Die Brücke* and other "prominent members of the BBC without Sgt. Moriarty or any other American sponsors." The sit-down strike began at 3:00 PM and Girschner made an address with corre-

222 Bremen Area Intelligence Office, Monthly Political Summary No. 3, Copy No. 37, May 1947, p. 13; Records of the Executive Office: Security-Classified General Records. 1945–49; OMGBR; Box 23; OMGUS; RG 260; NACP.

spondents present from "the 'Weser-Kurier,' LIFE, UP, Die Zeit, Die Welt, Das Ziel (?) [sic], and Stars & Stripes (?)," based on the advice of Moriarty to have journalists witness the strike. However, none of the newspapers ended up publishing about the club members' strike. Club members also displayed placards at the strike, which "stressed the points of the demonstration." According to Steinert in his testimony, Girschner was going to end the strike at 5:00 PM, but Steinert could not say for certain if Girschner did.[223]

That same day, on May 13, 1947, the *Stars and Stripes* published an article entitled "MG Investigating 'Anti-Soviet Tone' of Boys' Paper," which mentioned an investigation into whether Sergeant Patrick Moriarty had "sponsored an illegal club newspaper containing anti-Russian and anti-Polish articles," such as the report of a German in a Polish "internment" camp in 1945. The article mentioned that Moriarty had previously "been warned to limit his club's publication to the rules established for GYA publications," of publishing mimeographed texts of four pages exclusively about the activities of GYA and the club.[224] An official letter from May 13, 1947 from OMGBR headquarters to the Commanding Officer of the 104th Labor Supervision Center (Moriarty's unit) stated that the newspaper had made recent violations "of a serious nature," including "maliciously" criticizing the occupying powers and tending "to foster unrest and resistance to the Allies." The letter also mentioned that Moriarty had been previously warned about violating the rules, including that he had allowed 2,000 copies of the newspaper to circulate instead of 150 (the number of BBC members), as well as not submitting two copies of each issue to ICD for post-censorship, and printing six pages instead of four. The letter highlighted,

> It is not the intention of this headquarters to discourage army-sponsored [sic] groups from exploring the Four Freedoms. In fact it is our mission to give every aid and assistance in this important portion of German reorientation. However, malicious criticism of the Allied powers and rebellion against Allied policies cannot at this time be regarded as proper activities for German groups.

Moreover, it mentioned the October 5, 1946 directive for the Army Assistance to GYA program, which forbade political activities of the youth groups. The letter, however, indicated that the newspaper could be published again in consultation

223 Wolfgang Steinert testimony, May 14, 1947; Folder 17 Die Brücke; Records of the Information Control Division; OMGBR; Box 81; OMGUS; RG 260; NACP. See also Pedron, *Amerikaner vor Ort*, 291; Rode, "Zwischen Re-education und Freizeitvergnügen," 103–105.

224 "MG Investigating 'Anti-Soviet Tone' of Boys' Paper," *Stars and Stripes*, May 13, 1947, 3; Folder Bremen Boys Club; Records Relating to German Youth & Sports Clubs, 1947–49; OMGBR; Box 316; OMGUS; RG 260; NACP.

with ICD and if it followed the rules about publication, including containing "no National Socialistic, militaristic or expansionistic propaganda."[225] In addition, Moriarty had also violated another official regulation for GYA clubs, which required the Army-sponsored clubs to register with the American military government in the same manner as German-run clubs (this rule was put in place to try to reduce competition between American-sponsored and German-run clubs): so far, he had not officially registered the club.[226]

On May 14, 1947, the day after the boys' strike, reporter Al Gladding made a broadcast over American Forces Network (AFN) Bremen radio about the previous day's events, noting that "the most famous first sergeant in post war Germany [Moriarty] is fighting mad tonight":

> The six page printed paper, edited by six members of the boy's club, was suspended yesterday by Mr. Thomas Headen, local ICD Chief, on the grounds that it violated current MG directives governing German language publications and that it contained articles critical of America's Allies. When news of the paper's suspension reached club members, the editorial staff, headed by 16-year old Martin Girschner, club president[,] promptly made up placegards [sic], demanding freedom of the press, and picketed the ICD office. According to editor Girschner, when an attempted explanation of the move by one of Headen's assistants failed to impress the staff, they were told that their protest violated MG laws and that unless they left the building, MPs would be called. In language largely too colorful for direct quotation, Moriarty told reporters last night that the handling of the problem by local ICD officials had done untold damage to his work. He said he had taught his boys to sound off that injustice wherever he [sic] found it, that he had tried to instruct them in the Four Freedoms for which he had fought.
>
> "They called me a threat to international peace," said the usually jovial Irishman, "I don't know what to think." But apparently the folks back home did, for the state of Minnesota, Pat's home state, had passed a resolution commending him for inauguration [sic] a movement to further permanent world peace. And that's the news tonight at this gateway to the occupation and home.[227]

A letter from OMGBR headquarters from May 22, 1947 noted that Al Gladding's AFN broadcast was inaccurate and that "the impression left by its broadcast was detrimental to the US Army's mission in Germany." The letter clarified that the commanding officer of the 104th Labor Supervision Center and the military gov-

---

225 Letter from James R. Case, HQ OMGBR, "Boy's Club Publications," May 13, 1947; Folder 17 Die Brücke; Records of the Information Control Division; OMGBR; Box 81; OMGUS; RG 260; NACP.
226 Ladd, "Evaluation of the Achievement of 1st. Sgt. Moriarty," June 11, 1947, p. 3; Folder Bremen Boys Club; Records Relating to German Youth & Sports Clubs, 1947–49; OMGBR; Box 316; OMGUS; RG 260; NACP. See also Rode, "Zwischen Re-education und Freizeitvergnügen," 49–50, 72.
227 Broadcast over AFN, May 14, 1947; Folder 17 Die Brücke; Records of the Information Control Division; OMGBR; Box 81; OMGUS; RG 260; NACP.

ernment had "no difference of opinion." It also noted that misleading broadcasts, such as that of Al Gladding's, must "be prevented in the future," and that there was no intention by the military government "to deny the Bremen Boys' Club the right to publish a newspaper." In addition, the "so-called" picketers "were not told 'that unless they left the building, MPS [sic] would be called.'" The letter also stated that "the result of this broadcast has been to encourage the members of the Bremen Boys' Club to regard themselves as persecutees of Military Government, which is detrimental to the occupation mission and embarrasses our work."[228] In the end, however, the club members stopped writing a newspaper; only one more issue of *Die Brücke* appeared almost one year later in March 1948, highlighting the impact of the events on the youth activities within the club.[229]

Critique about *Die Brücke* even emerged from within the German Youth Activities clubs: The *Club Telegraph*, the newspaper of the Bremen Youth Club, stated that the articles in *Die Brücke* only served to split up youth, instead of building bridges.[230] In the last issue of *Die Brücke* from March 1948, Girschner explained the events of the last year, writing that in youthful exuberance the club members had overstepped the boundaries of what was allowed, thus losing their newspaper license. However, he wrote that they would continue to be political about the things they consider important for better understanding world affairs. However, the issue focused mainly on non-political topics in the old style of a club paper exclusively for members.[231] Additionally, the revoking of the club's paper did indeed cause Girschner to have doubts about American democratization attempts, showing that there were consequences from the military government restrictions on democratic practices such as freedom of speech.[232] However, despite the negative impact that the restrictions had on the boys' democratic attempts at freedom of press, the club as a whole played a major role in many of the members' experiences during the occupation. Decades later in 1998, over 50 of the Bremen Boys Club's members came together for a reunion. In an article written in the *Weser-Kurier* by Lutz Rode, the former club members stated that Americans had done a lot of good for them by creating a clubhouse full of activities for them and providing a place to stay warm, which was especially needed in

---

228 Letter from James R. Case, HQ OMGBR, "Radio Broadcast," May 22, 1947; Folder 17 Die Brücke; Records of the Information Control Division; OMGBR; Box 81; OMGUS; RG 260; NACP.

229 Rode, "Zwischen Re-education und Freizeitvergnügen," 106.

230 Rode, "Zwischen Re-education und Freizeitvergnügen," 106.

231 *Die Brücke* Nr. 21, March 1948, 2, quoted in Rode, "Zwischen Re-education und Freizeitvergnügen," 106–107.

232 See Rode, "Manche nannten sie nur 'Schokoladenclubs,'" 36; Rode, "Zwischen Re-education und Freizeitvergnügen," 118.

the cold winter of 1946–1947.[233] In addition, as Rode notes in his Master's thesis, club members' critiques about democracy were geared toward the strict regulations of the Allied occupation, rather than against the concept of democracy itself, showing a level of readiness for a democratic Germany among members.[234]

In May 1947 after the suspension of its newspaper license, the Bremen Boys Club faced yet another setback: Famous club sponsor and founder Patrick Moriarty was transferred to Frankfurt am Main. According to a letter on May 21, 1947 from Lieutenant General Clarence R. Huebner, Deputy Commander-in-Chief, EUCOM, the transfer was not a punishment but rather a way for Moriarty to reach a "larger field" for his activities, working under the EUCOM German Youth Assistance Section.[235] Starting in June 1947, 24-year-old First Sergeant Dale H. Fleming took over as sponsor of the BBC. He was accompanied by his 19-year-old wife Betty, who was already teaching the boys American dance moves, according to a June 1947 article in *The Port Reporter*. In response to a question about his inexperience in leading a youth club, Sgt. Fleming said, "I like boys and as much as I have seen of the club and its members, I know that I am going to enjoy my new job," while also noting, "My only hope is that I can do as good a job as Pat Moriarity [sic]."[236] By July 1947, however, the club had already received a new sponsor, Herbert Meyer.[237] It is uncertain what occurred in the club after the end of 1947, as the official OMGUS club records end, but in April of 1951, the BBC club home on Slevogtstrasse closed, and even before the closure, the BBC had shared the house with other clubs including the *Falken* (socialist youth), a reestablished *Wandervogel* group, a theater group, and a group of Silesian youth.[238]

---

233 Rode, "Zwischen Re-education und Freizeitvergnügen," 118; Lutz Rode, "Der Amerikaner hat viel Gutes getan," *Weser-Kurier*, January 25, 1998, 9.

234 Rode, "Zwischen Re-education und Freizeitvergnügen," 113.

235 Letter from Lt. General C.R. Huebner to Major General Frank A. Keating, May 21, 1947; Folder Bremen Boys Club; Records Relating to German Youth & Sports Clubs, 1947–49; OMGBR; Box 316; OMGUS; RG 260; NACP.

236 "1/Sgt. D.H. Fleming Named Leader of Bremen GYA Club," *The Port Reporter*, June 1947; Folder Bremen Boys Club; Records Relating to German Youth & Sports Clubs, 1947–49; OMGBR; Box 316; OMGUS; RG 260; NACP. See also Pedron, *Amerikaner vor Ort*, 292. The Army 323rd Military Intelligence Detachment became the new sponsors of the club.

237 Bremen Boys Club, German Youth Activities, Weekly Schedule from July 21st to July 27th 1947, July 21, 1947; Folder Bremen Boys Club 1946/47; Records Relating to German Youth & Sports Clubs, 1947–49; OMGBR; Box 316; OMGUS; RG 260; NACP. Also, Letter from Herbert A. Meyer to Maj. Marthinsson, September 30, 1947, same location as previous record.

238 "Slevogt-Heim wird aufgelöst," *Weser-Kurier*, March 22, 1951; Groth, "Bremer Jungs im Jahre Sechsundvierzig," in *Vom Trümmerkind zum Teenager*, ed. Foitzik, 27; Rode, "Zwischen Re-education und Freizeitvergnügen," 73.

The last GYA youth center in the Bremen Enclave existed at the Vahr barracks until 1955, when it closed.[239]

However, the Moriarty family continued to influence German Youth Activities even after Patrick Moriarty left Bremen: His father Joseph visited Germany in late 1947 and early 1948 to survey the conditions there. He also visited the Bremen Boys Club.[240] After his visit to Germany, Joseph Moriarty even wanted to personally call on President Truman to give him his report on conditions in Germany. He ended up leaving the report for Truman in the Executive Office.[241] Additionally, Minnesota Representative Joseph P. O'Hara read Joseph Moriarty's letter to President Truman in Congress on February 17, 1948. His letter reported on conditions in Germany. In the letter, Moriarty wrote that "the conscience of the German people is not dead," as churches and chapels have been rebuilt, and argued that Germany's "superhuman task of restoration" was "a sad fate not of the people's making but the fault of one Godless dictator whose name was Adolf Hitler." He painted the Germans as victims of both Hitler and the "racketeers" of the black market, describing Germany as an "unfortunate land." Additionally, Moriarty noted that Germany now "looks to America, and America alone, for security, liberty, and protection from now until the day it meets qualifications for national sovereignty." Meanwhile, he portrayed the displaced persons remaining in Germany as "lazy, worthless persons," and claimed that many of them "are avowed Communists and Nazi adherents." Furthermore, he also lauded the efforts of individual initiatives of soldiers in creating the GYA program, and remarked:

> The future hope of Germany lies in the mental and social attitudes of the German youth. Through no fault of their own they were doped and led to form pagan attitudes of cruelty and taught by the Nazis to hate God and every Christian concept of morality in order to wean German thought away from democratic channels of thought. This generation of German youth deserves guidance and fair treatment from America."[242]

---

239 "Wehmütiges Jubiläum in der Vahr," *Weser-Kurier*, April 30, 1955; Rode, "Manche nannten sie nur 'Schokoladenclubs,'" 34; Pedron, *Amerikaner vor Ort*, 287.

240 Handwritten note, "Bremen Boys Club," December 24, 1947; Folder Bremen Boys Club; Records Relating to German Youth & Sports Clubs, 1947–49; OMGBR; Box 316; OMGUS; RG 260; NACP.

241 Letter from William D. Hassett, Secretary to the President, to Joseph J. Moriarty, February 10, 1948; Folder OF 198 Misc. 1947 [1 of 2]; OF 198; Box 738; HSTP; HSTPL. Let. To Pres., 1-26-48 from Joseph J. Moriarty; same location as previous record.

242 Extension of Remarks of Hon. Joseph P. O'Hara, "Report on Conditions in Germany," in United States: Congress, Appendix to the Congressional Record (Bound), 80th Congress, 2nd Session, February 17, 1948, Vol. 94, Part 9 (January 6, 1948 to December 31, 1948), US Government Publishing Office, A896–A898.

Moriarty's visit to Germany and his report to the president illustrate the shift that occurred by 1948 in which German youth gained center stage in both occupation policies and in the increasing focus on anti-communism.[243] Displaced persons were no longer the targets of sympathy and positive attention; rather, it was young Germans who emerged as the future hope for American democratic aims in Europe. Assistance to youth would thus serve the dual purpose of democratization and anti-communism.

On April 6, 1948, Representative O'Hara made remarks in Congress about a newspaper account of a speech made by Joseph Moriarty on March 23, 1948 in New Ulm, Minnesota. He also remarked on a resolution adopted by over 1,000 people from the town, which recommended giving increased aid to Germany "as a means of stemming the western push of the Communists in Europe." Joseph Moriarty's speech in New Ulm again highlighted the supposed criminality of displaced persons remaining in Germany and characterized former Secretary of Treasury Morgenthau's plan as a "policy of extermination in Germany." He argued that the Morgenthau Plan of deindustrializing Germany was "exactly what Russia wants," and stated that "Morgenthau's hands are dripping with blood; but if we are called upon to fight Russia, more blood will be on his hands. If we are to survive, we must change hate and desire for extermination of people to rebuilding and rehabilitation of people." Thus, Joseph Moriarty painted an image of a Germany full of "starving" victims who were "not Godless" but rather were dutifully rebuilding and in need of material aid and currency stabilization in order to return to "normal and healthy lives." This would also ensure "the safety and security of the United States of America" by preventing the spread of communism. In addition, he accused the State Department of having "too many pink Communists," who should be replaced by "God-fearing people."[244] Thus, Joseph Moriarty's political engagement with reporting on conditions in Germany illustrates the deep shift that had taken place within a few years of the occupation: Germany was increasingly painted as an innocent victim in need of benevolence from the United States, which would not only help rehabilitate Germany, but would prevent the spread of communism and ensure the security of the United States, a shift that was furthered by the Truman Doctrine in 1947.[245] German youth had thus emerged as central figures in the geopolitical sphere of the emerging Cold War. For example, the Bremen Boys Club had evolved from a club for positive,

---

243 See Goedde, *GIs and Germans*, 152–153.

244 "Conditions in Germany," in United States: Congress, Appendix to the Congressional Record (Bound), 80th Congress, 2nd Session, April 6, 1948, Vol. 94, Part 10 (March 8, 1948 to December 31, 1948), US Government Publishing Office, A2156–A2158.

245 See Chapter 4 for more on the Truman Doctrine.

apolitical forms of fraternization to a site central to American political aims, based on aiding and democratizing youth in an attempt to prevent the spread of communism and World War III. Joseph Moriarty's aim in publicizing the Bremen Boys Club at high levels in the government was not just out of personal interest in assisting youth facing difficult situations but rather fit the larger American political project aimed at encouraging anti-communism and the rehabilitation of Germany for Cold War aims rather than punishment for Germany's National Socialist past.[246]

The Club Idol

Judge Joseph Moriarty's son Patrick J. Moriarty emerged as a major shaper in the development of Army Assistance to German Youth Activities during the occupation, yet his role as one of the founders and sponsors of the Bremen Boys Club was full of ambivalence. On June 11, 1947, after Moriarty's transfer to Frankfurt am Main, Edward Ladd, OMGBR Youth and Sports Officer, evaluated Moriarty's achievements, noting his "dramatic impact" on youth activities and "his tremendous enthusiasm and energy and his genius for attracting publicity." His work helped shape the "first-class activities" for youth in the Bremen Enclave. Ladd wrote, "His influence in this area has been particularly noticeable through the springing up of American-sponsored clubs [sic], a particular form of activity largely lacking in the rest of the US zone." Ladd commended Moriarty's "energies and endeavors," including the BBC's "public welfare projects" as well as, interestingly, the publication of the controversial club newspaper, *Die Brücke*. However, Ladd's assessment was not only full of praise for Moriarty's passion in the realm of youth activities: Ladd stated that according to reports from official intelligence and from American and German educators, Moriarty also evoked a sense of "hero-worship" among the club members, which was a clear danger for these teenagers who had lived under Hitler for 12 years. Moriarty claimed the club was his boys' yet he often focused on his own personal desire for fighting injustice where he himself saw it. Additionally, Ladd stated that Moriarty's attitude toward

246 Interestingly, the official presidential records regarding Joseph Moriarty's report to President Truman include a letter from H. P. Van Cleve, M.D. of Minnesota, who had heard Judge Moriarty speak and was "impressed by his viciousness" and wanted to do something to stop him. Van Cleve wrote the president's secretary, warning that Joseph Moriarty was "creating racial prejudice" and blaming the situation in Germany on the Jews, Morgenthau, and the current administration. Letter from H. P. Van Cleve, M.D., to the Secretary to the President, March 6, 1948; Folder OF 198 Misc. 1947 [1 of 2]; OF 198; Box 738; HSTP; HSTPL.

the military government was "unfortunate." He noted: "Apparently not realizing that Germany is a country under military occupation, he has acted with the freedom an American would expect to have at home, and he has encouraged his boys to follow him in this regard." Ladd wrote that attempts to get Moriarty to follow official directives were met with "frequent rudeness and personal abuse."[247] This included a phone call in January 1947 when Moriarty called Ladd, claiming that there were attacks on the BBC made during a meeting of the military government Youth Advisory Board. During the call, Moriarty even called Ladd a "Harvard communist" who was "not interested in the youth program."[248] Ladd's report also stated that Moriarty ignored the registration requirement for American-sponsored youth clubs, and that he ignored a Publications Control Branch directive regarding youth club bulletins, in addition to the Allied Control Council requirements for all German publications. Instead, Ladd wrote, Moriarty's club's newspaper *Die Brücke* printed 2,000 copies with "numerous articles attacking the Allied occupation and criticizing three members of the United Nations, Poland, Russia and France." Ladd noted that Sergeant Dale Fleming, Moriarty's successor, made a visit right away to the military government office to officially register the Bremen Boys Club.[249] In the club's registration application from June 1, 1947, one of the club's goals listed was for "practicing democratic self-government within the club as preparation for full-fledged citizenship in a new democratic Germany," marking the continuing importance of practicing democracy within the club.[250] Overall, Ladd wrote in his assessment that the future of the club was faced with the test of what would happen when Moriarty had departed, with Fleming facing a challenging task. Ladd concluded, "It is the hope of the undersigned that the good work done by Sgt. Moriarty will not suffer by his departure but become an even more solid foundation for educational work in the future."[251] Ladd's report hints at the tensions that could boil over regarding German youth initiatives due to the division of responsibilities for youth work between Ameri-

247 Edward T. Ladd, "Evaluation of the Achievement of 1st. Sgt. Moriarty," June 11, 1947; Folder Bremen Boys Club; Records Relating to German Youth & Sports Clubs, 1947–49; OMGBR; Box 316; OMGUS; RG 260; NACP. See also Rode, "Zwischen Re-education und Freizeitvergnügen," 71–72; Kleinschmidt, *Do Not Fraternize*, 227.

248 "Bremen Boys Club: Memo for the files," January 30, 1947; Folder Bremen Boys Club; Records Relating to German Youth & Sports Clubs, 1947–49; OMGBR; Box 316; OMGUS; RG 260; NACP.

249 Ladd, "Evaluation of the Achievement of 1st. Sgt. Moriarty"; Folder Bremen Boys Club; OMGBR; Box 316; OMGUS; RG 260; NACP.

250 "Application for Approval of Organization," June 1, 1947; Folder Bremen Boys Club; Records Relating to German Youth & Sports Clubs, 1947–49; OMGBR; Box 316; OMGUS; RG 260; NACP.

251 Ladd, "Evaluation of the Achievement of 1st. Sgt. Moriarty"; Folder Bremen Boys Club; OMGBR; Box 316; OMGUS; RG 260; NACP.

can military government officials, German youth authorities, and armed forces personnel active in assistance to GYA, such as Moriarty.

Moriarty indeed made an impact that influenced the sphere of youth life in the Bremen Enclave, initiating a club that spurred other American-sponsored groups to pop up on a large scale. However, his individual influence in the club was quite strong. Although he founded the club with other GIs, they were hardly ever mentioned. Moreover, he seemed to embody a father figure for the youth, with club members naming him "our Pat," and *Life* magazine stating that he was the boys' "idol."[252] *Life* magazine presented an image of him strolling the streets of Bremen with his "boys," depicting his strong influence despite the fact that he was supposed to be the club sponsor, not the leader. However, Moriarty provided a new type of role model: Although a military non-commissioned officer, he could portray a new type of masculinity based on democracy and non-fascist ways, providing new outlooks for boys amongst the rubble-strewn, desolate realities of postwar life. Yet the image of Moriarty leading "his" boys also provides an eerie continuity with the National Socialist past. A mass of young boys was following a uniformed military leader, hanging on to his every word.[253]

Additionally, there were uncertainties about the situation within the club itself. A report about youth activities in Bremen from January to March 1947 stated that there were rumors about conditions in boys clubs leading to dislike and mistrust about the clubs among the German population, although the report seems to be referring to German resentment over the food and fuel situation, since the club members had access to warm spaces and material goods.[254] There were also contradictory official reports about the quality of the activities being offered in

---

252 "Bremen Boys Club: U.S. Sergeant Finances a Lesson in Democracy," *Life*, December 9, 1946, 37; Girschner Jr., "Ziele des Bremen Boys Club," *Die Brücke* Nr. 19; Folder Bremen Boys Club; Records Relating to German Youth & Sports Clubs, 1947–49; OMGBR; OMGUS; Box 316; RG 260; NACP. See also Rode, "Zwischen Re-education und Freizeitvergnügen," 56.

253 "Bremen Boys Club: U.S. Sergeant Finances a Lesson in Democracy," *Life*, 36. Also, Sondern Jr., "GI Teachers for German Children," in Congressional Record, April 3, 1947, Vol. 93, Part 3, 3118–3119. See also Percy Knauth, Bremen Press Camp release, September 26, 1946; Folder YXXI Army Assistance Program A. Bremerhaven Military Community 1947 (formerly Grohn Military Community); Records of the Education Division: Gen Corresp & Rel Recs of Youth Activities Branch, 1945–47; OMGBR; Box 315; OMGUS; RG 260; NACP. Knauth's press release claimed that "Moriarty noticed [the] tendency on part of some to regard him as leader. So he stayed away several nights to emphasise [sic] point that [the] boys are on their own."

254 OMGBR, Civil Government Division, Youth Activities Branch, "Historical Report, January-March 1947," 5–6; Folder Historical Reports from Laender, 1946–48; Records RE the Work of the Youth Activities Section; Records of the Education and Cultural Relations Division: Records of the Community Education Branch; OMGUS; Box 146; RG 260; NACP.

the BBC. One confidential ICD report from April 1, 1947 about a visit to the club stated that the club home was well equipped, warm, and in excellent conditions, with rooms for music, theater, and table tennis. However, the report also noted that a club member complained that the program of activities was decided by the Americans, and that the boys were unable to do any activities that the Americans did not like. The report indicated that Moriarty showed concern for the boys' physical and spiritual state. Moriarty stated that he often went to church, and wanted the boys to learn religion again after having forgotten it under Hitler but in a way that was not forced. The report stated that Moriarty had said that not all Germans were happy with his work, and especially communists were against his youth work, hinting at the role of anti-communism in fueling his efforts. Additionally, the report gives a glimpse of the disillusioned condition among German youngsters: Two club members said that their fellow schoolmates were "too tired and disappointed by Hitler," while a third member said that, in his opinion, half of the boys in school were still Nazis who rejected anything new. One boy stated that he did not think Germany would improve in 40 years, so he was planning on emigrating. Additionally, the report noted that the club strictly enforced its rules. Around 30 to 40 boys had already been dismissed from the club since its founding due to bad behavior.[255] However, in contrast to the report, a letter from March 8, 1947 to Ladd about a GYA sergeant's visit to the BBC stated that the "place looked rather shabby and uninviting," with "little activity" and "very little to offer despite his [Moriarty's] big splash." Moreover, Moriarty also apparently spoke with "a lot of 'I.'"[256] This letter seems to contradict the official weekly reports of daily activities in the club, which showed a large variety of activities, as well as the April ICD report about the excellent club conditions.[257] However, it appears that Moriarty was especially motivated to be active in youth activities due to his anti-communism, which fit well in the heightening Cold War context that focused on educating youth to be anti-communist. Overall, however, it cannot be denied that Moriarty did indeed create initiatives that enabled some Bremen youth to practice democracy through discussions, debates, and even through writing articles in a critical, independent way, which in the end led the boys to get into trou-

255 Confidential ICD Intelligence Source, "Besuch beim Bremen Boys Club," April 1, 1947; Folder Bremen Boys Club; Records Relating to German Youth & Sports Clubs, 1947–49; OMGBR; Box 316; OMGUS; RG 260; NACP. Author's translation of quotations from German to English.

256 Letter to Edward Ladd from David Cozart, March 8, 1947; Folder Bremen Boys Club; Records Relating to German Youth & Sports Clubs, 1947–49; OMGBR; Box 316; OMGUS; RG 260; NACP.

257 For weekly reports of BBC activities in 1947, see Weekly Reports and Schedules; Folder Bremen Boys Club; OMGBR; Box 316; OMGUS; RG 260; NACP.

ble for pushing the limits of practicing democracy under a military government through their articles in *Die Brücke*.

In addition, yet another layer adds more complexity to the story of the Bremen Boys Club and the actions of the original club sponsor, Patrick Moriarty. Issues regarding the club may have not been limited to competition with German-run youth clubs or accusations of Americanization. Among the official OMGUS records about the club are two handwritten papers regarding potential sexual abuse occurring within the club. Unfortunately, the records are limited to these two notes, not allowing for a definite conclusion regarding this serious matter. The first note, marked as a confidential memorandum for the files on the Bremen Boys Club, was from July 25, 1947, and was most likely written by Edward Ladd of the military government youth activities office in Bremen. This note stated that an informant reported that two boys had said in a private conversation that they had left the Bremen Boys Club due to Moriarty making "improper advances" toward them.[258] The other document, from September 12, 1947, has different handwriting and stated that the same two boys had been dismissed from the club by Moriarty "'because they knew too much' [of] his affairs of homosexuality." These two boys also had stated that they heard from another boy that Moriarty was using homeless, fatherless boys who lived at the club house for "purposes of homosexuality." Furthermore, the document stated that the two boys had reported this information to the military police, as well as the former commanding officer and adjutant of the 104th Labor Supervision Center (Moriarty's unit until his transfer to Frankfurt). Despite this, according to this record, the two boys were "extremely interested in rejoining the Bremen Boys Club just as soon as it can be arranged for them to do so."[259]

Interestingly, these records are from the time after Moriarty had been sent to Frankfurt am Main in May 1947, but although he had left Bremen, it seems that he still remained connected to the club, and his father also visited the club during his trip to Germany in late 1947 and early 1948.[260] For his Master's thesis about the club written in 2002, Lutz Rode also examined the two handwritten docu-

---

258 "Confidential: Memorandum for the Files: Bremen Boys Club," July 25, 1947; Folder Bremen Boys Club; Records Relating to German Youth & Sports Clubs, 1947–49; OMGBR; Box 316; OMGUS; RG 260; NACP.

259 Handwritten note, September 12, 1947; Folder Bremen Boys Club; Records Relating to German Youth & Sports Clubs, 1947–49; OMGBR; Box 316; OMGUS; RG 260; NACP.

260 Handwritten note, "Bremen Boys Club," December 24, 1947; Folder Bremen Boys Club; Records Relating to German Youth & Sports Clubs, 1947–49; OMGBR; Box 316; OMGUS; RG 260; NACP. Also, Letter from William D. Hassett, Secretary to the President, to Joseph J. Moriarty, February 10, 1948; Folder OF 198 Misc. 1947 [1 of 2]; OF 198; Box 738; HSTP; HSTPL. Let. To Pres., 1-26-48 from Joseph J. Moriarty; same location as previous record.

ments and the uncertainty regarding the allegations about Moriarty. He notes that the military government itself felt competitive with Moriarty, which could have led to his transfer from Bremen. Rode argues that it is noteworthy that the military government records are meticulous in documenting Moriarty's various transgressions and that they also collected evidence for his alleged homosexuality.[261] However, Rode also states that it is possible that this feeling of competition between Moriarty and the military government may not have actually been a factor in Moriarty's transfer, as the Bremen Boys Club was long seen as the model club in the US zone and Moriarty's work thus also brought recognition to the American military government as well.[262] In the end, unfortunately, it is impossible to come to a conclusion about whether the accusations of the two former club members regarding sexual abuse are true, since the records only contain these two documents and no conclusion to the case.[263] It is particularly striking that the two boys reported the case to the military police and military officials, highlighting the level of attention they tried to reach with their statements. In addition, they were interested in rejoining the club again during the time when Moriarty was no longer sponsor. Overall, conditions in the immediate postwar era in Germany had the potential to lead to situations in which power could be misused. Although the allegations regarding abuse in the Bremen Boys Club remain inconclusive, there was certainly the potential for American soldiers to misuse their authority as occupiers and commit acts such as sexual abuse or other forms of abuse and violence against others including children and youth. This could cer-

---

261 Rode, "Zwischen Re-education und Freizeitvergnügen," 72–73, 114. Also relevant regarding accusations of homosexuality is the history of the Lavender Scare, the rise of a moral panic regarding homosexuality during the Cold War, which led to antigay purges of thousands of US federal government employees accused of being homosexual. Homosexuals, in addition to communists, were seen as a threat to national security. See David K. Johnson, *The Lavender Scare: The Cold War Persecution of Gays and Lesbians in the Federal Government* (University of Chicago Press, 2004). Moreover, during the era of World War II, homosexuality was seen as a mental illness, and military policy became increasingly anti-homosexual, with those targeted given undesirable discharges. See Allan Bérubé, *Coming Out Under Fire: The History of Gay Men and Women in World War II*, 20th Anniversary Edition (University of North Carolina Press, 2010). On homosexuality in postwar Germany, see Clayton J. Whisnant, *Male Homosexuality in West Germany: Between Persecution and Freedom, 1945–69* (Palgrave Macmillan, 2012); Samuel Clowes Huneke, *States of Liberation: Gay Men between Dictatorship and Democracy in Cold War Germany* (University of Toronto Press, 2022).

262 Rode, "Zwischen Re-education und Freizeitvergnügen," 114.

263 The author has been unable to find any more records regarding this case beyond the two handwritten notes in the folder on the Bremen Boys Club in the OMGUS records (RG 260) at the National Archives, College Park, Maryland. The records on the Bremen Boys Club end in December 1947.

tainly occur informally or in formal situations such as in the spaces of official youth clubs, where GIs had higher levels of power as both the club mentors of youth and as foreign occupiers.[264]

Overall, despite negative factors regarding GYA clubs in Bremen, such as rumors, competition with German-run youth clubs, and German resentment about the clubs, many German youngsters still went to GYA clubs, including the hundreds of members of the Bremen Boys Club. Motivated individual soldiers such as Moriarty certainly helped with this development in creating spaces designed for young Germans to have positive experiences, providing a respite from the challenging postwar circumstances. Moriarty appears to have remained motivated to continue working with the occupation youth activities program: He continued his engagement after he was transferred to Frankfurt in May 1947, working as part of the GYA Section of EUCOM. In September 1948, Moriarty participated in the Third Armed Forces Assistance Program to German Youth Activities training conference in Heidelberg. There he spoke about publicity for the program and highlighted the importance of spreading the story about GYA to three groups, the Germans, American military and civilian occupation personnel, and Americans at home, who were the ones "foot[ing] the bills." He argued that it was very important to tell "the people of our country" about "the tremendous effect that GYA is having on the youth of Germany." Moreover, he argued that "the millions we are sending to rebuild this country will be cheap insurance if these people [the Germans] will not be the instrument of another group such as the Nazis." Moreover, he emphasized the need for advertising GYA with compelling stories: "We have to have stories. You must advertize [sic] GYA. Get busy." He also stated that he had prepared a pamphlet entitled "Ambassadors in Khaki," which "tells the story of GYA and

---

264 Cases of child sexual abuse and the failure of institutions to respond have gained widespread attention in recent decades, including cases in the Catholic Church and the Boy Scouts of America. In October 2012, the Boy Scouts of America released files from 1959 to 1991 containing reports of child sexual abuse. See Michelle Anne Cubellis, "Sexual Victimization, Disclosure, and Accountability: Organizational Responses of the Boy Scouts of America to Child Sexual Abuse" (PhD diss., City University of New York, 2015), https://academicworks.cuny.edu/gc_etds/893. Cubellis notes, "Organizations that serve youth as their primary population have the responsibility of ensuring that the children are provided with safe and nurturing environments. One of the greatest responsibilities of these organizations is to ensure that the adults chosen to work with youth do not take advantage of their positions of power" (1). For an overview of institutional policies put in place to protect youth, see "Appendix A: Boy Scouts of America Youth Protection Policies," 206. Since 2011, mandatory reporting of child abuse has been required. See also Mitchell B. Mackinem and Deborah Laufersweiler-Dwyer, "A Deeper Look at the Boy Scouts of America 'Perversion' Files: Structural Factors Related to Access and Abuse," *Journal of Interpersonal Violence* 39, no. 15–16 (August 1, 2024): 3352–3372, https://doi.org/10.1177/08862605241230091.

the story of GI's [sic] in Germany," thus linking the experience of GIs to that of occupation activities for German youth. The plan was to send three million copies of this brochure to "every college and high school in our nation" with the assistance of the Armed Forces Recruiting Service, highlighting the central role of GYA had taken on in the occupation, even being used for recruitment of new occupation troops among young Americans.[265] Also in September 1948, Moriarty was commended by General Omar N. Bradley, Army Chief of Staff, who wrote to Moriarty that "much of the success of our GYA program has been due to your pioneering." Bradley connected the importance of GYA work to ensuring a positive future, stating that Moriarty's part in this "important undertaking . . . will pay us dividends in the future." In the *Stars and Stripes* article reporting on this commendation, Moriarty stated that he was extending his enlistment in order to assure "the people of Europe" that through a continued American occupation troop presence in Germany, they would be protected. He said, "We mean business when we say that we will oppose any threat or intimidation from forces that seek to destroy the right of men to govern themselves according to their own will and the dictates of their conscience." This indicates that he considered his work with German youth as playing an essential role in ensuring European security and requiring a continued American troop presence. Moriarty also claimed that the US was exceptional due to its focus on equality, stating, "It's a great government, our democracy. It's probably the only Army in the world where the Chief of Staff would sit down and write one of his men a personal letter."[266]

---

265 "The Armed Forces Assistance Program to German Youth Activities: Notes from the Third Training Conference," Heidelberg, September 16–19, 1948; Folder G.Y.A.; Records of the Education and Cultural Relations Division: Group Activities Branch Recs of German Youth Assoc. 1945–49; OMGBY; Box 45; OMGUS; RG 260; NACP.

266 "GI Commended for GYA Work: M Sgt, Lauded by Bradley, Urges Buddies to Re-Enlist," *Stars and Stripes*, October 10, 1948. Moriarty's official service records indicate that he was discharged in Heidelberg in November 1948. He did reenlist, serving in the Air Force and eventually ending up at Chanute Air Force Base in Illinois. On January 23, 1952 he was discharged early from Chanute Air Force Base due to his "unsuitability," but his discharge took place "under honorable conditions." For his 1948 discharge, see Enlisted Record and Report of Separation: Honorable Discharge, November 22, 1948; Enlistment Record: Regular Army, November 23, 1948. In 1947, Moriarty was awarded the Army Commendation Ribbon for meritorious service due to his engagement with GYA in Bremen during the period from August 1 to October 25, 1946. See General Orders No. 48, War Department, May 22, 1947; Citation, undated. For his discharge in 1952, see records including Request for Service Information, June 4, 1957; Report of Proceedings of Board of Officers, January 15, 1952; Charles A. Wunsch, M/Sgt Patrick Moriarty, December 6, 1951; Charles H. Kramer, Clinical Record, December 8, 1951. Also, Report of Separation from the Armed Forces of the United States, January 23, 1952. All records in Official Military Personnel File of Patrick Joseph Moriarty, 36707703; Official Military Personnel Files; RG 319; NASL.

Moriarty appeared in further press regarding his GYA engagement for EUCOM. An October 1948 report on GYA in the *National Geographic Magazine* included an image of Moriarty inspecting a water wheel project being built by a group of boys in Garmisch in Bavaria. The caption of the photo mentioned Moriarty's fame and expertise in GYA work: "Moriarty is one of the best-known Yankee soldiers in the American Zone, especially among young Germans. In off-duty hours, at his own expense, he has pioneered in GYA work. He knows almost every playground, summer camp, youth center, Army and Air Force library, and manual-art training school from Bremen to Munich." Moriarty also apparently worked closely with the *National Geographic* cameraman for the article, serving as his "guide, philosopher, and friend."[267] Thus, throughout his service in Germany, Moriarty remained passionate about GYA and the role of the GI in the occupation mission of democratizing German youth to help prevent future totalitarianism and war. Although his role as sponsor of the Bremen Boys Club was ambivalent and no conclusion can be made with certainty regarding potential misconduct documented in the records, Moriarty undoubtedly served as a role model of an individual benevolent GI sacrificing his own time and money to serve the greater mission of helping build GYA throughout the occupation zone. According to the *National Geographic* article, he had even achieved fame for his efforts among German youth themselves.

GYA and Girls

Moriarty's boys club focused on reeducating young men as future democratic leaders of Germany, thus highlighting gender roles of boys being future leaders, as well as the notion that men were seen as responsible for National Socialism while German women were passive bystanders, as Petra Goedde notes.[268] There also could have been fear among occupation officials of placing too much emphasis on clubs for girls due to worries that the clubs would be interpreted as spaces for negative forms of fraternization, mainly of underage females having sexual relations with GIs.[269] However, the role of girls was not completely overlooked in the youth activities program. Many GYA clubs were open to both girls and boys,

267 Frederick Simpich, "Uncle Sam Bends a Twig in Germany," *National Geographic Magazine*, October 1948, 540.
268 Goedde, *GIs and Germans*, 144.
269 See Goedde, *GIs and Germans*, 153.

such as the Bremen Baseball Club and the Bremen Liberty Club in Bremen.[270] Official records indicate engagement of the Bremen military government regarding gender equality: A Bremerhaven GYA club called the Club 48 (named after the year it was founded) was told it had to revise its application for approval with the military government, because in the constitution they had written that they preferred male members over female members in leadership positions, with three boys and one girl on the board. The club needed to revise this to have equal representation to prevent any discrimination between male and female members before they could be officially approved.[271] Female GYA clubs had to follow the same procedures as all GYA clubs, such as holding elections and writing a constitution, thus learning democratic practices. All-female clubs in Bremen such as the Bremen Girls Club and the Ann Fitzgerald Club did indeed often take on gendered activities such as handicrafts, but they also had other activities such as sports, discussions, and English lessons.[272] The Bremen Boys Club also collaborated with female GYA clubs including the Bremen Girls Club and the Ann Fitzgerald Club, holding dances and parties together as well as a quiz event in November 1947. The Bremen Boys Club also reported about elections in the Bremen Girls Club in their newspaper *Die Brücke*.[273] The Ann Fitzgerald Club was founded by Ann Fitzgerald, an American dependent volunteer, and sponsored by the AFN Bremen. However, the military government required the club to change its name to reduce the focus on Fitzgerald and increase its focus on the girls and their democratic

270 See Folder Baseball Club Bremen 1946–47; Records Relating to German Youth & Sports Clubs, 1947–49; OMGBR; Box 316; OMGUS; RG 260; NACP. Folder Liberty Club 1947; Records of the Education Division: Records Relating to German Youth & Sports Clubs, 1947–49; OMGBR; Box 319; OMGUS; RG 260; NACP.

271 Letter from Alexander F. Leith, OMGBR, to Magistrat der Stadt Bremerhaven Amt für Jugendpflege und Sport, July 2, 1948; Folder Club 48; Rcs of Bremerhaven Liasion & Security Detachment: Records of Clubs & Youth Activities, 1947–49; OMGBR; Box 594; OMGUS; RG 260; NACP. Verfassung des Klubs '48'; same location as previous.

272 Folder Bremen Girls Club, 1947; Records Relating to German Youth & Sports Clubs, 1947–49; OMGBR; Box 316; OMGUS; RG 260; NACP. The Bremen Girls Club also was engaged in community social work, for example knitting sweaters for orphans in 1947: "Bremen Girls Knit Sweaters German [sic] for Eleven Orphans," *Port Reporter*, October 17, 1947, in Folder Bremen Girls Club, same location as previous.

273 "Weekly report of German Youth Activities," June 13, 1947; Folder Bremen Boys Club; Records Relating to German Youth & Sports Clubs, 1947–49; OMGBR; Box 316; OMGUS; RG 260; NACP. "Report of Weekly Youth Activities," February 24, 1947; same location as previous. "Report of German Youth Activities," December 1, 1947; same location as previous. "In letzter Minute," *Die Brücke* Nr. 13, January 15, 1947; same location as previous.

agency; the club changed its name to the Unity Girls Club in December 1947.[274] The club's constitution stated that it aimed "to develop and maintain the high standards of culture and morale; to unite common interest of cooperative action between nations; to stimulate personal initiative; to acquire and instill self-reliance and self-responsibility for an everlasting peace."[275] The club's aims thus went beyond learning proper gender roles and preparing girls to be housewives and mothers. Petra Goedde argues that activities in GYA girls clubs were often based on such limited conceptions of female gender roles, doing "little to diminish the inequality between the sexes within German society."[276] However, the example of the Ann Fitzgerald Club/Unity Girls Club shows that, at least in theory, this club was based around democratic, international principles. Finally, the Girl Scouts also became active in postwar Germany, providing another way for German girls to belong to an internationally-oriented club, and many American women in Germany, including the wives of Military Governor Lucius Clay's two sons, were interested in playing an active role in the Girl Scouts in Germany.[277]

Officials especially wanted to encourage girls' participation in the clubs to prevent them from participating in negative forms of fraternization, such as having sexual relations with soldiers. A report about an informal discussion between

---

274 "AFN Girls Club," October 15, 1947; Folder Ann Fitzgerald Girls Club; Records of the Education Division: Records of Youth and Sports Clubs, 1947–49; OMGBR; Box 320; OMGUS; RG 260; NACP. Letter from Charles R. Jeffs to President of the Bremen Senate, Youth Service Office, "Ann Fitzgerald Girls Club," November 21, 1947; same location as previous. "Unity Girls Club," December 8, 1947; Folder Unity Girls' Club 1947; Records of the Education Division: Records of Youth and Sports Clubs, 1947–49; OMGBR; Box 319; OMGUS; RG 260; NACP.

275 Ann Fitzgerald Club Constitution; Folder Ann Fitzgerald Girls Club; Records of Youth and Sports Clubs, 1947–49; OMGBR; Box 320; OMGUS; RG 260; NACP. Also, Unity Girls Club, Constitution (in German), December 10, 1947; Records of the Education Division: Records of Youth and Sports Clubs, 1947–49; OMGBR; Box 319; OMGUS; RG 260; NACP.

276 Goedde, *GIs and Germans*, 154.

277 "Girl Scouts. American women interested in Scouting"; Folder Girl Scouts—Correspondence, Records RE the Work of the Youth Activities Section; Records of the Education and Cultural Relations Division: Records of the Community Education Branch; Box 141; OMGUS; RG 260; NACP. See also Folder Girl Scouts; The Education & Cultural Relations Division: Group Activities Branch: Recs of Organized Groups, 1946–49; Records of Office of Military Government, Hesse (OMGH); Box 713; OMGUS; RG 260; NACP. Also, Folder C9 Girl Scouts; Records of the Education and Cultural Relations Division: Community Activ Branch Chief: Corresp & Rel Recs, 1945–49; Office of Military Government, Wuerttemberg-Baden (OMGWB); Box 963; OMGUS; RG 260, NACP. Although organizations such as the Boy Scouts, Girl Scouts, and YMCA were indeed active, none of them met the scope of the GYA program. Scout uniforms were also a major issue, with scouting not allowed at first in the British zone. On the Boys Scouts of America, including on US military bases in Europe, see Mischa Honeck, *Our Frontier is the World: The Boy Scouts in the Age of American Ascendancy* (Cornell University Press, 2018).

Ladd and around 100 members of Wesermünde youth groups noted that club members believed that youth groups rarely reached teenaged girls (14 and up) who ran with GIs.[278] This highlights the supposedly deviant behavior of such young women and their lack of participation (or interest) in reeducative programs. However, the military government increasingly viewed young women as an important group in GYA. For example, beginning in 1946, the military government campaigned for increased WAC participation in GYA. In a message from November 1946, General McNarney emphasized the importance of having American women assist with youth activities for girls, writing that "although we are making great strides in handling boys, there is urgent need to place more emphasis upon activities for girls."[279] In addition, the October 5, 1946 official GYA directive required that "at least one qualified female advisor will be maintained at each of the above offices of Military Government," who would have the duty to recommend "procedures designed to intensify proper reeducation and rehabilitation of German females under age 18."[280] A report from December 1946 noted that so far, two WACs had been employed in the youth activities military government section in Greater Hesse and Bavaria.[281] In Bremen, the Women's Club GYA Auxiliary (made up of American dependent wives) played an active role in fundraising and assistance with youth activities and ran a variety show for the GYA clubs in August 1947, where GYA clubs performed to raise funds.[282] Military Governor Clay's wife, Marjorie, also urged American women to aid GYA, critiquing the fact that activities "for girls had lagged," since the program had mostly been in the hands of male military personnel. Additionally, she highlighted the role of the program as a reeducation program, not a recreational one, linking GYA to the

278 "Elements Not in Youth Groups," February 17, 1947; Folder YXI Incidents & Public Opinion; Rcs of Bremerhaven Liaison & Security Detachment: Records of Clubs & Youth Activities, 1947–49; OMGBR; Box 591; OMGUS; RG 260; NACP.

279 Unclassified Message from McNarney, November 4, 1946; Folder WAC Programs-1946/47; Records RE the Work of the Youth Activities Section; Box 148; OMGUS; RG 260; NACP.

280 5 October 1946 Directive, HQ USFET; Folder USFET Directive 5 October 1946; Records RE the Work of the Youth Activities Section; Box 148; OMGUS; RG 260; NACP.

281 "Summary of Youth Activities for the Directors' Meeting," December 20, 1946; Folder Weekly Summary 1946; Records RE the Work of the Youth Activities Section; Box 148; OMGUS; RG 260; NACP. See also Goedde, *GIs and Germans*, 153–154.

282 "The German Youth Activities Variety Show," August 29, 1947; Folder Liberty Club 1947; Records Relating to German Youth & Sports Clubs, 1947–49; OMGBR; Box 319; OMGUS; RG 260, NACP. See also Folder Bremen Women's Club GYA Auxiliary; Records Relating to German Youth & Sports Clubs, 1947–49; OMGBR; Box 320; OMGUS; RG 260; NACP. The Bremen Boys Club donated the funds they raised in the variety show to the "Stop the Polio" drive in Berlin.

wider occupation efforts.[283] A letter from November 5, 1946 from Elizabeth P. Lam of the OMGUS Youth Activities Section to Colonel Westray Battle Boyce, Director of WAC (see Figure 3.1), highlighted the importance of the GYA program in meeting the needs of German girls. Lam noted that there were "large areas of need among German girls which this assistance cannot meet as long as men only are appointed as GYA officers." She also noted the unique issues of German girlhood under military occupation:

> The problem of the German girls between fifteen and twenty is in many ways more difficult than that of the boys of the same age. Many girls are without family or relatives, and therefore without stabilizing influences of a home. The crowded and uncomfortable living conditions under which all families live provide no place for recreation or social intercourse in the homes. The lack of food and other necessities of life place hard pressure upon young girls to gain a livelihood by "fraternization." Even the earnings in [an] office or factory are not sufficient in many instances to keep body and soul together. Many thoughtful and decent German people see in this situation great potentialities of demoralization among German girls.[284]

Thus, Lam linked increasing girls' participation in GYA activities to helping mitigate societal issues such as preventing negative fraternization with GIs and decreasing the demoralization of young women.

Beginning in late 1946, official military government conferences took place in the American zone aiming at training women about the GYA program, including civilians, WACs, and dependents, focusing on clarifying the program's role as one of reeducation, not Americanization. A conference of WAC GYA officers on April 11, 1947 encouraged the development of friendships with German girls.[285] The summary report of the conference stated that participants (which included Elizabeth Lam of OMGUS, WACs, as well as other GYA Army personnel) discussed how young Germans have feelings of betrayal, because "they accepted Hitler's theory of race and nationalism, and it brought them poverty, want, and defeat." The summary also claimed that the "wrong girl" was being attracted to the GYA program, the "GI sweethearts" who wanted to practice their GI English and who

283 "Mrs. Clay Urges Women to Aid GYA," *Stars and Stripes*, September 4, 1947; in Folder Y.I. Policies and Directives, D. USFET and other US Army Units; Records of the Education Division: Gen Corresp & Rel Recs of Youth Activities Branch, 1945–47; OMGBR; Box 311; OMGUS; RG 260; NACP.

284 Letter from Elizabeth P. Lam to Colonel Westray Battle Boyce, "The Need of WACs in the German Youth Activities Program of the Army," November 5, 1946; Folder WAC Programs-1946/47; Records RE the Work of the Youth Activities Section; Box 148; OMGUS; RG 260; NACP.

285 "The Conference with WAC GYA Officers, Wiesbaden, April 11, 1947"; Folder WAC Programs-1946/47; Records RE the Work of the Youth Activities Section; Box 148; OMGUS; RG 260; NACP.

Figure 3.1: Women's Army Corps (WAC) Colonel Westray Battle Boyce (center) shares a Thanksgiving dinner with two German orphans during her visit to Frankfurt, Germany while on a tour of WAC European facilities, November 28, 1946 (US Army Signal Corps, Harry S. Truman Presidential Library).

"will not make much contribution toward the rehabilitation of Germany," in contrast to other more "serious-minded" girls. In addition, the report noted that participants discussed how Hitler had emphasized "Kinder, Kirche, and Kochen [sic] (children, church, and kitchen) as the duty of women," and that to combat these restrictive National Socialist gender roles, it was important to have "citizenship training of young women and girls."[286] Conference participants thus seemed to believe in the importance of wider societal roles for young women, pushing beyond traditional gender roles also common in the United States of women as housewives and mothers. Interestingly this report contradicted the statement from youth themselves in the Bremen Enclave, who claimed that so-called *Fräuleins* were often not members of GYA clubs, and it also demarcated girls' behavior and suitability for American reeducation goals based on their

286 *Kochen* is incorrectly used in the report; it should be *Küche*. "Summary Report of WAC German Youth Assistance Conference, Wiesbaden, April 11, 1947"; Folder WAC Programs-1946/47; Records RE the Work of the Youth Activities Section; Box 148; OMGUS; RG 260; NACP.

sexual relations.[287] Thus, for American officials, girls who were respectable and serious were seen as the future of Germany and were the focus of GYA activities, while those who behaved in a delinquent manner through sexual relations with GIs were not acceptable for the program. In this manner, the reeducative purpose of the program was contradicted: German girls who were fraternizing may have been doing so out of need, as Lam had noted, and youth clubs could serve as a space to provide positive activities and decrease demoralization of young women. Thus, girlhood under occupation was full of tension even within the sphere of youth activities. Gender roles impacted the level of attention that girls clubs received in comparison to boys clubs, and girls who were sexual partners of GIs were seen as simultaneously in need of guidance yet also unwanted due to their delinquency, as they were marked as not being able to make a positive contribution to future German society. Again, the focus of the issue of negative encounters of sexual fraternization tended to be about female misbehavior, rather than the misbehavior of GIs. In a way, the focus on male-centric GYA clubs such as the Bremen Boys Club also helped generate positive press in the US media, leading to a focus away from negative press about GIs encountering potentially dangerous, misbehaving *Fräuleins* and engaging in sexual activities. Thus, occupying GIs themselves with positive activities such as GYA could also help boost troop morale and lead to soldiers focusing less on negative behaviors common in the occupation such as drinking alcohol and having sex with *Fräuleins*.

Children at Play Across Nations

Late in 1946, the families of American military personnel began to arrive in Germany, beginning a new phase of the occupation. By the end of the decade, around 30,000 American dependent wives and children lived in Germany.[288] However, American dependent children were never completely protected from the grim realities of life in their new cities and towns, especially during the initial period of the occupation when Americans often lived within German communities, rather than in separate American, isolated military communities. According to Susan Carruthers, some service members were worried about exposing their children to shocking scenes of suffering and destruction, and also fretted about their families witnessing the debauchery present between GIs and *Fräuleins*. Husbands also

287 "Elements Not in Youth Groups," February 17, 1947; Folder YXI Incidents & Public Opinion; Rcs of Bremerhaven Liaison & Security Detachment: Records of Clubs & Youth Activities, 1947–49; OMGBR; Box 591; OMGUS; RG 260; NACP.

288 Willoughby, *Remaking the Conquering Heroes*, 120.

worried about their American wives being mistaken for German women and thus at risk of GIs harassing them, highlighting how sexualized the atmosphere in postwar Germany had become.[289] However, officials believed that bringing American wives and children would help bring stability. Domesticating the occupation would help provide families with much needed reunions, which would boost the military's popularity, and also clamp down on soldiers' inappropriate behavior, as John Willoughby notes.[290] Although this goal of improving the moral landscape of occupation Germany did not necessarily come to fruition, the presence of American wives and children did make a mark on everyday life and encounters during the occupation.[291]

American occupation officials specifically encouraged interactions between American civilians and German children. The April 11, 1947 WAC GYA conference placed emphasis on the role of American dependents, including those who had children of their own. Dependents who had children were encouraged to invite German children of the same age to their homes.[292] In addition, American children themselves were encouraged to become friendly and play with German children. Beginning in 1948, teachers and school administrators in Army schools were also encouraged to work together with local GYA officers and to organize special events that had the potential to promote positive relationships between American and German children such as school visits, programs, or parties. According to an official EUCOM report, which quoted the directive encouraging this engagement, the purpose of such undertakings was to "foster good will with the German populace." It noted that school was "one place to teach democracy in action; Germans are certain to be influenced in their estimation of the American way of life by observing the behavior of our children." Relationships between German and American families were thus "of fundamental importance in accomplishing the occupational mission."[293]

Thus, direct transatlantic encounters between children were encouraged as the American military presence in Germany took on a domestic, more permanent status with Americans in the role of protectors, especially in a heightened Cold War atmosphere. For some American officials, increasing the number of positive German and American encounters could serve "a political end" of facilitating "the

---

289 Carruthers, *The Good Occupation*, 269–279.

290 Willoughby, *Remaking the Conquering Heroes*, 117–119.

291 See Carruthers, *The Good Occupation*, 279–280.

292 "Summary Report of WAC German Youth Assistance Conference, Wiesbaden, April 11, 1947"; Folder WAC Programs-1946/47; Records RE the Work of the Youth Activities Section; Box 148; OMGUS; RG 260; NACP.

293 Geis and Gray Jr., *The Relations of Occupation Personnel*, 53–54.

acceptance of democracy in Germany," as Dewey A. Browder describes it.[294] As Donna Alvah argues, American dependent wives and children took on roles abroad as "unofficial ambassadors" of democracy and the American way.[295] American military family members became "representatives of American understanding and good will abroad."[296] In May 1947, according to a EUCOM report, dependents arriving in Germany took part in an information program that informed them that "as they represented the American way of life to a critical German audience, they should exert their best efforts to create a favorable impression on that audience and to illustrate, by their behavior, democracy in action."[297] According to Donna Alvah, with this increasing "civilianization" of the military, some family members actively promoted "American military and foreign relations goals in West Germany." Early in the occupation of Germany, wives and children were expected to "represent American family and home life, aid in establishing democracy, and demonstrate the intention of the occupation forces to help, not oppress, their former enemies."[298] American dependent children were thus also part of the wider Cold War aims of bolstering American global power and justifying the global American military presence.[299] Children were especially adaptable to foreign contexts, since they were able to quickly acclimate to new environments and easily learn other languages, thus being able to communicate with the local populations. Alvah notes that American children's friendships with local civilians served as a "resonant metaphor for ideal relations between the United States and other nations," with American children considered as "natural internationalists." In Germany, American children were informed that the German children would be watching their example. Despite the fact that dependent children were encouraged to show "respect and appreciation for other peoples and their ways of life," the fact remained that Americans were also simultaneously projecting notions of American superiority.[300] Thus, Alvah argues, "interpersonal encounters were always conditioned by geopolitical contexts which created fundamental power imbalances between Americans and non-Americans."[301]

---

294 Browder, *Americans in Post-World War II Germany*, 19.

295 Donna Alvah, *Unofficial Ambassadors: American Military Families Overseas and the Cold War, 1946–1965* (New York University Press, 2007), 2.

296 Alvah, *Unofficial Ambassadors*, 71.

297 Geis and Gray Jr., *The Relations of Occupation Personnel*, 7.

298 Donna Alvah, "American Military Families in West Germany: Social, Cultural, and Foreign Relations, 1946–1965," in *GIs in Germany*, ed. Maulucci Jr. and Junker, 161, 163.

299 Alvah, *Unofficial Ambassadors*, 2–3.

300 Alvah, *Unofficial Ambassadors*, 198–199.

301 Alvah, *Unofficial Ambassadors*, 233. See also Frederiksen, *The American Military Occupation*, 138.

By 1948, according to Alvah, the presence of military families in Germany served to show "the American military's commitment to stand its ground against the Soviet attempt to take over Berlin, as well as resistance to the feared encroachment of Soviet power in Western Europe in the 1950s and 1960s."[302]

Margaret Wood lived in Bremen and Bremerhaven from 1949 to 1952 as a young child while her father was stationed there as a master sergeant. Wood fondly remembers the friendships she created with local children (see Figure 3.2).[303] Wood was two years old when the family arrived in Germany and, at some point, she had been able to speak in German to her German friends, a language she easily picked up as a child but no longer remembers. Her older brother George often played "Cowboys and Indians" with German neighbor boys, most likely leading to a mix of cultural appropriations, as German children often had a positive image of Native peoples due to the popularity of Karl May's stories, where Natives were the heroes of the stories, in contrast with American views where Natives were typically portrayed as the "bad guys."[304] Thus, these children of American and German backgrounds found no issue in connecting over the universal language of fun and play. Wood stated that a German friend, Gunther, "often stayed for dinner at my parents' invitation. These German children and others were well integrated into the daily

302 Alvah, "American Military Families in West Germany," in *GIs in Germany*, ed. Maulucci Jr. and Junker, 161–162. In 1946, 7,500 military dependents were in the European Theater. In 1949, although the number of military personnel had decreased, the number of family members had grown to 33,000. In 1950, there were 44,337 US military and civilian dependents in Germany, and in 1960, there were 183,896. See Alvah, *Unofficial Ambassadors*, 139; Browder, *Americans in Post-World War II Germany*, 40. See also a 1947 account of the children of occupation personnel at Heidelberg High, "Life Visits 'Heidelberg High,'" *Life*, July 21, 1947, 92–94, 97. The cover of this issue featured the American teenagers outfitted in *Lederhosen*: "What happens when American bobby-soxers are transplanted to Germany is shown on LIFE's cover this week": 19.

303 Email from Margaret Wood to author, August 2, 2022; email from Margaret Wood to author, October 20, 2022. For a photo essay on American military families in Bremerhaven, see Friedrichs, *Bremerhaven und die Amerikaner*, 93–103. In the 1950s, a "James Dean look" was apparently especially popular among youth (98).

304 On Germans' "sense of affinity for American Indians," see H. Glenn Penny, *Kindred by Choice: Germans and American Indians since 1800* (University of North Carolina Press, 2013), xi. German novelist Karl May especially popularized stories of Native Americans. Even in Nazi Germany, children "played Indian." Hitler even read Karl May's work "for insights into crisis situations." Penny argues that "'Indians,' in short, became deeply ingrained in German cultures during the nineteenth century, their stories became ciphers for modern struggles during the twentieth century, and that long cultural history continued unabated through the post-war era" (3). See also Frank Usbeck, *Fellow Tribesmen: The Image of Native Americans, National Identity, and Nazi Ideology in Germany* (Berghahn Books, 2015).

Figure 3.2: Margaret Wood (front), her brother George, in cowboy gear (back row, second from left), and German friends in Bremerhaven, around 1949 (private records of Margaret Wood, Williamstown, Massachusetts).

fabric of our lives in Bremerhaven as were German children when we moved to Bremen in 1951."[305]

Wood's mother Lucile also wrote many letters home to her family in Tennessee describing the encounters between her children and local German children. In a letter written on Christmas in 1949, she argued that it was important to show German children how Americans are, and she noted that she often invited German children over to her home. She described the extreme politeness and even servility of the German children, who would shake hands and even bow to her. She wrote:

> If we don't treat them [German children] this way and make friends and show them our way of life then we will not accomplish our purpose here in Germany. Some American families call the MP's [sic] if a German child gets in their yard. I think that is defeating our purpose. If they can see that we Americans follow the Golden Rule and live in a peaceful, happy way then we are gaining something and we can accomplish much through these young German children who are coming along now. Their ideas are not formulated yet and we can show them the best way of life. So we encourage these children to come here.[306]

---

305 Email from Margaret Wood to author, October 20, 2022.
306 Letter from Lucile Hamlett to her parents and family in Bristol, TN, Bremerhaven, December 25, 1949, private records of Margaret Wood, Williamstown, Massachusetts.

Wood's mother was also active in developing the American military community in the Bremen Enclave, and was involved in founding an American Sunday School. However, according to Margaret Wood, her parents were often frustrated by the German mindset: On the one hand, they made close friendships with Germans, for example with the housekeepers, but on the other hand, they were disgusted by Germans' self-pity and avoidance of their complicity in the Nazi past. Her parents, however, saw German "children differently, as not yet set in their ways and ideologies and holding the promise of a Germany that could be free and democratic."[307] Margaret Wood's story of an early childhood shaped by transatlantic encounters portrays how ubiquitous personal encounters became during the occupation. Many Americans did develop strong personal friendships with German families, including in Bremen.[308] Since 1945, soldiers had been invited to celebrate Christmas with Bremen families, and in 1952, there was also a guest family program at Christmas for GIs in Bremen, in which they could spend Christmas with a German family.[309] Charles Jeffs, the last director of military government in Bremen, married a Bremen woman in 1953 and remained in Bremen until he passed away in 1959.[310] Thus, the American presence in Bremen was normalized, especially through direct personal encounters, including in local neighborhoods and the spaces of the GYA clubs. Germans and Americans exchanged ideas, play, and goods in an atmosphere marked by the power structures of the occupation, yet both sides made an impact on each other.

****

The GYA program especially encouraged personal encounters between Americans and young Germans and played a wide-ranging role in official occupation attempts at reeducating youth. Through GYA, German youth gained exposure to different ways of living, concepts of democracy, and an increased international outlook. However, an assessment of GYA's total impact on the reeducation of German youth leads to ambivalent conclusions. Instead of coming to definite conclusions about GYA's success or failure in terms of reeducating German youth into tolerant, peaceful democrats, it is more helpful to evaluate the impact of GYA

307 Email from Margaret Wood to author, October 20, 2022.

308 Jansen and Meyer-Braun, *Bremen in der Nachkriegszeit*, 31.

309 Pedron, *Amerikaner vor Ort*, 283–284.

310 Jansen and Meyer-Braun, *Bremen in der Nachkriegszeit*, 31; Pedron, 374–375. Jeffs' widower advocated for renaming Vahrerstrasse in Bremen to Jeffsallee, but this request was ultimately declined by Bremen Senate in 1967: see Pedron, 375–377. For photos of the couple, see Schmidt, *Als Bremen Amerikanisch war*. Before they married, both were widowers and they each had a son.

on the lives of its participants and on German society in the US zone. In general, personal encounters with GIs, including individual acts of kindness, could indeed transform children's views of the former enemy. The presence of Americans in the space of GYA clubs could also fundamentally impact youth's views, for example providing a model of a new and different way of living. GYA clubs could also have profound individual impacts. In a 2003 Radio Bremen filmed clip about the Bremen Boys Club, former member Walter Brandes stated that the members had been young Nazis when they joined the club; however, through the club, youth gained new conceptions about democracy in ways that challenged the beliefs learned in their National Socialist upbringing.[311] The democratic practices learned in the sphere of GYA clubs could indeed have a significant effect on reeducation of youth. Of course, however, this remained limited to those youth who were members of clubs.[312] Additionally, GYA clubs and youth centers were especially welcome for children most in need, such as children from low-income families and refugee children from the former German territories in the East.[313]

In contrast to most scholars, who are skeptical about GYA's long-term impact, Harald T. Leder argues that American youth programs and the presence of Americans in the occupation led to "a positive and long lasting effect which went beyond immediate material gains," contributing to shaping the "inner constitution of many young Germans in the American zone."[314] Moreover, he argues that American youth work impacted Germans, who "adopted American ideas and models for youth work and explored new ways of integrating young Germans into the international community."[315] Leder argues that many youngsters in the occupation took advantage of the various "opportunities to have a look at the outside world and to break out of the intellectual and spiritual isolation they had experienced during the Third Reich," with many of them seeming "to accept the new political system" and embracing basic democratic values including "freedom of expression, a higher degree of tolerance, and at least participation in the elec-

311 Susanne Brahms, *Bremen Boys Club*, in Buten un Binnen, Radio Bremen, January 19, 2003. The author wishes to thank Susanne Brahms for her assistance in providing information about this program. See also Markwort, "Wo Hitlerjungen zu Demokraten wurden," *Weser-Kurier*, November 5, 2015.

312 See Burschka, "Re-Education und Jugendöffentlichkeit," 23.

313 Rupieper, *Die Wurzeln der westdeutschen Nachkriegsdemokratie*, 161; Goedde, *GIs and Germans*, 157.

314 Leder, "Americans and German Youth," xii, 727.

315 Leder, xii. For an example of European and international exchange, the *Jugendamt* (Youth Welfare Office) Bremen and the *Freie Wohlfahrtsverbände* (official charity organizations) sponsored three-month long vacations to Switzerland for Bremen youth. Some 566 youth were able to take part in 1947: Peters, *Zwölf Jahre Bremen*, 105.

toral process." Leder also states that voter participation was high in the 1950s and 1960s, and notes how the next generation of youth of the 1960s took to the streets to protest in a demonstration of "an unequivocal commitment to democracy."[316] GYA did indeed provide an opportunity for young Germans to learn about another way of living and gain hands-on practice in democracy, but it is not possible to conclude whether the program fundamentally impacted German democracy, with a variety of reasons and contexts emerging that led to democratic engagement in the next decades after the youth program had ended. What is clear, however, is that the American occupation presence led to encounters that had the potential to make personal, political, and societal impacts, including through American reeducation programs such as GYA. Instead of focusing on the overarching success or failure of GYA and reeducation, this chapter has depicted the GYA program's centrality to American aims and the diverse effects of the program on individual Americans and Germans.

Criticisms of the GYA program highlighted the limitations and challenges of the program, including the fact that it did not reach all German youth, that regular soldiers instead of pedagogical experts (or Germans) took on the role of educators of youth, the negative effects of competition between military government, the Army, and German institutions, and the avoidance of challenging topics in clubs such as the recent National Socialist past.[317] Another major issue with GYA was frequent turnover: The quality of the GYA programs depended on the individual initiative of club sponsors.[318] The program was also dependent on the American military. After the end of the occupation statute in 1955, most GYA youth centers were shut down instead of turned over to the Germans, especially due to Germans' financial difficulties.[319] Overall, young Germans faced a particularly challenging time during the occupation, in which they not only were facing present challenges such as hunger but also had to confront deeper issues such as past experiences and future worries. GYA could provide a space of respite from the harsh realities of postwar, but youth remained in a difficult situation. According to an official report from 1948 on youth activities, "German youth is still in

316 Leder, 725–729.

317 See challenges of GYA in Rode, "Zwischen Re-education und Freizeitvergnügen," 23, 34, 47, 53, 110–111, 114–115.

318 Rode, "Manche nannten sie nur 'Schokoladenclubs,'" 25, 32–33; Rode, "Zwischen Re-education und Freizeitvergnügen," 46; Peterson, *The American Occupation of Germany*, 158–159.

319 See plans on phasing out GYA, The Foreign Service of the United States of America, Classified Telegram, May 29, 1953; Folder 572 Youth Activities 1953–1955; Security-Segregated General Records, 1953–55, 571–572.1; Box 233; HICOG, RG 466; NACP. See also *The U.S. Armed Forces German Youth Activities Program 1945–1955*, 49–59.

the transient stage between yesterday and tomorrow."[320] Additionally, the report concluded, "Until there is more assurance of a relatively stable future, German youth will remain with no sound 'today,' vacillating between his [sic] 'yesterday' and 'tomorrow.'"[321] German youth were thus still in a deep transition phase that would take more than a few years to reckon with. Many young Germans remained unable to reach a level of present contentedness in the wake of fears about the future and the background of the Nazi past. GYA could help provide positive experiences through encounters with GIs, learning about the benefits of American-style democracy, which included access to material plenty and gaining skills such as how to vote or participate in discussions. However, even those active in GYA clubs were impacted by the weight of the past and the uncertainty over the future.

Overall, Army Assistance to GYA did play a fundamental role in occupation goals of reeducation and democratization of youth. As the example of the Bremen Boys Club portrays, GYA impacted some young Germans in a positive manner, although GYA did not reach all young Germans. For example, the members of the Bremen Boys Club showed an ability to critically examine and form an opinion about current events in the articles of their club newspaper. Boys who joined the club had also trusted American soldiers enough to seek out a club with the potential for intensive contact with them.[322] However, the type of democracy that they learned came into tension with the limitations and contradictions inherent in practicing democracy within a military occupation, as the example of the revoking of permission for publishing the club newspaper *Die Brücke* portrayed.

The Bremen Boys Club benefited from the impressive engagement of soldiers stationed in Bremen such as Patrick Moriarty, who brought attention to the needs of the youngest Germans, impacting larger American policies towards German youth and shaping transatlantic aid. Spaces such as the Bremen Boys Club provided a youth-centric space in the midst of a destroyed city, where youth gained a chance to temporarily escape the misery and want common in postwar occupation Germany. Petra Goedde argues that GYA as a whole "succeeded best in areas where it filled a vacuum in children's social environment."[323] Through GYA, youth could gain connection with the wider world, which appears to have been a strong desire for many young Germans, as noted by an interest in pen pal pro-

320 *German Youth Between Yesterday and Tomorrow*, 1.
321 *German Youth Between Yesterday and Tomorrow*, 34.
322 See Rode, "Zwischen Re-education und Freizeitvergnügen," 116.
323 Goedde, *GIs and Germans*, 163. See also Rode, Manche nannten sie nur 'Schokoladenclubs,'" 35; Rode, "Zwischen Re-education und Freizeitvergnügen," 115; Füssl, *Die Umerziehung*, 167; Pedron, *Amerikaner vor Ort*, 280.

grams, the world language Esperanto, and trips abroad.[324] The clubs thus opened dialogue between German and American youth, and club life was shaped in a space of interaction between Germans and Americans, which could include exposure to American culture.[325] Journalist Peter Groth noted that the postwar "*Lebensgefühl*" of "Hey-Ba-Ba-Re-Bob" (a popular swing song from 1946 by Lionel Hampton) disappeared in 1951 when the Americans left Bremen in large numbers.[326] Reinald Ihler, who was 12 years old at the end of the war and often visited the Bremen Boys Club as a guest, mentioned in a 2015 interview that the boys in the club mostly preferred listening to American jazz and swing records, including the song "Hey-Ba-Ba-Re-Bop." In 1949, he founded the Astoria Club in Bremen but does not remember how exactly he and his friends chose that name for the new club. In the interview, he stated that they most likely thought it sounded chic and American, highlighting the positive view many youngsters held regarding American culture. In the club, the members held elections, had to write a constitution, played table tennis, did arts and crafts, and read American books.[327]

Thus, the GYA program impacted German society through its focus on youth work focused on democratic values, even if its direct impact on individual lives remained limited to those who had a positive experience in the clubs.[328] Overall,

324 *German Youth Between Yesterday and Tomorrow*, 28–32; Gerald C. Fisher, Report of German Youth Activities, December 15, 1947; Folder Bremen Boys Club; Records of the Education Division: Records Relating to German Youth and Sports Clubs, 1947–49; OMGBR; Box 316; OMGUS; RG 260; NACP. "Warum ich mir die Amerikanisierung gefallen lasse," *Die Brücke* Nr. 18, 2. Jahrgang, April 8, 1947, same location as previous record.

325 See Goedde, *GIs and Germans*, 163; Pedron, 13–14, 293.

326 Groth "Bremer Jungs im Jahre Sechsundvierzig," in *Vom Trümmerkind zum Teenager*, ed. Foitzik, 25–27. "Hey! Ba-Ba-Re-Bop" was a 1946 song by Lionel Hampton and His Orchestra and was a pop and R & B top hit. Heinrich Kupffer's book, Heinrich Kupffer, *Swingtime: Chronik einer Jugend in Deutschland 1937–1951* (Frieling, 1987), examines the role of swing music during the Third Reich as a way to retain connection and belonging with the wider world outside of Nazi Germany. Also see an oral history about swing and jazz in the Bremen Boys Club, Bruss, ed., *Mit Zuckersack und Heißgetränk*, 194.

327 Reinald Ihler, interview by Peter Strotmann, September 24, 2015; Peter Strotmann, "Als die Amerikaner einen 'Bremen Boys Club' gründeten," *Weser-Kurier*, August 5, 2023, 44. During the war, Reinald Ihler's mother was killed in an Allied bombing attack while on a train going to visit Reinald and his sister, who had been evacuated from Bremen through the *Kinderlandverschickung*. Ihler participated in GYA activities as early as 1946, when the Americans opened a GYA center. Besides his participation in youth activities, Ihler also worked for the Americans as a caddie at the country club, where he and the other boys were paid in Camels or Lucky Strikes, which he sold to black market dealers for Reichsmarks. In 1950, Ihler stopped participating in the Astoria Club, as he had to focus totally on school.

328 Kathleen J. Nawyn has provided a fascinating study into the impacts of German-run youth groups in occupation Württemberg-Baden. She argues that American efforts of demilitarization

however, the presence of American GIs as teachers, role models, benevolent providers, and father figures to youth, and their GYA role as youth club sponsors, helped shape German views of democracy, and also forged American views of Germans as people in need of aid and protection, which became especially relevant in the heightening Cold War. GYA aimed for a fundamental shift in the lives of young Germans: Through the youth activities program, club members who may have previously been part of the fascist Hitler Youth or *Bund Deutscher Mädel* now could work together to write a constitution, write articles in the club newspaper using critical analysis, or attend discussions on democracy in club rooms. Members of the most famous club, the Bremen Boys Club, even saw themselves in a pioneering role as agents of future German democracy, aiming to build bridges with the international community and rejecting National Socialist ideology for its emptiness and war-mongering.[329] Moreover, in articles written in the club newspaper, *Die Brücke*, and during the subsequent protest regarding the newspaper's license being revoked, the club members criticized the contradictions of democracy under a military occupation, rather than democracy in general.[330] Another young German, who had been the president of the first GYA club in Munich, provided a similar critique of the GYA program as to that of the Bremen Boys Club members' critique. He wrote in an article entitled "The German Youth—Guinea-Pigs for an Idea" that the occupation goal of teaching democracy with German youth as "guinea-pigs of a reeducation idea" was bound to be a failure, because democracy could not be taught nor forced, but rather, he argued, "you have to feel it, see it in action." What especially bothered this youth about American democracy was the irony of the mistreatment of African Americans, which Germans witnessed. The reasons for this mistreatment "did not seem rea-

---

impacted these clubs, even though "only a portion" of the youth were participating in these organized groups. She argues that Americans did make an impact on the demilitarization of youth activities, often receiving German support. She writes, "By 1949, military-style uniforms, soldier songs, and drill instruction were no longer key components of youth programs. Additionally, many groups had declared their opposition to militarism and war, and youth organizations would continue to reject militarism and advocate peace in the years that followed." Boys were thus no longer to be raised as soldiers, and a new "masculine ideal" appeared, a peaceful hero, who aimed to rebuild Germany. Kathleen J. Nawyn, "Banning the Soldier Hero: American Regulations, German Youth, and Changing Ideals of Manhood in Occupied Württemberg-Baden, 1945–1949," in *Gender and the Long Postwar: The United States and the Two Germanys, 1945–1989*, ed. Karen Hagemann and Sonya Michel (Woodrow Wilson Center Press, 2014), 136.

329 See "Application for Approval of Organization," June 1, 1947; Folder Bremen Boys Club; OMGBR; Box 316; OMGUS; RG 260; NACP. See also Rode, "Zwischen Re-education und Freizeitvergnügen," 112.

330 See Rode, "Zwischen Re-education und Freizeitvergnügen," 113.

sonable to us," he stated. He offered advice about how to rescue the program: "Above all, do not sell democracy like drummers. For us the form of democracy we see in Germany is hard to believe in anyway, but advertising will make it even harder. We heard a lot of advertisement for ideologies in recent years. Show us examples, let us be subject to democratic action. Then perhaps the guinea pigs will have some value."[331] GYA thus provided a basis for youth to grapple with questions of democracy and citizenship, even to the level that they would call into question the democratic limits of the GYA program itself, the contradictions of military occupation, and the fundamental tension inherent in American democracy, the treatment of its black citizens. Therefore, the occupation task that had emerged as most important, the reeducation of German youth to ensure future democracy, proved to be high stakes, with intergenerational, transatlantic encounters between German youth and American soldiers playing a major role in carving a path to a future German democratic state. GYA was flushed with ambivalence and contradiction, including soldiers teaching democracy and power imbalances between the conquerors and the conquered, yet it cannot be denied that the encounter between German youth and Americans molded German notions of democracy and spurred awareness of democracy's own limitations.

331 "The German Youth—Guinea-Pigs for an Idea"; Folder Germans on GYA; Records RE the Work of the Youth Activities Section; Box 140; OMGUS; RG 260; NACP. Letter Donald T. Shea, to OMGUS, Office of the Director of Intelligence, Subject: The Armed Forces Assistance Program, March 17, 1949; same location as previous record.

Chapter 4
Coca-Cola, Hershey Bars, and the Cold War Geopolitics of Gratitude

In such towns as Garmisch you may see American soldiers from Kansas, or any other State, with all the self-confidence of early Roman conquerors, riding about in carriages and holding fräuleins' hands, learning the German language, and spreading the gospel of private enterprise, individualism, and the streamlined American way.
–Frederick Simpich[1]

In *Life* magazine on February 17, 1941, Henry Luce declared that the American Century had dawned.[2] Nearly ten years later, on May 15, 1950, an article in *Time* magazine claimed that Coca-Cola had become an "empire" through a "peaceful near-conquest" of the world. The article mentioned that in occupied Japan, GIs had provided the locals with a sampling of the drink that had spread around the world by 1950, and that those who had a taste "have been pleased." Thus, the postwar presence of American soldiers ensured the simultaneous presence of the sweet soft drink Coca-Cola, "the Essence of America," as *Time* described the beverage.[3] Coca-Cola, in a way, came to mean the new, fresh postwar era; it came to mean "democracy," as Jeff R. Schutts notes.[4] Coca-Cola production was reintroduced in West Germany in October 1949, and according to Schutts, Germans, who were "no longer forced to rely on a friendly GI for an ice-cold Coke, overwhelmed Coca-Cola GmbH's initial limited supply," and the company even had to ration supplies for a time. By 1954, annual Coca-Cola sales were at over 24 million cases in West Germany, a 600% increase outpacing even the general rate of German economic recovery.[5] (West) Germany proved especially eager to become "Coca-Colonized," becoming the largest Coca-Cola market outside of the United States by 1965.[6] The type of freedom that American soldiers seemed to have brought to Ger-

---

1 Frederick Simpich, "Uncle Sam Bends a Twig in Germany," *National Geographic Magazine*, October 1948, 550.
2 Henry Luce, "The American Century," *Life*, February 17, 1941, 61–65.
3 "The Sun Never Sets on Cacoola," *Time*, May 15, 1950, 28–32.
4 Jeff R. Schutts, "Born Again in the Gospel of Refreshment? Coca-Cola and the Re-Making of Postwar German Identity," in *Consuming Germany in the Cold War*, ed. David F. Crew (Berg, 2003), 135.
5 Schutts, "Born Again in the Gospel of Refreshment?," in *Consuming Germany in the Cold War*, ed. Crew, 130.
6 Schutts, "Born Again in the Gospel of Refreshment?," in *Consuming Germany in the Cold War*, ed. Crew, 130, 143. See discussion of the term "Coca-Colonization" on page 131. Schutts notes that the usage of "Coca-Colonization" usually tends to see "globalization as a manifestation of cultural

https://doi.org/10.1515/9783111588155-005

many with the end of World War II was particularly sweet, embodied through individual acts of benevolence and turned into collective actions such as the candy bombing during the Berlin Airlift of June 1948 to September 1949.[7]

Exchanges of snacks and sugary products helped mold the US occupation of Germany, especially gifts of food to hungry German children from GIs. As benevolence towards German children became commonplace, official occupation policies shifted. This included an end to the ban on fraternization as well as increasing levels of humanitarian aid for Germans.[8] In 1946, President Truman officially approved sending aid to Germany, which included aid through the Council of Relief Agencies Licensed to Operate in Germany (CRALOG) and CARE packages. In 1947, the *Schulspeisung* school feeding program also began in the US zone.[9] President Truman himself even purchased 100 CARE packages at $15 each in May 1946.[10] As the Cold War heightened, aid to Germany intensified, especially during the Berlin

imperialism, where the largely American-based transnational corporations use their marketing power to clear-cut local cultural life in order to impose bland and invasive commercialized culture." Other scholars use the term "creolization" instead to understand processes of globalization, which "stresses the cross-currents and complexity of cultural transfer." See also Jeff R. Schutts, "Coca-Cola History: A 'Refreshing' Look at German-American Relations," *Bulletin of the German Historical Institute* 40 (Spring 2007): 132, 134–136; Willett, *The Americanization of Germany*, ix; Reinhold Wagnleitner, *Coca-Colonisation und Kalter Krieg: Die Kulturmission der USA in Österreich nach dem Zweiten Weltkrieg* (Verlag für Gesellschaftskritik, 1991). Wagnleitner discusses US cultural diplomacy in Austria but does not say much about Coca-Cola's impact.

7 See Kat Eschner, "The Sweet Story of the Berlin Candy Bomber," *Smithsonian Magazine*, October 10, 2017, https://www.smithsonianmag.com/smart-news/sweet-story-berlin-candy-bomber-180965156/. Chapter 5 discusses the Berlin Airlift in more detail.

8 See Peterson, *The American Occupation of Germany*, 155; Ziemke, *The U.S. Army in the Occupation*, 323, 327.

9 See O'Connell, "Weapon of War, Tool of Peace," 25–26; O'Connell, "Washington, D.C., 1946: Humanitarian Food Relief for Occupied Germany," in *Online Atlas on the History of Humanitarianism and Human Rights*, ed. Klose, Palen, Paulmann, and Thompson. For former President Herbert Hoover's role in developing the *Schulspeisung* school feeding program, see Hoover, *Freedom Betrayed*, 804–808; Clay, *Decision in Germany*, 268. For a history of CARE, see Morris, *A Gift from America*: "CARE, which emerged in response to World War II, became the humanitarian manifestation of America's leadership role in the postwar world. If the conflict and its aftermath convinced Americans that the world needed their help, then CARE gave them a way to act on that belief" (vii). For more on the *Schulspeisung* and CARE after World War II, see Werner, *Through the Eyes of Innocents*, 191–202. Werner argues that the arrival of the first CARE package in Le Havre in Normandy signified that "the second American 'invasion' of Europe had begun" (191). On the reasoning for American donors' desire to send humanitarian aid to Germany through CARE, see Klose, *Why They Gave*.

10 Wallace J. Campbell, *The History of CARE: A Personal Account* (Praeger, 1990), 34–35. Also, O'Connell, "Weapon of War, Tool of Peace," 302.

Airlift, and Germans were seen as victims in need of assistance, with Americans as their protectors. Encounters with children especially helped mold this shift.[11]

Personal actions of benevolence by US military personnel fit in with larger American geopolitical aims and actions under the Truman Doctrine, which arose from a speech in Congress by President Truman in March 1947 and helped lead to the development of the North Atlantic Treaty Organization (NATO) in 1949. Truman pledged American economic, political, and military assistance to any democracy under threat from authoritarianism. The Doctrine especially aimed to contain Soviet expansion.[12] Moreover, Marshall Plan aid for European recovery began in 1948, lasting four years and totaling $13 billion.[13] According to Maria Fritsche, the Truman Doctrine proved the "final departure from US isolationism," and provided a promise of US support for democratic nations under threat from totalitarian regimes, which would also help lead to security for the US itself. Fritsche notes that both the Marshall Plan and Truman Doctrine aimed at using "economic instruments" to achieve security for the US by bolstering free trade, strengthening the "liberal-capitalist system," and helping Europe recover from the war in order to create a "secure economic and political future." This would spur progress and spread prosperity in Europe, while also helping prevent the

11 See Goedde, "Gender, Race, and Power," in *The United States and Germany in the Era of the Cold War*, ed. Junker, 515–516; Goedde, *GIs and Germans*, 125–128, 149, 164–165, 167, 195. Also, O'Connell, "Hearts, Minds and Stomachs," in *The Berlin Airlift and the Making of the Cold War*, ed. Schuessler, Seipp, and Sullivan, 148–150.

12 See President Truman's address to Congress on March 12, 1947: "Truman Doctrine (1947)," Milestone Documents, National Archives, last modified February 8, 2022, https://www.archives.gov/milestone-documents/truman-doctrine.

13 See the Marshall Plan Speech, delivered by Secretary of State George C. Marshall at Harvard University on June 5, 1947, where he outlined the need for an economic aid plan for Europe and stated that the United States would play a role in European recovery: "The Marshall Plan Speech," The George C. Marshall Foundation, accessed December 20, 2024, https://www.marshallfoundation.org/the-marshall-plan/speech/. Marshall Plan aid was unique in the way that it sent goods. This also helped American business transition into a peacetime economy. Europeans also contributed to the recovery through the local "counterpart fund," in which they deposited the equivalent in costs. The local currency was then invested in even more infrastructure. See Sandra Schulberg and Ed Carter, *Selling Democracy: Films of the Marshall Plan: 1948–1953* (Academy Foundation, 2005), 10. See also Armin Grünbacher, "Cold-War Economics: The Use of Marshall Plan Counterpart Funds in Germany, 1948–1960," *Central European History* 45, no. 4 (December 2012): 698, https://doi.org/10.1017/S0008938912000659. For a more general overview of the Marshall Plan, see Benn Steil, *The Marshall Plan: Dawn of the Cold War* (Simon & Schuster, 2018); Michael J. Hogan, *The Marshall Plan: America, Britain, and the Reconstruction of Western Europe, 1947–1952* (Cambridge University Press, 1987).

spread of both communism and Soviet influence.[14] Germany was included in Marshall Plan aid, which served to strengthen the fundamental shift in American policy in Germany toward assistance to its former enemy, marking the formal end to attempts to punish the nation for its past crimes.

In 1946 and 1947, President Truman sent former President Herbert Hoover to study the food situation in Europe, including in Germany. Hoover's conclusions about the situation argued for long-range economic recovery over short-term relief.[15] Within a few years after the end of the war, wider American policies in Europe shifted toward a focus on ensuring long-term economic recovery, including through the Marshall Plan, which aimed for Europe to become economically prosperous and self-sufficient by 1952. Material prosperity and a high standard of living thus became equated with preventing the ideological onslaught of communism.[16] In postwar Germany, occupation policies became focused on individual and official acts of humanitarianism as a way to both improve young Germans' well-being and reach geopolitical goals. Thus, an American military occupation humanitarianism emerged, which ensured improved conditions for children and directly showed youngsters the benefits of American-style democracy, and simultaneously spurred gratitude among the recipients. A similar form of American humanitarianism spread throughout Western Europe, where improvements in economic conditions were linked to democracy. Moreover, spreading knowledge among the European population about the providers of the aid, the Americans, was essential, leading to a campaign to spread information about aid among Europeans, such as Marshall Plan films. Developments in postwar occupation Germany thus provided a foundation for wider Cold War humanitarian assistance to Western Europe.

---

14 Maria Fritsche, *The American Marshall Plan Film Campaign and the Europeans: A Captivated Audience?* (Bloomsbury Academic, 2018), 3–5, 17–19.

15 Hoover, *Freedom Betrayed*, 778–803. Also, Clay, *Decision in Germany*, 266–268; O'Connell, "Weapon of War, Tool of Peace," 26, 220. Hoover was also active in the aftermath of WWI and was a proponent then of a "novel strategic concept that linked security to social welfare," in which "he located the germ of future wars in reaction and revolution incubated by scarcity. Material abundance bred stability, he argued, but 'famine breeds anarchy.'" In Nick Cullather, "The Foreign Policy of the Calorie," *The American Historical Review* 112, no. 2 (April 2007): 350, http://www.jstor.org/stable/4136605.

16 See Cullather, 363. See also Fritsche, *The American Marshall Plan Film Campaign and the Europeans*, 4–5. Also, Victoria De Grazia, *Irresistible Empire: America's Advance through Twentieth-Century Europe* (The Belknap Press of Harvard University Press, 2005), 5. On the American standard of living, see De Grazia, Chapter 2: 75–129.

Cold War Military Humanitarianism

Individual and collective acts of American benevolence in Germany aligned with the greater American geopolitical aims of creating a unified, economically prosperous Europe as a bulwark against communism and to help ensure security for the United States. Germans had thus become allies in need of rehabilitation and protection. American aid including American products helped enable this shift, providing Germans with glimpses of American-style democracy, which came along with material benefits. Ralph Willett argues that it was "American goods which were to be the revolutionary missionaries for the American way of life."[17] By the end of the 1940s, Germans were not only drinking Coca-Cola but were also one of the main recipients of CARE packages.[18] During the occupation, children and young people, seen as the future of Germany, were often the main recipients of aid and the audience for democratization attempts. German children and youth were fundamental to molding occupation and geopolitical aims in the heightening Cold War context. The future of Europe as well as "the structure of world peace" and the very survival of "the civilization that Americans prize," as psychiatrist Bertram Schaffner termed it in 1948, were all at stake in the attempts to fundamentally change German culture, including the mindset of young Germans.[19]

In order to win over populations in the emerging Cold War, US policies focused on creating a stable and prosperous Europe, abandoning a punitive policy in Germany. This shifting focus also aimed to win over Germans to the American side. Scholars have focused on how the act of providing humanitarian assistance and food aid served American geopolitical aims, a connection that was forged during the occupation of Germany. According to Kaete O'Connell, American aid in occupied Germany, especially food aid, provided the "test case for Cold War era development programs. American food represented stability, prosperity, and strength; it was used to reward anti-communists while reinforcing the image of America as a land of plenty." Thus, she argues, food aid evolved from "emergency relief to propaganda tool and psychological weapon in America's Cold War arsenal."[20] Moreover, O'Connell notes that "food was a source of soft power," and

17 Willett, *The Americanization of Germany*, viii, 10, 27.

18 Baur, "From Victim to Partner: CARE and the Portrayal of Postwar Germany," in *Die Amerikanische Reeducation-Politik nach 1945*, ed. Gerund and Paul, 116. See also Weinreb, *Modern Hungers*, 113; Morris, *A Gift from America*, 21; Werner, *Through the Eyes of Innocents*, 193; Ehlers, *Die Ernährungssituation*, 38–39; Goedde, *GIs and Germans*, 121; Klose, *Why They Gave*, 16.

19 Schaffner, *Father Land*, 111–113.

20 O'Connell, "Weapon of War, Tool of Peace," 5–6.

food aid fulfilled "military and political objectives, reinforced notions of American exceptionalism, and encouraged emotional connections that won hearts and minds on both sides of the Atlantic."[21] In occupied Germany, she argues, food aid also provided a means to reinforce "democratic teachings." This was particularly important for occupation democratization aims, which often focused on young Germans, as "a full stomach not only made German children more receptive to reeducation, but food also conveyed the power of democracy."[22] O'Connell's findings thus show how Cold War American humanitarian actions and geopolitical aims had become intertwined, beginning with aid for occupied Germany.[23]

Alice Weinreb and Atina Grossmann have explored how food and hunger shaped relationships and forged new power structures in the occupation of Germany. Weinreb notes how rhetoric about German hunger occurred in the context of a "new language of human rights," which "cast concern over German hunger as emblematic of a new, modern, and progressive valuing of all human life regardless of political activity or personal history."[24] Grossmann notes that Allied language of rationing "calibrated new (and constantly shifting) standards of victimization, entitlement, and—very importantly—recognition among the many different groups present in the American occupation zone." Moreover, these groups, including "defeated Germans and surviving Jews," competed over the "favors of the 'good parent,' embodied by occupiers and international relief organizations."[25] In 1943, anthropologist Margaret Mead wrote about food policies in occupied territories, linking them to psychological effects. She stated:

> [The] giving of food is associated the world over with the cherishing of and responsible activities of parents toward dependent children; thus whenever a people feels that its food supply is in the hands of an authority, it tends to regard that authority as to some degree parental. As a matter of practice this means that feeding people adequately, either by the conspicuous regulation of commercially available supplies or by the provision of emergency mass feeding operations, is an efficient way of establishing the existing authority as a good parent toward whom the people assume an attitude of dependency. Probably no other operation, even the provision of hospitalization and emergency care, is so effective in proving to

21 O'Connell, "Weapon of War, Tool of Peace," 3. See also O'Connell, "The Taste of Defeat," in *Food, Culture and Identity*, ed. Benbow and Perry, 202–203, 214.

22 O'Connell, "Weapon of War, Tool of Peace," 28.

23 O'Connell, "Weapon of War, Tool of Peace," 4–5.

24 Weinreb, *Modern Hungers*, 111.

25 Atina Grossmann, "Grams, Calories, and Food: Languages of Victimization, Entitlement, and Human Rights in Occupied Germany, 1945–1949," *Central European History* 44, no. 1 (March 2011): 123, http://www.jstor.org/stable/41238390.

> an anxious and disturbed people that the powers that be are good and have their welfare at heart.[26]

Feeding the Germans thus played a central role in occupation policies, ranging from rationing policies to school feeding programs. Rationing played a balancing act between postwar food shortages, the initial punitive occupation policies, public health, and security. In June 1945, then Deputy Military Governor Lucius Clay noted that "some cold and hunger will be necessary to make the German people realize the consequences of a war which they caused," but that "this type of suffering should not extend to the point where it results in mass starvation and sickness."[27] However, in March 1946, Clay became increasingly worried about the potential wide-ranging effects of lowering rations and argued for food imports for Germany, writing,

> It is our belief that the Russian zone is feeding approximately 1500 calories and will continue to do so until the next harvest season. We have insisted on democratic processes in the U.S. zone and have maintained a strict neutrality between political parties. As a result the Communist Party has made little inroad. However, there is no choice between becoming a Communist on 1500 calories and a believer in democracy on 1000 calories. It is my sincere belief that our proposed ration allowance in Germany will not only defeat our objectives in middle Europe but will pave the road to a Communist Germany.[28]

Hunger, especially German hunger, thus became equated with the spread of communism in the postwar era.[29] In his inaugural speech on January 20, 1949, President Truman noted hunger's role as an enemy of democracy.[30] Therefore, the concept of limiting rations to Germans in order to teach a lesson about guilt disappeared in the Cold War context of preventing hunger to stop the spread of communism. Prosperity was needed, especially in Western Europe, including in West

---

26 Margaret Mead, "Food and Feeding in Occupied Territory," *The Public Opinion Quarterly* 7, no. 4 (Winter 1943): 619, https://www.jstor.org/stable/2745632. See also Grossmann, "Grams, Calories, and Food," 118–119; Goedde, *GIs and Germans*, 180; O'Connell, "The Taste of Defeat," in *Food, Culture and Identity*, ed. Benbow and Perry, 202.

27 "14. Conditions in Germany," Letter from Clay to McCloy, June 16, 1945, in Smith, ed., *The Papers of General Lucius D. Clay*, vol. 1, 24; "17. Conditions in Germany," Letter from Clay to McCloy, June 29, 1945, in Smith, ed., *Papers*, vol. 1, 42. See also O'Connell, "The Taste of Defeat," 211.

28 "103. Food Situation in U.S. Zone," Letter from Clay to Echols and Petersen, March 27, 1946, in Smith, ed., *The Papers of General Lucius D. Clay*, vol. 1, 184.

29 Weinreb, *Modern Hungers*, 112–113.

30 Harry S. Truman, Inaugural Address, January 20, 1949, online by Gerhard Peters and John T. Woolley, The American Presidency Project, University of California Santa Barbara, https://www.presidency.ucsb.edu/node/229929.

Germany, which would provide a bulwark against communism and serve to ensure the safety of the United States.

In his 1950 account of his time in Germany, General Clay argued that humanitarian efforts, especially the child feeding program, helped shift German views of Americans. For Clay, the *Schulspeisung* program "did more to convince the German people of our desire to recreate their nation than any other action on our part," and he received "expressions of gratitude from parents and children" for this program that he found "sincere and touching."[31] The Berlin Airlift of 1948 to 1949 served to substantiate this shift, with West Germans desiring American aid and protection. As Edward D. Peterson notes, Clay's role in postwar Germany went through a fundamental shift: Clay came to Germany as a conqueror in 1945 and when he left Germany four years later, he came to be regarded as a hero and the savior of Berlin.[32] Finally, the aid of the Marshall Plan provided crucial evidence for Germans about the American aim of rebuilding (West) Germany. For example, Marshall Aid signs on construction sites provided visual proof to Germans that US funds had played a role in reconstruction and that Germany was no longer seen as "a pariah," as Armin Grünbacher notes.[33]

Overall, postwar Germany became a site of Cold War military humanitarianism, with the Berlin Airlift especially spurring an acceptance of the link between the armed forces and humanitarian assistance.[34] As political scientist Thomas G. Weiss notes, the involvement of military forces in the relief of vanquished populations is not new, and was commonly used in the Napoleonic Wars and also predated Alexander the Great. Weiss writes, "Sometimes assistance was seen as a humane gesture to the vanquished, usually mixed with the desire to help secure loyalty from newly subject populations." Weiss also notes that the post-World War II occupations of Germany and Japan greatly expanded the military into the arena of humanitarian aid.[35] Since the 1990s, military intervention (especially American) has been commonplace in times of disasters, emergencies, and situa-

31 Clay, *Decision in Germany*, 268.

32 Peterson, *The American Occupation of Germany*, 58.

33 Grünbacher, "Cold-War Economics," 715.

34 On military humanitarianism, see Frederick Cuny, "Dilemmas of Military Involvement in Humanitarian Relief," in *Soldiers, Peacekeepers and Disasters*, ed. Leon Gordenker and Thomas G. Weiss (St. Martin Press, 1991), 52–54; Thomas G. Weiss, *Military-Civilian Interactions: Intervening in Humanitarian Crises* (Rowman & Littlefield Publishers, 1999), 17; Thomas G. Weiss and Kurt M. Campbell, "Military Humanitarianism," *Survival* 33, no. 5 (September/October 1991): 453, https://doi.org/10.1080/00396339108442612. See also John M. Schuessler and Adam R. Seipp, "Introduction," in *The Berlin Airlift and the Making of the Cold War*, ed. Schuessler, Seipp, and Sullivan, 4. The authors note how hard power was harnessed to humanitarian ends in the Berlin Airlift.

35 Weiss, *Military-Civilian Interactions*, 15–16.

tions of threats to global security.[36] Contemporary discussions of military humanitarianism include the concept of the "responsibility to protect" (R2P), which merges militaristic and humanist perspectives, uniting "the benevolent responsibility to intervene in times of suffering with an unquestionable right to employ force in the protection of global citizens."[37]

However, the blend of military involvement in humanitarian ventures is not without critique. For example, geographers Killian McCormack and Emily Gilbert argue that a militarized humanitarianism produces "violent geographies," which demonstrate "the ways political violence can be obscured through invocations of humanitarianism." They argue, "war and humanitarianism are thus intimately linked," and this became especially pronounced in the aftermath of World War II. Additionally, they claim, "Western forms of humanitarianism have always been entangled with militarism, and thus are inherently about violence."[38] Anthropologist Antonio De Lauri also argues that there is a "mutual relationship between compassion and violence," with militarized aid encompassing "values of benevolence and military ethos."[39] Moreover, SooJin Pate has researched the linkages of Korean adoption and US military intervention in Korea beginning in the 1940s, arguing that humanitarian rescue was linked to American Cold War-era expansion aims. She explores how Korean adoption was a product itself of military occupation, and also served American attempts to "rescue the image of the U.S. government by presenting the American soldier as a humanitarian," a "benevolent helper rather than neocolonial occupier."[40] American humanitarianism has thus been about more than benevolence toward needy populations: it is inherently tied up with the impacts of war and violence and is linked to American geopolitical aims and military strategies.

---

36 Anne Orford argues that the "centrality of the U.S. military to much humanitarian strategizing has not been seriously challenged." Anne Orford, "The Passions of Protection: Sovereign Authority and the Humanitarian War," in *Militarization: A Reader*, ed. Roberto J. González, Hugh Gusterson, and Gustaaf Houtman (Duke University Press, 2019), 208–209.

37 Mariella Pandolfi, "Laboratory of Intervention: The Humanitarian Governance of the Postcommunist Balkan Territories," in *Militarization: A Reader*, ed. González, Gusterson, and Houtman, 200.

38 Killian McCormack and Emily Gilbert, "Geopolitics of Militarism and Humanitarianism," *Progress in Human Geography* 46, no. 1 (2022): 179–180, 191, https://doi.org/10.1177/03091325211032267.

39 Antonio De Lauri, "Humanitarian Militarism and the Production of Humanity," *Social Anthropology/Anthropologie Sociale* 27, no. 1 (February 2019): 96, https://doi.org/10.1111/1469-8676.12507.

40 SooJin Pate, *From Orphan to Adoptee: U.S. Empire and Genealogies of Korean Adoption* (University of Minnesota Press, 2014), 16, 22–23. Pate notes that Korean orphans themselves became "militarized subjects" (40).

In postwar Germany, GIs shifted into a role as humanitarian agents within a military occupation. Moreover, Pate's argument about the occupation in Korea itself creating conditions in which humanitarian aid was needed is particularly relevant when looking at the occupation of Germany. The US had control over the politics of hunger in postwar Germany, determining rationing levels and food policies. These policies often led Germans to seek other sources of food, taking part in behavior such as "hamstering" (traveling to the countryside to attempt to trade goods for food) and black market participation.[41] However, rather than focusing on the stringent rationing policies of the military government, rhetoric regarding German hunger increasingly highlighted the benevolence of Americans, especially the US soldier as a humanitarian figure seeming to ensure a better future for Germans. The Candy Bomber of the Berlin Airlift, Lieutenant Gail Halvorsen, further cemented the image of the benevolent GI. Thus, occupation rhetoric shifted toward military humanitarianism, placing the role of the military as essential and even generous for taking care of a dependent population under occupation. This form of humanitarianism emerged as central in images of benevolence aimed at bolstering the United States' Cold War image, in Marshall Plan films that aimed at convincing Europeans about the promises of democracy and free trade, in organized aid toward German youth including the youth activities program, and in young Germans' own understandings of the occupation and their expressions of gratitude for aid. Thus, a geopolitics of gratitude emerged within a military occupation which aimed increasingly at feeding, taking care of, and refreshing the population with CARE packages, school feedings, sips of Coca-Cola, and airlifted supplies.[42]

Occupation Benevolence

Relatively quickly after the end of World War II, the occupation of (West) Germany had evolved into one based upon positive actions of providing, protecting, and giving aid to Germans. This shift occurred especially as a result of a focus on the situation of German children. For example, the plight of hungry children helped spur early occupation humanitarian developments toward Germans such

41 See Alexander Häusser and Gordian Maugg, *Hungerwinter: Deutschlands humanitäre Katastrophe 1946/47* (Propyläen, 2009), 65–84, for a discussion of "hamstering."

42 On the continuing significance of a "politics of gratitude" for German society and its gender logics, see Katharina Gerund, "Liberation, Re-Education, Democratisation: The Politics of Gratitude in German-American Relations after 1945," *Contemporary European History* (2024): 1–14, https://doi.org/10.1017/S0960777324000055.

as the school feeding program. German children emerged as the means of rehabilitating Germany, who needed to be helped and guided.[43] In addition, the figure of the US soldier had evolved into that of a benevolent figure, with a supposed universal appeal.[44] Ever since the first moments of encounter with Germans in mid-1944, GIs had been the first navigators of judgments about young Germans, and many soldiers responded with benevolence, focusing on the present-day needs of the children and youth they encountered.

Within the sphere of navigations between GIs and children, a power structure emerged, with GIs having access to material plenty as the occupiers, and Germans living within a context of great need. German society during the occupation tended to evolve around meeting everyday basic needs.[45] In contrast, GIs had access to plentiful supplies and food, receiving around 4,000 calories a day, while regular German ration levels remained between 1,000 and 1,500 a day, with the level often not being met in reality.[46] On the black market, prices favored those with plenty, the occupation troops.[47] Nazi-era souvenirs that GIs desired such as a *Ritterkreuz* would cost a carton of cigarettes, something that would not have been hard for soldiers to obtain.[48] In stark contrast to the prosperity of GIs stood the ubiquitous children playing in the rubble, often hungry and sometimes shoeless.

---

43 See O'Connell, "Hearts, Minds and Stomachs," in *The Berlin Airlift and the Making of the Cold War*, ed. Schuessler, Seipp, and Sullivan, 148–150.

44 See Willoughby, *Remaking the Conquering Heroes*, 113–114.

45 Laura J. Hilton, "Postwar Food Rumors: Security, Victimhood and Fear," in *Food, Culture and Identity in Germany's Century of War*, ed. Benbow and Perry, 186; Weinreb, *Modern Hungers*, 102.

46 Clay, *Decision in Germany*, 264–270; Goedde, *GIs in Germany*, 140; Enssle, "The Harsh Discipline," 487–489; O'Connell, "The Taste of Defeat," in *Food, Culture and Identity*, ed. Benbow and Perry, 208; O'Connell, "Weapon of War, Tool of Peace," 131, 168, 181, 183–184; Ziemke, *The U.S. Army in the Occupation*, 410; Werner, *Through the Eyes of Innocents*, 177; Willett, *The Americanization of Germany*, 3. Willett notes that in mid-1948, Bavarian students protested rationing, writing on placards, "Even a dog needs 1,700 calories." See also Judt, *Postwar*, 21: In June 1945, the daily ration for German *Normalverbraucher* was 860 calories. On calories, see Cullather, "The Foreign Policy of the Calories," 339. Cullather writes, "Europeans first measured food in calories, but Americans constructed the calorie by giving it practical value, standardizing it and embedding it in systems of distribution and administration."

47 For example, a 5 cent candy bar could bring in $5, a bottle of whiskey or gin $75–$100, and in the cigarette-fueled economy of the occupation, the going price for one pack of cigarettes was 100 Reichsmarks. See Bach Jr., *America's Germany*, 57–61; O'Connell, "The Taste of Defeat," in *Food, Culture and Identity*, ed. Benbow and Perry, 208; Georg Schmidt, *Als Bremen Amerikanisch war*. See also Häusser and Maugg, *Hungerwinter*, 87–88, for the going prices of the black market in Hamburg on April 20, 1946. Also, Judt, *Postwar*, 87–88: In Berlin a carton of American cigarettes on the black market ranged from $60 to $165. In the first four months of the occupation, US troops in Berlin sent home $11 million more than they had received in wages.

48 Georg Schmidt, *Als Bremen Amerikanisch war*.

As Martin Kalb notes, youth were often seen as a "clear symbol of Germany's larger decay," with children often seen begging, participating in black market activities, or left unaccompanied.[49] The visible need and hardship of young Germans helped lead to relationships between children and GIs centered around food. As O'Connell argues, American officials harnessed the "spontaneous food relationships that developed between children and the Army of Occupation," creating programs that aimed to both improve German children's welfare and serve occupation goals such as reeducation.[50] Soldiers' ability to befriend children served as a way to teach democracy, show the American way of life, and depict American goodwill in occupied Germany, as Donna Alvah notes.[51] These relationships also molded official occupation programs focused on children's welfare, such as GYA. Programs that centered around providing food for children gained support among GIs, including Christmas parties, summer camps for urban children to gain weight, and garden projects aimed at growing food. The October 1946 directive on German Youth Activities also allowed GIs to voluntarily donate food to GYA activities.[52] GIs were thus helping mold the future of German society, often using their own resources and free time. Their benevolence thus served the wider occupation aims of reeducation and democratization. Moreover, GI occupation benevolence could ensure American security and enhance long-range geopolitical goals, turning young Germans toward democracy and away from communism.

American geopolitical aims depended on German youngsters willingly receiving benevolence from Americans. For the most part, German youngsters proved willing to accept aid from Americans. However, occupation programs such as GYA could garner critique, including German accusations about the clubs being solely clubs for chocolate and sweets.[53] Americans at home were also initially frustrated about troop fraternization with guilty Germans, including helping children, but this changed later on as Germans became seen as a dependent, victim population.[54] The GYA program was just one instance of military-sponsored be-

---

49 Kalb, *Coming of Age*, 20. See also Steege, *Black Market, Cold War*, 121–122.

50 O'Connell, "Weapon of War, Tool of Peace," 232.

51 Alvah, *Unofficial Ambassadors*, 48.

52 5 October 1946 Directive, HQ USFET; Folder USFET Directive 5 October 1946; Records RE the Work of the Youth Activities Section; Records for the Community Education Branch; Records of the Education and Cultural Relations Division; Box 148; OMGUS; RG 260; NACP.

53 Rode, "Manche nannten sie nur 'Schokoladenclubs,'" 33; Rode, "Zwischen Re-education und Freizeitvergnügen," 48; Pedron, *Amerikaner vor Ort*, 285.

54 See Starr, *Fraternization with the Germans in World War II*, 19–20; Peterson, *The American Occupation of Germany*, 154–155.

nevolence towards German youth. As the occupation progressed, benevolence toward German youngsters, and, increasingly, to the entire German population, became commonplace. In addition, reports and images depicting benevolence toward young Germans helped serve as great propaganda for American Cold War geopolitical aims, including depictions of happy children at Army-sponsored Christmas parties, young recipients of CARE packages, or children running after candy falling from the sky during the Berlin Airlift.[55] Through exchanges of food and goods under a military occupation marked by the presence of GIs, young Germans learned a certain type of democracy in which freedom meant consumption and even luxury, with access to non-essential goods such as candy.[56]

This new form of American military occupation humanitarianism encouraged the participation of private citizens on the American home front. This included private initiatives of aid such as sending CARE packages to Germans and other humanitarian efforts.[57] Beginning in 1948, two prominent US citizens became active in promoting the cause of GYA with the American public. Catherine Filene Shouse and her husband Jouett Shouse had visited Germany during the occupation and gained an interest in aiding German youth. Jouett Shouse was a politician in the Democratic Party and his wife Catherine was a prominent member of Washington, DC society and had been the first woman ever appointed to the Democratic National Committee.[58]

---

55 See O'Connell, "Weapon of War, Tool of Peace," 22; O'Connell, "The Taste of Defeat," in *Food, Culture and Identity*, ed. Benbow and Perry, 212. On "America's first peacetime propaganda offensive," beginning in 1945 and spurred by the threats of communism and anti-Americanism, see Laura Belmonte, *Selling the American Way: U.S. Propaganda and the Cold War* (University of Pennsylvania Press, 2008), 4. For a discussion of the role of children in humanitarian imagery before 1945, see Heide Fehrenbach, "Children and Other Civilians: Photography and the Politics of Humanitarian Image-Making," in *Humanitarian Photography: A History*, ed. Heide Fehrenbach and Davide Rodogno (Cambridge University Press, 2015), 165–199.

56 See Goedde, *GIs and Germans*, 148, 158, 163–164, 170. Also, Willett, *The Americanization of Germany*, viii–ix, 1–2, 104.

57 See Klose, *Why They Gave.*

58 *The U.S. Armed Forces German Youth Activities Program*, 32–33; see Folder Shouse, Kay (Medal of Freedom); First Lady General Subject Files; Betty Ford White House Papers, 1973–1977; Box 45; Gerald R. Ford Presidential Library (GRFPL); online at https://catalog.archives.gov/id/81556866. Also, Sarah Booth Conroy, "The Wolf Trap Whirlwind," *The Washington Post*, July 30, 1984. In 1977, Catherine Shouse was awarded the Presidential Medal of Freedom from President Gerald Ford. Among many other accomplishments, she was the first woman to receive a M.Ed. from Harvard University (1923), published the book *Careers for Women* (1920), founded the Institute of Women's Professional Relations, and founded Wolf Trap outside of Washington, DC, now the Wolf Trap National Park for the Performing Arts (see "Catherine Filene Shouse," Wolf Trap National Park for the Performing Arts, National Park Service, May 6, 2021, https://www.nps.gov/

On December 22, 1948, Jouett Shouse wrote an article in *The Washington Post*, which aimed at calling attention to General Clay's "plea for CARE packages" for German children during the Christmas season. He also highlighted the GYA program and its youth centers, which he claimed were reaching an estimated 3,500,000 children. Mr. Shouse wrote, "in Germany last summer I had the opportunity to see the misery of these children and their dire needs." He argued that the bombings during the war "had to be done," and that "the German nation had to be taught the futility and the tragic consequences of the attempt at world conquest . . . But the children were not responsible for this policy. They will be the leaders of tomorrow, perhaps our first line of defense."[59] Shouse thus aimed to garner support for Germany by publicizing the innocence of German children and noting their simultaneous role as the reassurance of future support as American allies in potential conflict.

The Shouses' engagement in assisting German youth was especially spurred by Lieutenant General Clarence R. Huebner, who had asked Catherine Shouse to assist with raising publicity for GYA. As a result, in 1948, she created the General Lucius Clay Fund for German Youth Activities for the Army and Air Force Reorientation Program, which aimed at mobilizing American individuals to support the GYA program through monetary and material donations.[60] Lucius Clay served as Honorary Chairman, and in contrast to his hesitation about the program earlier in the occupation, he now seemed certain about GYA's central role in the occupation. According to Catherine Shouse in an October 1949 letter to President Truman, Clay believed that GYA had become "the most important effort of our Army of Occupation." Catherine Shouse's role in the realms of the Clay Fund was to "appeal to the American people for funds to support the splendid program being carried out by our Army men and women, known as German Youth Activi-

---

wotr/learn/historyculture/shouse.htm). Shouse also helped organize a humanitarian relief fund for Hungary in 1956 at the request of former President Hoover. Her decorations include the 1949 City of Paris Award, 1949 Vienna Medal of Honor for Assistance to Austrian Youth, 1954 US Army Patriotic Civilian Award, and in 1954 she was the first woman to receive the German Federal Republic's Commander's Cross of Merit. See "Decorations: Founder," Wolf Trap Foundation, accessed March 30, 2023, https://www.wolftrap.org/about/history/founder/decorations.aspx.

59 Jouett Shouse, "German Children," *The Washington Post*, December 22, 1948.

60 *The U.S. Armed Forces German Youth Activities Program*, 32–33; see Folder Shouse, Kay (Medal of Freedom); First Lady General Subject Files; Betty Ford White House Papers, 1973–1977; Box 45; GRFPL. Letter from Catherine Shouse to President Truman, October 11, 1949; Folder OF 198 1945–April 1950 [1 of 2] Germany; OF 198; Box 738; HSTP; HSTPL.

ties-GYA."[61] Initially, CARE was in charge of distributing the Clay Fund's packages and materials for the youth program. Later on, the Clay Fund directly collected and shipped materials to Germany.[62] In her October 1949 letter, Catherine Shouse described the GYA program to President Truman: "This program initiated by GI's [sic] now has 300 Centers and is reaching 800,000 German children and young people, trying to develop leadership and instill our ideas of fair play." She asked the president whether he was willing to receive a White House visit from the Fund's Committee, which included General Clay, Clay's wife, and the McCloys (although they were currently in Germany, where McCloy was High Commissioner). Catherine Shouse noted that the story of GYA about "the need of winning the friendship of German youth in this way" usually resonated with its audience, but they had trouble spreading the story as much as possible to the American public. She wrote to Truman, "I need not say that your receiving the Committee at the beginning of the campaign would be of immeasurable help."[63] In August 1950, Catherine's husband, Jouett Shouse, who was also active in the Clay Fund as a sponsor, requested an appointment with President Truman after returning from assisting "in a survey of German youth activities" with General Huebner.[64] This request highlights the Shouses' major role in raising attention to GYA within the highest spheres of American society, even as the occupation began to wind down through the 1949 transition from OMGUS to HICOG.

On September 21, 1951, Jouett Shouse wrote about the General Clay Fund for GYA in a memorandum to President Truman:

> Its purpose is to interest Americans in the splendid job being done by our officers and enlisted personnel and their wives in interpreting us to German youth. It raises money and ships various materials for bringing more young people to the GYA Centers for the many activities. Each year it has widened the interest State-side . . . The General Clay Fund campaign will start in November. A statement directed to our soldiers and airmen abroad which could be used in the campaign would be invaluable. As the interpreters of the United States they are giving the basic tenets of the Four Freedoms to a new generation.

61 Letter from Catherine Shouse to President Truman, October 11, 1949; Folder OF 198 1945–April 1950 [1 of 2] Germany; OF 198; Box 738; HSTP; HSTPL. See also "Funds Sought for Youth Centers in Germany," *The Washington Post*, October 22, 1949.

62 *The U.S. Armed Forces German Youth Activities Program*, 32.

63 Letter from Catherine Shouse to President Truman, October 11, 1949; Folder OF 198 1945–April 1950 [1 of 2] Germany; OF 198; Box 738; HSTP; HSTPL.

64 Requests to see the President, August 17, 1950; Folder OF 198 May–December 1950; OF 198; Box 738; HSTP; HSTPL.

Furthermore, he noted GYA's Cold War significance: "Through the many activities carried on, such as handicraft, discussion groups, debates, English classes, election of officers, and sports, German youth have been learning, through doing, the difference between our ideals and those of the East." GYA thus had reached a major transatlantic level of significance, playing a major role not only in continuing to reorient German youth toward democracy but also in promoting "good relations between our two nations," as Jouett Shouse put it.[65] Crafting good relations was thus essential within the Cold War atmosphere, as the focus turned toward the threat of Soviet Union, rather than on Germany's Nazi past. Mr. Shouse's memorandum included attachments from major figures praising the initiative, including a statement from Chancellor Konrad Adenauer, noting his "own sincere thanks and the heartful thanks of the German people." Adenauer wrote that "innumerable German children" had benefited from the Fund, which "promotes human relationships between American soldiers and German youth" in a time of "common defence [sic] against Communism." In addition, Adenauer wrote, "The G.Y.A. [sic] institutions to whose support the General Clay Fund contributes, are one of the most valuable means for the promotion of mutual understanding."[66] Furthermore, Shouse's memorandum included a statement from General Thomas T. Handy, Commander in Chief of the European Command, who wrote:

> The European Command is proud of its GYA program. It is a unique project in the history of military occupations. A great part in bettering American-German relations has been undertaken and accomplished through this program. The General Clay Fund for German Youth Activities serves as an invaluable link to bring the expressions of good will of the American people to the German people at this important stage in international relations.[67]

Handy's statement highlights the militarized nature of the aid toward German youth, marking this American military occupation humanitarianism as a special phase in history. General L. Mathewson, Major General and US Commander in Berlin, also wrote about the importance of and centrality of GYA in ensuring future allies:

> In answer to the hypothetical question which might well arise in the mind of the average American, "What do we Americans get out of time and money spent on German Youth Ac-

65 Memorandum to The President from Jouett Shouse, September 21, 1951; Folder OF 198 1951–1953 Germany; Box 738; HSTP; HSTPL.
66 Statement by Chancellor Adenauer, attachment to Memorandum to The President from Jouett Shouse, September 21, 1951; Folder OF 198 1951–1953 Germany; Box 738; HSTP; HSTPL.
67 Letter from Thomas T. Handy to Mrs. Jouett Shouse, September 4, 1951, attachment to Memorandum to The President from Jouett Shouse, September 21, 1951; Folder OF 198 1951–1953 Germany; Box 738; HSTP; HSTPL.

> tivities?" we might reply in the following sense. We are faced with two choices—we can either do nothing, or we can support a program which is designed to bring some order out of chaos in the minds of the youth that has been conceived under Nazism, brought up in time of war, and left to flounder in the rubble heaps and mental confusion of the post-war period.
>
> Is it not in our national interest to attempt to enlighten this youth and orient his [sic] thinking in the ways of democracy, as against any one of the many other ideologies to which he might fall prey? I think the answer is inescapable. With no final assurance in the matter whatsoever, we can only hope that by doing something of a positive nature, such as the GYA, we are giving these children a feeling that they as individuals have a real place in Western society. We are giving them a better understanding of Americans, and perhaps gaining some long-range friends for the United States when these children will have reached their maturity and when we may need friends very badly.[68]

On September 24, 1951, President Truman responded to Jouett Shouse's memorandum and a recent visit Shouse had made to the White House, stating, "I don't know what I can do about it but I may be able to be helpful."[69] Thus, as President Truman's engagement shows, humanitarianism toward German youth had reached the highest level of attention within the US political sphere, and military and civilian relationships were linked together across the Atlantic. Americans provided humanitarian aid for a former enemy population under occupation, a population which became increasingly dependent on US protection and assistance in the Cold War context. This dynamic had come far from the early days of benevolent individual actions of GIs such as spontaneous gifts of candy bars and Sergeant Ballard's early organized youth group in the Bremen Enclave in 1945.

Private occupation-era aid to Germans even included the participation of the most powerful member of the American public: in late 1951, President Harry Truman secretly donated $500 for sporting goods for GYA. This was not his first act of private aid to Germans, as he had previously purchased CARE packages in 1946. In a November 5, 1951 personal letter to Fred Bowman, President of Wilson Sporting Goods Company in Chicago, President Truman wrote about GYA and its need for sporting goods supplies through the Clay Fund. He wrote, "Jouett Shouse and his wife have been supporting and promoting it [GYA] and it is a wonderful proposition. They have nearly 500,000 German children, between the ages of ten and eighteen, who are learning our brand of sports and who are in line to become

68 L. Mathewson, Memorandum for Mrs. Shouse, September 5, 1951, attachment to Memorandum to the President from Jouett Shouse, September 21, 1951; Folder OF 198 1951–1953 Germany; Box 738; HSTP; HSTPL.

69 Letter from Truman to Jouett Shouse, September 24, 1951; Folder OF 198 1951–1953 Germany; Box 738; HSTP; HSTPL.

really good citizens of a Republic [sic].” He explained that the organization needed sporting goods, including “sixty basketballs, about forty soccerballs [sic] and as many ping-pong sets as we can get within that figure.” Truman enclosed a $500 check with the request to get the “sporting goods houses in Chicago and the wholesale manufacturers to go together and make that $500 spread very thin and get quite a bit of equipment for these people.” A note at the bottom of the letter stated, “President added in longhand — ‘I don’t want to be known in the transaction,’” noting his desire that the transaction not be publicized.[70] On November 8, 1951, Fred Bowman responded that he would be glad to provide the sporting goods, writing, “We all realize the importance of athletics and games in building good-will and you may be sure everyone will cooperate in every way.” He also stated that he had contacted four other manufacturers who could provide more goods. Bowman also returned Truman’s check, writing, “It certainly will not be necessary for you to personally take care of any of this, so I am returning the check you made out to me.”[71] Truman responded on November 13, 1951, writing to Bowman,

> How kind and generous you are in returning my check in the amount of $500.00 . . . I am deeply interested in athletics in Germany as a genuine morale builder and surely all who supply the necessary equipment are contributing to a highly constructive work. You are, therefore, performing a genuinely patriotic act in donating the volleyballs, basketballs, soccerballs [sic], footballs and ping pong sets for use in Germany.[72]

On December 31, 1951, Catherine Shouse wrote a thank you letter to President Truman, noting the numbers of basketballs, volleyballs, soccer balls, footballs, and table tennis sets that were sent to Germany due to Truman’s advocacy. Wilson Sporting Goods in Chicago along with Rawlings in St. Louis, Spalding in New York, MacGregor-Goldsmith in Cincinnati, and Universal in Cambridge, Massachusetts had all donated materials. She wrote, “I know how heartening it is for those in charge of the Youth Reorientation Program to have your interest. On instructions from Miss Conway [the president’s secretary], I have asked that no publicity be

70 Letter from Truman to Fred J. Bowman, November 5, 1951; Folder Germany: General [2 of 2]; Subject File, 1940–1953: Foreign Affairs File, 1940–1953; Box 151; President’s Secretary’s Files (PSF); HSTP; HSTPL.
71 Letter from Fred J. Bowman to Truman, November 8, 1951; Folder Germany: General [2 of 2]; Subject File, 1940–1953: Foreign Affairs File, 1940–1953; Box 151; PSF; HSTP; HSTPL.
72 Letter from Truman to Fred J. Bowman, November 13, 1951; Folder Germany: General [2 of 2]; Subject File, 1940–1953: Foreign Affairs File, 1940–1953; Box 151; PSF; HSTP; HSTPL.

given to your part in making this shipment possible."[73] Another note to President Truman from Catherine Shouse included a photo from Augsburg Military Post GYA of the post commander giving a soccer ball to a group of German orphan boys who had won the first prize in a group contest. She wrote, "This is one of the balls sent at your request."[74]

In November 1952, Catherine Shouse again wrote to the president regarding a similar contribution for GYA as last year's donation, noting "all of it was used to further American-German relations." She also mentioned the GYA Meistersinger Contest, one of the main cultural activities of GYA, which was held in Nuremberg, with 2,800 boys and girls between age 18 and 25 competing in 1952. The winner of the contest, Herman Prey from Berlin, was arriving in the US on November 17, 1952. As part of his prize, he was to sing with the National Symphony on December 3, 1952. Catherine Shouse wrote to Truman, "He is a fine young man and his coming will help to create interest in what our Army is doing for the youth in his country." She also asked the president whether she could bring Prey "to call on you and Mrs. Truman" during his visit to Washington, DC. She concluded the letter noting that she and her husband "appreciate all you have done towards better international understanding."[75] However, Truman had to decline her request to "receive the young man to whom you referred, much to my regret," as he was "completely tied up with the transfer of the Government to the new Administration [Dwight D. Eisenhower]," writing that he did not even have a minute to see his own family. He also wrote that the suggestion of sporting goods to Bowman of the Wilson Sporting Goods company was "a personal matter," and "since I am going out of office I don't feel as if I should be asking him for further donations. You can use your own judgment on it."[76] After Truman left office and the occupation statute approached its end, GYA seemed to receive less of a priority, and the last of the GYA centers largely shut down in 1955

73 Letter from Catherine Jouett Shouse to President Truman, December 31, 1951; Folder Germany: General [2 of 2], Subject File, 1940–1953: Foreign Affairs File, 1940–1953; Box 151; PSF; HSTP; HSTPL.

74 Photo of Col. James J. Pirtle presenting a soccer ball to a group of German orphans, c. 1952, and handwritten note from Catherine Shouse to Truman; Folder OF 198 1951–1953 Germany; Box 738; HSTP; HSTPL.

75 Letter to Truman from Catherine Shouse, November 7, 1952; Folder OF 198 1951–1953 Germany; HSTP; Box 738; HSTPL. For more on the GYA Meistersinger contest and other cultural programs such as the "Soap Box Derby," see *The U.S. Armed Forces German Youth Activities Program 1945–1955*, 34–36.

76 Letter to Catherine Shouse from Truman, November 14, 1952; Folder OF 198 1951–1953 Germany; Box 738; HSTP; HSTPL.

instead of being passed over to the Germans.[77] Although the support for GYA from prominent Americans such as the Shouses occurred relatively late, moving into the period of the West German state under the supervision of HICOG from 1949 to 1955, it ensured the continued funding of and awareness about GYA. Moreover, support for GYA continued despite drops in personnel assigned to GYA or helping as volunteers.[78] According to an official report, Catherine Shouse's advocacy through the Clay Fund enabled GYA projects including CARE packages for GYA Christmas parties, a candy caravan, book collections for GYA Libraries, toy drives organized by the American Legion, fundraising through the General Federation of Women's Clubs, donations of items through businesses, and donations of sewing and arts and crafts materials through the Girl Scouts in the US. GYA centers would even send the Girl Scouts "samples of the finished products, for which the American materials had been used" to be displayed.[79] Thus, GYA had reached center stage in the Cold War politics of aid to Germany, and the stakes of the reorientation of youth were high in the heightening atmosphere. Aid toward Germans forged an image of a benevolent United States whose citizens participated in private and collective acts of kindness. In addition, aid served to ensure that the youngest German generation would be molded in an atmosphere of American generosity as recipients who would never forget the American kindness they received. This kindness came in the form of CARE packages, fun evenings in the GYA center playing sports, or receiving a gift of a soccer ball, which actually happened to be gifted as a result of the engagement of the president of the United States, even if the children might not have been aware of that fact.

The Benevolent Empire, Hungry Children, and the Marshall Plan

American acts of occupation benevolence led to a major shift in which (West) Germans accepted and even welcomed American aid and the protective nature of the American presence. During the Blockade of Berlin, Military Governor Lucius Clay even chose to keep American dependents in Berlin in order to prevent hysteria and "a rush of Germans to Communism for safety," as he stated in March 1948.[80] Thus, the physical presence of Americans in Berlin during the Blockade was to

77 See Chapter 3; *The U.S. Armed Forces German Youth Activities Program 1945–1955*, 49–59.
78 *The U.S. Armed Forces German Youth Activities Program 1945–1955*, 33–34.
79 *The U.S. Armed Forces German Youth Activities Program 1945–1955*, 32–33.
80 "349. Evacuation of Dependents," March 17, 1948, Telecon TT-9218, in Smith, ed., *The Papers of General Lucius D. Clay*, Vol. 2, 580; see also 579–583. See also Clay, *Decision in Germany*, 358, 386.

serve as part of the proof that the Americans were not abandoning Berliners.[81] The American presence, American support, and American material aid also had the potential to make profound impacts on German inner thoughts and emotions, with the Berlin Airlift ultimately leading West Berliners to feel reassured that Americans were present as parental-type protectors.[82] As Kaete O'Connell notes, benevolent acts by Americans, especially those based on food, imprinted West German mindsets and created a bond between Germans and Americans.[83] Emmy E. Werner, who was age 16 in 1945, reflected on her strong memories about receiving CARE packages: "After all the misery and dying, compassion was alive: It came in a sturdy brown box!"[84] As James F. Tent notes in his study of the work of the American Friends Service Committee (AFSC) in postwar Germany, "Gratitude is a fleeting emotion although the generation that experienced acts of moral and material support after the war retain[s] memories of gratitude for what occurred."[85] German hunger had evolved from being part of an occupation politics of punishment for past Nazi crimes into part of an American foreign policy revolving around compassion, which served American Cold War aims of creating a strong democratic partner out of West Germany. Children's hunger played a central role in this shift. Even in the early days of the occupation, children usually responded in an extremely positive manner after receiving gifts from GIs such as chocolate bars, acts which could shatter their images of Americans as dangerous enemies. Some youngsters even noted that they essentially fell in love with American soldiers, highlighting the level of positive emotive responses that actions such as gifts of sweets or the Airlift candy bombing created.[86] A focus on the youngest Germans also helped mold the shift in American views about aid to Ger-

---

81 Alvah, *Unofficial Ambassadors*, 72.

82 On emotions in diplomacy and foreign contact, see Frank Costigliola, "'Mixed Up' and 'Contact': Culture and Emotion among the Allies in the Second World War," *The International History Review* 20, no. 4 (December 1998): 791–805, http://www.jstor.org/stable/40107996; Frank Costigliola, "'I Had Come as a Friend': Emotion, Culture, and Ambiguity in the Formation of the Cold War, 1943–45," *Cold War History* 1, no. 1 (2000): 103–128, https://doi.org/10.1080/713999913; Todd H. Hall, *Emotional Diplomacy: Official Emotion on the International Stage* (Cornell University Press, 2015).

83 O'Connell, "Weapon of War, Tool of Peace," 28; O'Connell, "Benevolent Diplomacy," *Perspectives on History*.

84 Werner, *Through the Eyes of Innocents*, 194.

85 James F. Tent, "Simple Gifts: The American Friends Service Committee and the Establishment of Neighborhood Centers in Post-1945 Germany," *Kirchliche Zeitgeschichte* 2, no. 1 (May 1989): 81, https://www.jstor.org/stable/43098025.

86 Willett, *The Americanization of Germany*, 2–3; Weiss, *A Nazi Childhood*, 171, 196; Edward N. Peterson, *The Many Faces of Defeat: The German People's Experience in 1945* (Peter Lang, 1990), 49; O'Connell, "Weapon of War, Tool of Peace," 1–2; O'Connell, "Hearts, Minds, and Stomachs," in

many into widespread acceptance and even support, with citizens including President Truman taking part in private actions of benevolent aid to Germany.

Aid to Germany continued during the first decades of the Cold War. CARE operated until 1960, and CRALOG sent its final shipments in 1961, marking the continued importance of aid, especially food aid, to American foreign policy goals of containing communism and encouraging liberal democracy's spread. Large-scale benevolent efforts in Europe not only assisted European recovery but also served American aims by enhancing American status and painting Americans as inherently good.[87] Assistance such as GYA also provided a rationale for the continued presence of occupation troops in Germany years beyond the end of the war.

Rhetoric about aid in postwar Germany focused on positive aspects of rebuilding, including ensuring freedom and prosperity in a way that stood in stark contrast to Soviet communism. Moreover, it cast GIs as positive agents of assistance, who granted bits of the American plenty to Germans. As Kaete O'Connell argues, "food relief in Germany was rooted in a desire to appear compassionate." Furthermore, aid to the former enemy was never due to "purely altruistic" reasons, she argues.[88] Stephen R. Porter writes that the rise of the US in the twentieth century to that of "a position of elite global power was significantly justified and fueled by the proposition that the country's objects of philanthropic concern might potentially include any vulnerable people across the globe." In addition, he notes that this aid to vulnerable populations was the "way in which both the American state and civil society staked a claim for their country as a truly global power." Thus, "America's influence over foreign populations" was often justified by "its benevolent intentions for the most vulnerable and needy among them."[89] In postwar Germany, American benevolence was part of a politics centered around compassion, which was used in a way that served American interests. Aid toward young Germans remained central in American plans for selling the benefits of democratic plenty to Germans, as children and youth were the future of the country. American strength and benevolence thus had to be imprinted into the experiences of young Germans.[90] The young German generation also needed to realize where aid was coming from, which would spur them to feel gratitude for the unique American way that was enabling these gifts. American policy to-

---

The Berlin Airlift and the Making of the Cold War, ed. Schuessler, Seipp, and Sullivan, 146–147, 158, 160–161.

87 O'Connell, "Weapon of War, Tool of Peace," 302–303. See also De Grazia, *Irresistible Empire*, 5.

88 O'Connell, "Weapon of War, Tool of Peace," 27.

89 Stephen R. Porter, *Benevolent Empire: U.S. Power, Humanitarianism, and the World's Dispossessed* (University of Pennsylvania Press, 2017), 1–2.

90 See O'Connell, "Weapon of War, Tool of Peace," 28.

ward Germany thus became centered around a geopolitics of gratitude, which aimed to harness awareness and positive responses among the German population due to the Americans' compassionate acts.

American kindness toward Germany played a role in Cold War propaganda, which required young Germans to play the double-edged role of being the beneficiaries of aid and also serve as the audience who needed to learn how to craft a future Germany in a way that Americans desired.[91] For example, images of soldiers' benevolence in Germany served as great propaganda that supported American geopolitical aims of portraying benevolent power, which overlapped with the tactics of Marshall Plan films. These films aimed at selling the Marshall Plan to European audiences and were first produced through the Information Division of the European Cooperation Administration (ECA) in Paris and in 17 other country missions beginning in 1948.[92] American postwar benevolence had thus spread beyond postwar occupation Germany, and Americans developed tactics to ensure Europeans would view propaganda to learn about the important messages behind American material assistance, including the Marshall Plan films. By March 1951, over two million people in West Germany and Berlin had seen the films, in addition to millions of other Europeans.[93] The films included a conscious effort to ensure that young Europeans would admire the American way of life.[94]

---

91 During the Cold War, the term "information" was often used to avoid the negative connotations of "propaganda." See Fritsche, *The American Marshall Plan Film Campaign and the Europeans*, 11. See also Belmonte, *Selling the American Way*, 7. See also a discussion of tensions within the Marshall Plan publicity campaign regarding use of the term "propaganda," in Hans-Jürgen Schröder, "Marshall Plan Propaganda in Austria and Western Germany," in *The Marshall Plan in Austria*, ed. Günter Bischof, Anton Pelinka, and Dieter Stiefel (Transaction Publishers, 2000), 234–235.

92 See Schulberg and Carter, *Selling Democracy*, 8, 11–13, 15–16; Fritsche, *The American Marshall Plan Film Campaign and the Europeans*, 5; Maria Fritsche, "Das Schiff und der Strom—Subtiles Werben für Europa in den Marshallplan-Filmen," in *Werben für Europa: Die mediale Konstruktion europäischer Identität durch Europafilme*, ed. Gabriele Clemens (Ferdinand Schöningh, 2016), 471, 488. The films were not able to be shown to American audiences due to the 1948 Smith-Mundt Act, because Americans "were not to be 'propagandized' with their own tax dollars." In 1990 this ban was lifted. The "Selling Democracy" series were the first screenings of the films in early 2000s in the United States led by Sandra Schulberg, daughter of Marshall Plan Motion Picture Section chief Stuart Schulberg (Schulberg and Carter, 8).

93 Frank Mehring, "The Promises of 'Young Europe': Cultural Diplomacy, Reeducation, and Youth Culture in the Films of the Marshall Plan," in *Die amerikanische Reeducation-Politik nach 1945*, ed. Gerund and Paul, 67.

94 See Alexandra Schenke, "Targeting the Next Generation: How Marshall Plan Films Urged Young Europeans to Rebuild—and Rethink," *Transatlantic Studies: A Student Research Blog*, July 24, 2020, https://transatlanticmoment.wordpress.com/2020/07/24/children/.

American Marshall Plan propaganda aimed at spreading information about democracy, free trade, and the American model, attempting both to explain the purpose of the aid and to persuade Europeans of all ages about the benefits of a society based around liberal democracy.[95] Europeans were also encouraged to integrate in a way that would serve American policy aims, including the containment of Soviet power, the revival of international trade, and the financial benefits of a prosperous Western European economy.[96] According to Maria Fritsche, Marshall Plan publicity often took place on subtle and indirect levels, with films aiming at "indirect persuasion."[97] European children also played a central role in the Marshall Plan goal of an integrated Europe, formed especially by young, cosmopolitan, consumerist, democratic Europeans who did not carry the baggage of the past generation.[98] Moreover, these youngsters would try to emulate the American way of life, which was already often admired in Germany by young Germans who encountered American plenty through encounters with GIs during the occupation.[99] A future democratic "United States of Europe" was therefore a young one.[100]

The Marshall Plan film *Let's Be Childish* portrayed children as the center protagonists of navigations of attempts for European unity.[101] The 1950 film, produced in France and written and directed by George Freedland, a Russian-born filmmaker, portrays children of various European nationalities on vacation at an

95 See Fritsche, *The American Marshall Plan Film Campaign and the Europeans*, 11–12. Also, Mehring, "The Promises of 'Young Europe'" in *Die amerikanische Reeducation-Politik nach 1945*, ed. Gerund and Paul, 63. Mehring notes that "the Marshall Plan films represent the first transnational effort in American cultural diplomacy to use the audio-visual medium to promote citizenship education."

96 See Fritsche, *The American Marshall Plan Film Campaign and the Europeans*, 129.

97 Fritsche, "Das Schiff und der Strom—Subtiles Werben für Europa in den Marshallplan-Filmen," in *Werben für Europa*, ed. Clemens, 488.

98 See Fritsche, *The American Marshall Plan Film Campaign and the Europeans*, 3, 129, 140–141; Mehring, "The Promises of 'Young Europe'" in *Die amerikanische Reeducation-Politik nach 1945*, ed. Gerund and Paul, 61–62; Schenke, "Targeting the Next Generation," *Transatlantic Studies: A Student Research Blog*.

99 See Fritsche, *The American Marshall Plan Film Campaign and the Europeans*, 234; Willett, *The Americanization of Germany*, 104; Stephan, "A Special Case of Cultural Americanization," in *The Americanization of Europe*, ed. Stephan, 78–80, 85.

100 See Mehring, "The Promises of 'Young Europe'" in *Die amerikanische Reeducation-Politik nach 1945*, ed. Gerund and Paul, 61–62, 64, 73, 86–87; Fritsche, *The American Marshall Plan Film Campaign and the Europeans*, 141; Schenke, "Targeting the Next Generation," *Transatlantic Studies: A Student Research Blog*.

101 George Freedland, *Let's Be Childish*, USIS, 1950, available in Mediathek of bpb: Bundeszentrale für politische Bildung, https://www.bpb.de/mediathek/video/206880/let-s-be-childish/.

alpine resort. The plot includes a contest in the snow, and at first, the children do not understand each other and nationalism rises as they compete against each other. However, a newcomer, Toni, an English girl, is accidentally hurt in a snowball fight, and all the children try to work together to buy her chocolates from the local pastry shop. Finally, the children decide to band together instead of competing against each other in the contest, creating a town out of snow called "Toniville," and they all share the contest's grand prize, a four-pound box of sweets. The film concludes, "May it be a lesson to our adult world." In contrast to the cooperative children, the children's parents are seen arguing at the end of the film, with the captions appearing: "but that's another story . . . "[102] The film was especially unique as it is filmed completely from the perspective of the children, with only the legs and torsos of the adults shown until the final scene when the full bodies of the adults are shown. The film's message about European cooperation and unity is communicated without a mention of the Marshall Plan. The film was simultaneously propaganda aimed at a young audience as well as a call for the promises of a unified Europe.[103]

Children and youth made up a large part of the audience of Marshall Plan film screenings.[104] Children were thus not only the protagonists of propaganda films such as *Let's Be Childish*, but they also were the target audience, as they were the symbolic future of Europe.[105] In contrast to the previous generation, whose nationalism had led to war, this new generation was capable of coming together and finding "intercultural and international understanding," as the film *Let's Be Childish* denoted, according to Frank Mehring.[106] Young Europeans were navigators of the societal processes and negotiations of the transfer of American culture, which the Marshall Plan propaganda played a role in, as Fritsche highlights.[107] In addition, young people played a role in creating international link-

102 Freedland, *Let's Be Childish*, 18:09–18:12, 19:02–19:12.

103 See Anne Bruch, Gabriele Clemens, Jeanpaul Goergen, and Thomas Tode, "'Cooperation Means Prosperity'—Das Werben für die Integration Europas in den Marshallplan-Filmen," in *Werben für Europa*, ed. Clemens, 225–226; Schenke, "Targeting the Next Generation," *Transatlantic Studies: A Student Research Blog*; Schulberg and Carter, *Selling Democracy*, 22; Mehring, "The Promises of 'Young Europe'" in *Die amerikanische Reeducation-Politik nach 1945*, ed. Gerund and Paul, 71–74.

104 Fritsche, *The American Marshall Plan Film Campaign and the Europeans*, 186.

105 See Schenke, "Targeting the Next Generation," *Transatlantic Studies: A Student Research Blog*; Mehring, "The Promises of 'Young Europe'" in *Die amerikanische Reeducation-Politik nach 1945*, ed. Gerund and Paul, 61–62.

106 Mehring, "The Promises of 'Young Europe'" in *Die amerikanische Reeducation-Politik nach 1945*, ed. Gerund and Paul, 71.

107 Fritsche, *The American Marshall Plan Film Campaign and the Europeans*, 8–9, 239.

ages. As the example of GYA in occupation Germany has shown, young Germans themselves often wished for European and international cooperation, showing an interest in exchange programs, pen pal programs with American children, and the world language Esperanto.

Thus, American aid had become part of the wider Cold War policy goal of crafting a prosperous, democratic postwar Western Europe (which included West Germany) with the United States "at the helm," as Fritsche notes.[108] As had developed in occupation Germany, the United States emerged as model, protector, and even as a teacher to Europeans during the budding Cold War, providing lessons on the new way to live based on the American way of life.[109] Through propaganda such as the Marshall Plan films, Europeans learned the message that Frank Mehring highlights, that "You too, can be like us," if only they accepted what Americans offered.[110] Overall, as Fritsche argues, the Marshall Plan is remembered very positively, which could partially be a result of the propaganda campaign, which aimed at convincing Europeans that the Marshall Plan was necessary for recovery.[111] The Cold War geopolitics of gratitude ensured the provider of this aid, the United States, was not to be forgotten. In (West) Germany, Americans and American culture undoubtably made a profound impact following the days of the occupation and Marshall Plan. As Philipp Gassert argues, the United States has fundamentally impacted German society, even more than other nations have, such as England or the Soviet Union.[112] Moreover, as Maria Fritsche claims, "Whether we describe the rapid economic, cultural and political changes Europe experienced in the twentieth century, particularly after 1945, as modernization, Westernization or Americanization, it is undeniable that the United States played an influential role in this process, both through active intervention and through indirect promotion."[113] However, this development occurred in the context of a complex and selective process of transfer of American culture. The recipients also played an active role in this process, such as the members of GYA clubs or Marshall Plan

---

108 Fritsche, 129.

109 See Fritsche, 19.

110 Mehring, "The Promises of 'Young Europe'" in *Die amerikanische Reeducation-Politik nach 1945*, ed. Gerund and Paul, 66.

111 Fritsche, *The American Marshall Plan Film Campaign and the Europeans*, 240.

112 Philipp Gassert, "Amerikanismus, Antiamerikanismus, Amerikanisierung: Neue Literatur zur Sozial-, Wirtschafts- und Kulturgeschichte des amerikanischen Einflusses in Deutschland und Europa," *Archiv für Sozialgeschichte* 39 (1999): 531. See also De Grazia, *Irresistible Empire*, 552–556 for a literature review on the topic of Americanization. See also Wagnleitner, *Coca-Colonisation*, 352.

113 Fritsche, *The American Marshall Plan Film Campaign and the Europeans*, 235.

film audiences.[114] Above all, the Marshall Plan helped mold the context of a European-wide geopolitics of gratitude for American assistance in European recovery. Moreover, the military occupation of Germany was integral in setting up this position of Americans as benevolent suppliers and caretakers, while local citizens served as recipients of the promises of the American way. German youngsters were the first to play the postwar role of both recipient and audience within the budding American Cold War geopolitics of gratitude.

Products of Luxury: Selling the American Way of Life

Throughout the postwar occupation in Germany, GIs served as representatives of the American way, and Germans noted the material plenty that GIs possessed in contrast to German need. The presence of GIs thus fundamentally shaped the German impression of the United States.[115] As Manfred J. Enssle has noted in his study of hunger in occupied postwar Stuttgart, the scarcity present in the German society under occupation, which stood in contrast to the prosperity of the occupiers, caused the accumulation of "great unsatisfied wants" among German children and adults. After the currency reform of 1948, this led Germans to especially focus on "materialistic concerns," Enssle notes.[116] During and after the occupation, (West) Germans often welcomed consumer products central to the American lifestyle, including Coca-Cola, which became a booming market in West Germany by the mid-1960s.[117] Occupation transactions between Germans and Americans created the foundation for Germany's acceptance of a consumer-style democracy, which especially emerged with the rise of German affluence in the 1950s. As Victoria de Grazia argues, consumption practices in Europe helped lead to the United States' rise as a globally active empire, noting that when this "Market Empire," as she terms it, "did impose itself militarily elsewhere, it promised to follow up with substantial aid to rebuild the ruins in its own image."[118] This occurred especially following the end of World War II in Europe, when encounters with American products and the American way provided a tempting glimpse into the benefits of a consumer democracy for Germans.

---

114 See Fritsche, 8–9, 239.
115 See Willett, *The Americanization of Germany*, viii–ix, 1–3.
116 Enssle, "The Harsh Discipline," 501.
117 Schutts, "Born Again in the Gospel of Refreshment?," in *Consuming Germany in the Cold War*, ed. Crew, 130, 143. See also Willett, *The Americanization of Germany*, 103–106.
118 De Grazia, *Irresistible Empire*, 9. See also, 4–5.

For many young Germans during the occupation, American soldiers proved particularly enticing, with friendly GIs providing recreational activities and access to food. Youngsters also gained a tantalizing glimpse of the luxury and abundance that these GI ambassadors of the American way had access to. German youth got their first tastes of products such as Coca-Cola in encounters with GIs.[119] From Hershey bars to Lucky Strikes, German youngsters directly witnessed the irresistible nature of prosperity in a mass consumer society. To many young Germans, democracy came to mean access to non-essential goods such as chocolate.[120] These glimpses of the temptations of the American way of life created a promise of a future of plenty, which stood in contrast with the present stark needs of occupation life and the crimes of the Nazi past.

Among the first American products of democratic luxury that German youngsters encountered were chewing gum and candy bars, especially Hershey's chocolate.[121] Although chocolate had of course been produced in Germany by companies such as Ritter Sport, many children did not have access to chocolate during the war. Many youngsters experienced their first taste of chocolate through a GI's gift of a Hershey bar or from the chocolate inside of a CARE package. This first taste often imprinted their experiences of the occupation era. Eva Goslar, who in 1947 was a five-year-old refugee in Einbeck in Lower Saxony, recollected the arrival of a CARE package for her family. The package contained many goods that she had never encountered before, such as powdered milk and white flour, and it included two huge bars of chocolate. Eva's mother had warned her children to be frugal with the food, but she did give them all a small piece of chocolate. Eva described the first taste of the chocolate:

> I had never tasted anything so wonderful in my life. Very slowly, I moved the sweet, melting delicacy around in my mouth, and kept my mouth closed tight for a while in order to preserve the taste. (*Ich hatte noch nie in meinem Leben etwas so Wunderbares geschmeckt. Ganz langsam hatte ich die süße, schmelzende Köstlichkeit in meinem Mund hin und her geschoben und noch lange den Mund fest verschlossen gehalten, um den Geschmack zu bewahren.*)

That night, Eva kept recalling the taste of the chocolate and snuck to the cupboard where the chocolate was stored with the idea of smelling or licking the chocolate,

---

119 Willett, *The Americanization of Germany*, 104; Fritsche, *The American Marshall Plan Film Campaign and the Europeans*, 234; Stephan, "A Special Case of Cultural Americanization," in *The Americanization of Europe*, ed. Stephan, 78–79.

120 See O'Connell, "Hearts, Minds, and Stomachs," in *The Berlin Airlift and the Making of the Cold War*, 146–147; Goedde, *GIs and Germans*, 158.

121 About the invention of M&M's during World War II, see Constance L. Hays, "Forrest Mars, 95, Creator of the M & M and a Candy Empire," *New York Times*, July 3, 1999.

which she thought no one would notice. However, when she reached for the chocolate, the powdered milk package fell down and exploded all over the ground, and she was discovered by her family holding a chocolate bar while standing in the powder. The memory of the taste of chocolate had been starkly imprinted in Eva's mind, and even led the young girl to act against the wishes of her mother. In addition, the memory of the CARE package and the chocolate incident proved particularly noteworthy for Eva, enough for her to include it decades later in a collection of stories on postwar occupation childhood, published in 2000.[122] The taste of chocolate and being the recipient of a benevolent act from a stranger were thus linked in many personal memories of occupation.

CARE packages usually contained American candy, such as Hershey bars that had originally been rations for US military usage, including wartime supplies that had been for the planned troop invasion of the Japanese mainland.[123] Candy had developed into a central part of early twentieth century American consumption, including for military usage. Starting around the turn of the twentieth century, the consumption of candy had become linked with American masculinity and the military, with the War Department commissioning candy companies to supply the troops. GIs and sailors were often featured in ads beginning in the 1920s. Candy became viewed as an essential good for quick energy, beyond just being a delicious treat.[124] In April 1937, The Hershey Company, then known as Hershey Chocolate Corporation, became involved in the production of chocolate ration bars for the military. The Hershey D-Ration bar was developed as an emergency ration that could be consumed in any temperature with a taste "a little better than a boiled potato." A four-ounce bar contained 600 calories.[125] In addition, candy helped boost troop morale, with the Hershey's D-Ration bar being replaced in 1943 by the better tasting Hershey's Tropical Bar, which was heat resistant for one hour in 120 degrees Fahrenheit.[126] According to the Encyclopedia of the Hershey Community Archives, "by the end of World War II, almost 380,000,000 two ounce Tropical bars had been produced for the United States military."[127] Hershey Chocolate Corporation received five Army-Navy "E" Production awards beginning

122 Eva Goslar, "Schokolade," in *Lebertran und Chewing Gum*, ed. Kleindienst, 246, 248.
123 Werner, *Through the Eyes of Innocents*, 191.
124 O'Connell, "The Taste of Defeat," in *Food, Culture and Identity*, ed. Benbow and Perry, 210.
125 "Ration D Bars," Encyclopedia, Hershey Community Archives, September 7, 2018, https://hersheyarchives.org/encyclopedia/ration-d-bars/.
126 "Hershey's Tropical Chocolate Bar," Encyclopedia, Hershey Community Archives, September 6, 2018, https://hersheyarchives.org/encyclopedia/hersheys-tropical-chocolate-bar/. See also O'Connell, "The Taste of Defeat," in *Food, Culture and Identity*, ed. Benbow and Perry, 210.
127 "Hershey's Tropical Chocolate Bar." The Tropical Bar also went to the moon with Apollo 15 in July 1971.

in 1942 for "exceeding all production expectations in the manufacturing of an Emergency Field Ration." According to Major General Edmund Gregory during the awards ceremony in 1942, "the men and women of Hershey Chocolate Corporation have every reason to be proud of their great work in backing up our soldiers on the fighting fronts."[128] Kaete O'Connell remarks on chocolate's particular place in the contrast between American plenty and German need during the occupation: "Scarce in postwar Germany, chocolate was an American luxury that conveyed the affluence of the victors and the rewards of democracy."[129] In addition, chewing gum, a non-necessity, also portrayed American material prosperity and played a role in the GI persona. Soldiers were often seen swaggering about and chewing gum, while Germans often did not understand the point of chewing gum.[130] Sweets and the US military had become intertwined, which emerged at the forefront in occupation encounters.

In addition to Hershey bars and chewing gum, Coca-Cola also moved into the frontline in postwar German society. Coca-Cola had been produced in Germany since 1929, and the company had even been sponsors of the 1938 Olympics. During the war, the German producers of Coca-Cola had invented Fanta.[131] Once Coca-Cola was produced again in Germany in 1949, it proved extremely popular, with sales skyrocketing.[132] In Tokyo, according to *Time*, the Japanese got their first sampling from GIs, encountering the taste of first love, as a Tokyo waitress characterized the taste of Coca-Cola.[133] Coca-Cola in postwar societies could thus provoke strong positive emotions such as love and happiness, while simultaneously serving as a symbol of freedom and democracy.[134] However, no product proved more controversial than this soft drink. Critics claimed that it had the potential to corrupt youth and some were not happy about its role as a symbol of an American-

128 "Ration D Bars," Encyclopedia, Hershey Community Archives.
129 O'Connell, "The Taste of Defeat," in *Food, Culture and Identity*, ed. Benbow and Perry, 214.
130 See O'Connell, "The Taste of Defeat," 210.
131 See Willett, *The Americanization of Germany*, 8, 12–13, 99–103; Schutts, "Born Again in the Gospel of Refreshment?," in *Consuming Germany in the Cold War*, ed. Crew, 125–127; Stephan, "A Special Case of Cultural Americanization," in *The Americanization of Europe*, ed. Stephan, 79; Volker R. Berghahn, *American Big Business in Britain and Germany: A Comparative History of Two "Special Relationships" in the 20th Century* (Princeton University Press, 2014), 259.
132 See Schutts, "Born Again in the Gospel of Refreshment?," in *Consuming Germany in the Cold War*, ed. Crew, 129–130, 143; Schutts, "Coca-Cola History," 132; Willett, *The Americanization of Germany*, 104–106.
133 "The Sun Never Sets on Cacoola," *Time*, 29.
134 See Schutts, "Born Again in the Gospel of Refreshment?," in *Consuming Germany in the Cold War*, ed. Crew, 122, 135; "The Sun Never Sets on Cacoola" 28–29; Willett, *The Americanization of Germany*, 103.

style "consumer-capitalist way of life," as Jeff Schutts depicts it.[135] For many Europeans, according to Schutts, Coca-Cola became "an easy symbol for whatever one did not like about the postwar European society then under construction via the Marshall Plan," with France even attempting to ban the fizzy drink.[136] In Austria, there were also rumors that atomic bombs were being made at Coca-Cola bottling plants.[137]

In a similar manner to Hershey Chocolate Corporation, the Coca-Cola Company had developed a relationship with the World War II military. Robert Woodruff, CEO of the company, had declared that every man in uniform would be able to get a Coke for five cents.[138] The 1950 *Time* article on the world empire of Coca-Cola explained how its spread around the world was linked to the US military presence: "The Coke bottling plants which moved along with the invading U.S. armies and brought the sight and taste of Coke to millions of people who had never heard of it before were actually the biggest impetus of Coca-Cola's present international boom."[139] The Coca-Cola Company attempted to spread a concept of Coke's universal appeal, "international 'good will,'" and friendship, even linking the soft drink to the friendliness of GIs, according to Jeff Schutts.[140] The focus was on the future, on democratization and a raising of living standards, thus moving away from the dark past of war and fascism. In addition, the company co-opted the "language of democracy to promote sales," creating a type of "soft-drink diplomacy," for example donating the soft drink "to forums that fostered actual democratic discourse," notes Schutts.[141] Schutts also argues that West Germans seemed to buy in to the desires of Coca-Cola and "recreate[d] themselves as 'consumer-democrats' in the new West-oriented German state." Interestingly, he argues, Germans for the most part proved to be gladly "Coca-Colonized," but not "Americanized," using an image of Coca-Cola that fit their own needs.[142] Germans thus liked Coca-Cola even if they did

---

135 Schutts, "Born Again in the Gospel of Refreshment?," 125. See also Willett, 99–100, 103–106.
136 Schutts, "Born Again in the Gospel of Refreshment?," 123–125. Also, Schutts, "Coca-Cola History," 132; "The Sun Never Sets on Cacoola," *Time*, 28.
137 See Schutts, "Born Again in the Gospel of Refreshment?," 123. Also, Ulf Biedermann, *Ein amerikanischer Traum: Coca-Cola: Die unglaubliche Geschichte eines 100jährigen Erfolges* (Rasch und Röhring, 1985), 114.
138 See Schutts, "Born Again in the Gospel of Refreshment?," 122; Biedermann, 63; "The Sun Never Sets on Cacoola," *Time*, 32; Willett, *The Americanization of Germany*, 102.
139 "The Sun Never Sets on Cacoola," 32.
140 Schutts, "Born Again in the Gospel of Refreshment?," in *Consuming Germany in the Cold War*, ed. Crew, 133; Schutts, "Coca-Cola History," 137.
141 Schutts, "Born Again in the Gospel of Refreshment?," 135–136.
142 Schutts, "Born Again in the Gospel of Refreshment?," 142–143. See also Schutts, "Coca-Cola History," 136–137.

not necessarily like the United States. In postwar occupation Germany and beyond, the ubiquitous presence of Coca-Cola served as concrete evidence perhaps even more than the Marshall Plan or Voice of America that "the U.S. has gone out into the world to stay," as the *Time* article put it.[143] Even if global consumers including Germans did not interpret the United States in a positive manner, they still gladly consumed the products of democratic luxury.

Coca-Cola beverages were arguably not essential products for children in postwar occupation Germany. They were not beneficial drinks that could help improve the health of the often-undernourished children. Coca-Cola mainly consists of sugar, which is free of any essential vitamins and minerals.[144] As the example of GYA made clear, many children who participated in the American-sponsored clubs and other GYA activities often came for material goods, including food and Coca-Cola.[145] Some eyewitnesses remembered drinking Coca-Cola in combination with dancing swing and listening to jazz music as the best part of the clubs such as the Bremen Boys Club.[146] One boy who played swing music for the Americans was paid in a case of Coca-Cola and a carton of cigarettes.[147] In addition, according to a contemporary witness, in the Bremen Boys Club during club dances, the boys often preferred to drink the free Coke than dance with the girls.[148] Coca-Cola and other sweet products played a central role in navigations in GYA clubs, providing a taste of what all American plenty and democracy could mean.

In Austria, which was also under occupation by the four Allied nations, the linkages between Coca-Cola, reeducation efforts, and the youth activities program were even stronger. The Austrian Youth Activities program (AYA), which was essentially the Austrian version of GYA, consisted of Army-sponsored youth clubs, summer camping programs, sport events, Christmas parties, and youth centers, which were supported by Good Neighbor Societies with Austrian representatives. According to a historical outline of the program, these youth centers developed as demonstration projects "to promote the idea of community responsibility for the

143 "The Sun Never Sets on Cacoola," *Time*, 28.

144 On sugar and nutrition, see Ehlers, *Die Ernährungssituation*, 46. The military government sometimes substituted fats for sugar in ration distributions.

145 Report No. 56 (26 April 1947), German Children Appraise the Youth Program, in Merritt and Merritt, eds., *Public Opinion in Occupied Germany*, 155–157.

146 Bruss, ed., *Mit Zuckersack und Heißgetränk*, 194–195; Groth, "Bremer Jungs im Jahre Sechsundvierzig," in *Vom Trümmerkind zum Teenager*, ed. Foitzik, 25–26.

147 Gunther Joe Kirchhoff (former musician, played swing and blues music for the GIs and in the Bremen Boys Club), interview by Peter Strotmann, Bremen, November 5, 2015.

148 Reinald Ihler, interview by Peter Strotmann. Also, Groth, "Bremer Jungs im Jahre Sechsundvierzig," in *Vom Trümmerkind zum Teenager*, ed. Foitzik, 26.

constructive utilization of the leisure time of youth free of partisan, political or secular exploitation." The outline noted that the "democratic reorientation of Austrian youth and its leaders" was considered "a primary concern in accomplishing its mission in the reconstruction of the economic, political and social life of Austria." Austrian youth were central to this aim and the future of the country: "The future of Austria is dependent to a great extent upon the development of a clean living, democratic-minded generation of Austrian youth. From the youth of today will come Austria's leaders of the future." In addition, AYA would "stimulate the development of constructive recreational and informal education activities for Austrian Youth [sic] regardless of race, religion, political affiliations or other such requirements, where they can exercise the democratic concepts of freedom, fair play, tolerance and team work." The program included Austrian participation in order to "eventually permit complete, autonomous operation by the Austrians themselves with American aid being advisory and supplementary in nature." AYA thus introduced a new type of "non-political and non-partisan" community recreation in Austria.[149]

Lieutenant General Geoffrey Keyes, the US High Commissioner of Austria from 1947 to 1950, actively supported AYA. Keyes had previously played a major role in the development of Army assistance for youth activities in Germany with his issuance of the Seventh Army youth activities directive in 1945. His engagement with Austrian youth included visits to AYA summer camps, and he gave a keynote address at the opening events for AYA swimming pools in Salzburg and Linz. During the ceremony in Salzburg, his wife "unveiled an engraved marble tablet with the inscription:- 'Dedicated to Austrian Youth by the American Peo-

149 Historical Outline The Armed Forces Assistance Program to Austrian Youth; Folder AYA Reports-Consolidated. USACA. 1950; Records Relating to Austrian Youth Activities 1946–1952; Box 1; Department of State/Office of the U.S. High Commissioner for Austria; RG 260, NACP. According to the outline, youth center projects were "integrated into the Austrian organizational structure through the formation of Good Neighbor Societies, composed of individuals representing a cross section of the community including Land and City governments, Trade Unions, Schools, Churches and welfare agencies." Each center was managed by a local board of directors, which was elected by Society members. The board was formed as a result of an aim to continue the youth program after the end of American support, and to avoid having one political party take over the program for its own gain. AYA special events included soap box derbies and Golden Gloves boxing tournaments. For the first two years, the program had operated with no government funds. In 1949, the program received government funds from the Reorientation Branch in Washington. Activities in youth centers included handicrafts, sports, movies, and ice skating. Also, William K. Purdy, Youth Activities Specialist, "Formal opening of the Austrian 'Good Neighbor' settlement house," November 26, 1947; Folder AYA Correspondence (Lt. Karlstrom) [Folder 2 of 2]; Records Relating to Austrian Youth Activities 1946–1952; Box 18; Department of State/Office of the U.S. High Commissioner for Austria; RG 260; NACP. The first "Good Neighbor" youth center opened in Linz in 1947.

ple.'"[150] Keyes' April 1, 1947 directive regarding assistance to Austrian youth noted the purpose of the program for "reducing juvenile delinquency, providing worthwhile leisure time activities, and assisting in the development of a training program for the responsibilities of Austrian citizenship."[151] According to an official summary from 1949, an average of around 25,000 Austrians between ten and 25 were the recipients of direct assistance, and many others had benefited in ways such as receiving loans of equipment.[152] In 1947, 10,000 young Austrians had taken part in summer camps and over 30,000 had attended Christmas parties. In addition, by 1949, over 10,000 Austrian youth were enrolled as active members of youth centers. AYA emerged as central to "the attainment of the aims of the mission of the United States Forces in Austria," according to an official report.[153] In June 1947, John B. Schwertman, a Youth Activities Specialist, wrote in a report that he read at a Youth Activities conference that month about the importance of having an "American type i.e. unpolitical, youth program" that would win over the political and confessional groups. He noted that the stakes were high and mentioned, "Has it occurred to you how closely related our tiny little youth program is to the whole so-called 'Truman Doctrine'?" Thus, he linked AYA to wider American geopolitical goals. He also remarked on the tremendous importance of youth activities, arguing, "our government has given us a terrific assignment." Moreover, he commented on the importance of not just copying the GYA program in Germany, which he critiqued, describing it as a "baseball coca cola [sic] . . . 'razzle dazzle' the give 'em bread and circuses direction," and noted reports about doubtful results of the GYA program. Instead, he believed that it was essential to gain the support from both the US Forces and from the Austrian *Länder*

---

150 Historical Outline The Armed Forces Assistance Program to Austrian Youth; Folder AYA Reports-Consolidated. USACA. 1950; Records Relating to Austrian Youth Activities 1946–1952; Box 1; Department of State/Office of the U.S. High Commissioner for Austria; RG 260; NACP. AYA Report for Quarter Ending 30 September 1950, October 5, 1950; same location as previous record.

151 Historical Outline; Folder AYA Reports-Consolidated. USACA. 1950; Records Relating to Austrian Youth Activities 1946–1952; Box 1; RG 260; NACP. See directive: Howard V. Judson, Asst Adj General, "Assistance to Austrian Youth Activities," April 1, 1947; Folder AYA Directives-Old, Records Relating to Austrian Youth Activities 1946–1952; Box 1; Department of State/Office of the U.S. High Commissioner for Austria; RG 260; NACP.

152 Samuel H. Williams, Summary of AYA Program, August 1949; Folder AYA-Directives-Current; Records Relating to Austrian Youth Activities 1946–1952; Box 1; Department of State/Office of the U.S. High Commissioner for Austria; RG 260, NACP.

153 Historical Outline; Folder AYA Reports-Consolidated. USACA. 1950; Records Relating to Austrian Youth Activities 1946–1952; Box 1; Department of State/Office of the U.S. High Commissioner for Austria; RG 260; NACP.

governments, who had to be persuaded about the importance of a non-political youth program that could reach all youth.[154]

According to Reinhold Wagnleitner, AYA gave out gifts of the GIs' Coca-Cola rations to young participants at a time when Coca-Cola was not yet available for Austrian consumers to purchase.[155] Wagnleitner argues that this action provided a twofold benefit: it improved Austrian youth's opinions of the US Army and also prepared a new market group for the consumption of Coca-Cola.[156] In addition, working in agreement with the Coca-Cola Company, the AYA directly received funds through the sale of Coca-Cola to Austrians in locations such as Austrian employee cafeterias, ice rinks, public pools, and movie theaters.[157] For example, this source of income brought in an average of 15,000 Schillings a month for AYA's Good Neighbor Club Fund in Linz in 1949.[158] The beverages were from the Coca-Cola bottling plant, Plant Thirteen in Lambach, Austria.[159] Thus, Coca-Cola beverages offered not only a tempting reason for Austrian youths to attend AYA programs but also contributed to the funding of the youth program itself.

---

154 Report by John B. Schwertman, Youth Activities Specialist, Folder AYA Directives-Old; Records Relating to Austrian Youth Activities 1946–1952; Box 1; Department of State/Office of the U.S. High Commissioner for Austria; RG 260; NACP.

155 Wagnleitner, *Coca-Colonisation*, 329–330. Also, Schutts, "Born Again in the Gospel of Refreshment?," in *Consuming Germany in the Cold War*, ed. Crew, 128.

156 Wagnleitner, 330.

157 Samuel H. Williams, Chief, Education Division, Selling of Coca Cola to Austrians, 11 April 1949; Folder AYA-1949-General; Records Relating to Austrian Youth Activities 1946–1952; Box 1; Department of State/Office of the U.S. High Commissioner for Austria; RG 260; NACP. Sale of Coca Cola to Austrians, John D. Coney, Adjutant, to Commanding General United States Forces in Austria, February 10, 1949; same location as previous record. Expansion of Coca-Cola Sales to Raise A.Y.A. Funds in Vienna and Salzburg Area Commands, R. L. Novarine, Chief, Public Welfare Branch, to Col. H. C. Dellert, Chief Civil Affairs, March 2, 1949; same location as previous. Letter from William K. Purdy, Youth Activities Specialist, August 21, 1948; Folder Coco [sic] Cola Operational Expenses (1 Sept. 48–31 Dec. 48) [Folder 4 of 4]; Records Relating to Austrian Youth Activities 1946–1952; Box 15; Department of State/Office of the U.S. High Commissioner for Austria; RG 260; NACP.

158 Austrian Youth Activities, 3; Folder AYA-1949-General; Records Relating to Austrian Youth Activities 1946–1952; Box 1; Department of State/Office of the U.S. High Commissioner for Austria; RG 260; NACP.

159 See Cash Sale Tickets, Coca-Cola Bottling Plant, Lambach Austria, in Folders Coco [sic] Cola Operational Expenses (1 Sept 48–31 Dec 48) [Folders 1 through 4 of 4]. Folders 1 through 3 in Records Relating to Austrian Youth Activities 1946–1952; Box 14; Department of State/Office of the U.S. High Commissioner for Austria; RG 260. Folder 4 in Records Relating to Austrian Youth Activities 1946–1952; Box 15; Department of State/Office of the U.S. High Commissioner for Austria; RG 260.

In 1948, an Austrian youth named Helmut Liebl wrote to General Keyes regarding a desire to watch movies at the US Army theaters. Liebl wanted to go to these theaters, since they showed more "thrilling films" than those in Austrian cinemas. He received a response from the Special Services Staff Section stating that he could go to the US Army theaters only if he was accompanied by an American and if he paid in US scrip. He also was informed about AYA and the opportunities for hobbies and exchange with GIs. The youth wrote back that he had not heard about the AYA but that he was familiar with Austrian political youth associations. However, he did not wish to join those, "as I know that from the 'Hitler-Youth,'" he wrote.[160] Therefore, this boy was interested in learning more about what the Americans had to offer such as exciting movies, but he was tired of the way Austrian youngsters had been mobilized for political purposes by adults. It is unclear if Liebl decided to join AYA, but he seemed open to joining a club run by Americans. His tentative response about Austrian youth associations depicts that some youngsters remained skeptical about joining youth clubs, which had been used in the past to serve political purposes. The officials claimed that AYA could serve his interests in following his hobby of watching movies, but in the end, AYA did indeed also serve a political purpose based on American Cold War aims, which encouraged the reorientation of Austrian youth in a manner fitting American goals. In addition, the American authorities saw young Austrians as being important to the fabric of the occupation, and responding to Liebl's letters with "a nice answer" was essential, according to George R. Barker, Chief of Staff of the Headquarters of the Zone Command in Austria.[161]

160 Letter from Helmut Liebl, March 3, 1948, Folder Correspondence (Lt. Karlstrom) [Folder 1 of 2]; Records Relating to Austrian Youth Activities; Box 18; Department of State/Office of the U.S. High Commissioner for Austria; RG 260; NACP. Letter from J.E. Tarrant, Executive Officer, US Forces in Austria Special Services Staff Section, March 2, 1948; same location as previous record. Liebl wrote his letter on February 25, 1948 to General Keyes, then he wrote on March 3, 1948 to J.E. Tarrant at the Special Services Staff Section, who had replied to his first letter. On March 4, 1948, he also wrote a letter describing his family situation: his father had died in 1940, his family had been bombed out twice, and they were living with his aunt. He wrote, "Times are very hard and the Austrian government do [sic] not care about the victims of the last war." He also wrote, "If you have time, please write to me again. I always enjoy it to get letters." Liebl's friend Ferdinand K. Durnhofer in Linz also wrote a letter on March 3, 1948. Durnhofer had apparently also previously sent a letter to President Truman and heard back from the Vice-Consul of the Legation in Vienna. Letters in Folder Correspondence (Lt. Karlstrom) [Folder 1 of 2]; same location as previous record.

161 George R. Barker to Commanding General, Land Upper Austria Area Command, March 12, 1948; Folder Correspondence (Lt. Karlstrom) [Folder 1 of 2]; Records Relating to Austrian Youth Activities; Box 18; Department of State/Office of the U.S. High Commissioner for Austria; RG 260; NACP.

Attention to the plight of Austrian youth even interested wealthy and famous Americans across the Atlantic. In 1948, the philanthropic organization "Save Austria's Children Inc." was founded in New York City. In 1949, they held a fundraising ball in Vienna, "A Night in Vienna in Aid of Save Austria's Children Inc." The event included patronesses Marlene Dietrich, Greta Garbo, Gloria Vanderbilt, and Millicent Hearst. The program cover design for the aid event was donated by Salvador Dali, and the famous Vienna Choir Boys, the *Sängerknaben*, performed. The event's program also included an image of an Austrian child eating bread, ads for products including New York City jewelers, tailors, perfume, and more, and had space for autographs.[162] Thus, saving the most innocent members of Austrian society had reached the highest echelons of Western society and was bound up in philanthropic benevolence on the part of the attendees, with hungry children juxtaposed with the luxury of diamonds and Viennese palaces. Powerful American citizens such as the Vanderbilts and President Truman were personally interested in helping young Europeans, including Austrians and Germans, whose hunger or need for sporting goods fit with wider American political and societal aims of anti-communism, democratization, and even with the philanthropic goals of the wealthy.

Thank You, Mr. Truman: Narratives of Gratitude

On September 12, 1947, Rosemaria Kleingeist wrote a letter of thanks for the *Schulspeisung* as part of a class assignment. She was a ten-year-old "thankful school pupil" of the fourth grade in Bickenbach, a town south of Darmstadt in the state of Hesse. She wrote:

> But the best day [at school] is Saturday. That is when we have chocolate. I see to it that I can always be the first one [in line]. And how happy I am when I have my chocolate in my hands. Then I hurry to my seat, beaming with happiness. But there are also even more sweets. For example: cookies, drops, and also fruit juice. We all can hardly wait for Saturday. But unfortunately, for some time now, the good chocolate has been boiled down to hot cocoa. That is a shame. Now I want to conclude. (*Doch der schönste Tag [in der Schule] ist der Samstag. Da gibt es nämlich Schokolade. Ich sehe zu, daß ich immer die Erste sein kann.*

162 "A Night in Vienna in Aid of Save Austria's Children Inc.," March 8, 1949; Folder "A Night in Vienna in Aid of Save Austria's Children Inc." Program 1949; Records Relating to Austrian Youth Activities 1946–1952; Box 1; Department of State/Office of the U.S. High Commissioner for Austria; RG 260; NACP. See also "Night in Vienna Planned," *The New York Times*, February 9, 1949; "Fete for Austria's Young," *New York Times*, March 9, 1949; "Austrian Aid Ball Splits Group Here," *New York Times*, August 30, 1949.

> *Und wie bin ich froh, wenn ich meine Schokolade in den Händen habe. Dann eile ich glückstrahlend an meinem Platz. Doch gibt es auch noch andere Süßigkeiten. Zum Beispiel: Plätzchen, Drops und auch Fruchtsaft. Den Samstag konnten wir alle kaum erwarten. Doch leider wird seit einiger Zeit die gute Schokolade zu Kakao verkocht. Das ist sehr schade. Jetzt will ich schleißen.)*[163]

Scattered throughout the official records of the American occupation of Germany are thank you letters and thank you drawings from young Germans, providing an often colorful contrast to the official documents and correspondence about the military occupation.[164] The vast majority of the thank you narratives and drawings revolve around gratitude for American gifts of food, including the *Schulspeisung* school feeding program. Rosemaria Kleingeist's letter was part of a school project to thank American donors for the program, which included letters and drawings. Her letter is one of many materials by German schoolchildren found in the Official File at the Harry S. Truman Presidential Library, which include the thank you letters and drawings from the *Volkschule* Bickenbach and many letters from school pupils in Eltville am Rhein. In May 1947, Clarence E. Pickett, the Executive Secretary of the AFSC in Philadelphia, also sent President Truman thank you letters from "children who have received food and clothing from agencies concerned with relief in Germany."[165]

The German children recipients of this aid were very aware that the source of food assistance was the United States, and they were grateful for the food's role in the lessening of their hunger, even though some noted a yearning to be in the United States to have access to such food. The Eltville school pupils addressed their thank you letters for the *Schulspeisung* to American children, most likely as a school assignment. Some of the pupils even practiced their English in the letters. Rosemarie Lange wrote, "When you have there such good meals always, then I wish, I could also be once in America [sic]."[166] Anni Lange, who was perhaps Rosemarie's sister, wrote, "We get every day American schol-feeding [sic]. I like it very much. For this charity we say our heartiest thanks. We are very glad, that you have to spare something [sic] for us German children then we don't have to

163 Rosemaria Kleingeist, "Von der Schulspeisung," September 12, 1947; Folder OF 198 Misc. 1947 [1 of 2]; OF 198; Box 738; HSTP; HSTPL.
164 See also O'Connell, "Benevolent Diplomacy," *Perspectives on History*.
165 Memo about letter from Clarence E. Pickett, May 7, 1947; Folder OF 198 Misc. 1947 [2 of 2] Germany; OF 198; Box 739; HSTP; HSTPL.
166 Rosemarie Lange, Letter to American children, November 5, 1947; Folder OF 198 Misc. 1947 [2 of 2] Germany; OF 198; Box 739; HSTP; HSTPL.

suffer from hunger."[167] Lydia Breitmoser, who noted that she was 11 years old, also wrote in English and included a photograph of herself with skis, and wrote that her parents extended their thanks too: "To all American children . . . We all thank you very much for the schoolfeeding [sic] which you give us. Every day we have to think on you, when we have your lunch at school. You all have such good meals and it is very kind of you, that you give also something to us [sic]. The winter will be very hard for us Germans."[168] Thus, she linked the daily activity of eating a meal to knowledge of the prosperity of the American people, who had access to such meals, in contrast to the German people, who would especially be suffering from hunger in the coming winter.

In the Bremen Enclave in Wesermünde, local orphans sent a thank you letter to the director of the Wesermünde Liaison Group of OMGBR. The orphans had been able to attend an Army-sponsored camp event in December 1946. In a letter to the director, James R. Bartholomew, Adjutant for OMGBR Wesermünde Liaison Group, recorded the thank you letter from the orphans. Thirty-five children had signed the letter, writing,

> Dear Mr. Oberst (Colonel),
>
> To-morrow [sic] we have to say good-bye to our dear camp Barkhausen, where we have been having a wonderful time. One of the great joys here was the wonderful chocolate we got. – Last night we put our shoes behind our bedroom doors, and when we got up this morning, we found them filled with the most wonderful chocolate. Dear Santa Claus had brought it. You cannot imagine how delighted we were. We were singing and dancing with joy. Fräulein Lohmann told us that you have been so kind to send Santa Claus to our camp Barkhausen. Thank you every so much for doing so. It was really very kind of you to think of us; you have given us much joy.

According to Bartholomew, the orphanage was a place specifically for undernourished children, who "normally do not have parents nor friends and do not know the taste of candy or sweets." He wrote, "The German officials do not have the material nor personnel to care for them that is available in America, therefore these children very sincerely appreciate the little things the American Army has been doing and contemplates doing for them."[169] Occupation soldiers thus will-

167 Anni Lange, Letter to American children, November 5, 1947; Folder OF 198 Misc. 1947 [2 of 2] Germany; OF 198; Box 739; HSTP; HSTPL.

168 Lydia Breitmoser, Letter to American children, November 5, 1947; Folder OF 198 Misc. 1947 [2 of 2] Germany; OF 198; Box 739; HSTP; HSTPL.

169 James R. Bartholomew, "Sponsoring of German Youth Groups," December 13, 1946; Folder Y XXI Army Assistance Program B. Wesermünde Military Units; Rcs of Bremerhaven Liaison & Security Detachment: Records of Clubs and Youth Activities, 1947–49; OMGBR; Box 591; OMGUS; RG 260; NACP.

ingly took on a Santa Claus-type role in acts of benevolence for needy children such as throwing holiday parties and giving Christmas gifts, highlighting how they had become providers for Germans.[170] In the case of the orphans, the Army camp event made an impact by creating an experience where orphans woke up to chocolate in their shoes, something that German adults would not have been able to do for the children during the postwar time of scarcity.

Most Germans were aware that the aid they received was from the United States. Occupation aid including CARE packages, the *Schulspeisung*, holiday parties, and other GYA initiatives all contributed to narratives of German gratitude. For the German recipients of benevolence, it was obvious that the United States was clearly a land of material plenty and abundance, with access to chewing gum and chocolate. Children's thank you letters for American aid were sent and addressed to various American individuals, including American citizens in general, American children, military personnel including General Lucius Clay, former President Herbert Hoover, the Quakers (or the AFSC), the Candy Bomber Gail Halvorsen, and President Truman.[171] Most letters were "laudatory, a chorus of praise—'Schmeckt gut!,'" according to Kaete O'Connell.[172] In October 1948, Bavarian Minister President Dr. Hans Ehard and *Staatsminister* Dr. Alois Hundhammer sent President Truman the best 50 drawings made by Bavarian schoolchildren in a drawing competition that took place among over a million pupils in Bavaria, which was undertaken as a measure of thanks for the American *Schulspeisung*.[173] In response to the drawings, President Truman wrote, "This token of gratitude to the people of America from the Bavarian school children impressed me deeply."[174] These drawings were also put on display at the Grand Rapids Art Gallery in Grand Rapids, Michigan in March 1949, providing an "interesting exhibit for the school children of Grand Rapids," as a letter to the gallery's director

170 See Goedde, *GIs and Germans*, 149; Dana Adams Schmidt, "German Children to Have Big Yule," *The New York Times*, December 16, 1946.

171 See O'Connell, "Weapon of War, Tool of Peace," 1, 237. Letters to Hoover were addressed, for example, to "*Onkel Hoover*" (237). See also O'Connell, "Benevolent Diplomacy," *Perspectives on History*.

172 O'Connell, "Weapon of War, Tool of Peace," 241. Also, O'Connell, "Benevolent Diplomacy."

173 Dr. Hans Ehard and Dr. Alois Hundhammer to President Truman, September 17, 1948; Folder OF 198 Misc. 1948–May 1949 [1 of 2]; OF 198; Box 739; HSTP; HSTPL.

174 Harry Truman to Murray D. Van Wagoner, Land Director, Military Government for Bavaria, October 16, 1947; Folder OF 198 Misc. 1948–May 1949 [1 of 2]; OF 198; Box 739; HSTP; HSTPL. Van Wagoner was the former Governor of Michigan and was now the US Land Director in Bavaria. He was the one who presented the collection of drawings to President Truman at the White House.

stated.[175] The drawings, now part of the museum collections of the Truman Library, often depict the two geographical sites of the food aid, representing the providers and the recipients, with the charitable United States appearing with skyscrapers and as a land of plenty, while the receiving German side included villages, castles, cathedrals, and even rubble. These two sides were bridged through ships on the Atlantic Ocean that connected the two countries or via airplanes, with one drawing depicting a plane dropping goods from the sky, in the style of the Berlin Airlift. Thus, separate events were bridged in the imagination of German youngsters, with American *Schulspeisung* food aid linked to the benevolent actions of the Berlin Airlift. Moreover, the United States and Germany were interconnected, despite being an ocean away from each other. The drawings thanked the United States in general, the individual GI, and even Uncle Sam, marking an awareness of who was behind the goods.[176] As Kaete O'Connell argues, children were sometimes even aware of the value of this food aid for American propaganda, with one of the Bavarian schoolchildren drawings depicting a GI taking a picture of the school feeding in a classroom.[177] It was imprinted in young German minds that this was American food, and that it was provided by and paid for by Americans. One drawing (Figure 4.1) featured a package with the words "Made in U.S.A. [sic]" written on it, portrayed a girl giving flowers in thanks to two GIs, and also depicted the food being served by a female Red Cross employee and a nun. Sugary foods and beverages featured heavily in the drawings, such as hot chocolate, chocolate bars, and raisins. In addition, not everything in the drawings was happy-go-lucky: one drawing depicted chaos in the classroom as a fistfight over the food took place, and another drawing with children weighing themselves on scales hints that German children were often undernourished (Figure 4.2). Only through the *Schulspeisung* did they gain weight.[178] These drawings hint at a more complex reality, highlighting the fact that occupation food policies impacted the health of the youngest Germans in ways beyond benevolence.

These narratives of gratitude often served adult needs, including military government goals of raising awareness about American support of Germany, which was important for creating an ally out of West Germany for Cold War aims. American officials and aid workers welcomed letters and drawings of grati-

---

175 Eben A. Ayers to Jan Vander Heide, March 1, 1949; OF 198 Misc. 1948–May 1949 [1 of 2]; OF 198; Box 739; HSTP; HSTPL.

176 Collection of Bavarian schoolchildren drawings, Museum Artifact number 3025, HSTPL.

177 O'Connell, "Benevolent Diplomacy," *Perspectives on History*; O'Connell, "Weapon of War, Tool of Peace," 241.

178 Collection of Bavarian schoolchildren drawings, Museum Artifact number 3025, HSTPL.

Figure 4.1: Thank you drawing by a 16-year-old Bavarian schoolgirl (Museum collections, Harry S. Truman Presidential Library).

tude, according to O'Connell.[179] Reports of American benevolence helped serve Cold War propaganda aims of advertising the fundamental role of the United States in European recovery. Recovery in Germany was also of central importance to American goals, and concerns about children and nutrition thus merged with concerns about a future democratic Germany.[180] A focus on aid toward German children also helped shift American opinions about providing aid to a former enemy. In addition, in a way, German gratitude for American assistance had become compulsory in the heightening Cold War atmosphere. O'Connell also explores how American "concern for gratitude extended to [German] adults as well." Military government officials in Bavaria even held "mandatory meetings in villages across Bavaria, where they explained bread was a gift from America," with the wheat used to make the bread originating in Kansas and ending up on Bavarian tables.[181] Additionally, spreading awareness about American food aid

179 O'Connell, "Weapon of War, Tool of Peace," 240.
180 See O'Connell, "Benevolent Diplomacy," *Perspectives on History*.
181 O'Connell, "Weapon of War, Tool of Peace," 241.

Figure 4.2: Thank you drawing by a 17-year-old Bavarian schoolgirl. The text reads, "One year ago, so light, but now the weight is achieved" (author's translation) (Museum collections, Harry S. Truman Presidential Library).

highlighted American compassion to Germans in need, helping mold positive German-American relations.[182] Some of the pupils in the sixth grade at the *Volksschule* Bickenbach created a booklet to thank Americans for the *Schulspeisung*, and a poem concluded their creative work: "We the children of Bickenbach will never forget you. We thank you all very much for the good food! (*Wir Bickenbacher Kinder werden Euch nie vergessen. Wir danken alle sehr fürs gute Essen!*)"[183] Thus, American aid made a major impact on the young German beneficiaries, with the children themselves noting quite accurately that they would never forget the childhood experience of receiving American aid. American benevolence fundamentally molded relations with Germany, remaining relevant over the decades since the occupation.

182 See O'Connell, "Benevolent Diplomacy," *Perspectives on History*; O'Connell, "Weapon of War, Tool of Peace," 28.

183 Booklet, "Unseren Helfern aus Amerika in Dankbarkeit Volksschule Bickenbach"; Folder OF 198 Misc. 1947 [1 of 2]; OF 198; Box 738; HSTP; HSTPL.

German adults also played a role in the construction of narratives of gratitude. For example, German teachers assigned the task of writing thank you letters. Rosemaria Kleingeist's thank you letter included corrections (most likely by the teacher), who she mentioned in her letter. She wrote, "Our teacher is also happy along with us and he always says: 'We have to be very grateful to the Americans for this blessing.' But all the children agree. (*Auch unser Herr Lehrer freut sich mit uns und er sagt auch immer: 'Wir müssen den Amerikanern für diese Wohltat sehr dankbar sein.' Da stimmen aber auch alle Kinder bei.*)"[184] Thus, Germans of all ages were linked in their gratitude. Although German schoolchildren were often assigned by teachers to create narratives of gratitude, children appeared open to such creations, enriching the texts with their personal backgrounds, opinions about American food, and colorful art.[185] Sonja Leukel of Eltville, whose "Daddy died 8 years ago," wrote in her thank you letter (all in English) that she was happy about her school assignment: "Dear children of the United States of America, When our teacher said to us, please write a letter to the American children, I was very glad. I'm now 11 years old and hope that an 11 years old American girl receive [sic] my letter. Now I wait week for week for an answer from America."[186] Even though adults played a role in the creation of narratives of gratitude, for example being the driving force behind their creation, including schoolteachers assigning and correcting the texts, children often shaped them to fit their opinions and also embedded them with their own creativity, including, for example, humor, poetry, art, photographs of themselves, and more. Thank you notes and drawings thus confirm the gratitude of German children for US aid.[187]

European adults also indicated their own gratitude for American assistance, which often centered around aid that positively impacted their children. In Austria, reports on hungry children attending Austrian Youth Activities summer camps indicate the role that the camps played in improving the health of children. The camps provided children with as many as five meals and 5,000 calories a day, with children sometimes gaining over two kilograms during their time at

184 Kleingeist, "Von der Schulspeisung"; Folder OF 198 Misc. 1947 [1 of 2]; OF 198; Box 738; HSTP; HSTPL.

185 See O'Connell, "Benevolent Diplomacy," *Perspectives on History*.

186 Sonja Leukel, Letter to American children, November 4, 1947; Folder OF 198 Misc. 1947 [2 of 2] Germany; OF 198, Box 739; HSTP; HSTPL.

187 O'Connell, "Benevolent Diplomacy," *Perspectives on History*.

the camps.[188] An AYA quarterly report from October 5, 1950 stated that the camps provided not only food but also "a democratic experience in group living to over 1,100 youths" in the summer of 1950. Thus, improving the health of children was linked to wider democratization goals. The report also noted that "numerous letters have been received from parents of the children expressing their appreciation for the opportunity given their children to attend the camps."[189] Mary J. Fabian, a WAC Assistant AYA Officer at the Austrian Youth Center in Vienna, wrote a letter about children who had attended an AYA summer camp in Ebensee. She wrote that she "heard nothing but praises from them and their parents of the wonderful treatment, food and good times they had there." Thus, she thanked First Lieutenant Einar J. Karlstrom, an AYA Officer in Linz, and his "co-workers, school board and employees for giving so much pleasure, health and happiness to the children of Vienna." In addition, she asked Lt. Karlstrom whether it would be possible to help a woman employed at the youth center, who was a 37-year-old widow and mother of a nine-year-old boy and a 20-month-old baby. Apparently, the woman's sister had been assisting with childcare but had to leave Vienna due to illness, leaving the children home alone all day. The city authorities had warned the widower that she was required to arrange a way in which the children were "adequately taken care of," or else they might be sent away. The younger child had been sent to a home "for the present," and the mother hoped that the older boy, Fritz, "who is frightfully undernourished and thin, might be sent away for several months in a camp similar to yours in Ebensee," according to Fabian. WAC Officer Fabian then asked Lt. Karlstrom, "Won't you please do all in your power to aid this child and woman, they are in desperate need of immediate help."[190] Unfortunately, the records on this case are lacking about whether Karlstrom did follow up and assist them. Overall, this letter not only depicted the pleasure of the children and the relief of the parents regarding American assistance but also included an American female military personnel's request for further assistance for a needy child, highlighting adult concerns

---

188 "One half a millino [sic] of calories per day (US AYA takes care of Upper Austrian Children)," *Upper Austria Nachrichten*, July 17, 1950; Folder AYA Reports-Consolidated. USACA. 1950; Records Relating to Austrian Youth Activities 1946–1952; Box 1; Department of State/Office of the U.S. High Commissioner for Austria; RG 260; NACP. "Youth Summer Camp at Mattsee," *Salzburger Nachrichten*, July 29, 1950, same location as previous record.

189 AYA Report for Quarter Ending 30 September 1950, October 5, 1950; Folder AYA Reports-Consolidated. USACA. 1950; Records Relating to Austrian Youth Activities 1946–1952; Box 1; Department of State/Office of the U.S. High Commissioner for Austria; RG 260; NACP.

190 Letter from Mary J. Fabian to Lt. Karlstrom, August 10, 1948; Folder AYA Correspondence (Lt. Karlstrom) [Folder 2 of 2]; Records Relating to Austrian Youth Activities 1946–1952; Box 18; Department of State/Office of the U.S. High Commissioner for Austria; RG 260; NACP.

regarding children's conditions, in addition to the central role that US officials came to play in attempts to improve the welfare of children. The Welfare Office of the Upper Austrian government also sent Lt. Karlstrom a thank you letter "on behalf of all 900 children for the invitation on the 20 August 1948 to an excursion trip on the Danube River." According to the letter, not only was the trip a success with excellent hospitality, but the many orphans who attended the event would remember it, since many of them had never seen a boat in their lives.[191]

Moreover, in the case of GYA engagement, the father of Bremen Boys Club President Girschner, Martin Girschner Sr., also noted his gratitude for the engagement and assistance of club founder and sponsor Sergeant Patrick Moriarty. He made a speech during a parents' visit to the club on December 22, 1946, noting how German children had not been spared from the war, with "their conception of the term of fatherland" broken into pieces. Thus, "the fate of our children" often preoccupied parents' thoughts during this time of German need. German youth were poorly dressed and nourished, with shattered nerves from the nights of bombings. However, "just as bad . . . is the fact that the young have hardly any organization to foster social life and comradeship and to serve ideal goals." Girschner continued, thanking Moriarty for providing for the boys in ways that the parents did not have the resources to do:

> You, dear Sergeant Moriarty, must have felt this need and this gap, when you offered your sympathetic hand and heart to part of the Bremen youth, in order to unite the German boys and to create the first ties of understanding. Therefore we parents can only thank you by means of words and by our good intentions to support you in your selfless ideal and material efforts regarding our boys, and we wish you success and personal satisfaction.[192]

Thus, direct actions that impacted young German and Austrian lives led to expressions of gratitude from parents, who often did not have the resources to adequately take care of their children in a society marked by the consequences of the war. American efforts such as AYA and GYA were often most welcome for many parents in providing organized activities, material benefits, and a reprieve from the postwar atmosphere of need, even if just for one summer or a few hours in the evening.

---

191 Letter from Zemlizka of the Oberoesterreichische Landesregierung to Lt. Einar J. Karlstrom, August 21, 1948; Folder AYA Correspondence (Lt. Karlstrom) [Folder 2 of 2]; Records Relating to Austrian Youth Activities 1946–1952; Box 18; Department of State/Office of the U.S. High Commissioner for Austria; RG 260; NACP.

192 Author's translation. "Klubangelegenheiten," *Die Brücke* Nr. 13; Folder Bremen Boys Club 1946/47; Records of the Education Division: Records Relating to German Youth and Sports Clubs, 1947–49; OMGBR; Box 316; OMGUS; RG 260; NACP. For more on parent's opinions of GYA, see Goedde, *GIs and Germans*, 158–160.

German adults were also concerned about children's nutrition in the occupation. A pamphlet from the town government of Mühlheim am Main in Hesse from March 1947 included statistics about a study of the local schoolchildren, including their social situation, measurements, weight, and the results of physical examinations. *Bürgermeister* Anton Dey wrote in the foreword to the pamphlet, "The future of our people rests on a healthy youth spent in joyful childhood. (*Die Zukunft unseres Volkes ruht auf einer gesunden, in froher Kindheit verlebten Jugend.*)" In addition, he mentioned worries about the nutrition crisis and its effects on the development of the town's children. The mayor encouraged the support of all citizens, and noted the local government's gladness that the *Schulspeisung* had been introduced. At the time of the study, there were 1,378 children of ages six to 14 registered in the local schools. Two years after the end of the war, 15% of the children were without fathers. In the age six to ten range, 30.5% of boys and 24.7% of girls were underweight. From ages 11 to 14, 17.2% of boys and 11.7% of girls were underweight. Thus, the food crisis had led to dangerous weight loss for many children. The physical examinations indicated that 75.2% of the children examined were "*krankhaft*," unhealthy, with at least one or more "*Schäden*," damages to the body. These conditions included ailments and difficulties such as tonsil problems, bronchitis, asthma, heart issues, weakness, anemia, rickets, dental problems, eczema, and more. Thus, the report concluded, the results portrayed the severity of the current crisis situation in their town, with the health situation of children much worse than they had thought. In order to achieve a healthy population and a happy youth, the report concluded, the nutrition situation needed to be improved as first step.[193] American food aid was thus essential to meeting this need, linking the state of German children's health to American benevolence.

On October 23, 1947, Mühlheim am Main held a Parents Meeting in which *Bürgermeister* Dey presented a leather-bound Letter of Thanks book to Major William R. Sheehan, Commanding Officer of Liaison and Security Office Offenbach. The book had been created by the citizens in response to the *Schulspeisung* and was to be "passed on to the American people." Dey thanked the military government and "its higher headquarters," and mentioned statistics relating to the *Schulspeisung*, which provided young Germans with 300 to 400 calories per meal. Another local government representative expressed thanks to the military government and the American people, stating that "he believes that still in later days the children will think of this help and contribution and carry on in the same tendency." Major Sheehan responded, noting his "pleasure to be the recipient of

---

193 Johann Wack, "Die Schulkinduntersuchung in Mühlheim a. M. März 1947," Stadtverwaltung Mühlheim am Main; Folder OF 198 Misc. 1947 [2 of 2] Germany; OF 198; Box 739; HSTP; HSTPL.

thanks for the School Feeding Program." He explained that the program was applied based on former President Hoover's recommendations, and that it had been approved by President Truman. He also closed with the promise that "the Germans can be certain that the American people have always and will always continue to support a humantarian [sic] plan and will never forget the children of any nation in need. This was one of many ways the American people are giving assistance to the German people."[194]

Other areas in Hesse, the state where the first American school feedings took place, also sent their thanks for the *Schulspeisung*, including the *Landkreis* Darmstadt, a school in Marburg, Gießen, and Dudenhofen.[195] These letters were often written with the combined thanks of the community, including local government officials, teachers, parents, and children. In addition, the letters indicated that the *Schulspeisung* was having a positive effect on children, who were growing healthier. They also sometimes hinted at the growing dependence of Germany on the United States, for example in the Gießen "Vote of Thanks," written in the name of the 5,600 schoolchildren receiving the *Schulspeisung* and signed by the *Oberbürgermeister* and the *Schulrat*. It stated, "Our hope is combined with the expectation of the Gießen population that this work of aid might be continued until we are able to procure the quantities of food necessary for our children by our own power." Furthermore, the school feeding was seen as "an action of humanity, which is a contribution to attain a real understanding and a real peace."[196] The mayor of Bickenbach also indicated his request that these American "Quaker shipments" not be ended, because they were having such an effect on the preser-

194 William R. Sheehan, "Report of Parents-Meeting in Muhlheim [sic] a.M.," October 24, 1947; Folder OF 198 Misc. 1947 [1 of 2]; OF 198; Box 738; HSTP; HSTPL. William R. Sheehan to Director, Office of MG for Hesse, Attn. Dr. Wann, Chief of Education and Religious Affairs, "Letter of Transmittel [sic]," October 24, 1947; same location as previous record. Memo to Director OMGH, Attn. Dr. Wann, Chief of Education and Religious Affairs, about William R. Sheehan, October 24, 1947; same location as previous. Stadt Mühlheim am Main, Leather book (copy); same location as previous.

195 Der Landrat des Landkreises Darmstadt, an die Militärregierung für Hessen, "Eating for the pupils/Speisung der Schulkinder," September 23, 1947; Folder OF 198 Misc. 1947 [1 of 2]; OF 198; Box 738; HSTP; HSTPL. Parents' Council of the Marburg/Lahn Süd-Schule, "Decision/Entschliessung," September 23, 1947; same location as previous. Letter from the Oberbürgermeister der Stadt Gießen, "Schulkinderspeisung," October 15, 1947; same location as previous. Dankadresse and Vote of Thanks certificates (German and English) from the Oberbürgermeister and Schulrat of Gießen, October 15, 1947; same location as previous. Letter from the Teachers' College of the Volksschule Dudenhofen (Kr. Offenbach a. M.) to the Military Government Wiesbaden, December 2, 1947, same location as previous.

196 Vote of Thanks certificate (English) from the Oberbürgermeister and Schulrat of Gießen, Folder OF 198 Misc. 1947 [1 of 2], OF 198, Box 738, HSTP, HSTPL.

vation of the health and wellness of the children.[197] American benevolence thus had become linked to ensuring the well-being of German children. German adults of various relationships to young Germans thus noted the impact of American humanitarian aid on children's health, marking the intertwined relationship between Americans and Germans that had emerged through this benevolence.

Letters from Germans of all ages often mentioned German "*Not*," need, contrasting American material plenty with the challenging situation in German society. The letter of thanks from the Marburg school also noted that the pupils were innocent and not to blame for the tyranny of National Socialism.[198] In addition, the hungry schoolchildren were "poor children," according to the Teachers' College of the *Volksschule* Dudenhofen, emphasizing notions of children's innocence.[199] Eltville school pupil Lydia Breitmoser's thank you letter to American children noted her desire to give Americans something, "at least with a letter, because we have'nt [sic] got anything else" that she could give as a gift for the American children to enjoy.[200] A thank you letter was usually all that German youngsters were able to give in return for American benevolence.

****

The need of the youngest, most innocent-seeming members of German society thus contributed to the shift in American views of Germans, creating a transatlantic system of humanitarian aid that led to West German dependence on and alliance with Americans. This relationship molded personal experiences of the occupation, with memories of the taste of the *Schulspeisung* or Hershey bars serving as a reminder of American benevolence. Simultaneously, this system of aid crafted a transatlantic politics of gratitude and served wider American geopolitical aims of spreading both democracy and anti-communism in Europe. Acts of benevolence humanized both Americans and Germans on a personal basis, with wider geopolitical impacts. Sometimes Germans were spurred to give something in return in their own act of benevolence, whether through sending a book of thanks or a thank you drawing. In 1946 in Darmstadt, where children were among the first to receive the *Schulspeisung*,

197 Letter from the Bürgermeister der Gemeinde Bickenbach to the military government via the Kreisschulamt Darmstadt, September 17, 1947, Folder OF 198 Misc. 1947 [1 of 2], OF 198, Box 738, HSTP, HSTPL.
198 Parents' Council of the Marburg/Lahn Süd-Schule, "Decision/Entschliessung," Folder OF 198 Misc. 1947 [1 of 2] Germany, OF 198, Box 738, HSTP, HSTPL.
199 Letter from the Teachers' College of the Volksschule Dudenhofen (Kr. Offenbach a. M.) to the Military Government Wiesbaden, December 2, 1947, Folder OF 198 Misc. 1947 [1 of 2] Germany, OF 198, Box 738, HSTP, HSTPL.
200 Breitmoser, Letter to American children, Folder OF 198 Misc. 1947 [2 of 2] Germany, OF 198, Box 739, HSTP, HSTPL.

9,800 children aged six to 16, working on their own initiative, created thousands of handmade toys. The toys were to be gifts for American dependent children for Christmas. The American dependent children were invited to an exhibition of the toys, dolls, and games, and they could choose which item they wanted to bring home. The leftover items were then sent to orphanages in the US.[201] In 1947, Darmstadt children also sent homemade gifts to American children through the AFSC in thanks for American contributions "of buy[ing] milk for the children of our wartime enemy," as *The Washington Post* noted. Instead of sending the toys and homemade gifts to every contributor, which was impossible due to the impressive number of people who had contributed funds, the AFSC sent "the gifts on a tour to all of the schools and churches which had contributed, so that all of the [American] children could know of the 'thank you' gift."[202] Even the youngest of the German population thus aimed to return the favor to Americans and serve as actors of benevolence themselves. The bridge created between West Germany and the United States through humanitarian aid especially for German children thus ensured a strong relationship on personal and political levels, at least as long as the emotional impacts of American postwar occupation benevolence were remembered among the German population.

Moreover, this bridge provided the foundation stone for the emerging transatlantic development of the United States as benevolent protector of Western Europeans. Occupation benevolence in Germany helped lead to the wider development of Cold War benevolence to Europe. Not only were young Germans seen as the future of an anti-communist, democratic future, but young Europeans all over could ensure the future would be one to the liking of Americans. Youth in Austria could learn the promises of American-style democracy while receiving its benefits through the AYA program, and European youngsters all over the continent could receive material assistance through the Marshall Plan, which they were taught about through posters or Marshall Plan films. This material help was most needed for many, including youngsters who often remained hungry in the postwar years, but it did not come without strings attached. Young Europeans were to note the providers of this aid, the Americans, and to link the humanitarian assistance including the tastes of consumer products to the promises of a democratic future. Moreover, they needed to show their gratitude for such help,

---

201 OMGUS, "Darmstadt Toy Project," *Weekly Information Bulletin*, no. 73, December 23, 1946, 18–19, Germany under Reconstruction, University of Wisconsin-Madison Libraries, https://digital.library.wisc.edu/1711.dl/KVREI7QUAMG2O8C. Also, *The U.S. Armed Forces German Youth Activities Program 1945–1955*, 26; O'Connell, "Weapon of War, Tool of Peace," 240.

202 "Children of Germany Send Toys," *The Washington Post*, August 2, 1947. See also O'Connell, "Weapon of War, Tool of Peace," 240.

which would serve to convince Americans about the righteousness of their cause, which fed hungry stomachs, ensured future democracy, prevented the spread of communism, and kept the United States safe. The stakes of Cold War benevolence and the geopolitics of gratitude were high, and they were forged in the aftermath of war, with young Europeans emerging as the centerpiece to these aims.

Chapter 5
Memories of Occupation: Candy Rains Down from the Sky

We stay in Berlin, period.
–President Harry S. Truman[1]

On May 12, 2019, Berlin celebrated the seventieth anniversary of the end of the Soviet Blockade of Berlin with a family-friendly festival on the grounds of the historic Tempelhof Airport. Along with the mayor of Berlin, Michael Müller, veterans of the Berlin Airlift were in attendance, including Lieutenant Gail S. Halvorsen, then 98 years old, the most famous of the Berlin Airlift pilots.[2] At the anniversary celebration, Halvorsen told Müller, "It's good to be home," depicting his personal feelings of closeness to the city. During the event, which had tens of thousands of attendees, a baseball field at Tempelhof was named in his honor, the "Gail S. Halvorsen Park—Home of the Berlin Braves."[3] Halvorsen became famous during the Berlin Airlift of June 1948 to September 1949 due to his decision to drop homemade parachutes of candy for the children of Berlin. His spontaneous decision to do so was made after meeting a group of 30 young Germans behind a fence at the end of the runway at Tempelhof Airport in July 1948.

Then 27 years old, Halvorsen was visiting Berlin as a tourist, having hitched a ride on another Airlift flight rather than sleep back at Rhein-Main Air Base in-between his own flights. At Tempelhof, Halvorsen was waiting for his jeep ride to take him on his sightseeing tour through Berlin and, while waiting, as he was filming the planes landing, a group of children behind the barbed wire fence

1 Richard Reeves, *Daring Young Men: The Heroism and Triumph of the Berlin Airlift, June 1948–May 1949* (Simon & Schuster, 2010), 30.

2 "Fest der Luftbrücke," Berlin.de: Das offizielle Hauptstadtportal, Presse- und Informationsamt des Landes Berlin/BerlinOnline, May 12, 2019, https://www.berlin.de/kultur-und-tickets/archiv/5713996-2805649-fest-der-luftbruecke-70-jahre-luftbrueck.html. See the event's program at "Fest der Luftbrücke—70 Jahre Luftbrücke in Tempelhof," Tempelhof Projekt (2019), https://www.fest-der-luftbruecke.de/.

3 Kirsten Grieshaber, "Baseball field dedicated to 98-year-old US WWII veteran as Germans recall Berlin Airlift," *Air Force Times*, May 12, 2019, https://www.airforcetimes.com/2019/05/12/baseball-field-dedicated-to-98-year-old-us-wwii-veteran-as-germans-recall-berlin-airlift/. The May 12, 2019 festivities in Berlin attracted around 50,000 visitors. See Frank Bachner, "Luftbrücken-Legende Gail Halvorsen: Berliner Baseballer ehren den Candy-Bomber," *Tagesspiegel*, May 11, 2019, https://www.tagesspiegel.de/berlin/luftbruecken-legende-gail-halvorsen-berliner-baseballer-ehren-den-candy-bomber/24331028.html.

https://doi.org/10.1515/9783111588155-006

caught his attention. Halvorsen, who "loved kids," went over to speak with them.[4] According to Halvorsen in his memoir, most of the children were between the ages of eight and 14, and some could speak English quite well. The children were very interested in learning more about the American aircraft and facts about the Airlift supplies. In addition, they spoke to Halvorsen about freedom and the struggles of their relatives living in East Berlin, also noting their fear that "if they lost their freedom they feared they would never get it back." Thus, according to Halvorsen, these children gave him "the most meaningful lesson in freedom I ever had." To the children, freedom seemed more important than food. They also did not mention the fact that he "wore the [American] uniform they had been taught to hate; a symbol of death from the skies" during the war, nor did they ask if he participated in the wartime bombing of Berlin. Halvorsen wrote: "What they referred to as freedom was the idea that they could be what they wanted to be, to choose their course in life without being told what they would be, that they could really have open access to a free press, and speak freely their thoughts on a subject without fear. Very high on their priority was to be able to travel if and when they had the means." Halvorsen started to leave to catch his jeep for the sightseeing tour, but then realized that the children were different than most of the children he had encountered in his time as a supply pilot in South America, Africa, and other countries, where an "American in uniform was fair game on the street for kids with a sweet tooth." Halvorsen wrote, "They [the children at Tempelhof] were so grateful for freedom and our desire to help them with these meager food supplies that they refused to tarnish their feelings of gratitude for something so nonessential and so extravagant" as a stick of gum or a candy bar.[5] This "silent gratitude" was what spurred Halvorsen to turn back to the children at the fence, reach into his pocket, and pull out the remaining two sticks of gum he had.[6] He broke the sticks of gum in half and gave the four pieces to the children who had served as translators. As Halvorsen looked on amazed, the children then tore up the gum wrappers and passed them around for the rest of the children to smell; some even put the wrappers in their pockets like treasures. At that moment, Halvorsen came up with the idea to drop gum and chocolate to all the children on his next daylight flight to Tempelhof, as long as the children promised to share the sweets equally among themselves, which they heartily agreed to do. He told the children that he would wiggle his wings so they would know which plane was his, an action he had previously done when flying over his family's farm in Gar-

4 Reeves, *Daring Young Men*, 88.
5 Halvorsen, *The Berlin Candy Bomber*, 92–97.
6 Halvorsen, 243.

land, Utah.[7] What then ensued was at first a private (and non-approved) measure upon the part of Gail Halvorsen and his crew, who tied their candy rations to parachutes made out of handkerchiefs (so the falling candy would not injure the children below) and dropped them over the children near the end of the runway shortly before landing at Tempelhof. Halvorsen's effort eventually became an official part of the Berlin Airlift, with organized candy parachute drops occurring throughout Berlin. Gail Halvorsen even dropped candy in East Berlin until the Soviets demanded an end to the measure, which they viewed as capitalist propaganda.[8]

Gail Halvorsen stated, "Because not one of 30 children begged for chocolate, thousands of children in Berlin received over 20 tons of chocolate, gum and other goodies, delivered on the ground, or dropped from C-54 Skymaster aircraft over a 14 month [sic] period."[9] Halvorsen's interaction with the grateful and well-behaved German children at the fence thus enabled thousands of other children to receive the benefits of his benevolent action. Although Halvorsen was rotated back to the US from Berlin in January 1949, the Airlift candy bombing action continued on, and Halvorsen had gained fame among the children of Berlin, having received thousands of letters from children requesting candy, addressed to the Chocolate Uncle, *Onkel Wackelflügel* (Uncle Wiggly Wings), Bon Bon Pilot, the *Schokoladenflieger* (chocolate flier), and the Lollipop Pilot.[10] The encounter between Halvorsen and the 30 German children at the fence of Tempelhof in July 1948 thus changed the history of the Airlift and molded transatlantic memory of the entire occupation period.

The memory of the Berlin Airlift has been strongly imprinted in German collective memory, as noted by the tens of thousands of attendees at Airlift anniversary events in recent times. However, collective memory of the Airlift within the United States has had less of a hold than in Germany. Even though Halvorsen obtained a high level of fame in the United States during the Airlift due to a public relations campaign featuring him in order to increase American support of the Airlift, the Berlin Airlift as a whole has been relatively forgotten in American col-

7 Halvorsen, 99–101.
8 Halvorsen, 128.
9 Halvorsen, quoted on website of The Candy Bomber Foundation, "Gail's Story," The Candy Bomber Foundation, accessed January 5, 2025, https://www.thecandybomber.org/gails-story/.
10 O'Connell, "Weapon of War, Tool of Peace," 266. See also Kaete M. O'Connell, "'Uncle Wiggly Wings': Children, Chocolates, and the Berlin Airlift," *Food and Foodways* 25, no. 2 (2017): 142–159, https://doi.org/10.1080/07409710.2017.1311163. For images of many of these letters from German children as well as letters to Halvorsen from contemporary children, see Halvorsen's website, "Children's Letters," The Berlin Candy Bomber," accessed July 2, 2023, http://wigglywings.weebly.com/childrens-letters.html.

lective memory regarding the immediate postwar era in Germany.[11] Many Americans in contemporary times think that the Airlift happened during the 1960s after the construction of the Berlin Wall.[12] Andrei Cherny, who in 2008 published a book about the "untold story of the Berlin Airlift," argues that certain aspects of the story of the Berlin Airlift are remembered to some extent in the US, such as the story of Gail Halvorsen, the "kind American pilot who dropped candy to the children of Berlin." However, he claims that the history of the Airlift as a whole "is the forgotten foundation tale of America in the modern world." Cherny argues that the Airlift represented a turning point, the moment when "America came to fully accept the mantle of leader of the free world," as well as being seen throughout the world "as a source of decency and good."[13] He notes that Halvorsen remained famous in the United States for a few years after the Airlift. For example, Halvorsen's engagement to his sweetheart Alta in February 1949 was even featured in the newsreel in American movie theaters. Halvorsen's life after the Airlift, however, soon went back to normal, and he continued to serve in the Air Force, flying transport planes to Puerto Rico. According to Cherny, "Within a few years, however, he would be only dimly remembered by his countrymen, an offhand sentence in most histories of the era, a memory clattering about in America's consciousness."[14]

Thus, when the wider efforts of the Berlin Airlift are remembered in the United States, it often is in combination with patriotic narratives about the greatness of the United States in assuming the post-World War II mantle of protecting the free world, an action that was exemplified through the noble humanitarian efforts of the Air Force during the Airlift. For example, Cherny writes that the Berlin Airlift "is a story of America at her best."[15] Richard Reeves also claims that

---

11 See Andrei Cherny, *The Candy Bombers: The Untold Story of the Berlin Airlift and America's Finest Hour*, Berkley Caliber trade paperback ed. (Berkley Pub. Group, 2009), 6, 547. The Berlin Airlift Historical Foundation aims to push back against the trend toward forgetting the Berlin Airlift, being "dedicated to preserving the memory and legacy of the greatest humanitarian aviation event in history." The Foundation aims to "acquire several aircraft used in the great event and create 'Flying Memorials and Classrooms' with the purpose of educating the public about this pivotal, yet forgotten, event in world history." The C-54 "Spirit of Freedom" is their most famous aircraft, converted into a "flying Airlift museum." See Pavan Mohan and Kevin Kearny, "Spirit of Freedom," Berlin Airlift Historical Foundation, accessed July 2, 2023, http://www.spiritoffreedom.org/. In 2011, Timothy Chopp, the founder and president of the Foundation, was awarded the German Order of Merit by Ambassador Klaus Scharioth.

12 Reeves, *Daring Young Men*, xv.

13 Cherny, *The Candy Bombers*, 6.

14 Cherny, 547.

15 Cherny, 6.

the Berlin Airlift ensured that "America was engaged with the world again," and that "Americans were being seen as they saw themselves, as crusaders for the right and true."[16] American memory narratives regarding the Airlift thus usually focus on the heroism of the pilots, the resounding victory of the American way over communism, and the role of the Airlift in cementing the central global role of the United States during the American Century. However, these broad-sweeping narratives are limiting and avoid the complexities of the Airlift and the wider occupation context, not to mention the role of the other Western Allies including the British and French. The British Royal Air Force (RAF) also flew Airlift flights, flying from their occupation zone into Gatow in Berlin.[17] The French enabled the construction of another airport in its sector of Berlin, Tegel, with construction of the first runway completed in less than 90 days, even though it was mostly done by hand.[18]

In contrast to the fading memory in the United States, in Germany, the Berlin Airlift has remained a staple part of (West) German identity and memory culture throughout the second half of the twentieth century until the present day. This is reflected by continuous reenactment and anniversary events, which have taken place throughout the decades. The 2019 events took place not only in Berlin but also in Faßberg and Wiesbaden, drawing crowds of tens of thousands.[19] Andrei

---

16 Richard Reeves, "The Greatest Opportunity We Ever Had: The Airlift in American Global Politics," in *Die Berliner Luftbrücke: Ereignis und Erinnerung*, ed. Helmut Trotnow and Bernd von Kostka (Frank & Timme, 2010), 59. See also Reeves, *Daring Young Men*.

17 The British called the Airlift "Operation Plainfare." Moreover, Canadian, Australian, New Zealander, and South African crews also assisted the British RAF during the Airlift.

18 On the construction of Tegel, see Roger G. Miller, *To Save a City* (US Government Printing Office, Air Force History and Museums Program, 1998), 59–62.

19 Faßberg celebrations on June 15, 2019 were combined with the "*Tag der Bundeswehr*," Day of the German Armed Forces. Faßberg Air Base was one of the bases for British Royal Air Force flights during the Berlin Airlift. Today there is a Berlin Airlift Museum located in Faßberg. See "Luftbrückenmuseum Faßberg," accessed January 4, 2025, https://www.luftbrueckenmuseum.de/. Plans for a June 16, 2019 reenactment of the Airlift in Berlin with flights over the Brandenburger Gate and landings at Tempelhof were rejected by the Berlin government. Pilots were able to fly over Tempelhof but were unable to land due to regulations forbidding landing at Tempelhof. In addition, flying over the Brandenburg Gate was also not approved. The city claimed that the May 12, 2019 celebrations were the main Berlin Airlift anniversary celebrations. See Jannik Waidner, "Rosinenbomber in der Schwebe," *Frankfurter Allgemeine Zeitung*, June 8, 2019, https://www.faz.net/aktuell/gesellschaft/menschen/rosinenbomber-in-der-schwebe-16226638.html; "70 Jahre Berliner Luftbrücke: Big Lift," Berlin.de: Das offizielle Hauptstadtportal, June 16, 2019, https://www.berlin.de/kultur-und-tickets/archiv/5086913-2805649-big-lift-70-jahre-berliner-luftbruecke.html. A July 4, 2019 Independence Day celebration at Tempelhof also attracted 2,000 guests. Elisabeth Binder, "Independence Day in Berlin: Amerikaner feiern auf dem Flughafen

Cherny argues that "in Germany, and especially in Berlin, the pilot from Utah [Gail Halvorsen] would become part of the national lore."[20] The *Rosinenbomber* (raisin bombers), as the Airlift planes are known among Germans, have not been forgotten to this day. They remain a staple and even beloved part of German collective memory of the immediate postwar era. As Stefanie Eisenhuth notes, the Berlin Airlift became stamped in collective memory as the birth of the special relationship between Berlin and the Western world.[21] Petra Goedde also argues that the "metamorphosis of war planes into Rosinenbomber during the year-long airlift epitomized the dramatic turnabout in American-German relations since the end of the war."[22] This shift toward strong relations with the United States has remained a central part of the (West) German state since the events of the Airlift, and the heroism of the Airlift pilots in bringing food and supplies to West Berliners has continued to be referenced in official commemoration up to the present day. The Berlin Airlift cemented the strong bond that was already developing during the occupation, and ensured (West) Germany's role as an ally of the United States over the decades since, despite some phases of geopolitical challenges. Americans during the Cold War also identified with the struggles of the West Berliners and were inspired by the courage of the population in staying committed to democracy despite hardship. As Daniel F. Harrington writes, "The crisis, the shared sense of sacrifice, and the growing sense of mutual obligation and admiration eroded the earlier distance between victor and vanquished."[23] Moreover, as Jared Donnelly notes, the Airlift cemented the Cold War border between East and West Germany and allowed West Germans to feel connected to West Berliners, confirming rhetoric about common Western values such as freedom and democracy.[24] This connection has ensured decades-long ties between Americans, (former) West Germans, and (former) West Berliners, creating a strong German-American relationship which has continued beyond the fall of the Berlin Wall.

****

Tempelhof," *Tagesspiegel*, July 4, 2019, https://www.tagesspiegel.de/berlin/amerikaner-feiern-auf-dem-flughafen-tempelhof-6604888.html.

20 Cherny, *The Candy Bombers*, 547. Also, Michael O. Tunnell, *Candy Bomber: The Story of the Berlin Airlift's "Chocolate Pilot"* (Charlesbridge, 2010), 83.

21 Eisenhuth, *Die Schutzmacht*, 137.

22 Goedde, *GIs and Germans*, xiv.

23 Daniel F. Harrington, *Berlin on the Brink: The Blockade, the Airlift, and the Early Cold War* (University Press of Kentucky, 2012), 227.

24 Jared Donnelly, "The Airlift: 'The Air Force Can Deliver Anything,'" *in The Berlin Airlift and the Making of the Cold War*, ed. Schuessler, Seipp, and Sullivan, 36.

Gail Halvorsen's candy bombing initiative was just one part of the massive effort of the Airlift, in which the US Air Force and British RAF supplied 2.3 million tons of food and supplies to Berlin through around 277,000 flights after the Soviets blockaded road, railroad, and water supply routes to Berlin on June 24, 1948. The Soviets acted in response to the introduction of the *Deutsche Mark* currency in the British, French, and American occupation Trizone, which the Soviets claimed undermined the four-power rule of Germany and interpreted as a provocation.[25] After the start of the Blockade, General Clay quickly realized he needed to explore different options and buy some time for possible negotiations with the Soviets. Air Force commanders including Curtis LeMay agreed to Air Force participation in an Airlift via the air corridors between West Berlin and the British and US zones of occupation. In creating the Blockade, the Soviets hoped that the Western Allies would either leave the city or reach an agreement with them that would end the Blockade.[26] The Soviets did not expect the events to unfold as they did, nor did they anticipate the resounding victory that the Airlift provided for the Western Allies. The Airlift lasted from June 26, 1948 to September 30, 1949, providing supplies even after the Soviets ended the Blockade on May 12, 1949. The remaining months of deliveries were undertaken in order to ensure West Berliners would have enough supplies stockpiled in case of further unrest.

Despite most of the Airlift supplies being supplies such as canned or packaged food (including CARE packages), coal, and medicine, it was Gail Halvorsen's act of individual benevolence of dropping candy that especially shaped the entire Airlift and impacted the history and memory of the occupation period. Halvorsen's actions became the public face of the Airlift measure, and were taken on as a collective military effort in the Airlift. His efforts also became "a massive public relations success for the Airlift," and the story of the candy bombing became "iconic," according to Donnelly.[27] Andrei Cherny argues that Halvorsen, an "ordinary

25 Donnelly, "The Airlift," 16; Corine Defrance, "Die Berliner Luftbrücke zwischen Geschichte und Erinnerung: Einleitende Überlegungen," in *Die Berliner Luftbrücke: Erinnerungsort des Kalten Krieges*, ed. Corine Defrance, Bettina Greiner, and Ulrich Pfeil (Ch. Links Verlag, 2018), 20; Alexej M. Filitow, "Defensive Taktik oder Offensive Strategie?: Die Entscheidung zur Blockade auf sowjetischer Seite," in *Die Berliner Luftbrücke*, ed. Trotnow and von Kostka, 30. Roger G. Miller describes the currency reform in the Western zone as the "pretext for Soviet Action." See Miller, *To Save a City*, 18–19.

26 See Donnelly, "The Airlift," in *The Berlin Airlift and the Making of the Cold War*, ed. Schuessler, Seipp, and Sullivan, 16–17. For more on Air Force General Curtis LeMay, see Miller, 11. LeMay apparently responded to Clay's question about whether he had planes that could carry coal by stating, "The Air Force can deliver anything" (in Donnelly, 16). In 1968, LeMay ran as Alabama Governor George Wallace's running mate in the presidential election.

27 Donnelly, "The Airlift," 32.

young pilot, would almost single-handedly transform how the citizens of defeated Germany's capital saw the United States."[28] Berlin children from that time never forgot about the Chocolate Uncle, as they called Halvorsen, and many tried to meet him later in their lives, with some breaking down in tears of gratitude when they met him even decades later at events such as the Airlift anniversaries.[29] Ever since Halvorsen's first encounter with those 30 children at Tempelhof in Berlin, his life and the lives of the children he impacted have remained linked, symbolizing the bond between Americans and Germans that the candy bombing helped forge.

During the May 12, 2019 Airlift commemoration in Berlin, Gail Halvorsen stated, "The heroes of the Berlin Airlift were not the pilots, the heroes were the Germans." This included parents and their children, who were the future "of the free world" and "were free to make choices." To Halvorsen, "They were the heroes, not the guys bringing in the food."[30] Halvorsen thus claims that it was the Berliners' embrace of freedom that emerged during the Airlift (represented through children and their parents), not the actions of the British and American pilots, that most shaped the time. This included the children he met at the Tempelhof fence who cared more about freedom than food. German children and their apparent embrace of freedom thus forged an unbreakable bond between Germans and Americans through the Airlift. Berliner children emerged as central figures in memory narratives regarding the Airlift, having navigated the challenges of postwar occupation under the four powers in addition to Cold War geopolitics. According to these narratives, West Berlin's children apparently unequivocally chose to be members of the Western alliance over Soviet communism. Berlin's children thus fundamentally impacted transatlantic political navigations during the Airlift, and they remain central figures to this day in memory culture about the time.

---

28 Cherny, *The Candy Bombers*, 8.

29 For an example of German reactions at the 1998 Berlin Airlift fiftieth anniversary, see Cherny, 547.

30 "Rosinenbomber-Pilot Gail Halvorsen gestorben," *Zeit Online*, February 17, 2022, https://www.zeit.de/gesellschaft/zeitgeschehen/2022-02/rosinenbomber-gail-halvorsen-pilot-berliner-luftbruecke-gestorben. Author's translation. See also Jessica Marie Ryan, "Americans, Germans memorialize airlift personnel 70 years later," *U.S. Army News*, June 14, 2019, https://www.army.mil/article/223087/americans_germans_memorialize_airlift_personnel_70_years_later. Also, see an interview with Gail Halvorsen on the heroes of the Airlift, Gail S. Halvorsen, "Helden der Luftbrücke," Gedächtnis der Nation, Zeitzeugen Portal, Stiftung Haus der Geschichte der Bundesrepublik Deutschland, accessed June 20, 2023, https://www.zeitzeugen-portal.de/zeitraeume/jahrzehnte/1940/luftbruecke-die-rosinenbomber/TBqo4Y-eDuY.

Halvorsen's candy bombing action fit perfectly into the Cold War power struggle, playing a major role as a valuable source of propaganda and a show of American power and values. The Airlift was essential in the Cold War struggle of winning over hearts and minds, because it illustrated the values that America stood for, including standing up for freedom and democracy. In his memoir, Harry Truman described the achievements of the Air Force during the Airlift as proving "a beacon light of hope for the peoples of Europe." He wrote, "When we refused to be forced out of the city of Berlin, we demonstrated to the people of Europe that with their co-operation we would act, and act resolutely, when their freedom was threatened. Politically it brought the peoples of western Europe more closely to us."[31] The Airlift thus molded Cold War alliances between Western Europe and the United States.

Gail Halvorsen exemplified the good, kindly, all-American soldier, and his encounter with Berlin's children fit into wider Cold War aims.[32] However, although his "candy diplomacy" perfectly aligned with American Cold War goals, the children themselves also shaped the Airlift through their desire for the candy that fell from the sky in parachutes.[33] The children were apparently hungry for food and for freedom, fitting perfectly with Cold War narratives that aimed to portray the goodness of the American side. Yet young Berliners' roles in the Airlift moved beyond that of innocent recipients. They undertook personal action, which included the conversations at Tempelhof with Gail Halvorsen and the writing of letters in support of the candy bombing. Overall, as Kaete O'Connell argues, the children of Berlin "were the most ardent supporters of the Airlift."[34] She also claims that the personal relationships forged between Germans and Americans during the Airlift are what helped win over German hearts and minds the most.[35] Berliner children's lives were shaped by a geopolitical crisis and the wonder of candy falling from the sky, and their encounters with American pilots and American products helped cement the postwar shift in German-American relations. The actions of Gail Halvorsen also helped humanize the Airlift and the wider occupation of Germany, turning the focus to the present-day needs of German children. Young Germans emerged central to the occupation and the Airlift. Moreover, the Airlift and the candy bombing were part of a wider trend of personal aid from Americans to Germans, especially children, which during the occupation included

31 Truman, *Memoirs of Harry S. Truman*, vol. 2, 131.

32 See O'Connell, "Weapon of War, Tool of Peace," 258, 267; O'Connell, "Uncle Wiggly Wings," 7–8.

33 See "candy diplomacy" in O'Connell, "Weapon of War, Tool of Peace," 267.

34 O'Connell, "Weapon of War, Tool of Peace," 266.

35 O'Connell, "Uncle Wiggly Wings," 15.

not only Airlift deliveries and candy parachutes but also CARE packages, the *Schulspeisung* school feeding program, GYA clubs aimed at assisting German youth, and holiday parties for German children. In addition, the candy bombing has molded the collective memory of the American occupation after World War II and also has impacted (West) German identity even until today.

The Big Lift: The *Rosinenbomber* and America's Greatest Moment

Memory culture regarding the Berlin Airlift often embraces a black and white narrative of the Berlin Blockade, which focuses on the Soviets as a force of evil trying to starve West Berliners and the Americans as the saviors, bringing candy and democracy via air. This narrative parallels collective memory of the wider US occupation of Germany after World War II, which often focuses on the "goodness" of the American occupation, usually focusing on the American role as liberators from fascism and portraying the Soviets as a destructive force, who for example reaped destruction, tried to starve West Berlin through the Blockade, and committed violent acts at the end of the war, such as mass rape.[36] This narrative simplifies Americans into a benevolent source of liberation, freeing Germans from fascism (and the new enemy, communism). Such a simplified story glosses over the complexity of the immediate postwar years and tends to paint Germans as victims. Moreover, memory of the occupation and the Berlin Airlift also highlights the great actions of the Americans, ignoring the role that other Western Allies played during both the occupation and the Airlift.

36 See Carruthers, *The Good Occupation*, 5. For an example of American descriptions of Soviet actions, see Frank Howley, *Berlin Command* (G.P. Putnam's Sons, 1950), 3–4. Frank Howley, Commandant of the American sector of Berlin during the Airlift, noted in his 1950 account of the Airlift that "the cold, inhuman minds in the Kremlin had reached a wicked decision, the most barbarous in history since Ghengis [sic] Khan reduced conquered cities to pyramids of skulls." He described the decision to blockade Berlin as an "atrocious crime" and a decision "to starve the Germans into revolt against the Western powers and thus drive us out." A few days before the Blockade was imposed, his medical officer notified him that "the Russians have cut off our milk supply. Unless we get that fresh milk, six thousand German babies in our sector will be dead by Monday." Howley, who was a "family man," noted that he "could share the anguish of the German mothers and fathers who were faced with this dreadful calamity." When the Blockade occurred, he was "ready for them," having brought in "200 tons of condensed milk and 150 tons of powdered milk" which could be used "as a substitute for fresh milk." Howley wrote, "Not one of my babies died!"

Recent scholarship on the Berlin Blockade and Airlift aims at complicating the narrative of good Americans versus evil Soviets, noting that this narrative itself was part of the Cold War fight for the hearts and minds of the Berliners. For example, Paul Steege argues that the Blockade itself "emerged not primarily as a battle for material control of access to Berlin but as a contest between competing 'spin doctors' who sought to shape popular understanding of what was happening."[37] However, American memory narratives about the Airlift often continue to focus on the goodness and heroism of the pilots, who were committing actions as part of the "Greatest Generation," the conquering heroes who had won World War II and willingly came back to Germany to prevent their former enemy from starving. For example, Richard Reeves claims that the Berlin Airlift could be considered "the last act of . . . 'The Greatest Generation.'"[38]

Even Gail Halvorsen's role in the Airlift was more complicated than the triumphant tales of his candy bombing action indicate. In July 1948, while stationed at Brookley Air Force Base in Mobile, Alabama, Gail Halvorsen volunteered to be a pilot in the Berlin Airlift in the place of his friend who had been selected to serve, because this friend had a wife and twin babies at home, while Halvorsen was still single. The day he left for Germany to serve in the Airlift, he parked his new red car under the trees at Brookley Air Force Base; he would never see that car again. The car had played a major role in his desire to integrate back into regular American life after his service during World War II as a transport pilot. For example, he could aim to impress girls by driving them on dates in his new car. Halvorsen described in his memoir, "Most of the pilots had been overseas during the war and were not expecting or hoping to return this soon. A similar situation existed with the crew chiefs and ground personnel. The call to leave home again so soon on behalf of a former mortal enemy was not a popular one."[39] Halvorsen did not expect that the Blockade would last more than 25 days. When he finally returned home over half a year later, he never saw his car again, having sold it through the mail to a lieutenant at the Brookley Air Force Base while he was still in Germany serving in the Airlift. For Halvorsen, selling the car during his service in the Airlift thus had confirmed that he "was more firmly committed to the airlift than ever before."[40] Thus even the famous Candy Bomber was initially not entirely enthusiastic about returning to active military service in a foreign country, just years after the end of the war. Through his decision to volunteer in place of his friend, Halvorsen had been able to ensure that his friend

37 Steege, *Black Market, Cold War*, 210.
38 Reeves, *Daring Young Men*, xvi.
39 Halvorsen, *The Berlin Candy Bomber*, 20.
40 Halvorsen, 127.

would not have to leave his wife and young children for an unknown amount of time, although other Airlift service personnel certainly had families waiting eagerly for their return, perhaps for the second time in just a few years.

Service in the Airlift and the wider US occupation forces could be messy and ambiguous, with tensions arising regarding navigating feelings about German guilt and witnessing the harsh realities of devastation and hardship on the ground for the German people. Although Halvorsen did not serve in combat or in Germany during the war, but instead in air transport in the South Atlantic Theater, he grappled with his feelings about Germans, and he initially did not like them, especially because they shot down one of his best friends during the war.[41] Although he knew some people of German descent in his hometown in Utah, he wrote in his memoir that he had been conditioned by the American media regarding "the hardness of the Germans, the atrocities, and the claims of superiority."[42] Some of the Berlin Airlift pilots did indeed serve during the war in the bombing of Germany. In his memoir, Halvorsen recorded a conversation he had with a pilot who had been a B-17 bomber pilot who had flown bombing missions over Berlin and other bombing targets in Germany, during which two of his crew members had been killed. This pilot noted his frustration with being called to duty a second time, getting in the way of his plans to get on with his life after the end of World War II. However, the pilot claimed that the Airlift changed his views, enabling him to realize "that these people [the Germans] wanted to be free just like we in America were free." The pilot stated, "When defenseless women and children are involved, it cancels out a lot of the past. Things during the war were based on a whole different set of rules. Somehow that faceless mass of two million people suddenly became individuals just like my mother and sister. From then on I could handle it." He also told Halvorsen, "I didn't feel good about dropping the bombs. Now maybe I can do something about the food." Halvorsen concluded his reflections on the conversation with the bomber pilot by writing, "The cloud from the gas chambers and the ghosts of six million innocent victims were impossible to set aside, but the barely living called and begged [for] a response."[43]

Nevertheless, Halvorsen grappled with his own reaction upon meeting Germans for the first time on his first flight into Tempelhof. These Germans were working at the airport unloading the plane, and some of them had even previously been Luftwaffe pilots. Halvorsen wrote, "Mixed emotions were going

41 Halvorsen, 18.
42 Halvorsen, 34.
43 Halvorsen, 38–39.

through me as I sized up this heterogeneous crew through my stereotyped eyes. As I looked from one to another to find the monster, the hardened stare, the 'superior' eye, or the defiant look, it wasn't there." In addition, the German men closest to him had their hands extended out to shake his hand, and they had a certain look in their eyes as they gazed at the sacks of flour they were unloading and then looked at the American pilots as if "we were angels from heaven delivering the news of the resurrection." Halvorsen noted their "expression of humble gratitude," as well as "the moist eye, and the sincere thrusting forward of the hand of friendship," an exchange that took place for a brief moment as they unloaded the sacks of flour into trucks. Halvorsen argued that this brief moment forever changed his mindset about Germans:

> There was so much communicated in that short moment that it seemed more like ten minutes as I went back over the things that had gone through my mind as a young man and later during the war. The look in their eyes was unmistakable. No matter what had gone on before or for whatever reasons, they were individuals—human beings. We were friends working for a common goal: freedom.

He also wrote, "A wave of emotion came over me. We were trying to bomb each other into oblivion just a few years before, and now a tremendous feeling of working together, united for a common cause, replaced my search for stereotype reinforcement." Halvorsen wrote that this shift in his views "didn't come easily," and that this first encounter with the former enemy taught him an important lesson "about prejudging individuals because they belong to a certain nation, race, or color."[44]

Kaete O'Connell argues that the narrative of the Candy Bomber helped act "as a cleansing agent, mollifying lingering hostilities and sanitizing past promiscuities" of an occupation that had become highly sexual.[45] Relationships between GIs and their German *Fräuleins* often served as a central focal point and a major source of criticism about the occupation from Americans at home. In contrast, the "human-interest narrative" and Gail Halvorsen's child-friendly, humble, altruistic persona helped mold American support for both the occupation and the Airlift, as "the confusion and anxiety of the occupation" was replaced instead "with overwhelming support and pride in the US presence abroad," O'Connell writes.[46] The narrative of the Candy Bomber thus contributed to smoothing over the continuing complexities of the Allied presence in Germany as occupiers. It also helped further American support of a continued active military presence in foreign

44 Halvorsen, 52–53.
45 O'Connell, "Uncle Wiggly Wings," 11.
46 O'Connell, "Uncle Wiggly Wings," 11, 14.

lands. The focus on Gail Halvorsen and on German children thus helped shift collective American views of Germans, enabling a high level of support for the humanitarian efforts aimed at rehabilitating a former enemy, efforts that included the Berlin Airlift and other aid such as CARE packages. According to an official OMGUS survey, which surveyed 300 West Berliners about the Airlift in July 1948, 98% of the survey respondents believed that the Western Allies were correct in their decision to stay in Berlin. Moreover, 84% were confident that the Airlift could provide enough food supplies to maintain the current rationing level.[47] In addition, the Airlift shaped the Western Allies' views about Germany's return to the so-called "civilized nations," as West Berliners had proven that they undoubtedly chose freedom and democracy over communism. Focus thus turned away from discussions about the Nazi past or about the level of success of occupation measures such as the denazification process.[48] Instead, attention turned to abstract notions about (West) Germans' embrace of notions of freedom, as denoted by their resounding support of the Airlift.

The Berlin Airlift proved a major success, both logistically and symbolically, with American and British pilots supplying West Berliners. The Airlift portrayed the might of the Western Allies, as well as tangible proof of their values in action, such as freedom and democracy, spread through benevolent aid. In addition, according to Dewey A. Browder, the Airlift "vividly demonstrated" the growing partnership of Germans and Americans, who worked together during the Airlift in a "spirit of cooperation," with Germans working to unload the supplies from the planes that Americans flew in to Tempelhof.[49] Gail Halvorsen helped personify the effort of the Airlift, demonstrating values of self-sacrifice and kindness. As Daniel F. Harrington notes, Halvorsen "became a world-famous symbol of the humanitarian essence of the airlift," whose story "epitomized the deepening bonds between Berliners and the Western powers."[50] Halvorsen often mentioned a saying of his father's, "From little things come big things," which impacted his decision to do something for the children at Tempelhof.[51] Halvorsen was also religious, practicing Mormonism, which impacted his belief in the importance of service to others. He wrote in his memoir, "Service to others, as the Savior taught, provides those magical moments. The exhortation to serve, to love, is so simple

47 Report No. 130 (23 July 1948): "Berlin Reactions to the Air Lift and the Western Powers," in Merritt and Merritt, eds., *Public Opinion in Occupied Germany*, 248.
48 See Goedde, *GIs and Germans*, 170.
49 Browder, *Americans in Post-World War II Germany*, 21.
50 Harrington, *Berlin on the Brink*, 226–227.
51 Tunnell, *Candy Bomber*, 41.

but its blessing is so complex."[52] Halvorsen thus provided a figure of an exemplary Cold War American serviceman, willing to sacrifice and kind enough to help the needy children of a former enemy.

In addition, Halvorsen made an impression on young Berliners at the time, who were intrigued by the figure of the Airlift pilot. American military personnel such as Halvorsen provided youngsters a new type of adult figure to look up to, one that was easy-going, generous, and yet still a military figure.[53] Moreover, common childhood role models in the twentieth and twenty-first century have often included pilots, which seems to have extended to Berliner children during the Airlift, who saw the pilots as especially heroic, bringing them food and candy through the skies. Berlin Airlift pilots thus became heroes to many of Berlin's children.[54] Some children in Berlin were even photographed "playing Airlift," although a photo showing a group of boys among the ruins of Berlin while playing with model C-54s may have been staged due to the obvious uncomfortable stance of the children, according to Wilhelm van Kampen.[55] Mercedes Wild, who as a child wrote to Halvorsen during the Airlift asking him to drop candy parachutes in her yard by searching for her white chickens, later indeed trained to become a pilot, showing the life-long impact that the Airlift pilots could make on the lives of young Berliners.[56]

Gail Halvorsen also played a central role in making the Airlift the largest American media event since the end of the war.[57] After conducting a few secret candy parachute drops after meeting the children at the fence at Tempelhof, he and his crew decided to stop, because the crowd of children at Tempelhof had become so large that they were sure they would be caught undertaking their secret drops. However, it was too late: letters addressed to "the Chocolate Pilot of Tempelhof" piled up on a desk at Tempelhof Base Operations, and one day Halvorsen was summoned at Rhein-Main Air Base to meet with his commander, Colonel James R. Haun. Haun asked Halvorsen, "What in the world have you been doing?" to which Halvorsen responded, "Flying like mad, sir." It became clear during their conversation that Halvorsen's candy bombing had been discovered. Haun showed Halvorsen an article in the *Frankfurter Zeitung* about a reporter

52 Halvorsen, *The Berlin Candy Bomber*, 142.
53 See Sollors, *The Temptation of Despair*, 217.
54 Tunnell, *Candy Bomber*, vii, 61.
55 Wilhelm van Kampen, "Was bleibt, sind die Bilder: Die Luftbrücke als 'Medienereignis,'" in *Auftrag Luftbrücke: Der Himmel über Berlin 1948–1949*, ed. Uwe Förster et al. (Nicolai, 1998), 334–335.
56 See Halvorsen, *The Berlin Candy Bomber*, 159–160, 162–163.
57 See van Kampen, "Was bleibt, sind die Bilder," in *Auftrag Luftbrücke*, ed. Förster et al., 332.

almost getting hit in the head with a candy bar the day before in Berlin. The story had already spread all over Europe. In addition, Lieutenant General William H. Tunner, Commander of the Airlift, had called Colonel Haun with congratulations, but Colonel Haun had not known what Tunner was talking about. Halvorsen thought his flying days were over after being caught doing something without permission, but after Colonel Haun gave him a scolding for not asking permission first, Haun said, "Keep flying, keep dropping, and keep me informed." He also told Halvorsen that General Tunner wanted to see him in Frankfurt, where an international press conference was set up for him.[58] Candy bombing thus became an official part of the Airlift effort. General Tunner had realized the public relations and propaganda value of Halvorsen's candy bombing action and its potential wide-ranging psychological impact on boosting Airlift goals, increasing morale among both Berliners and airmen and furthering American public approval of the Airlift. Moreover, the action also helped advertise the newly created Air Force as a benevolent force.[59] In September 1948, Tunner sent Halvorsen on a media tour in the US, which included interviews on the newly popular media of television, where he was interviewed on the "We the People" show, in addition to appearing on the radio and in newspaper coverage.[60] Halvorsen's candy bombing action thus forged a connection between US military personnel, the American public, and West Berliners, as Jared Donnelly notes.[61]

While in New York during his media tour, Halvorsen was invited to lunch by John S. Swersey, a member of the American Confectioners Association, who asked him how many sweets he needed for Operation Little Vittles (OLV), as the candy bombing action became known as. Halvorsen told him a huge number, the exact

---

58 Halvorsen, *The Berlin Candy Bomber*, 112–114. Tunner had already become famous for being an airlift expert, having served as commander of the India-China Division of the Air Transport Command. The airlift there was known as "The Hump" and carried supplies across the Himalayas in India into China during World War II. See Walter H. Waggoner, "Gen. William H. Tunner Dies; Directed Berlin Airlift in 1948," *New York Times*, April 8, 1983.

59 See Donnelly, "The Airlift," in *The Berlin Airlift and the Making of the Cold War*, ed. Schuessler, Seipp, and Sullivan, 31–32; O'Connell, "Weapon of War, Tool of Peace," 246–247, 257–258, 270–273, 278; O'Connell, "Uncle Wiggly Wings," 7–8. In 1947, the United States Air Force (USAF) was established as a separate branch by the National Security Act. See also Tunner's account of Halvorsen's actions, in William H. Tunner, *Over the Hump*, Berlin Airlift 50th Anniversary Commemorative Edition (U.S. Government Printing Office, Air Force History and Museums Program, 1998), 207–208, https://purl.access.gpo.gov/GPO/LPS48694.

60 Halvorsen, *The Berlin Candy Bomber*, 129–130. See also Halvorsen's report on the New York trip, Gail S. Halvorsen, "Halvorsen New York Trip Report to General Tunner," September 29, 1948, in Halvorsen, 262–263. Also, Cherny, *The Candy Bombers*, 384–387.

61 Donnelly, "The Airlift," in *The Berlin Airlift and the Making of the Cold War*, ed. Schuessler, Seipp, and Sullivan, 32.

sum of which he could not remember. Later on, two boxcars of candy totaling 6,500 pounds were then shipped by Swersey from New York via Bremerhaven to Rhein-Main.[62] According to Halvorsen, Swersey, who was Jewish, explained to him at the lunch that he believed "that kids were the hope of the future and whatever had gone on before was now in the past."[63] The candy shipment was guarded by armed guards, since it was "almost enough stuff to buy King Ludwig's castle on the black market," according to the officer who showed Halvorsen the shipment. The shipment was so large that they could not drop it all during flights, but instead it was shipped into Berlin in segments on Airlift planes to later be distributed at Christmas parties organized by the Air Force and German Youth Activities. Before the parties, the candy was kept safe locked in Berlin jail cells.[64]

American contributions of sweets and homemade parachutes flooded into Germany after radio stations reported on the operation's lack of handkerchiefs and after Halvorsen's media appearances in the US. Some handkerchief contributions had the names and addresses of the donors, and some even were made of black lace or were perfumed, containing the contact information of the women who sent them, as media reports had mentioned that Halvorsen was single.[65] Armed forces personnel stationed in Germany also helped donate supplies.[66] Donations arrived from Great Britain and even Australia, according to Halvorsen. In addition, American military wives and service clubs in Germany also assisted with logistics and created assembly lines for Operation Little Vittles.[67] After running out of handkerchiefs and before the flood of donations came in, Halvorsen had started using reusable silk parachutes, on which he added a written request in German to return them to the local Military Police, who would then bring them to Tempelhof. The vast majority of parachutes with these requests for returning them were indeed returned by the children. Some children sent along their own homemade parachute contributions with maps or letters requesting a candy drop at their house.[68] One man even brought a donated homemade handkerchief para-

62 Halvorsen, *The Berlin Candy Bomber*, 130–131, 135.
63 Halvorsen, 131.
64 Halvorsen, 135–136. Also, Cherny, *The Candy Bombers*, 495–497. That Christmas in 1948, Halvorsen received 1,400 Christmas cards.
65 Halvorsen, 121. One couple had responded to a radio station's report, and had sent three parachutes with their names and addresses. Two of the children who caught the parachutes wrote back to them, and the couple informally adopted the children, sending 77 CARE packages to them over the years and providing the one with her wedding dress when she grew up and got married. In Tunnell, *Candy Bomber*, 74–76.
66 Halvorsen, 114–115.
67 Halvorsen, 123.
68 Halvorsen, 115–116.

chute to finally return to Halvorsen at the 1998 fiftieth anniversary Airlift celebration in Berlin, noting his apologies about not returning it, stating, "I just couldn't part with my parachute, my personal symbol of freedom." Halvorsen made a copy of the parachute and returned it to the man to allow him to keep his symbol of freedom. This particular handkerchief had been donated by a couple from Pennsylvania, who had written "Best wishes" on the handkerchief below their names.[69] For this Berliner citizen, the parachute still symbolized the linkages between freedom and personal acts of American benevolence, including Halvorsen's candy bombing and the personal act of kindness from an American couple.

As the candy bombing progressed, the crowd of children at Tempelhof grew so large that it became too dangerous to drop next to the airfield in case of a mad dash to retrieve the candy. Instead, the candy bombing actions were changed to drops over open areas such as playgrounds, parks, schools, and church yards all over West Berlin, without any announcement.[70] Halvorsen received many letters from West Berlin children who requested drops over their homes or schools, including a memorable request from nine-year-old Peter Zimmerman, who included a homemade parachute and a map with instructions of how to fly to his house. "Please note the map," he wrote. "As you see, after takeoff fly along the big canal to the second highway bridge, turn right one block. I live in the bombed-out house on the corner. I'll be in the backyard every day at 2 p.m., drop it there."[71] Halvorsen tried multiple times to find Zimmerman's house but was unable to, leading the child to write follow up letters, including one that stated, "Have not received any chocolate yet! But I also want thank you for your good will and it all! Here I am presenting you a few draws [sic] in remembrance to Berlin and me!" The letter included drawings of a tiger and also of an Airlift plane conducting a candy drop, with the plane's tail end reading, "No chocolate yet" to further his point.[72] Drops to Zimmerman were never successful, and one time after a drop he wrote Halvorsen, "Didn't get any gum or candy, a bigger kid beat me to it." Later on, he wrote yet another disappointed letter to Halvorsen stating, "You

---

69 Halvorsen, 229. See image of Halvorsen's request to return the parachute, 228.

70 Halvorsen, 122.

71 Halvorsen, 116. See images of Zimmerman's letters and drawings to Halvorsen on Halvorsen's website, "Children's Letters," The Berlin Candy Bomber, accessed July 2, 2023, http://wigglywings.weebly.com/childrens-letters.html. See also interview of Gail S. Halvorsen, "Kinderwünsche," Gedächtnis der Nation, Zeitzeugen Portal, Stiftung Haus der Geschichte der Bundesrepublik Deutschland, accessed June 20, 2023, https://www.zeitzeugen-portal.de/zeitraeume/jahrzehnte/1940/luftbruecke-die-rosinenbomber/gcdVy2ksdjg. Gail stated in this interview that he became friends with Peter. Peter was an orphan and Halvorsen also sent him shoes. He said that Peter ended up immigrating to the United States.

72 Image of Peter's letter and drawing, in Halvorsen, 118.

are a pilot? I gave you a map. How did you guys win the war?" He also suggested he might build a fire so Halvorsen could be guided to his house by the smoke. Instead, Halvorsen ended up mailing sweets to Zimmerman to guarantee he actually got the candy he wanted so badly.[73]

Children at a polio hospital with limited mobility also wrote letters to Halvorsen, requesting that he conduct a candy drop over the hospital grounds, since they could not walk or run to catch the candy parachutes. The children claimed that their doctors would not mind a drop and that the adults could run out and then bring them the candy to their hospital beds. However, instead of making a drop at the hospital, Halvorsen decided to come visit in person, bringing candy bars and bubble gum. Photos of the visit show children and the hospital staff responding with happiness at meeting the Chocolate Pilot. An American health officer, James J. Gibson Jr., also taught the children how to chew gum during the visit.[74] Not all of the letters to Halvorsen were requests for special candy drops, and most were letters of gratitude, which often addressed Halvorsen with affectionate nicknames, such as "*Onkel.*" Adults also wrote to Halvorsen, including parents who had nothing to give to their children for their birthday except candy from his parachutes.[75] One letter from a Berlin elementary school teacher read, "My best thanks for the 'Sky-Food,'" attached with letters and drawings from her pupils.[76] By December 1948, according to Michael O. Tunnell, Gail Halvorsen and all of the pilots of the Airlift had thus undoubtedly become heroes to the children of West Berlin.[77]

In addition to West Berliner children, the children of East Berlin also vied for a part of the candy action. They also wrote to Halvorsen, stating that sometimes they went over to West Berlin to catch some of the parachutes. According to Halvorsen, they hoped that it was okay with him that they were "collecting bounty intended for the Free Berliners." In their letters, they assured him that it was not their choice to live in East Berlin, but that they had to live there since their parents lived there. According to Halvorsen, "an admiration was often expressed for the Americans."[78] Most of these letters included the request that Halvorsen drop candy for them as he approached Tempelhof, since he flew right over them while preparing to land. Halvorsen then did do so after receiving their requests. He noted that dropping candy for East Berliners was easy for him even though

73 Halvorsen, 117–118; Tunnell, *Candy Bomber*, 55.
74 Halvorsen, 116–120. See photos, 119–120.
75 Tunnell, *Candy Bomber*, 56, 60–61.
76 In Halvorsen, *The Berlin Candy Bomber*, 269–271.
77 Tunnell, *Candy Bomber*, 61.
78 Halvorsen, *The Berlin Candy Bomber*, 125–126.

they were in the communist Soviet sector, since he had grappled with his "own stereotyped prejudices." He wrote in his memoir that he believed that it was "the system, not the people, that causes miscommunication and misunderstanding between nations."[79] Halvorsen's candy bombing over East Berlin took place until the Soviets launched a complaint with the State Department, saying that his candy drops "on their side of the border is a capitalist trick to influence the minds of the young people against them," according to the officer who reported this to Halvorsen.[80] Interestingly, in 1971, a former East Berliner told Halvorsen that Russian children had also caught some of the candy parachutes during the time when he was dropping them over East Berlin. Apparently, "these children were as thrilled as any others who were surprised by a small parachute descending above their heads," Halvorsen wrote in his memoir.[81] The candy bombing had thus attained fame in Berlin, throughout Germany, and across the Atlantic in the United States. Halvorsen's actions also helped mold American public opinion towards Germany, convincing many about their role as protectors of values such as freedom and democracy in the Cold War era.[82] Germans were thus no longer the enemy, they were friends to be protected, helped, and saved, and West Berliners proved willing to sacrifice for values core to Americans such as freedom. In addition, encounters between German children and the representatives of the United States, the Berlin Airlift pilots, as well as the products of the Airlift, including Hershey bars delivered via the sky, shaped Berliner youngsters' early lives.

Young American citizens also played a central role in Operation Little Vittles. An American elementary school publication included information about the candy bombing, leading young Americans to volunteer in candy drives and parachute-making campaigns. After hearing of the candy bombing, they also sent letters to Germany requesting addresses of young Germans for pen pal exchanges.[83] The town of Chicopee, Massachusetts (home to Westover Air Force Base) converted their old firehouse into a 24-hours-a-day assembly station for Operation Little Vittles. Mary Connors, a local college student, served as chairwoman. The Chicopee fire station became the Center for Little Vittles in the United States. Twenty-two local schools processed candy and parachute donations and shipped them to Germany, and the Center reached a peak production of 800 pounds shipped every other day by January 21, 1949.[84] Chicopee schoolchildren volun-

79 Halvorsen, 126–127.
80 Halvorsen, 128.
81 Halvorsen, 183.
82 See O'Connell, "Weapon of War, Tool of Peace," 251, 260, 273–274, 277–278.
83 Halvorsen, *The Berlin Candy Bomber*, 121–122.
84 Halvorsen, 122–123.

teered at the Center outside of their school hours, and they stamped the parachutes with a message in German that said, “This candy is sent to you from the school children [sic] of America,” highlighting their focus on promoting goodwill between German and American children.[85] Gail Halvorsen’s candy bombing ensured American participation in Cold War humanitarian efforts, including the participation of young American citizens.[86] Kaete O’Connell argues that Operation Little Vittles “eased Americans into the Cold War in the service of humanitarianism, while simultaneously illustrating that power need not be measured by weaponry alone.”[87] Despite the apparently benevolent nature of Operation Little Vittles, the effort was inherently tied to the American military presence in Germany, a presence which increasingly served American Cold War geopolitical aims. Only a few years after the end of the war, instead of bombs, candy was falling from the sky, but the specter of the Cold War loomed over Germany, with fears that tensions could erupt into the next world war.[88]

Gail Halvorsen was rotated from Berlin in January 1949, but before he departed, he ensured that he found an ideal successor to take over as Candy Bomber. Captain Lawrence Caskey and then Captain Eugene T. Williams took over the efforts. Halvorsen noted in his memoir that Captain Williams actually “dropped more than Caskey and I put together,” and also organized drops to “needy children” on Peacock Island in Berlin every two weeks.[89] Even though Halvorsen departed Berlin before the end of the Airlift and his successors dropped more candy than he had, Halvorsen remains remembered as the official Candy Bomber. Moreover, he has remained the most active in Airlift commemoration events, thus remaining the official face of the benevolent efforts, reflecting the linkage between his actions and the projection of the goodness of American values, which Halvorsen shaped.

****

One of the most iconic images of the Airlift is the so-called “*Rosinenbomber-Foto*” (raisin bomber photo) by Henry Ries, which shows a group of children standing

---

85 Halvorsen, 128–129. Also, Cherny, *The Candy Bombers*, 410; O’Connell, “Weapon of War, Tool of Peace,” 260.

86 See O’Connell, “Uncle Wiggly Wings,” 2.

87 O’Connell, “Uncle Wiggly Wings,” 14.

88 In the July 1948 OMGUS survey of West Berliners, 82% believed that there would be war within a decade. Report No. 130, in Merritt and Merritt, eds., *Public Opinion in Occupied Germany*, 249.

89 Halvorsen, *The Berlin Candy Bomber*, 138–139. See also a flyer made by Captain Williams, Halvorsen, 146.

on a pile of rubble as they watch a C-54 Skymaster Airlift plane crossing overhead. Wilhelm van Kampen states that this image has become synonymous with the Airlift, and has frequently been shown over the years, including at the Airlift anniversaries, becoming stamped into German memory.[90] Such an image of American military benevolence thus enhances the common collective memory trope of Americans as democracy bringers and providers of material aid in the immediate postwar years. Moreover, Berlin children are often mentioned in the collective memory of the Airlift, for example as the recipients of the candy bombing. However, although children are often placed at the center of Airlift memory narratives, it is often in ways that ignore their complex lived experiences, instead focusing on how children fit into wider aims within the Cold War geopolitics of the Berlin Airlift. These collective memory narratives also impact individual memories. For example, most individual German memories of Americans during the postwar years focus on their generosity through food-based aid, and mention the Americans' greatness and heroism, which was especially exemplified by the Berlin Airlift pilots.

When speaking of the Airlift, Germans usually refer to the *Rosinenbomber*, raisin bombers. Airlift supplies included many raisins, because California had a surplus crop of raisins, and the raisin growers' cooperative donated one million pounds of raisins to CARE. CARE packages sent for the Airlift were loaded into any leftover space on flights, with a total of a quarter of a million packages delivered to Berlin during the Airlift. CARE co-founder Wallace J. Campbell wrote in his memoir that the raisins "brought not only food but joy to children who had very little in the way of sweets during the airlift crisis."[91] Wolfgang J. Huschke explains that the term *Rosinenbomber* became the unofficial popular German language term for the Airlift aircraft as a whole, while the American press at the time dubbed the term "Candy Bomber" to refer to the fact that a few years ago during the war, pilots were throwing bombs over Berlin, and now they were bombing the city with candy.[92] The term "Candy Bomber" also usually references Gail Halvorsen himself rather than the wider Airlift. However, these terms can lead to confusion as to what exactly the Airlift was, with the term *Rosinenbomber* making it seem as if the entire Airlift was about delivering sweet food such as raisins and candy, while the "Candy Bomber" term could lead to English speakers

90 Van Kampen, "Was bleibt, sind die Bilder," in *Auftrag Luftbrücke*, ed. Förster et al., 332–334. See obituary of Henry Ries: Douglas Martin, "Henry Ries, 86, Photographer Who Captured Berlin Airlift," *New York Times*, May 26, 2004.

91 Campbell, *The History of CARE*, 60.

92 Wolfgang J. Huschke, *Die Rosinenbomber: Die Berliner Luftbrücke 1948/49, ihre technischen Voraussetzungen und deren erfolgreiche Umsetzung* (Berliner Wissenschafts-Verlag, 2008), 270.

to think that the Airlift was just what Gail Halvorsen initiated, namely, the dropping of candy over Berlin, rather than a wider effort that supplied Berlin with millions of tons of supplies in response to the Soviet Blockade. The term *Rosinenbomber* also connotes the entire Airlift as a benevolent effort to feed Berliners, providing a contrast to the Soviet aims of blockade. Corine Defrance explores how the Airlift also made linguistic impacts, with the term "airlift" itself being cemented in usage in English as a way to describe the Western Allied response to the Soviet Blockade. Germans tend to use the term "*Luftbrücke*," air bridge, which derived from the English "airlift" but used another metaphor of a bridge rather than a lift.[93] The Airlift has thus had profound, long-lasting impacts, including impacts on languages and on individual and collective memory.

Germans who witnessed the Airlift were also often emotionally impacted. Some of them refer to the Airlift pilots as "angels from heaven," terminology that Halvorsen also used when he described in his memoir how German workers at Tempelhof reacted to the pilots.[94] Richard Reeves notes that the actions of the Airlift pilots led German mothers to tell their children that Americans were "angels in uniform."[95] Christel Jonge Vos, who was 11 during the Airlift, was one of the children who stood behind the fence at the Tempelhof waiting for candy parachutes after school, which she unfortunately never caught, because the boys were faster. One time she also brought a gift for Halvorsen, a small wreath of wild flowers, but she did not get close enough to him to deliver it. However, she was able to meet Halvorsen in Arizona in 2014 after starting correspondence with him. She stated before the meeting took place that this was her dream, and that she would probably cry when she met him.[96] Vos, now a resident of Oregon, remembered the "daily ritual" of waiting at Tempelhof hoping for a candy parachute "as a symbol of hope and fun at a time when such things were thin on the ground."[97] Another one of the Berlin Airlift children, Ursula Yunger, whose mother was Jewish and who had survived the war in hiding with her mother and siblings, met Halvorsen in 2003 in Arizona for the first time. He gave her a hug

93 Defrance, "Die Berliner Luftbrücke zwischen Geschichte und Erinnerung," in *Die Berliner Luftbrücke*, ed. Defrance, Greiner, and Pfeil, 18.

94 O'Connell, "Hearts, Minds and Stomachs," in *The Berlin Airlift and the Making of the Cold War*, ed. Schuessler, Seipp, and Sullivan, 161; Halvorsen, *The Berlin Candy Bomber*, 52.

95 Reeves, *Daring Young Men*, xvii.

96 Eschner, "The Sweet Story of the Berlin Candy Bomber," *Smithsonian Magazine*, October 10, 2017, https://www.smithsonianmag.com/smart-news/sweet-story-berlin-candy-bomber-180965156/; Capi Lynn, Ore. Woman to Meet 'Candy Bomber,' her Cold War Hero," *USA Today*, November 8, 2014, https://www.usatoday.com/story/news/nation/2014/11/08/candy-bomber-her-cold-war-hero/18740429/.

97 Eschner, "The Sweet Story of the Berlin Candy Bomber."

and a Hershey bar while she stood there "just shaking." Yunger said that "Gail Halvorsen enchanted the children of Berlin," noting that, "It wasn't the candy" but rather that "it was his profound gesture, showing us that somebody cared."[98] Thus, gifts such as a candy bar from a GI and especially the collective action in Berlin of the candy bombing led to the creation of a high level of positive emotional responses, especially among young Germans, potentially impacting an individual's entire life and remaining never forgotten.

Many of these former children of Berlin thus contacted Halvorsen in their later years, wrote or spoke about their experiences, or attended Airlift anniversary events. Dagmar Weiss Snodgrass, who was 11 during the Airlift, stated that the Airlift pilots "were heroes, angels with metal wings," and her main lifetime wish was to meet Gail Halvorsen, which she did in 2015 at a school in Kansas. She apparently "hugged him, held his face in her hands and thanked him for everything he had done." She also told Halvorsen, "I've been waiting a lifetime to meet you," and said, "I'm here to say thank you, not just for me, but for all of the kids of West Berlin because you were the Santa Claus, the Easter Bunny, all of the things we had been missing in the years that were wartime."[99] Halvorsen's actions thus reached deeply into the emotional experiences of young Berliners whose early lives had been shaped by war, bombings, hunger, and now a Blockade. The efforts of the Berlin Airlift and especially Halvorsen's candy bombing spurred lifelong ties between these Germans and Halvorsen and the other Airlift pilots, even if they had never met in person.

For some young children, the candy parachutes provided messages of hope and even love, showing that someone cared and was trying to help them. They were the neediest of Berlin, the children who seemed hungry for not just candy but also hope. The story of Gail Halvorsen is in a way a story of lifelong connection based on a paternal type of benevolence, with both sides seeming to embrace

98 Richard Goldstein, "Gail Halvorsen, 'Candy Bomber' in Berlin Airlift, Dies at 101," *New York Times*, February 17, 2022. See also Ursula Erika Yunger, *The Healing Presence* (Ruth Publications, 1995). Ursula immigrated to the United States.

99 Kimberly Barker, "Berlin woman shares stories of 'Candy Bomber,'" *Joplin Globe*, November 8, 2018, https://www.joplinglobe.com/news/local_news/berlin-woman-shares-stories-of-candy-bomber/article_0c5a6f8b-9a96-5bad-9eaf-443a93319da6.html. Also, Steve Pokin, "She will never forget 'Berlin candy bomber' and the determination of a great, kind nation," *Springfield News-Leader*, October 22, 2019, https://www.news-leader.com/story/news/local/ozarks/2019/10/23/pokin-around-springfield-woman-85-never-forget-berlin-airlift-world-war-ii/4022826002/. Snodgrass married an American soldier and immigrated to the United States. For more on Snodgrass and Christel Jonge Vos, see O'Connell, "Weapon of War, Tool of Peace," 1; O'Connell, "Hearts, Minds, and Stomachs," in *The Berlin Airlift and the Making of the Cold War*, ed. Schuessler, Seipp, and Sullivan, 146–147, 158–161.

this relationship. For some West Berliner children, Halvorsen's actions spurred a familial-type of bond, filling a void left by the war and its aftermath.[100] During the Airlift, children such as Christel Jonge Vos and their parents brought gifts of gratitude to Tempelhof for Halvorsen and the other pilots, including flowers. Halvorsen described in his memoir a scene at Tempelhof that was often repeated: "Two little girls, dressed in heavy winter coats, bearing a bouquet of fresh flowers and accompanied by a grandmother, were crossing the windswept ramp toward some airlift pilots," giving the flowers to the pilots "as an offering of friendship and appreciation." Halvorsen wrote that the flowers provided a "delicate symbol of something beyond their physical needs. A token of hope, of peace, of beauty, of things to come. How necessary, how important these symbols to the hunger of the spirit."[101] Halvorsen received many homemade gifts, including one from two brothers, Manfred and Klaus Meisner, who constructed a set of book ends from broken pieces of marble from the ruins around the Reichstag, setting them in metal bases and inscribing, "Lt. Halvorsen USA AIRPORT Thankful and as a Remember [sic] from a Berlin boy," with their names inscribed below.[102] For Halvorsen, these tokens of gratitude gained more meaning due to his direct encounter with the provider of the gift. He wrote, "In every case the meaning beyond intrinsic value was the look [in the child's eyes] from the depths of the soul . . . In every case the experience left me a more humble and grateful pilot." These gifts were all "genuine," and showed how the children wished "to share something of themselves, something that had some special value or meaning to them personally." For Halvorsen, a gift from a ten-year-old especially moved him. He described this gift in his memoir:

> None was more genuine than a ten-year-old girl whose name I never learned but who brought with her the greatest gift that she could give, her most cherished and perhaps last remaining personal possession, her little fuzzy teddy bear. It had been her constant companion in the cellar during the British and American bombing raids. She had explained in her school English that it had been a comfort to her during the last battle for Berlin. It was this fuzzy reassurance that she cuddled as the Russian rockets tore away the last of the city's defenses. It was a small, brown, Berlin bear with the fuzz worn off the elbows. "Please take my teddy bear," she said in halting English, looking up at me with big brown, expressive eyes rapidly filling with tears.

---

100 See Huschke, *Die Rosinenbomber*, 275; O'Connell, "Weapon of War, Tool of Peace," 267. Also, O'Connell, "Uncle Wiggly Wings," 13. O'Connell argues that Halvorsen personified a type of "avuncularism," as he was an "affable bachelor with a genuine interest in children."

101 Halvorsen, *The Berlin Candy Bomber*, 138–139.

102 Halvorsen, 139.

Halvorsen tried to return the bear to her, realizing its importance to her, but she did not allow him. She told him to take good care of the bear, and that the bear would now bring good luck to him and his friends on their flights to Berlin. For Halvorsen, the bear was especially meaningful not just because of the "obvious love with which it was given" but also because the girl gave it to him without awareness that he was the original Candy Bomber. She had come to Tempelhof to give it to any Airlift pilot and Halvorsen happened to be the closest to her. According to Halvorsen, this experience of receiving gifts from Germans was common among the Airlift aircrew, and they "had been touched as I had been," he wrote.[103] For Halvorsen, the acts of service to others, even to a former enemy, provided more fulfilment than the honors, gifts, and "other worldly things" he received from his efforts.[104] Halvorsen's many honors over the years have included the German Order of Merit, awarded to him in 1974.

The Airlift Lives On: Post-1949 Narratives of Candy, Raisins, and Freedom

The Airlift has lived on in both the United States and especially in Germany, spurring transatlantic memorialization practices, books, TV shows, and more. Corine Defrance argues that it is important not just to consider the events of the Airlift in 1948 and 1949 but to also examine the "*Nachgeschichte*," the post-history of the Airlift, which continues to the present day.[105] During the Cold War, the Airlift remained relevant especially for its symbolic value, with Airlift commemoration fitting with the "politics of visibility" in a similar manner to President John F. Kennedy's visit to Berlin in 1963, as Dominik Geppert argues.[106] Over the decades, there has been continuous memorialization centered around the history of the Airlift, and the Airlift has remained relevant symbolically even until today. For example, according to Defrance, in today's memory culture, the Airlift remains relevant as a way to depict solidarity narratives.[107] Continuous practices of

103 Halvorsen, 140–141.
104 Tunnell, *Candy Bomber*, ix.
105 Defrance, "Die Berliner Luftbrücke zwischen Geschichte und Erinnerung," in *Die Berliner Luftbrücke*, ed. Defrance, Greiner, and Pfeil, 15.
106 Dominik Geppert, "Symbolische Politik: Berliner Konjunkturen der Erinnerung an die Luftbrücke," in *Die Berliner Luftbrücke*, ed. Trotnow and von Kostka, 139. On the "politics of visibility," see Andreas W. Daum, *Kennedy in Berlin* (German Historical Institute; Cambridge University Press, 2008), 10.
107 Defrance, "Die Berliner Luftbrücke zwischen Geschichte und Erinnerung," in *Die Berliner Luftbrücke*, ed. Defrance, Greiner, and Pfeil, 27.

Airlift memorialization and events centered around Tempelhof have included Open House celebrations (*Tag der offenen Tür*) at Tempelhof Airport from 1950 to 1992, the creation of an Airlift monument at Tempelhof in 1951, and Airlift anniversary commemoration events, including yearly events on May 12, the day of the lifting of the Soviet Blockade. In 1959, at the tenth year Airlift anniversary, British Prime Minister Clement Attlee, General Lucius Clay, General William Tunner, and Willy Brandt (then mayor of West Berlin) were in attendance. Tens of thousands of Berliners came to this commemoration event, which made up a very visible presence in West Berlin, as it included a parade through the streets of West Berlin.[108] On June 26, 1963, as part of the fifteenth anniversary of the beginning of the Airlift, President John F. Kennedy made his (in)famous speech, in which he stated, *"Ich bin ein Berliner."*[109] In 1969 for the twentieth anniversary, Gail Halvorsen was present and reenacted the candy bombing. Many children of the original children of 1948 and 1949 were in attendance, and they learned how it had felt for their parents to capture candy parachutes that fell from the sky when they were children.[110] These events, which continue on until the present day, have had millions of attendees over the decades. This has ensured that the Airlift has remained in the public discourse, has impacted personal experiences, and also has allowed for continuous positive German-American encounters, including encounters between German civilians and US military personnel such as Halvorsen or other Air Force members.[111]

---

108 On Open Houses (known initially as "Armed Forces Day"), see Matthias Heisig, "Der 'Tag der offenen Tür' auf dem amerikanischen Luftwaffenstützpunkt Tempelhof: Ein Beitrag zum Erinnerungsdiskurs der Berliner Luftbrücke," in *Die Berliner Luftbrücke*, ed. Defrance, Greiner, and Pfeil, 202–224. On the 1951 monument, known among Berliners as the "*Hungerharke*," the hunger rake, due to its appearance, see Axel Dreischner, "Chronik eines Wettbewerbs: Der Streit um das Luftbrückendenkmal für Berlin 1949–1951," in *Die Berliner Luftbrücke*, ed. Defrance, Greiner, and Pfeil, 176–201. In May 1949, the square in front of Tempelhof was renamed the Platz der Luftbrücke. Also, Paul Steege, "Looking for German Resistance: The Berlin Blockade from 20 July and 17 June," in *The Berlin Airlift and the Making of the Cold War*, ed. Schuessler, Seipp, and Sullivan, 167, 176–179. The Airlift monument has three arches reaching westward to symbolize the three Airlift airports in Berlin, Tempelhof, Tegel, and Gatow, and the three air corridors. A plaque at the base honors the Allied and German personnel who "gave their lives for Berlin's freedom," mostly due to crashes and accidents during the Airlift. On the 1959 Airlift anniversary, see Geppert, "Symbolische Politik," in *Die Berliner Luftbrücke*, ed. Trotnow and von Kostka, 139.

109 Defrance, "Die Berliner Luftbrücke zwischen Geschichte und Erinnerung," in *Die Berliner Luftbrücke*, ed. Defrance, Greiner, and Pfeil, 14.

110 Halvorsen, *The Berlin Candy Bomber*, 163–165.

111 On Open House German-American encounters, see Heisig, "Der 'Tag der offenen Tür' auf dem amerikanischen Luftwaffenstützpunkt Tempelhof," in *Die Berliner Luftbrücke*, ed. Defrance, Greiner, and Pfeil, 202.

During the Airlift, West Berliners on the whole accepted their role as dependents of Western Allied military support, with the vast majority of citizens choosing "personal freedom" over an offer of food shipments from the Soviets, as Halvorsen wrote in his memoir.[112] In addition, Berliners showed their solidarity during Berlin mayor Ernst Reuter's speech on September 9, 1948, which Corine Defrance argues is etched into the collective memory of Germans.[113] Gail Halvorsen described the speech as "one of the most stirring events of the Blockade," when around 300,000 East and West Berliners gathered in front of the Reichstag at the Platz der Republik while Airlift planes flew above. According to Halvorsen in his memoir:

> Westerner and Easterner joined ranks to cry out to the free world of the Stalinist's [sic] injustice to humanity on both sides of the border. The magnificent Mayor, Ernst Reuter, displayed the throb of the bruised Berliner's heart for all to hear: "We cannot be bartered, we cannot be negotiated, we cannot be sold . . . Whoever would surrender the people of Berlin, would surrender a world . . . more, he would surrender himself."

Halvorsen describes how Reuter finished his speech, calling out to the world, as the crowd of Berliners roared its approval: Reuter proclaimed, "People of the world, look upon this city! You cannot, you must not, forsake us! There is only one possibility for all of us: to stand jointly together until this fight has been won."[114] A few moments after the speech, a 20-year-old German man tore the Soviet flag from the top of the Brandenburger Tor and in the tumult, a 15-year-old was shot.[115] In his memoir, Halvorsen described the moment of the "Red flag" being torn down: "The heart of Berlin had spoken, and so it was to be."[116] Thus, Berliners chose to take on the mantle as defenders of freedom, in need of protection through the Western Allies, including the Americans. West Berliners and as a

112 Halvorsen, *The Berlin Candy Bomber*, 66. See also Finell, *Good-bye to the Mermaids*, 274. Karin Finell, a teenager during the Airlift, noted in her memoirs that few West Berliners took the Russian offer to buy rations in their sector. Instead, "We knew we would be playing into their hands, and they would use our purchases for their propaganda. We, and 97 percent of the population, preferred our meager rations of dried egg powder and milk powder to anything the Russians might have to offer."

113 Defrance, "Die Berliner Luftbrücke zwischen Geschichte und Erinnerung," in *Die Berliner Luftbrücke*, ed. Defrance, Greiner, and Pfeil, 14.

114 Halvorsen, *The Berlin Candy Bomber*, 127. See German version of speech in Defrance, "Die Berliner Luftbrücke zwischen Geschichte und Erinnerung," *Die Berliner Luftbrücke*, ed. Defrance, Greiner, and Pfeil, 14. See also Andreas-Friedrich, *Battleground Berlin*, 243–244.

115 See Edward A. Morrow, "German is Shot Defying Russians: Wounded as He Shouts 'Back to Moscow' as Crowd Mills About Brandenburg Gate," *New York Times*, September 10, 1948; Halvorsen, 127.

116 Halvorsen, 127.

whole, West Germans, had accepted their position as Cold War allies with the West, also accepting the potentially indefinite presence of American troops to serve in the role as their protectors.

In contrast to the widespread acceptance of the West German population of their role as allies of the West in the Cold War, the Soviets never managed to win over the German population in East Berlin and in their occupation zone on the scale of the Western Allies, as Helmut Trotnow argues.[117] Overall, memory culture about the Airlift has depended on the contrast provided by the Soviets, and after the reunification of Germany, the Airlift still retained significance as a symbol of a moment in history when freedom and Western values triumphed. The role of East Berliners in the memory culture of the Airlift remains an underexamined topic, but overarching German narratives accept the Airlift as part of the story of Germany's reemergence into the fold of the Western world. Any East Berliner narratives that challenged that have been drowned out in the face of the strength of the bond between Germans and Americans.[118]

In addition, another side of memory culture surrounding the Berlin Airlift has transatlantic connections. For many Americans, the Berlin Airlift serves as a great positive moment in American history, when military power through the newly created Air Force was harnessed for the good of others, sending not only food but allowing American values such as freedom to persevere in foreign lands. From its earliest days as a separate branch of the US military, the Air Force thus became tied to notions of benevolence through its actions in the Berlin Airlift. The Airlift shaped the image of the US Air Force into a force of military humanitarianism, a trend that has continued with Air Force humanitarian actions over the decades, including during the 1990s in the Balkans, which Gail Halvorsen also contributed to, making candy drops.[119] In addition, in 2014, Air Force members serving in Iraq dropped food supplies and gifts of sweets to Iraqis under siege by Islamic State militants. Sgt. Emily Edmunds of the 816th Expeditionary Airlift Squadron stated about the action, "We are definitely not at the level of the Candy

117 Helmut Trotnow, "Einleitung," in *Die Berliner Luftbrücke*, ed. Trotnow and von Kostka, 12.

118 See Geppert, "Symbolische Politik," in *Die Berliner Luftbrücke*, ed. Trotnow and von Kostka, 146. Geppert notes that East Berliners remembered the noise of the planes, not the coal and candy bomber. Also, Defrance, "Die Berliner Luftbrücke zwischen Geschichte und Erinnerung," *Die Berliner Luftbrücke*, ed. Defrance, Greiner, and Pfeil, 21. Defrance reflects on the fact that Germans were being portrayed as the victims of the Soviet Blockade. She notes that the Soviet perception needs to be embedded more with the context of the recently ended war, in which the Soviet Union suffered enormous losses.

119 See Halvorsen, *The Berlin Candy Bomber*, 232. Tunnell, *Candy Bomber*, 90, 92–94.

Bomber, but I'd give us an 'almost' for our modern version of it."[120] Gail Halvorsen concluded his memoir stressing the positive nature of American Air Force power: "The American flag on the aircraft tail is the symbol of hope to those in deep despair from whatever the source of oppression."[121] The memory of the Berlin Airlift thus provides Americans with a story that validates prominent American values such as the importance of freedom, democracy, and inherent goodness. It allows a way for Americans to view a major Cold War event in a way that is less complex and challenging in comparison to other major conflicts that took place in the context of the Cold War, such as the Korean War and the Vietnam War. Even in recent times, the complexities of the Iraq War can be glossed over through kind actions such as food drops to Iraqis in need, thus using a historic action of American benevolence, a candy drop, to serve to justify the US presence as a benevolent force.

Moreover, commemorations of the Airlift have also highlighted the acceptance of Germans of the permanent presence of American troops since the end of World War II. After the end of the war, life in Berlin thus became a militarized everyday existence marked by the presence of Allied troops, which began as a punitive occupation force with the end of the war and evolved into a protective presence for West Berlin as the Cold War took shape. The fact that the Berlin Airlift took place within the context of the continued occupation of Germany is often forgotten. The presence of American military personnel in Berlin was not new, and borders between the zones had been relevant since the early days of the occupation, not just since the Blockade beginning in 1948. Narratives of the Airlift tend to focus on the context in the air and at Tempelhof, where heartwarming encounters often occurred, such as exchanges of gifts from German children to the Airlift pilots. However, the context in Berlin in 1948 and 1949 was in fact more ambivalent than the triumphant narratives proclaim, with the presence of Western Allied troops in the city, including American troops, not just symbolizing positive protective notions such as freedom but also potentially chaos or danger. Memory narratives about the Airlift tend to minimize the context of the occupation, focusing on the healing embrace of former enemies, tending to avoid any discussion of challenges beyond Airlift logistical issues and the tragic crashes that led to losses of life.

Gail Halvorsen has remained central to collective memory practices over the decades, attending multiple commemoration events. Moreover, he also returned

120 Goldstein, "Gail Halvorsen, 'Candy Bomber' in Berlin Airlift, Dies at 101," *The New York Times*, February 17, 2022.

121 Halvorsen, *The Berlin Candy Bomber*, 244.

to Berlin in the early 1970s for official duties, spurring further commemoration and discourses about the Airlift and candy bombing, and he also had more encounters with the children of 1948 and 1949 as adults. In 1970, Gail Halvorsen was assigned as Commander of Tempelhof, and he returned to Berlin for a few years, with his wife and children in tow. Although Berlin remained a special place to him, he was not totally enthusiastic about uprooting his family, selling his new house, and moving to Germany. He also had to ensure that the bar was removed from the Tempelhof Commander's house: due to his religious beliefs as a Mormon, Halvorsen did not drink alcohol, preferring beverages such as orange juice.[122] According to Halvorsen in his memoir, during Open House celebrations at Tempelhof while Commander, some of the German visitors would come up to him "with tears in their eyes" and would recount to him "how much the flour, coal, and medicine meant to them during the airlift times." He wrote that the level of gratitude in the early 1970s was the same as those of the first Germans he met at Tempelhof in 1948.[123] In 1971, Halvorsen also had a C-54 plane, an "airlift veteran" just like him, transported to Tempelhof as a memorial, which the people of Berlin named the "*Rosinenbomber*."[124]

During Halvorsen's time as Commander at Tempelhof in the early 1970s, he received multiple dinner invitations from a woman who was a child during the Airlift. Eventually, he accepted the request and met Mercedes Wild, her husband Peter Wild, and their children in September 1972, bringing his own two youngest sons to the dinner based on the invitation's request: the Wilds also had two boys the same age.[125] Mercedes Wild was seven years old during the Airlift and was one of the letter writers who had decided to reach Halvorsen directly in order to try another way of getting a candy parachute. Wild had tried to catch a parachute at Tempelhof, but a larger boy had grabbed the parachute before she could. In the fall of 1948, she had written to Halvorsen describing her situation at home in her garden, where she had white chickens that were no longer laying eggs, probably due to their fear of the noise from the Airlift planes. She requested that Halvorsen drop some candy parachutes at her house, writing, "When you fly over the garden and see the white chickens, please drop some candy there and all will

122 On the Halvorsen family's move to Berlin and his preference for orange juice, see Halvorsen, 168, 172–181.
123 Halvorsen, 182.
124 Halvorsen, 182–183.
125 Halvorsen, 186.

be ok. I don't care if you scare them. Your little friend, Mercedes."[126] Unfortunately Halvorsen did not have time to fly around searching for the chickens, so instead he sent her a letter and a package of sweets in the mail. At the dinner in 1972, Mercedes Wild showed Halvorsen the original letter she had received from him on November 4, 1948, signed "*Dein Schokoladenonkel*" (Your Chocolate Uncle). She treasured the letter and kept it in her china cabinet. In the letter, Halvorsen had written, "I didn't know that in Hahnelstrasse there lived such a nice little girl. If I could fly a few rounds over Friedenau, I surely would find the garden with the white chickens but for this there is not enough time. I hope that through what is with this letter I give you a little joy."[127] During his visit in 1972, Halvorsen added a new message to the original letter. Wild also showed Halvorsen where the white chickens had been in the yard. The two became friends, and every time Halvorsen visited her, he added more messages to the original letter. Halvorsen and his family continued to visit the Wilds over the years, and even "slept in the bedroom from which Mercedes wrote that 1948 letter," wrote Halvorsen in his memoir. In addition, Mercedes' husband Peter Wild was a teacher. During a visit to Halvorsen in Provo, Utah, he met with a local high school German teacher, Brent Chambers, and together they created "a new airlift, an airbridge of understanding from West Berlin to Provo, Utah," which was an exchange program between high school students in Utah and Berlin. Halvorsen's official assignment as Tempelhof Commander in Berlin came to an end in February 1974, and as he wrote in his memoir, the assignment in Berlin, "rather than being one to dread, was one of the most moving human experiences that we could have imagined," especially due to his personal experiences of friendship with Germans such as the Wilds.[128]

Mercedes Wild and Gail Halvorsen both appeared together at Airlift anniversary events throughout the decades, including in 2019, and Wild's story is featured alongside Halvorsen's in his memoir.[129] Halvorsen and Wild's friendship portrays how the Airlift and candy bombing linked the lives of the American Airlift participants and its German recipients, as well as the depths that such friendships could reach. The Airlift thus forged a strong connection between Germans and Americans, with both Airlift veterans and the German recipients of their be-

126 Margot Theis Raven, *Mercedes and the Chocolate Pilot: A True Story of the Berlin Airlift and the Candy that Dropped from the Sky* (Sleeping Bear Press, 2002); Tunnell, *Candy Bomber*, 56; Halvorsen, 117.

127 English translation and original German letter in Halvorsen, 186–187.

128 Halvorsen, 188–189.

129 See Halvorsen, *The Berlin Candy Bomber*. See also Interview with Gail S. Halvorsen, "Kinderwünsche," Zeitzeugen Portal. Halvorsen states that he seen Mercedes at least 35 times since 1972.

nevolence usually never forgetting that connection. On a wider geopolitical scale, the Airlift ensured a long-term bond, with the United States guaranteeing West Berlin and West Germany that they would stand by as protectors, friends, and allies in the Cold War. The Airlift thus provided a powerful narrative of a (West) Berlin that had transformed from the capital of the Third Reich into a bulwark of freedom and a symbol of the free world's fight against anti-communism.[130] The Airlift events also served to humanize Germans to Americans. As Susan Carruthers notes, "As plucky underdogs in this confrontation between unarmed democrats and armed dictators, Berliners appeared thoroughly deserving of Americans' sympathy and support."[131] Thus, the Airlift remains a useful memory to turn to in order to prove (West) Germany's embrace of democratic values in the postwar era despite the fact that the Nazi past lay just a few years back.

Gail Halvorsen embodied the Allied soldier who was able to move past the history of World War II to embrace Germans as people in need of assistance to save their freedom, especially that of the youngest of the Germans. The attention to Halvorsen's actions and his personal decision to aid young Berliners played a fundamental role in the molding of shifting Cold War dynamics and also ensured American support for intervention on behalf of Germans and their fight for freedom. Halvorsen and the Berlin children of the Airlift thus shaped the history of the Cold War, furthering developments that were already occurring during the occupation, including GIs' encounters with German children and their strong desire to assist them, which impacted American views of Germans. A whole infrastructure of American aid for Germany developed especially due to American benevolence toward German children. Halvorsen's initiatives cemented the benevolent nature of the encounter between US military personnel and German children. The candy bombing combined the American desire to help young Germans with wider geopolitical Cold War aims, allowing for the American embrace of West Germans as friends to be helped and protected to ensure that their freedom was preserved.

---

130 See Geppert, "Symbolische Politik," in *Die Berliner Luftbrücke*, ed. Trotnow and von Kostka, 137. See also Jason Johnson, "There is No Closing Time: Tourism to Cold War Berlin," in *The Berlin Airlift and the Making of the Cold War*, ed. Schuessler, Seipp, and Sullivan, 190. Berlin continues to see itself and even market itself to tourists as "The City of Freedom."
131 Carruthers, *The Good Occupation*, 309.

Tell the Children: Narratives of the Airlift in Juvenile Literature

American narratives of the candy bombing have also been written for young audiences, providing young readers with a human-centric story that can simultaneously teach the history of the Cold War, illustrate American values, and provide emotional interest in the stories of a foreign population. In 2002, the children's book *Mercedes and the Chocolate Pilot* was published. The illustrated non-fiction book depicts the story of Mercedes Wild of Berlin. The book begins with a historical note about the Berlin Airlift, noting that despite the human cost of the operation of 31 Americans, 39 British, and nine Germans losing their lives in Airlift-related accidents, "In Berlin today, the memory of the beautiful 'bridge' is cherished by the people who love their freedom, and remember the brave pilots and the countries who did not forsake them in their time of need." The story starts with Mercedes checking for eggs from her chickens who had stopped laying them as frequently since the Airlift began. That day, they had only produced one small egg. Meanwhile, in the sky above Mercedes the "silver-winged planes flew above like guardian angels." As Mercedes walks back "up the bomb-splintered steps to her apartment," the story explains that even though her chickens were no longer laying eggs, "Mercedes would never complain about the great soaring grocery stores that everyone called *Raisinbombers*," since they bring tasty raisins as well as "flour and clothing and coal too." The story also features Mercedes' mother and her struggles. For example, the book mentions that Mercedes knew her mother cried at night, because Mercedes' father had not returned from the war. In addition, her mother's dresses still smelled of smoke "from the time when the bombs had fallen during the war."[132] Thus, the book's narrative fits in the feminized and infantilized version of Germany that Petra Goedde argues became dominant in postwar occupation Germany: Germans were depicted as mostly suffering women and innocent children, trying to make the most of their desperate circumstances, which helped shift views of Germans from enemies to friends.[133] The postwar occupation era ensured a major, long-lasting shift toward focusing on garnering sympathy for Germans. Narratives such as *Mercedes and the Chocolate Pilot* could serve to further this mindset among young American readers in the twenty-first century, who would be able to empathize with Mercedes and her mother in dealing with the challenging circumstances of the Blockade. The occupation development in viewing Germans as friends to be helped was a founda-

132 Raven, *Mercedes and the Chocolate Pilot.*
133 Goedde, *GIs and Germans*, xxii–xxiii, 126, 164.

tional shift, one that has lasted until the present day and is furthered through books such as children's literature about the Airlift.

In the book's narrative, Mercedes learns about Gail Halvorsen one day when her mother reads a newspaper article to her about Halvorsen's candy bombings. After hearing about the Chocolate Pilot, Mercedes asks her mother if she could go to Tempelhof to catch some candy, and her mother allows her to go as long as she accompanies her. Her mother tells Mercedes, "The streets are too dangerous with soldiers and rubble everywhere." Interestingly, this hints at the fact that Berliners were living in a highly militarized atmosphere, with occupation soldiers all over Berlin, including American soldiers. Mercedes' mother's fear implies that GIs on the ground were not always seen as behaving in a positive light in the way that the Airlift pilots were. The American presence in Berlin was therefore not an unequivocally benevolent and celebrated circumstance as narratives surrounding the Airlift seem to imply.

Unfortunately, while at Tempelhof, a "large boy" catches the parachute closest to Mercedes: "And oh, the look in his eyes as he bit into the silky, smooth chocolate! It was all Mercedes could think about the whole sad way home . . . If only she had caught the chocolate it wouldn't matter if the chickens laid eggs. The candy would make her and Mama so happy! But what should she do?" The story mentions that "Mercedes remembered from the newspaper that children wrote letters to the Chocolate Pilot," so she decides to write one too, requesting a candy drop when he sees the chickens. The story notes Mercedes' dream of receiving a candy parachute after mailing her letter to Halvorsen: "Mercedes now waited in the garden with the white chickens every day, wishing on each angel-plane above, for her candy to fall from the sky." The story also mentions Peter Zimmerman and his failure to catch candy, since apparently "his legs were too short to run fast for the candy." Instead, he sent his letters and maps requesting a drop at his house. The story notes that Halvorsen received hundreds of such letters "with crayon-colored drawings," which were translated by his two German secretaries. Some he even replied to personally. According to the story, "But all the letters touched his heart—some even made Lt. Halvorsen laugh 'til he cried." While reading Mercedes' letter, Halvorsen "laughed and fought back a tear . . . His little friend's sweet hope was as fragile as the eggs and as precious to him as the white chickens were to her." Instead of attempting a candy drop, the story notes how Halvorsen mailed Mercedes a package from Tempelhof. Mercedes opened the package with delight as the "sweet smell of candy" spread through the room. The package had "chocolate bars! Packs of white and green mint gum! Pink bubble gum too! And Life Saver rolls, colored like the rainbow! Her Chocolate Pilot had found her at last!" Her mother was also "blinking back happy tears," and Mercedes gave her a chocolate bar, showing her own kindness and generosity, as well as her concern for her mother's suffering. In the story, Mercedes reads the letter from Halvorsen, which is the one she showed him in 1972 when he visited. The story notes, "The memory of this day would stay with her for the rest of her life." This appears to be true in real life, since Mercedes Wild has continued to play a central role in Airlift commemoration practices alongside Halvorsen.

The book ends with the story of Halvorsen's return as Tempelhof Commander in 1970 and his visit to Mercedes "at an old apartment building near Tempelhof Air Field." Mercedes brought Halvorsen's 1948 letter from her china cabinet. As "her eyes welled with tears of love and gratitude," she told Halvorsen that back in 1948 she "ate the candy little by little," but that she "will keep the letter forever." According to the story, as she "tried to tell him how much his gift had meant to her," Halvorsen's "eyes misted over. Oh yes, he knew! But how could he tell Mercedes the joy that had come to him from two sticks of gum? He'd seen a World War go by, and a Cold War begin, but he'd always found in the children's eyes the hope for a better tomorrow." Instead of trying to explain further about what he felt, Halvorsen wrote a new message on the original letter, wishing Mercedes "many sweet things to come!" The letter is "still Mercedes' most precious possession," and, according to the story, is now kept in a bank vault, only to be brought out during a visit by her "beloved Chocolate Pilot." The story concludes, "Every day when Mercedes walks under the skies of a free Berlin, the sweet memory of his gift stills soars in her heart like the great silver planes of hope." The end of the book includes a note about Gail Halvorsen's accomplishments in dropping over 20 tons of candy to Berlin's 100,000 children, and how the citizens of Chicopee, Massachusetts aided in the cause. In addition, it mentions Halvorsen's continued candy activities: he conducted candy bombings to the children and grandchildren of the original Berliners who were at the fence, and "he has flown candy to refugee camps in Bosnia in 1994 and in 1999 to Camp Hope, the U.S.-built shelter for Albanians fleeing from Kosovo," in addition to making candy drops to his own 24 grandchildren and also for the four children of Mercedes and her husband Peter.[134] The dust jacket of the book includes a statement from Halvorsen, who states that he "was a simple pilot" during the Airlift, and it was enough to him that people needed help, without knowing "the full significance of what was being played out in the skies over East Germany." Halvorsen notes, "I learned that hope is the essential ingredient for a child to recover from tragedy, whether it is in Berlin, Camp Hope in Albania, or in homes across the United States." In addition, Halvorsen mentions his encounter with a Berliner in 1998, who told him, "It wasn't the chocolate you gave us that was important, it was what it meant, that someone in America cared, that someday

134 All quotations from Raven, *Mercedes and the Chocolate Pilot*.

things would be alright. Without hope, the soul dies."[135] Thus, Halvorsen wishes that the story can serve as "inspiration" in "every child's and every person's search for his [sic] own source of hope."[136]

Overall, the story of *Mercedes and the Chocolate Pilot* provides young readers with a heartwarming historical account of the candy bombing and the encounter between Halvorsen and Mercedes. The two were connected over the decades not only through the original candy delivery and the letter exchange but also through the wider act of gifting itself. Mercedes received a candy package and a letter, giving her hope, and Gail Halvorsen has stated that he also received joy originating from his gift of the two sticks of gum to the group of children at Tempelhof.[137] The "silent gratitude" and good behavior of the original 30 children at the fence is what spurred Halvorsen to take action and drop candy, reaching thousands of children, and changing his own life as well.[138] In his memoir, Halvorsen writes in the Epilogue, "Gratitude, integrity, and service to the unfortunate provide more rewards than all things material. They are the foundation upon which hope is born. They provide the strength by which hope endures."[139] The children's book *Mercedes and the Chocolate Pilot* highlights the deep emotional bond that had been created between the young Berliner witnesses of history and Halvorsen, as well as the gratitude garnered among Germans such as Mercedes and her mother due to the efforts of the candy bombing. The story is all the more heartwarming due to the fact that it is a true story. It gives today's children a glimpse into the historical moment of the Airlift as a triumph for Cold War-era American values such as the protection of freedom in foreign lands, a narrative that has remained relevant even after the end of the Cold War. In addition, the story humanizes the encounter between Germans and Americans in the aftermath of World War II.

Besides *Mercedes and the Chocolate Pilot*, other juvenile literature has been published about Gail Halvorsen and the candy bombing, including a Christmas book, *Christmas from Heaven*, made in collaboration with the Mormon Tabernacle choir and narrated by Tom Brokaw, the author of *The Greatest Generation*. The illustrated book, published in 2013, is based off the December 2012 performance of the Mormon Tabernacle Choir Christmas Concert, where Brokaw narrated the story and the Choir provided a musical accompaniment to Brokaw's narration. Hal-

135 Dust jacket of Raven, *Mercedes and the Chocolate Pilot*. Also in Halvorsen, *The Berlin Candy Bomber*, 244; Tunnell, *Candy Bomber*, 67.

136 Dust jacket of Raven, *Mercedes and the Chocolate Pilot*.

137 Tunnell, *Candy Bomber*, ix.

138 Halvorsen, *The Berlin Candy Bomber*, 243.

139 Halvorsen, 244.

vorsen also made a guest appearance during the live performance.[140] The Mormon Tabernacle Choir Christmas concert is popular among Americans and is aired around Christmastime on TV through the Public Broadcasting Service (PBS). Millions of viewers watch the concert yearly, and 80,000 attend live in Salt Lake City, Utah, according to the book.[141] *Christmas from Heaven* features a story of Halvorsen making an Airlift flight on Christmas Eve in 1948 and thinking back to the day six months before, when the candy bombing idea came to his mind as he met the 30 children behind the fence at Tempelhof: "Although the children had been on meager rations, they were more concerned with freedom than with flour. They wanted what Hal [Halvorsen] always had—the opportunity to pursue their dreams." According to the story, "Their gratitude melted Hal's heart," and the look on the children's faces as they passed the gum wrappers around were "such expressions of joy and wonder," more than he had ever seen before. Thus, the candy bombing began, and "day by day, the parachutes brought peace and the candy renewed hope. The children made friends of their former enemies, and their parents' hearts were softened. The wounds of war began to heal." The book features historical images of the Airlift as well as some of the actual letters German children sent to Halvorsen. The book notes that in December 1948, tons of candy came in from American candy companies and from private American donors, highlighting that "the spirit of Christmas was descending on people everywhere, lifting them up in the joy of giving." For Halvorsen on board an Airlift plane to Berlin on Christmas Eve, "The stars overhead could not be more beautiful than skies overflowing with parachutes, tumbling to earth in a brilliant display of Christmas generosity and joy." The story thus connects Halvorsen's giving to the "real spirit of Christmas." The story concludes, "In that moment Hal Halvorsen prayed for the courage to never give anything less." The book includes a historical note about the Candy Bomber and a craft guide to making a homemade candy parachute, as well as information about the "wonders" of the annual Christmas concert of the Mormon Tabernacle Choir and an image of the 2012 concert featuring Halvorsen.[142] The book thus connects the importance of giving and generosity, the central role of children in the Airlift, Halvorsen's candy bombing, and the Christmas season. As Stefanie Eisenhuth notes, the appearance of Gail Halvorsen during the live performance portrayed him as

---

140 David T. Warner, *Christmas from Heaven* (Shadow Mountain, 2013). Also, David Burger, "Alfie Boe and Tom Brokaw bring star power to Mormon Tabernacle Choir concert," *The Salt Lake Tribune*, December 7, 2012.
141 Warner, *Christmas from Heaven.*
142 Warner, *Christmas from Heaven.*

the embodiment of "the spirit of Christmas," complete with his Air Force uniform.[143] The audiences of the book and the live performance learned that Christmas was not just about receiving but giving. The 2012 live performance included children dressed up as 1948/49 Berliner children, ensuring another level of connection that ensured the audience would feel sympathy for the historic plight of the children of Berlin, who celebrated Christmas just like the viewers of the Christmas concert.

Overall, Soviets do not tend to feature in the narratives in these children's books about the candy bombing except as a silent foil to the Americans, with their goal of blockading Berlin contrasting with the generosity of Americans in Berlin. For example, the Soviets do not feature at all in the narrative of *Mercedes and the Chocolate Pilot*, except in the historical overview at the beginning of the book, which emphasizes Stalin's desire to obtain more territory for the Soviets and his role in the decision for the Blockade: "At first, all four Allies ruled Germany in friendship, but on the fateful day of June 24, 1948, Josef [sic] Stalin tried to take both East and West Berlin for himself so he could eventually put all of Germany, then all of Europe, under his communist government." According to the book, Stalin thus played the major role in blockading "the roads, railroads, and canal routes coming in and out of the city to cut off West Berliners from food, clothing, heat, and electricity." The book notes that the Airlift was a "rescue mission," and that one difficulty for the pilots was that "Russian planes harassed the exhausted fliers in the air corridors." In these narratives, Russians do not garner any sympathy for their behavior, and the focus of the book is on the heroic American pilot, Halvorsen. The end of the story indicates the victory of the Americans (and the Western Allies) and, thus, freedom.[144] *Christmas from Heaven* similarly focuses on Stalin's role in the Blockade, with the US and Britain responding with the Airlift "to preserve freedom and keep two and a half million West Berliners from starving." The historical note in the book states, "Following the end of World War II, Russia laid siege to Berlin, cutting off the flow of food and supplies into the city."[145] Narratives about the Berlin Airlift in children's literature tend to stay focused on the candy bombing story rather than examine the story of the entire Airlift, highlighting the heartwarming decision of Gail Halvorsen to drop candy as a result of him meeting the children at the fence. The candy bombing effort did indeed impact the entire Airlift and contributed to reconciliation among former enemies, but these narratives, although of course written for

143 Eisenhuth, *Die Schutzmacht*, 137.
144 Raven, *Mercedes and the Chocolate Pilot.*
145 Warner, *Christmas from Heaven.*

young readers, tend toward mythic narratives of American goodness, avoiding the complexities of an event that played a role in the challenging time of the division of Berlin and Germany. The candy bombing was just one aspect of the Airlift's efforts, but it proves the easiest part of the history to retell. This is understandable for children's literature aimed mostly at an American audience, but an intense focus on the goodness of Gail Halvorsen and the candy bombing furthers a black and white narrative and simplifies the history of the Airlift and the wider occupation context. In addition, the focus on the goodness and innocence of German children such as Mercedes further enhances the simplistic view of Germans as innocent victims under protection of a paternalist force, the Americans.

Michael O. Tunnell's juvenile non-fiction book *Candy Bomber: The Story of the Berlin Airlift's "Chocolate Pilot"*, published in 2010, provides a more detailed look into the candy bombing than the other two, shorter works aimed at younger children, but the emphasis in the book remains on the heroism of the Americans involved in the Airlift. Tunnell, who worked closely with Halvorsen and his personal collections, argues that "Gail and the other men of Operation Little Vittles [were] true American heroes—heroes as much for their compassion as their bravery and moral strength."[146] The book also focuses on the role of the Berliner children in seeming to choose freedom over the Soviets' offers of food. Gail Halvorsen writes in the Prologue,

> This book is special to me because it tells about the people of Berlin who valued freedom over food. The Russians promised them food if they agreed to live under Soviet rule, but they refused. They wanted to be free, even if that meant going hungry. Children felt this way, too. "I can live on thin rations but not without hope," one ten-year-old boy told me.[147]

Tunnell includes the fact that, to Halvorsen, the children at the Tempelhof fence were the ones responsible for spurring his decision to drop candy, giving him a lesson in freedom.[148] Helping them brought him joy and fulfilment from serving others, even those who were former enemies.[149] Enemies thus became friends, aided by the good behavior and yearning for freedom of the Berliner children at the fence at Tempelhof, in addition to kind, benevolent acts of American military personnel such as Halvorsen. Tunnell does include discussion of communism but in a way that enhances the black and white nature of the story. He mentions the story of a girl at the Tempelhof fence who was about 12 years old and had "wistful blue eyes." She was one of the English speakers in the group who translated for

146 Tunnell, *Candy Bomber*, 104.
147 Tunnell, vii–viii.
148 Tunnell, 21.
149 Tunnell, ix.

the others. This girl spoke about the wartime bombings, and mentioned that the "Communist system" was even worse.[150]

In his book, Tunnell highlights the denial of "civil liberties" in East Berlin, thus making the stakes of the situation clear to his young readers and highlighting the importance of freedom and democracy.[151] Although it cannot be certain whether the children at the Tempelhof fence specifically talked to Halvorsen about the role of communism, the encounter that was depicted fit directly with the Cold War fight over hearts and minds, which Gail Halvorsen profoundly impacted during the Airlift. In addition, more recent narratives such as Tunnell's book make clear that the Berliner children played a central role in this struggle as well, and they were the ones who became enamored by the Airlift pilots, marking the pilots as heroes. However, the 30 children at the fence who figure in various narratives of the Airlift, including Halvorsen's memoir and Tunnell's juvenile non-fiction book, serve more as symbols for the wider values of the Airlift struggle: They tend to be portrayed as saying what they are supposed to say in a way that fits Cold War narratives of good versus evil, representing the innocence of Berliners in contrast to the cruelty of the Soviets. Innocent Berliner children chose the Americans; they chose democracy and freedom. It cannot be denied that children played an active, major role in the shaping of the Airlift by impacting Gail Halvorsen so much that he decided to create candy parachutes, but it is limiting to depict the children in ways that enhance simplistic narratives of American heroism versus Soviet cruelty, and to depict them without a critical analysis for young audiences today. Moreover, the inclusion of children's real experiences and voices is of central importance to crafting narratives about the past, enabling a closer look at lived realities rather than focusing on the role that children played in adult developments.

In addition, the focus of recent narratives about the Candy Bomber often center around the story of reconciliation between Germans and Americans, with the contact between a kind, even "boyish" 27-year-old Airlift pilot and innocent and well-behaved Berlin children providing a good story of understanding between the two former enemy nations.[152] Michael O. Tunnell argues that the memory of the candy bombing remains a staple part of German memory: "Although many years have passed since the Berlin Airlift—and even since Uncle Wiggly Wings finally met the little girl with the frightened chickens [Mercedes]—the memory of candy parachutes hasn't faded from German memory." For example, Gail Hal-

150 Tunnell 19. Also, Halvorsen, *The Berlin Candy Bomber*, 93.
151 Tunnell, 18.
152 Warner, *Christmas from Heaven.*

vorsen, Tunnell notes, was called to serve at the request of the Germans to lead the German Olympics Team into the stadium in Salt Lake City, Utah at the 2002 Olympics.[153] These narratives accurately depict the central role of Gail Halvorsen in contributing to long-term positive relations between the United States and Germany, in addition to the important role that the Airlift continues to play in German memory culture. Special events and ceremonies have kept the memory alive, including the Tempelhof Open Houses, memorials, and Airlift anniversary events up to the present day. For Halvorsen's one hundredth birthday, German President Frank-Walter Steinmeier sent a message to Halvorsen stating that he had "built a bridge of humanity and compassion between Americans and Berliners."[154] On February 16, 2022, Gail Halvorsen passed away at the age of 101. Overall, Halvorsen did indeed leave behind a remarkable legacy, one "of kindness and compassion that stands as a true testament to humanitarianism, even in times of conflict and uncertainty," in the words of an obituary of Gail Halvorsen, written by The National WWII Museum in New Orleans.[155] His legacy and that of the children who were there with him in 1948 and 1949 deserve to be examined with honesty and in the context of the complexities of the time of the postwar era and the multifarious range of encounters that occurred.

We Remember Together: Contemporary Commemoration of the Berlin Airlift

Commemoration of the Berlin Airlift has thus remained a decades-long transatlantic practice, attracting figures including American presidents, military personnel, German politicians, and the remaining Airlift veterans. Even after the fall of the Berlin Wall and the collapse of the Soviet Union, remembrance of the Berlin Airlift has maintained its relevance. Moreover, memorialization practices have taken place beyond the sphere of Tempelhof Airport and (West) Berlin. Airlift events continue to attract large audiences in a reunified Germany, both in Berlin and in former West Germany, and the memory of the Airlift has become nation-

153 Tunnell, *Candy Bomber*, 83.

154 Goldstein, "Gail Halvorsen, 'Candy Bomber' in Berlin Airlift, Dies at 101," *New York Times*, February 17, 2022.

155 "In Memoriam: Colonel Gail S. Halvorsen, USAF (Ret.) (1920–2022)," The National WWII Museum, accessed June 10, 2023, https://www.nationalww2museum.org/about-us/notes-museum/memoriam-colonel-gail-s-halvorsen-usaf-ret-1920-2022.

ally relevant.[156] Five-year and ten-year anniversaries of the Airlift have taken place since 1959. Moreover, in 1994, half a million people attended commemoration events at the Olympic Stadium in Berlin, which also served as a goodbye party for the Western Allies, who were leaving the city after a 45-year presence.[157] In 1998, Chancellor Helmut Kohl, President Bill Clinton, and Gail Halvorsen were present at the anniversary events. The Allied Museum in Berlin also opened shortly thereafter on Clayallee (named after Lucius Clay), with former President George H.W. Bush participating in the opening ceremony.[158] In former West Germany, celebrations of the anniversary of the Airlift have been large events, especially since the sixtieth anniversary in 2008, when an anniversary event took place in Wiesbaden, indicating the continuing relevance of narratives of solidarity and freedom, which the Airlift memory culture depicts. The seventy-fifth anniversary included an open-air exhibition entitled "Blocked Victors—Divided Berlin: 75 Years of the Airlift" in front of the former departure hall at Tempelhof. The exhibition ran from June 28, 2023 until May 12, 2024, and it was developed in collaboration between the Allied Museum, the Museum Berlin-Karlshorst, and the Bundeswehr Military History Museum Airfield Berlin-Gatow. The information at the exhibition was provided in English, French, German, and Russian, in addition to a handout available in Ukrainian.[159] Moreover, there is a website dedicated to the seventy-fifth anniversary, which provides information about the Airlift and its relevance today. The website was created as a collaborative project between the Allied Museum, the Bundeswehr Military History Museum Airfield Berlin-Gatow, the National Museum of the United States Air Force, and the Royal Air Force Museum.[160] Memorialization and commemoration of the Berlin Airlift has thus continued on even during shifting spheres of global geopolitical contexts. In addition, Germans often display a fascination and even a nostalgia for the technological aspects of the Airlift, with historic displays of the Airlift planes such as C-

---

156 On the Berlin Airlift as a national memory since the end of the Cold War, see Torben Giese, ". . . der Erinnerung an jene große Zeit ist in diesem Tagen kein Ende," in *Die Berliner Luftbrücke*, ed. Defrance, Greiner, and Pfeil, 137–139.

157 See Geppert, "Symbolische Politik," in *Die Berliner Luftbrücke*, ed. Trotnow and von Kostka, 145.

158 Geppert, 145.

159 "Blocked Victors-Divided Berlin: 75 Years of the Airlift," Berlin.de: The Official Website of Berlin, September 4, 2023, https://www.berlin.de/en/exhibitions/8122028-5202331-blocked-victors-divided-berlin-airlift.en.html.

160 Ewan Burnet, Bernd von Kostka, Witali Gerber, William McLaughlin, eds., "Berlin Airlift Remembered: People, Places and Objects 75 Years On," Royal Air Force Museum, Allied Museum, Bundeswehr Military History Museum Airfield Berlin-Gatow, National Museum of the United States Air Force, accessed September 15, 2023, https://www.berlinairlift75.org/en/.

54s drawing crowds who come to look at the machines known as *Rosinenbomber*.[161]

Tempelhof has remained a central site for commemoration of the Berlin Airlift. Since the airport closed in 2008, Berliners have debated about what to do with this site that serves as a symbol of freedom. The former runway space opened as a public park in 2010. Plans to develop the site in 2014 into housing and retail development were voted down. Berliners have also argued that the site should include information about its history during National Socialism, including as the site of an early Nazi concentration camp and as housing for forced laborers during the war.[162] The Allied Museum, which examines the history of the Western Allies in Berlin, will also be moving to Tempelhof Hangar Seven within the next ten years. The move highlights the power of the symbolism of the Airlift and the multi-layered meanings behind Tempelhof, which evolved from a space constructed by the Nazis to "a symbolic site of freedom and a space for creativity, encounter and cooperation," according to the Allied Museum website.[163] The history of the Berlin Airlift thus retains a central relevance in twenty-first century public historical spaces. In the future, Tempelhof will surely remain a central location in commemoration of the Airlift through special events and the permanent presence of the Allied Museum, enabling continuing discourse around the values of freedom and democracy and the role of the Western Allies (especially Americans) in guaranteeing that these values persisted in 1948 and 1949.

The seventieth anniversary of the Berlin Airlift in 2019 bridged German memory culture and German-American friendship, with the focus of memorialization especially concentrating on American efforts during the Airlift. The June 10, 2019 anniversary event in Wiesbaden took place at the Lucius D. Clay Kaserne, the US Army Garrison Wiesbaden, which is still currently a US military base, adding another dimension to the events.[164] The US military presence in Germany has be-

161 On American military technology on display at the Tempelhof Open Houses, see Heisig, "Der 'Tag der offenen Tür' auf dem amerikanischen Luftwaffenstützpunkt Tempelhof," in *Die Berliner Luftbrücke*, ed. Defrance, Greiner, and Pfeil, 205–217. In 1967 and 1972, there were protests against the Vietnam War during the Open Houses (214–216).

162 See Steege, "Looking for German Resistance," *The Berlin Airlift and the Making of the Cold War*, ed. Schuessler, Seipp, and Sullivan, 185. See the latest development plans for Tempelhof at "Flughafen Tempelhof: Tempelhof Airport," Tempelhof Projekt, accessed September 26, 2024, https://www.thf-berlin.de/en/.

163 "A Twenty-First Century Museum: The Allied Museum at Tempelhof Airport," Allied Museum/Alliierten Museum, accessed September 15, 2023, https://www.alliiertenmuseum.de/en/museum/refounding-the-museum-in-tempelhof/.

164 On the Wiesbaden 2019 commemoration, see Kane Farabaugh, "'Candy Bomber' Honored in Germany 70 Years After Historic Berlin Airlift," *Voice of America*, June 22, 2019, https://www.voa

come an accepted fact in Germany over the decades since 1945 until today. The event in Wiesbaden attracted around 33,000 visitors, and portrayed the continuing strength and relevance of German memory narratives of the *Rosinenbomber* and the notion of American military humanitarianism toward Germans in the immediate postwar era.[165] The celebration was a mix of official speeches from American and German officials, technological nostalgia with the presence of historic World War II-era planes, American military culture including paratrooper demonstrations, exhibits with historic Airlift images, family fun, entertainment, and food. There was even a Bob Hope show reenactment with swing and jazz music. Some of the historic planes had also recently been used in the seventy-fifth anniversary D-Day events atg Normandy, where they flew before heading to Germany for the Airlift events. Interestingly, some of the planes on display at the event in Wiesbaden were Douglas C-47s, which not only played a role in the Airlift but also carried paratroopers into battle during World War II. During the Airlift, their usage was phased out by the larger Douglas C-54.[166] This means that the German visitors to the Airlift commemoration were able to tour the planes that had once been used in combat situations against Germans during the war. Also present at the Wiesbaden event was Gail Halvorsen, still sprightly at age 98 and wearing his uniform and his German Order of Merit, in addition to relatives of Lucius Clay, Mercedes Wild, and other Berliners who were children at the time of the Airlift. Vera Mitschrich, who was five years old when the Airlift began, was in attendance and noted her gratitude toward the pilots. She thanked Halvorsen, stating, "I'm so proud of you. You gave us hope. You gave us food. I never, never will forget you."[167] American military personnel and their families were also present, creating a space that allowed for moments of German-American interactions.

The moment everyone was waiting for was the candy drop and flight program, which Halvorsen took part in (see Figure 5.1). Multiple planes flew over the base's field as the crowd waited in anticipation. The drop was a sensory and emotive experience, with the noise of the historic plane engines creating excitement

---

news.com/a/candy-bomber-honored-in-germany-70-years-after-historic-berlin-airlift/4969527.html; Ryan, "Americans, Germans memorialize airlift personnel 70 years later," *U.S. Army News*.

165 Jennifer H. Svan, "'Candy bomber' joins tens of thousands on base for 70th anniversary of Berlin Airlift's end," *Stars and Stripes*, June 10, 2019, https://www.stripes.com/theaters/europe/2019-06-10/'candy-bomber'-joins-tens-of-thousands-on-base-for-70th-anniversary-of-berlin-airlift%E2%80%99s-end-1483040.html.

166 See Bob van der Linden, "Supplying a City by Air: The Berlin Airlift," Smithsonian National Air and Space Museum, September 14, 2018, https://airandspace.si.edu/stories/editorial/supplying-city-air-berlin-airlift.

167 Svan, "'Candy bomber' joins tens of thousands on base for 70th anniversary of Berlin Airlift's end," *Stars and Stripes*.

Figure 5.1: A *Rosinenbomber* in action dropping candy, Wiesbaden, June 10, 2019 (photo by author).

in the audience below. The audience was lined up in a straight line by the field, and when the parachutes began to drop, there were cries of joy among the crowd, and the children sprinted to get their loot, which were parachutes with Jelly Belly jelly beans attached. In an unintentional parallel to the postwar period, after the candy drop, some children ended up losing track of their parents and guardians, and announcements were made over the loudspeaker for missing children to come to a certain location where their parents or guardians were waiting for them. This moment brought back the reality of present-day childhood in comparison to that of childhood in Berlin during the Airlift: In the aftermath of World War II, many children had lost at least one parent and often played unsupervised in the ruins of Berlin. For example, the crowd of the 30 original children at Tempelhof who had spurred Gail Halvorsen's decision to make candy drops were without supervision, watching the planes taking off and landing.

In the end, the candy bombing reenactment provided a glimpse of the fact that the action of one man could change history, spur widespread joy, and make children's dreams come true. Halvorsen's benevolent act continues to be reenacted even decades after the original event, highlighting its wide-ranging impact. Halvorsen's act had also fit perfectly with American Cold War goals, helping serve as Cold War propaganda that aimed at winning over hearts and minds, but its effect on individual children also deserves to play an important role in the history of the time. Without a doubt, despite Gail Halvorsen's passing on in February 2022, the memory of his benevolent feat will live on and continue to be reenacted. It was a singular action that was spurred by an encounter with German children, and it deserves to be looked at with clarity and in the context of the wider developments of the Airlift in ways that move beyond simplistic narratives of good and evil. To do so will ensure that the complex lived experiences and ambivalent navigations of the conquered and the conquerors in the aftermath of a terrible war are examined with honesty, unclouded by sentiments of the righteousness of one's cause or by mythological narratives. Instead, the human side of history needs to be highlighted, including the roles of children. Their lives were shaped by history yet they also shaped history, such as the history of the Berlin Airlift. The Berlin Airlift cemented developments already in place during the occupation that increasingly saw Germans as friends to be protected and aided, with German children often emerging at the forefront of these developments. This impacted young Germans' lives growing up in the shadow of war, and they themselves continued on, trying to make the most of the historical moment they grew up in, a complex and often ambivalent moment that could include Christmas parties with soldiers of the former enemy, memories of bombings, a missing parent, and candy raining down from the sky. Once they became adults, some of them could never let those memories fade. The former children of the Berlin Airlift seem to have been especially impacted by their early years, with some of these witnesses attending commemorations even decades on, highlighting the lifelong impacts of the historical events, especially regarding the actions of the Candy Bomber. Their childhood dreams about candy raining down from the sky never did fade.

Conclusion

On April 13, 1945 in Darmstadt, Lieutenant Melvin J. Lasky lamented in his diary about the state of German society: “How could there be a new Germany when the tragedy of the old was not fully deeply understood?”[1] Young Germans, who had grown up only knowing life under Nazism, had been “subjected willingly or unwillingly to a ten-year intellectual blackout, to the depreciation of moral values, to the substitution of Nazism for religion, and to the master race concept,” as Dr. Alonzo G. Grace, OMGUS Director of the Education and Cultural Relations Division, wrote in the US military government magazine the *Information Bulletin* in July 1949, concluding his article arguing that the “ultimate test” of the US occupation’s effort to help “German youth to help themselves,” was simple:

> Will [German] youth develop the character, the moral-spiritual power to resist the nationalistic trend? Will youth fall for anything? I believe that the youth of the world will help the youth of Germany to create a world of law and order, humanity, social justice, and peace. I believe that a large number of German youth, in spite of the Hitler era, are ready, willing and eager to do their part, but the change will not be accomplished overnight.[2]

German youth had emerged as important actors for the future of Germany, and American occupation efforts were continuously designed to help youth shift away from the “tragedy of the old” (as Lasky termed it) toward the promise of the new, a world of peace, justice, and respect. Even as OMGUS approached its end, turning over controls to the State Department through HICOG in September 1949, young Germans remained central figures for American efforts in Germany. The young generation thus had been given the mantle of Germany’s future freedom, and even youth throughout the world had a role to play in ensuring this hope for a peaceful Germany would become the truth, as Dr. Grace had noted.

Young Germans had thus emerged as central figures in American occupation policies, as they had the power to determine the course of the coming future of Germany. Official occupation navigations regarding young Germans were continuously in flux and dynamic, with American policies evolving from the early days

1 Lerg, ed., *The Diary of Lt. Melvin J. Lasky*, 153.
2 Alonzo G. Grace, “The Coming Generations,” in OMGUS, *Information Bulletin*, no. 166, July 26, 1949, 3–4, Germany under Reconstruction, University of Wisconsin-Madison Libraries, https://digital.library.wisc.edu/1711.dl/2RFLRGJCPAAQP83. Before arriving in Germany in 1948, Dr. Grace was the Connecticut State Education Commissioner. After his return to the United States, he served in various posts in the department of education at University of Chicago, New York University, and University of Illinois. See obituary, “Alonzo G. Grace, an Educator, 76,” *New York Times*, October 23, 1971.

https://doi.org/10.1515/9783111588155-007

of fear and punishment of all Germans, including radicalized youngsters, due to their taint of Nazism; to on-the-ground, individual encounters aimed at assisting young Germans, from Sergeant Wilson Ballard's early youth clubs in the Bremen Enclave in summer of 1945 to the official embrace in 1946 of occupation programs aimed at reeducating youth from Hitler Youths into democrats, including German Youth Activities; to the provision of protection and aid which culminated in the actions of the Berlin Airlift, where the Candy Bomber ensured a central role for German children in the transatlantic geopolitical sphere. Above all, however, young Germans were central actors in these occupation navigations, because they were not simply silent recipients of the shifting American policies. Their experiences fundamentally shaped and molded the fabric of the US occupation of Germany as young Germans navigated the transition from the old toward the visions of a new, democratic Germany. The personal encounter between young Germans and American military personnel undoubtedly forged the sphere of the occupation of Germany from the very first moments of contact beginning in September of 1944 as the war continued to rage on. Encounters between Americans and young Germans moved to the forefront of occupation developments, especially as Germany became increasingly seen as a land in need of rehabilitation, and as a place where German-American friendship became essential within the heightening Cold War atmosphere. Young Germans could thus ensure the future strength of German democracy and freedom.

The shifting realms of occupation policies under a rapidly changing geopolitical context especially affected the lives of youngsters, but they were no mere observers or silent witnesses of occupation developments. Young Germans were simultaneously affected by and aware of the occupation circumstances they were growing up in. Some of them wrote down their observations in diaries, including those as young as seven years old, such as Theodor Wild of Amberg, who later in his life gave copies of his diaries to the Deutsches Tagebucharchiv in Emmendingen, Germany, ensuring future generations a glimpse into his past. These sources from the youngest of Germans are especially fascinating, and also portray a level of clarity about life events that only children can attain, for example having adventures around the town and viewing American antics with child-like curiosity. Witness Hilde Herzmann, who at age seven lost her memory of all previous events in her life due to injuries from a bombing attack in Remagen in March 1945, stated about her childhood, "Although that life seems awful in retrospect, at the time I didn't perceive it as especially painful. I didn't know anything else. I had no memory of a better past, and also children see things differently. They tend to take the world the way they find it."[3]

In addition, later on in life, some of these former children desired to reflect on the unique experience of growing up under a military occupation after the complete defeat of National Socialist ideology. Mercedes Wild has proved particularly active in revisiting her childhood growing up in Berlin during the occupation and Airlift, repeatedly appearing over the years with Candy Bomber Gail Halvorsen at commemoration events. She also had her story published as a children's book for future generations to learn about the impacts of German-American encounters during the geopolitical crisis of the Berlin Blockade of 1948 to 1949.[4] However, the experiences of the young Germans featured in this work cannot and do not speak for an entire generation, nor are their stories to be considered representative of all young Germans in all locations under American occupation. The work is also limited in its exploration of the experiences of those Germans who were victims of the horrors of the Nazi regime, instead mostly focusing on non-victim German citizens who were undergoing the navigations of transition from Nazism to democracy, faced with life under a military government enforced with soldiers of the former enemy troops. Moreover, many young Germans did not record their stories for future generations, or if they did, the records may have been lost, remained within the family, were never shared with anyone else, or never made their way into an archive. Many Germans may not have wanted to remember the immediate postwar years, for example if they experienced traumatic incidents or if they struggled with grappling with the end of National Socialism. In the immediate decades following World War II, most Germans remained unwilling to delve into potentially uncomfortable truths about wartime participation or belief in National Socialism, instead choosing repression over openness about past experiences and their roles in a fascist regime. In addition, many Germans believed the myth of the clean Wehrmacht, believing that regular Germans, such as ordinary soldiers in the Wehrmacht, did not play a central role in the atrocities of the Holocaust and in other war crimes.[5] However, generations following those of World War II began to question the roles of their parents and, later on, their grandparents. This included the generation of young people in 1968, who protested against their parents, although the focus of these protests on a detailed examination of their parents' generation's roles in National Socialism remained limited, according to Harald Jähner.[6] However, as formerly young Ger-

3 Samuel, *The War of Our Childhood*, 125.
4 Raven, *Mercedes and the Chocolate Pilot*.
5 See Wolfram Wette, *The Wehrmacht: History, Myth, Reality* (Harvard University Press, 2006).
6 Jähner, *Aftermath*, 323–326.

man witnesses of the war and its aftermath began to share their stories, especially by the early 2000s, it became more of a norm in German society for others to share their stories, breaking the taboo about discussing personal experiences of the National Socialist past.

Although German society today faces challenges including disturbing instances of antisemitism such as synagogue attacks as well as racially motivated violence, for example directed at refugees, it is a widely accepted truth that Nazism and the Holocaust were horrors that Germany perpetrated and that they are never to be repeated. Young Germans today in the twenty-first century gain an education about the Holocaust and the crimes of National Socialism, often taking school trips to concentration camp memorial sites or Holocaust museums. Practices of memorialization also ensure that history is presented for the public, including memorials such as those to Holocaust victims, museums such as the Jewish Museum in Berlin, or the NS-Dokumentationszentrum in Munich, and through other initiatives such as the *Stolpersteine*, stumbling stones, which are cobblestones placed on the street in front of the former residence of victims of the National Socialist regime.

In addition, increasing scholarly interest in the unique dynamics of the postwar occupation sphere in Germany has emerged in recent years, with research being conducted into understudied aspects of the occupation such as the French occupation zone and more.[7] With the simultaneous rising interest in the history of children and youth, there will hopefully be more studies that explore the unique blend of military occupation, childhood, and the aftermath of World War II in Germany in the various zones, including a focus on populations such as German refugee children, DP children, and children born of occupied soldiers. Interesting will also be studies that look into the role of young people in other locations and time periods, such as the occupation of Japan after World War II, the occupation of Korea, or even the Iraq War. It is essential to consider youngsters as major players in the history of war and its aftermath, as they are a part of the population that cannot simply be disregarded as unimportant nor seen simply as silent victims of circumstances out of their own making. Their voices in sources from the time, as well as the reflections of these former children later in life, can play an important role in gaining a better understanding of past events. This work has only broached the surface of the wide range of lived experiences of young Germans in the American occupation, but it has shown that these children

7 For a report on a 2023 conference on the Western Allied occupations, see Emanuel Marx, "Tagungsbericht: Occupied Everyday Life—New Perspectives on the Western Allied Occupations 1945–1955," H-Soz-Kult, August 16, 2023, www.hsozkult.de/conferencereport/id/fdkn-137722.

and youth were unequivocally important in personal experiences of the occupation, for example during informal encounters between children and GIs. Moreover, youngsters also played a central role in impacting occupation developments, from policies of reeducation to humanitarian aid such as the *Schulspeisung* and CARE packages, as well as during the geopolitical Cold War crisis of the Berlin Airlift.

The intersections of age, society, crisis, war, and childhood remain ever relevant in today's world.[8] Although the United Nations Convention on the Rights of the Child came into effect on September 2, 1990, and has been ratified by all eligible states except the United States, children's rights remain negatively impacted by various factors throughout the world including due to armed conflict.[9] War has again returned to the European continent with the Russian invasion of Ukraine on February 24, 2022. Age has emerged as central to these navigations, with young men being called to serve in combat in the brutal war, and with Ukrainian children and youth being victims of bombing attacks on residential areas and schools. There are also reports that Russia has forcibly taken some Ukrainian children into Russia for purposes of "reeducation."[10] The plight of Ukrainian children has been leveraged as a way to highlight the destructive nature of the war and motivate support and solidarity for Ukrainians, as well as for humanitarian aid purposes by highlighting the most innocent victims of the war, the children. A May 2023 outdoor display at the Ukraine House in Washington, DC, a cultural center, included a slide riddled with bullet holes. Stuffed animals and toys scattered about the slide and the surrounding grass, with caution tape surrounding the scene, seem to represent the children whose lives have been disrupted by the war. The display included a sign about "War Crimes Committed Against Children (as of May 2023)," which noted that 480 Ukrainian children had been killed, 968 injured, 17 subjected to sexual violence, 1,709 children's educational, medical, and

---

8 See Baard Herman Borge, Elke Kleinau, and Ingvill Constanze Ødegaard, eds., *Children and Youth at Risk in Times of Transition: International and Interdisciplinary Perspectives* (De Gruyter, 2024), https://doi.org/10.1515/9783111010649.

9 See text of the treaty at "11. Convention on the Rights of the Child," United Nations, New York, November 20, 1989, https://treaties.un.org/pages/ViewDetails.aspx?src=TREATY&mtdsg_no=IV-11&chapter=4&clang=_en.

10 Helen Sullivan, "Thousands of Ukrainian children put through Russian 're-education' camps, US report finds," *The Guardian*, February 14, 2023; Friederike Kind-Kovács and Anna Oksiutovych. "Reflecting on the Present through the Past: Children's Displacement from Ukraine," *The Journal of the History of Childhood and Youth* 17, no. 2 (Spring 2024): 254–271, https://dx.doi.org/10.1353/hcy.2024.a926867.

recreational facilities damaged or destroyed, and 19,390 Ukrainian children in Russian captivity.[11] In August 2023, the United Nations and the government of Ukraine signed a "joint prevention plan" which aims "to end and prevent grave violations against children" due to the war.[12]

Beyond Ukraine, children throughout the world remain impacted by wars, including in the Middle East region. The Israel-Gaza war began on October 7, 2023, and the Syrian Civil War has gone on since March 2011.[13] Throughout the world, children are still recruited and directly used in armed conflicts in combat and support roles, and the United Nations has developed initiatives that aim to increase the protection of children faced with life in areas of armed conflict, including the Office of the Special Representative of the Secretary-General for Children and Armed Conflict, which was created by UN mandate in December 1996.[14] This Office notes that children become involved with armed forces and groups in various ways, stating on their website, "Some children are abducted and beaten into submission, others join military groups to escape poverty, to defend their communities, out of a feeling of revenge or for other reasons."[15] Their roles in combat can vary, for example ranging from actual combatants to cooks, spies, messengers, or sex slaves. The United Nations Children's Fund (UNICEF) notes that between 2005 and 2022, over 105,000 children were verified to have been recruited

11 Display at Ukraine House, Washington, DC, viewed by author on May 13, 2023.

12 Office of the Special Representative of the Secretary-General for Children and Armed Conflict, "The Government of Ukraine signs plan to end and prevent grave violations against children, with the support of the United Nations," United Nations, August 23, 2023, https://childrenandarmedconflict.un.org/2023/08/the-government-of-ukraine-signs-plan-to-end-and-prevent-grave-violations-against-children-with-the-support-of-the-united-nations/.

13 For an example of children and war in Syria, see Aeham Ahmad, *The Pianist from Syria: A Memoir*, trans. Emanuel Bergmann (Atria Books, an imprint of Simon & Schuster, Inc., 2019). During the Syrian Civil War, Ahmad played piano and sang with children on the streets in the besieged district of Yarmouk, a Palestinian refugee camp in the south of Damascus, creating the group "The Yarmouk Kids" to bring joy and music to the local children. After his family's escape in 2015, someone offered his son candy; his son, "who had spent his entire life in a city under siege, said, 'Papa, what's candy?'" (228). Ahmad fled to Germany in 2015. His wife and children joined him in 2016.

14 Office of the Special Representative of the Secretary-General for Children and Armed Conflict, "About Us," United Nations, accessed August 25, 2023, https://childrenandarmedconflict.un.org/about/.

15 Office of the Special Representative of the Secretary-General for Children and Armed Conflict, "Child Recruitment and Use," United Nations, accessed August 25, 2023, https://childrenandarmedconflict.un.org/six-grave-violations/child-soldiers/. See also "The Paris Principles: The Principles and Guidelines on Children Associated with Armed Forces or Armed Groups," United Nations, February 2007, https://childrenandarmedconflict.un.org/publications/ParisPrinciples_EN.pdf.

and used by parties in conflict; the actual number of children involved in combat is most likely much more.[16]

In addition, the US military continues to play a role in Germany, with a troop presence that rose under the presidency of Joe Biden during a time of heightening tensions on the continent.[17] The globally extended American forces have thus remained relevant since the end of World War II, a time when Americans by and large accepted playing a major role in global affairs, especially through having a military presence in locations in East Asia and Germany. The notion of an American Century has also continued to be relevant, as the United States has often professed to be the protector of democracy and freedom throughout the globe, and has been willing to intervene in conflicts far removed from the United States, linking the security of democracy in foreign countries to the security of the United States. In Iraq, this played a role in the reasoning for American military intervention in 2003, with politicians pointing to Germany as a model of a "good occupation" that led to positive democratic transformation, without delving into the context or differences between a Middle Eastern, formerly colonized nation and a European country in ruins and under occupation after waging the largest war in global history.[18] Since the Russian invasion of Ukraine in 2022, the US has provided abundant military aid to Ukraine, and NATO has expanded its membership. The United States under the administration of Joe Biden aimed to hold up the promise of being defenders of values such as freedom and democracy when under threat in Europe in regards to Ukraine, a rhetoric similar to that of the Truman Doctrine of 1947, which, although focused on containing the spread of communism, aimed to support democratic nations that were under threat from totalitarian regimes through American military, political, and economic assistance.

In addition, Ukrainian President Volodymyr Zelenskyy has displayed a politics of gratitude for American aid to Ukraine, remarking in the US Congress on December 21, 2022 that he is incredibly thankful for all that the American people have done to support his country. He stated, "Your money is not charity. It's an investment in the global security and democracy that we handle in the most responsible way." In addition to his profusive thanks to the United States, Presi-

16 "Children Recruited by Armed Forces or Armed Groups," UNICEF, accessed August 25, 2023, https://www.unicef.org/protection/children-recruited-by-armed-forces.

17 Ben Knight, "US Military in Germany: What You Need to Know," *Deutsche Welle*, February 29, 2024, https://www.dw.com/en/us-military-in-germany-what-you-need-to-know/a-49998340.

18 See George W. Bush, The President's Radio Address, March 1, 2003, The American Presidency Project, University of California Santa Barbara, https://www.presidency.ucsb.edu/node/216097. Also, Carruthers, *The Good Occupation*, 1–3.

dent Zelenskyy in his speech linked the conflict in Ukraine to the fate of the democratic future of the world:

> This battle is not only for the territory, for this or another part of Europe. The battle is not only for life, freedom and security of Ukrainians or any other nation which Russia attempts to conquer. This struggle will define in what world our children and grandchildren will live, and then their children and grandchildren.
>
> It will define whether it will be a democracy of Ukrainians and for Americans — for all.[19]

Zelenskyy's visit and speech thus highlighted the continuing significance of debates around security and democracy in Europe, with the United States playing a major role under the policies of the Biden administration.

Beyond war in Ukraine, the Middle East, and conflicts elsewhere, the world faces numerous present-day global challenges, such as the fragility of many democracies, including in the United States itself, rapidly changing technology including social media, as well as the major uncertainty of climate change and its effects. Adult-made decisions surrounding war, education, technology, and climate, for example, are of great significance for the lives of today's young people. Children and youth emerge as central in times of crisis, seen both as victims of effects such as those caused by violence or climate change and also as a group in need of assistance. In addition, crisis narratives often focus on the role of an uncertain future for the future generations. However, these narratives tend to be from an adult lens and ignore the fact that young people themselves can also use their status as future global citizens to voice their own opinions and mark their own places in present-day navigations around crisis. For example, in August 2023, 16 young people in Montana from the ages of five to 22 successfully sued the state for willingly conducting practices that worsened climate change by promoting fossil fuels, which has violated their right to a "clean and healthful environment," as is stated in the Montana state constitution.[20] Greta Thunberg of Sweden has emerged as a global voice on the effects of climate change and the unwillingness of most adults to take present-day action to help combat it.[21] In addition, children have played a central role in activism around human rights in the past. For exam-

---

19 "Full Transcript of Zelensky's Speech Before Congress," *New York Times*, December 21, 2022, https://www.nytimes.com/2022/12/21/us/politics/zelensky-speech-transcript.html.

20 Kate Selig, "Youths sued Montana over climate change and won. Here's why it matters," *The Washington Post*, August 16, 2023. On the intersections of childhood studies and youth climate activism using the case study of Australia, see Lucy Hopkins, "'The Ice is Melting and I Don't Want Santa to Drown!': Reflections on Childhood, Climate Action, and Futurity," *Journal of Childhood Studies* 48, no. 1 (January 2023): 85–98, https://doi.org/10.18357/jcs202320484.

21 See for example quotes from her speech at the 2019 UN Climate Summit in Hopkins, 90.

ple, during the US civil rights movement in the 1960s, the "Children's Crusade" occurred beginning on May 2, 1963, in which thousands of schoolchildren skipped class in Birmingham, Alabama to march for civil rights and an end to segregation. Protestors the next day were blasted by high pressure fire hoses and attacked by police dogs, creating shocking images printed in newspapers around the world. The events played a role in impacting President John F. Kennedy and spurring the passing of the Civil Rights Act of 1964.[22] Young people, although mostly not yet of age to vote, still have a voice and can advocate for issues that affect their daily lives and their futures in ways that may impact global geopolitics and have the potential to create positive changes that may help mitigate the effects of the various crises. Some states in the US are even conducting a program called "Kid Governor," created by The Connecticut Democracy Center, in which fifth graders elect a kid governor, who runs on a specific platform, giving young children practical experience in democratic behavior and teaching youngsters the importance of being active in a democracy.[23] Above all, young people are thus central societal figures who need to be seen as such in both present-day politics and in historical studies of the past. Without their voices, opinions, and ideas, both then and now, something fundamental is missing. Discourse about the present and the past should not just speak for and about children and youth, but must include them and their stories. Young people today continue to document their lives in various formats, including in traditional diaries, for example describing life during the Covid-19 pandemic lockdowns, or by using newer forms of technology such as social media.[24]

Overall, young Germans imprinted the core of the US occupation of Germany. American military members encountered German youngsters from the very first moments of stepping on to German territory in September of 1944 with boots muddied from combat. This encounter, extending into the years of the US occupation of Germany, proved all the more complicated, because these were two former enemy population groups taking up the same space, and one of them was

---

22 National Museum of African American History and Culture, "On This Day: The Children's Crusade," Smithsonian Institution, accessed August 25, 2023, https://nmaahc.si.edu/explore/stories/childrens-crusade.

23 "What is Kid Governor?" Kid Governor, accessed August 25, 2023, http://kidgovernor.org/about kidgovernor.

24 For an example of a diary written by a child during the Covid-19 lockdown measures in Austria in 2020, see "Tagebuch eines auf soziale Betreuung angewiesenen Kindes, April 2020," Corona Sammeln—Ein Krisenjahr in Objekten, Haus der Geschichte Österreich, accessed August 25, 2023, https://hdgoe.at/tagebuch_corona. On young people's recordings of life experiences using new technologies, see Honeck and Moore, "War and Conflict," in *A Cultural History of Youth in the Modern Age*, ed. Alexander and Sleight, 216.

young, perhaps waving amidst the rubble of his or her home, hiding from the former enemy, or stretching a hand out for some chewing gum. Both young Germans and Americans were active participants in the navigations of the time, as they came to terms with the shifting modes of life in the occupation. Moreover, moving beyond a generalized, cliched view of innocent children and kind soldiers is essential to grasp at the lived realities of the occupation. Personal experiences of this exchange between populations proved complex yet essential to the sphere of the occupation, having the potential to shape a military member's experience, for example, or on the other side, planting a never to be forgotten memory in a German child's mind. GIs were placed in the role as early navigators of judgments about German children. However, German youngsters were also viewing the behaviors of soldiers with awareness and often curiosity. In turn, both GIs and German children served as mediators between the two former enemies in a time of chaos and confusion. Young Germans could be aware of the privilege and power of the military conquerors but also notice acts of kindness. These German children and youth viewed GIs in diverse and shifting ways, for example as business partners for bartering, as a source to steal from, as potential sources for food, as powerful occupiers, or as generous soldiers handing out candy. Although the complexity of this exchange has been lost in the sanitized, reconstructed versions of the occupation that have emerged, the voices of both Americans and Germans within the occupation remain recorded in the pages of diaries and within the folds of personal memories. Occupation-era childhood was not an easy or protected status but a complicated, often painful venture, full of bizarre mixtures of experiences, people, and challenges. It was an experience ever-shifting and dependent on time, place, language skills, wartime experience, and family situation. For some German youngsters, the GI could provide hope amidst loss, although many were aware that this hope was occurring under the realms of American military power. In addition, for some GIs, German children became their children for a brief moment in time. Above all, the central role of children and youth in the American occupation deserves deep examination. Their voices emerge in unexpected ways, ways that sear through the ease of a narrative without pain and loss, a narrative convinced at its utter goodness. They paint the complexity of the occupation and the role of the soldier among challenging tasks and judgments undertaken in the rubble.

In addition, young Germans fundamentally impacted the geopolitical sphere of occupation developments, especially as their encounters with Americans became an official part of reeducation policies. For example, the Army Assistance to the German Youth Activities program became an essential tool for reeducating the future democrats of Germany, as well as to motivate the often bored and disgruntled occupation troops that their presence could serve a tangible, positive purpose. The benevolence of average soldiers toward young Germans became a central instrument in the occupation, as German youth became seen as the future of a free, democratic Germany and even the guardians of world peace. Young Germans noted the positive actions of Americans that served to enrich their lives, becoming often willing participants in a transatlantic geopolitics of gratitude, which thanked American citizens for not forsaking them and providing them with CARE packages, school meals, and more. The Berlin Airlift of 1948 and 1949 again placed children at the center of geopolitical events: Gail Halvorsen, the Candy Bomber, decided to take an action that changed history by dropping candy parachutes to the German children at Tempelhof who seemed to care so much about freedom. Americans were thus there for those in need of assistance in times of crisis over (West) German democracy. Through it all, young Germans of various ages and backgrounds understood, reckoned with, and described the events of the times. They became central figures in the immediate postwar sphere in Germany, and they forged their own paths within the shifting encounters made among the looming mounds of rubble. From the rubble-strewn streets of postwar Germany, there even was the possibility for hope and common humanity to emerge strong among these transatlantic, multilingual, intergenerational contacts.

Bibliography

Archival Collections

AACVR: The Civil Rights Struggle, African-American GIs, and Germany

Interview of Lawrence Johnson. Digitized. http://digitales-archiv.aacvr-germany.org/

Amerikahaus Munich Archives, Munich

Amerikahaus programs, 1948.

Newspaper clippings, 1948.

Deutsches Tagebucharchiv, Emmendingen

Edeltraud Großjohann, Reg-Nr. 185/I,1–4 Abschrift

Wolfgang K., in "Vereinte Tagebücher 1945–46," Reg.-Nr. 1414-I

Ingrid Picker, Signatur-Nr. 3853,1

Dietrich Volker (Pseudonym), Signatur-Nr. 1950,1

Theodor Wild (Gruschka), Reg.-Nr. 540,1–3

Gerald R. Ford Presidential Library, Grand Rapids, Michigan

Betty Ford White House Papers, 1973–1977. Digitized. https://catalog.archives.gov/id/573379.

Harry S. Truman Presidential Library, Independence, Missouri

Executive Orders. Digitized. https://www.trumanlibrary.gov/library/executive-orders.

Harry S. Truman Papers:

Harry S. Truman Papers Pertaining to Family, Business and Personal Affairs. Digitized. https://catalog.archives.gov/id/1195.

President's Secretary's Files

White House Central Files: Official File

Museum Artifact number 3025

Paul L. Webb Papers

Harvard Divinity School Library, Harvard University, Cambridge, Massachusetts

Unitarian Service Committee, Administrative Records, 1946–1950. Digitized. https://hollisarchives.lib.harvard.edu/repositories/12/resources/1138.

https://doi.org/10.1515/9783111588155-008

Indiana University Archives, Bloomington, Indiana
Image Collection Online. Malcolm Fleming World War II Photographs. Digitized. https://webapp1.dlib.indiana.edu/images/splash.htm?scope=archives/VAD2888.

Lebendiges Museum Online: Stiftung Haus der Geschichte der Bundesrepublik Deutschland, Deutsches Historisches Museum, das Bundesarchiv
Christa Ronke. Zeitzeugen. Digitized. https://www.dhm.de/lemo/zeitzeugen.

The Library of Congress, Washington, DC
Manuscript Collection
Interview of Lawrence Norrie. Frontline Diplomacy: The Foreign Affairs Oral History Collection of the Association for Diplomatic Studies and Training. Digitized. https://www.loc.gov/collections/foreign-affairs-oral-history/.
Veterans History Project (VHP), American Folklife Center
Robert Walter Baird (AFC/2001/001/73816)
Bernard R. Bolf (AFC/2001/001/25786)
Richard W. Fabian (AFC/2001/001/62498)
Malcolm L. Fleming (AFC 2001/001/27926)
John Junji Katsu (AFC/2001/001/89308)
Robert Allen Macon (AFC/2001/001/90477)
James Gustavus Smith (AFC/2001/001/106804)
Robert Edward Wilson (AFC/2001/001/2210)

Margaret Wood, Private Records, Williamstown, Massachusetts
Private family documents and photographs.

National Archives and Records Administration, National Archives at College Park, Maryland
Record Group 260: Records of U.S. Occupation Headquarters, World War II
Record Group 407: Records of the Adjutant General's Office
Record Group 466: Records of the U.S. High Commissioner for Germany

National Archives and Records Administration, National Archives at St. Louis, Missouri
Record Group 319: Records of the Army Staff. Official Military Personnel Files.

Stadtarchiv Nürnberg
E 10/1 Nachlass Otto Barthel

United States Army Heritage and Education Center (USAHEC), Carlisle, Pennsylvania
Bion C. Welker Papers

United States Holocaust Memorial Museum Collections, Washington, DC
Photographs. Digitized. https://collections.ushmm.org/search/.

Zeitzeugen Portal: Stiftung Haus der Geschichte der Bundesrepublik Deutschland
Gail S. Halvorsen. Zeitzeugen. Digitized. https://www.zeitzeugen-portal.de/.

Periodicals

Air Force Times
Amberger Zeitung
The Atlantic
Chicago Defender
Deutsche Welle
FOCUS Magazin
Frankfurter Allgemeine Zeitung
The Guardian
Harper's
Jet
Joplin Globe
Life
Mittelbayerische Zeitung
National Geographic Magazine
New York Times
Oberpfalz Medien
Perspectives on History
Prologue Magazine
The Salt Lake Tribune
Santa Barbara Independent
Smithsonian Magazine
Der Spiegel
Der Spiegel Geschichte
Springfield News-Leader
Stars and Stripes

Tagesspiegel
Taz, die Tageszeitung
Time
U.S. Army News
USA Today
Voice of America
The Washington Post
Weser-Kurier
Yank, the Army Weekly
Zeit Online

Videos and Films

Bremen Boys Club (2003)
Let's Be Childish (1950)
Your Job in Germany (1945)

Websites, Blogs, and Other Digital Materials

Allied Museum/Alliierten Museum. https://www.alliiertenmuseum.de/en/.
Amerikahaus Munich. https://www.amerikahaus.de/en/.
Berlin Airlift Historical Foundation. http://www.spiritoffreedom.org/.
Berlin Airlift Remembered. Royal Air Force Museum, Allied Museum, Bundeswehr Military History Museum Airfield Berlin-Gatow, National Museum of the United States Air Force. https://www.berlinairlift75.org/en/.
The Berlin Candy Bomber. http://wigglywings.weebly.com.
Berlin.de: Das offizielle Hauptstadtportal. https://www.berlin.de.
Die Bundesregierung. Pressemitteilungen. https://www.bundesregierung.de/breg-de/aktuelles/pressemitteilungen.
The Candy Bomber Foundation. https://www.thecandybomber.org.
The George C. Marshall Foundation. https://www.marshallfoundation.org/.
German Historical Institute, Washington, DC. German History in Documents and Images. https://ghdi.ghi-dc.org/index.cfm.
Haus der Bayerischen Geschichte. Biografien Menschen aus Bayern. https://hdbg.eu/biografien/.
Haus der Geschichte Österreich. Corona Sammeln—Ein Krisenjahr in Objekten. https://hdgoe.at/category/corona_sammeln.
Hershey Community Archives. Encyclopedia. https://hersheyarchives.org/online-resources/encyclopedia/.
Historisches Lexikon Bayerns. https://www.historisches-lexikon-bayerns.de/Lexikon/Startseite.
H-Soz-Kult. Conference Reports. https://www.hsozkult.de/conferencereport/page.

Kid Governor. http://kidgovernor.org/.
Luftbrückenmuseum Faßberg. https://www.luftbrueckenmuseum.de/.
Maneuver Center of Excellence Libraries, Fort Benning, Georgia. World War II Student Papers Collection. https://www.benning.army.mil/Library/Donovanpapers/wwii/index.html.
National Archives. Milestone Documents. https://www.archives.gov/milestone-documents/list.
National Park Service. Wolf Trap National Park for the Performing Arts. https://www.nps.gov/wotr/index.htm.
The National WWII Museum. https://www.nationalww2museum.org/.
Online Atlas on the History of Humanitarianism and Human Rights. https://hhr-atlas.ieg-mainz.de/.
Smithsonian National Air and Space Museum. https://airandspace.si.edu/.
Smithsonian National Museum of African American History and Culture. https://nmaahc.si.edu/.
Southern Methodist University Libraries. Historical Government Publications from World War II Collection. https://www.smu.edu/libraries/digitalcollections/hgp.
Tempelhof Projekt. Fest der Luftbrücke. https://www.fest-der-luftbruecke.de/.
Tempelhof Projekt. https://www.thf-berlin.de/en/
Transatlantic Studies: A Student Research Blog. https://transatlanticmoment.wordpress.com/.
United Nations Children's Fund (UNICEF). https://www.unicef.org.
United Nations. Office of the Special Representative of the Secretary-General for Children and Armed Conflict. https://childrenandarmedconflict.un.org/.
United Nations Treaties. https://treaties.un.org/.
University of California Santa Barbara. The American Presidency Project. https://www.presidency.ucsb.edu/.
University of Wisconsin-Madison Libraries. Germany under Reconstruction Collection. https://search.library.wisc.edu/digital/AGerRecon.
Wolf Trap Foundation. https://www.wolftrap.org/.

Published Memoirs, Diaries, and Other Personal Materials

Ahmad, Aeham. *The Pianist from Syria: A Memoir*. Translated by Emanuel Bergmann. Atria Books, an imprint of Simon & Schuster, Inc., 2019.
Andreas-Friedrich, Ruth. *Battleground Berlin: Diaries, 1945–1948*. Paragon House, 1990.
Anonymous. *A Woman in Berlin: Eight Weeks in the Conquered City: A Diary*. Translated by Philip Boehm. Picador/Henry Holt, 2005.
Bach Jr., Julian. *America's Germany: An Account of the Occupation*. Random House, 1946.
Beissel, Henry. *Coming to Terms with a Child: Ein Kind Kommt Zur Sprache*. Verlag LiteraturWissenschaft.de, 2015.
Bernstein, Barton J., ed. "Truman at Potsdam: His Secret Diary." *Foreign Service Journal* 57, no. 7 (July/August 1980): 29–34, 36.
Bourke-White, Margaret. *"Dear Fatherland, Rest Quietly": A Report on the Collapse of Hitler's "Thousand Years."* Simon & Schuster, 1946.
Brandl, Friedrich. *Ziegelgassler: eine Kindheit nach dem Krieg*. Ed. Lichtung, 2009.
Brockway, Fenner. *German Diary*. Victor Gollancz, 1946.
Bruss, Regina, ed. *Mit Zuckersack und Heissgetränk: Leben und Überleben in der Nachkriegszeit, Bremen 1945–1949*. Hefte des Focke-Museums, Nr. 83. Bremer Landesmuseum für Kunst- und Kulturgeschichte, 1989.

Campbell, Wallace J. *The History of CARE: A Personal Account*. Praeger, 1990.
Clay, Lucius D. *Decision in Germany*. Doubleday, 1950.
Dagerman, Stig. *German Autumn*. Translated by Robin Fulton Macpherson. University of Minnesota Press, 2011.
Dudman, Helga. *Letters Home to San Francisco from Occupied Germany, 1945–1946*. Carta, 2007.
Finell, Karin. *Good-Bye to the Mermaids: A Childhood Lost in Hitler's Berlin*. University of Missouri Press, 2006.
Fleming, Malcolm L. *From War to Peace in 1945 Germany: A GI's Experience*. Indiana University Press, 2016.
Frank, Anne. *Anne Frank: The Diary of a Young Girl*. Translated by B. M. Mooyaart-Doubleday. Bantam Books, 1993.
Geve, Thomas. *Es gibt hier keine Kinder: Auschwitz, Gross-Rosen, Buchenwald: Zeichnungen eines kindlichen Historikers*. Wallstein Verlag, 1997.
Giles, Janice Holt, ed. *The G.I. Journal of Sergeant Giles*. Houghton Mifflin, 1965.
Granzow, Klaus. *Tagebuch eines Hitlerjungen, 1943–1945*. C. Schünemann, 1965.
Habe, Hans. *Our Love Affair with Germany*. Putnam, 1953.
Halvorsen, Gail S. *The Berlin Candy Bomber*. Horizon Publishers, 2017.
Haß, Kurt, ed. *Jugend unterm Schicksal: Lebensberichte junger Deutscher 1946–1949*. Aare-Verlag, 1950.
Heer, Hannes, ed. *Als ich 9 Jahre alt war, kam der Krieg: Schüleraufsätze 1946: ein Lesebuch gegen den Krieg*. Prometh, 1980.
Hirschfeld, Gerhard, and Irina Renz, eds. *Vormittags die ersten Amerikaner: Stimmen und Bilder vom Kriegsende 1945*. Klett-Cotta, 2005.
Holliday, Laurel, ed. *Children in the Holocaust and World War II: Their Secret Diaries*. Pocket Books, 1995.
Horrocks, Brian. *A Full Life*. L. Cooper, 1974.
Howley, Frank L. *Berlin Command*. G.P. Putnam's Sons, 1950.
Keller, Sven, ed. *Kriegstagebuch einer jungen Nationalsozialistin: Die Aufzeichnungen Wolfhilde von Königs 1939–1946*. De Gruyter, 2015. https://doi.org/10.1515/9783110405378.
Kleindienst, Jürgen, ed. *Hungern und hoffen: Jugend in Deutschland 1945–1950: 48 Geschichten und Berichte von Zeitzeugen*. JKL Publikationen, 2000.
Kleindienst, Jürgen, ed. *Lebertran und Chewing Gum: Kindheit in Deutschland 1945–1950: 55 Geschichten und Berichte von Zeitzeugen*. JKL Publikationen, 2000.
Kleindienst, Jürgen, ed. *Nachkriegs-Kinder: Kindheit in Deutschland 1945–1950: 67 Geschichten und Berichte von Zeitzeugen*. JKL Publikationen, 1998.
Kleindienst, Jürgen, ed. *Der Traum ist aus: Jugend im Zusammenbruch 1944–1945: 31 Geschichten und Berichte von Zeitzeugen*. Zeitgut, 2005.
Knauth, Percy. *Germany in Defeat*. Alfred A. Knopf, 1946.
Köhler, Rosemarie. *Brennesselsuppe und Rosinenbomber: das Berliner Notkochbuch: Rezepte, Erfahrungen und Hintergründe 1945–1949*. Eichborn, 1999.
Krause, Walter C. *So I Was a Sergeant: Memoirs of an Occupation Soldier*. Exposition Press, 1978.
Kupffer, Heinrich. *Swingtime: Chronik einer Jugend in Deutschland 1937–1951*. Frieling, 1987.
Lepman, Jella. *A Bridge of Children's Books*. Translated by Edith McCormick. O'Brien Press, 2002.
Lepman, Jella. *Die Kinderbuchbrücke*. S. Fischer, 1964.
Lerg, Charlotte A., ed. *The Diary of Lt. Melvin J. Lasky: Into Germany at the End of World War II*. Berghahn Books, 2023.
Miller, Lee. *Lee Miller's War: Beyond D-Day*. Thames & Hudson, 2014.
Museum Schloß Schönebeck, ed. *Kriegsende 1945: Vegesack und umzu: das Kriegsende erlebt und aufgeschrieben von Bewohnern aus Vegesack und umliegenden Ortschaften*. J.H. Döll, 1994.

Padover, Saul K. *Experiment in Germany: The Story of an American Intelligence Officer*. Duell, Sloan and Pearce, 1946.
Pogue, Forrest C. *Pogue's War: Diaries of a WWII Combat Historian*. University Press of Kentucky, 2001.
Pollock, James K. *Besatzung und Staatsaufbau nach 1945: Occupation Diary and Private Correspondence 1945–1948*. Edited by Ingrid Krüger-Bulcke. R. Oldenbourg, 1994.
Samuel, Wolfgang W. E. *German Boy: A Refugee's Story*. University Press of Mississippi, 2000.
Samuel, Wolfgang W. E. *The War of Our Childhood: Memories of World War II*. University Press of Mississippi, 2002.
Scheper, Burchard. *". . .You Must Learn Democracy": Ende Und Anfang, 1944–1945*. Nordwestdeutsche Verlagsgesellschaft, 1995.
Schmidt, Georg. *Als Bremen amerikanisch war: zwischen Krieg und Wirtschaftswunder: Bilder von 1945 bis 1950*. Johann Heinrich Döll Verlag, 1989.
Shirer, William L. *End of a Berlin Diary*. Alfred A. Knopf, 1947.
Spitta, Theodor. *Neuanfang auf Trümmern: Die Tagebücher des Bremer Bürgermeisters Theodor Spitta 1945–1947*. Edited by Ursula Büttner and Angelika Voß-Louis. R. Oldenbourg, 1992.
State Jewish Museum. *Children's Drawings from the Concentration Camp of Terezín*. [Praha]: n.d.
Tomikel, John. *A German Journal: The Diary of a Soldier in the Army of Occupation of Germany Shortly After World War II: The Occupation Diary of Cpl. John Tomikel*. Allegheny Press, 2000.
Truman, Harry S. *Memoirs of Harry S. Truman: Years of Trial and Hope*. Vol. 2. Da Capo Press, 1956.
Tunner, William H. *Over the Hump*. Berlin Airlift 50th Anniversary Commemorative Edition. U.S. Government Printing Office, Air Force History and Museums Program, 1998. https://purl.access.gpo.gov/GPO/LPS48694.
Vaccaro, Tony. *Entering Germany: 1944–1949*. Taschen, 2001.
Wallis, Sarah, and Svetlana Palmer. *We Were Young and at War: The First-Hand Story of Young Lives Lived and Lost in World War II*. Collins, 2009.
Weiss, Winfried. *A Nazi Childhood*. Capra Press, 1983.
White, Osmar. *Conquerors' Road: An Eyewitness Report of Germany 1945*. Cambridge University Press, 2003.
Wild, Theodor. *Wo der "Müde" war, war immer was los*. Verlag Leben in der Sprache, 2015.
Yunger, Ursula Erika. *The Healing Presence*. Ruth Publications, 1995.
Zapruder, Alexandra, ed. *Salvaged Pages: Young Writers' Diaries of the Holocaust*. Yale University Press, 2002.

Other Primary Source Publications

Boyle, Kay. *The Smoking Mountain: Stories of Germany During the Occupation*. Knopf, 1963.
Bremen Port Command's "GI Paradise." Public Relations Office, Bremen Port Command, 1946.
Brickner, Richard M. *Is Germany Incurable?* J.B. Lippincott Co., 1943.
Frederiksen, Oliver J. *The American Military Occupation of Germany, 1945–1953*. Historical Division, Headquarters, United States Army, 1953.
Freud, Anna, and Dorothy T. Burlingham. *War and Children*. Ernst Willard, 1943.
Geis, Margaret L., and George J. Gray Jr. *The Relations of Occupation Personnel with the Civil Population, 1946–1948*. Occupation Forces in Europe Series. Historical Division, European Command, 1951.
German Youth Activities: Army Assistance Program Guide. United States Army, European Command, OPOT Division, Training and Education Branch, 1948.

German Youth Activities of the United States Army. Occupation Forces in Europe Series. Office of the Chief Historian, European Command, 1947.

German Youth Between Yesterday and Tomorrow, 1 April 1947–30 April 1948. Office of Military Government, Education and Cultural Relations Division, 1948.

Gollancz, Victor. *In Darkest Germany*. Henry Regnery Company, 1947.

Hoover, Herbert. *Freedom Betrayed: Herbert Hoover's Secret History of the Second World War and Its Aftermath*. Edited by George H. Nash. Hoover Institution Press, Stanford University, 2011.

Instructions for British Servicemen in Germany 1944. Bodleian Library, 2007.

Jaspers, Karl. *Die Schuldfrage: von der politischen Haftung Deutschlands*. Piper, 2012.

Kurz, Karl. *Lebensverhältnisse der Nachkriegsjugend, eine soziologische Studie*. F. Trüjen, 1949.

Liddell, Helen. "Education in Occupied Germany: A Field Study." *International Affairs* 24, no. 1 (January 1, 1948): 30–62. https://doi.org/10.2307/3016951.

Merritt, Anna J., and Richard L. Merritt. *Public Opinion in Occupied Germany: The OMGUS Surveys, 1945–1949*. Urbana: University of Illinois Press, 1970.

Merritt, Anna J., and Richard L. Merritt. *Public Opinion in Semisovereign Germany: The HICOG Surveys, 1949–1955*. University of Illinois Press, 1980.

Minear, Richard H. *Dr. Seuss Goes to War: The World War II Editorial Cartoons of Theodor Seuss Geisel*. The New Press, 2001.

Morgenthau, Henry. *Germany Is Our Problem*. Harper & Brothers Publishers, 1945.

Nalty, Bernard C., and Morris J. MacGregor, eds. *Blacks in the Military: Essential Documents*. Scholarly Resources, 1981.

Patri, Angelo. *Your Children in Wartime*. Doubleday, Doran & Co., 1943.

Schaffner, Bertram. *Father Land: A Study of Authoritarianism in the German Family*. Columbia University Press, 1948.

Smith, Jean Edward, ed. *The Papers of General Lucius D. Clay: Germany, 1945–1949*. Vol. 1. Indiana University Press, 1974.

Smith, William Gardner. *The Last of the Conquerors*. Farrar, Straus, 1948.

Spock, Benjamin. *Baby and Child Care*. E.P. Dutton, 1985.

Starr, Joseph R. *Fraternization with the Germans in World War II*. Office of the Chief Historian, European Command, 1947.

The U.S. Armed Forces German Youth Activities Program, 1945–1955. Historical Division, Headquarters, United States Army, Europe, 1956.

United States: Congress. "Appendix - Congressional Record (Bound), Volume 94, Part 9 (January 6, 1948 to December 31, 1948)." U.S. Government Publishing Office, December 31, 1948.

United States: Congress. "Appendix - Congressional Record (Bound), Volume 94, Part 10 (March 8, 1948 to December 31, 1948)." U.S. Government Publishing Office, December 31, 1948.

United States: Congress. "Congressional Record (Bound), Volume 93, Part 3 (March 31, 1947 to April 29, 1947)." U.S. Government Publishing Office, April 29, 1947.

United States Department of State. *Occupation of Germany, Policy and Progress 1945–46*. Washington, DC: U.S. Government Printing Office, 1947.

Secondary Literature

Adams, Bianka J. *From Crusade to Hazard: The Denazification of Bremen, Germany*. Scarecrow Press, Inc., 2009.

Alexander, Kristine, and Simon Sleight, eds. *A Cultural History of Youth in the Modern Age*. Bloomsbury Academic, 2022. https://doi.org/10.5040/9781350033085.

Alvah, Donna. *Unofficial Ambassadors: American Military Families Overseas and the Cold War, 1946–1965*. New York University Press, 2007.

Aresin, Jana, and Katharina Gerund. "Civilization, Democratization, Containment: Strategies of Re-Education in Imperial Settings and Beyond." *The International History Review* 46, no. 3 (2024): 263–270. https://doi.org/10.1080/07075332.2024.2298035.

Ariès, Philippe. *Centuries of Childhood: A Social History of Family Life*. Vintage Books, 1962.

Assmann, Aleida. *Erinnerungsräume: Formen und Wandlungen des kulturellen Gedächtnisses*. Fünfte, Durchgesehene Auflage. C.H. Beck, 2010.

Baker, Anni P. *Wiesbaden and the Americans 1945–2003: The Social, Economic, and Political Impact of the U.S. Forces in Wiesbaden*. Magistrat der Landeshauptstadt Wiesbaden, Kulturamt-Stadtarchiv, 2004.

Baumert, Gerhard. *Jugend der Nachkriegszeit: Lebensverhältnisse und Reaktionsweisen*. Eduard Roether Verlag, 1952.

Belmonte, Laura A. *Selling the American Way: U.S. Propaganda and the Cold War*. University of Pennsylvania Press, 2010.

Benbow, Heather Merle, and Heather R. Perry, eds. *Food, Culture and Identity in Germany's Century of War*. Palgrave Macmillan, 2019.

Bentley, Amy. *Eating for Victory: Food Rationing and the Politics of Domesticity*. University of Illinois Press, 1998.

Berghahn, Volker R. *American Big Business in Britain and Germany: A Comparative History of Two "Special Relationships" in the 20th Century*. Princeton University Press, 2014.

Bérubé, Allan. *Coming Out Under Fire: The History of Gay Men and Women in World War II*. 20th Anniversary Edition. University of North Carolina Press, 2010.

Bessel, Richard. *Germany 1945: From War to Peace*. Harper Perennial, 2009.

Biddiscombe, Perry. *Werwolf!: The History of the National Socialist Guerrilla Movement, 1944–1946*. University of Toronto Press, 1998.

Biedermann, Ulf. *Ein amerikanischer Traum: Coca-Cola, die unglaubliche Geschichte eines 100jährigen Erfolges*. Rasch und Röhring, 1985.

Bischof, Günter, Anton Pelinka, and Dieter Stiefel, eds. *The Marshall Plan in Austria*. Transaction Publishers, 2000.

Bius, Joel Richard. "The Soldier and the Cigarette: 1918–1986." PhD diss., University of Southern Mississippi, 2015. https://aquila.usm.edu/dissertations/63.

Bode, Sabine. *Die vergessene Generation: die Kriegskinder brechen ihr Schweigen*. 2. Aufl. Klett-Cotta, 2004.

Boghardt, Thomas. *Covert Legions: U.S. Army Intelligence in Germany, 1944–1949*. Center of Military History, United States Army, 2022. https://purl.fdlp.gov/GPO/gpo183492.

Borge, Baard Herman, Elke Kleinau, and Ingvill Constanze Ødegaard, eds. *Children and Youth at Risk in Times of Transition: International and Interdisciplinary Perspectives*. De Gruyter, 2024. https://doi.org/10.1515/9783111010649.

Borries, Achim von. *Quiet Helpers: Quaker Service in Postwar Germany*. Quaker Home Service and the American Friends Service Committee, 2000. https://afsc.org/sites/default/files/documents/Quiet%20Helpers%20%28Quaker%20Service%20in%20Postwar%20Germany%202000.pdf.

Brauerhoch, Annette. *"Fräuleins" und GIs: Geschichte und Filmgeschichte*. Stroemfeld, 2006.

Brokaw, Tom. *The Greatest Generation*. Random House trade pbk. ed. Random House Trade Paperbacks, 2005.

Browder, Dewey A. *Americans in Post-World War II Germany: Teachers, Tinkers, Neighbors and Nuisances*. The Edwin Mellen Press, 1998.

Burgard, Antoine. "Contested Childhood: Assessing the Age of Young Refugees in the Aftermath of the Second World War." *History Workshop Journal* 92 (Autumn 2021): 174–193. https://doi.org/10.1093/hwj/dbab016.

Burschka, Manfred H. "Re-education und Jugendöffentlichkeit: Orientierung und Selbstverständnis deutscher Nachkriegsjugend in der Jugendpresse, 1945–1948: ein Beitrag zur politischen Kultur der Nachkriegszeit." PhD diss., Georg-August-Universität Göttingen, 1987.

Buss, Wolfgang. "Reeducation Durch Sport - Ein Gescheiterter Versuch Amerikanischer Besatzungspolitik im Nachkriegsdeutschland?" *STADION* 37, no. 1 (2011): 109–126. https://doi.org/10.5771/0172-4029-2011-1-109.

Carruthers, Susan L. *The Good Occupation: American Soldiers and the Hazards of Peace*. Harvard University Press, 2016.

Chambers II, John Whiteclay. "Conference Review Essay: The New Military History: Myth and Reality." *The Journal of Military History* 55, no. 3 (1991): 395–406. https://doi.org/10.2307/1985686.

Cherny, Andrei. *The Candy Bombers: The Untold Story of the Berlin Airlift and America's Finest Hour*. Berkley Caliber trade paperback ed. Berkley Pub. Group, 2009.

Childers, Thomas. *Soldier from the War Returning: The Greatest Generation's Troubled Homecoming from World War II*. Houghton Mifflin Harcourt, 2009.

Chudacoff, Howard P. *How Old Are You?: Age Consciousness in American Culture*. Princeton University Press, 1989.

Citino, Robert M. "Military Histories Old and New: A Reintroduction." *The American Historical Review* 112, no. 4 (October 2007): 1070–1090. https://doi.org/10.1086/ahr.112.4.1070.

Clemens, Gabriele B., ed. *Werben für Europa: die mediale Konstruktion europäischer Identität durch Europafilme*. Ferdinand Schöningh, 2016.

Clifton, Denzil Tim. "Bremen under U.S. Military Occupation: 1945–1949, the Reform of Education." Microfilm facsimile. 1974. PhD diss., University of Delaware, 1973.

Coerper, Carl. *Deutsche Nachkriegskinder: Methoden und erste Ergebnisse der deutschen Längsschnittuntersuchungen über die körperliche und seelische Entwicklung im Schulkindalter*. Thieme, 1954.

Collins, Ross F. *Children, War & Propaganda*. Peter Lang, 2011.

Costigliola, Frank. "'I Had Come as a Friend': Emotion, Cultural, and Ambiguity in the Formation of the Cold War, 1943–45." *Cold War History* 1, no. 1 (2000): 103–128. https://doi.org/10.1080/713999913.

Costigliola, Frank. "'Mixed Up' and 'Contact': Culture and Emotion among the Allies in the Second World War." *The International History Review* 20, no. 4 (December 1998): 791–805. http://www.jstor.org/stable/40107996.

Cox, Caroline. *Boy Soldiers of the American Revolution*. University of North Carolina Press, 2016.

Crew, David F. "Alltagsgeschichte: A New Social History 'From Below'?" *Central European History* 22, no. 3/4 (Sep.-Dec. 1989): 394–407. http://www.jstor.org/stable/4546159.

Crew, David F, ed. *Consuming Germany in the Cold War*. Leisure, Consumption, and Culture. Berg, 2003.

Cubellis, Michelle Anne. "Sexual Victimization, Disclosure, and Accountability: Organizational Responses of the Boy Scouts of America to Child Sexual Abuse." PhD diss., City University of New York, 2015. https://academicworks.cuny.edu/gc_etds/893.

Cullather, Nick. "The Foreign Policy of the Calorie." *The American Historical Review* 112, no. 2 (April 2007): 337–364. http://www.jstor.org/stable/4136605.

Dack, Mikkel. *Everyday Denazification in Postwar Germany: The Fragebogen and Political Screening during the Allied Occupation*. Cambridge University Press, 2023. https://doi.org/10.1017/9781009216326.

Daum, Andreas W. *Kennedy in Berlin*. German Historical Institute; Cambridge University Press, 2008.

De Grazia, Victoria. *Irresistible Empire: America's Advance through Twentieth-Century Europe*. The Belknap Press of Harvard University Press, 2005.

De Lauri, Antonio. "Humanitarian Militarism and the Production of Humanity." *Social Anthropology* 27, no. 1 (February 2019): 84–99. https://doi.org/10.1111/1469-8676.12507.

Defrance, Corine, Bettina Greiner, and Ulrich Pfeil, eds. *Die Berliner Luftbrücke: Erinnerungsort des Kalten Krieges*. Ch. Links Verlag, 2018.

Delmont, Matthew F. *Half American: The Epic Story of African Americans Fighting World War II at Home and Abroad*. Viking, 2022.

Dichter, Heather L. "Sporting Democracy: The Western Allies' Reconstruction of Germany through Sport, 1944–1952." PhD diss., University of Toronto, 2008. https://central.bac-lac.gc.ca/.item?id=NR57981&op=pdf&app=Library&oclc_number=755208434.

Domentat, Tamara. *Coca-Cola, Jazz & AFN: Berlin und die Amerikaner*. Schwarzkopf & Schwarzkopf, 1995.

Domentat, Tamara. *Hallo Fräulein: deutsche Frauen und amerikanische Soldaten*. Aufbau-Verlag, 1998.

Drechsel, Wiltrud Ulrike, and Andreas Röpcke, eds. *"Denazification": zur Entnazifizierung in Bremen*. Edition Temmen, 1992.

Ehlers, Imke. *Die Ernährungssituation nach dem Zweiten Weltkrieg am Beispiel des Landes Bremen*. Universitätsbuchhandlung, 1995.

Eisenhuth, Stefanie. *Die Schutzmacht: die Amerikaner in Berlin 1945–1994*. Wallstein Verlag, 2018.

Engehausen, Frank, Marie A. Muschalek, and Wolfgang Zimmermann, eds. *Deutsch-französische Besatzungsbeziehungen im 20. Jahrhundert*. Verlag W. Kohlhammer, 2018.

Enssle, Manfred J. "The Harsh Discipline of Food Scarcity in Postwar Stuttgart, 1945–1948." *German Studies Review* 10, no. 3 (Oct. 1987): 481–502. https://doi.org/10.2307/1430898.

Erlichman, Camilo, and Christopher Knowles, eds. *Transforming Occupation in the Western Zones of Germany: Politics, Everyday Life and Social Interactions, 1945–55*. Bloomsbury Academic, 2018.

Evans, Jennifer V. "Bahnhof Boys: Policing Male Prostitution in Post-Nazi Berlin." *Journal of the History of Sexuality* 12, no. 4 (October 2003): 605–636. https://doi.org/10.1353/sex.2004.0026.

Evans, Jennifer V. *Life among the Ruins*. Palgrave Macmillan, 2011.

Ewers, Hans-Heino, Jana Mikota, Jürgen Reulecke, and Jürgen Zinnecker, eds. *Erinnerungen an Kriegskindheiten: Erfahrungsräume, Erinnerungskultur und Geschichtspolitik unter sozial- und kulturwissenschaftlicher Perspektive*. Kinder des Weltkrieges. Juventa, 2006.

Fass, Paula S., ed. *The Routledge History of Childhood in the Western World*. Routledge, 2013.

Faure, Laura Hobson. "Exploring Political Rupture through Jewish Children's Diaries: Kindertransport Children in France, 1938–1942." *Journal of Modern European History* 19, no. 3 (August 2021): 258–273. https://doi.org/10.1177/16118944211017765.

Fehrenbach, Heide. *Race after Hitler: Black Occupation Children in Postwar Germany and America*. Princeton University Press, 2005.

Fehrenbach, Heide. “Rehabilitating Fatherland: Race and German Remasculinization.” *Signs* 24, no. 1 (Autumn 1998): 107–127. http://www.jstor.org/stable/3175674.

Fehrenbach, Heide, and Davide Rodogno, eds. *Humanitarian Photography: A History*. Cambridge University Press, 2015.

Field, Corinne T., and Nicholas L. Syrett, eds. *Age in America: The Colonial Era to the Present*New York University Press, 2015.

Fieldston, Sara. *Raising the World: Child Welfare in the American Century*. Harvard University Press, 2015.

Fisher, Jaimey. *Disciplining Germany: Youth, Reeducation, and Reconstruction after the Second World War*. Wayne State University Press, 2007.

Foitzik, Doris, ed. *Vom Trümmerkind zum Teenager: Kindheit und Jugend in der Nachkriegszeit*. Edition Temmen, 1992.

Förster, Uwe, Stephanie von Hochberg, Ulrich Kubisch, and Dietrich Kuhlgatz, eds. *Auftrag Luftbrücke: der Himmel über Berlin 1948–1949*. Nicolai, 1998.

Foucault, Michel. *The History of Sexuality*. 1st American ed. Vol. 1. Pantheon Books, 1978.

Friedrich, Carl J., and Associates. *American Experiences in Military Government in World War II*. Rinehart, 1948.

Friedrichs, Horst-Eberhard. *Bremerhaven und die Amerikaner: Stationierung der U.S. Army 1945–1993: eine Bild-Dokumentation*. Wirtschaftsverlag NW, Verlag für neue Wissenschaft, 2008.

Fritsche, Maria. *The American Marshall Plan Film Campaign and the Europeans: A Captivated Audience?* Bloomsbury Academic, 2018.

Fulbrook, Mary. *Power and Society in the GDR, 1961–1979: The “Normalisation of Rule”?* Berghahn Books, 2009.

Fussell, Paul. *Wartime: Understanding and Behavior in the Second World War*. Oxford University Press, 1989.

Füssl, Karl-Heinz. *Die Umerziehung der Deutschen Jugend und Schule unter den Siegermächten des Zweiten Weltkriegs 1945–1955*. 2., Unveränd. Aufl. Schöningh, 1995.

Füssl, Karl-Heinz, and Gregory Paul Wegner. “Education under Radical Change: Education Policy and the Youth Program of the United States in Postwar Germany.” *History of Education Quarterly* 36, no. 1 (Spring 1996): 1–18. https://doi.org/10.2307/369298.

Gassert, Philipp. “Amerikanismus, Antiamerikanismus, Amerikanisierung: Neue Literatur zur Sozial-, Wirtschafts- und Kulturgeschichte des amerikanischen Einflusses in Deutschland und Europa.” *Archiv Für Sozialgeschichte* 39 (1999): 531–561.

Gebhardt, Miriam. *Als die Soldaten kamen: die Vergewaltigung deutscher Frauen am Ende des Zweiten Weltkriegs*. 3. Auflage. Deutsche Verlags-Anstalt, 2015.

Gergel, Richard. *Unexampled Courage: The Blinding of Sgt. Isaac Woodard and the Awakening of President Harry S. Truman and Judge J. Waties Waring*. Sarah Crichton Books/Farrar, Straus and Giroux, 2019.

Gerund, Katharina. “Liberation, Re-Education, Democratisation: The Politics of Gratitude in German-American Relations after 1945,” *Contemporary European History* (2024): 1–14, https://doi.org/10.1017/S0960777324000055.

Gerund, Katharina, and Heike Paul, eds. *Die amerikanische Reeducation, Politik nach 1945: interdisziplinäre Perspektiven auf “America’s Germany.”* Transcript, 2015.

Gimbel, John. *A German Community under American Occupation: Marburg, 1945–52*. Stanford University Press, 1961.

Goedde, Petra. *GIs and Germans: Culture, Gender and Foreign Relations, 1945–1949*. Yale University Press, 2003.

González, Roberto J., Hugh Gusterson, and Gustaaf Houtman, eds. *Militarization: A Reader.* Duke University Press, 2019.
Gordenker, Leon, and Thomas G. Weiss, eds. *Soldiers, Peacekeepers, and Disasters*. St. Martin's Press, 1991.
Grossmann, Atina. "Grams, Calories, and Food: Languages of Victimization, Entitlement, and Human Rights in Occupied Germany, 1945–1949." *Central European History* 44, no. 1 (March 2011): 118–148. http://www.jstor.org/stable/41238390.
Grossmann, Atina. *Jews, Germans, and Allies: Close Encounters in Occupied Germany*. Princeton University Press, 2007.
Grossmann, Atina. "A Question of Silence: The Rape of German Women by Occupation Soldiers." *October* 72 (1995): 43–63. https://doi.org/10.2307/778926.
Grünbacher, Armin. "Cold-War Economics: The Use of Marshall Plan Counterpart Funds in Germany, 1948–1960." *Central European History* 45, no. 4 (December 2012): 697–716. https://doi.org/10.1017/S0008938912000659.
Guglielmo, Thomas A. *Divisions: A New History of Racism and Resistance in America's World War II Military*. Oxford University Press, 2021.
Hagemann, Karen, and Sonya Michel, eds. *Gender and the Long Postwar: The United States and the Two Germanys, 1945–1989*. Woodrow Wilson Center Press, 2014.
Hagen, Wilhelm. "Deutsche Nachkriegskinder." *Sozialer Fortschritt* 4, no. 7/8 (Juli/August 1955): 169–171. https://www.jstor.org/stable/24498368.
Hájková, Anna. "Sexual Barter in Times of Genocide: Negotiating the Sexual Economy of the Theresienstadt Ghetto." *Signs* 38, no. 3 (Spring 2013): 503–533. https://doi.org/10.1086/668607.
Halbwachs, Maurice. *On Collective Memory*. University of Chicago Press, 1992.
Hall, Todd H. *Emotional Diplomacy: Official Emotion on the International Stage*. Cornell University Press, 2015.
Harrington, Daniel F. *Berlin on the Brink: The Blockade, the Airlift, and the Early Cold War*. University Press of Kentucky, 2012.
Häusser, Alexander, and Gordian Maugg. *Hungerwinter: Deutschlands humanitäre Katastrophe 1946/47*. Propyläen, 2009.
Herget, Winfried, ed. *Amerika in Rheinland-Pfalz: Beiträge zu einem halben Jahrhundert deutsch-amerikanischer Nachbarschaft*. Wissenschaftlicher Verlag, 1996.
Herwig, Malte. *Die Flakhelfer: wie aus Hitlers jüngsten Parteimitgliedern Deutschlands führende Demokraten wurden*. Deutsche Verlags-Anstalt, 2013.
Hesse, Hans. *Konstruktionen der Unschuld: die Entnazifizierung am Beispiel von Bremen und Bremerhaven, 1945–1953*. Selbstverlag des Staatsarchivs Bremen, 2005.
Heywood, Colin. *A History of Childhood: Children and Childhood in the West from Medieval to Modern Times*. Polity Press, 2001.
Hogan, Michael J. *The Marshall Plan: America, Britain, and the Reconstruction of Western Europe, 1947–1952*. Cambridge University Press, 1987.
Höhn, Maria. *GIs and Fräuleins: The German-American Encounter in 1950s West Germany*. University of North Carolina Press, 2002.
Höhn, Maria. "'We Will Never Go Back to the Old Way Again': Germany in the African-American Debate on Civil Rights." *Central European History* 41, no. 4 (December 2008): 605–637. https://doi.org/10.1017/S0008938908000861.
Höhn, Maria, and Martin Klimke. *A Breath of Freedom: The Civil Rights Struggle, African American GIs, and Germany*. Palgrave Macmillan, 2010.

Honeck, Mischa. *Our Frontier Is the World: The Boy Scouts in the Age of American Ascendancy*. Cornell University Press, 2018.

Honeck, Mischa, and James Alan Marten, eds. *War and Childhood in the Era of the Two World Wars*. Cambridge University Press, 2019.

Hopkins, Lucy. "'The Ice Is Melting and I Don't Want Santa to Drown!': Reflections on Childhood, Climate Action, and Futurity." *Journal of Childhood Studies* 48, no. 1 (January 2023): 85–98. https://doi.org/10.18357/jcs202320484.

Höschler, Christian. *Home(less): The IRO Children's Village Bad Aibling, 1948–1951*. Epubli, 2017.

Huneke, Samuel Clowes. *States of Liberation: Gay Men between Dictatorship and Democracy in Cold War Germany*. University of Toronto Press, 2022.

Huschke, Wolfgang J. *Die Rosinenbomber: Die Berliner Luftbrücke 1948/49, ihre technischen Voraussetzungen und deren erfolgreiche Umsetzung*. Berliner Wissenschafts-Verlag, 2008.

Jähner, Harald. *Aftermath: Life in the Fallout of the Third Reich, 1945–1955*. Translated by Shaun Whiteside. Alfred A. Knopf, 2022.

Jansen, Hans G., and Renate Meyer-Braun. *Bremen in der Nachkriegszeit: 1945–1949: Politik, Wirtschaft, Gesellschaft*. Steintor, 1990.

Johnson, David K. *The Lavender Scare: The Cold War Persecution of Gays and Lesbians in the Federal Government*. University of Chicago Press, 2004.

Judt, Tony. *Postwar: A History of Europe since 1945*. The Penguin Press, 2005.

Junker, Detlef, ed. *The United States and Germany in the Era of the Cold War, 1945–1990: A Handbook*. Vol. 1. Cambridge University Press, 2004.

Kalb, Martin. *Coming of Age: Constructing and Controlling Youth in Munich, 1942–1973*. Berghahn Books, 2016.

Kalb, Martin. "'The Youth Is a Threat!' Controlling the Delinquent Boy in Post-WWII Munich." *The Journal of the History of Childhood and Youth* 6, no. 2 (Spring 2013): 263–290. https://doi.org/10.1353/hcy.2013.0022.

Kater, Michael H. *Hitler Youth*. Harvard University Press, 2004.

Kebbedies, Frank. *Ausser Kontrolle: Jugendkriminalität in der NS-Zeit und der frühen Nachkriegszeit*. Klartext, 2000.

Kehoe, Thomas J. *The Art of Occupation: Crime and Governance in American-Controlled Germany, 1944–1949*. Ohio University Press, 2019.

Kind-Kovács, Friederike, and Anna Oksiutovych. "Reflecting on the Present through the Past: Children's Displacement from Ukraine." *The Journal of the History of Childhood and Youth* 17, no. 2 (Spring 2024): 254–271. https://dx.doi.org/10.1353/hcy.2024.a926867.

Kleinau, Elke, and Ingvill C. Mochmann, eds. *Kinder Des Zweiten Weltkrieges: Stigmatisierung, Ausgrenzung, Bewältigungsstrategien*. Campus Verlag, 2016.

Kleinschmidt, Johannes. *Do Not Fraternize: die schwierigen Anfänge deutsch-amerikanischer Freundschaft, 1944–1949*. WVT Wissenschaftler Verlag, 1997.

Klose, Maximilian. *Why They Gave: CARE and American Aid for Germany after 1945*. Franz Steiner Verlag, 2024.

Knowles, Christopher. *Winning the Peace: The British in Occupied Germany, 1945–1948*. Bloomsbury Academic, 2017.

Laqueur, Walter. *Young Germany: A History of the German Youth Movement*. Basic Books, 1962.

Leder, Harald Thomas Oskar. "Americans and German Youth in Nuremberg, 1945–1956: A Study in Politics and Culture." PhD diss., Louisiana State University, 1997. https://digitalcommons.lsu.edu/gradschool_disstheses/6430.

Lee, Sabine. "A Forgotten Legacy of the Second World War: GI Children in Post-War Britain and Germany." *Contemporary European History* 20, no. 2 (2011): 157–181. https://www.jstor.org/stable/41238351.

Lorenz, Hilke. *Kriegskinder: Das Schicksal Einer Generation*. List, 2003.

Lüdtke, Alf, ed. *Alltagsgeschichte: zur Rekonstruktion historischer Erfahrungen und Lebensweisen*. Campus Verlag, 1989.

Maase, Kaspar. *BRAVO Amerika: Erkundungen zur Jugendkultur der Bundesrepublik in den fünfziger Jahren*. Junius, 1992.

Mackinem, Mitchell B., and Deborah Laufersweiler-Dwyer. "A Deeper Look at the Boy Scouts of America 'Perversion' Files: Structural Factors Related to Access and Abuse." *Journal of Interpersonal Violence* 39, no. 15–16 (August 1, 2024): 3352–3372. https://doi.org/10.1177/08862605241230091.

Marten, James Alan, ed. *Children and Youth during the Civil War Era*. New York University Press, 2012.

Martin, Peter, and Christine Alonzo, eds. *Zwischen Charleston und Stechschritt: Schwarze im Nationalsozialismus*. Dölling und Galitz, 2004.

Matthews, Corrine. "The Right to Resist: Childhood Agency in Julian Kulski's World War II Diary." *The Journal of the History of Childhood and Youth* 16, no. 1 (Winter 2023): 134–150. https://doi.org/10.1353/hcy.2023.0012.

Maul, Daniel. *The Politics of Service: US-amerikanische Quäker und internationale humanitäre Hilfe 1917–1945*. De Gruyter, 2021.

Maulucci Jr., Thomas W., and Detlef Junker, eds. *GIs in Germany: The Social, Economic, Cultural and Political History of the American Military Presence*. German Historical Institute; Cambridge University Press, 2013.

May, Antoinette. *Witness to War: A Biography of Marguerite Higgins*. Beaufort Books, 1983.

McCormack, Killian, and Emily Gilbert. "The Geopolitics of Militarism and Humanitarianism." *Progress in Human Geography* 46, no. 1 (2022): 179–197. https://doi.org/10.1177/03091325211032267.

McDougall, Alan. *Youth Politics in East Germany: The Free German Youth Movement, 1946–1968*. Clarendon, 2004.

Mead, Margaret. "Food and Feeding in Occupied Territory." *The Public Opinion Quarterly* 7, no. 4 (1943): 618–628. https://www.jstor.org/stable/2745632.

Merritt, Richard L. *Democracy Imposed: U.S. Occupation Policy and the German Public, 1945–1949*. Yale University Press, 1995.

Miller, Roger G. *To Save a City*. U.S. Government Printing Office, Air Force History and Museums Program, 1998.

Mintz, Steven. "Children's History Matters." *The American Historical Review* 125, no. 4 (October 2020): 1286–1292. https://doi.org/10.1093/ahr/rhaa382.

Mintz, Steven. *Huck's Raft: A History of American Childhood*. The Belknap Press of Harvard University Press, 2004.

Mintz, Steven. "Why the History of Childhood Matters." *The Journal of the History of Childhood and Youth* 5, no. 1 (Winter 2012): 15–28. https://doi.org/10.1353/hcy.2012.0012.

Möckel, Benjamin. *Erfahrungsbruch und Generationsbehauptung: die "Kriegsjugendgeneration" in den beiden deutschen Nachkriegsgesellschaften*. Wallstein Verlag, 2014.

Mörchen, Stefan. *Schwarzer Markt: Kriminalität, Ordnung und Moral in Bremen, 1939–1949*. Campus-Verlag, 2011.

Morris, David. *A Gift from America: The First 50 Years of CARE*. Longstreet Press, 1996.

Morrow, John H. "Black Africans in World War II: The Soldiers' Stories." *The Annals of the American Academy of Political and Social Science* 632 (November 2010): 12–25. https://www.jstor.org/stable/27895945.

Motley, Mary Penick. *The Invisible Soldier: The Experience of the Black Soldier, World War II*. Wayne State University Press, 1987.

Mouton, Michelle. "Missing, Lost, and Displaced Children in Postwar Germany: The Great Struggle to Provide for the War's Youngest Victims." *Central European History* 48, no. 1 (March 2015): 53–78. https://doi.org/10.1017/S0008938915000035.

Müller, Beate. "'Der Mann, den ich vergötterte, hat uns ins Unglück geführt': The Post-War Crisis of Consciousness as Mirrored in Essays and Questionnaires by Nuremberg's Schoolchildren in 1946." *German Life and Letters* 69, no. 4 (October 2016): 453–467. https://doi.org/10.1111/glal.12130.

Müller, Christa. *Schatten des Schweigens, Notwendigkeit des Erinnerns: Kindheiten im Nationalsozialismus, im Zweiten Weltkrieg und in der Nachkriegszeit*. Psychosozial-Verlag, 2014.

Müller, Hartmut, and Günther Rohdenburg, eds. *Kriegsende in Bremen: Erinnerungen, Berichte, Dokumente*. Edition Temmen, 1995.

Muniz de Faria, Yara-Colette Lemke. "'Germany's 'Brown Babies' Must Be Helped! Will You?': U.S. Adoption Plans for Afro-German Children, 1950–1955." *Callaloo* 26, no. 2 (2003): 342–362. http://www.jstor.org/stable/3300857.

Naimark, Norman M. *The Russians in Germany: A History of the Soviet Zone of Occupation, 1945–1949*. The Belknap Press of Harvard University Press, 1995.

Nalley, Kim. "GI Jazz: African Americans as Artists and Occupiers in Post-World War II Germany." PhD diss., University of California, Berkeley, 2021. https://escholarship.org/uc/item/9wx3s83d.

Nelson, Daniel J. *A History of U.S. Military Forces in Germany*. Westview Press, 1987.

Nelson, Keith L. "The 'Black Horror on the Rhine': Race as a Factor in Post-World War I Diplomacy." *The Journal of Modern History* 42, no. 4 (December 1970): 606–627. https://doi.org/10.1086/244041.

Neumann, Brian F., and Shane D. Makowicki. *Occupation and Demobilization, 1918–1923*. Center of Military History, United States Army, 2019.

O'Connell, Kaete M. "'Uncle Wiggly Wings': Children, Chocolates, and the Berlin Airlift." *Food and Foodways* 25, no. 2 (2017): 142–159. https://doi.org/10.1080/07409710.2017.1311163.

O'Connell, Kaete M. "Weapon of War, Tool of Peace: U.S. Food Diplomacy in Postwar Germany." PhD diss., Temple University, 2019. http://dx.doi.org/10.34944/dspace/489.

Olick, Jeffrey K., Vered Vinitzky-Seroussi, and Daniel Levy, eds. *The Collective Memory Reader*. Oxford University Press, 2011.

Olsen, Stephanie, Kristine Alexander, Susan Miller, Ville Vuolanto, Simon Sleight, Mischa Honeck, Sarah Emily Duff, and Karen Vallgårda. "A Critical Conversation on Agency." *The Journal of the History of Childhood and Youth* 17, no. 2 (Spring 2024): 169–187. https://dx.doi.org/10.1353/hcy.2024.a926862.

Pate, SooJin. *From Orphan to Adoptee: U.S. Empire and Genealogies of Korean Adoption*. University of Minnesota Press, 2014.

Pedron, Anna-Maria. *Amerikaner vor Ort: Besatzer und Besetzte in der Enklave Bremen nach dem Zweiten Weltkrieg*. Selbstverlag des Staatsarchivs Bremen, 2010.

Penny, H. Glenn. *Kindred by Choice: Germans and American Indians since 1800*. University of North Carolina Press, 2013.

Peters, Fritz. *Zwölf Jahre Bremen: 1945–1956: eine Chronik*. H.H. Hauschild, 1976.

Peterson, Edward N. *The American Occupation of Germany: Retreat to Victory*. Wayne State University Press, 1977.
Peterson, Edward N. *The Many Faces of Defeat: The German People's Experience in 1945*. Peter Lang, 1990.
Pfau, Ann Elizabeth. *Miss Yourlovin: GIs, Gender and Domesticity during World War II*. Columbia University Press, 2008. http://www.gutenberg-e.org/pfau/.
Phillips, David. *Educating the Germans: People and Policy in the British Zone of Germany, 1945–1949*. Bloomsbury Academic, 2018.
Poiger, Uta G. *Jazz, Rock, and Rebels: Cold War Politics and American Culture in a Divided Germany*. University of California Press, 2000.
Pommerin, Reiner, ed. *The American Impact on Postwar Germany*. Berghahn Books, 1995.
Porter, Stephen R. *Benevolent Empire: U.S. Power, Humanitarianism, and the World's Dispossessed*. University of Pennsylvania Press, 2017.
Puaca, Brian M. *Learning Democracy: Education Reform in West Germany, 1945–1965*. Berghahn Books, 2009.
Rathfelder, Gerhard, Ulrich Schubert, and Margarethe Wild. *GYA das Jugendarbeitsprogramm der amerikanischen Armee im Nachkriegsdeutschland*. Verlag Burkhard Fehrlen, 1987.
Raven, Margot Theis. *Mercedes and the Chocolate Pilot: A True Story of the Berlin Airlift and the Candy that Dropped from the Sky*. Sleeping Bear Press, 2002.
Reese, Dagmar, ed. *Die BDM-Generation: weibliche Jugendliche in Deutschland und Österreich im Nationalsozialismus*. Verlag für Berlin-Brandenburg, 2007.
Reeves, Richard. *Daring Young Men: The Heroism and Triumph of the Berlin Airlift, June 1948–May 1949*. Simon & Schuster, 2010.
Reinisch, Jessica. *The Perils of Peace: The Public Health Crisis in Occupied Germany*. Oxford University Press, 2013. https://doi.org/10.1093/acprof:oso/9780199660797.001.0001.
Rempel, Gerhard. *Hitler's Children: The Hitler Youth and the SS*. University of North Carolina Press, 1989.
Retzlaff, Birgit, and Jörg-Johannes Lechner. *Bund Deutscher Mädel in der Hitlerjugend: fakultative Eintrittsgründe von Mädchen und jungen Frauen in den BDM*. Kovač, 2008.
Ritter, Rüdiger. *Vorort von New York?: die Amerikaner in Bremerhaven : Ergebnisse einer Studie am Museum der 50er Jahre Bremerhaven*. Wirtschaftsverlag NW, Verlag für neue Wissenschaft, 2010.
Rode, Lutz. "Manche nannten sie nur 'Schokoladenclubs': Die Jugendarbeit der US-Armee in der Besatzungszeit." *Arbeiterbewegung und Sozialgeschichte. Zeitschrift für die Regionalgeschichte Bremens im 19. und 20. Jahrhundert* 13/14 (2004): 22–38.
Rode, Lutz. "Zwischen Re-Education und Freizeitvergnügen: Die Jugendarbeit der US-Armee in der Besatzungszeit, der Bremen Boys Club und seine Zeitschrift 'Die Brücke.'" Magisterarbeit, Universität Bremen, 2002.
Rudeck, Lena. *Vergnügen in Besatzungszeiten: Begegnungen in Westalliierten Offiziers- und Soldatenclubs in Deutschland, 1945–1955*. Transcript Verlag, 2023.
Ruhl, Klaus-Jörg. *Neubeginn und Restauration: Dokumente zur Vorgeschichte der Bundesrepublik Deutschland 1945–1949*. Deutscher Taschenbuch Verlag, 1982.
Rupieper, Hermann-Josef. *Die Wurzeln der westdeutschen Nachkriegsdemokratie: der amerikanische Beitrag 1945–1952*. Westdeutscher Verlag, 1993.
Sahrakorpi, Tiia. "Memory, Family, and the Self in Hitler Youth Generation Narratives." *Journal of Family History* 45, no. 1 (January 1, 2020): 88–108. https://doi.org/10.1177/0363199019880254.
Samet, Elizabeth D. *Looking for the Good War: American Amnesia and the Violent Pursuit of Happiness*. Farrar, Straus and Giroux, 2021.

Satjukow, Silke, and Rainer Gries. *Bankerte!: Besatzungskinder in Deutschland nach 1945*. Campus, 2015.

Schissler, Hanna, ed. *The Miracle Years: A Cultural History of West Germany, 1949–1968*. Princeton University Press, 2001.

Schmidt, Oliver R. *Afroamerikanische GIs in Deutschland 1944 bis 1973: Rassekrieg, Integration und globale Protestbewegung*. Monsenstein und Vannerdat, 2013.

Schörken, Rolf. *Die Niederlage als Generationserfahrung: Jugendliche nach dem Zusammenbruch der NS-Herrschaft*. Juventa, 2004.

Schroer, Timothy L. *Recasting Race after World War II: Germans and African Americans in American-Occupied Germany*. University Press of Colorado, 2007.

Schuessler, John M., Adam R. Seipp, and Thomas D. Sullivan, eds. *The Berlin Airlift and the Making of the Cold War*. Texas A&M University Press, 2022.

Schulberg, Sandra, and Ed Carter. *Selling Democracy: Films of the Marshall Plan: 1948–1953*. Academy Foundation, 2005.

Schulgeschichtliche Sammlung Bremen, ed. *Am Roland hing ein Hakenkreuz: Bremer Kinder und Jugendliche in der Nazizeit: Katalog zur Ausstellung*. Hauschild, 2002.

Schumann, Dirk, ed. *Raising Citizens in the "Century of the Child": The United States and German Central Europe in Comparative Perspective*. Berghahn Books, 2010.

Schutts, Jeff R. "Coca-Cola History: A 'Refreshing' Look at German-American Relations." *Bulletin of the German Historical Institute* 40 (Spring 2007): 127–142.

Schwartz, Thomas Alan. *America's Germany: John J. McCloy and the Federal Republic of Germany*. Harvard University Press, 1991.

Seegers, Lu. "'Dead Dads': Memory Narratives of War-Related Fatherlessness in Germany." *European Review of History: Revue Européenne d'histoire* 22, no. 2 (2015): 259–276. https://doi.org/10.1080/13507486.2015.1008417.

Seegers, Lu. *"Vati blieb im Krieg": Vaterlosigkeit als generationelle Erfahrung im 20. Jahrhundert, Deutschland und Polen*. Wallstein Verlag, 2013.

Seipp, Adam R. *Strangers in the Wild Place: Refugees, Americans, and a German Town, 1945–1952*. Indiana University Press, 2013.

Shukert, Elfrieda Berthiaume, and Barbara Smith Scibetta. *War Brides of World War II*. Presidio Press, 1988.

Sollors, Werner. *The Temptation of Despair: Tales of the 1940s*. The Belknap Press of Harvard University Press, 2014.

Sommer, Karl-Ludwig. *Wilhelm Kaisen: eine politische Biographie*. 2., Durchges. Aufl. Dietz, 2000.

Stargardt, Nicholas. "Children's Art of the Holocaust." *Past & Present* 161, no. 1 (November 1, 1998): 191–235. https://doi.org/10.1093/past/161.1.191.

Stargardt, Nicholas. *Witnesses of War: Children's Lives Under the Nazis*. Alfred A. Knopf, 2006.

Steege, Paul. *Black Market, Cold War: Everyday Life in Berlin, 1946–1949*. Cambridge University Press, 2007.

Steil, Benn. *The Marshall Plan: Dawn of the Cold War*. Simon & Schuster, 2018.

Stephan, Alexander, ed. *The Americanization of Europe: Culture, Diplomacy, and Anti-Americanism after 1945*. Berghahn Books, 2006.

Taylor, Frederick. *Exorcising Hitler: The Occupation and Denazification of Germany*. Bloomsbury Press, 2011.

Taylor, Lynne. *In the Children's Best Interests: Unaccompanied Children in American-Occupied Germany, 1945–1952*. University of Toronto Press, 2017.

Tent, James F. *Mission on the Rhine: Reeducation and Denazification in American-Occupied Germany*. University of Chicago Press, 1982.

Tent, James F. "Simple Gifts: The American Friends Service Committee and the Establishment of Neighborhood Centers in Post-1945 Germany." *Kirchliche Zeitgeschichte* 2, no. 1 (May 1989): 64–82. https://www.jstor.org/stable/43098025.

Treber, Leonie. *Mythos Trümmerfrauen: von der Trümmerbeseitigung in der Kriegs- und Nachkriegszeit und der Entstehung eines deutschen Erinnerungsortes*. Klartext, 2014.

Trotnow, Helmut, and Bernd von Kostka, eds. *Die Berliner Luftbrücke: Ereignis und Erinnerung*. Frank & Timme, 2010.

Tunnell, Michael O. *Candy Bomber: The Story of the Berlin Airlift's "Chocolate Pilot."* Charlesbridge, 2010.

Turner, Ian D., ed. *Reconstruction in Post-War Germany: British Occupation Policy and the Western Zones, 1945–55*. Berg, 1989.

Tuttle, William M. *Daddy's Gone to War: The Second World War in the Lives of America's Children*. Oxford University Press, 1993.

Usbeck, Frank. *Fellow Tribesmen: The Image of Native Americans, National Identity, and Nazi Ideology in Germany*. Berghahn Books, 2015.

Vaizey, Hester. *Surviving Hitler's War*. Palgrave Macmillan, 2010.

Venken, Machteld, and Maren Röger. "Growing up in the Shadow of the Second World War: European Perspectives." *European Review of History: Revue Européenne d'histoire* 22, no. 2 (March 4, 2015): 199–220. https://doi.org/10.1080/13507486.2015.1008410.

Vogelsang, German, ed. *Sie Kommen!: Die Letzten Kriegstage in Der Oberpfalz 1945*. Buch & Kunstverlag Oberpfalz, 2005.

Wagnleitner, Reinhold. *Coca-colonisation und Kalter Krieg: die Kulturmission der USA in Österreich nach dem Zweiten Weltkrieg*. Verlag für Gesellschaftskritik, 1991.

Warner, David T. *Christmas from Heaven: The True Story of the Berlin Candy Bomber*. Shadow Mountain, 2013.

Weinreb, Alice. *Modern Hungers: Food and Power in Twentieth-Century Germany*. Oxford University Press, 2017.

Weiss, Thomas G. *Military-Civilian Interactions: Intervening in Humanitarian Crises*. Rowman & Littlefield, 1999.

Weiss, Thomas G., and Kurt M. Campbell. "Military Humanitarianism." *Survival* 33, no. 5 (September/October 1991): 451–465. https://doi.org/10.1080/00396339108442612.

Weisz, Christoph, ed. *OMGUS-Handbuch: die amerikanische Militärregierung in Deutschland 1945–1949*. 2. Aufl. Quellen und Darstellungen zur Zeitgeschichte. Oldenbourg, 1994. https://doi.org/10.1524/9783486587777.

Werner, Emmy E. *Through the Eyes of Innocents: Children Witness World War II*. Westview Press, 2000.

Wette, Wolfram. *The Wehrmacht: History, Myth, Reality*. Harvard University Press, 2007.

Whisnant, Clayton J. *Male Homosexuality in West Germany: Between Persecution and Freedom, 1945–69*. Palgrave Macmillan, 2012.

Willett, Ralph. *The Americanization of Germany, 1945–1949*. Routledge, 1989.

Willis, F. Roy. *The French in Germany, 1945–1949*. Stanford University Press, 1962.

Willoughby, John. *Remaking the Conquering Heroes: The Social and Geopolitical Impact of the Post-War American Occupation of Germany*., 2001.

Zahra, Tara. *The Lost Children: Reconstructing Europe's Families after World War II*. Harvard University Press, 2011.

Ziemke, Earl F. *The U.S. Army in the Occupation of Germany 1944–1946*. Army Historical Series. Center of Military History, United States Army, 1990. https://purl.fdlp.gov/GPO/LPS33225.

Zierenberg, Malte. *Berlin's Black Market, 1939–1950*. Palgrave Macmillan, 2015.

Index

https://doi.org/10.1515/9783111588155-009